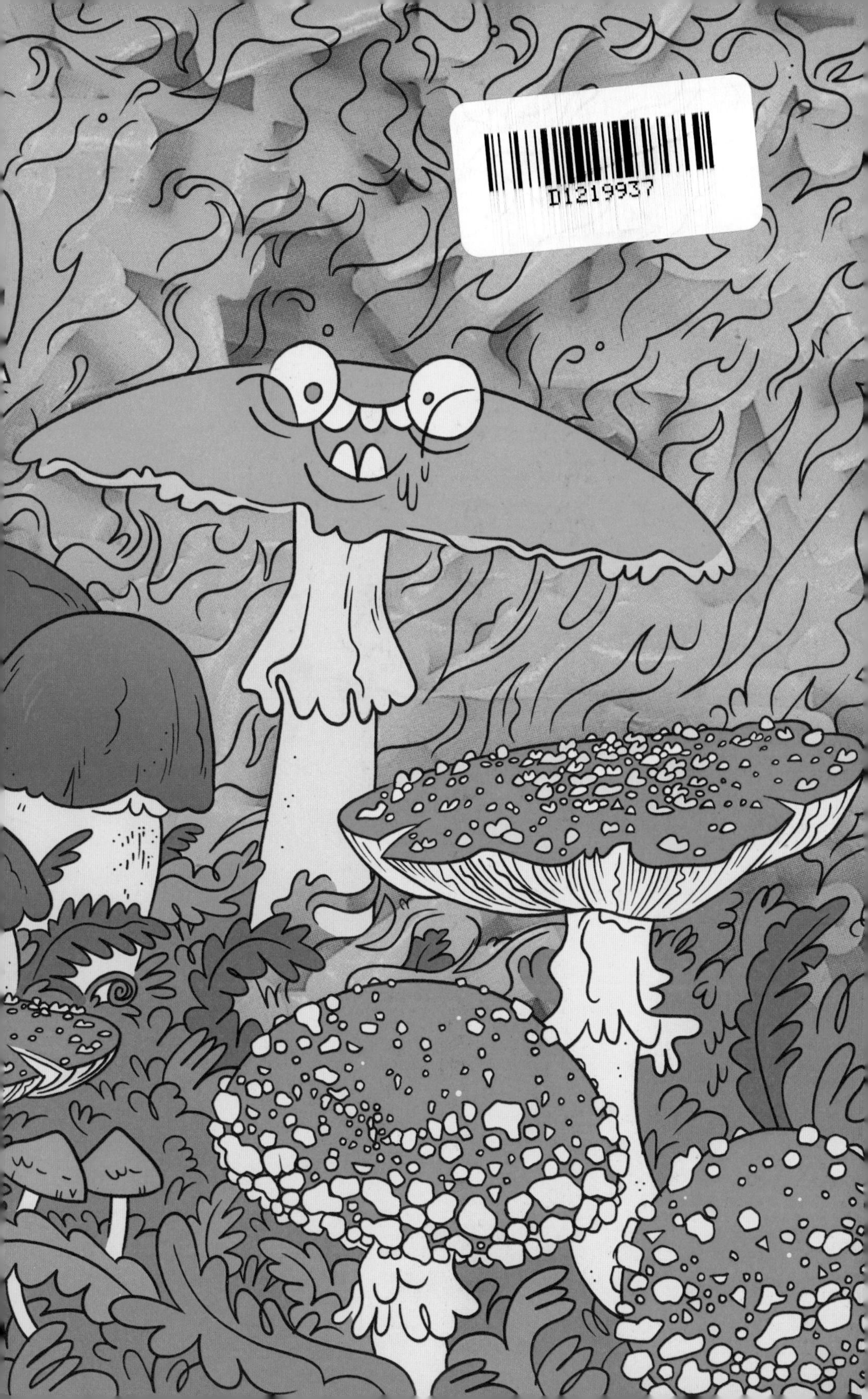

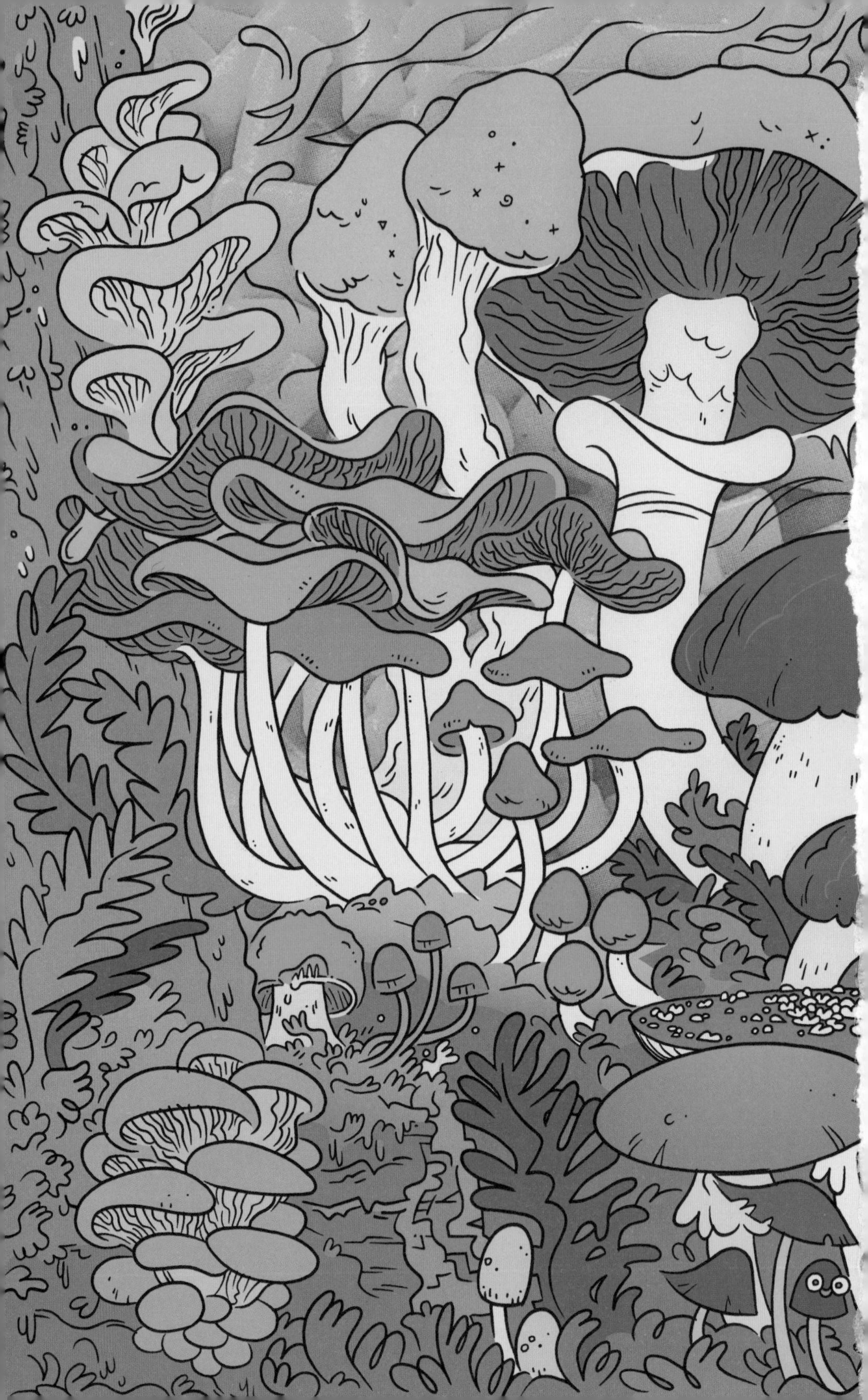

GNARTOONS

JAMES the STANTON

JAMES STANTON - COVER ART
KAT WONG - BOOK LAYOUT DESIGNER

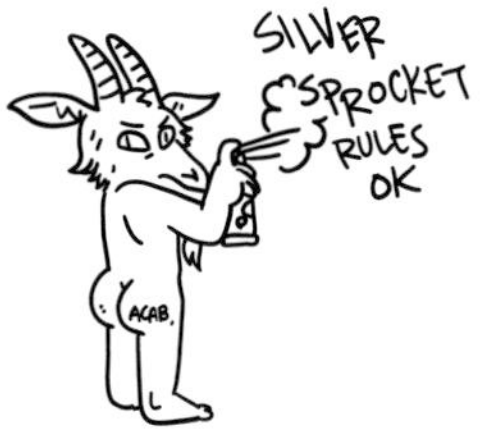
SILVER SPROCKET RULES OK
ACAB

SILVER SPROCKET
AVI EHRLICH - PUBLISHER
JOSH PM - GENERAL MANAGER
ARI YARWOOD - MANAGING EDITOR
CARINA TAYLOR - PRODUCTION DESIGNER
SIMON JANE CROWBROCK - SHOP GOBLIN
DANIEL ZHOU - SHOP RAT
RAUL HIGUERA-CORTEZ - BIG HEAD BANDIT
YASMEEN ABEDIFARD - SHOP SHROOM
SARAH MALONEY - SHOP CAT
SOL CINTRON - FRUIT BAT
WWW.SILVERSPROCKET.NET

ISBN 978-1-945509-41-4 FIRST PRINTING, MARCH 2022. PUBLISHED BY SILVER SPROCKET. 1018 VALENCIA ST, SAN FRANCISCO, CA 94110, USA.

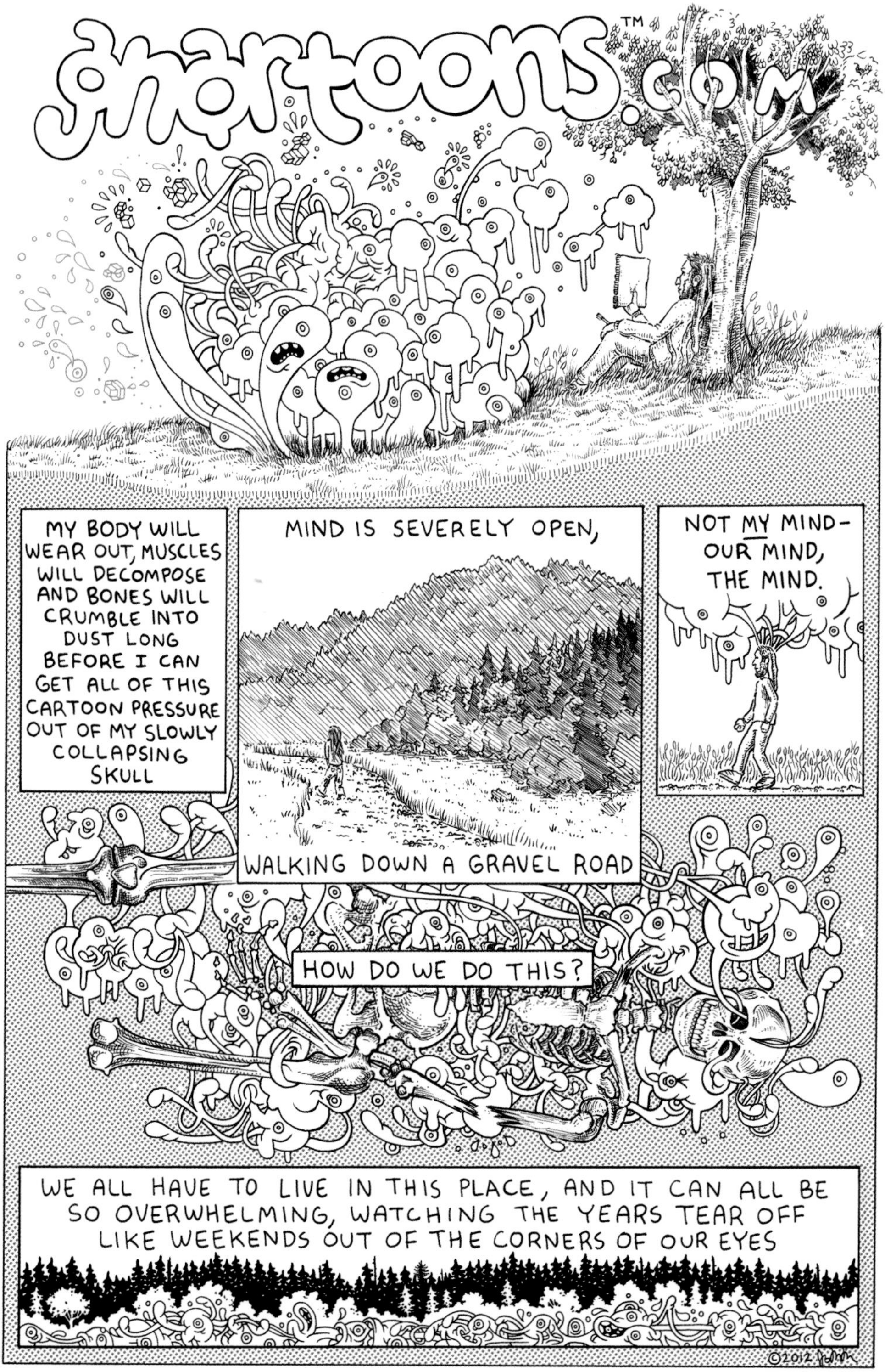
shartoons.com
TM
MY BODY WILL WEAR OUT, MUSCLES WILL DECOMPOSE AND BONES WILL CRUMBLE INTO DUST LONG BEFORE I CAN GET ALL OF THIS CARTOON PRESSURE OUT OF MY SLOWLY COLLAPSING SKULL
MIND IS SEVERELY OPEN,
WALKING DOWN A GRAVEL ROAD
NOT MY MIND- OUR MIND, THE MIND.
HOW DO WE DO THIS?
WE ALL HAVE TO LIVE IN THIS PLACE, AND IT CAN ALL BE SO OVERWHELMING, WATCHING THE YEARS TEAR OFF LIKE WEEKENDS OUT OF THE CORNERS OF OUR EYES
©2012

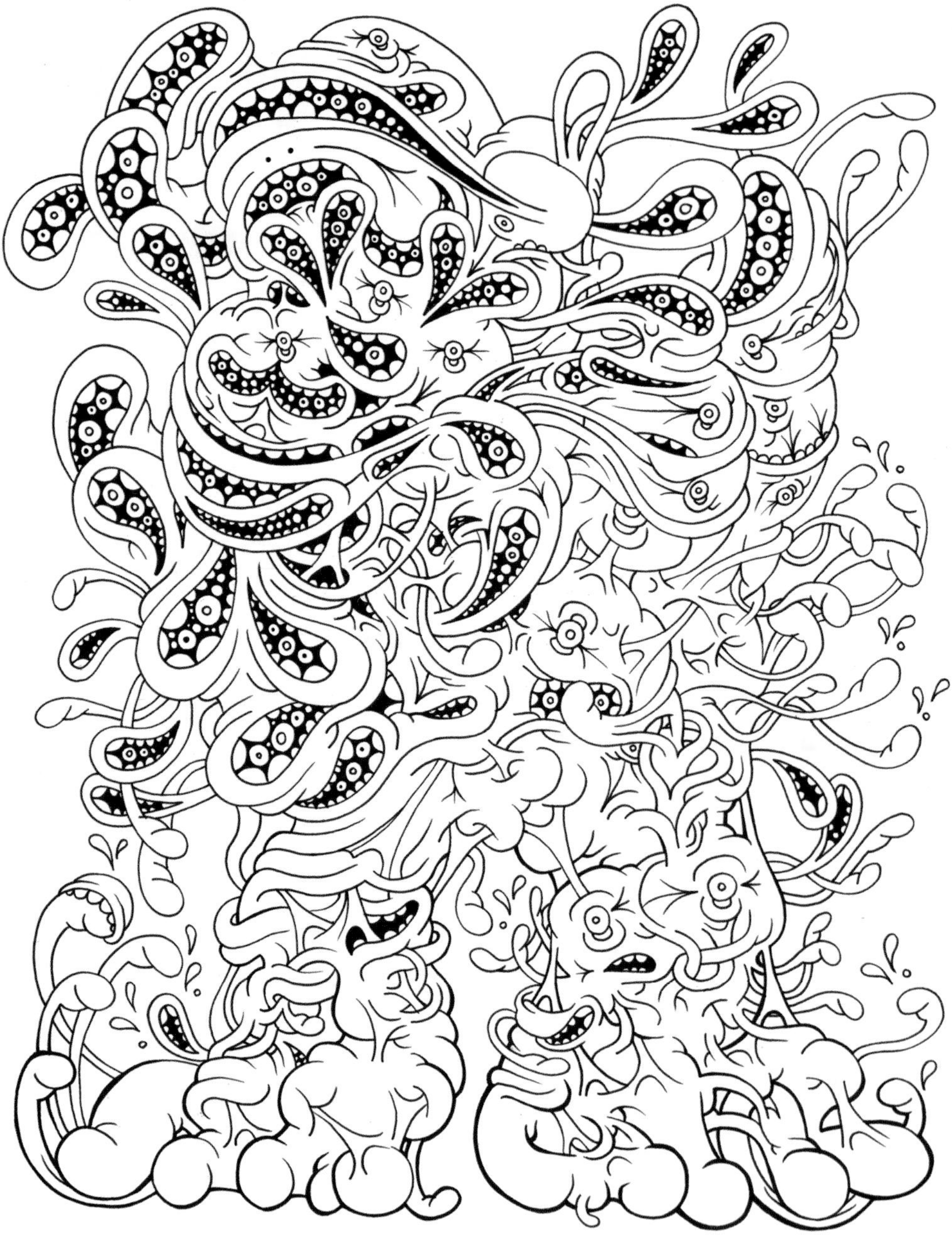

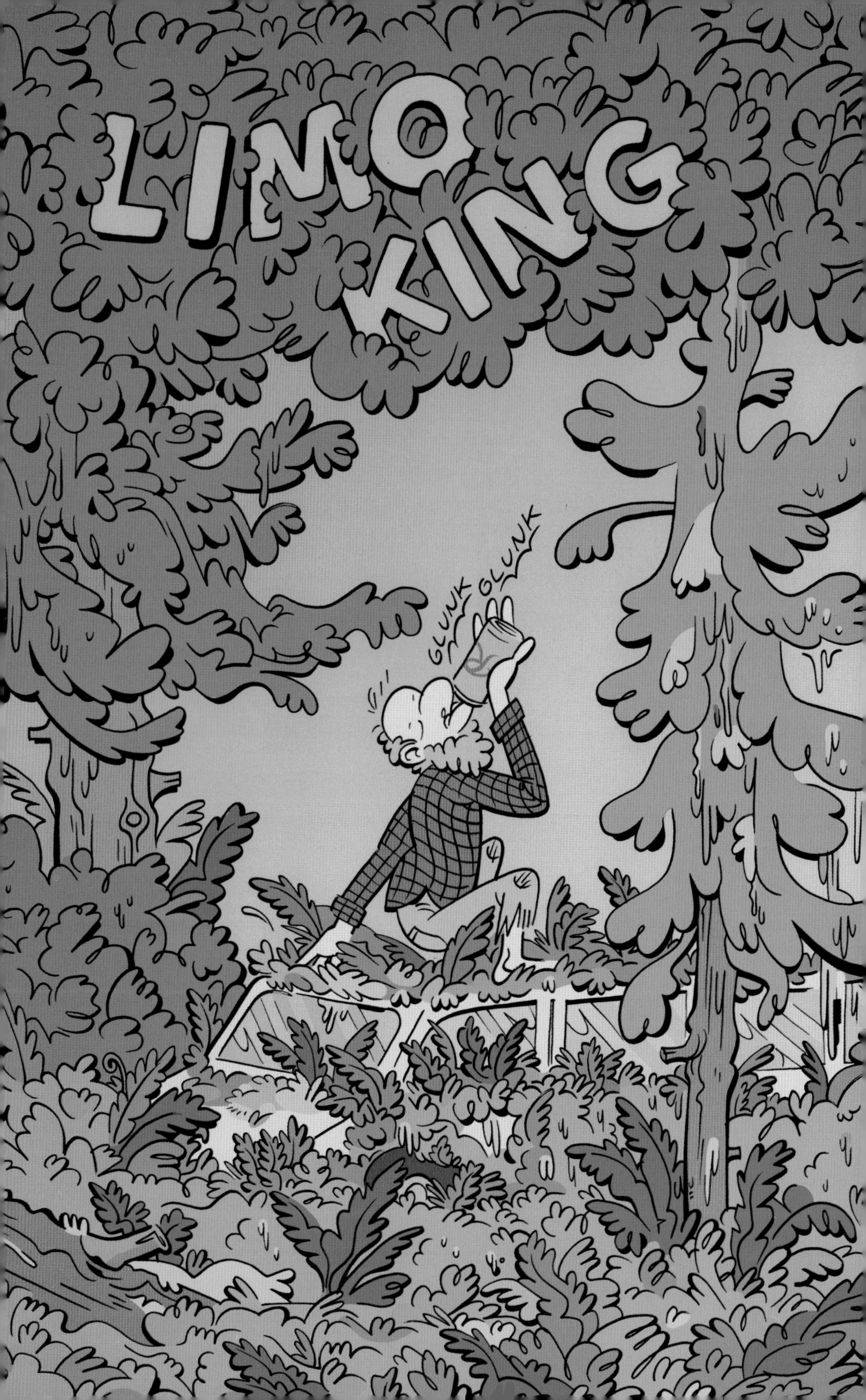
LIMO KING
GLUNK GLUNK

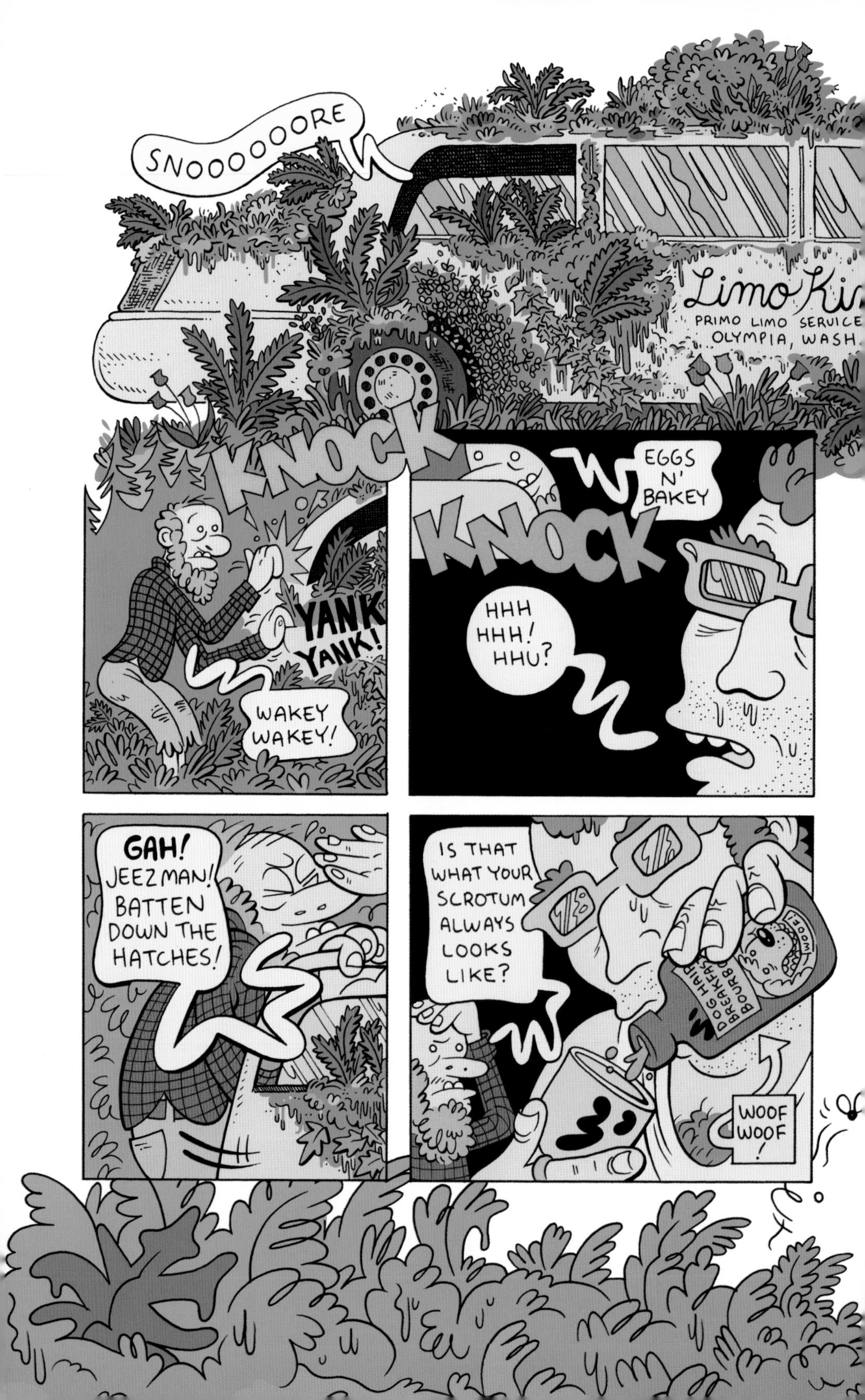
SNOOOOOORE
Limo Kin
PRIMO LIMO SERVICE
OLYMPIA, WASH
KNOCK
YANK
YANK!
WAKEY WAKEY!
EGGS N' BAKEY
KNOCK
HHH HHH! HHU?
GAH! JEEZMAN! BATTEN DOWN THE HATCHES!
IS THAT WHAT YOUR SCROTUM ALWAYS LOOKS LIKE?
DOG HAIR BREAKFAST BOURBON
WOOF!
WOOF WOOF!

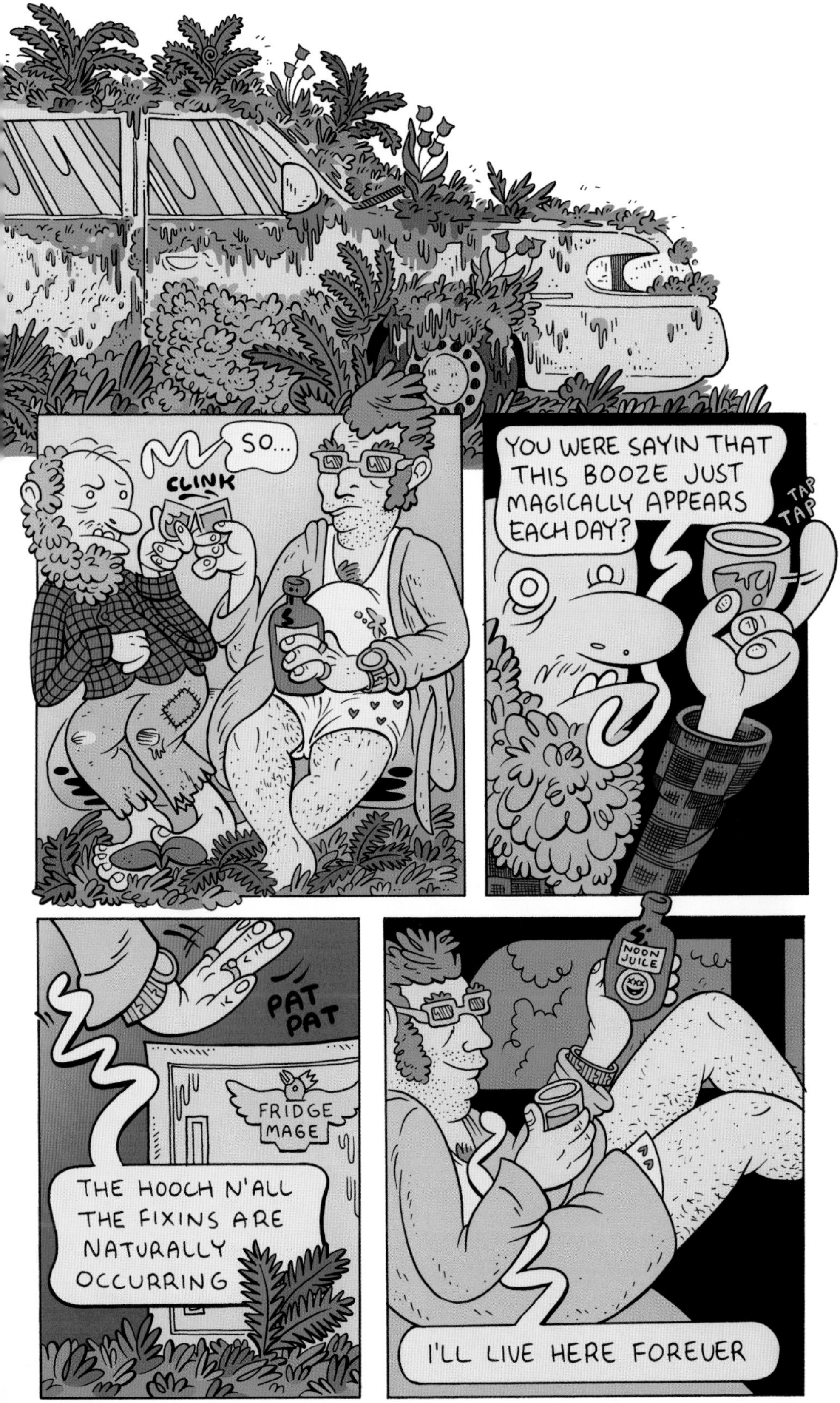
SO...
CLINK
YOU WERE SAYIN THAT THIS BOOZE JUST MAGICALLY APPEARS EACH DAY?
TAP TAP
PAT PAT
FRIDGE MAGE
THE HOOCH N'ALL THE FIXINS ARE NATURALLY OCCURRING
NOON JUICE
I'LL LIVE HERE FOREVER

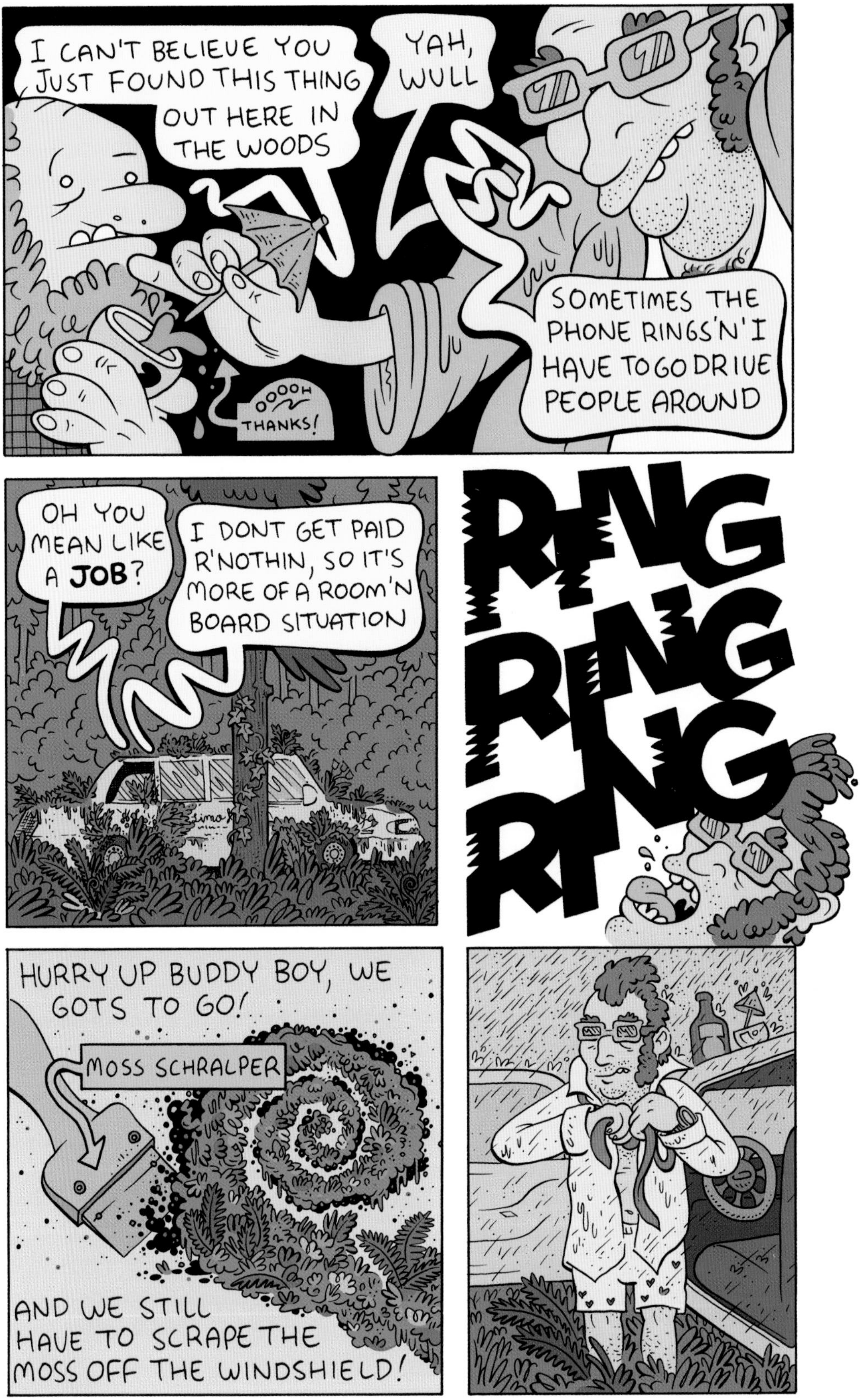
I CAN'T BELIEVE YOU JUST FOUND THIS THING OUT HERE IN THE WOODS
YAH, WULL
OOOOH THANKS!
SOMETIMES THE PHONE RINGS'N' I HAVE TO GO DRIVE PEOPLE AROUND
OH YOU MEAN LIKE A **JOB**?
I DONT GET PAID R'NOTHIN, SO IT'S MORE OF A ROOM'N BOARD SITUATION
RING RING RING
HURRY UP BUDDY BOY, WE GOTS TO GO!
MOSS SCHRALPER
AND WE STILL HAVE TO SCRAPE THE MOSS OFF THE WINDSHIELD!

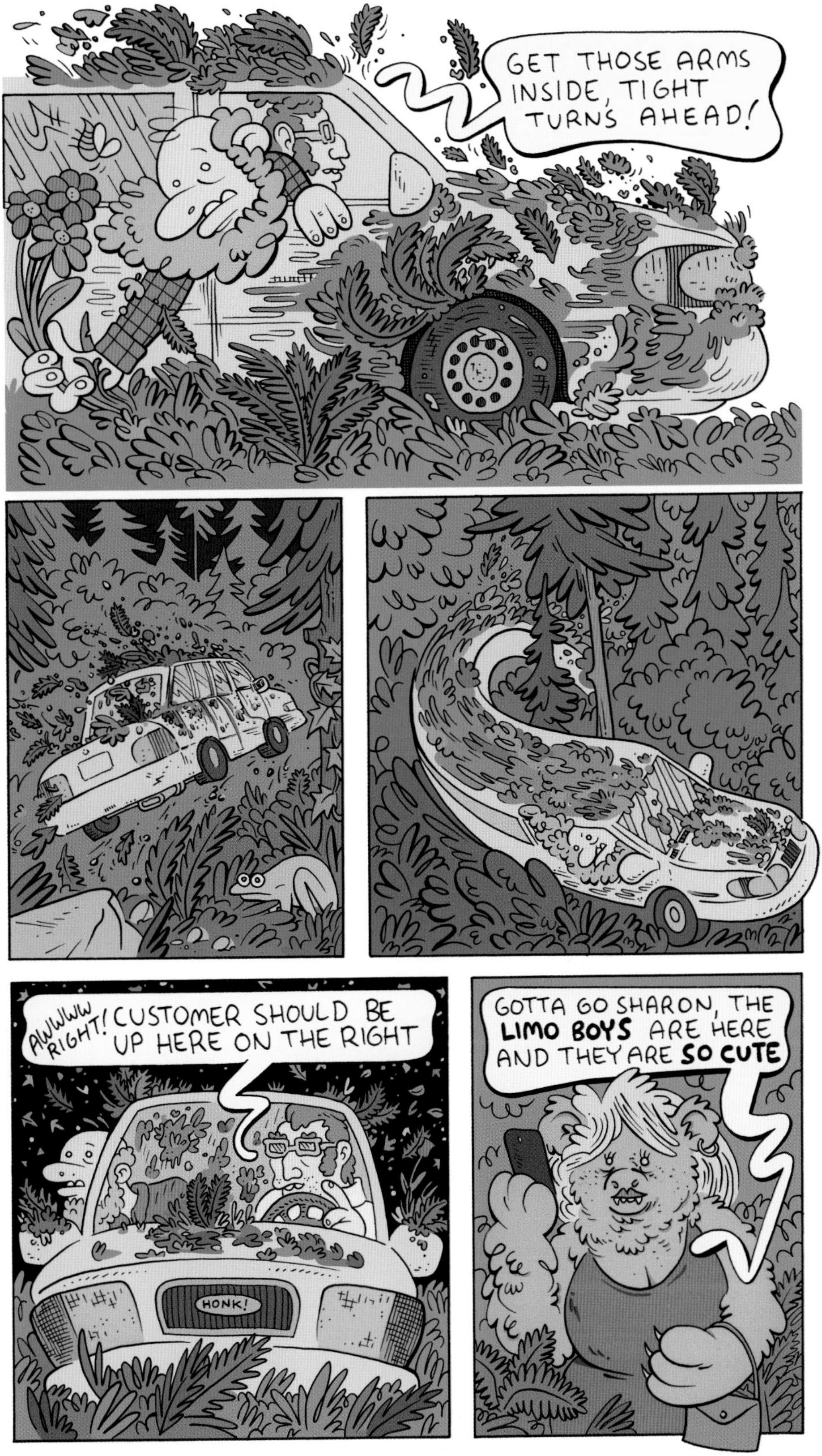
GET THOSE ARMS INSIDE, TIGHT TURNS AHEAD!
AWWWW RIGHT!
CUSTOMER SHOULD BE UP HERE ON THE RIGHT
HONK!
GOTTA GO SHARON, THE **LIMO BOYS** ARE HERE AND THEY ARE **SO CUTE**

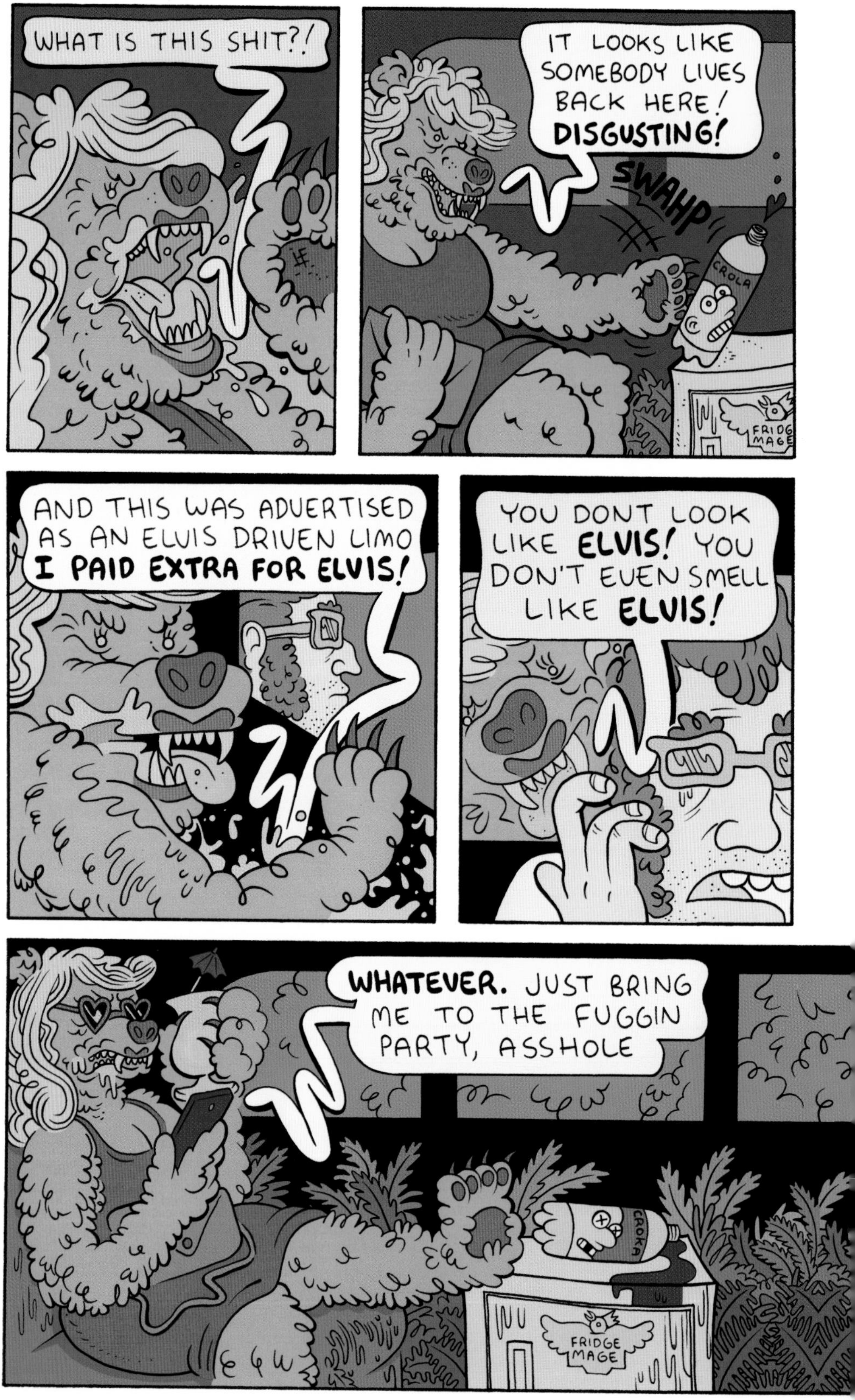
WHAT IS THIS SHIT?!
IT LOOKS LIKE SOMEBODY LIVES BACK HERE! DISGUSTING!
SWAHP
CROLA
FRIDGE MAGE
AND THIS WAS ADVERTISED AS AN ELVIS DRIVEN LIMO I PAID EXTRA FOR ELVIS!
YOU DONT LOOK LIKE ELVIS! YOU DON'T EVEN SMELL LIKE ELVIS!
WHATEVER. JUST BRING ME TO THE FUGGIN PARTY, ASSHOLE
CROKA
FRIDGE MAGE

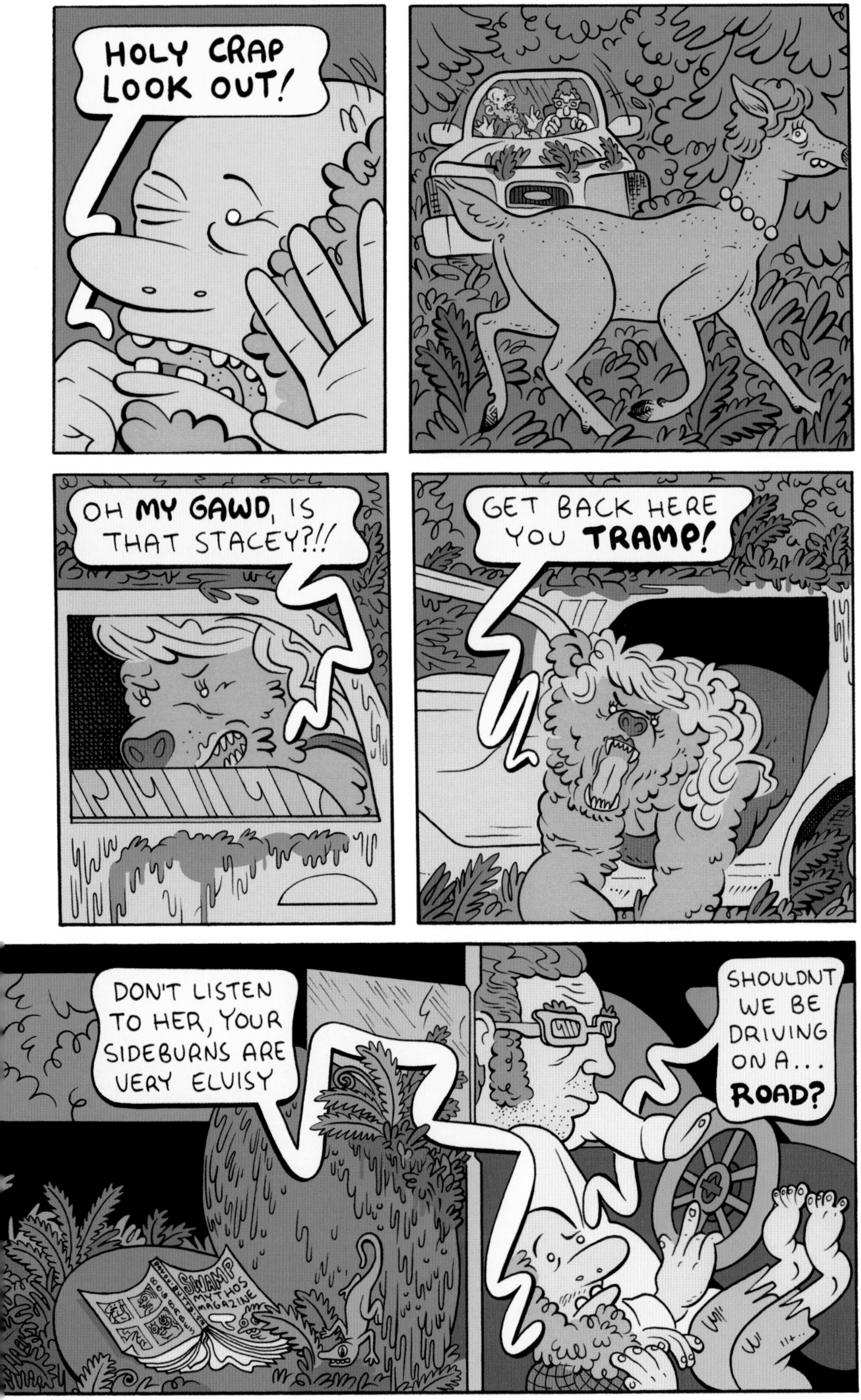
HOLY CRAP LOOK OUT!
OH MY GAWD, IS THAT STACEY?!!
GET BACK HERE YOU TRAMP!
DON'T LISTEN TO HER, YOUR SIDEBURNS ARE VERY ELVISY
SHOULDNT WE BE DRIVING ON A... ROAD?
SWAMP MYTHOS MAGAZINE

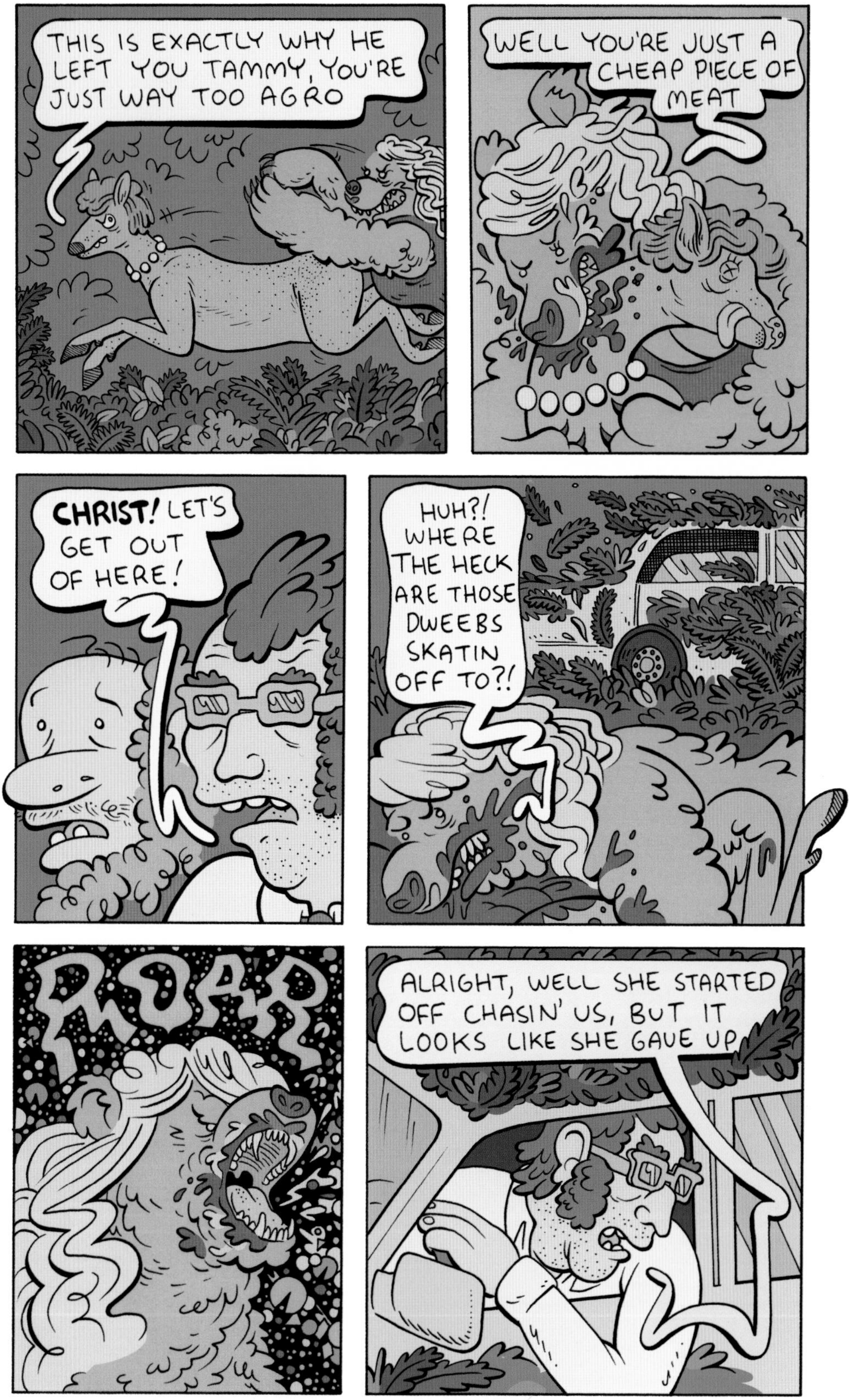
THIS IS EXACTLY WHY HE LEFT YOU TAMMY, YOU'RE JUST WAY TOO AGRO
WELL YOU'RE JUST A CHEAP PIECE OF MEAT
CHRIST! LET'S GET OUT OF HERE!
HUH?! WHERE THE HECK ARE THOSE DWEEBS SKATIN OFF TO?!
ROAR
ALRIGHT, WELL SHE STARTED OFF CHASIN' US, BUT IT LOOKS LIKE SHE GAVE UP

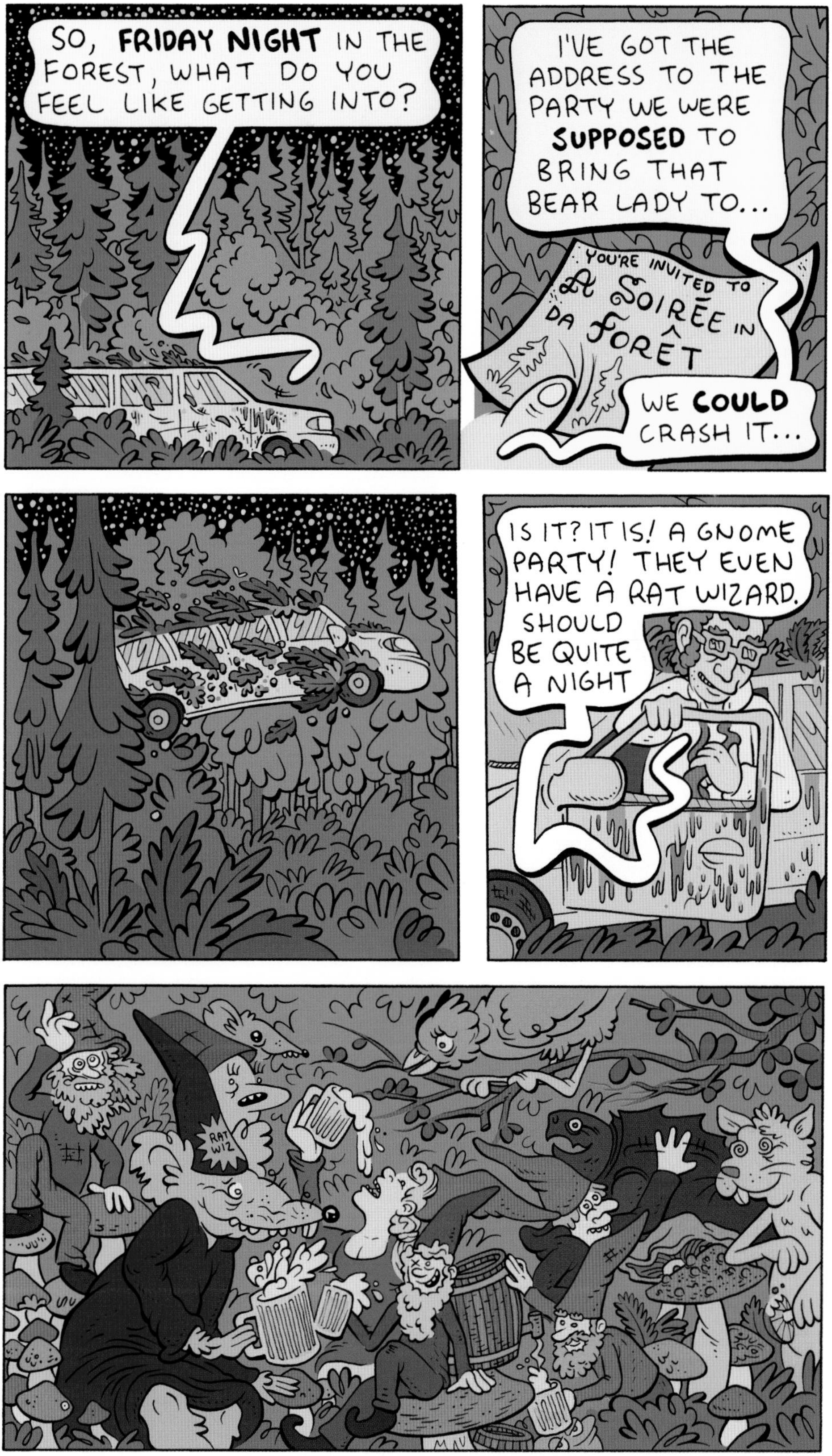
SO, **FRIDAY NIGHT** IN THE FOREST, WHAT DO YOU FEEL LIKE GETTING INTO?
I'VE GOT THE ADDRESS TO THE PARTY WE WERE **SUPPOSED** TO BRING THAT BEAR LADY TO...
YOU'RE INVITED TO A SOIRÉE IN DA FORÊT
WE **COULD** CRASH IT...
IS IT? IT IS! A GNOME PARTY! THEY EVEN HAVE A RAT WIZARD. SHOULD BE QUITE A NIGHT
RAT WIZ

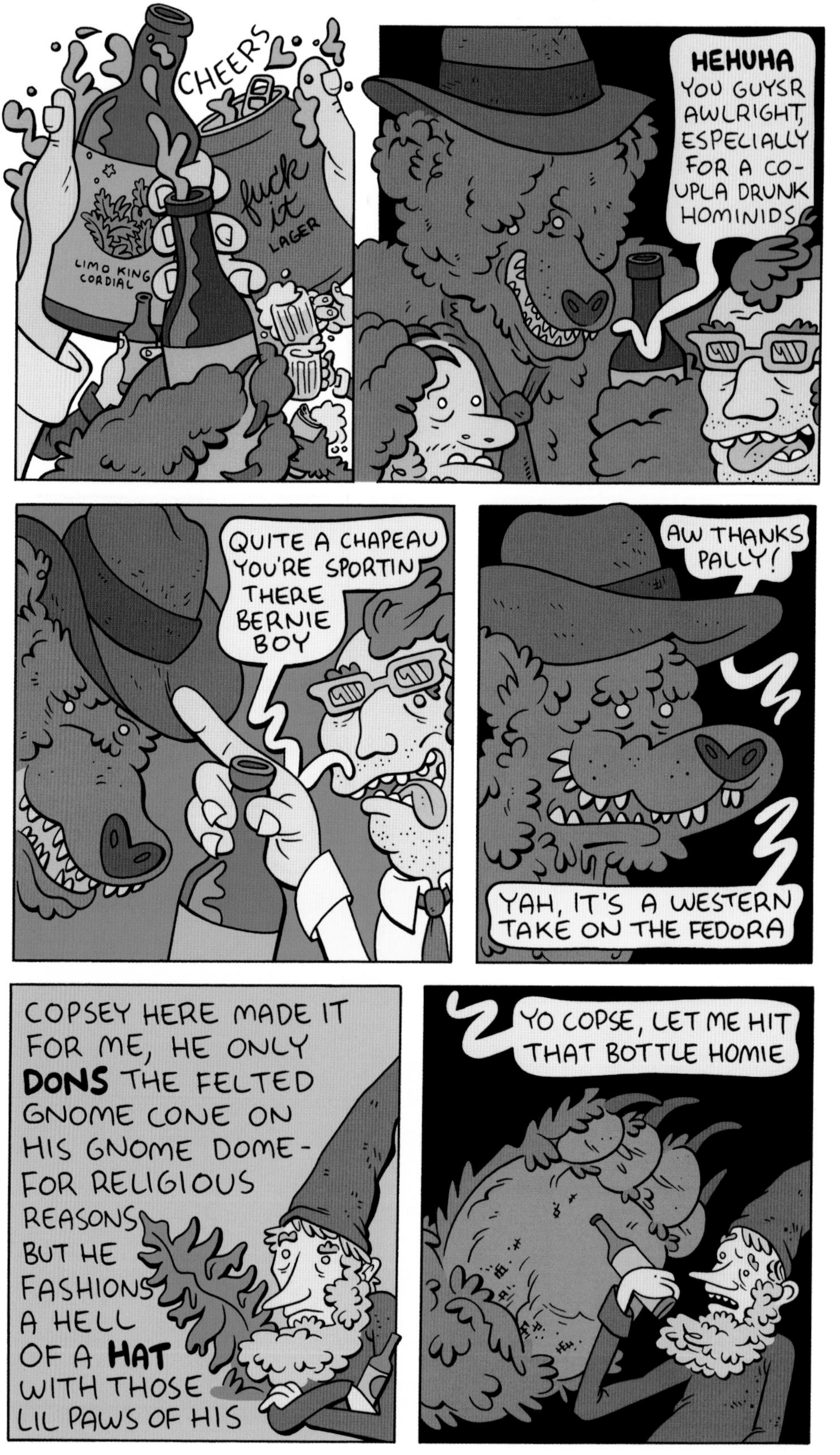
CHEERS
LIMO KING CORDIAL
fuck it LAGER
HEHUHA YOU GUYSR AWLRIGHT, ESPECIALLY FOR A CO-UPLA DRUNK HOMINIDS
QUITE A CHAPEAU YOU'RE SPORTIN THERE BERNIE BOY
AW THANKS PALLY!
YAH, IT'S A WESTERN TAKE ON THE FEDORA
COPSEY HERE MADE IT FOR ME, HE ONLY **DONS** THE FELTED GNOME CONE ON HIS GNOME DOME- FOR RELIGIOUS REASONS BUT HE FASHIONS A HELL OF A **HAT** WITH THOSE LIL PAWS OF HIS
YO COPSE, LET ME HIT THAT BOTTLE HOMIE

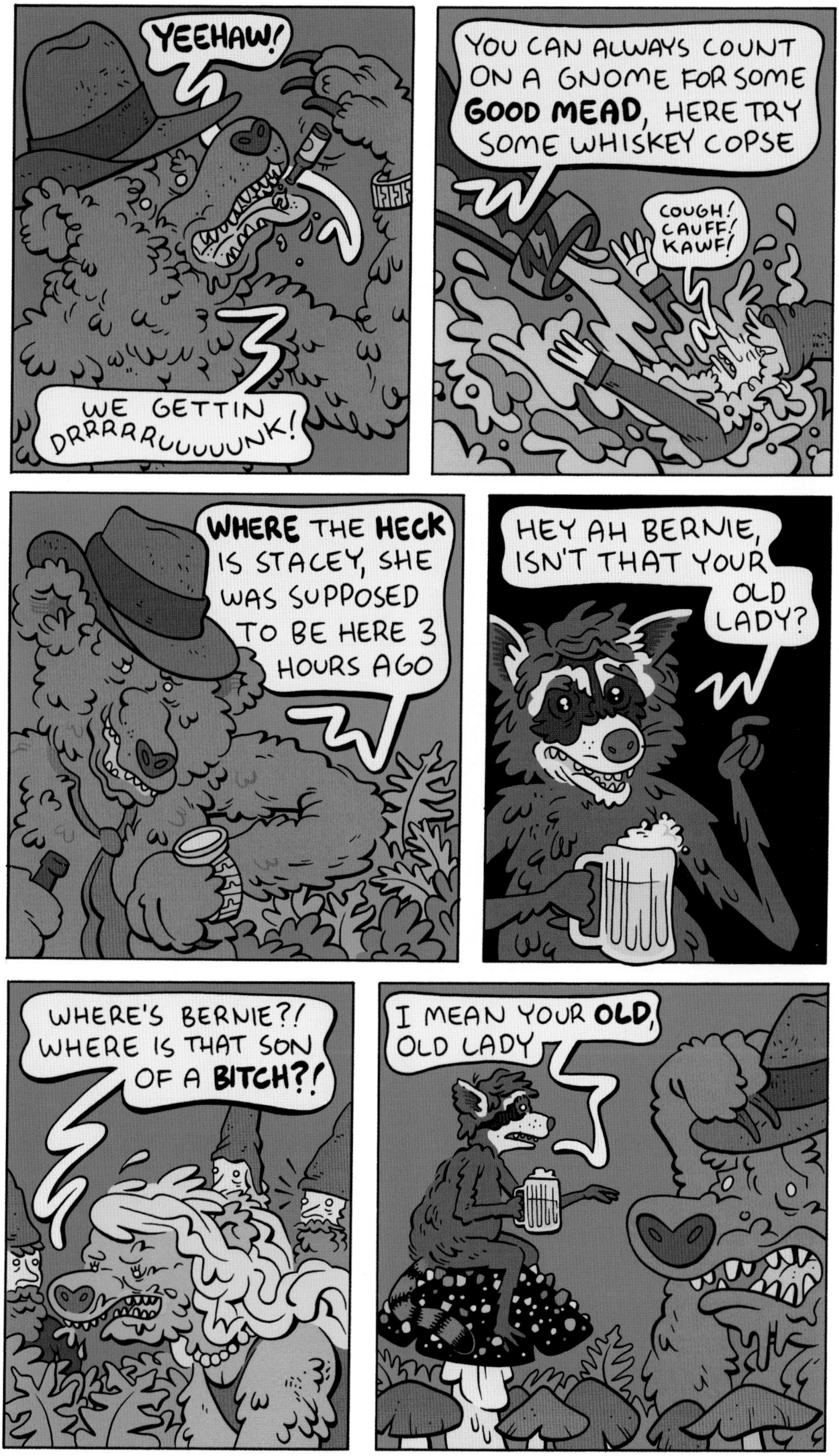
YEEHAW!
WE GETTIN DRRRRRRUUUUUUNK!
YOU CAN ALWAYS COUNT ON A GNOME FOR SOME **GOOD MEAD**, HERE TRY SOME WHISKEY COPSE
COUGH! CAUFF! KAWF!
WHERE THE **HECK** IS STACEY, SHE WAS SUPPOSED TO BE HERE 3 HOURS AGO
HEY AH BERNIE, ISN'T THAT YOUR OLD LADY?
WHERE'S BERNIE?! WHERE IS THAT SON OF A **BITCH?!**
I MEAN YOUR **OLD**, OLD LADY

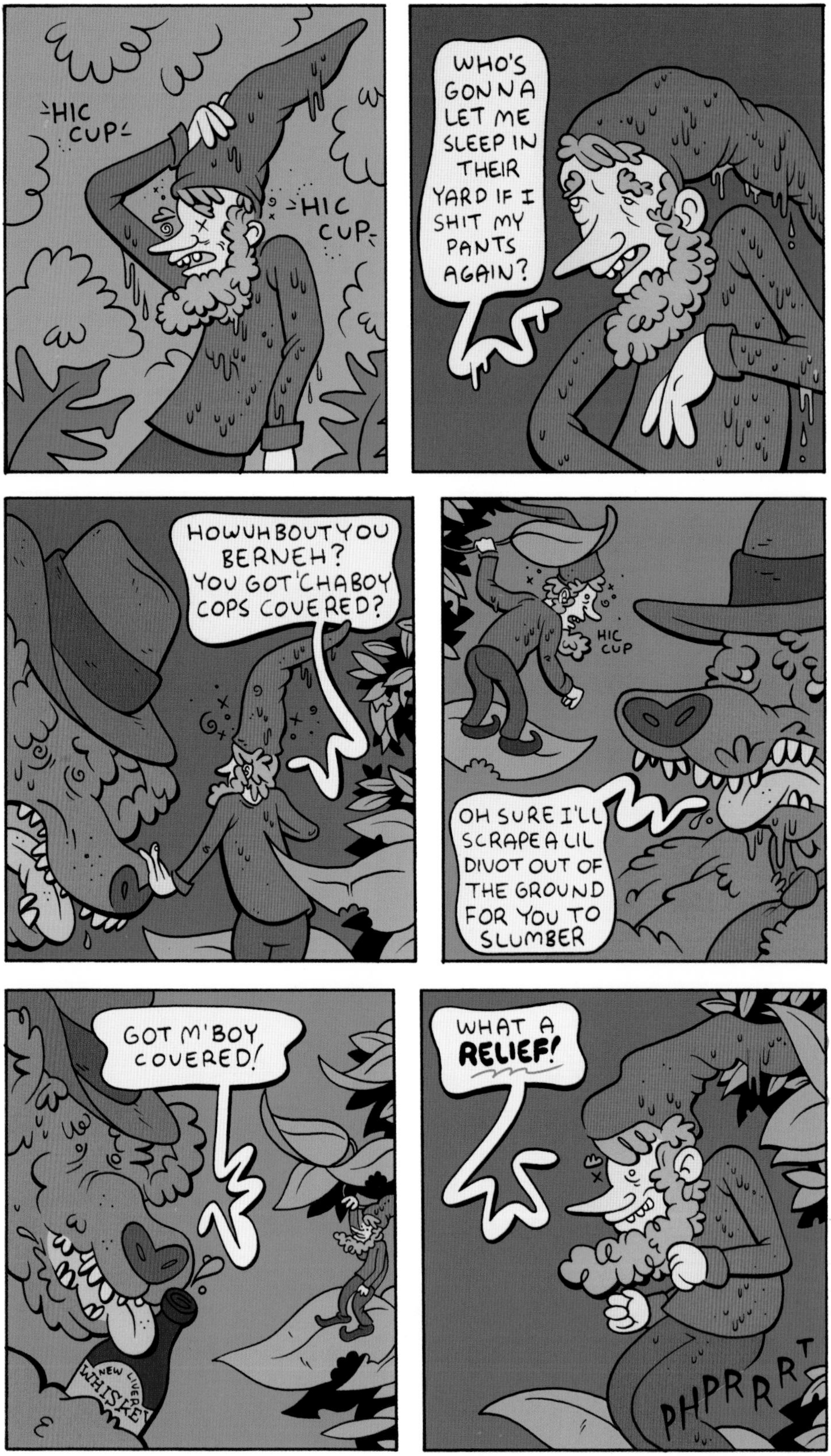
HIC CUP
HIC CUP
WHO'S GONNA LET ME SLEEP IN THEIR YARD IF I SHIT MY PANTS AGAIN?
HOWUHBOUTYOU BERNEH? YOU GOT'CHABOY COPS COVERED?
HIC CUP
OH SURE I'LL SCRAPE A LIL DIVOT OUT OF THE GROUND FOR YOU TO SLUMBER
GOT M'BOY COVERED!
NEW LIVER WHISKEY
WHAT A **RELIEF!**
PHPRRRRT

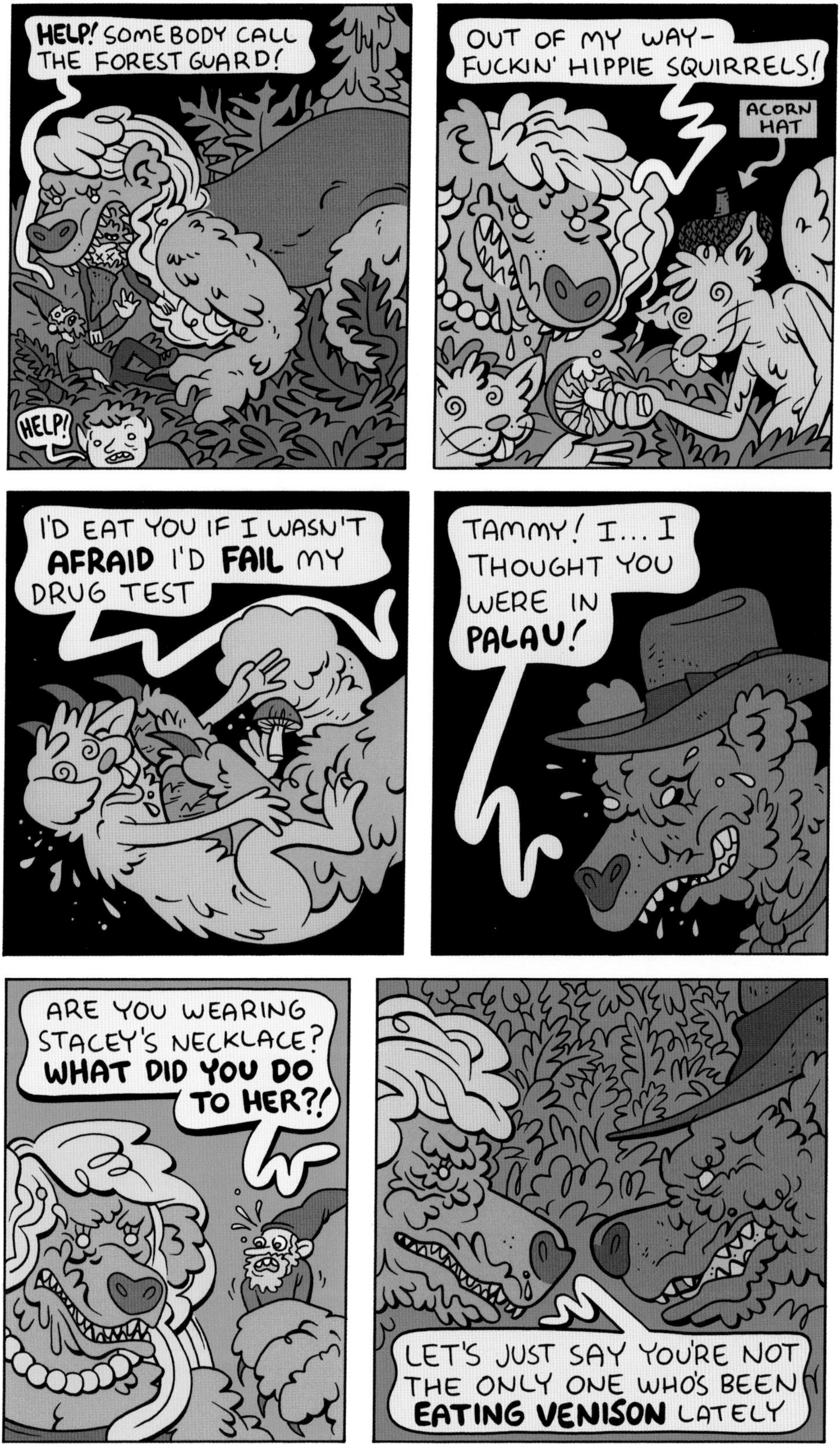
HELP! SOMEBODY CALL THE FOREST GUARD!
HELP!
OUT OF MY WAY- FUCKIN' HIPPIE SQUIRRELS!
ACORN HAT
I'D EAT YOU IF I WASN'T AFRAID I'D FAIL MY DRUG TEST
TAMMY! I... I THOUGHT YOU WERE IN PALAU!
ARE YOU WEARING STACEY'S NECKLACE? WHAT DID YOU DO TO HER?!
LET'S JUST SAY YOU'RE NOT THE ONLY ONE WHO'S BEEN EATING VENISON LATELY

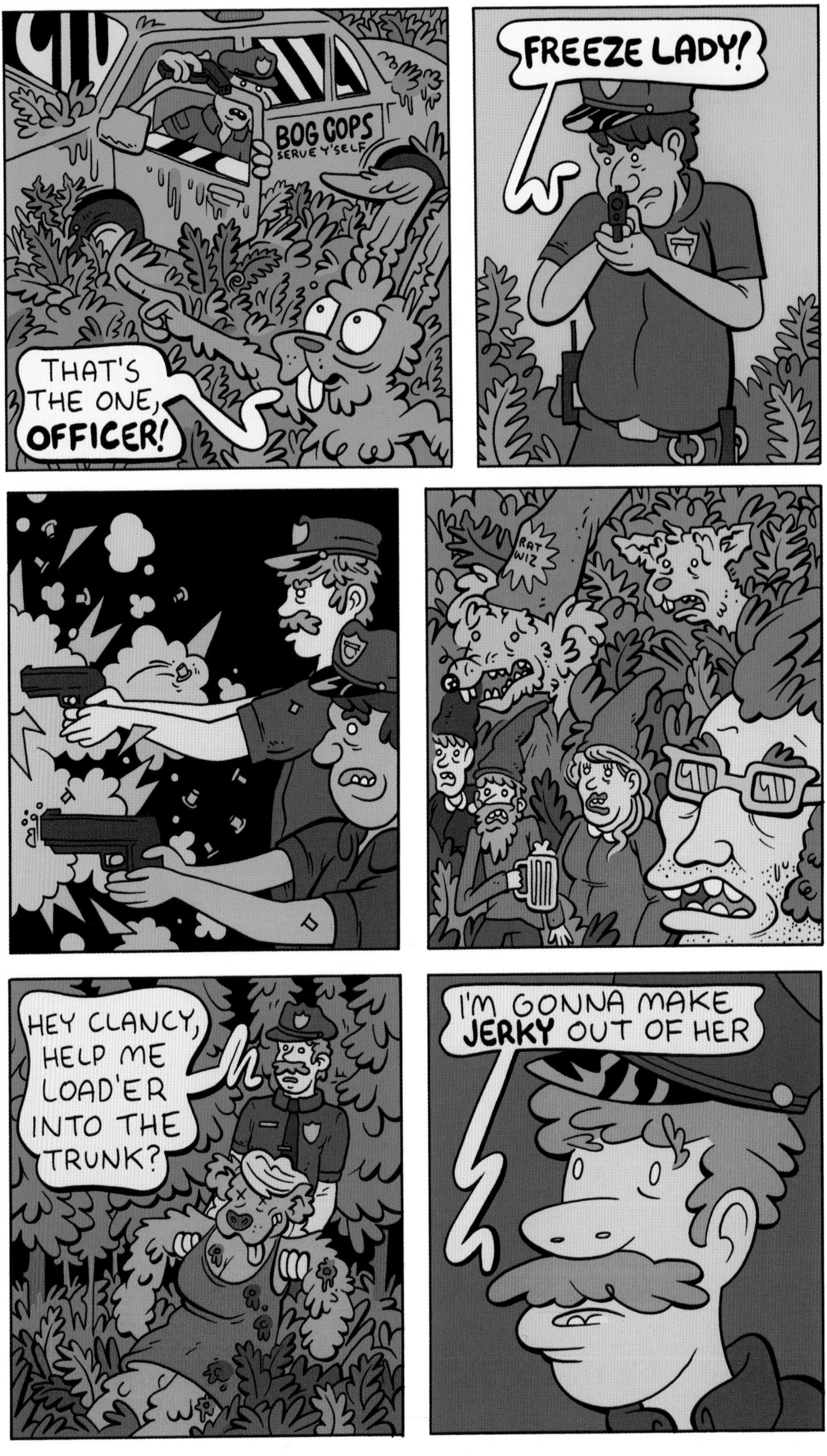
BOG COPS
SERVE Y'SELF
THAT'S THE ONE, OFFICER!
FREEZE LADY!
RAT WIZ
HEY CLANCY, HELP ME LOAD'ER INTO THE TRUNK?
I'M GONNA MAKE JERKY OUT OF HER

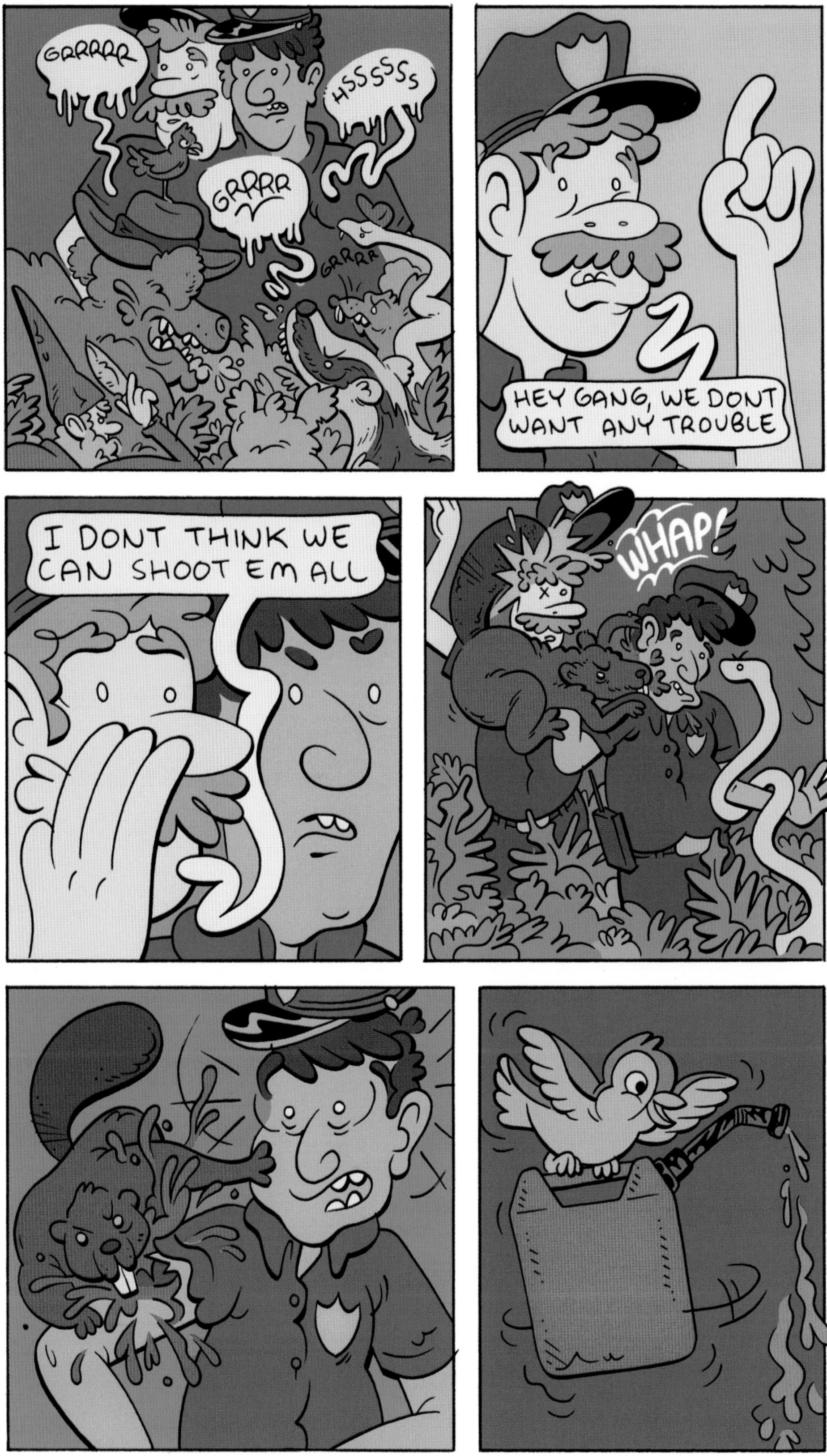
GRRRRR
HSSSSSS
GRRRR
GRRRR
HEY GANG, WE DONT WANT ANY TROUBLE
I DONT THINK WE CAN SHOOT EM ALL
WHAP!

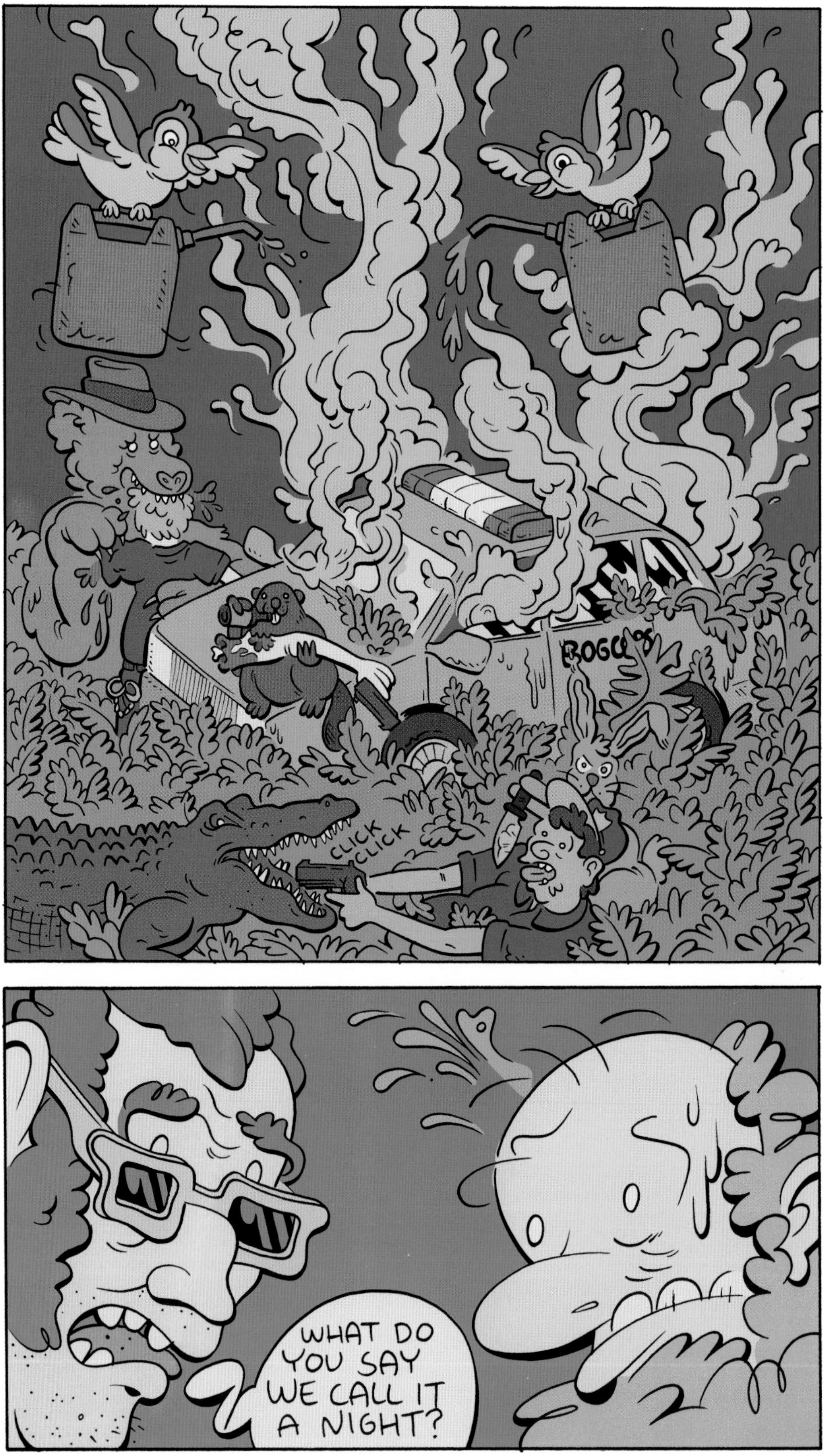
CLICK CLICK
WHAT DO YOU SAY WE CALL IT A NIGHT?

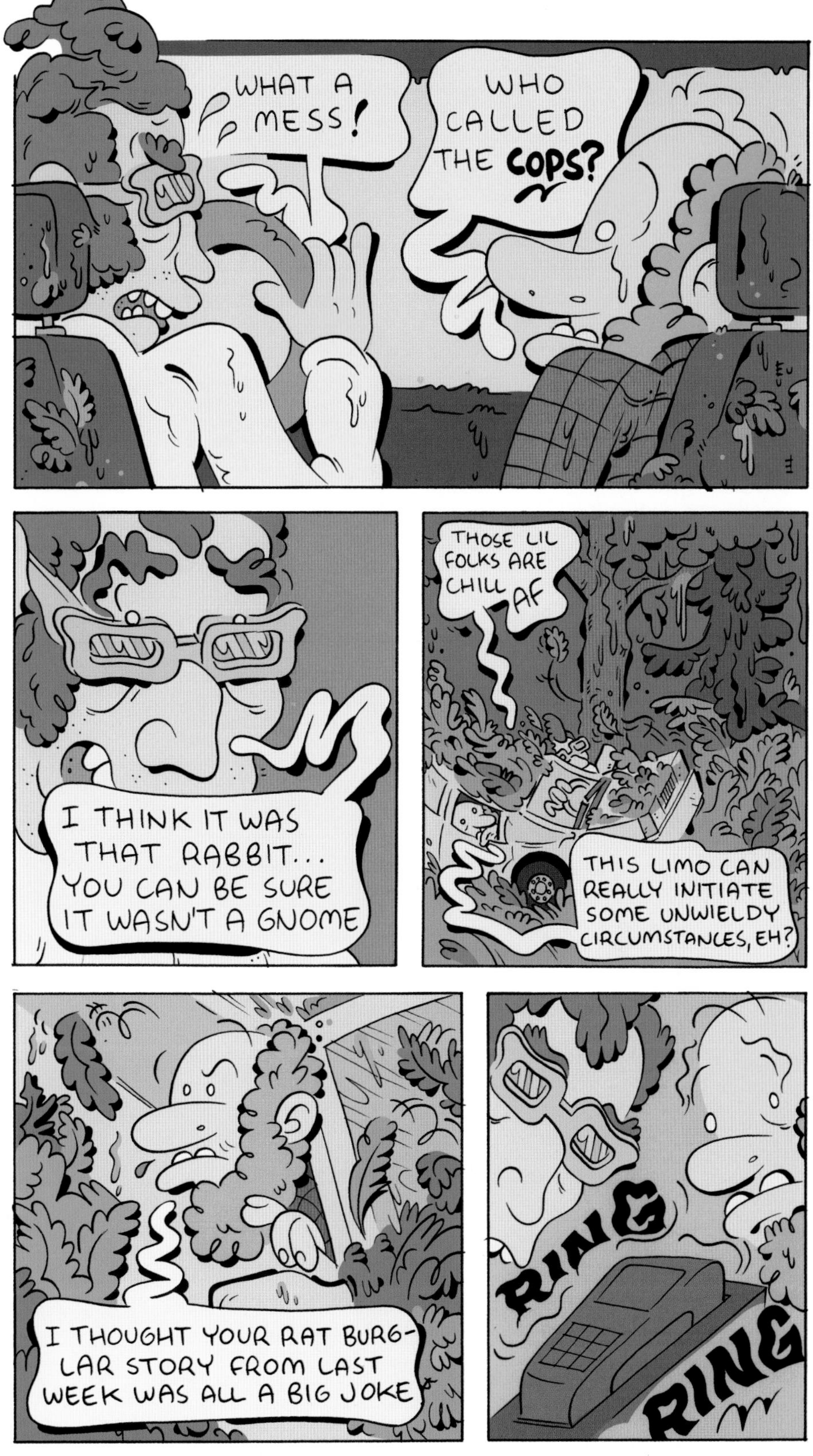
WHAT A MESS!
WHO CALLED THE COPS?
I THINK IT WAS THAT RABBIT... YOU CAN BE SURE IT WASN'T A GNOME
THOSE LIL FOLKS ARE CHILL AF
THIS LIMO CAN REALLY INITIATE SOME UNWIELDY CIRCUMSTANCES, EH?
I THOUGHT YOUR RAT BURG-LAR STORY FROM LAST WEEK WAS ALL A BIG JOKE
RING
RING

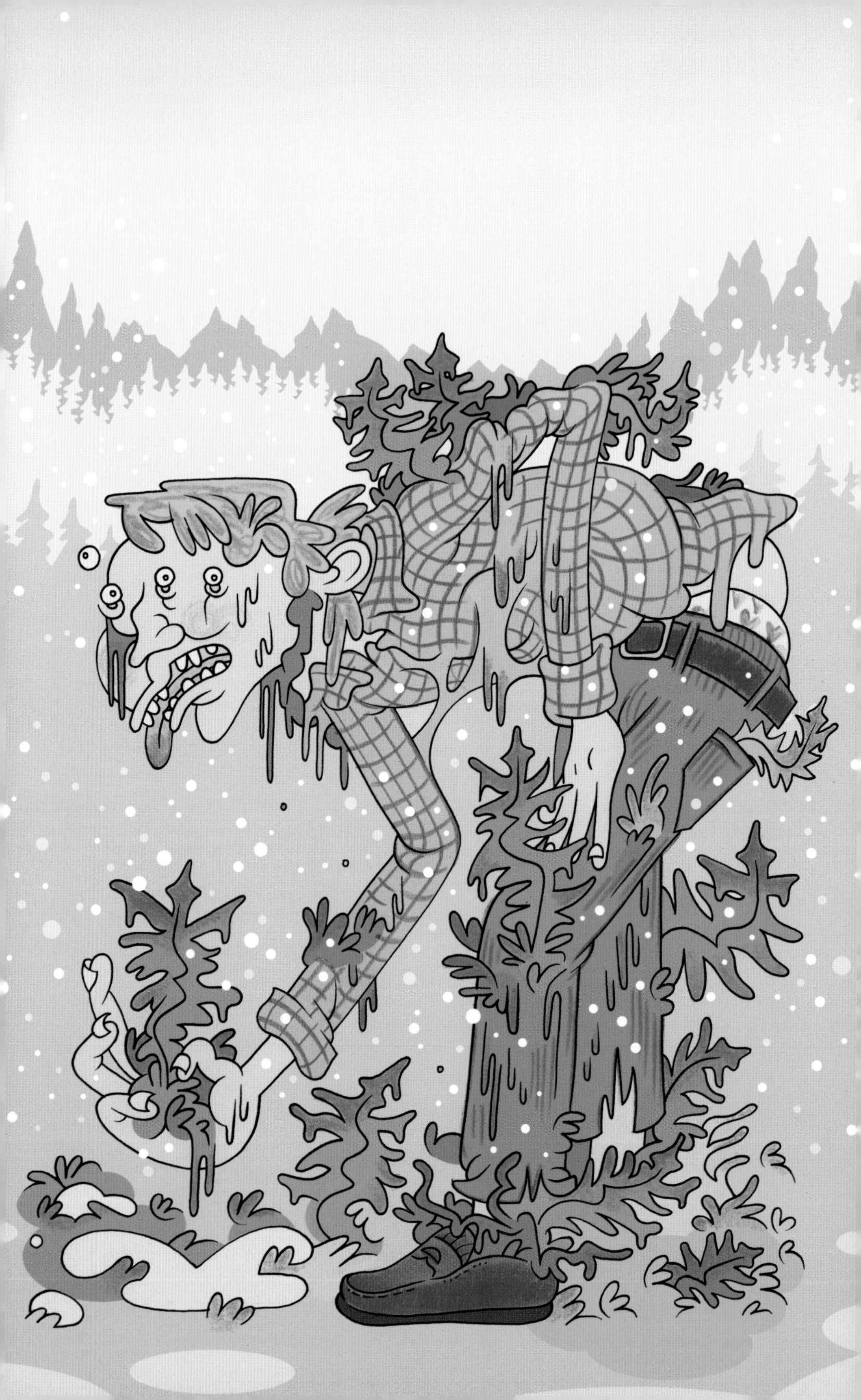

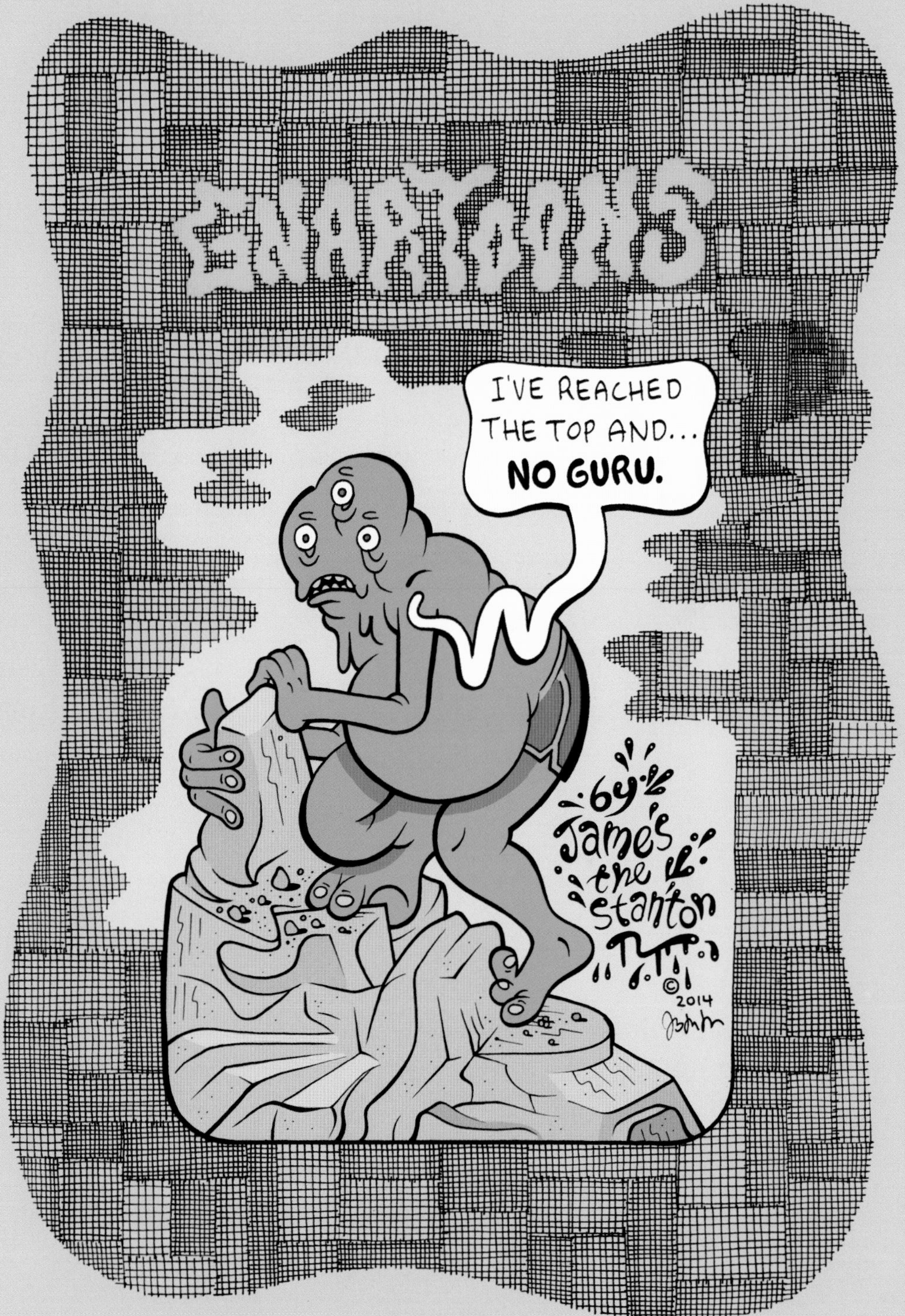
ENARTOONS
I'VE REACHED THE TOP AND... **NO GURU.**
by James the stanton
© 2014

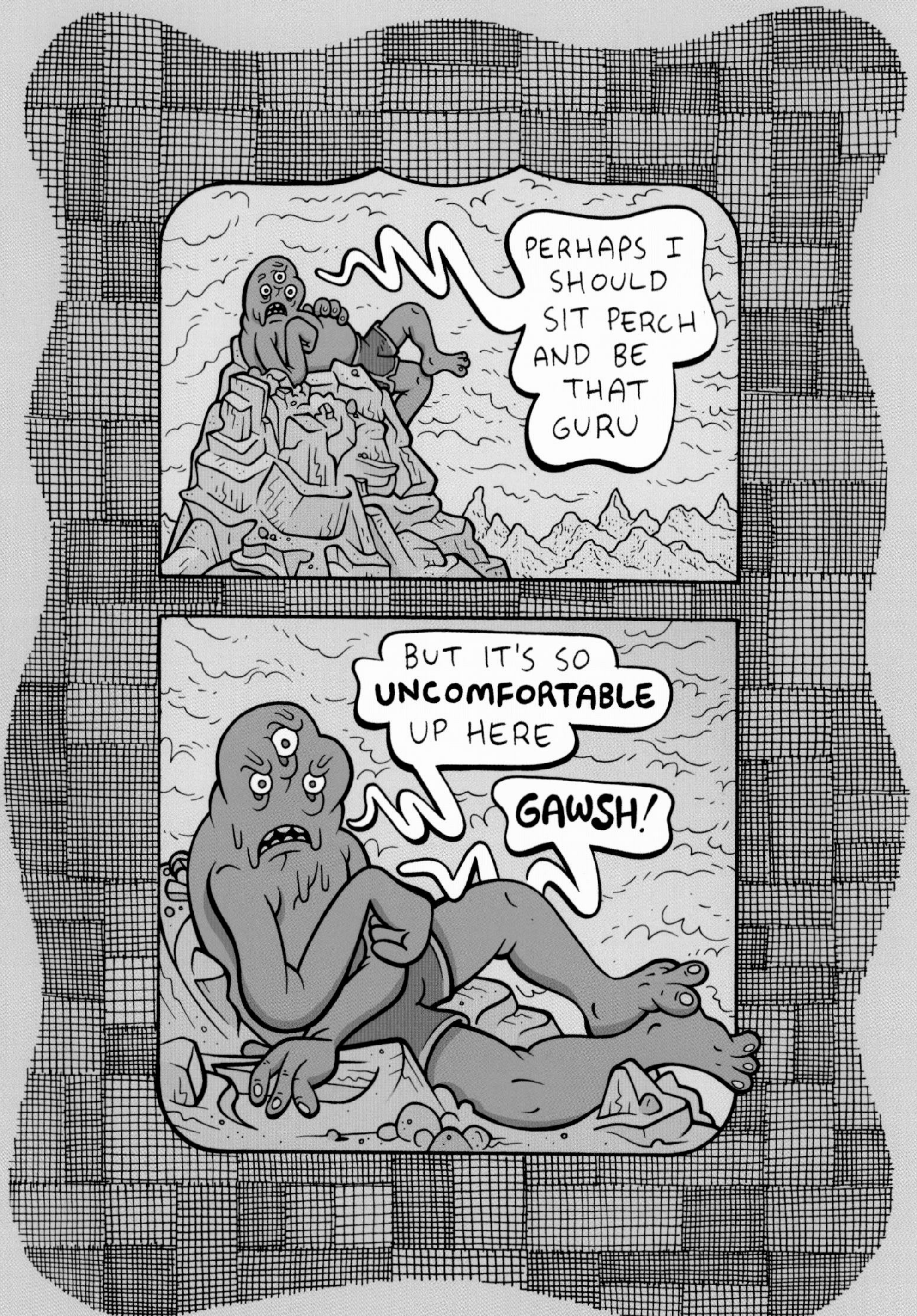
PERHAPS I SHOULD SIT PERCH AND BE THAT GURU
BUT IT'S SO **UNCOMFORTABLE** UP HERE
GAWSH!

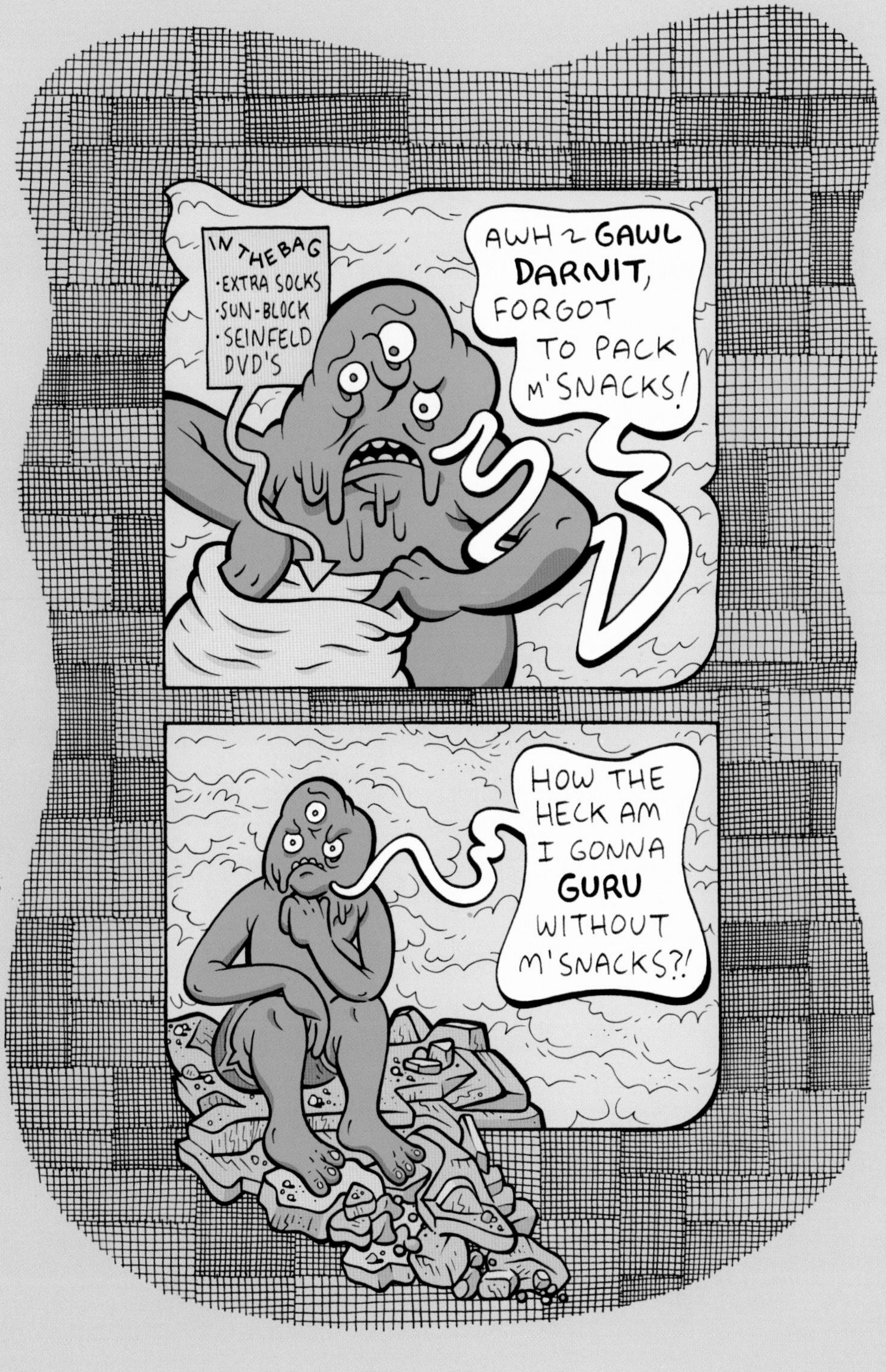
IN THE BAG
·EXTRA SOCKS
·SUN-BLOCK
·SEINFELD DVD'S
AWH 2 GAWL DARNIT, FORGOT TO PACK M'SNACKS!
HOW THE HECK AM I GONNA GURU WITHOUT M'SNACKS?!

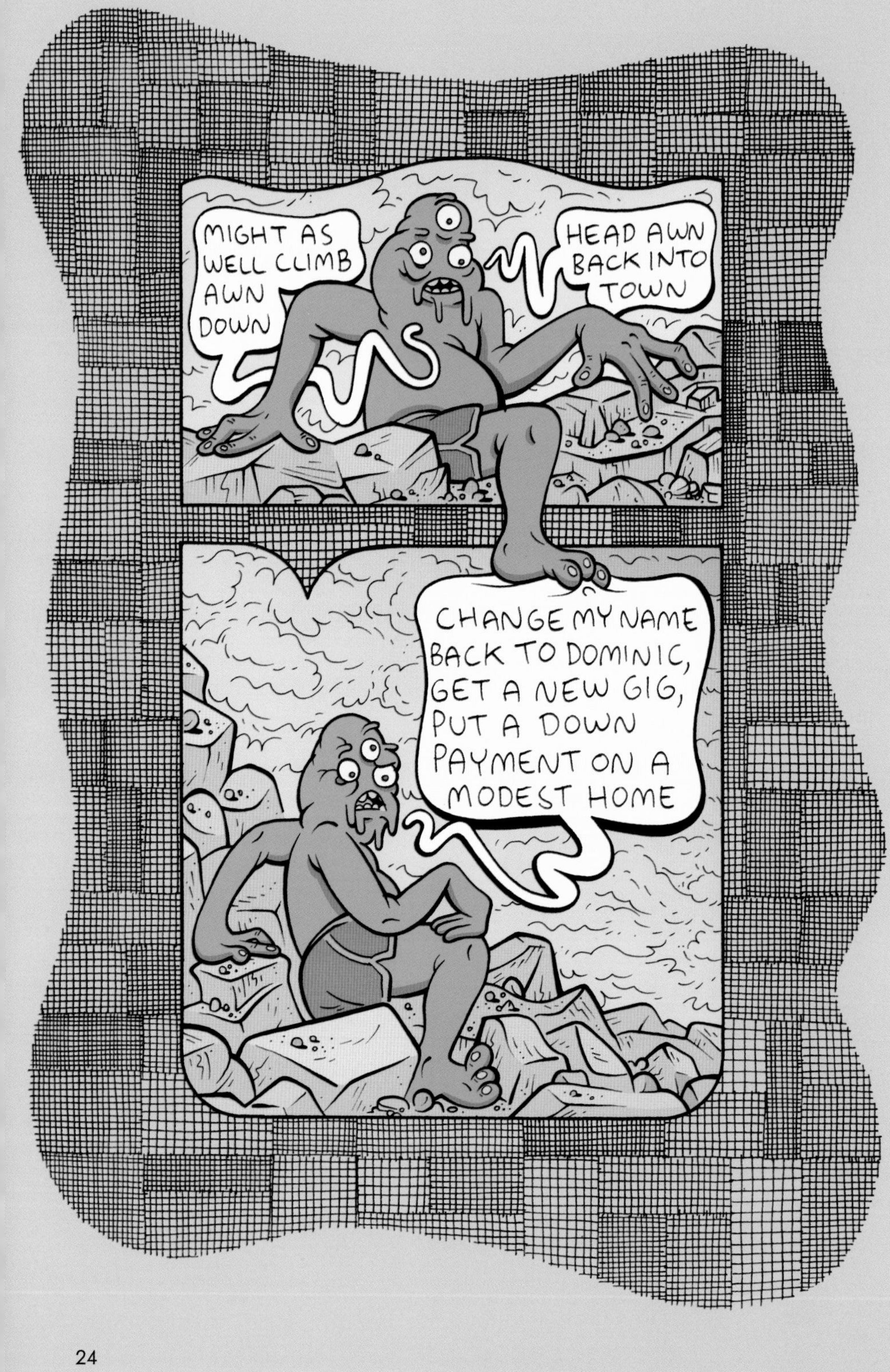
MIGHT AS WELL CLIMB AWN DOWN
HEAD AWN BACK INTO TOWN
CHANGE MY NAME BACK TO DOMINIC, GET A NEW GIG, PUT A DOWN PAYMENT ON A MODEST HOME

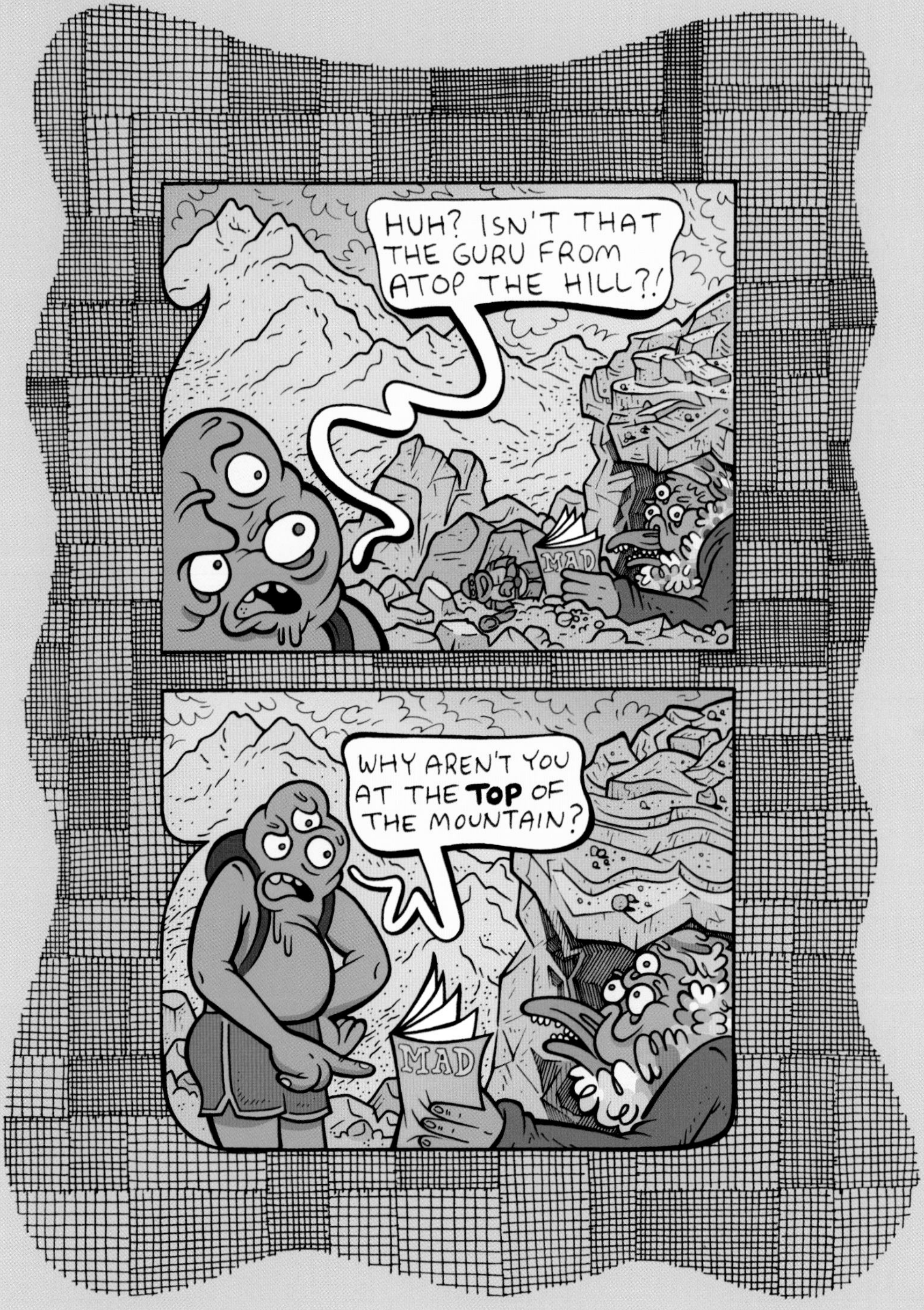
HUH? ISN'T THAT THE GURU FROM ATOP THE HILL?!
MAD
WHY AREN'T YOU AT THE **TOP** OF THE MOUNTAIN?
MAD

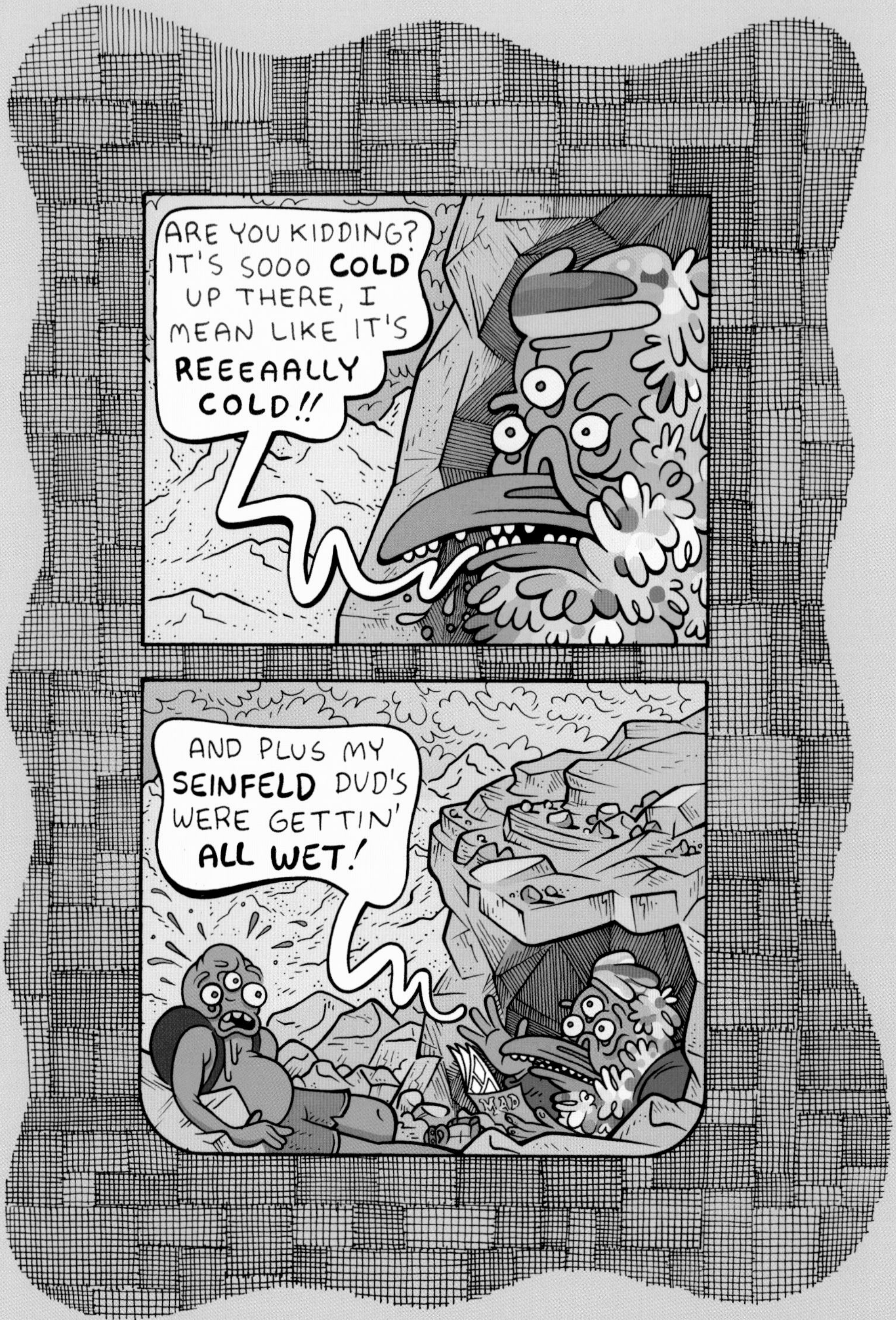
ARE YOU KIDDING? IT'S SOOO COLD UP THERE, I MEAN LIKE IT'S REEEAALLY COLD!!
AND PLUS MY SEINFELD DUD'S WERE GETTIN' ALL WET!

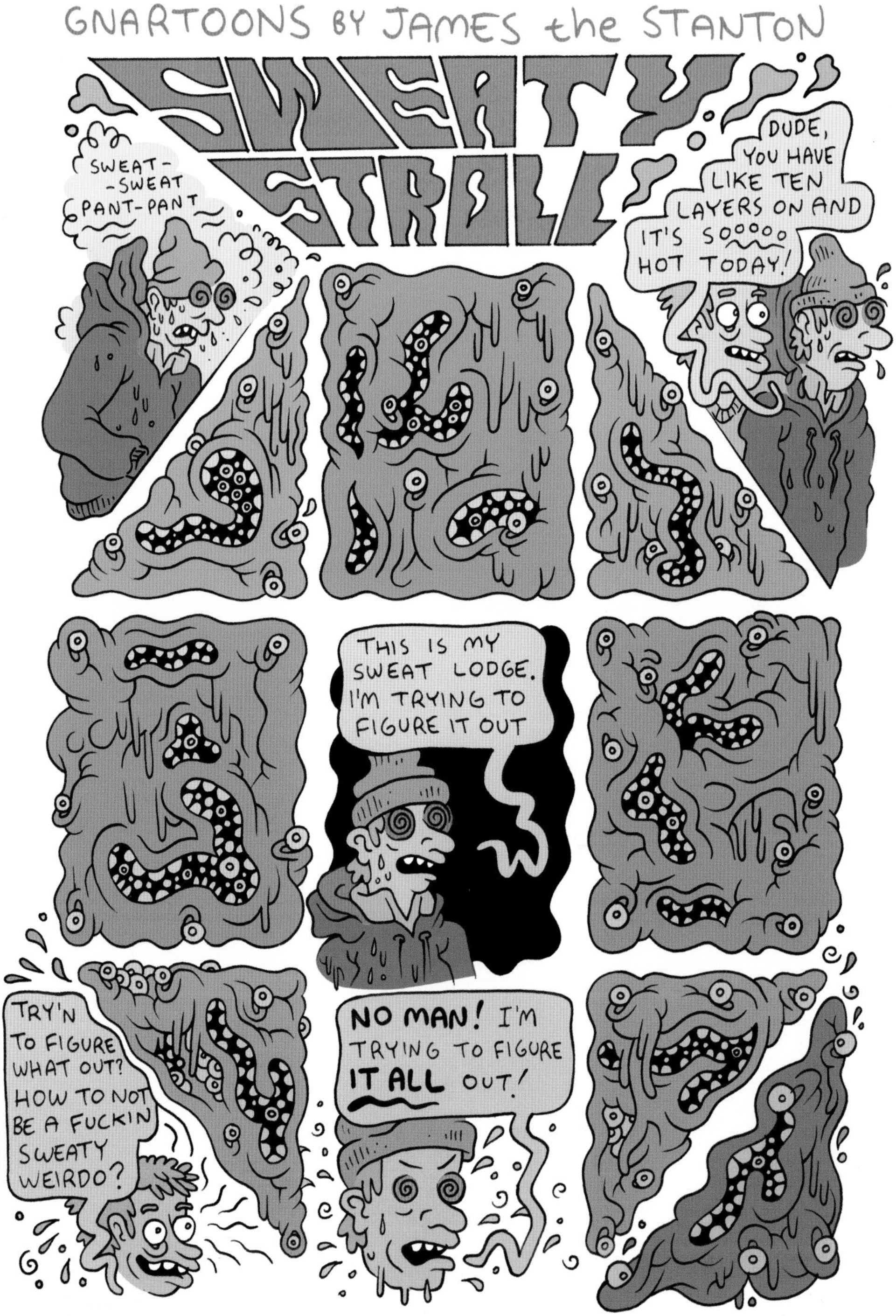
GNARTOONS BY JAMES the STANTON
SWEATY STROLL
SWEAT- -SWEAT PANT-PANT
DUDE, YOU HAVE LIKE TEN LAYERS ON AND IT'S SOOOOO HOT TODAY!
THIS IS MY SWEAT LODGE. I'M TRYING TO FIGURE IT OUT
TRY'N TO FIGURE WHAT OUT? HOW TO NOT BE A FUCKIN SWEATY WEIRDO?
NO MAN! I'M TRYING TO FIGURE IT ALL OUT!

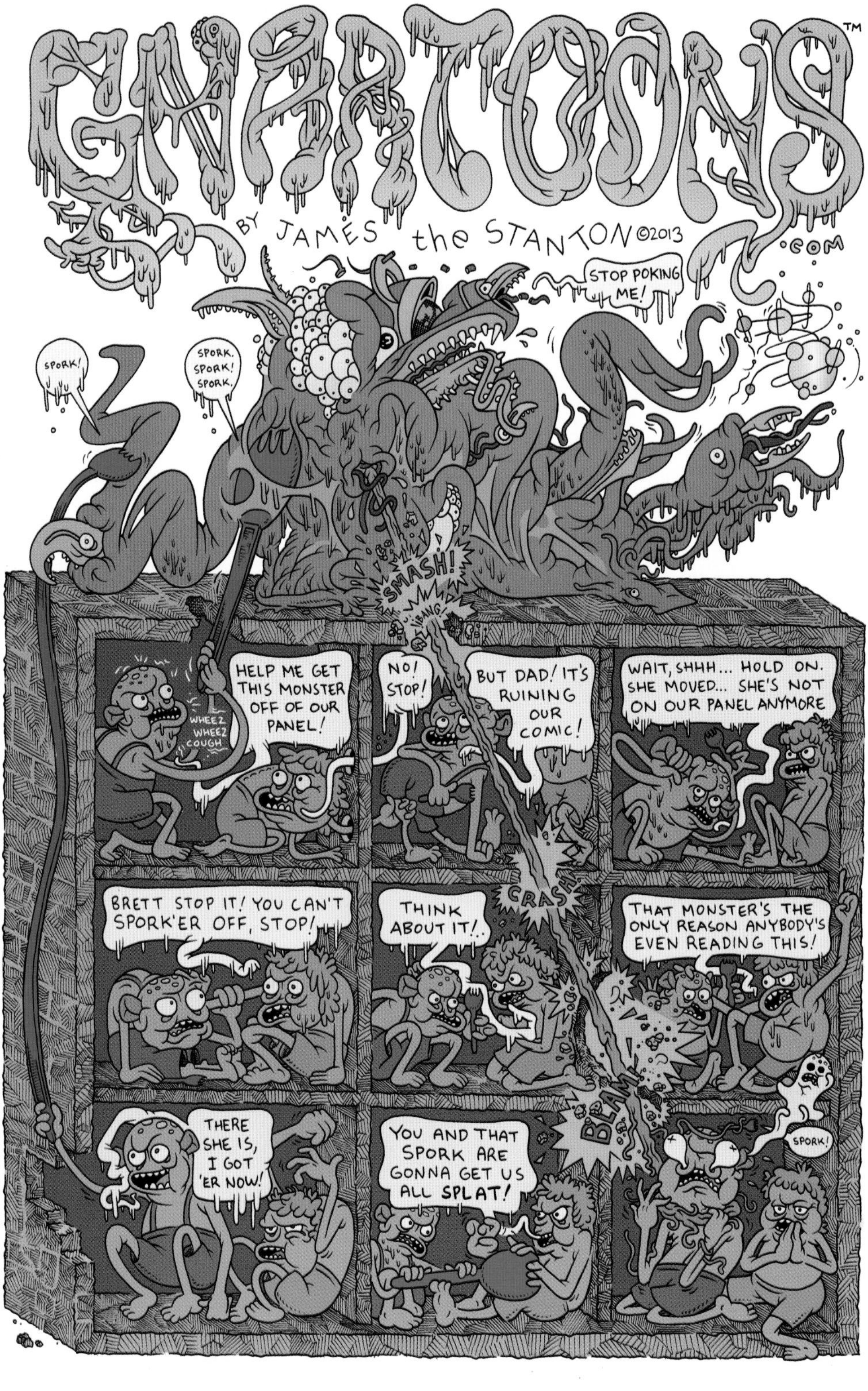
GNARTOONS™
BY JAMES the STANTON ©2013 .COM
STOP POKING ME!
SPORK!
SPORK. SPORK! SPORK.
SMASH!
BANG!
HELP ME GET THIS MONSTER OFF OF OUR PANEL!
WHEEZ WHEEZ COUGH
NO! STOP!
BUT DAD! IT'S RUINING OUR COMIC!
WAIT, SHHH... HOLD ON. SHE MOVED... SHE'S NOT ON OUR PANEL ANYMORE
CRASH
BRETT STOP IT! YOU CAN'T SPORK'ER OFF, STOP!
THINK ABOUT IT!
THAT MONSTER'S THE ONLY REASON ANYBODY'S EVEN READING THIS!
THERE SHE IS, I GOT 'ER NOW!
YOU AND THAT SPORK ARE GONNA GET US ALL SPLAT!
BLAM
SPORK!

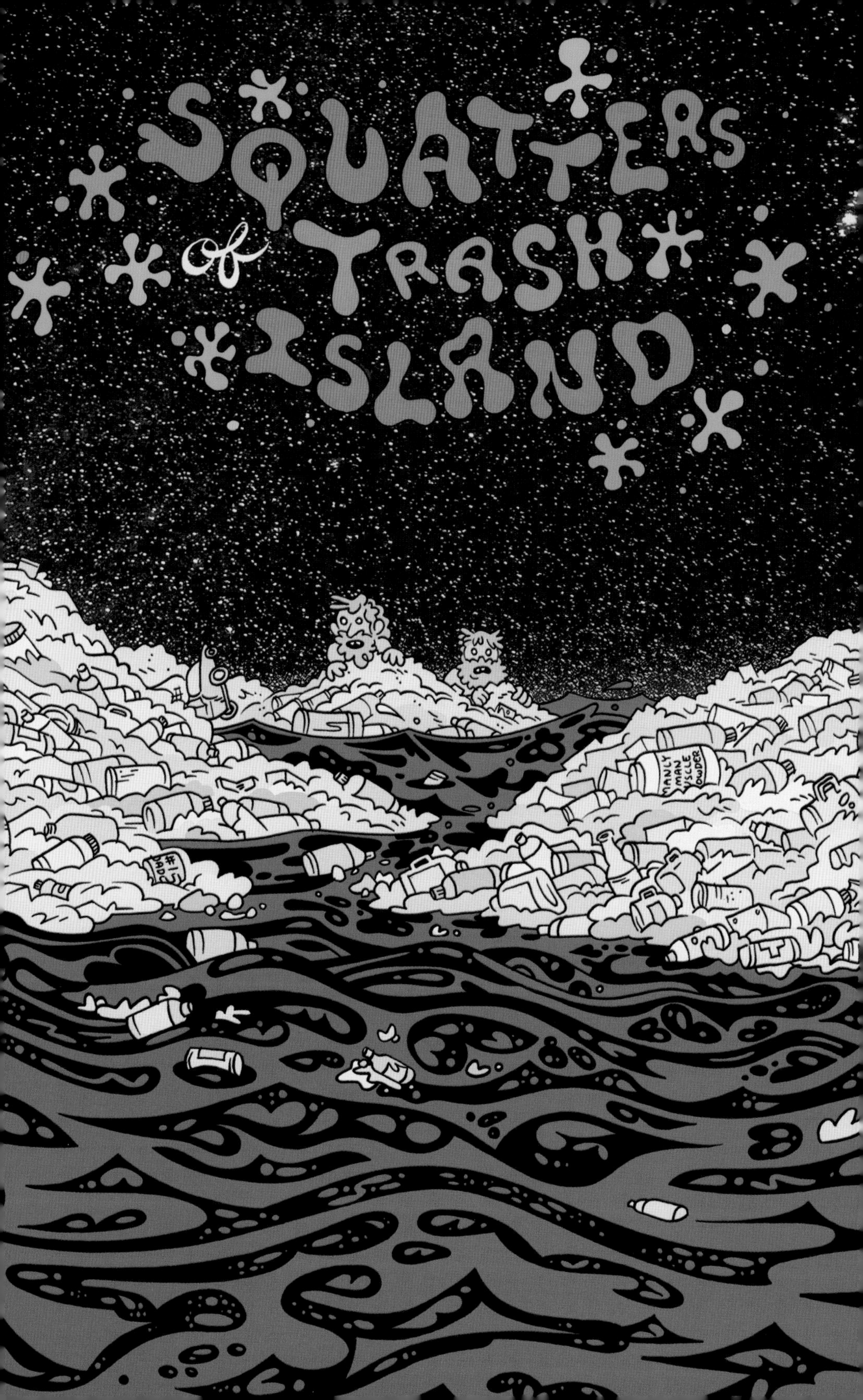
SQUATTERS
of
TRASH
ISLAND
MANLY
MAN

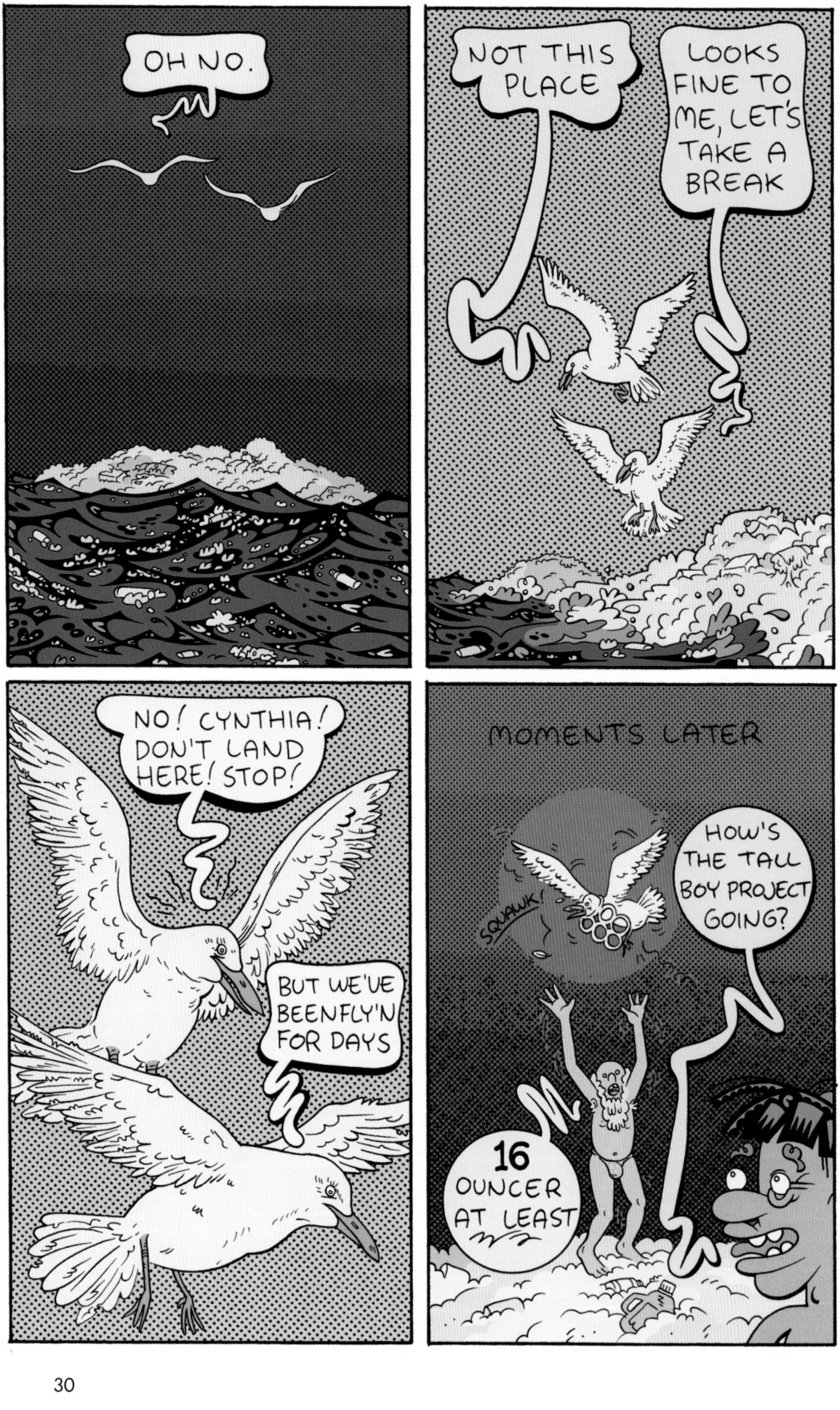
OH NO.
NOT THIS PLACE
LOOKS FINE TO ME, LET'S TAKE A BREAK
NO! CYNTHIA! DON'T LAND HERE! STOP!
BUT WE'VE BEENFLY'N FOR DAYS
MOMENTS LATER
SQUAWK!
HOW'S THE TALL BOY PROJECT GOING?
16 OUNCER AT LEAST

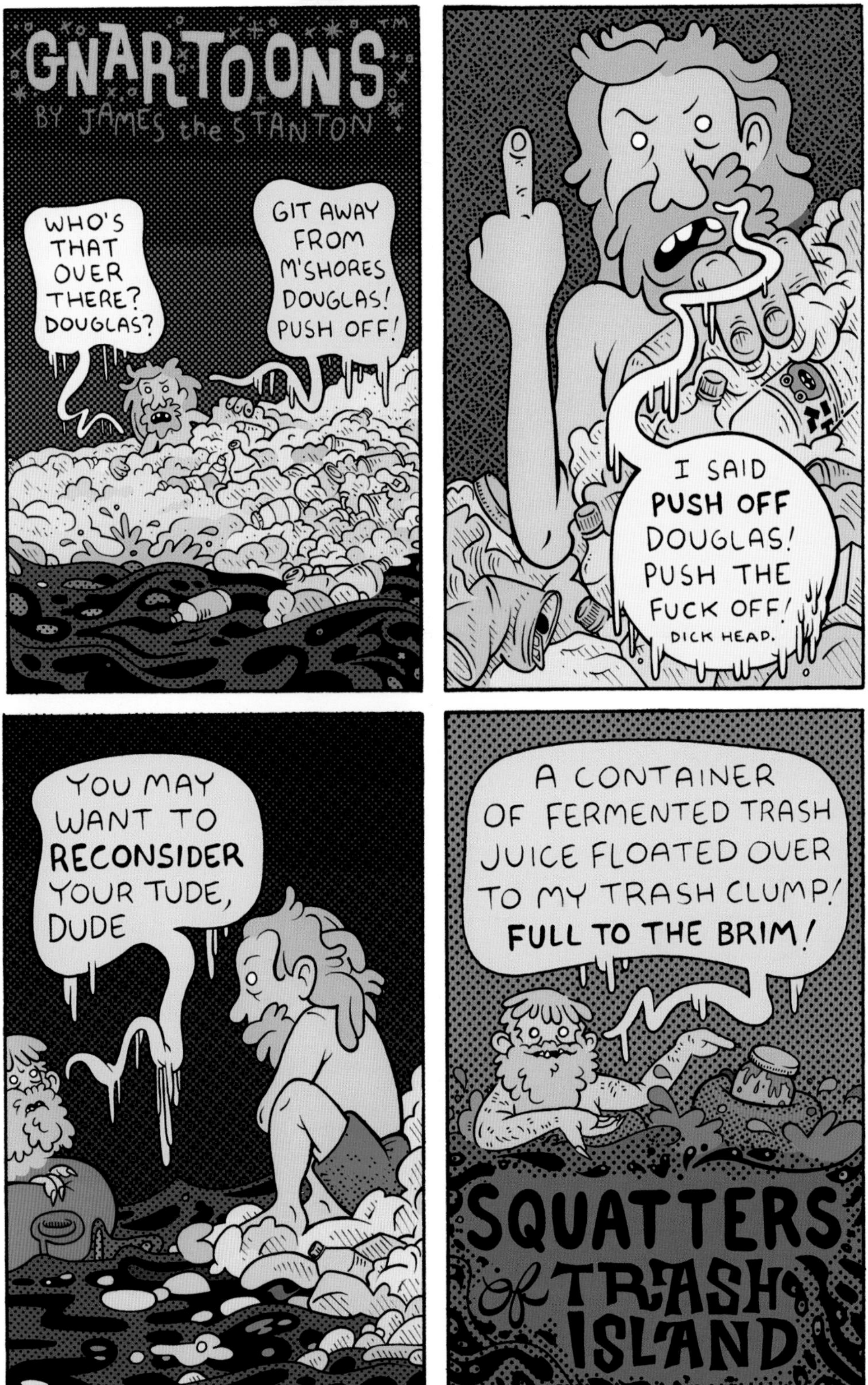
GNARTOONS
BY JAMES the STANTON
WHO'S THAT OVER THERE? DOUGLAS?
GIT AWAY FROM M'SHORES DOUGLAS! PUSH OFF!
I SAID PUSH OFF DOUGLAS! PUSH THE FUCK OFF! DICK HEAD.
YOU MAY WANT TO RECONSIDER YOUR TUDE, DUDE
A CONTAINER OF FERMENTED TRASH JUICE FLOATED OVER TO MY TRASH CLUMP! FULL TO THE BRIM!
SQUATTERS of TRASH ISLAND

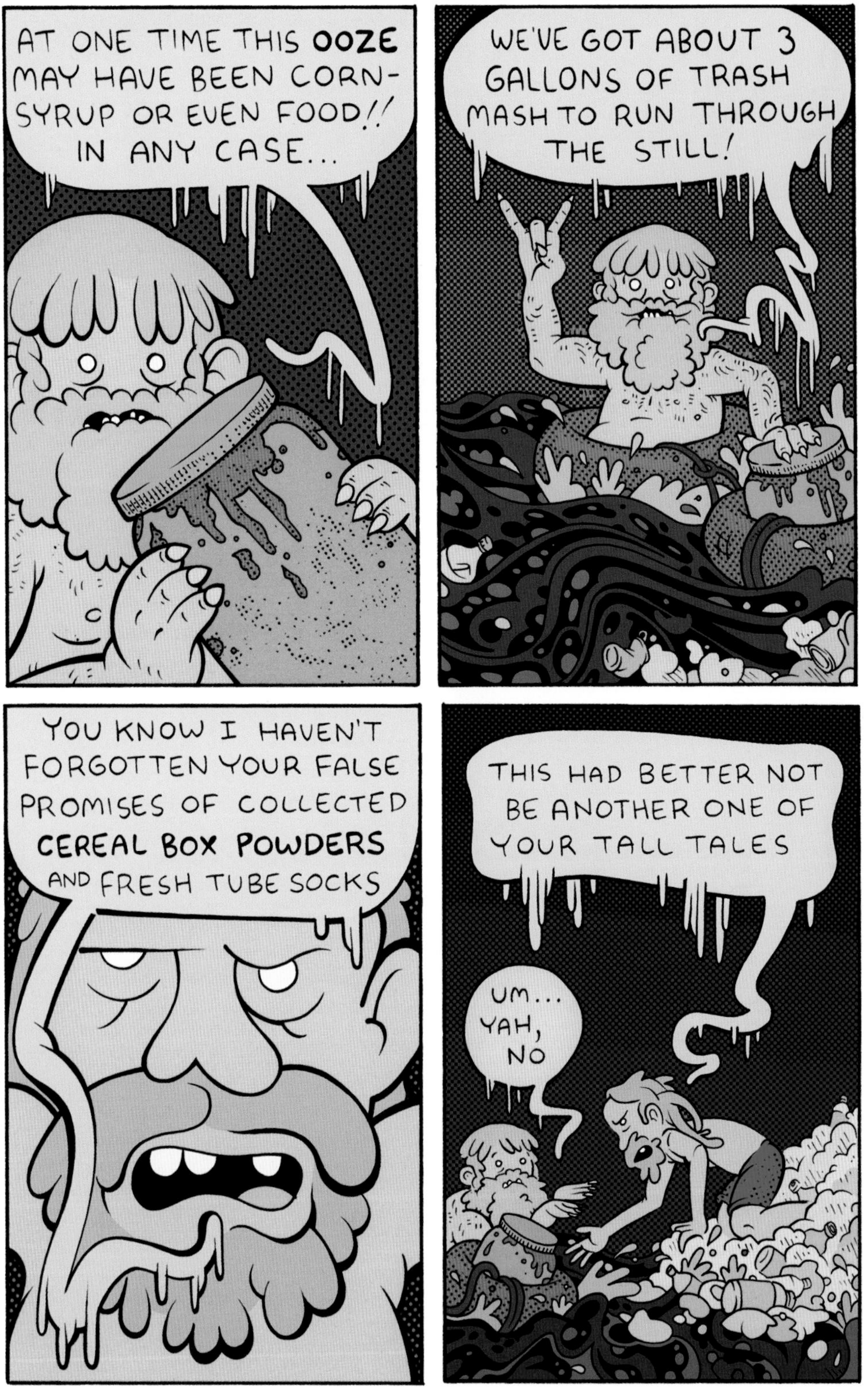
AT ONE TIME THIS OOZE MAY HAVE BEEN CORN-SYRUP OR EVEN FOOD!! IN ANY CASE...
WE'VE GOT ABOUT 3 GALLONS OF TRASH MASH TO RUN THROUGH THE STILL!
YOU KNOW I HAVEN'T FORGOTTEN YOUR FALSE PROMISES OF COLLECTED CEREAL BOX POWDERS AND FRESH TUBE SOCKS
THIS HAD BETTER NOT BE ANOTHER ONE OF YOUR TALL TALES
UM... YAH, NO

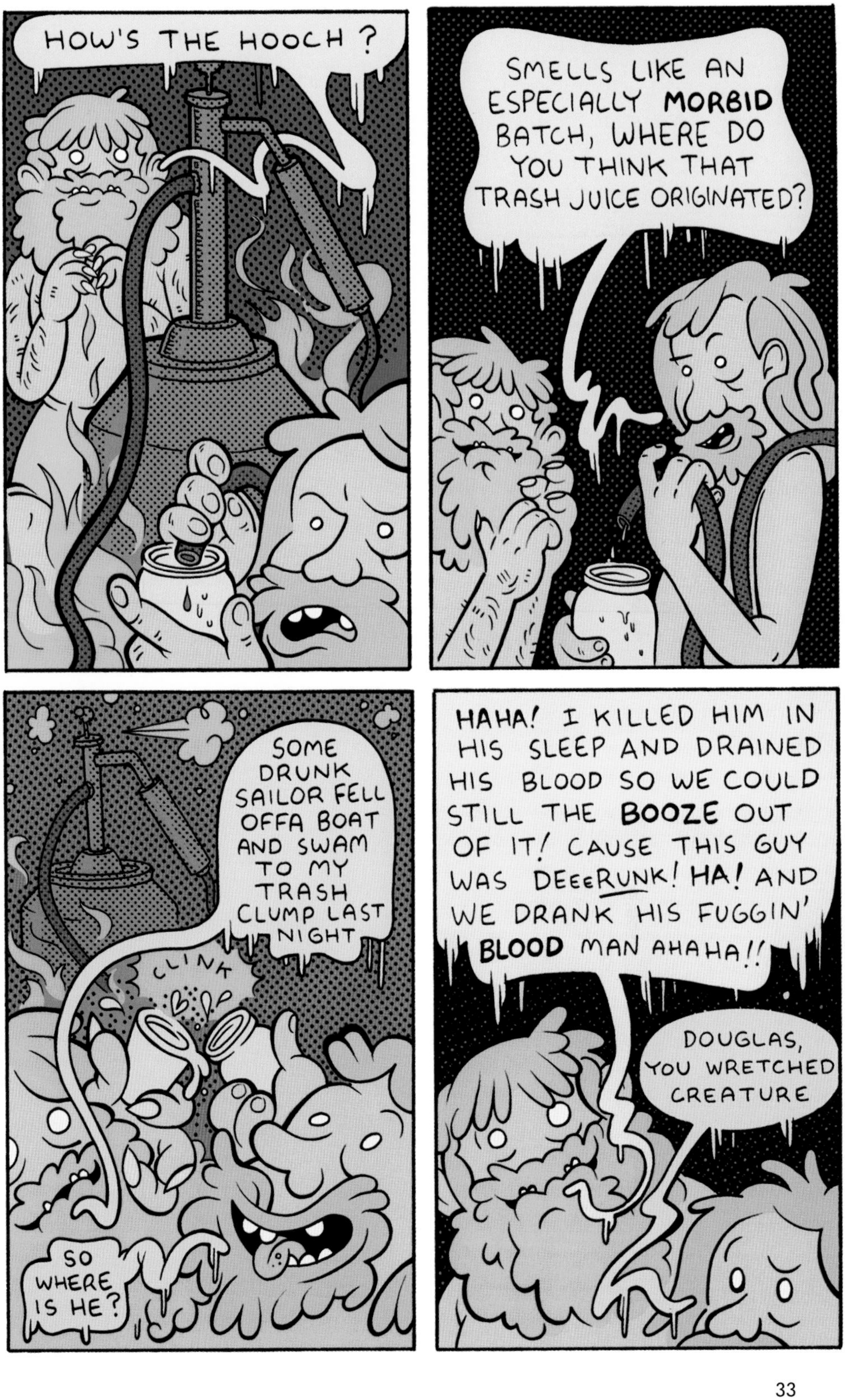
HOW'S THE HOOCH?
SMELLS LIKE AN ESPECIALLY MORBID BATCH, WHERE DO YOU THINK THAT TRASH JUICE ORIGINATED?
SOME DRUNK SAILOR FELL OFFA BOAT AND SWAM TO MY TRASH CLUMP LAST NIGHT
CLINK
SO WHERE IS HE?
HAHA! I KILLED HIM IN HIS SLEEP AND DRAINED HIS BLOOD SO WE COULD STILL THE BOOZE OUT OF IT! CAUSE THIS GUY WAS DEEeRUNK! HA! AND WE DRANK HIS FUGGIN' BLOOD MAN AHAHA!!
DOUGLAS, YOU WRETCHED CREATURE

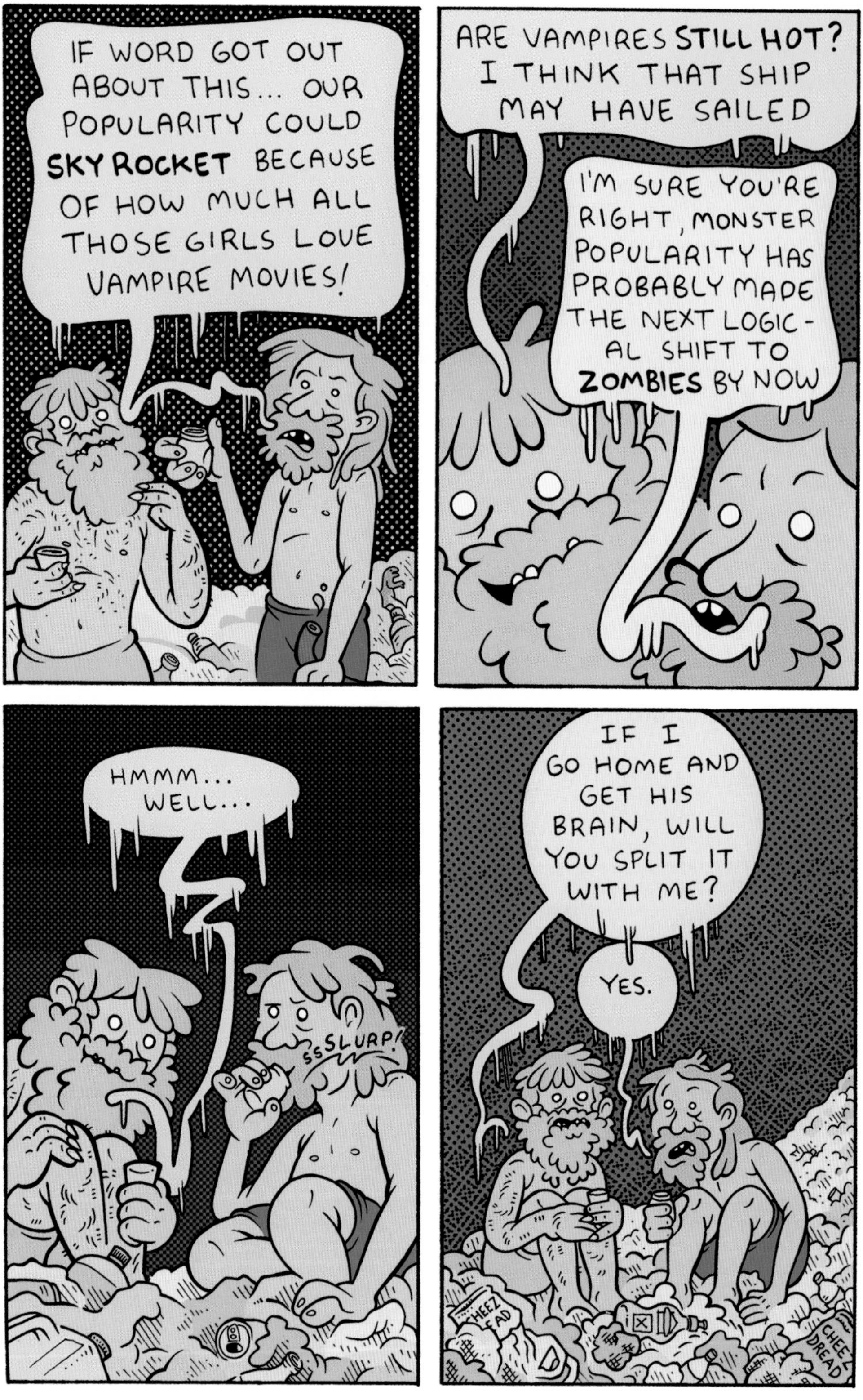
IF WORD GOT OUT ABOUT THIS... OUR POPULARITY COULD SKYROCKET BECAUSE OF HOW MUCH ALL THOSE GIRLS LOVE VAMPIRE MOVIES!
ARE VAMPIRES STILL HOT? I THINK THAT SHIP MAY HAVE SAILED
I'M SURE YOU'RE RIGHT, MONSTER POPULARITY HAS PROBABLY MADE THE NEXT LOGICAL SHIFT TO ZOMBIES BY NOW
HMMM... WELL...
SSSLURP!
IF I GO HOME AND GET HIS BRAIN, WILL YOU SPLIT IT WITH ME?
YES.

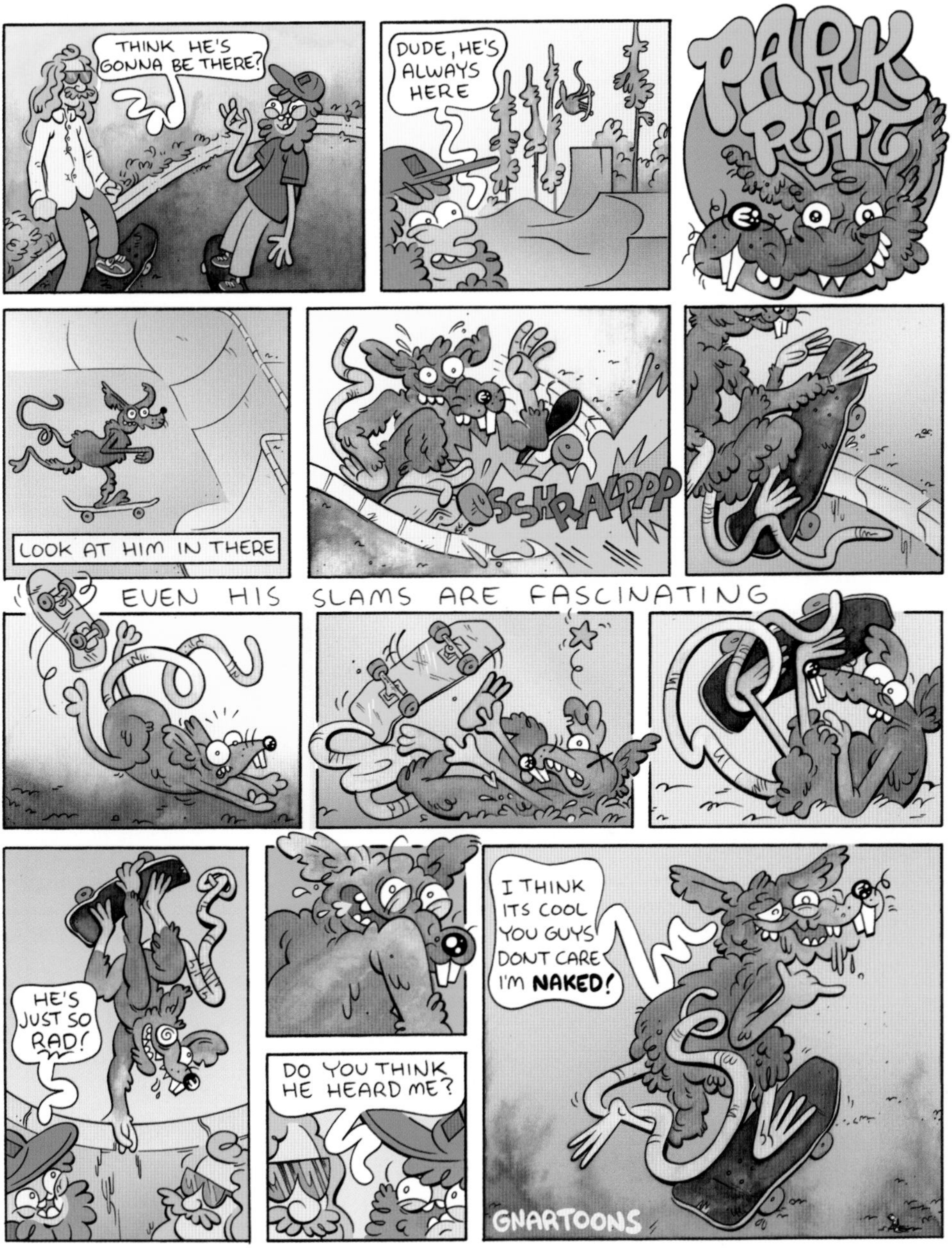
THINK HE'S GONNA BE THERE?
DUDE, HE'S ALWAYS HERE
PARK RAT
LOOK AT HIM IN THERE
SSSHRALPPP
EVEN HIS SLAMS ARE FASCINATING
HE'S JUST SO RAD!
DO YOU THINK HE HEARD ME?
I THINK ITS COOL YOU GUYS DONT CARE I'M **NAKED!**
GNARTOONS

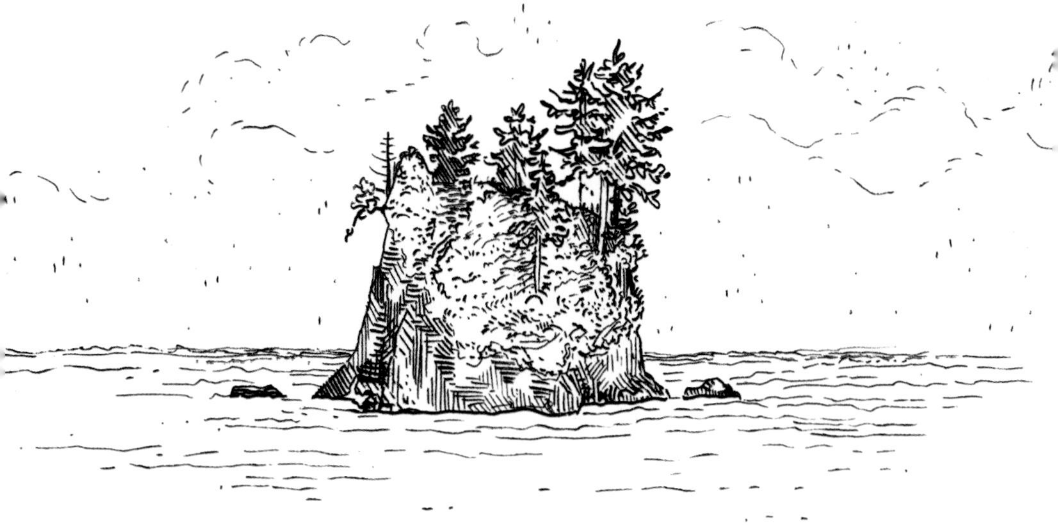

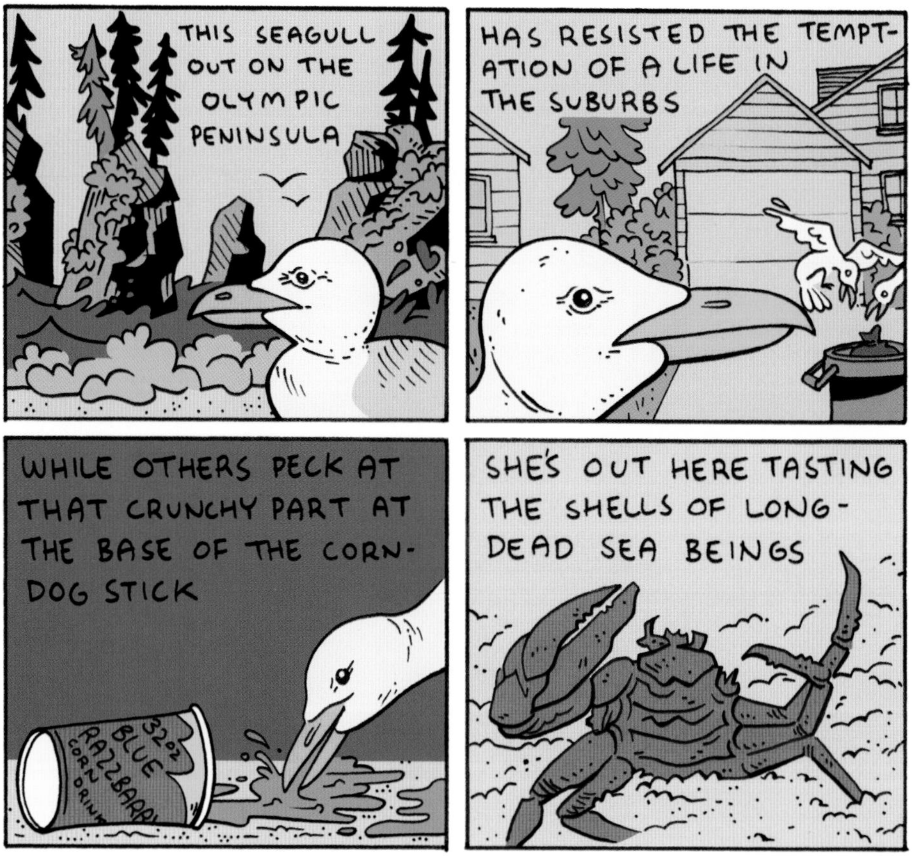
THIS SEAGULL OUT ON THE OLYMPIC PENINSULA
HAS RESISTED THE TEMPT-ATION OF A LIFE IN THE SUBURBS
WHILE OTHERS PECK AT THAT CRUNCHY PART AT THE BASE OF THE CORN-DOG STICK
32oz
BLUE
SHE'S OUT HERE TASTING THE SHELLS OF LONG-DEAD SEA BEINGS

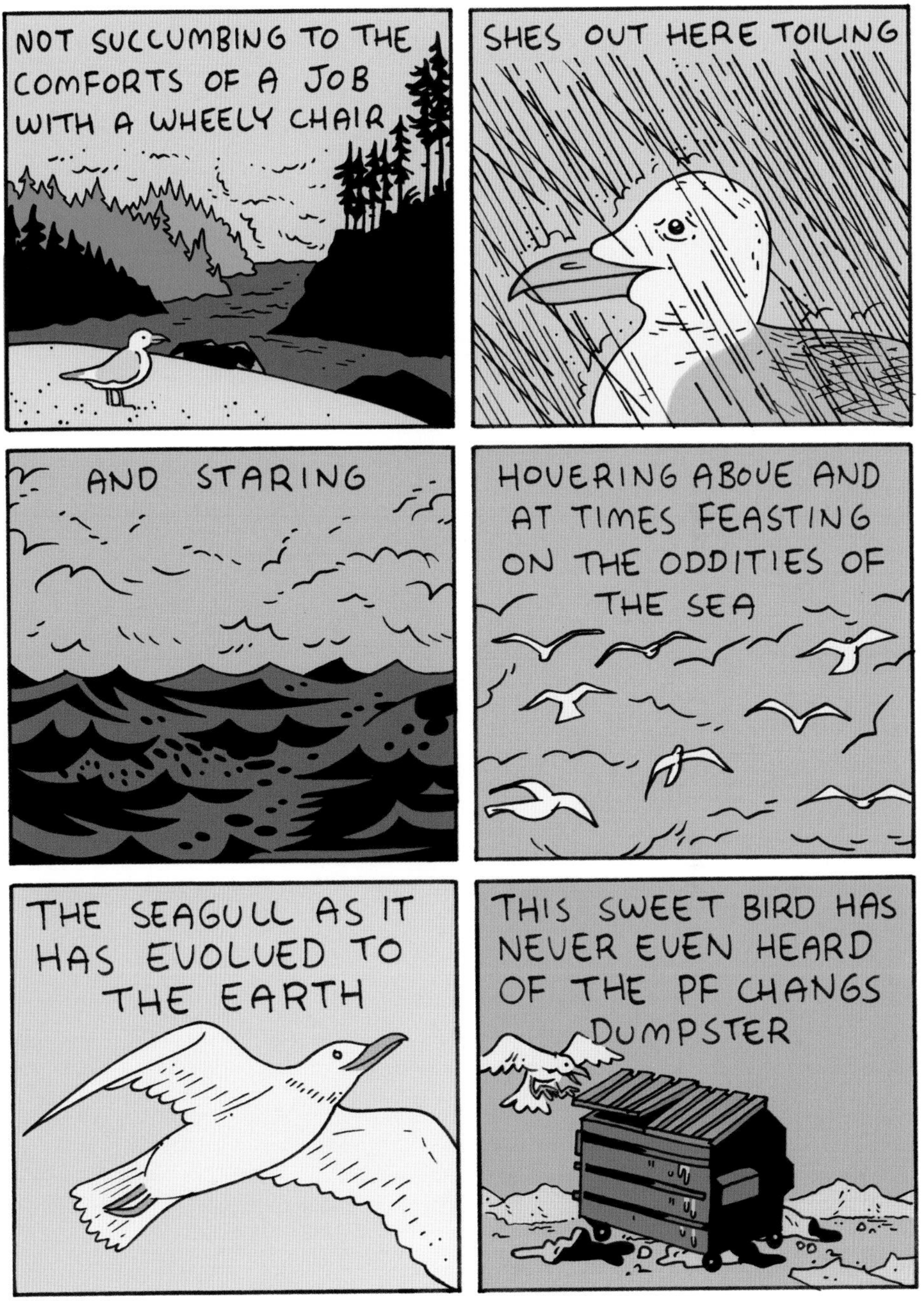
NOT SUCCUMBING TO THE COMFORTS OF A JOB WITH A WHEELY CHAIR
SHES OUT HERE TOILING
AND STARING
HOVERING ABOVE AND AT TIMES FEASTING ON THE ODDITIES OF THE SEA
THE SEAGULL AS IT HAS EVOLVED TO THE EARTH
THIS SWEET BIRD HAS NEVER EVEN HEARD OF THE PF CHANGS DUMPSTER

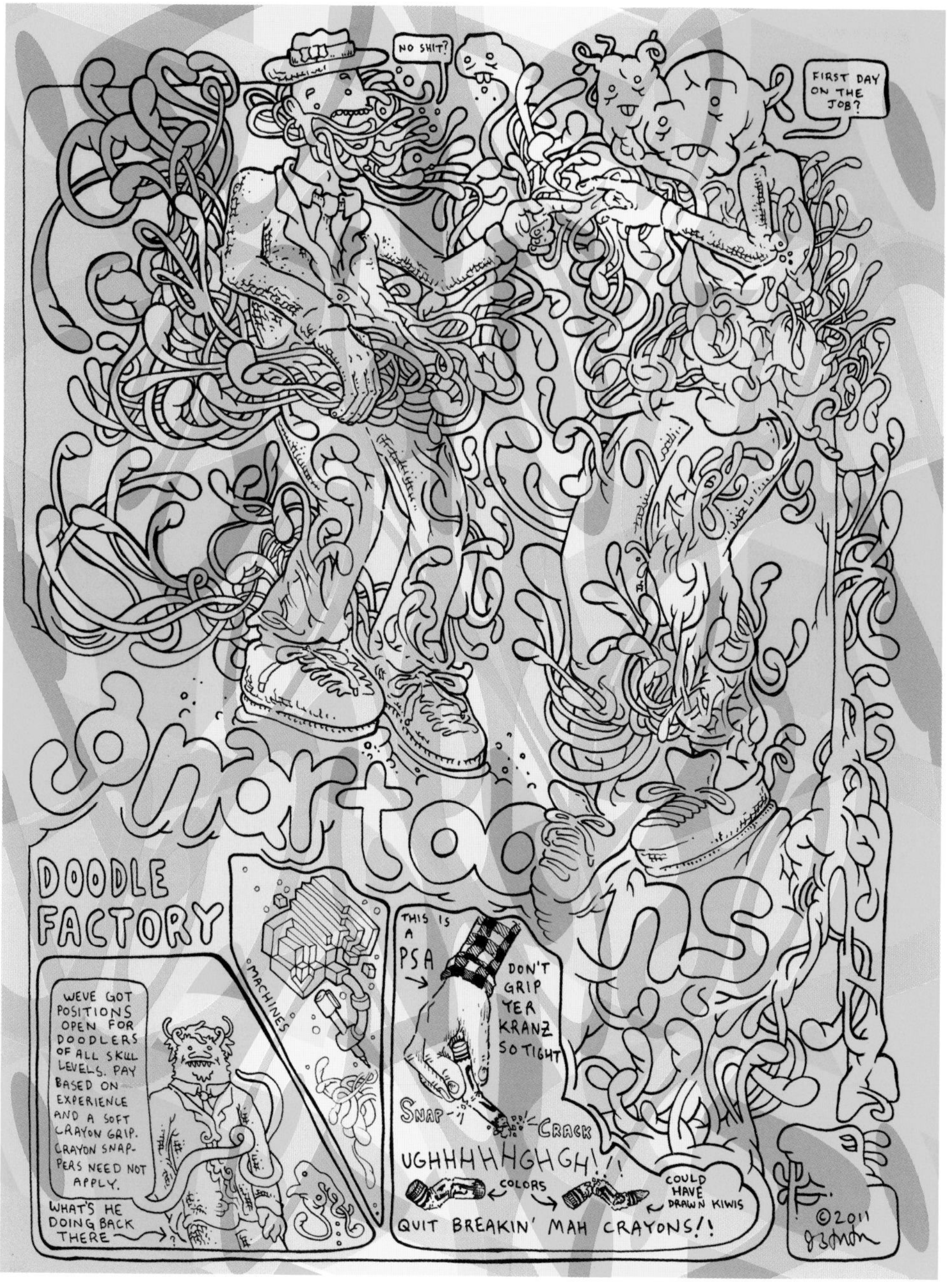
NO SHIT?
FIRST DAY ON THE JOB?
DOODLE FACTORY
WEVE GOT POSITIONS OPEN FOR DOODLERS OF ALL SKILL LEVELS. PAY BASED ON EXPERIENCE AND A SOFT CRAYON GRIP. CRAYON SNAP-PERS NEED NOT APPLY.
WHAT'S HE DOING BACK THERE
MACHINES
THIS IS A PSA
DON'T GRIP YER KRANZ SO TIGHT
SNAP
CRACK
UGHHHHHGHGH!!
COLORS
COULD HAVE DRAWN KIWIS
QUIT BREAKIN' MAH CRAYONS!!
©2011

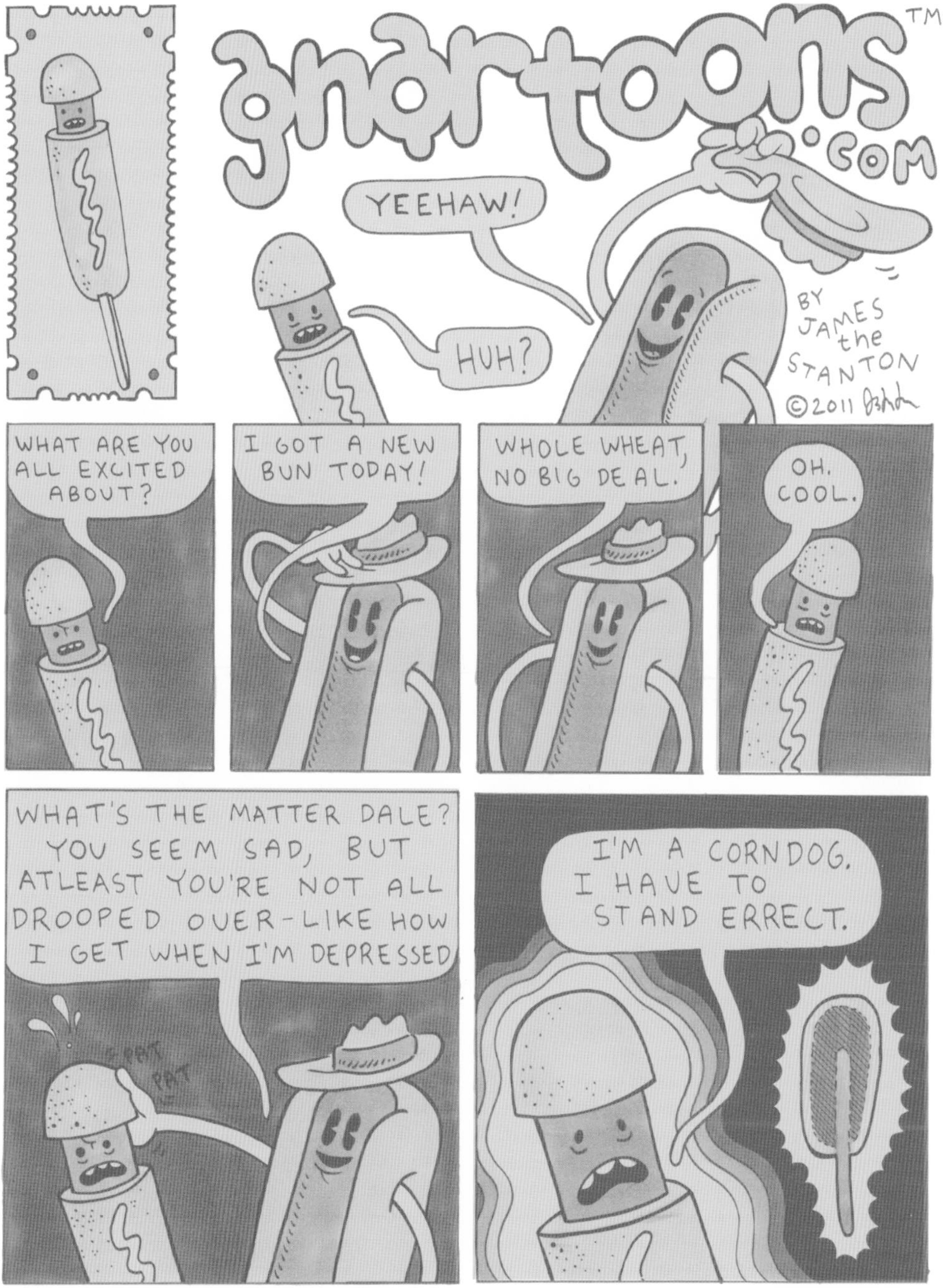
gnartoons.com™
YEEHAW!
HUH?
BY JAMES the STANTON ©2011
WHAT ARE YOU ALL EXCITED ABOUT?
I GOT A NEW BUN TODAY!
WHOLE WHEAT, NO BIG DEAL.
OH. COOL.
WHAT'S THE MATTER DALE? YOU SEEM SAD, BUT ATLEAST YOU'RE NOT ALL DROOPED OVER-LIKE HOW I GET WHEN I'M DEPRESSED
PAT PAT
I'M A CORNDOG. I HAVE TO STAND ERRECT.

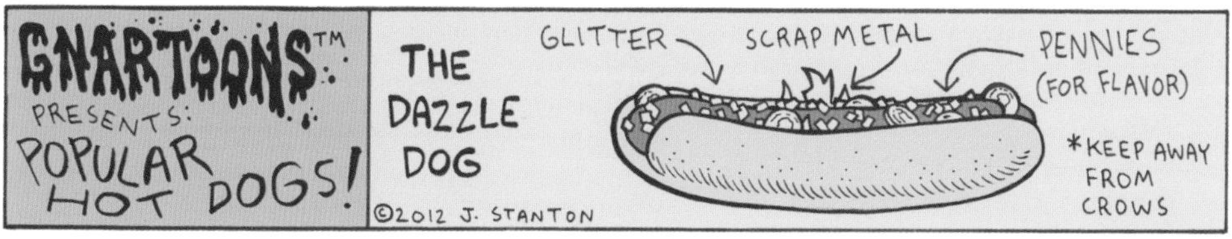
GNARTOONS™ PRESENTS: POPULAR HOT DOGS!
THE DAZZLE DOG
GLITTER
SCRAP METAL
PENNIES (FOR FLAVOR)
*KEEP AWAY FROM CROWS
©2012 J. STANTON

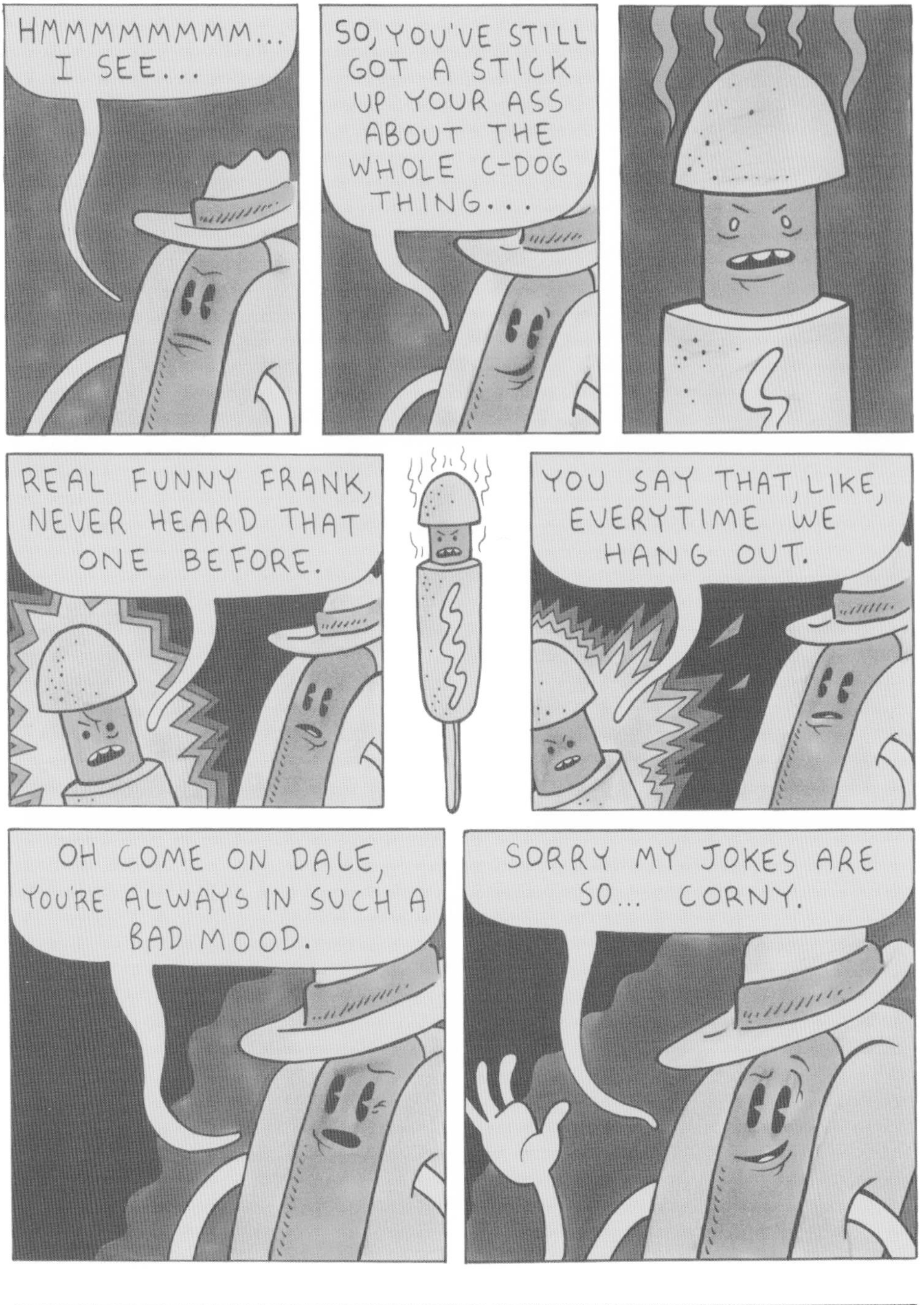
HMMMMMMMM... I SEE...
SO, YOU'VE STILL GOT A STICK UP YOUR ASS ABOUT THE WHOLE C-DOG THING...
REAL FUNNY FRANK, NEVER HEARD THAT ONE BEFORE.
YOU SAY THAT, LIKE, EVERYTIME WE HANG OUT.
OH COME ON DALE, YOU'RE ALWAYS IN SUCH A BAD MOOD.
SORRY MY JOKES ARE SO... CORNY.

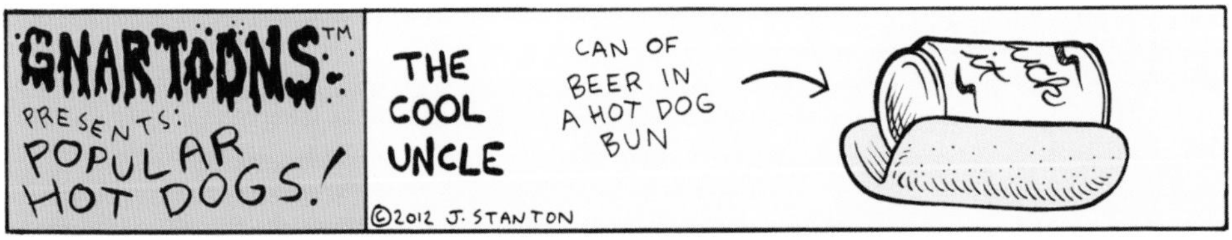
GNARTOONS™
PRESENTS: POPULAR HOT DOGS!
THE COOL UNCLE
CAN OF BEER IN A HOT DOG BUN
©2012 J. STANTON

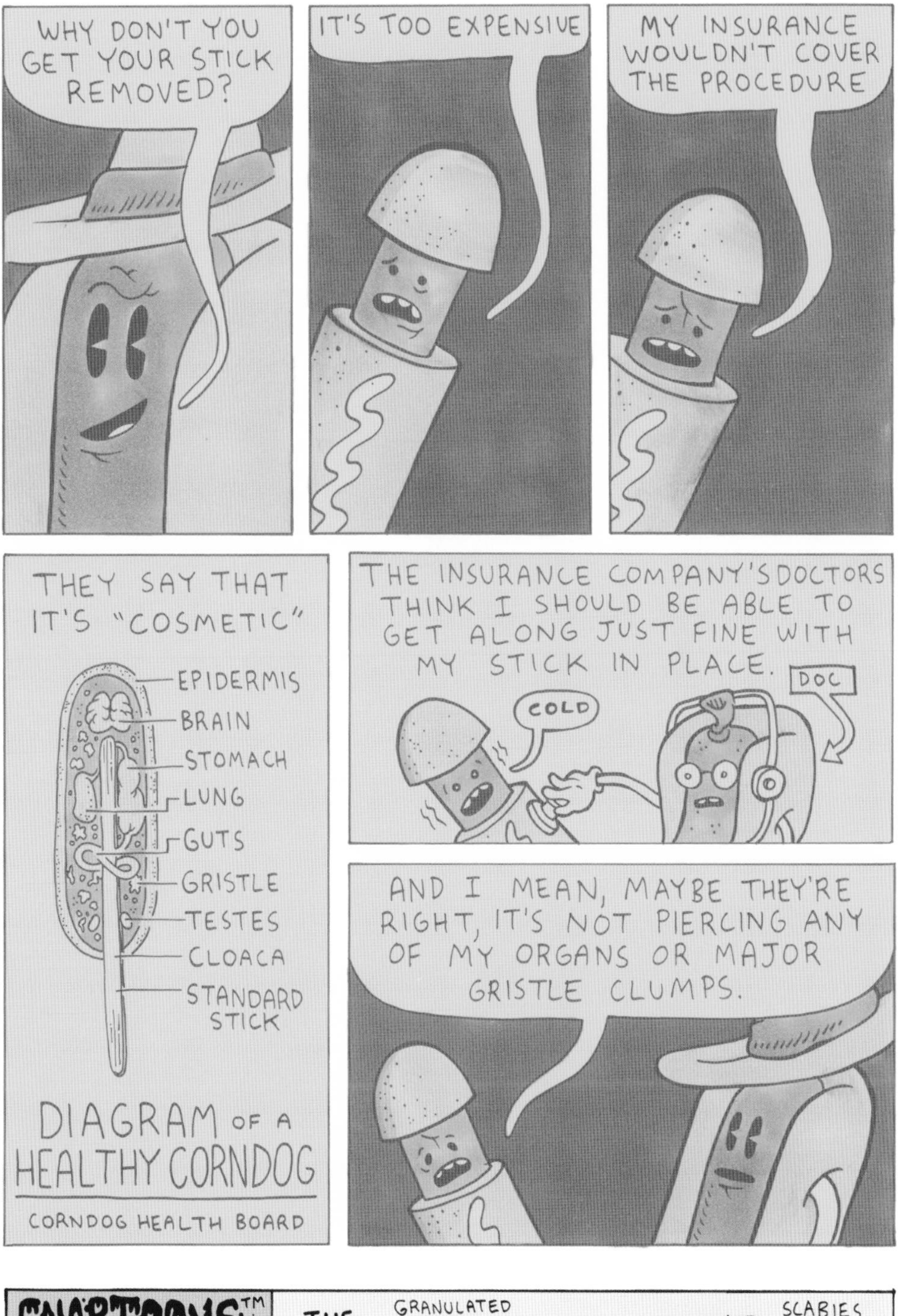
WHY DON'T YOU GET YOUR STICK REMOVED?
IT'S TOO EXPENSIVE
MY INSURANCE WOULDN'T COVER THE PROCEDURE
THEY SAY THAT IT'S "COSMETIC"
EPIDERMIS
BRAIN
STOMACH
LUNG
GUTS
GRISTLE
TESTES
CLOACA
STANDARD STICK
DIAGRAM OF A HEALTHY CORNDOG
CORNDOG HEALTH BOARD
THE INSURANCE COMPANY'S DOCTORS THINK I SHOULD BE ABLE TO GET ALONG JUST FINE WITH MY STICK IN PLACE.
COLD
DOC
AND I MEAN, MAYBE THEY'RE RIGHT, IT'S NOT PIERCING ANY OF MY ORGANS OR MAJOR GRISTLE CLUMPS.

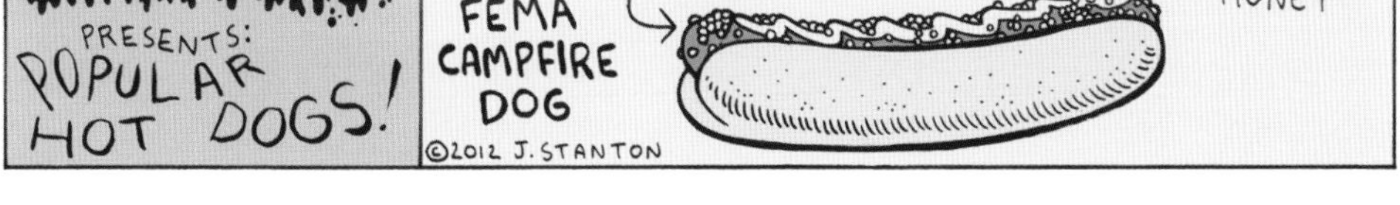
GNARTOONS™
PRESENTS:
POPULAR HOT DOGS!
THE FEMA CAMPFIRE DOG
GRANULATED RAT SKULLS
SCABIES "HONEY"
©2012 J. STANTON

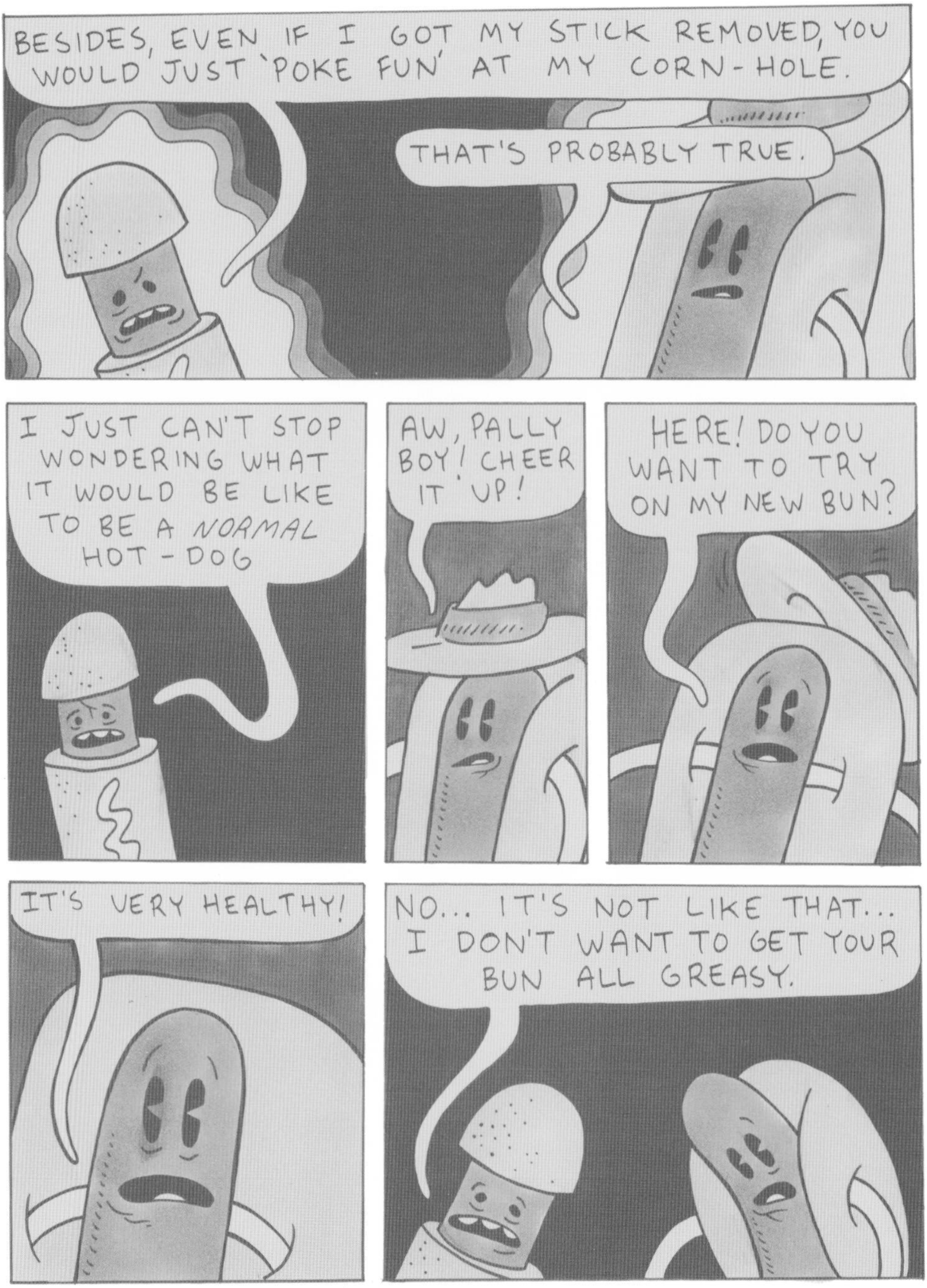
BESIDES, EVEN IF I GOT MY STICK REMOVED, YOU WOULD JUST 'POKE FUN' AT MY CORN-HOLE.
THAT'S PROBABLY TRUE.
I JUST CAN'T STOP WONDERING WHAT IT WOULD BE LIKE TO BE A *NORMAL* HOT-DOG
AW, PALLY BOY! CHEER IT UP!
HERE! DO YOU WANT TO TRY ON MY NEW BUN?
IT'S VERY HEALTHY!
NO... IT'S NOT LIKE THAT... I DON'T WANT TO GET YOUR BUN ALL GREASY.

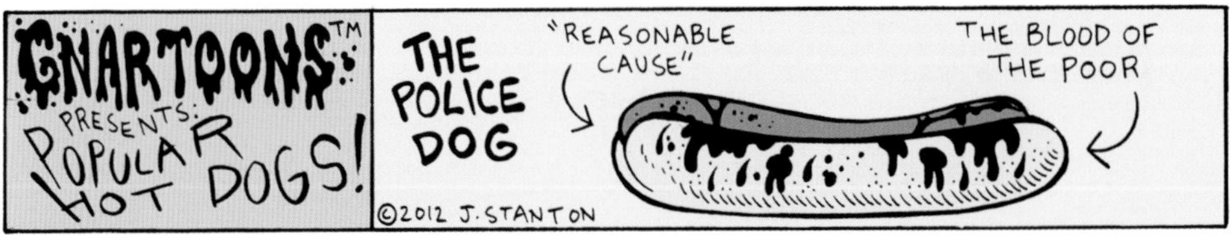
GNARTOONS™
PRESENTS:
POPULAR HOT DOGS!
THE POLICE DOG
"REASONABLE CAUSE"
THE BLOOD OF THE POOR
©2012 J. STANTON

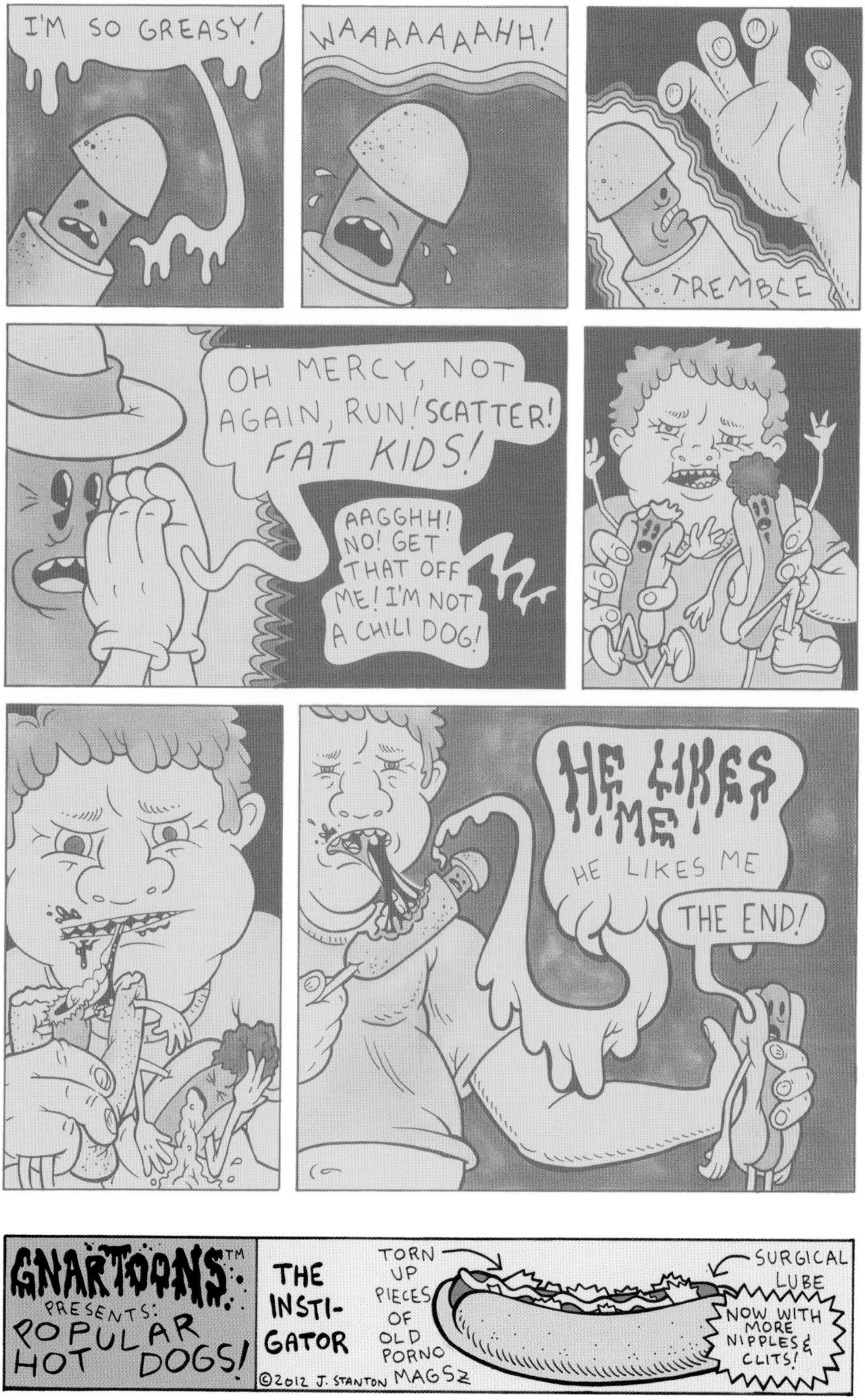
I'M SO GREASY!
WAAAAAAAHH!
TREMBLE
OH MERCY, NOT AGAIN, RUN! SCATTER! FAT KIDS!
AAGGHH! NO! GET THAT OFF ME! I'M NOT A CHILI DOG!
HE LIKES ME!
HE LIKES ME
THE END!
GNARTOONS™ PRESENTS: POPULAR HOT DOGS!
THE INSTI-GATOR
TORN UP PIECES OF OLD PORNO MAGSZ
SURGICAL LUBE
NOW WITH MORE NIPPLES & CLITS!
©2012 J. STANTON

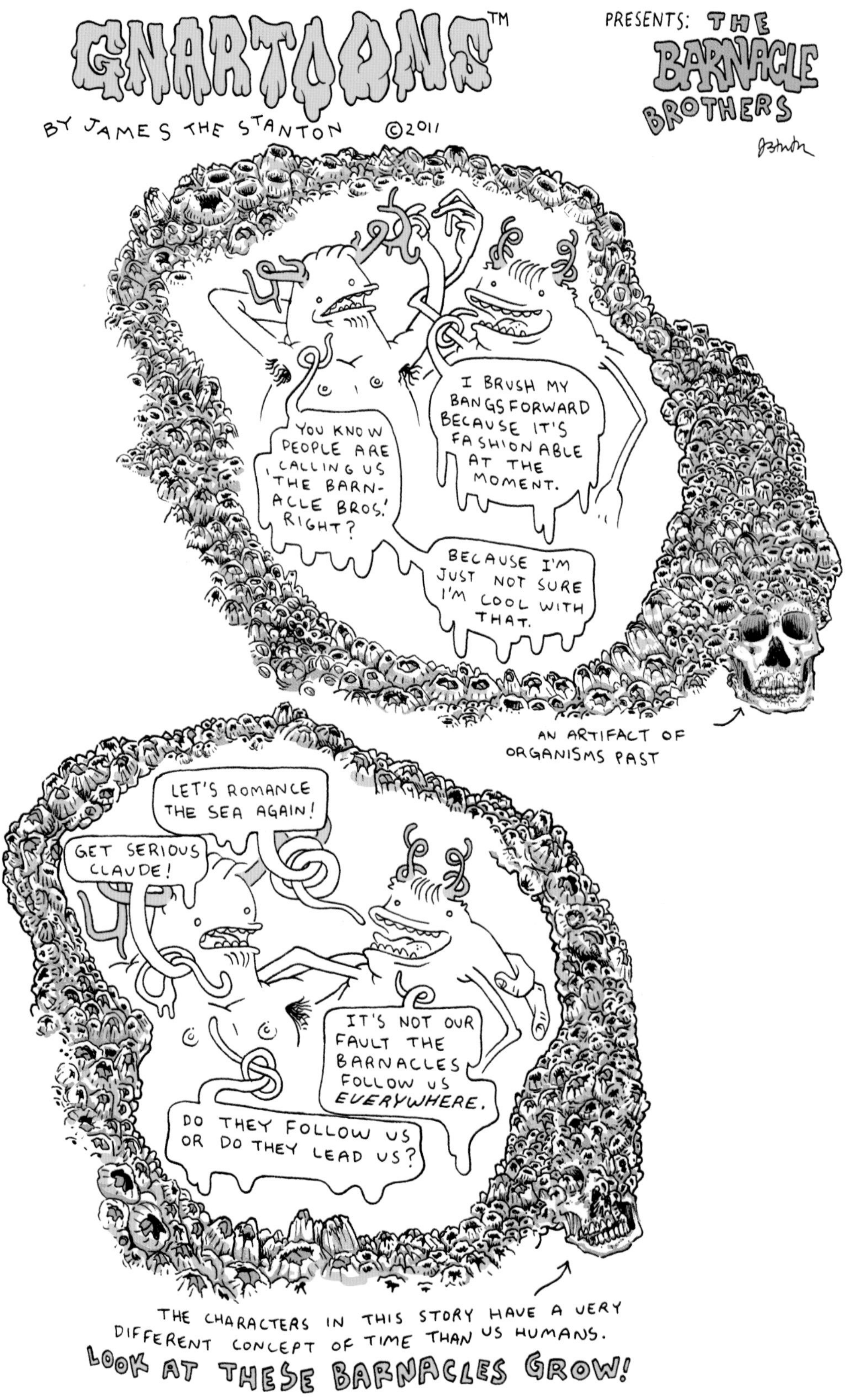
GNARTOONS™
BY JAMES THE STANTON ©2011
PRESENTS: THE BARNACLE BROTHERS
YOU KNOW PEOPLE ARE CALLING US 'THE BARN-ACLE BROS.' RIGHT?
I BRUSH MY BANGS FORWARD BECAUSE IT'S FASHIONABLE AT THE MOMENT.
BECAUSE I'M JUST NOT SURE I'M COOL WITH THAT.
AN ARTIFACT OF ORGANISMS PAST
LET'S ROMANCE THE SEA AGAIN!
GET SERIOUS CLAUDE!
IT'S NOT OUR FAULT THE BARNACLES FOLLOW US EVERYWHERE.
DO THEY FOLLOW US OR DO THEY LEAD US?
THE CHARACTERS IN THIS STORY HAVE A VERY DIFFERENT CONCEPT OF TIME THAN US HUMANS.
LOOK AT THESE BARNACLES GROW!

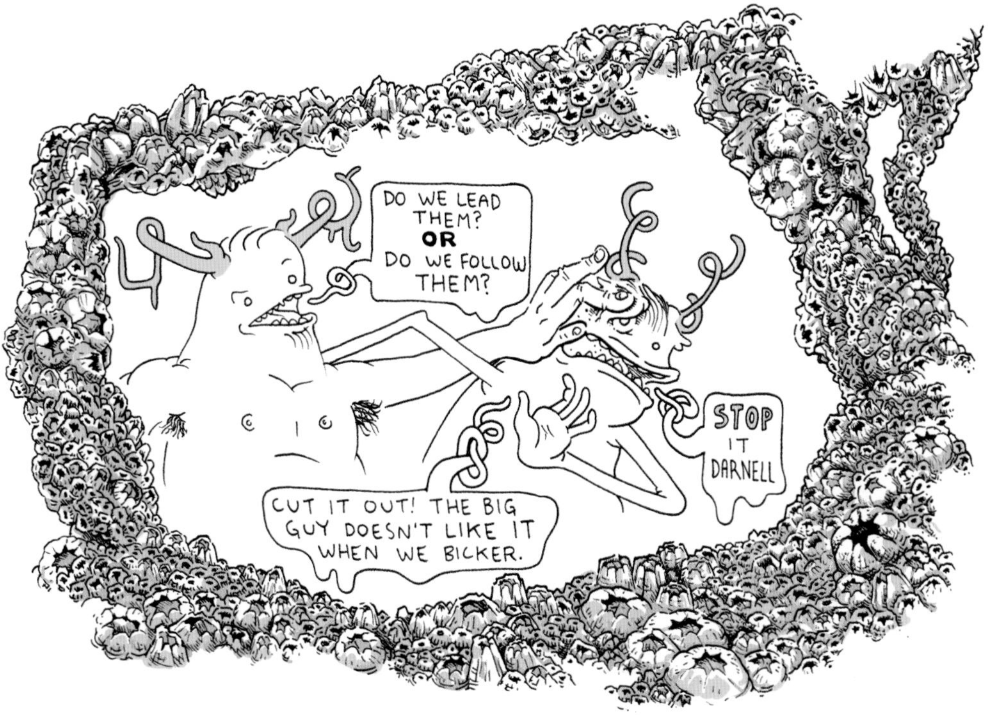
DO WE LEAD THEM? OR DO WE FOLLOW THEM?
STOP IT DARNELL
CUT IT OUT! THE BIG GUY DOESN'T LIKE IT WHEN WE BICKER.

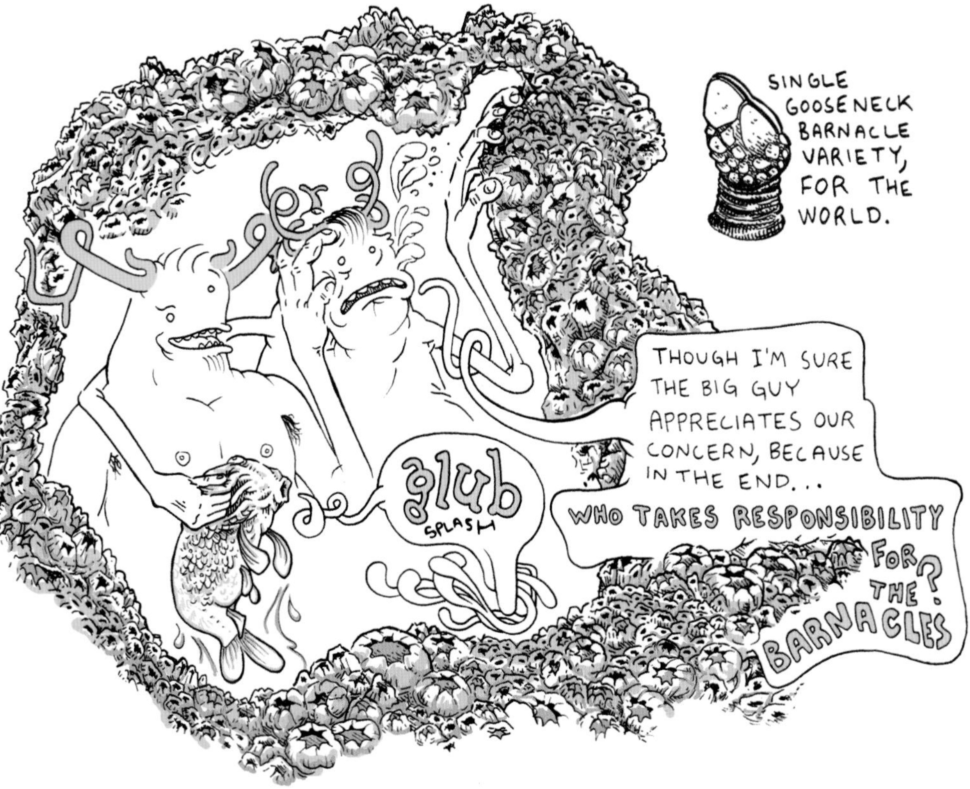
SINGLE GOOSENECK BARNACLE VARIETY, FOR THE WORLD.
glub
SPLASH
THOUGH I'M SURE THE BIG GUY APPRECIATES OUR CONCERN, BECAUSE IN THE END...
WHO TAKES RESPONSIBILITY FOR THE BARNACLES?

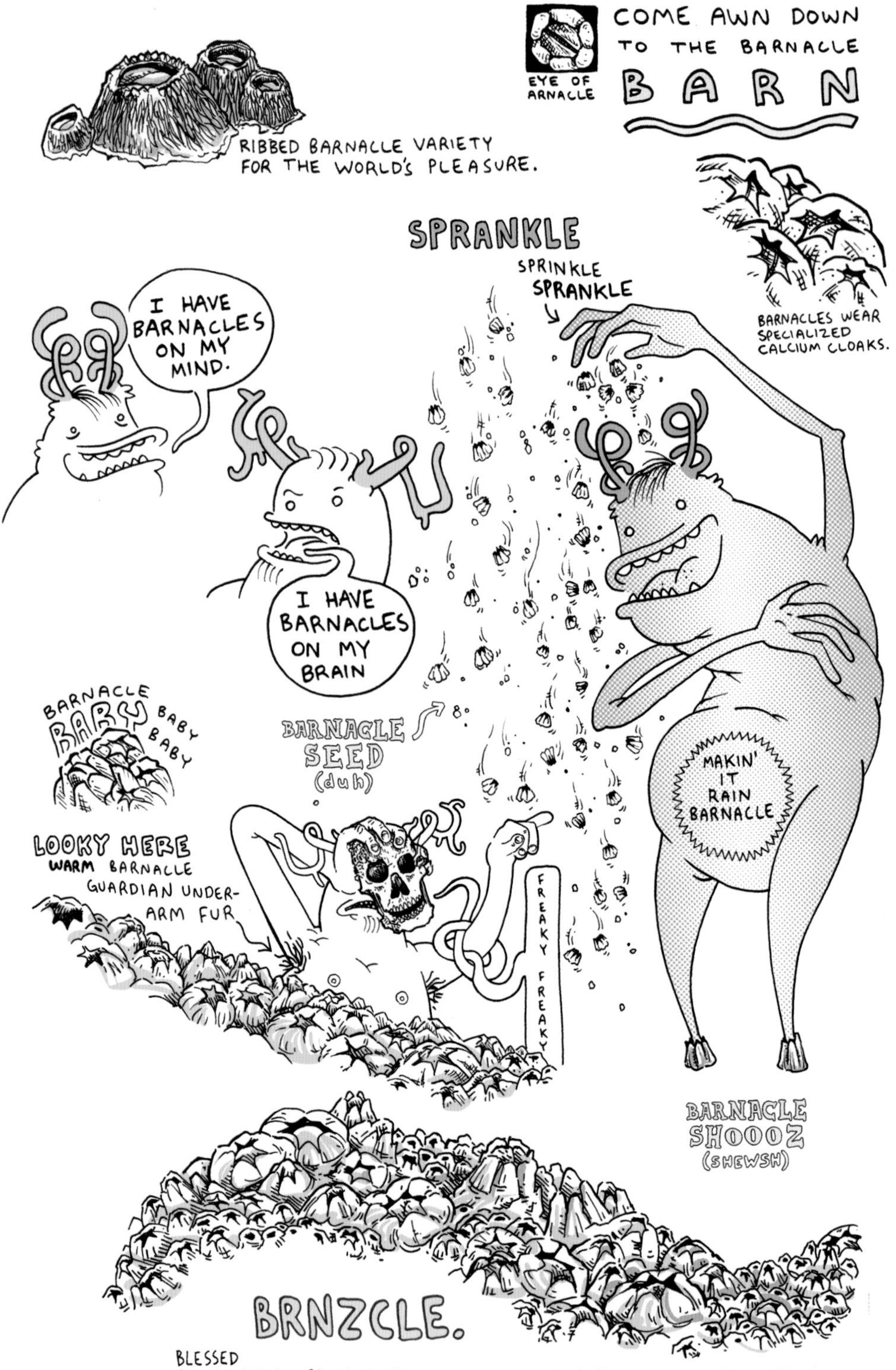
COME AWN DOWN TO THE BARNACLE BARN
EYE OF ARNACLE
RIBBED BARNACLE VARIETY FOR THE WORLD'S PLEASURE.
SPRANKLE
SPRINKLE SPRANKLE
BARNACLES WEAR SPECIALIZED CALCIUM CLOAKS.
I HAVE BARNACLES ON MY MIND.
I HAVE BARNACLES ON MY BRAIN
BARNACLE BABY BABY BABY
BARNACLE SEED (duh)
MAKIN' IT RAIN BARNACLE
LOOKY HERE WARM BARNACLE GUARDIAN UNDER-ARM FUR
FREAKY FREAKY
BARNACLE SHOOOZ (SHEWSH)
BRNZCLE.
BLESSED BE THE BARNACLES AS THEY COMMITTEDLY CLING TO THEIR CHOSEN SURFACE.

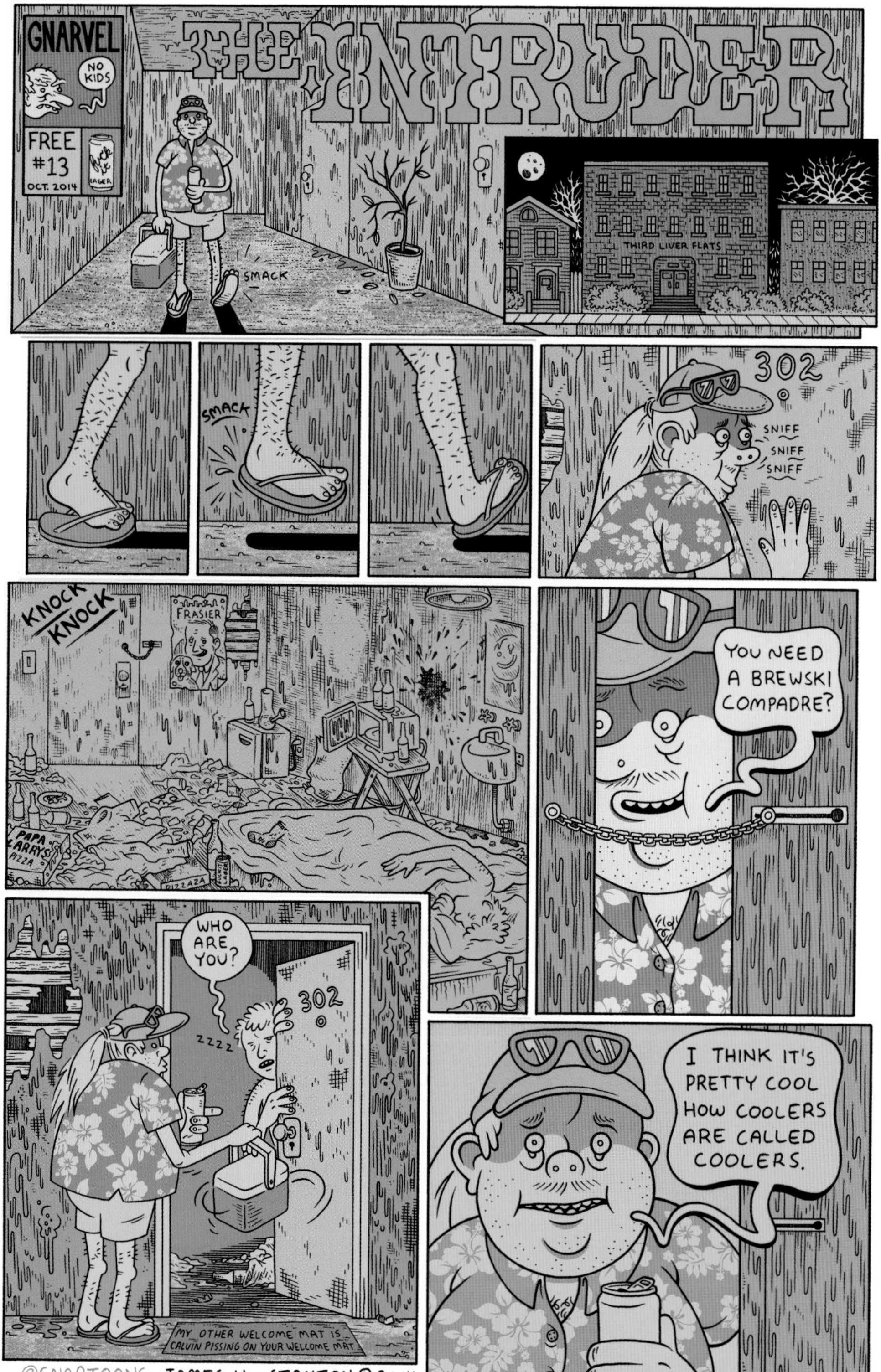
GNARVEL
NO KIDS
FREE #13
OCT. 2014
THE INTRUDER
THIRD LIVER FLATS
SMACK
SMACK
302
SNIFF SNIFF SNIFF
KNOCK KNOCK
FRASIER
PAPA LARRYS PIZZA
PIZZAZA
YOU NEED A BREWSKI COMPADRE?
WHO ARE YOU?
ZZZZ
302
MY OTHER WELCOME MAT IS CALVIN PISSING ON YOUR WELCOME MAT
I THINK IT'S PRETTY COOL HOW COOLERS ARE CALLED COOLERS.
@GNARTOONS JAMES the STANTON © 2014

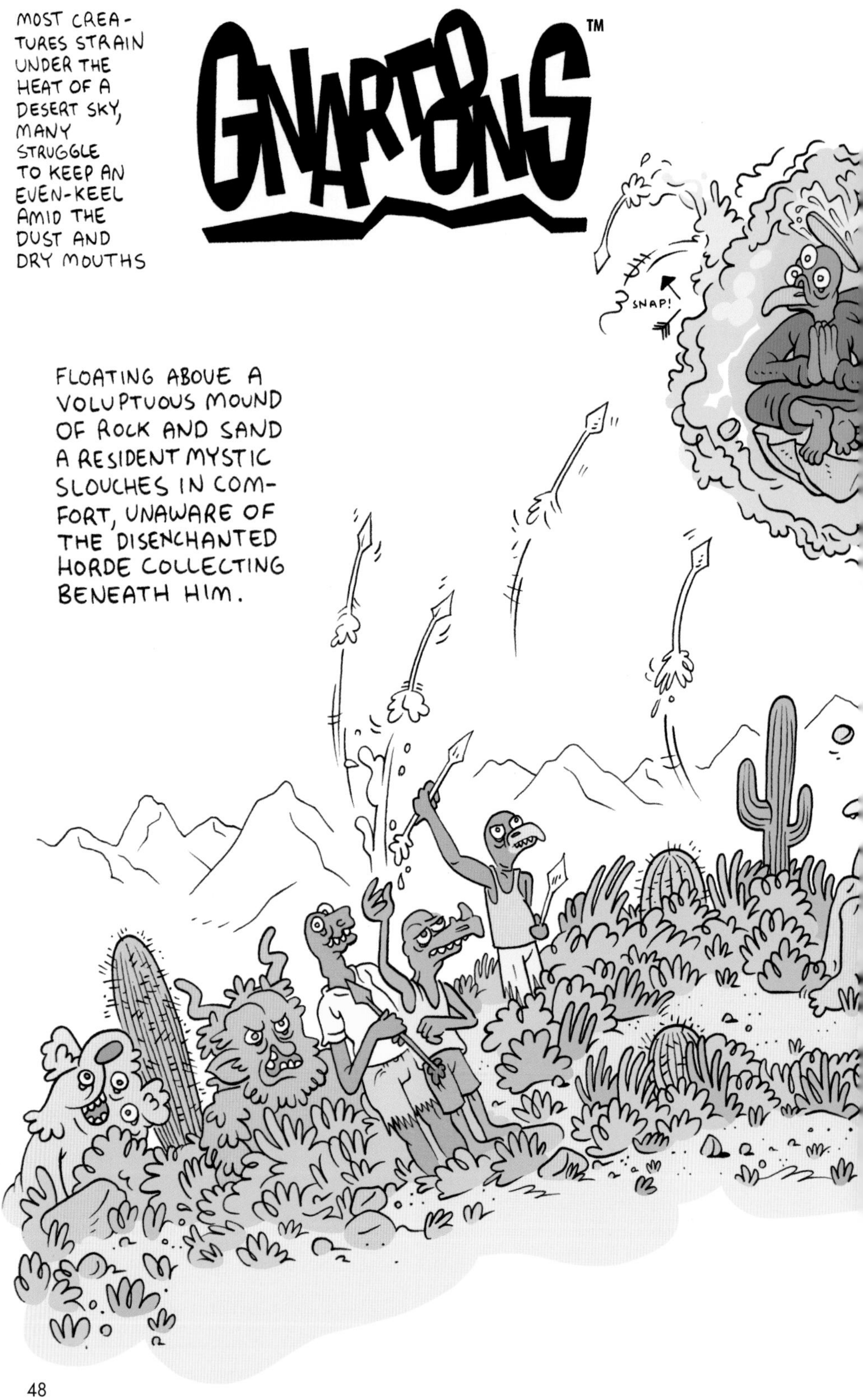
MOST CREATURES STRAIN UNDER THE HEAT OF A DESERT SKY, MANY STRUGGLE TO KEEP AN EVEN-KEEL AMID THE DUST AND DRY MOUTHS
GNARTOONS™
SNAP!
FLOATING ABOVE A VOLUPTUOUS MOUND OF ROCK AND SAND A RESIDENT MYSTIC SLOUCHES IN COMFORT, UNAWARE OF THE DISENCHANTED HORDE COLLECTING BENEATH HIM.

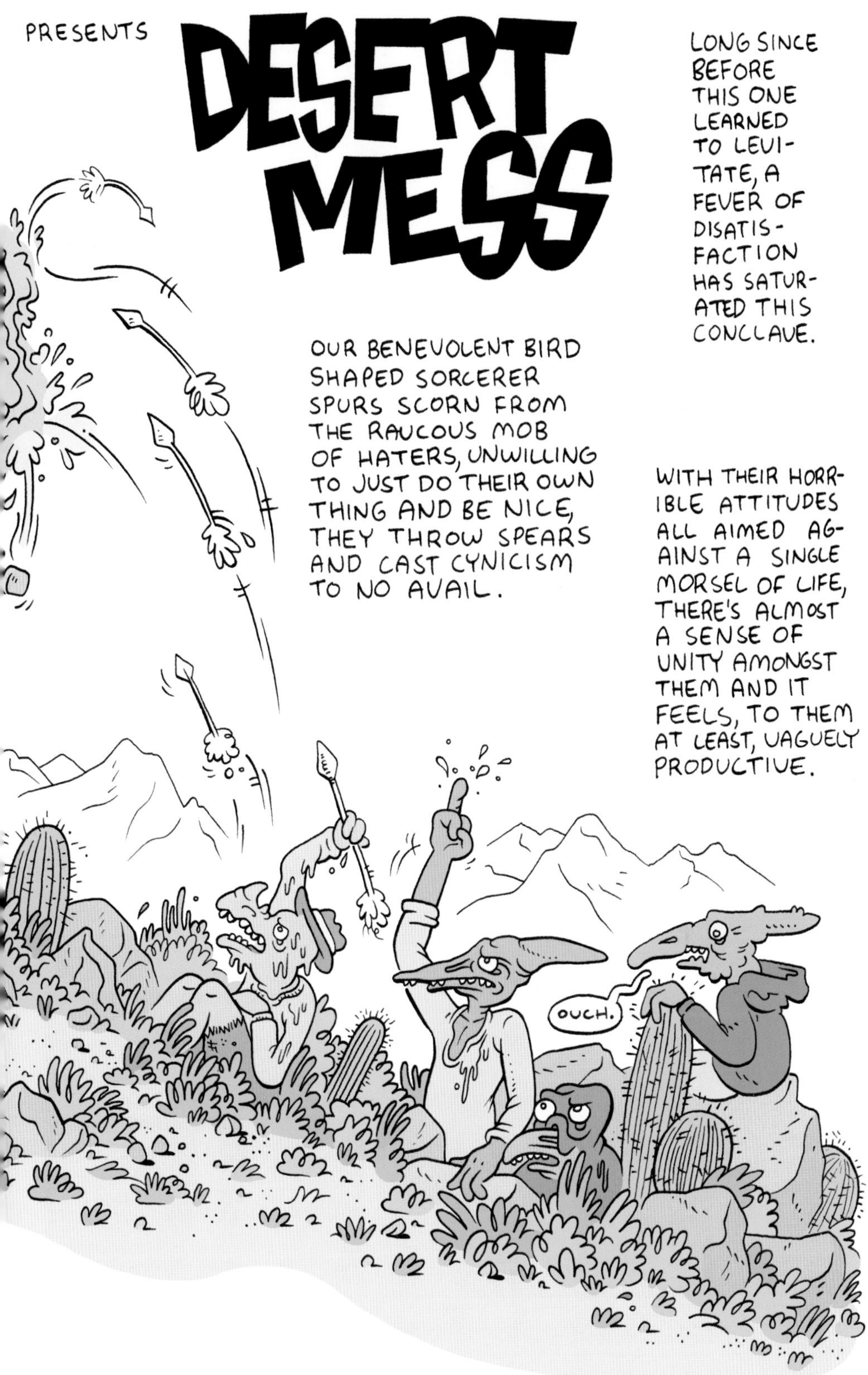
PRESENTS
DESERT MESS
LONG SINCE BEFORE THIS ONE LEARNED TO LEVI- TATE, A FEVER OF DISATIS- FACTION HAS SATUR- ATED THIS CONCLAVE.
OUR BENEVOLENT BIRD SHAPED SORCERER SPURS SCORN FROM THE RAUCOUS MOB OF HATERS, UNWILLING TO JUST DO THEIR OWN THING AND BE NICE, THEY THROW SPEARS AND CAST CYNICISM TO NO AVAIL.
WITH THEIR HORR- IBLE ATTITUDES ALL AIMED AG- AINST A SINGLE MORSEL OF LIFE, THERE'S ALMOST A SENSE OF UNITY AMONGST THEM AND IT FEELS, TO THEM AT LEAST, VAGUELY PRODUCTIVE.
OUCH.

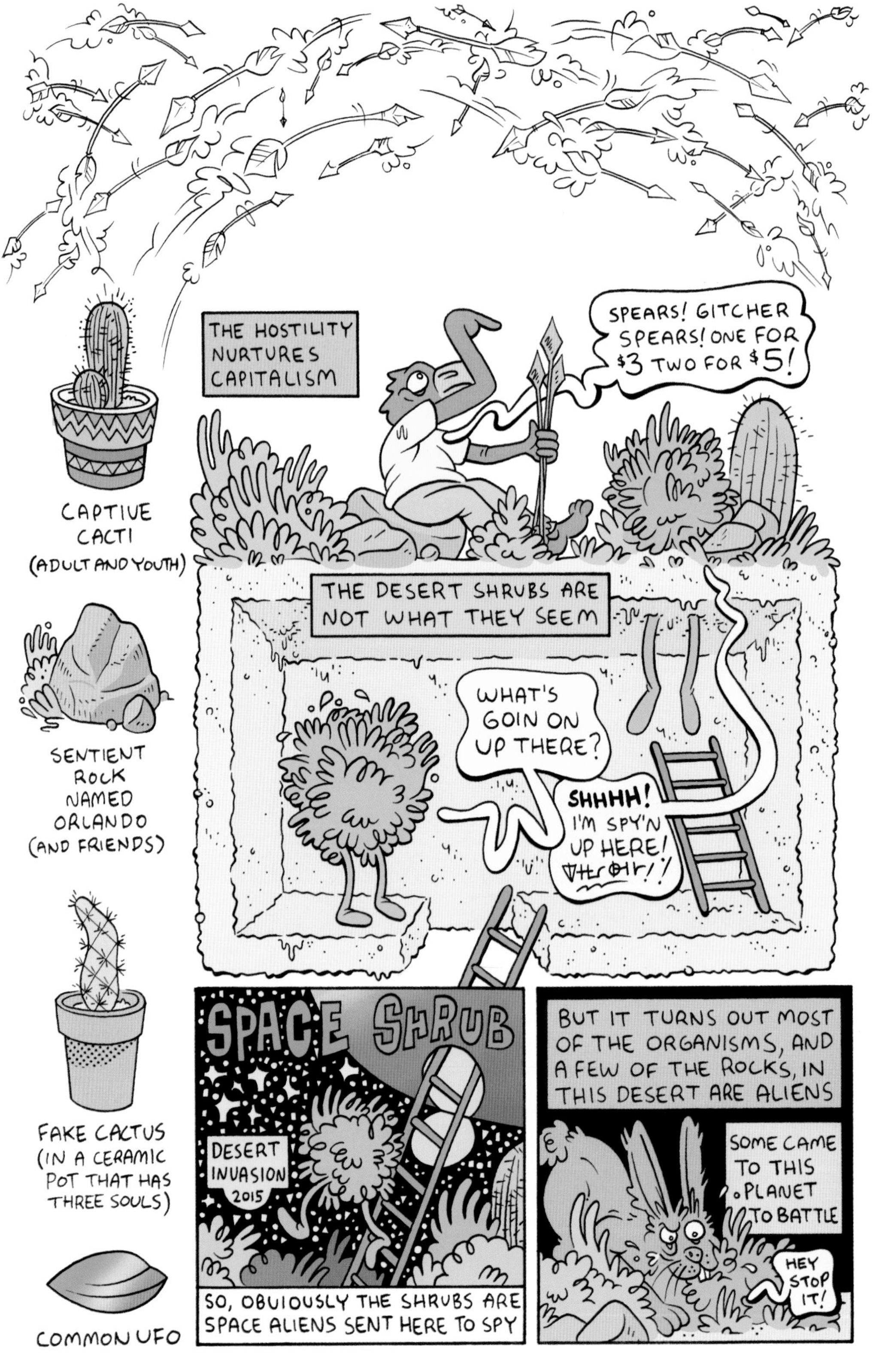
CAPTIVE CACTI (ADULT AND YOUTH)
THE HOSTILITY NURTURES CAPITALISM
SPEARS! GITCHER SPEARS! ONE FOR $3 TWO FOR $5!
SENTIENT ROCK NAMED ORLANDO (AND FRIENDS)
THE DESERT SHRUBS ARE NOT WHAT THEY SEEM
WHAT'S GOIN ON UP THERE?
SHHHH! I'M SPY'N UP HERE!
FAKE CACTUS (IN A CERAMIC POT THAT HAS THREE SOULS)
SPACE SHRUB
DESERT INVASION 2015
SO, OBVIOUSLY THE SHRUBS ARE SPACE ALIENS SENT HERE TO SPY
BUT IT TURNS OUT MOST OF THE ORGANISMS, AND A FEW OF THE ROCKS, IN THIS DESERT ARE ALIENS
SOME CAME TO THIS PLANET TO BATTLE
HEY STOP IT!
COMMON UFO

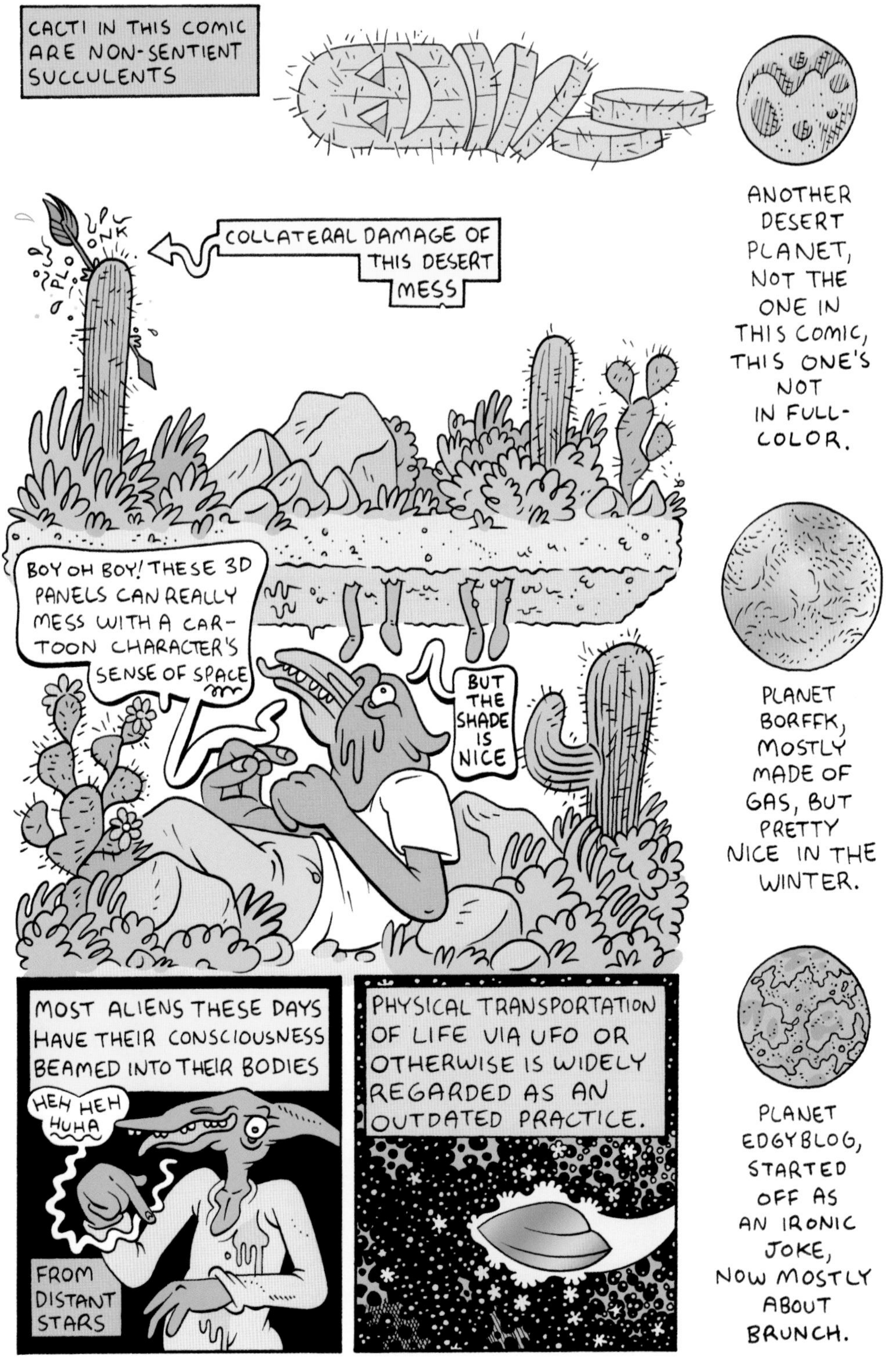

CACTI IN THIS COMIC ARE NON-SENTIENT SUCCULENTS
ANOTHER DESERT PLANET, NOT THE ONE IN THIS COMIC, THIS ONE'S NOT IN FULL-COLOR.
COLLATERAL DAMAGE OF THIS DESERT MESS
BOY OH BOY! THESE 3D PANELS CAN REALLY MESS WITH A CARTOON CHARACTER'S SENSE OF SPACE
BUT THE SHADE IS NICE
PLANET BORFFK, MOSTLY MADE OF GAS, BUT PRETTY NICE IN THE WINTER.
MOST ALIENS THESE DAYS HAVE THEIR CONSCIOUSNESS BEAMED INTO THEIR BODIES
HEH HEH HUHA
FROM DISTANT STARS
PHYSICAL TRANSPORTATION OF LIFE VIA UFO OR OTHERWISE IS WIDELY REGARDED AS AN OUTDATED PRACTICE.
PLANET EDGYBLOG, STARTED OFF AS AN IRONIC JOKE, NOW MOSTLY ABOUT BRUNCH.

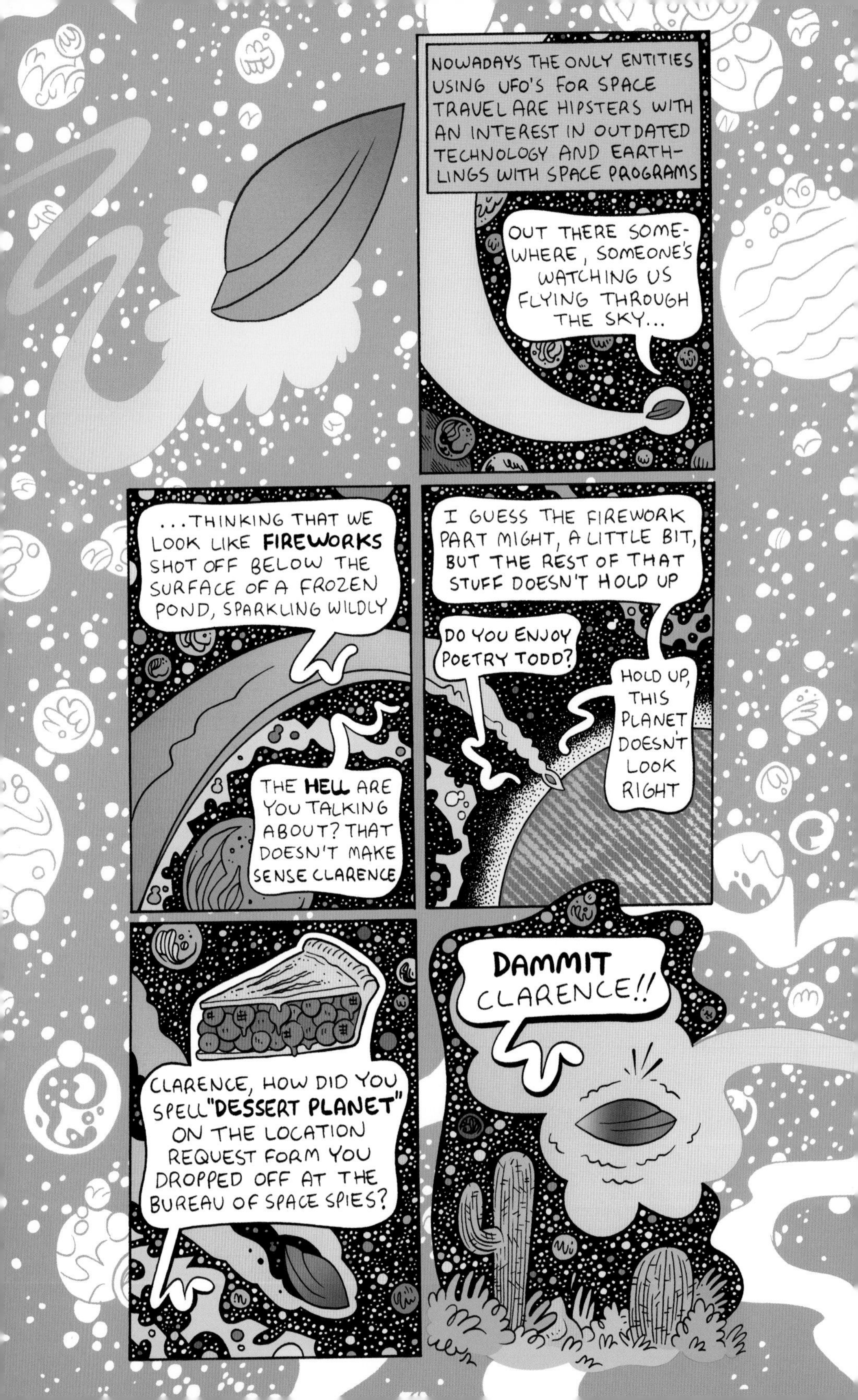

NOWADAYS THE ONLY ENTITIES USING UFO'S FOR SPACE TRAVEL ARE HIPSTERS WITH AN INTEREST IN OUTDATED TECHNOLOGY AND EARTHLINGS WITH SPACE PROGRAMS
OUT THERE SOMEWHERE, SOMEONE'S WATCHING US FLYING THROUGH THE SKY...
...THINKING THAT WE LOOK LIKE FIREWORKS SHOT OFF BELOW THE SURFACE OF A FROZEN POND, SPARKLING WILDLY
THE HELL ARE YOU TALKING ABOUT? THAT DOESN'T MAKE SENSE CLARENCE
I GUESS THE FIREWORK PART MIGHT, A LITTLE BIT, BUT THE REST OF THAT STUFF DOESN'T HOLD UP
DO YOU ENJOY POETRY TODD?
HOLD UP, THIS PLANET DOESN'T LOOK RIGHT
CLARENCE, HOW DID YOU SPELL "DESSERT PLANET" ON THE LOCATION REQUEST FORM YOU DROPPED OFF AT THE BUREAU OF SPACE SPIES?
DAMMIT CLARENCE!!

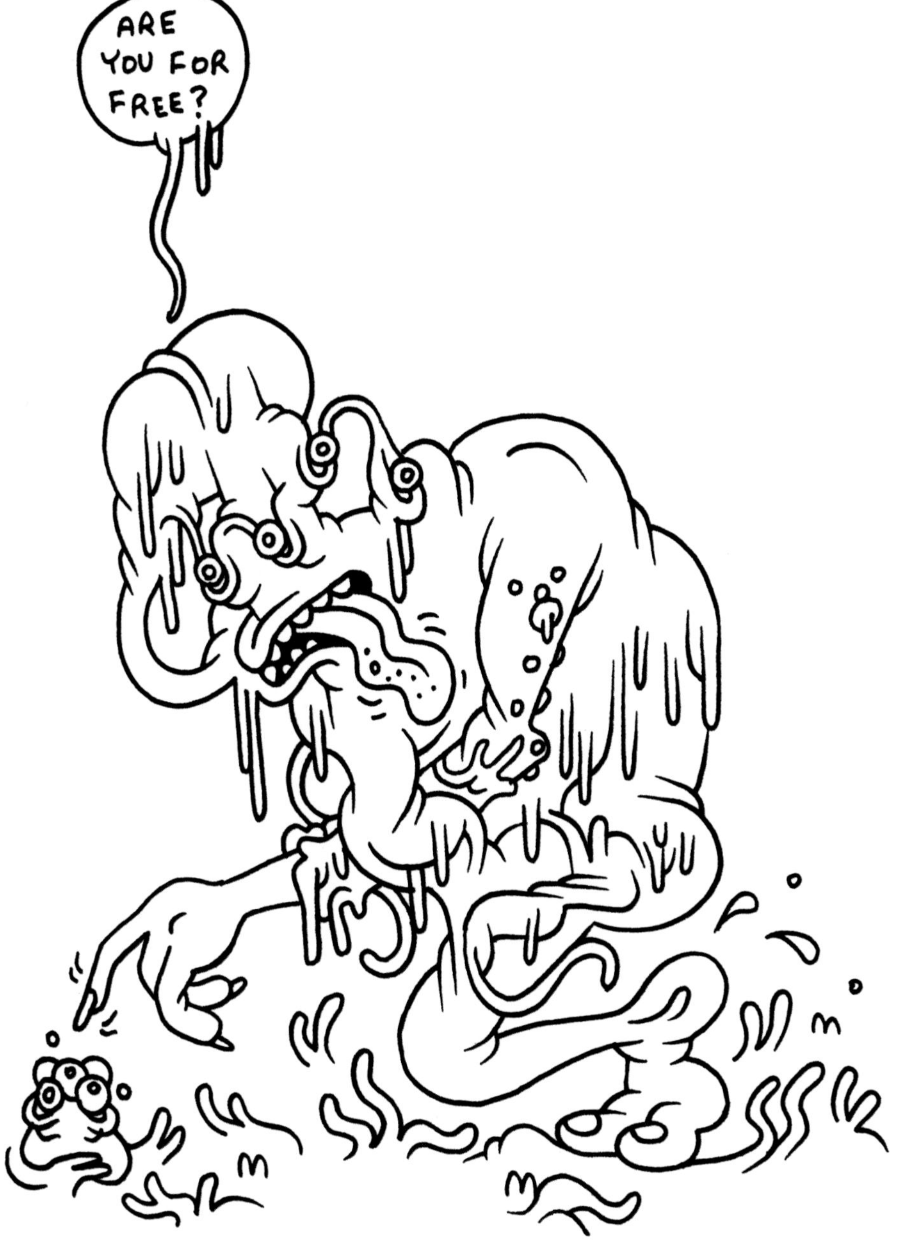
ARE YOU FOR FREE?

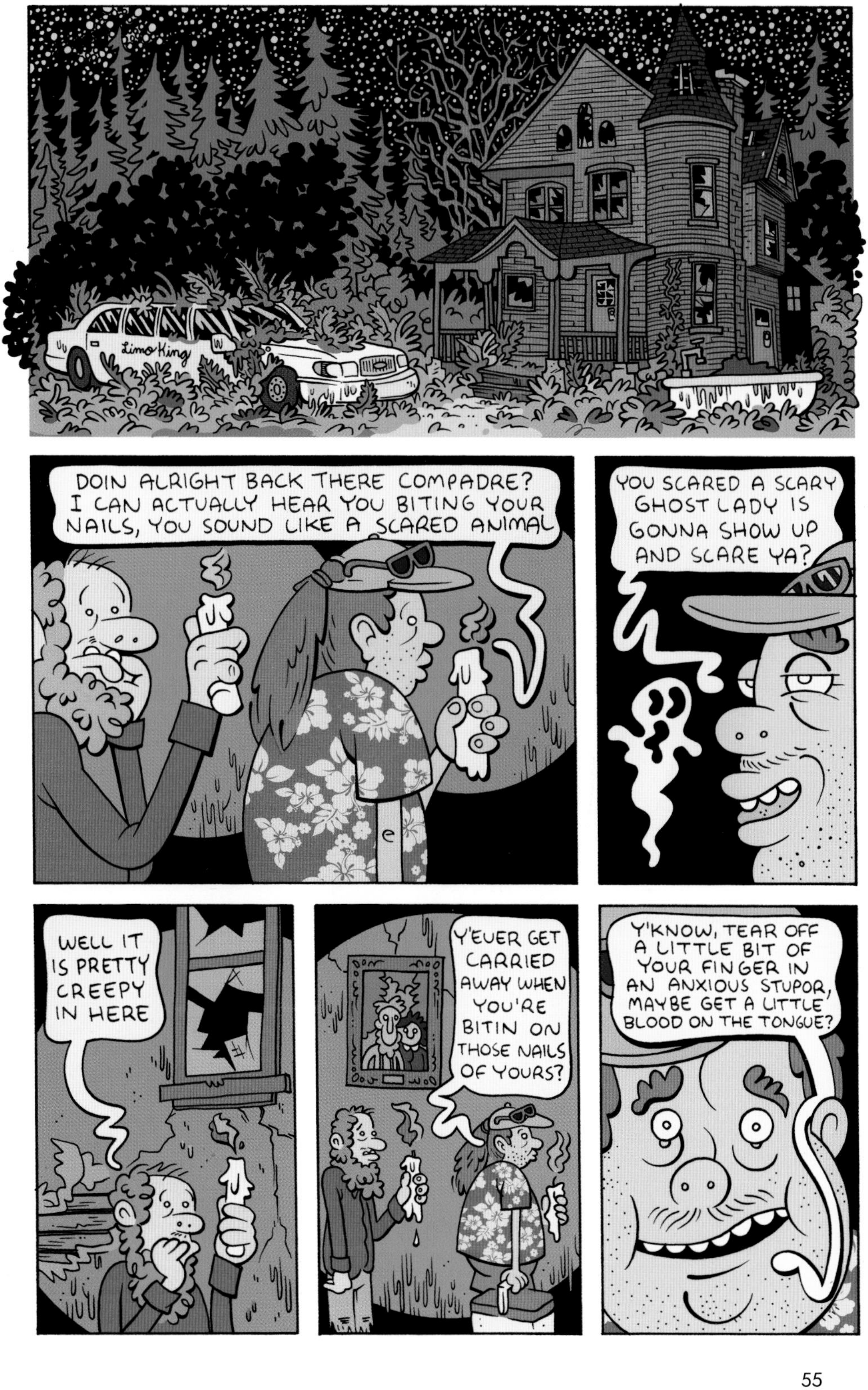
Limo King
DOIN ALRIGHT BACK THERE COMPADRE? I CAN ACTUALLY HEAR YOU BITING YOUR NAILS, YOU SOUND LIKE A SCARED ANIMAL
YOU SCARED A SCARY GHOST LADY IS GONNA SHOW UP AND SCARE YA?
WELL IT IS PRETTY CREEPY IN HERE
Y'EVER GET CARRIED AWAY WHEN YOU'RE BITIN ON THOSE NAILS OF YOURS?
Y'KNOW, TEAR OFF A LITTLE BIT OF YOUR FINGER IN AN ANXIOUS STUPOR, MAYBE GET A LITTLE BLOOD ON THE TONGUE?

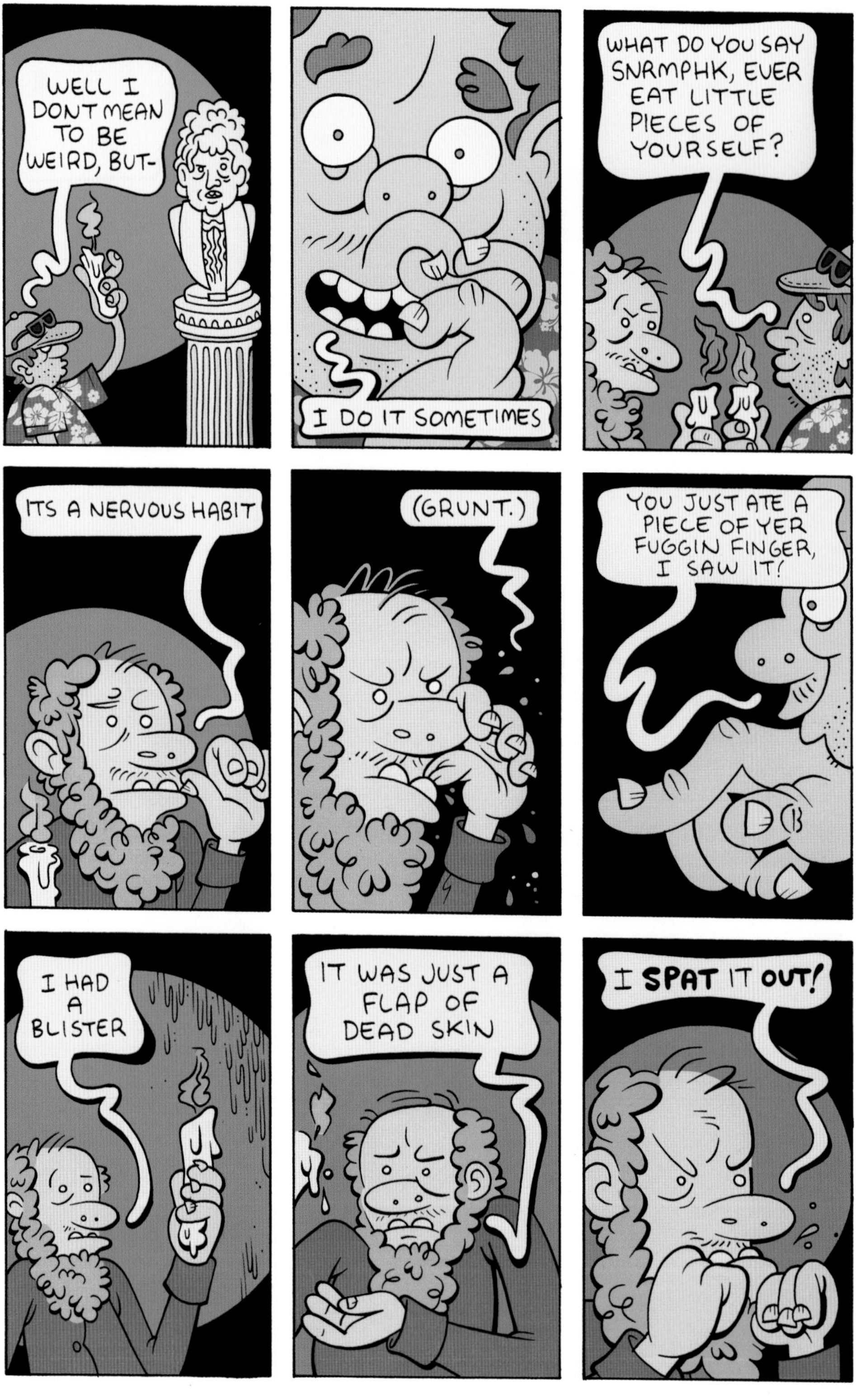
WELL I DONT MEAN TO BE WEIRD, BUT-
I DO IT SOMETIMES
WHAT DO YOU SAY SNRMPHK, EVER EAT LITTLE PIECES OF YOURSELF?
ITS A NERVOUS HABIT
(GRUNT.)
YOU JUST ATE A PIECE OF YER FUGGIN FINGER, I SAW IT!
I HAD A BLISTER
IT WAS JUST A FLAP OF DEAD SKIN
I SPAT IT OUT!

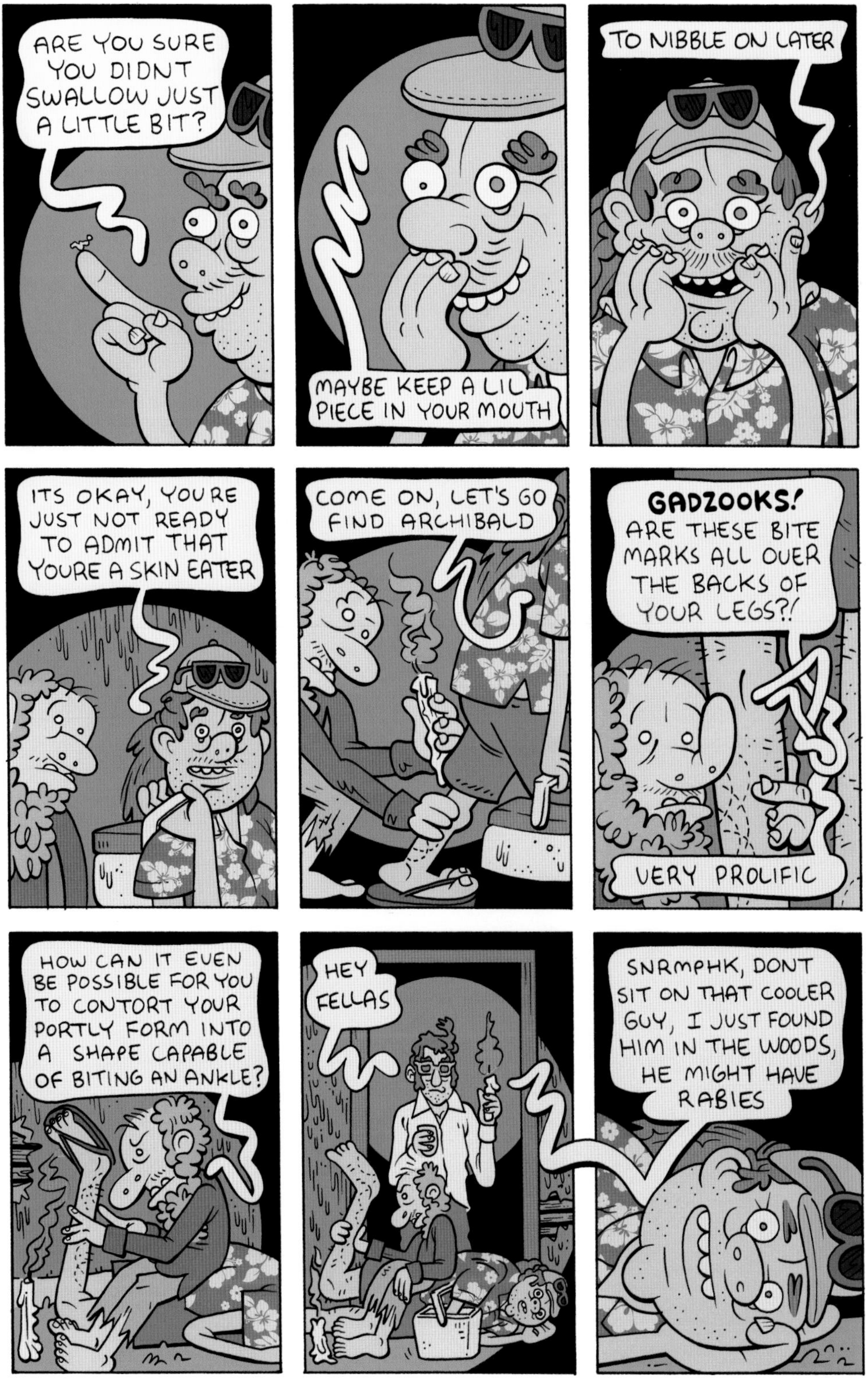
ARE YOU SURE YOU DIDNT SWALLOW JUST A LITTLE BIT?
MAYBE KEEP A LIL PIECE IN YOUR MOUTH
TO NIBBLE ON LATER
ITS OKAY, YOURE JUST NOT READY TO ADMIT THAT YOURE A SKIN EATER
COME ON, LET'S GO FIND ARCHIBALD
GADZOOKS! ARE THESE BITE MARKS ALL OVER THE BACKS OF YOUR LEGS?!
VERY PROLIFIC
HOW CAN IT EVEN BE POSSIBLE FOR YOU TO CONTORT YOUR PORTLY FORM INTO A SHAPE CAPABLE OF BITING AN ANKLE?
HEY FELLAS
SNRMPHK, DONT SIT ON THAT COOLER GUY, I JUST FOUND HIM IN THE WOODS, HE MIGHT HAVE RABIES

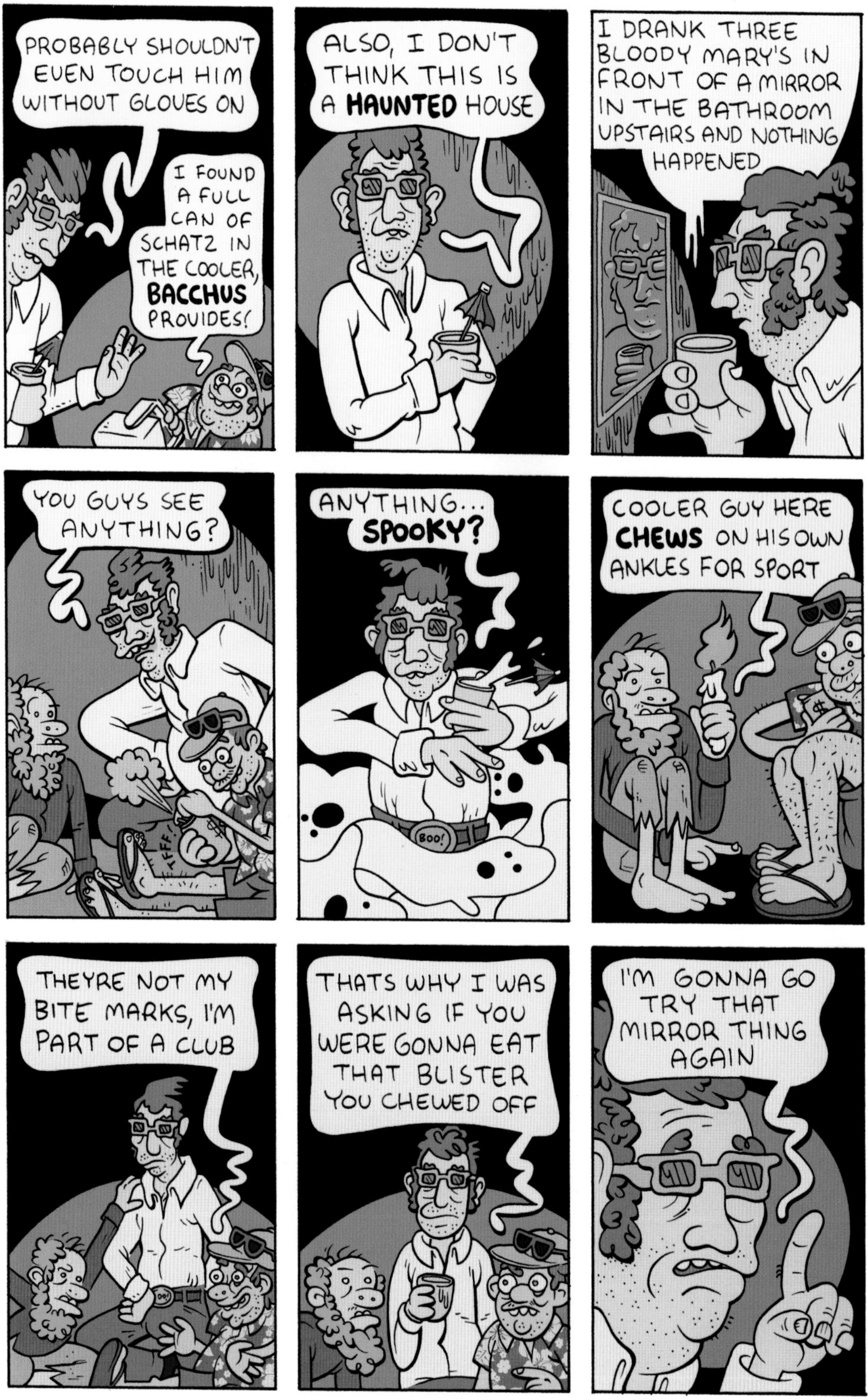
PROBABLY SHOULDN'T EVEN TOUCH HIM WITHOUT GLOVES ON
I FOUND A FULL CAN OF SCHATZ IN THE COOLER, BACCHUS PROVIDES!
ALSO, I DON'T THINK THIS IS A HAUNTED HOUSE
I DRANK THREE BLOODY MARY'S IN FRONT OF A MIRROR IN THE BATHROOM UPSTAIRS AND NOTHING HAPPENED
YOU GUYS SEE ANYTHING?
TFFF!
ANYTHING... SPOOKY?
BOO!
COOLER GUY HERE CHEWS ON HIS OWN ANKLES FOR SPORT
THEYRE NOT MY BITE MARKS, I'M PART OF A CLUB
THATS WHY I WAS ASKING IF YOU WERE GONNA EAT THAT BLISTER YOU CHEWED OFF
I'M GONNA GO TRY THAT MIRROR THING AGAIN

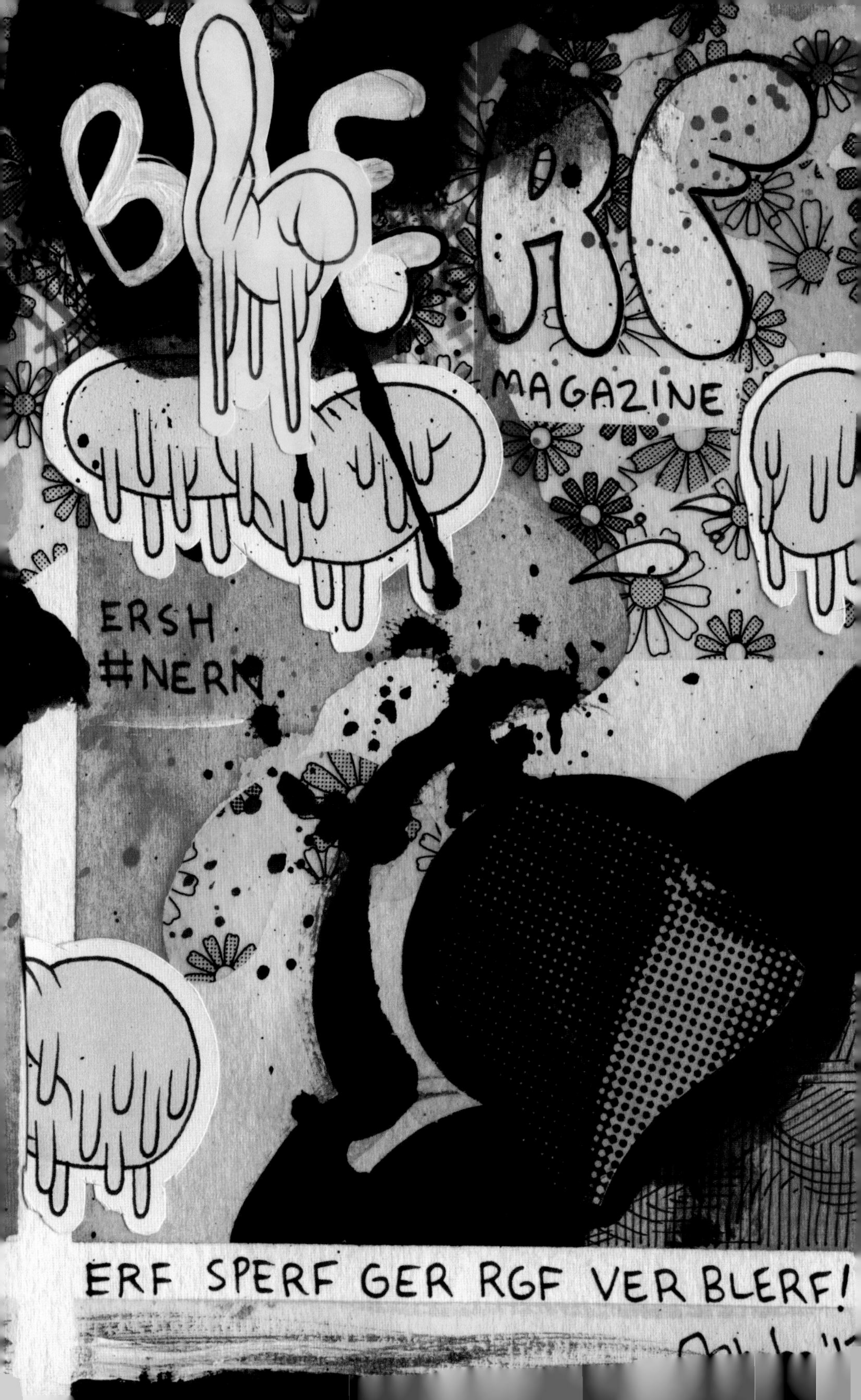
MAGAZINE
ERSH
#NERN
ERF SPERF GER RGF VER BLERF!

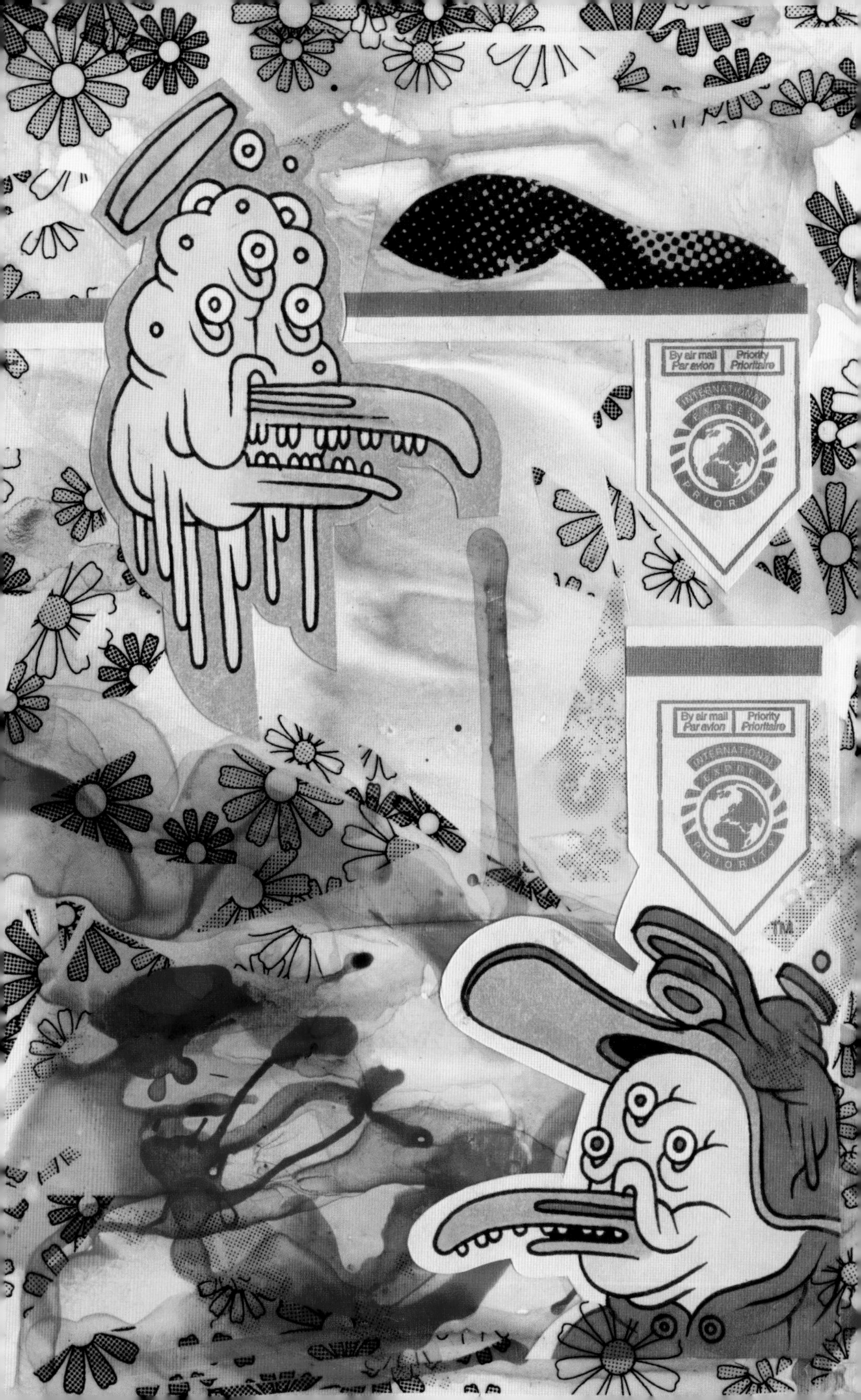

By air mail
Par avion
Priority
Prioritaire
INTERNATIONAL
EXPRESS
PRIORITY
By air mail
Par avion
Priority
Prioritaire
INTERNATIONAL
EXPRESS
PRIORITY
TM

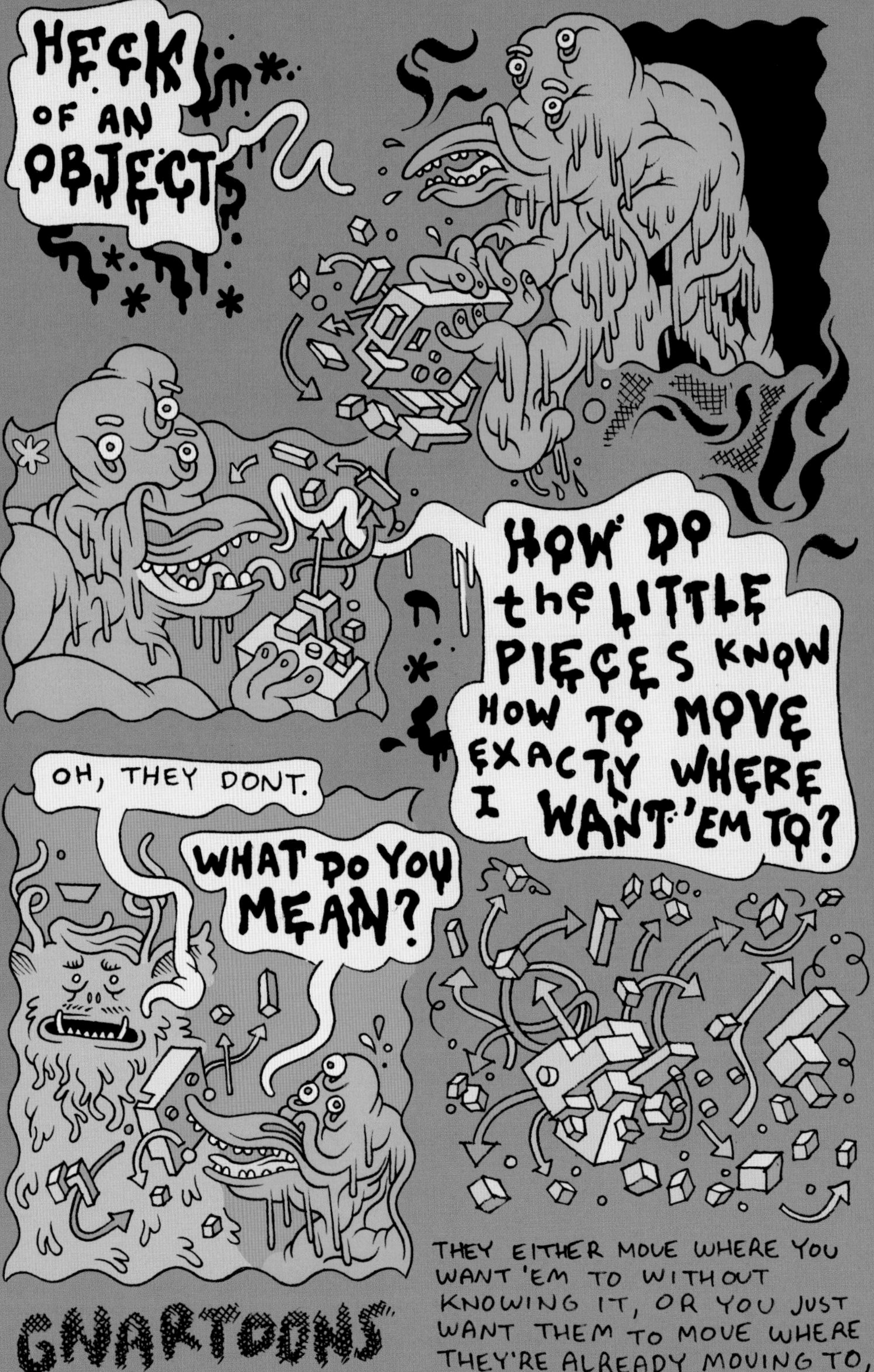

HECK OF AN OBJECT
HOW DO the LITTLE PIECES KNOW HOW TO MOVE EXACTLY WHERE I WANT 'EM TO?
OH, THEY DONT.
WHAT DO YOU MEAN?
THEY EITHER MOVE WHERE YOU WANT 'EM TO WITHOUT KNOWING IT, OR YOU JUST WANT THEM TO MOVE WHERE THEY'RE ALREADY MOVING TO, EITHER WAY, IT ALL WORKS OUT IN THE END.
GNARTOONS
BY JAMES the STANTON

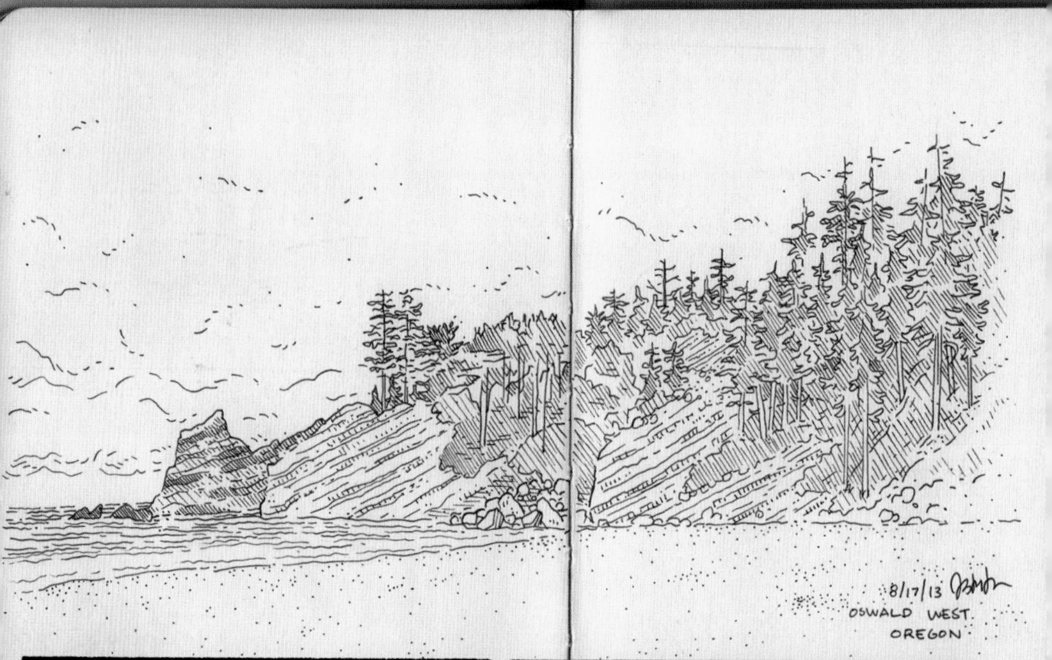
8/17/13
OSWALD WEST.
OREGON

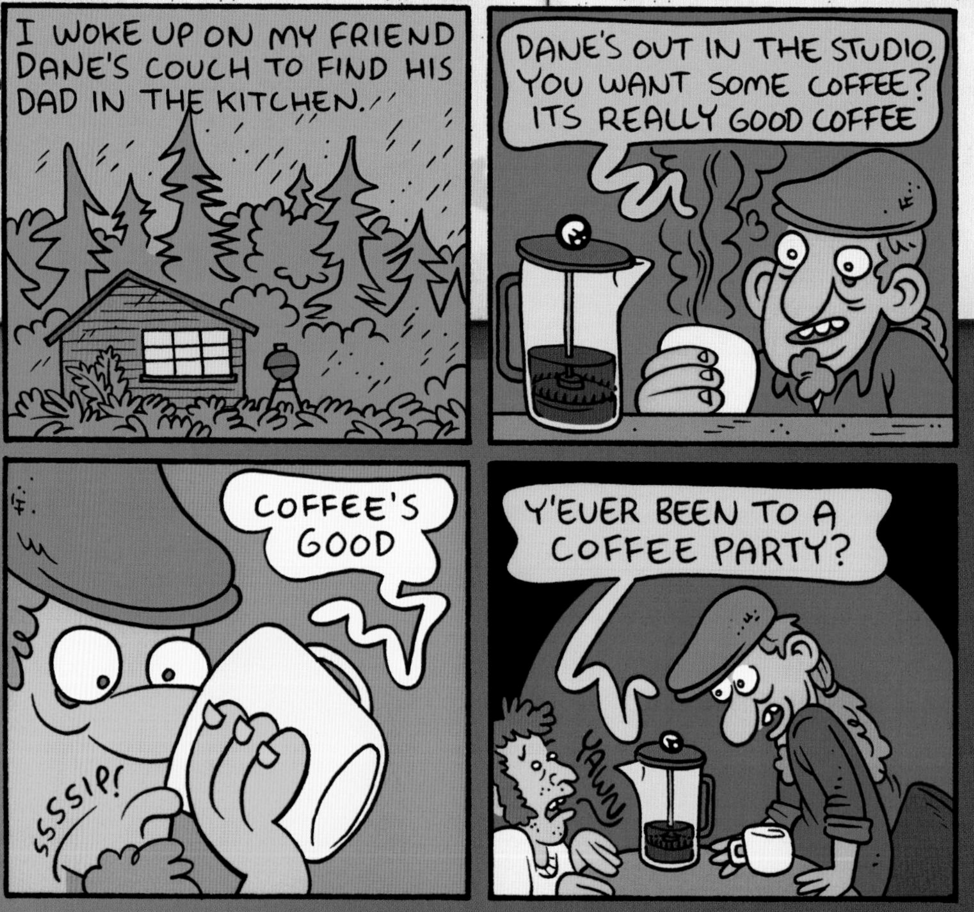
I WOKE UP ON MY FRIEND DANE'S COUCH TO FIND HIS DAD IN THE KITCHEN.
DANE'S OUT IN THE STUDIO, YOU WANT SOME COFFEE? ITS REALLY GOOD COFFEE
COFFEE'S GOOD
SSSSIP!
Y'EVER BEEN TO A COFFEE PARTY?
YAWN

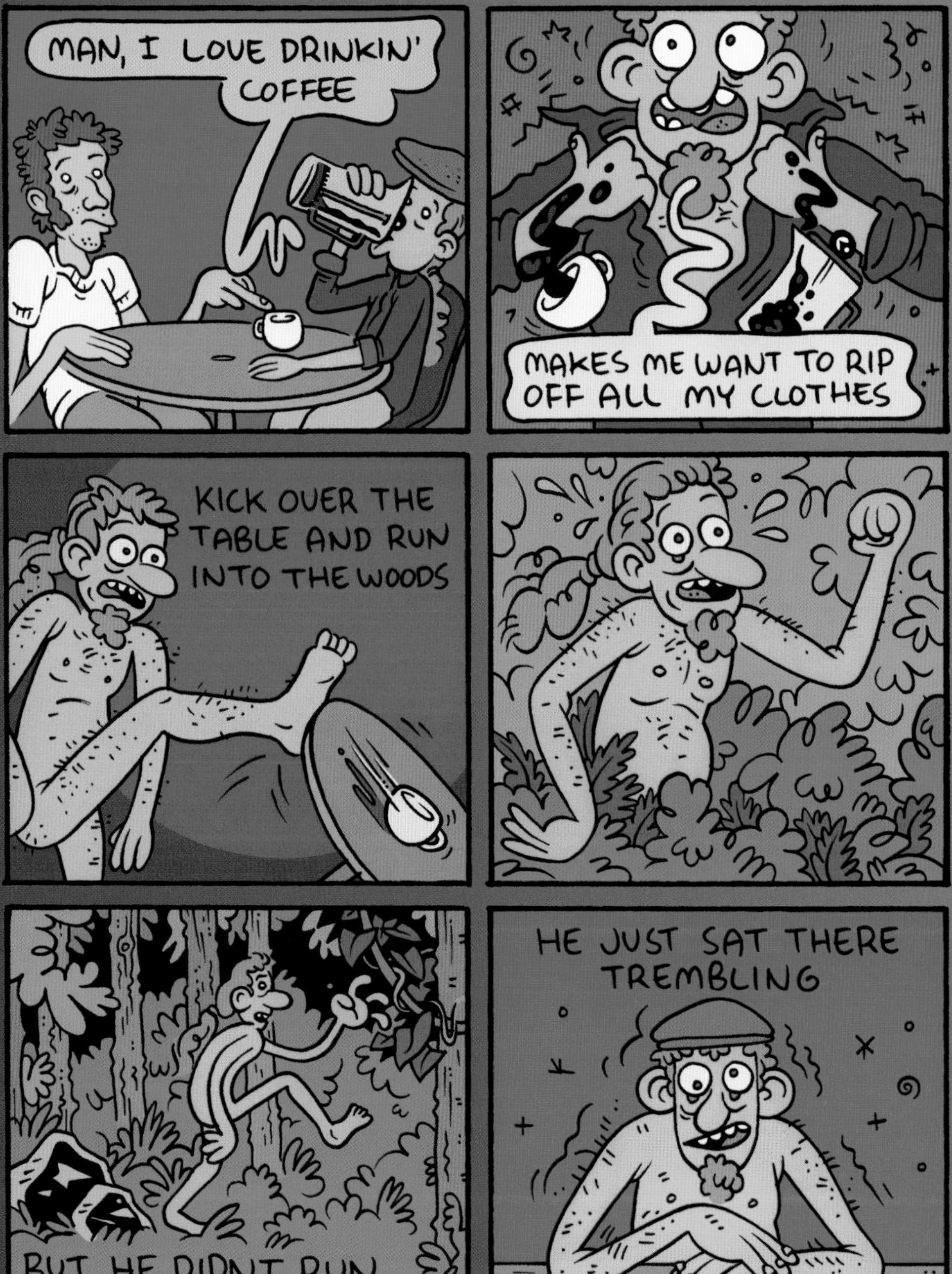
MAN, I LOVE DRINKIN' COFFEE
MAKES ME WANT TO RIP OFF ALL MY CLOTHES
KICK OVER THE TABLE AND RUN INTO THE WOODS
BUT HE DIDNT RUN OFF INTO THE WOODS.
HE JUST SAT THERE TREMBLING

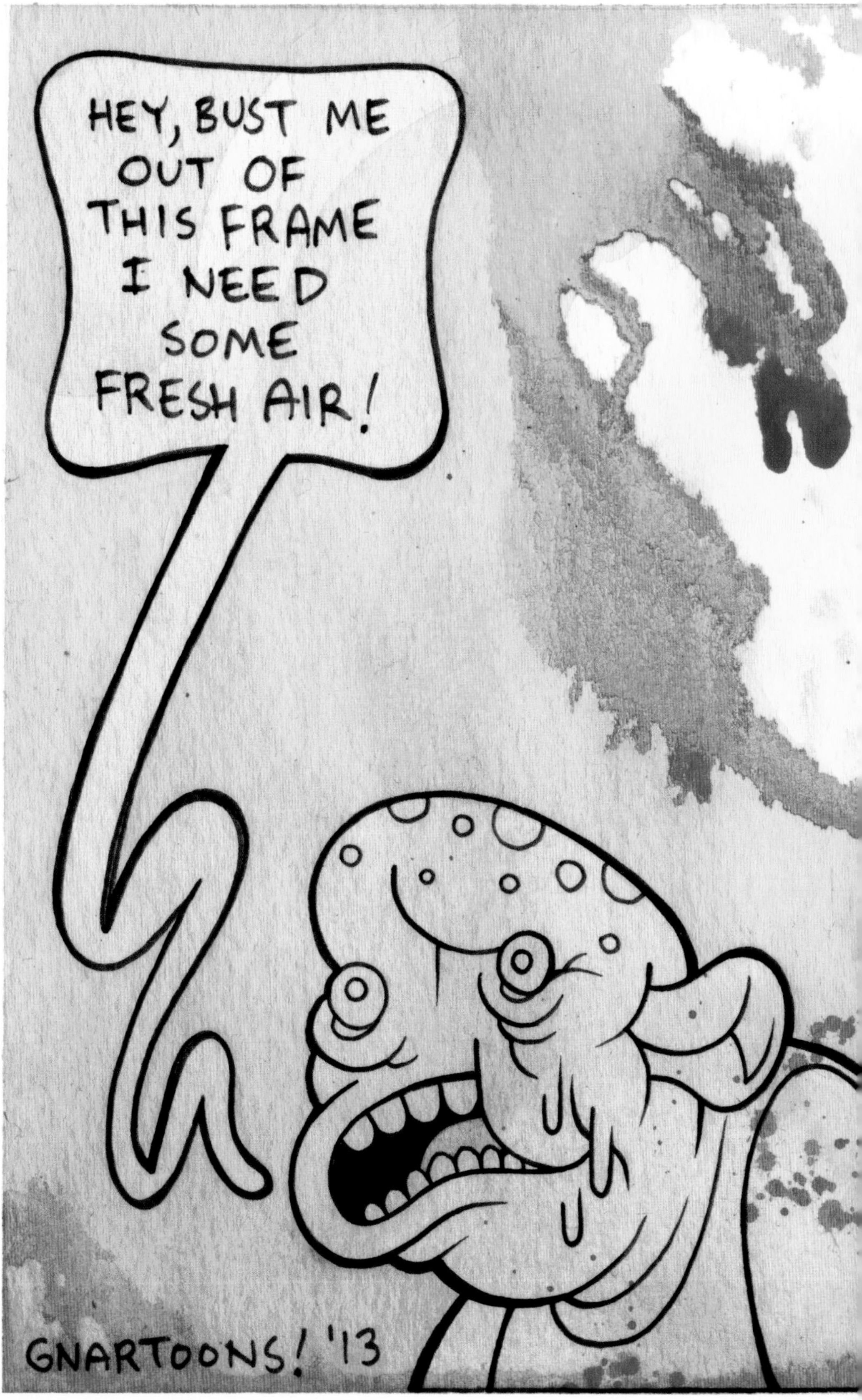
HEY, BUST ME OUT OF THIS FRAME I NEED SOME FRESH AIR!
GNARTOONS! '13

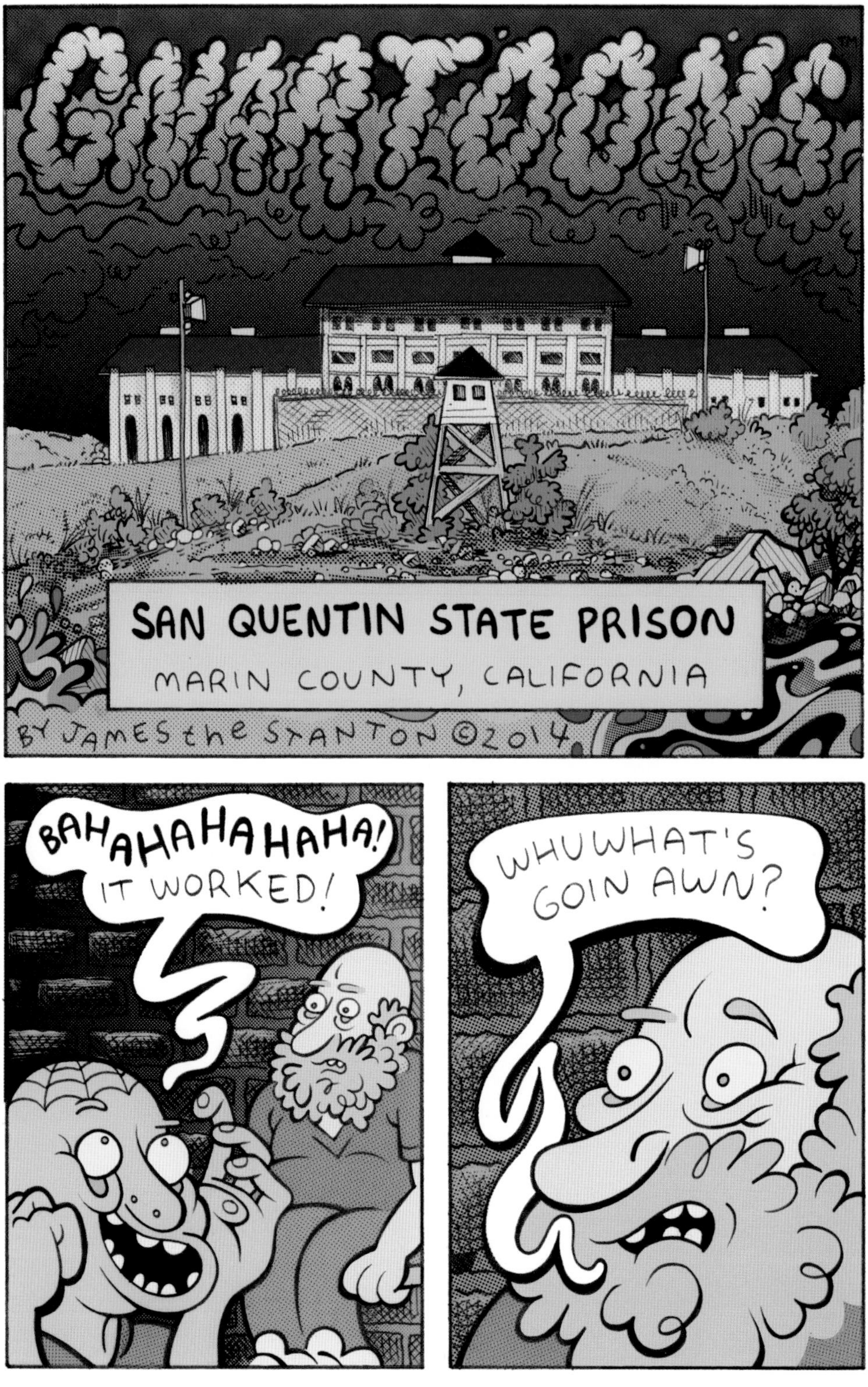
SAN QUENTIN STATE PRISON
MARIN COUNTY, CALIFORNIA
BY JAMES the STANTON ©2014
BAHAHAHAHAHA! IT WORKED!
WHUWHAT'S GOIN AWN?

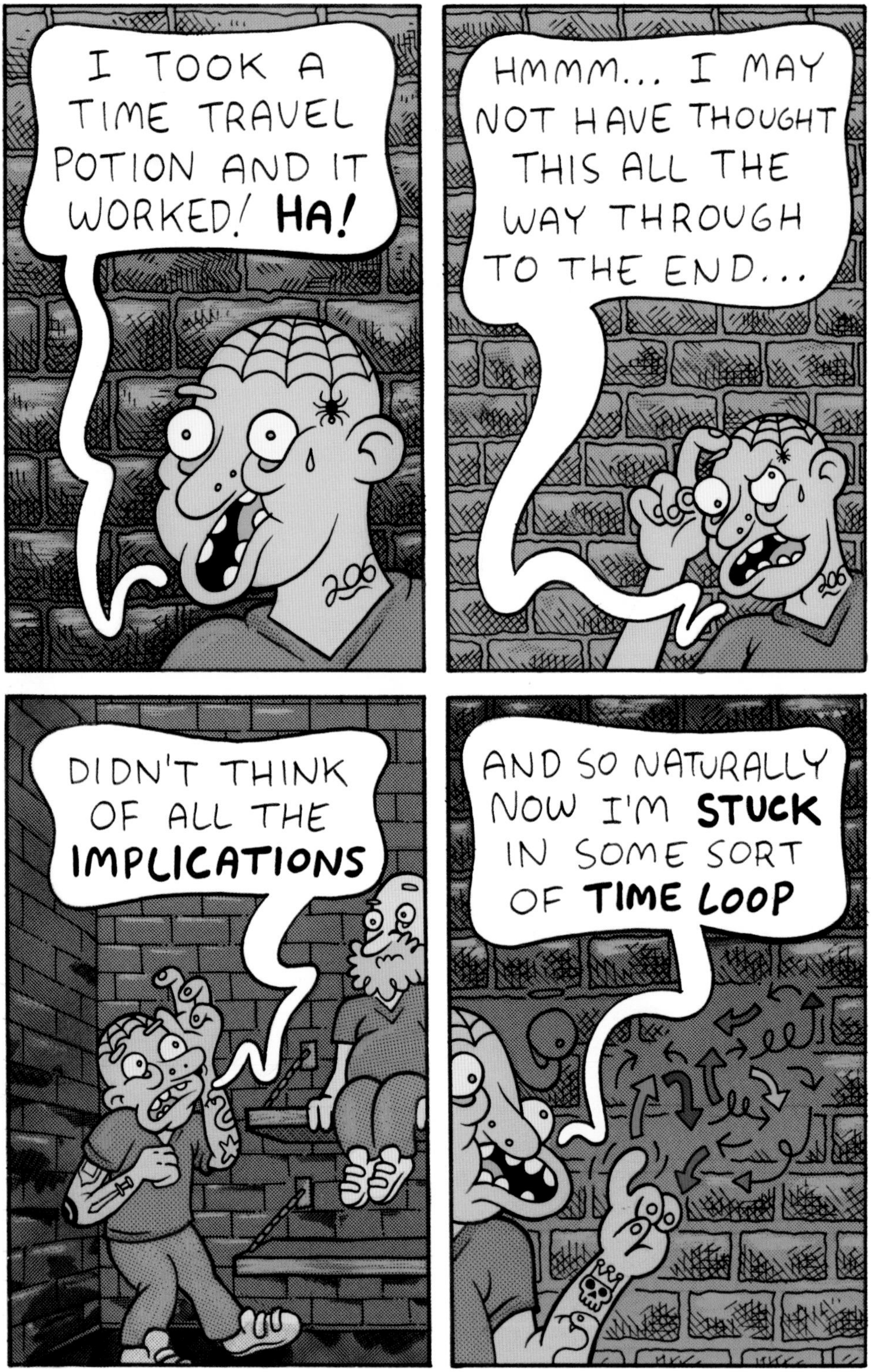

I TOOK A TIME TRAVEL POTION AND IT WORKED! HA!
HMMM... I MAY NOT HAVE THOUGHT THIS ALL THE WAY THROUGH TO THE END...
DIDN'T THINK OF ALL THE IMPLICATIONS
AND SO NATURALLY NOW I'M STUCK IN SOME SORT OF TIME LOOP

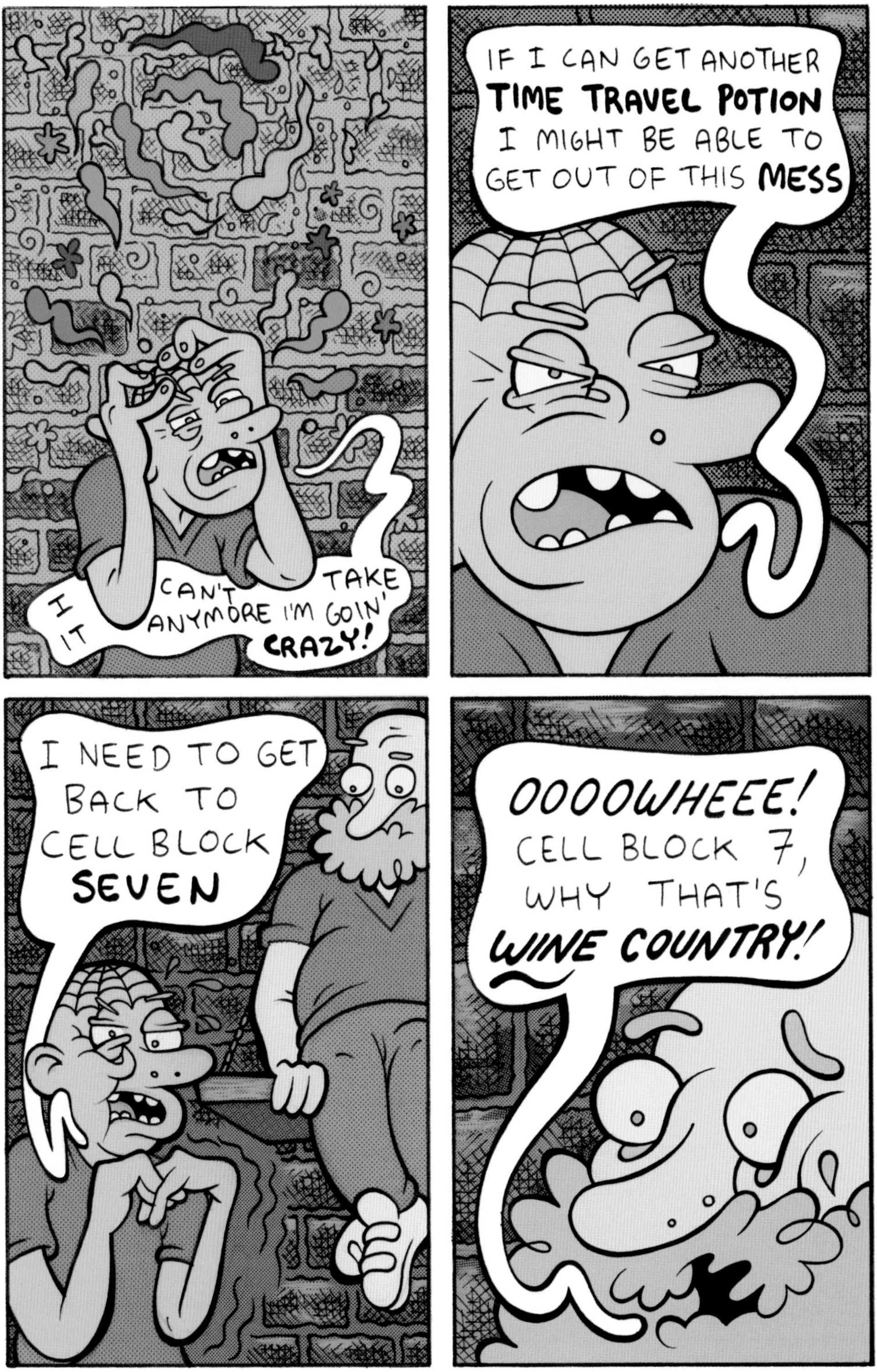
I CAN'T TAKE IT ANYMORE I'M GOIN' CRAZY!
IF I CAN GET ANOTHER TIME TRAVEL POTION I MIGHT BE ABLE TO GET OUT OF THIS MESS
I NEED TO GET BACK TO CELL BLOCK SEVEN
OOOOWHEEE! CELL BLOCK 7, WHY THAT'S WINE COUNTRY!

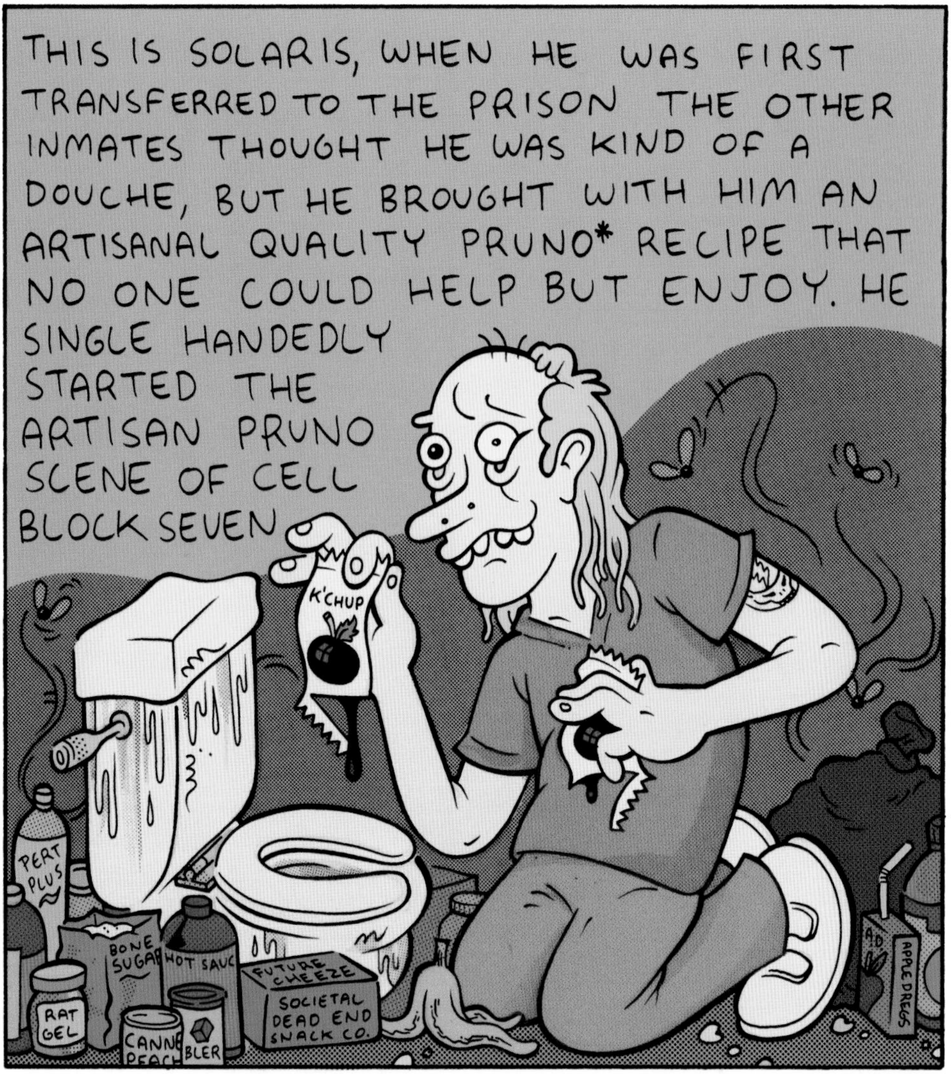
THIS IS SOLARIS, WHEN HE WAS FIRST TRANSFERRED TO THE PRISON THE OTHER INMATES THOUGHT HE WAS KIND OF A DOUCHE, BUT HE BROUGHT WITH HIM AN ARTISANAL QUALITY PRUNO* RECIPE THAT NO ONE COULD HELP BUT ENJOY. HE SINGLE HANDEDLY STARTED THE ARTISAN PRUNO SCENE OF CELL BLOCK SEVEN
K'CHUP
PERT PLUS
BONE SUGAR
HOT SAUC
FUTURE CHEEZE
SOCIETAL DEAD END SNACK CO.
RAT GEL
CANNE PEACH
BLER
AD
APPLE DREGS

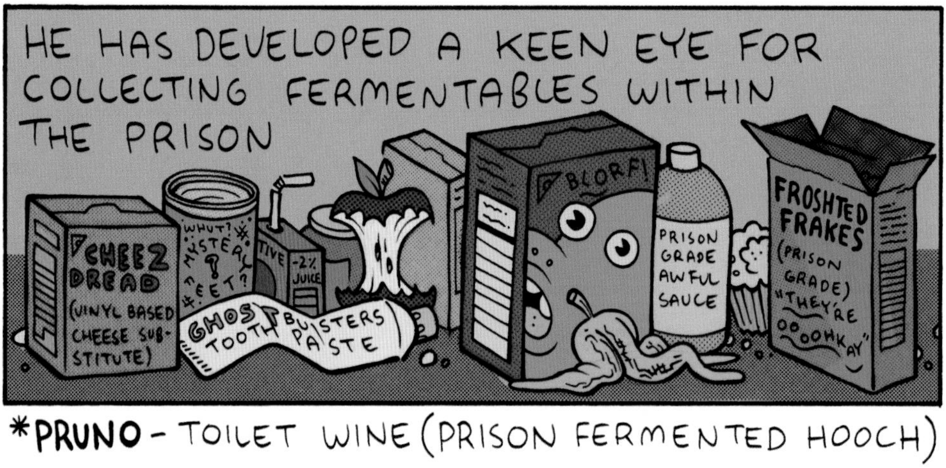
HE HAS DEVELOPED A KEEN EYE FOR COLLECTING FERMENTABLES WITHIN THE PRISON
CHEEZ DREAD (VINYL BASED CHEESE SUBSTITUTE)
WHUT?! MYSTERY FEET?
TIVE -2% JUICE
GHOST BUSTERS TOOTH PASTE
BLORF!
PRISON GRADE AWFUL SAUCE
FROSHTED FRAKES (PRISON GRADE) "THEY'RE OOOOHKAY"

***PRUNO** - TOILET WINE (PRISON FERMENTED HOOCH)

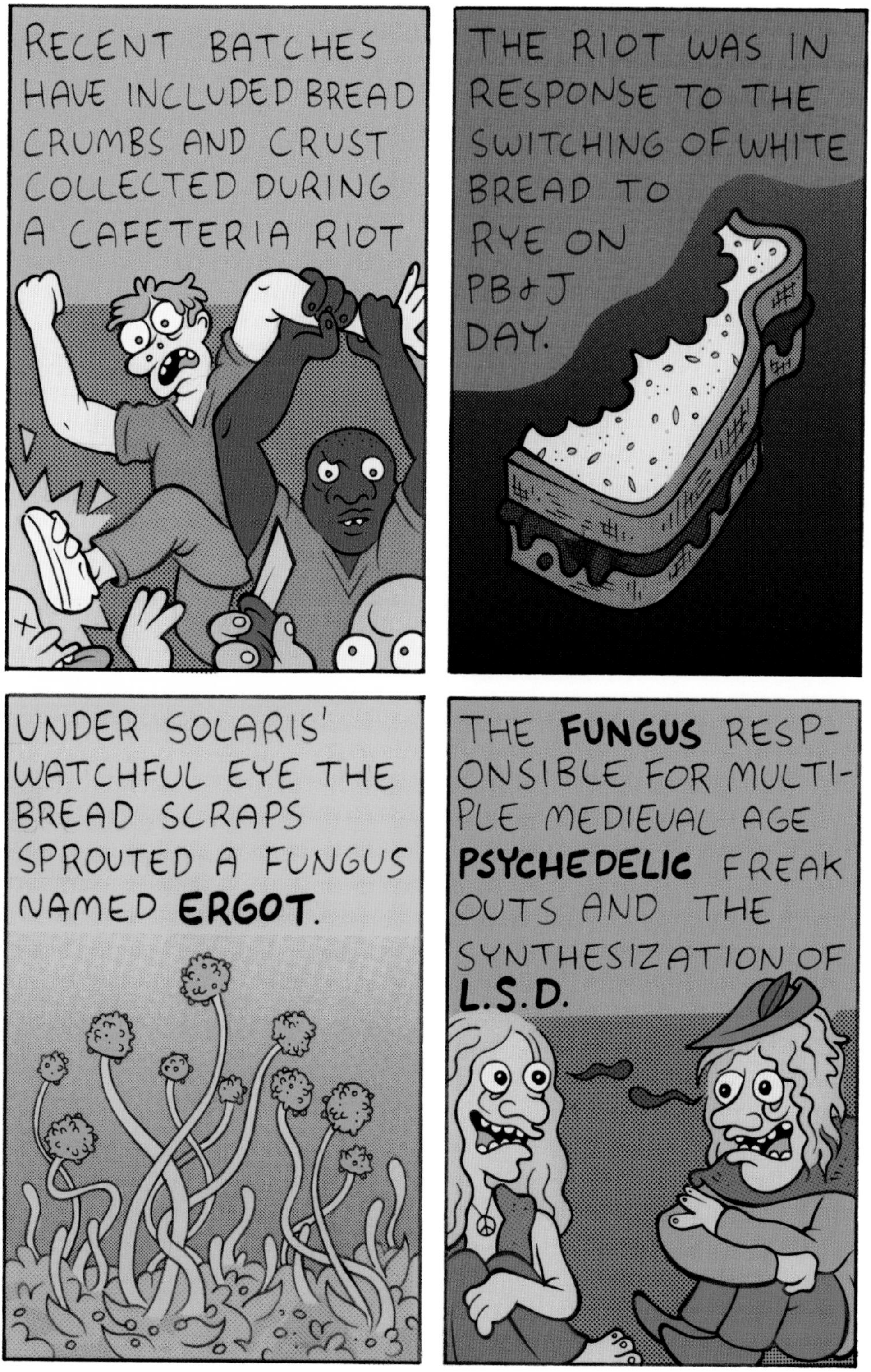
RECENT BATCHES HAVE INCLUDED BREAD CRUMBS AND CRUST COLLECTED DURING A CAFETERIA RIOT
THE RIOT WAS IN RESPONSE TO THE SWITCHING OF WHITE BREAD TO RYE ON PB&J DAY.
UNDER SOLARIS' WATCHFUL EYE THE BREAD SCRAPS SPROUTED A FUNGUS NAMED **ERGOT**.
THE **FUNGUS** RESPONSIBLE FOR MULTIPLE MEDIEVAL AGE **PSYCHEDELIC** FREAK OUTS AND THE SYNTHESIZATION OF **L.S.D.**

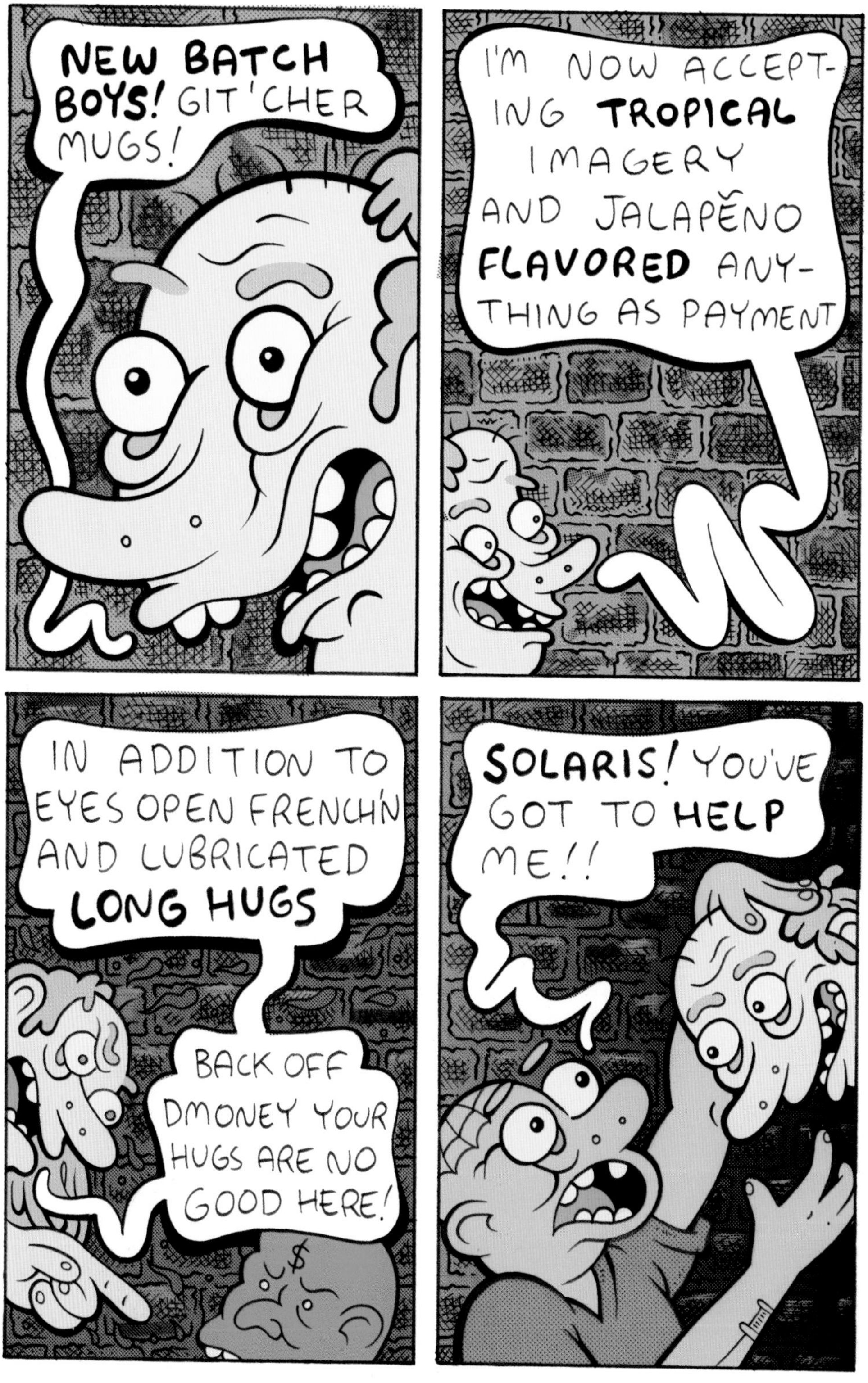
NEW BATCH BOYS! GIT'CHER MUGS!
I'M NOW ACCEPT-ING TROPICAL IMAGERY AND JALAPĔNO FLAVORED ANY-THING AS PAYMENT
IN ADDITION TO EYES OPEN FRENCH'N AND LUBRICATED LONG HUGS
BACK OFF DMONEY YOUR HUGS ARE NO GOOD HERE!
SOLARIS! YOU'VE GOT TO HELP ME!!

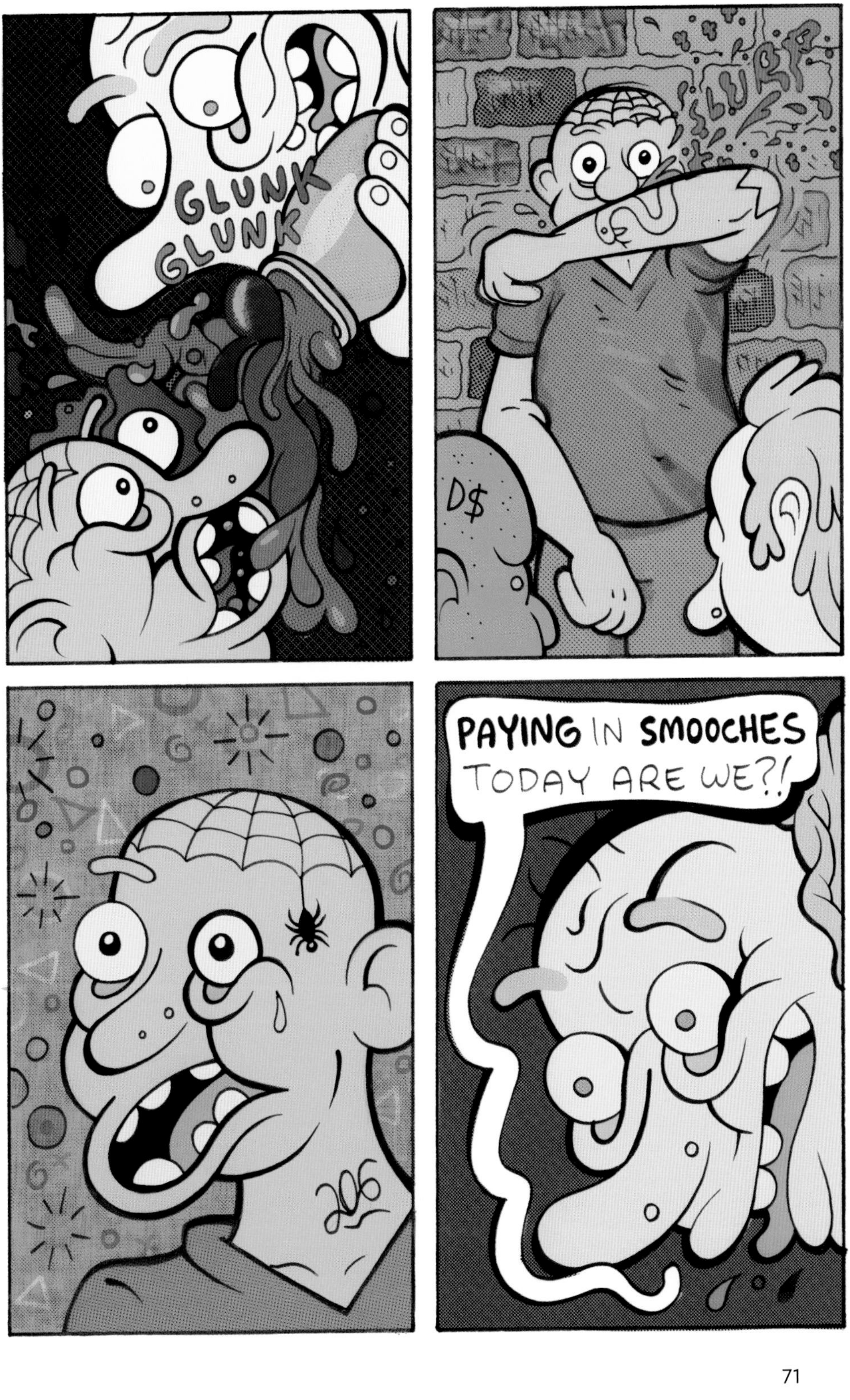
GLUNK
GLUNK
SLURP
D$
PAYING IN SMOOCHES TODAY ARE WE?!

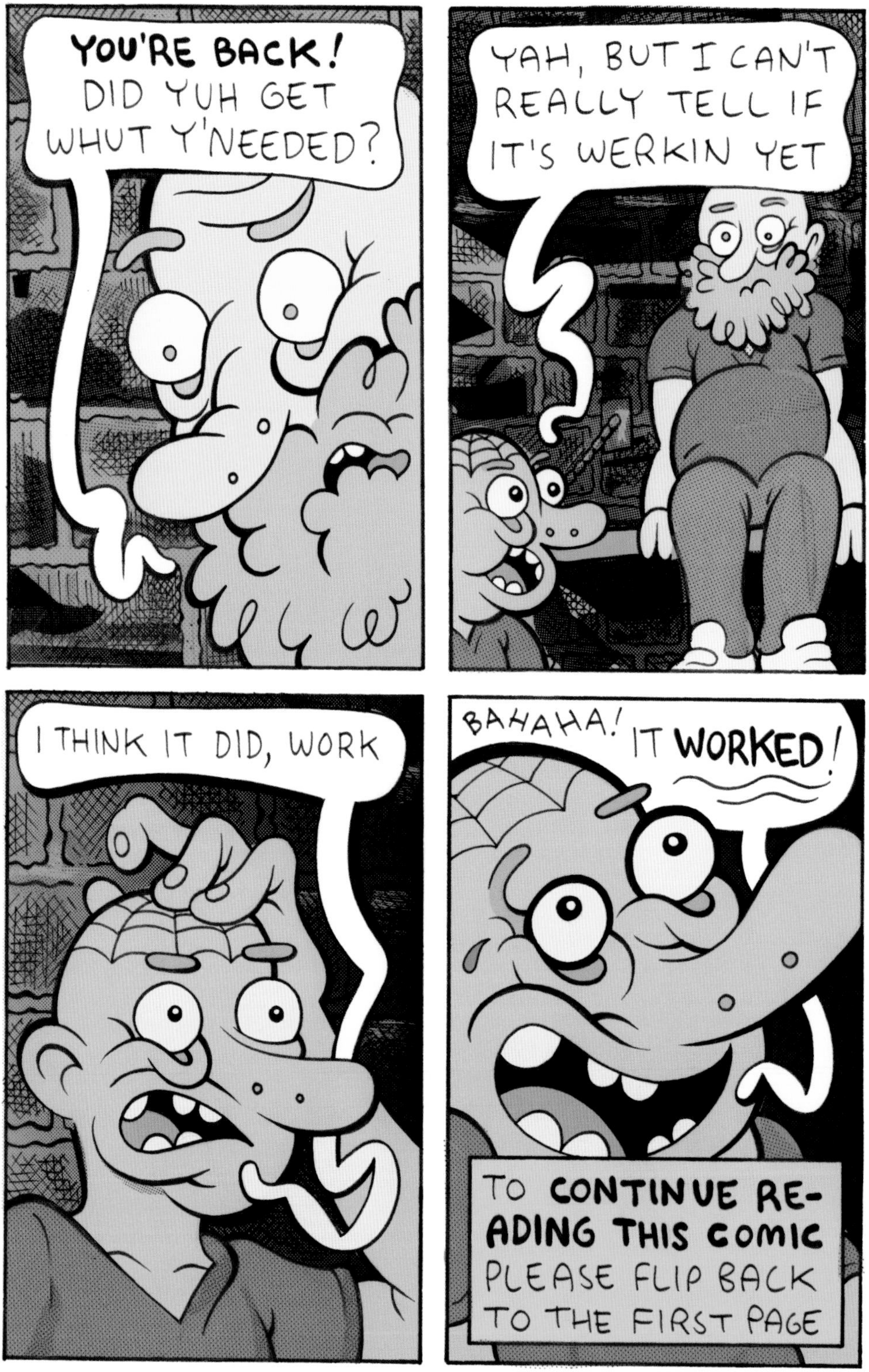
YOU'RE BACK! DID YUH GET WHUT Y'NEEDED?
YAH, BUT I CAN'T REALLY TELL IF IT'S WERKIN YET
I THINK IT DID, WORK
BAHAHA! IT WORKED!
TO CONTINUE READING THIS COMIC PLEASE FLIP BACK TO THE FIRST PAGE

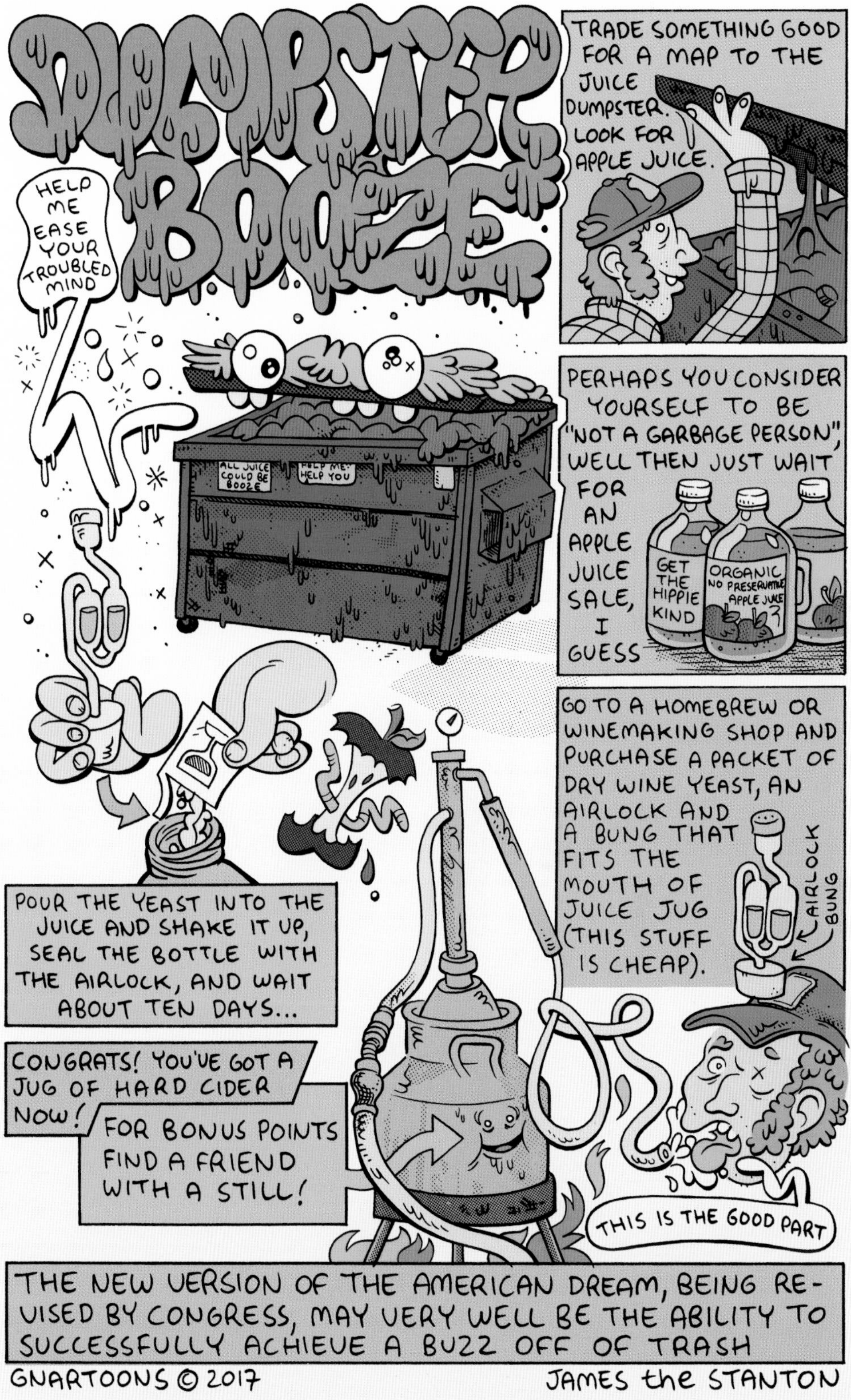
DUMPSTER BOOZE
HELP ME EASE YOUR TROUBLED MIND
TRADE SOMETHING GOOD FOR A MAP TO THE JUICE DUMPSTER. LOOK FOR APPLE JUICE.
ALL JUICE COULD BE BOOZE
HELP ME HELP YOU
PERHAPS YOU CONSIDER YOURSELF TO BE "NOT A GARBAGE PERSON", WELL THEN JUST WAIT FOR AN APPLE JUICE SALE, I GUESS
GET THE HIPPIE KIND
ORGANIC NO PRESERVATIVES APPLE JUICE
GO TO A HOMEBREW OR WINEMAKING SHOP AND PURCHASE A PACKET OF DRY WINE YEAST, AN AIRLOCK AND A BUNG THAT FITS THE MOUTH OF JUICE JUG (THIS STUFF IS CHEAP).
AIRLOCK
BUNG
POUR THE YEAST INTO THE JUICE AND SHAKE IT UP, SEAL THE BOTTLE WITH THE AIRLOCK, AND WAIT ABOUT TEN DAYS...
CONGRATS! YOU'VE GOT A JUG OF HARD CIDER NOW!
FOR BONUS POINTS FIND A FRIEND WITH A STILL!
THIS IS THE GOOD PART
THE NEW VERSION OF THE AMERICAN DREAM, BEING REVISED BY CONGRESS, MAY VERY WELL BE THE ABILITY TO SUCCESSFULLY ACHIEVE A BUZZ OFF OF TRASH

 JAMES the STANTON

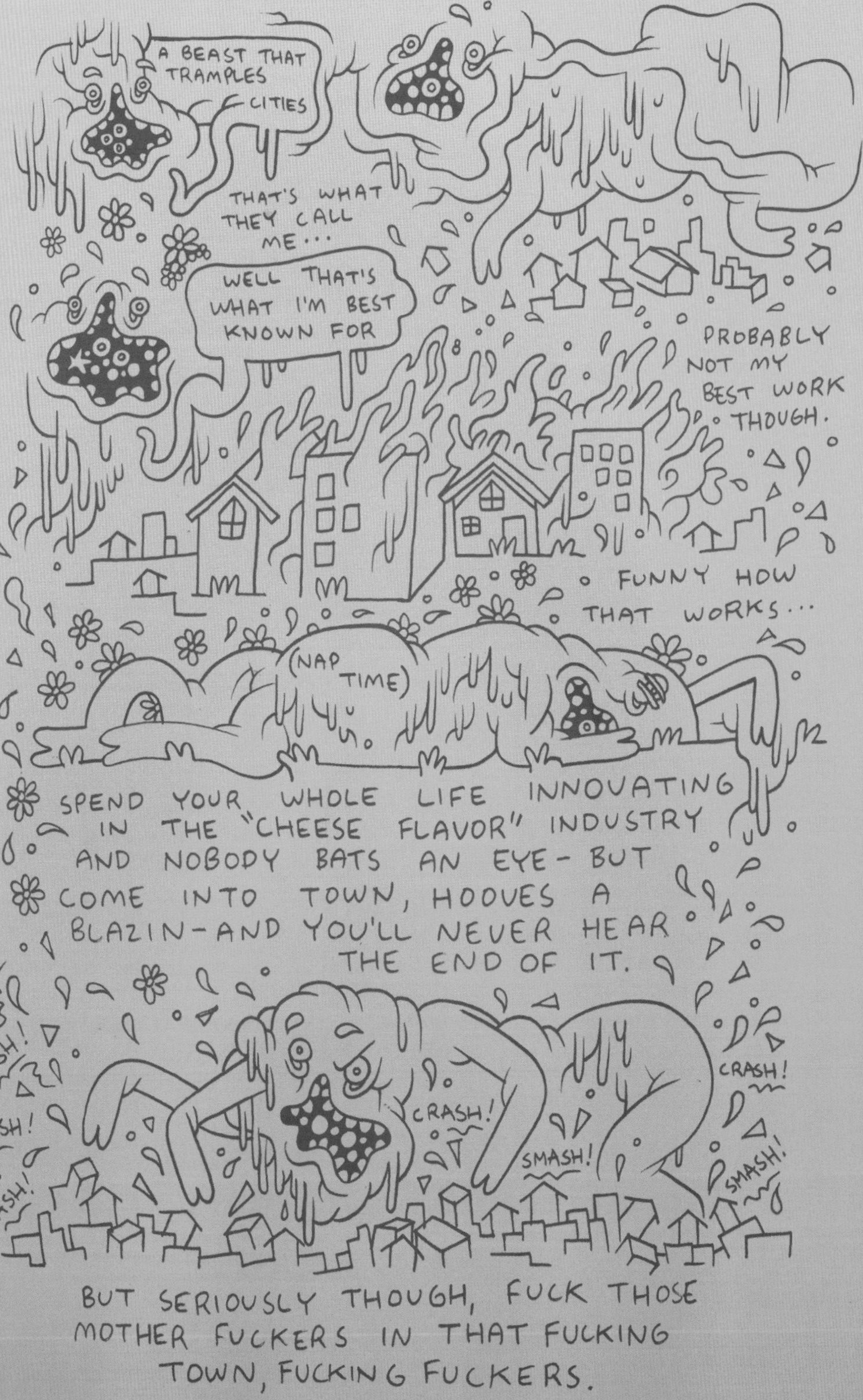
A BEAST THAT TRAMPLES CITIES
THAT'S WHAT THEY CALL ME...
WELL THAT'S WHAT I'M BEST KNOWN FOR
PROBABLY NOT MY BEST WORK THOUGH.
FUNNY HOW THAT WORKS...
(NAP TIME)
SPEND YOUR WHOLE LIFE INNOVATING IN THE "CHEESE FLAVOR" INDUSTRY AND NOBODY BATS AN EYE- BUT COME INTO TOWN, HOOVES A BLAZIN- AND YOU'LL NEVER HEAR THE END OF IT.
SHMASH!
CRASH!
SMASH!
CRASH!
SMASH!
CRASH!
SMASH!
BUT SERIOUSLY THOUGH, FUCK THOSE MOTHER FUCKERS IN THAT FUCKING TOWN, FUCKING FUCKERS.

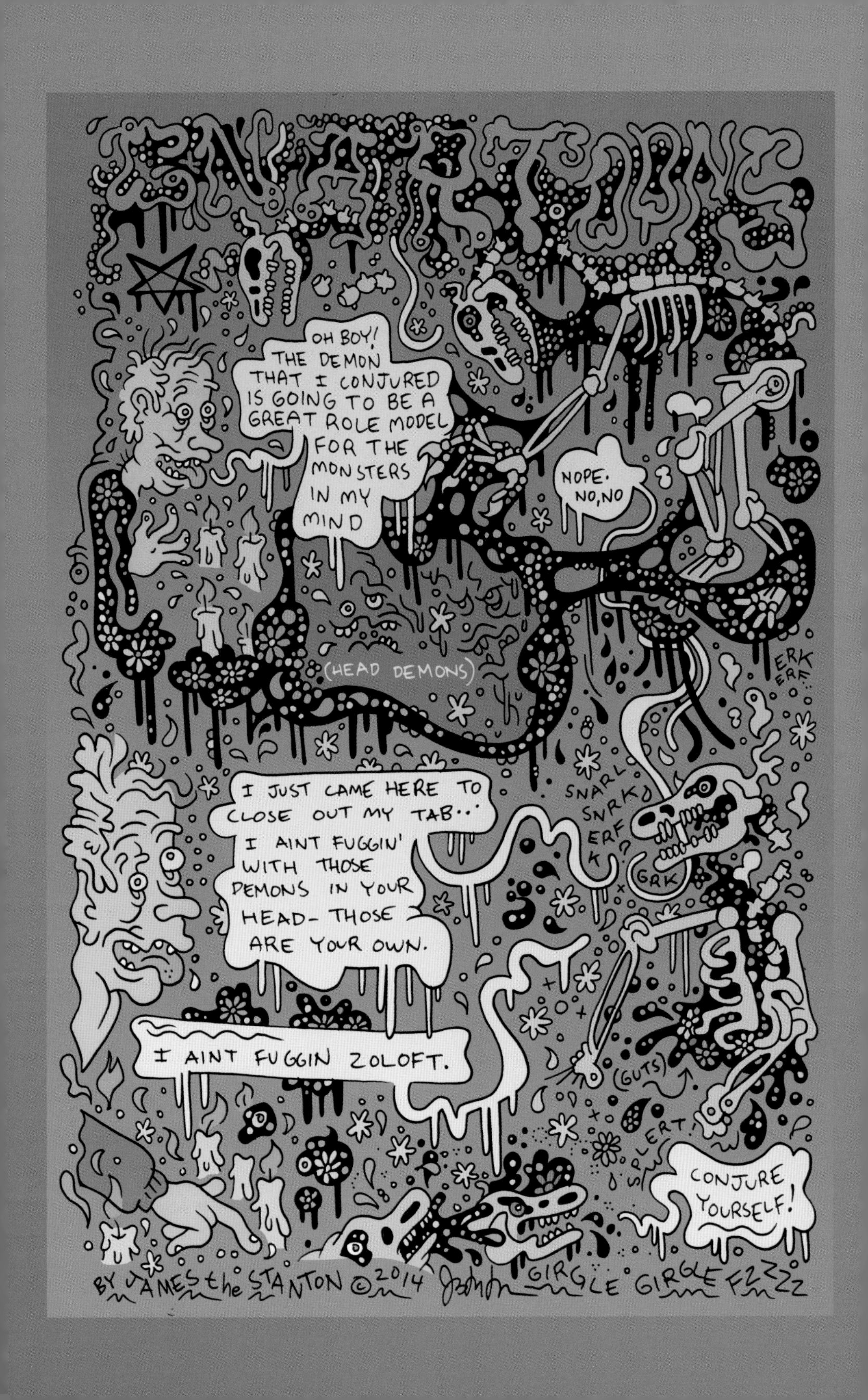
OH BOY! THE DEMON THAT I CONJURED IS GOING TO BE A GREAT ROLE MODEL FOR THE MONSTERS IN MY MIND
NOPE. NO, NO
(HEAD DEMONS)
ERK ERF
SNARL SNRK ERF K?
GRK
I JUST CAME HERE TO CLOSE OUT MY TAB.. I AINT FUGGIN' WITH THOSE DEMONS IN YOUR HEAD- THOSE ARE YOUR OWN.
I AINT FUGGIN ZOLOFT.
(GUTS)
SPLERT!
CONJURE YOURSELF!
BY JAMES the STANTON © 2014
GIRGLE GIRGLE FZZZZ

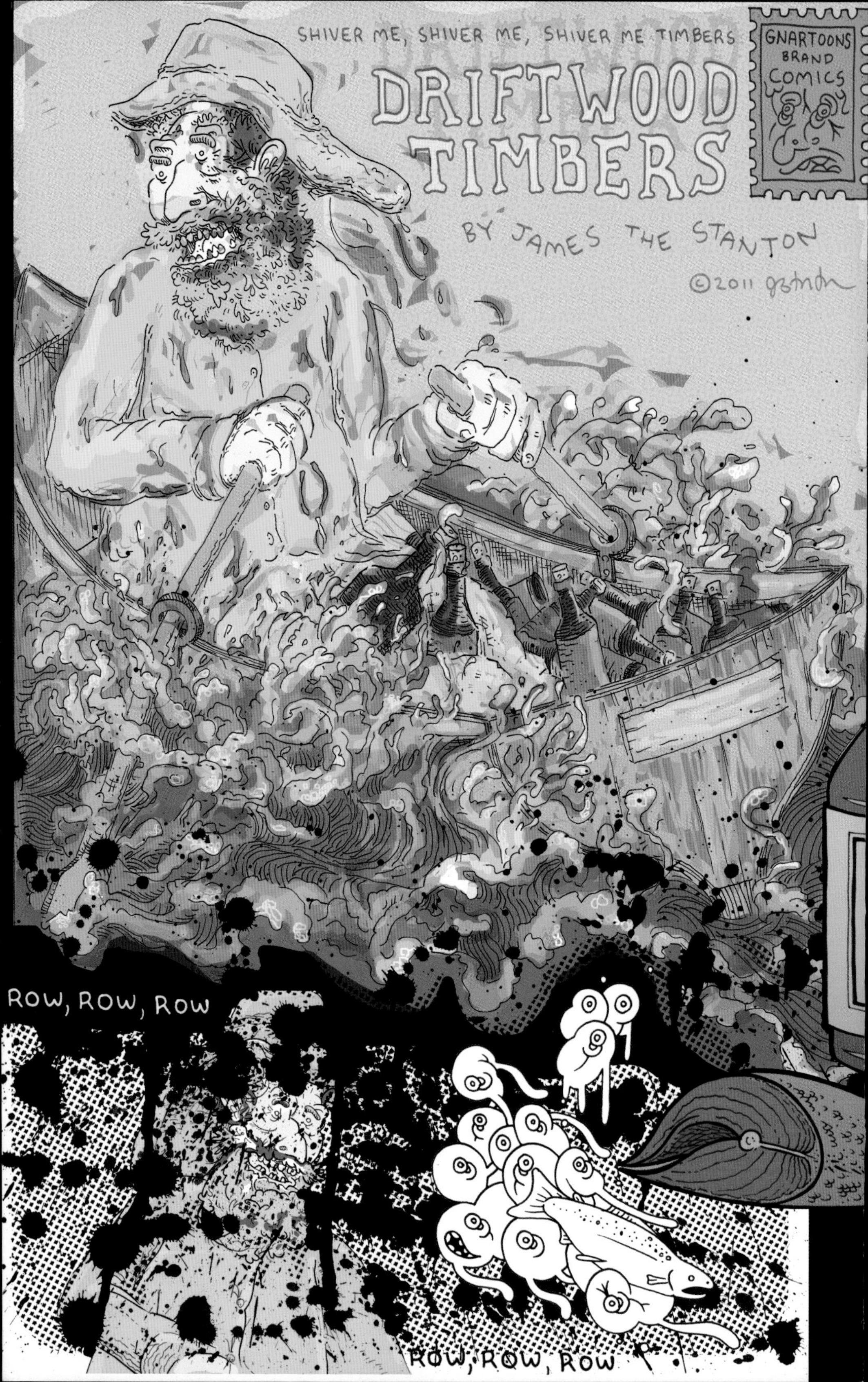

SHIVER ME, SHIVER ME, SHIVER ME TIMBERS
DRIFTWOOD TIMBERS
GNARTOONS BRAND COMICS
BY JAMES THE STANTON
©2011
ROW, ROW, ROW
ROW, ROW, ROW

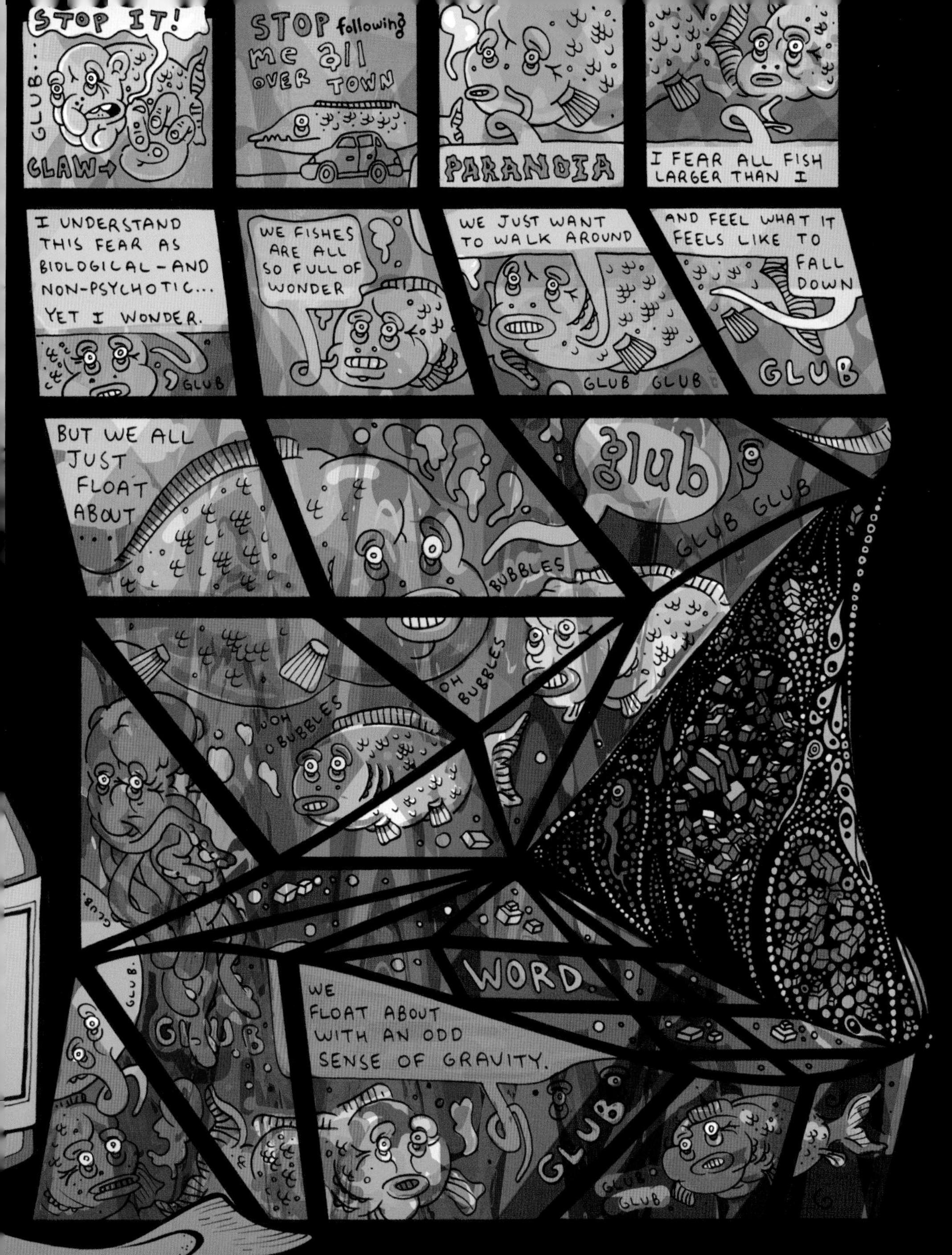
STOP IT!
GLUB...
CLAW→
STOP following me all OVER TOWN
PARANOIA
I FEAR ALL FISH LARGER THAN I
I UNDERSTAND THIS FEAR AS BIOLOGICAL - AND NON-PSYCHOTIC... YET I WONDER.
GLUB
WE FISHES ARE ALL SO FULL OF WONDER
WE JUST WANT TO WALK AROUND
GLUB GLUB
AND FEEL WHAT IT FEELS LIKE TO FALL DOWN
GLUB
BUT WE ALL JUST FLOAT ABOUT ...
glub
GLUB GLUB
BUBBLES
OH BUBBLES
OOH BUBBLES
GLUB.
GLUB.
GLUB
WORD
WE FLOAT ABOUT WITH AN ODD SENSE OF GRAVITY.
GLUB
GLUB
GLUB GLUB

We can handle it

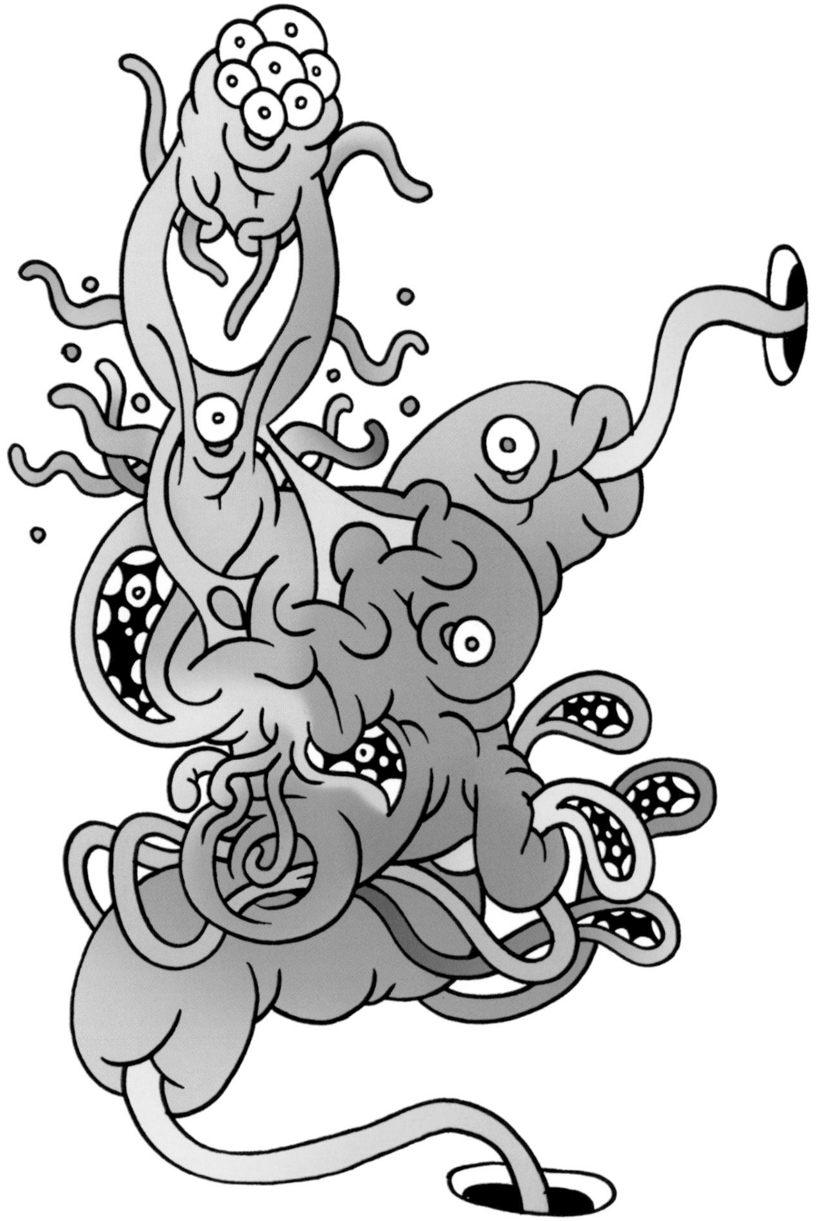

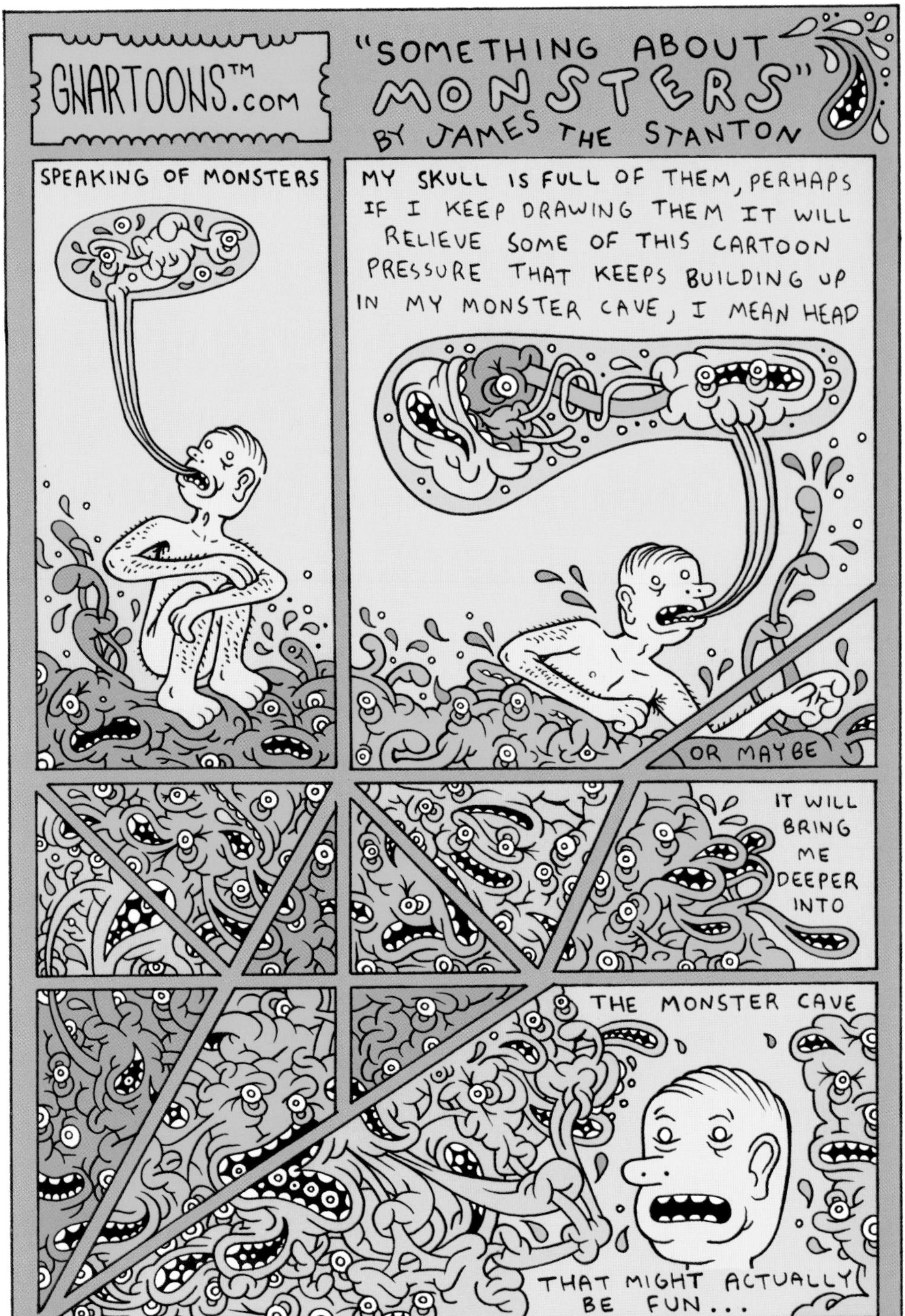
GNARTOONS™.com
"SOMETHING ABOUT MONSTERS"
BY JAMES THE STANTON
SPEAKING OF MONSTERS
MY SKULL IS FULL OF THEM, PERHAPS IF I KEEP DRAWING THEM IT WILL RELIEVE SOME OF THIS CARTOON PRESSURE THAT KEEPS BUILDING UP IN MY MONSTER CAVE, I MEAN HEAD
OR MAYBE
IT WILL BRING ME DEEPER INTO
THE MONSTER CAVE
THAT MIGHT ACTUALLY BE FUN...

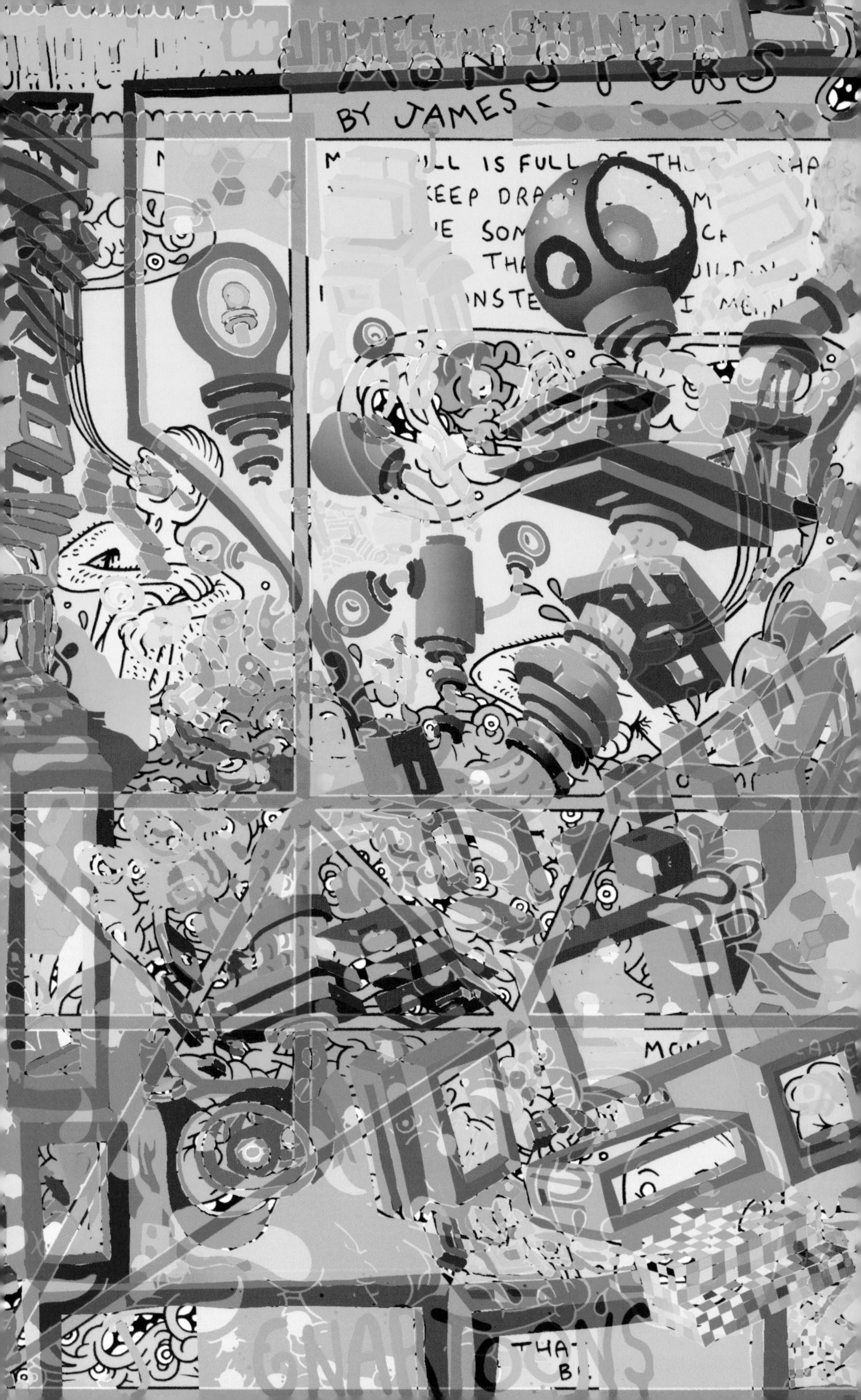
JAMES STANTON
MONSTERS
BY JAMES
GNARTOONS

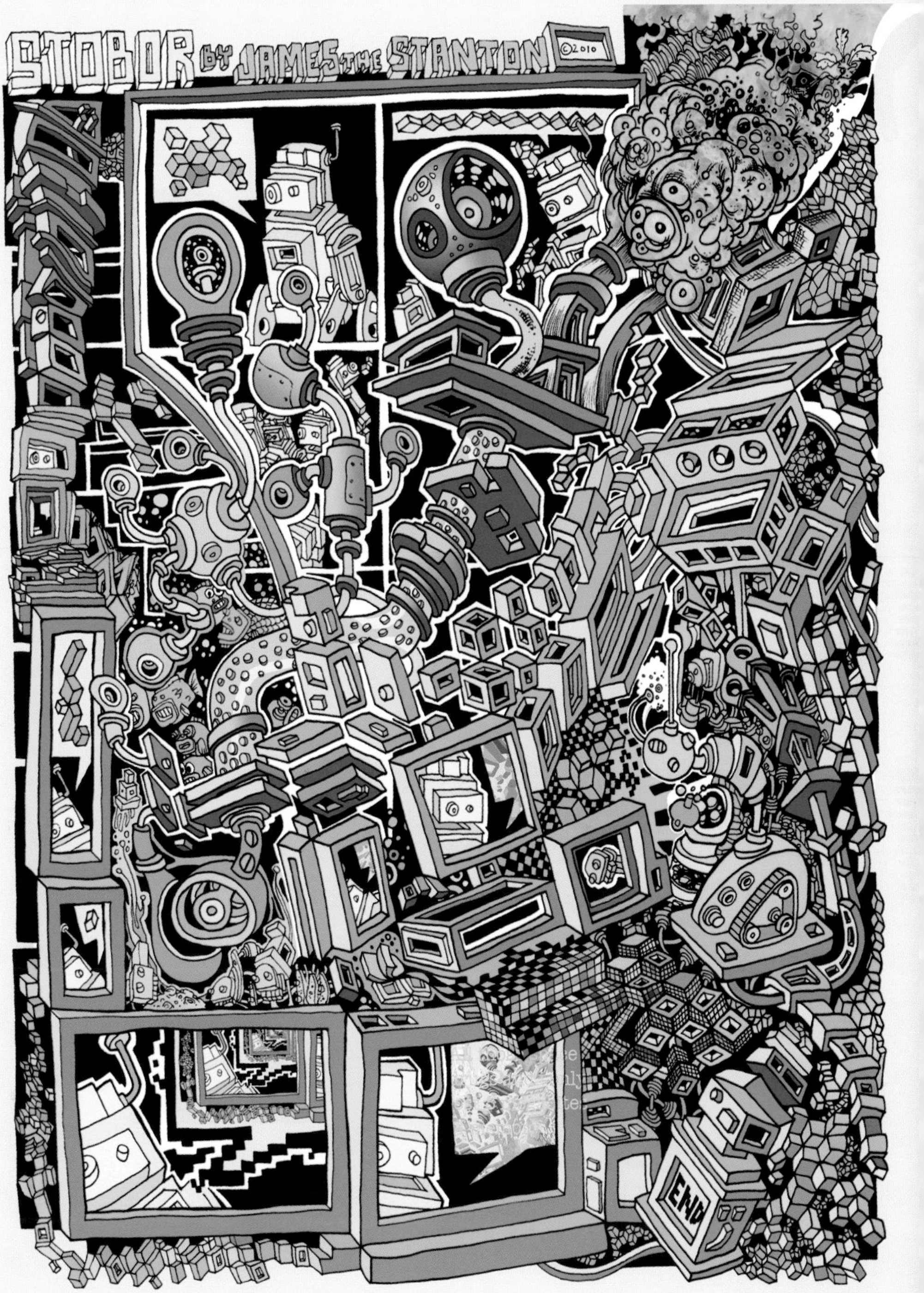
STOBOR by JAMES the STANTON
©2010
END

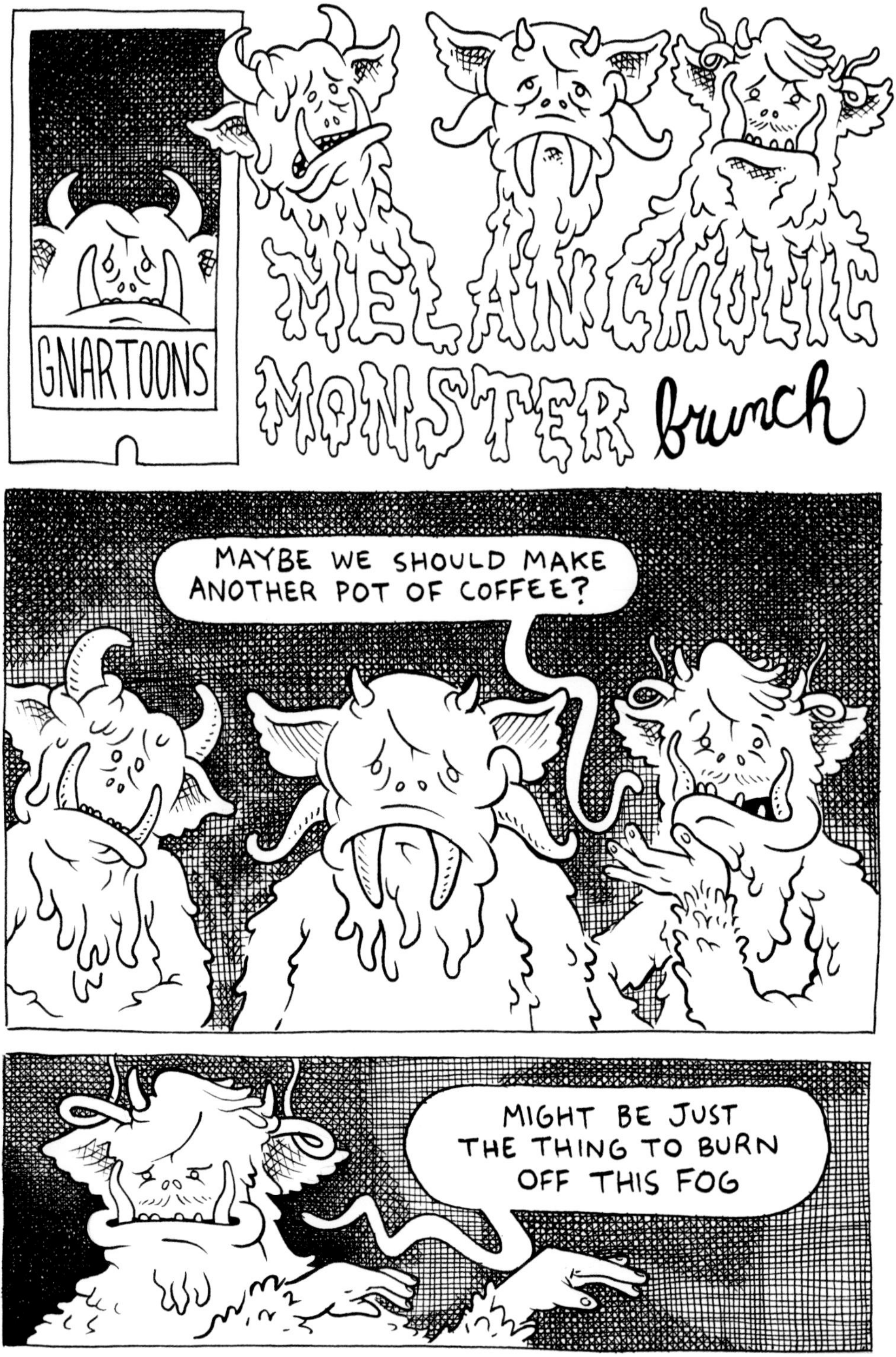
GNARTOONS
MELANCHOLIC MONSTER brunch
MAYBE WE SHOULD MAKE ANOTHER POT OF COFFEE?
MIGHT BE JUST THE THING TO BURN OFF THIS FOG

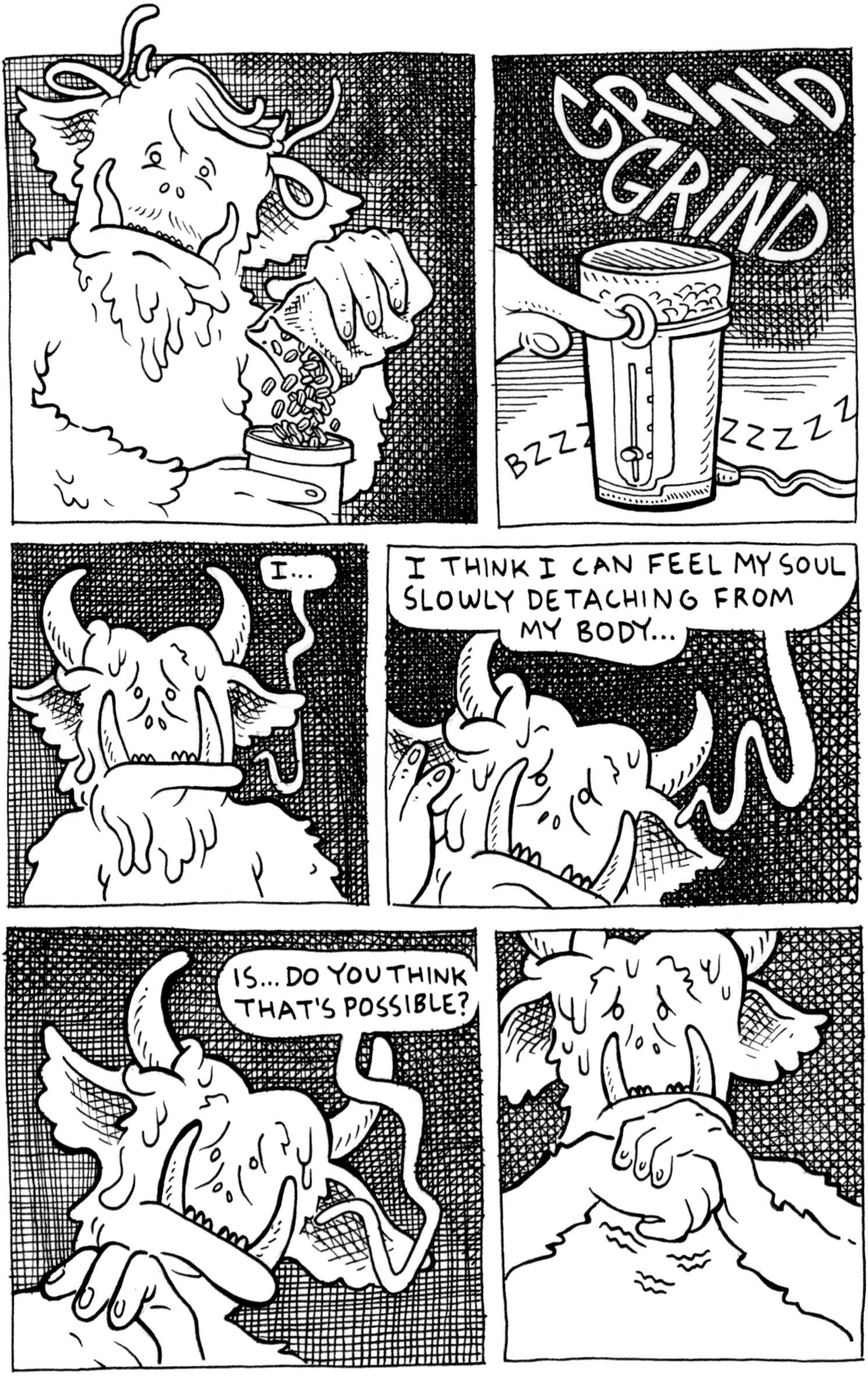
GRIND
GRIND
BZZZZZZZZZ
I...
I THINK I CAN FEEL MY SOUL SLOWLY DETACHING FROM MY BODY...
IS... DO YOU THINK THAT'S POSSIBLE?

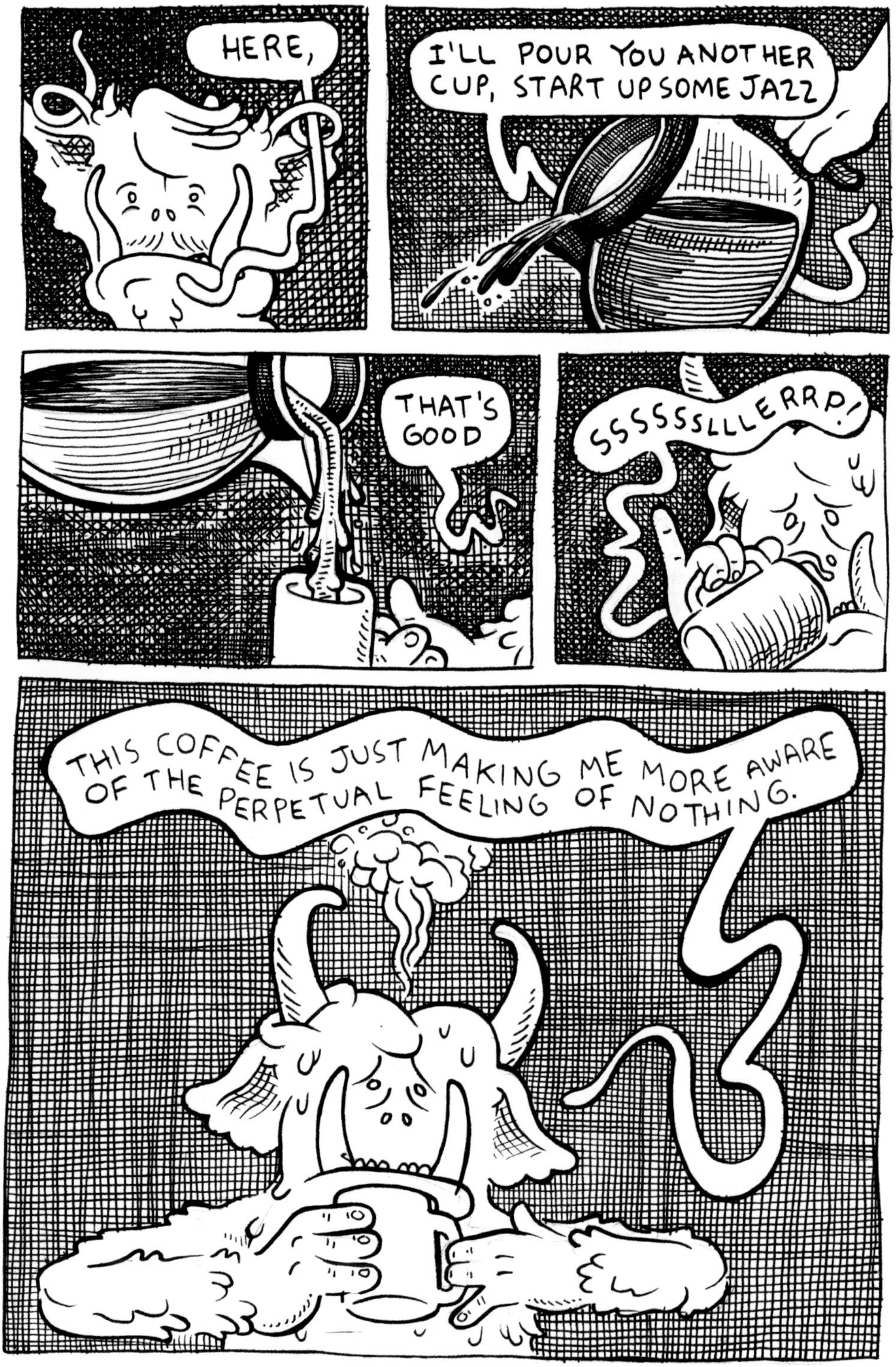
HERE,
I'LL POUR YOU ANOTHER CUP, START UP SOME JAZZ
THAT'S GOOD
SSSSSSLLLERRP!
THIS COFFEE IS JUST MAKING ME MORE AWARE OF THE PERPETUAL FEELING OF NOTHING.

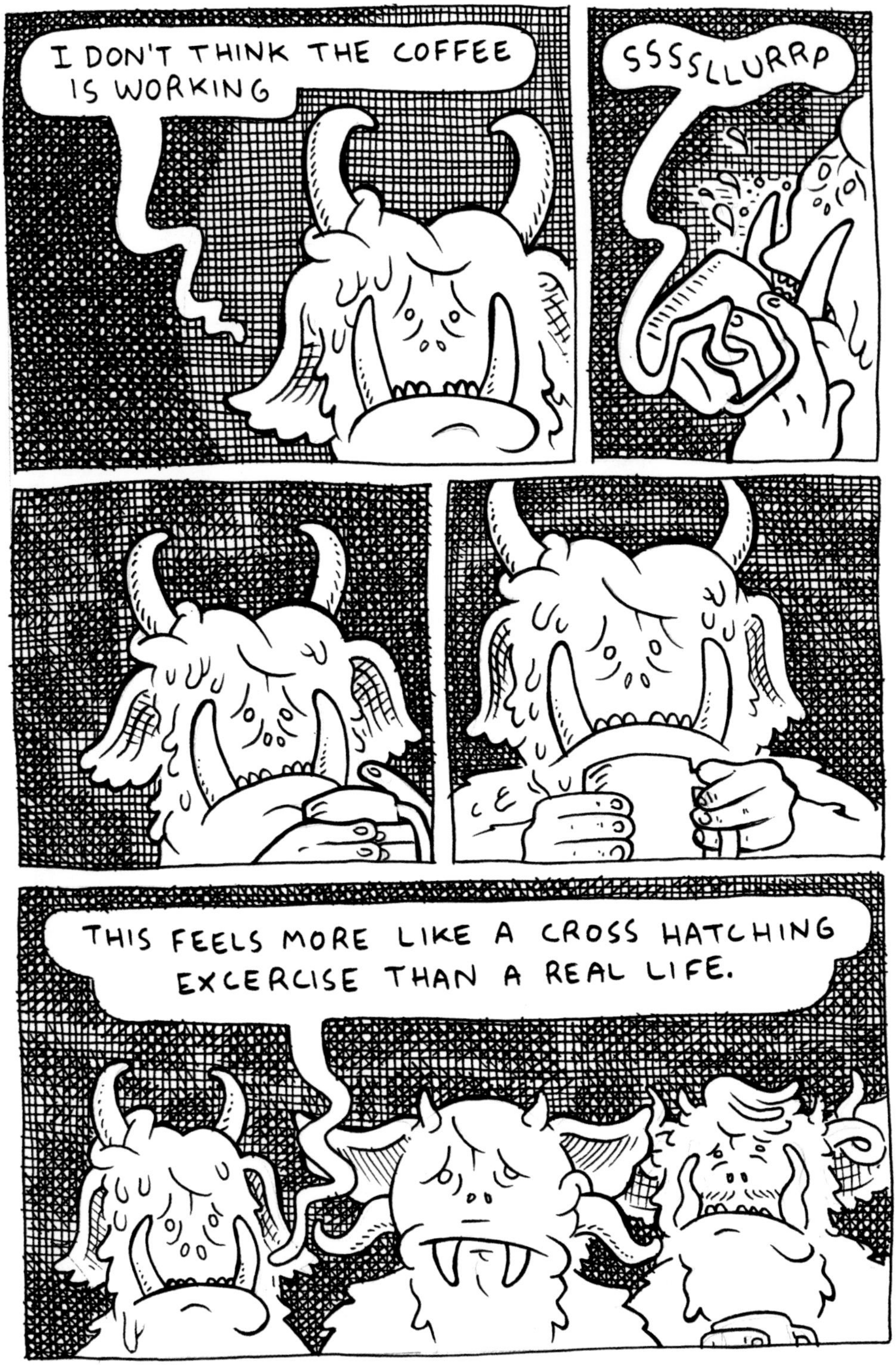
I DON'T THINK THE COFFEE IS WORKING
SSSSLLURRP
THIS FEELS MORE LIKE A CROSS HATCHING EXCERCISE THAN A REAL LIFE.

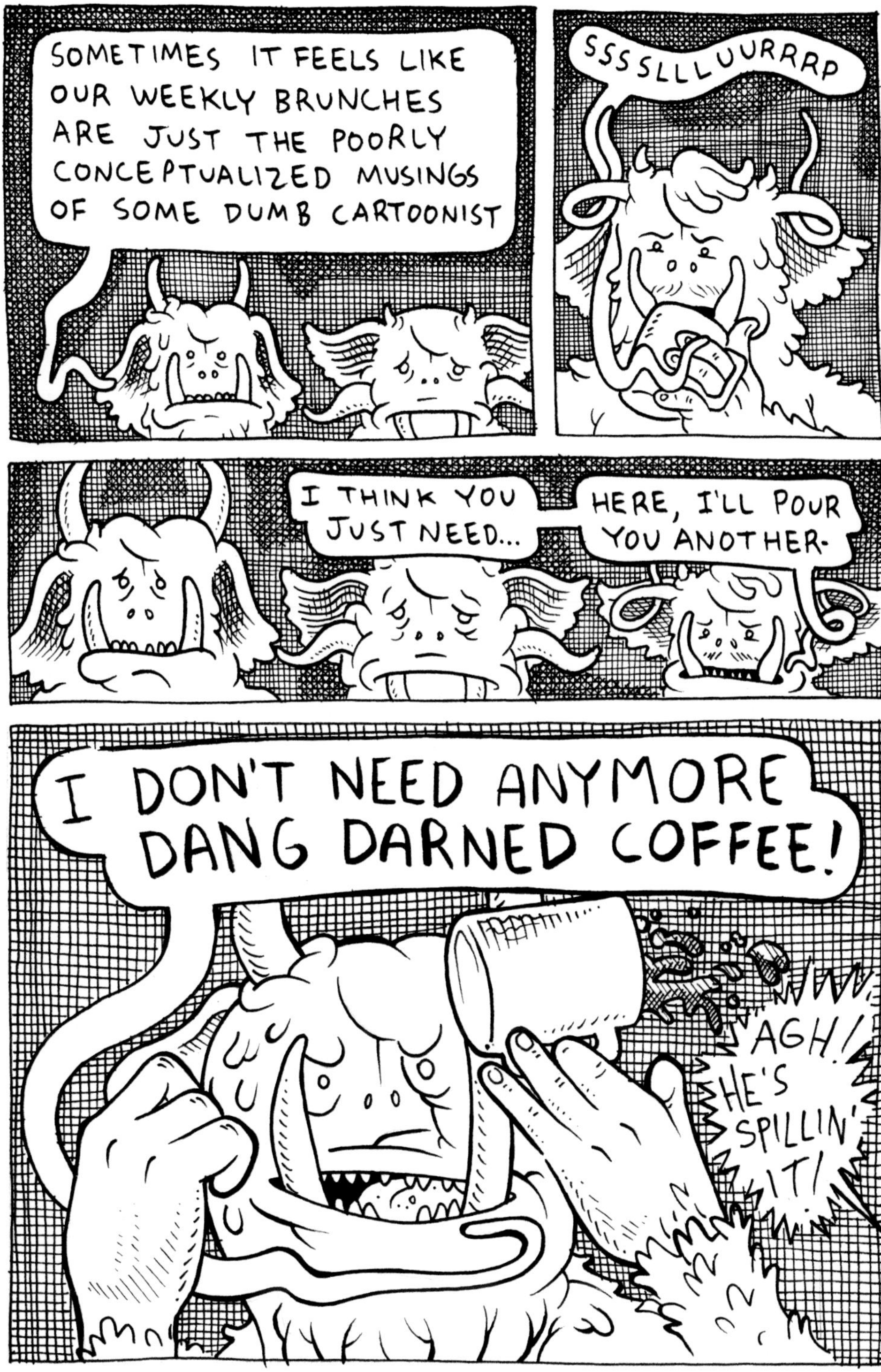
SOMETIMES IT FEELS LIKE OUR WEEKLY BRUNCHES ARE JUST THE POORLY CONCEPTUALIZED MUSINGS OF SOME DUMB CARTOONIST
SSSSLLLUURRRP
I THINK YOU JUST NEED...
HERE, I'LL POUR YOU ANOTHER-
I DON'T NEED ANYMORE DANG DARNED COFFEE!
AGH! HE'S SPILLIN' IT!

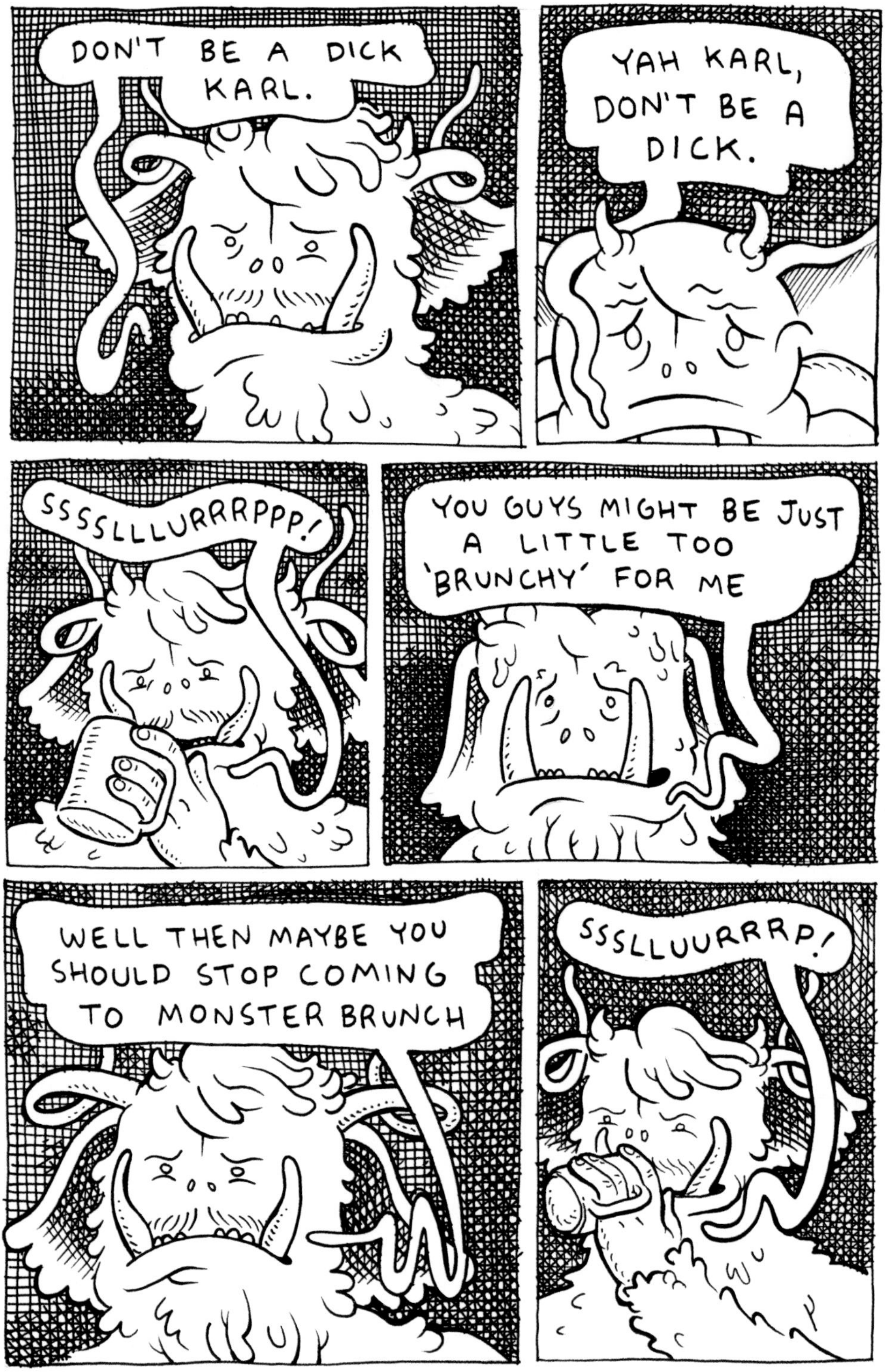
DON'T BE A DICK KARL.
YAH KARL, DON'T BE A DICK.
SSSSLLLURRRPPP!
YOU GUYS MIGHT BE JUST A LITTLE TOO 'BRUNCHY' FOR ME
WELL THEN MAYBE YOU SHOULD STOP COMING TO MONSTER BRUNCH
SSSLLUURRRP!

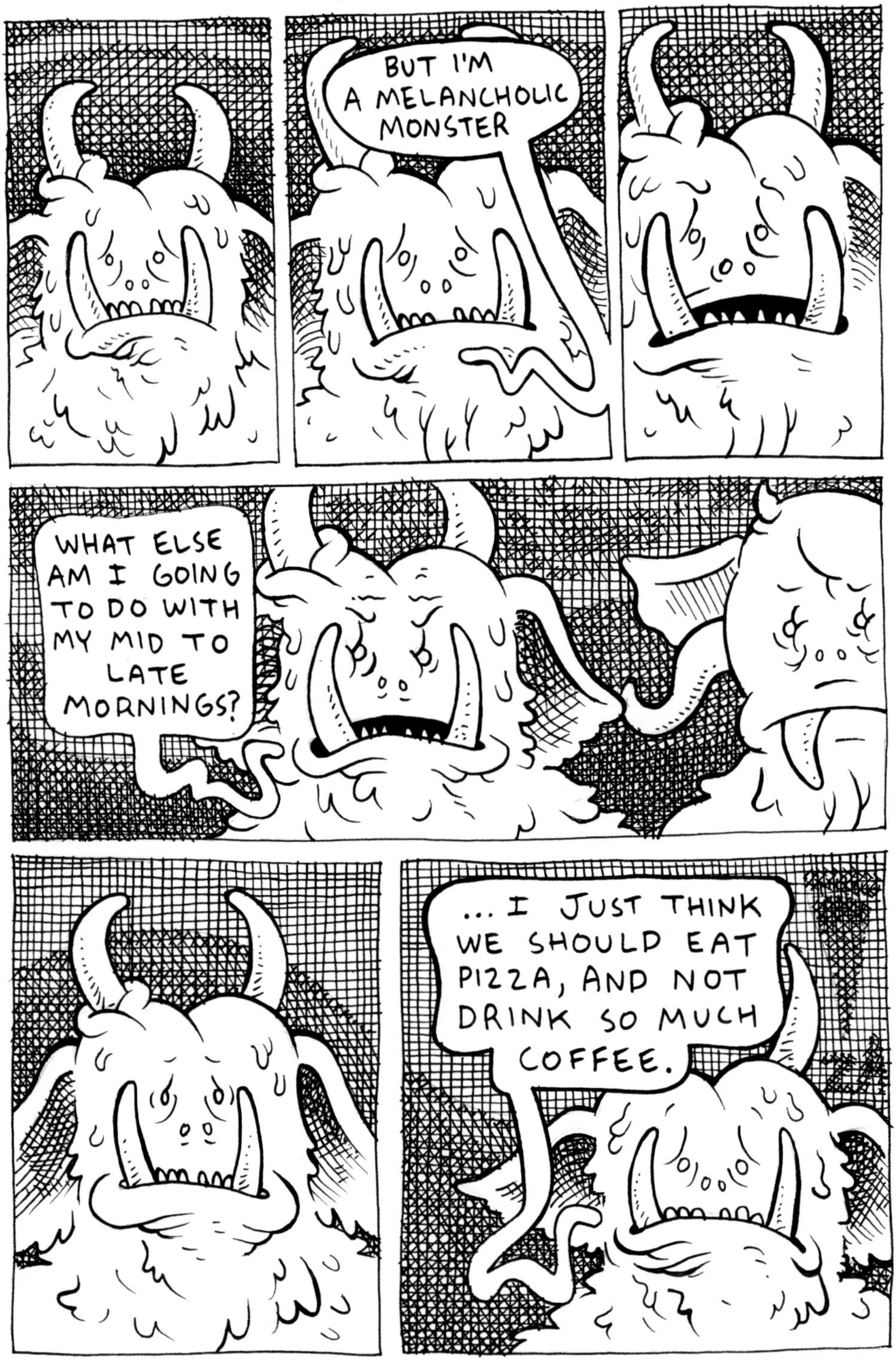
BUT I'M A MELANCHOLIC MONSTER
WHAT ELSE AM I GOING TO DO WITH MY MID TO LATE MORNINGS?
... I JUST THINK WE SHOULD EAT PIZZA, AND NOT DRINK SO MUCH COFFEE.

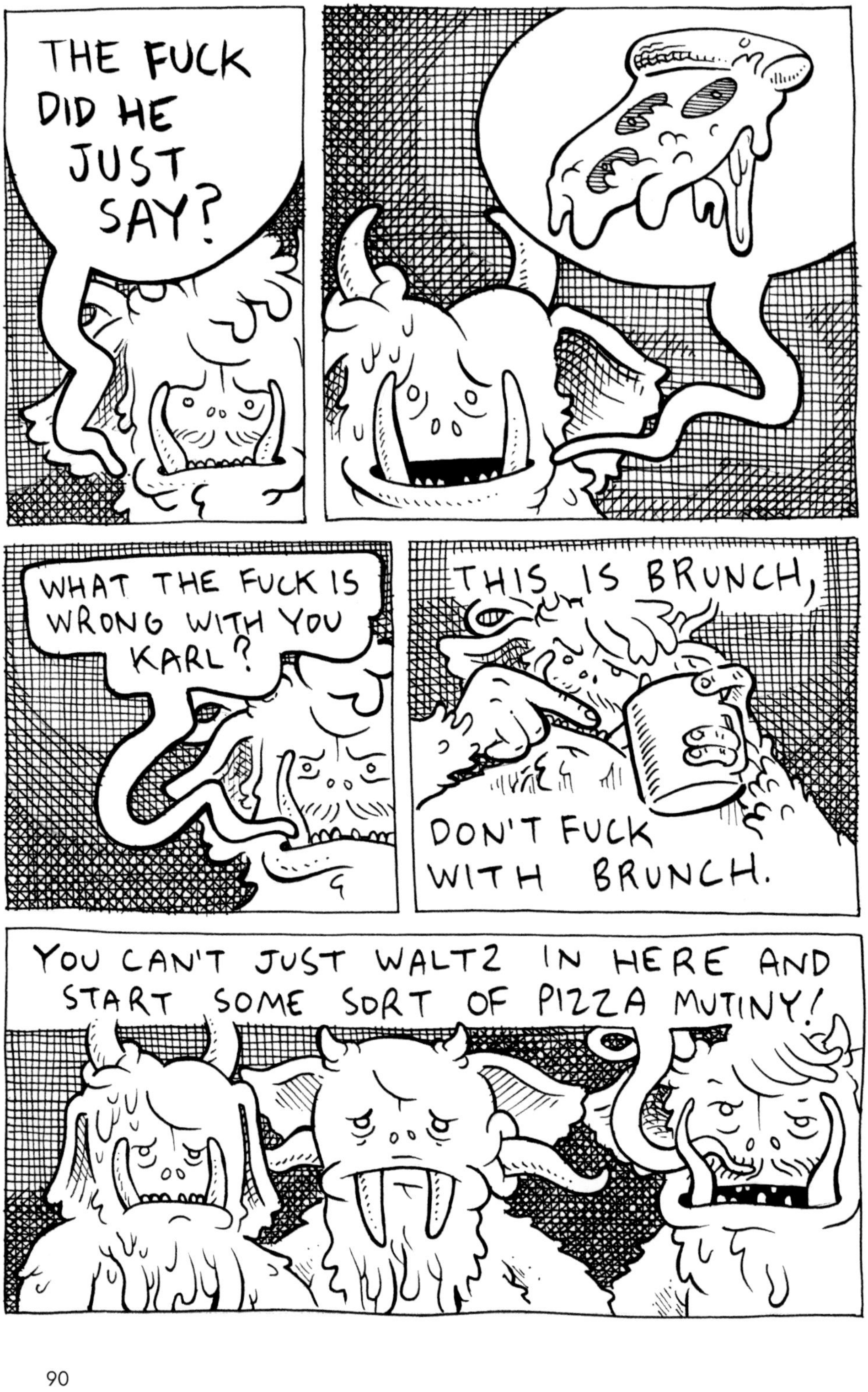

THE FUCK DID HE JUST SAY?
WHAT THE FUCK IS WRONG WITH YOU KARL?
THIS IS BRUNCH,
DON'T FUCK WITH BRUNCH.
YOU CAN'T JUST WALTZ IN HERE AND START SOME SORT OF PIZZA MUTINY!

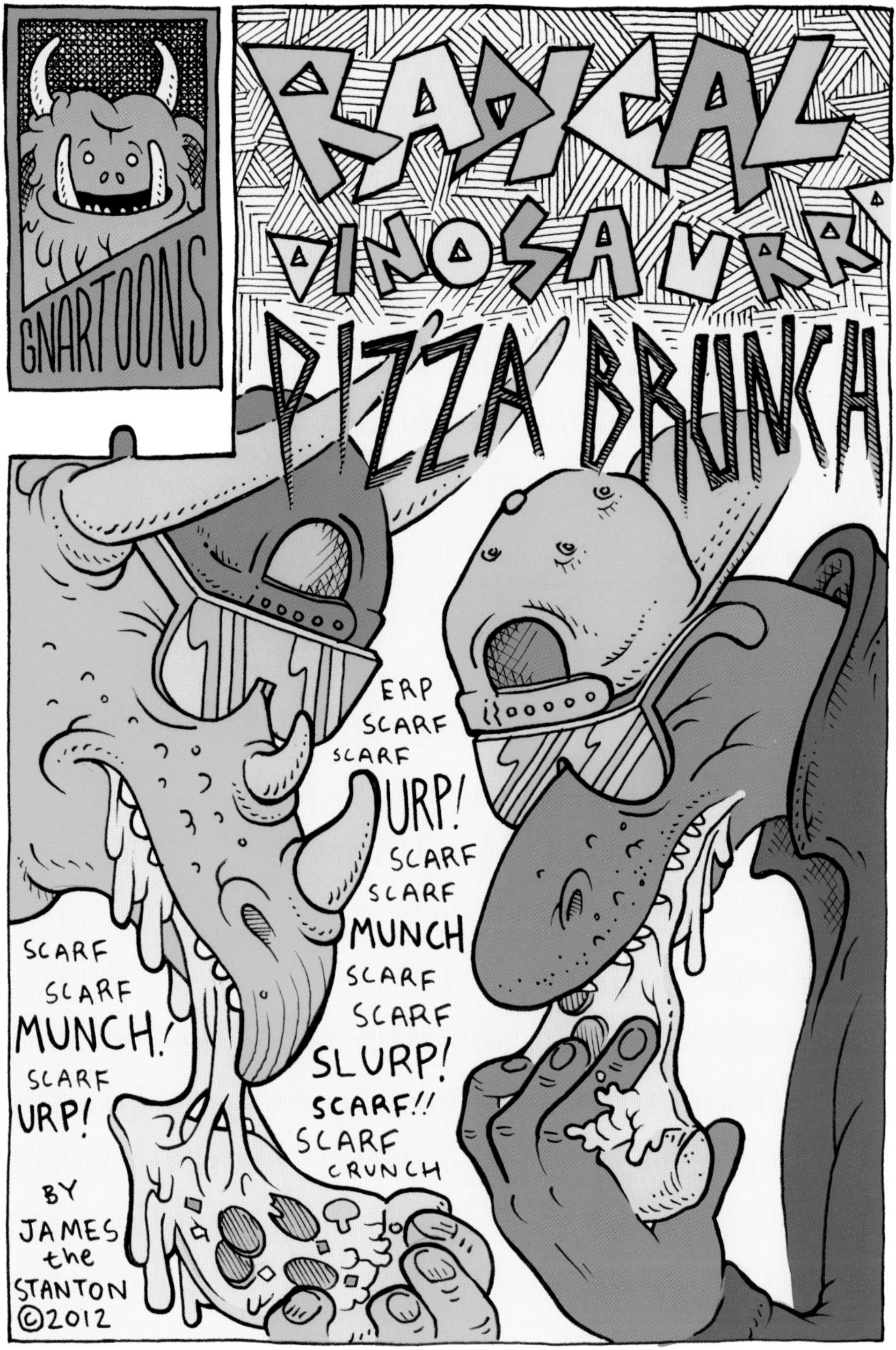
GNARTOONS
RADICAL DINOSAURR PIZZA BRUNCH
ERP
SCARF
SCARF
URP!
SCARF
SCARF
MUNCH
SCARF
SCARF
SLURP!
SCARF!!
SCARF
CRUNCH
SCARF
SCARF
MUNCH!
SCARF
URP!
BY JAMES the STANTON ©2012

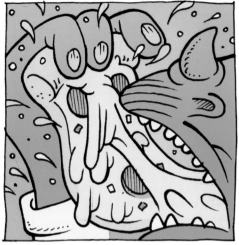

UM... HELLO? EXCUSE ME?

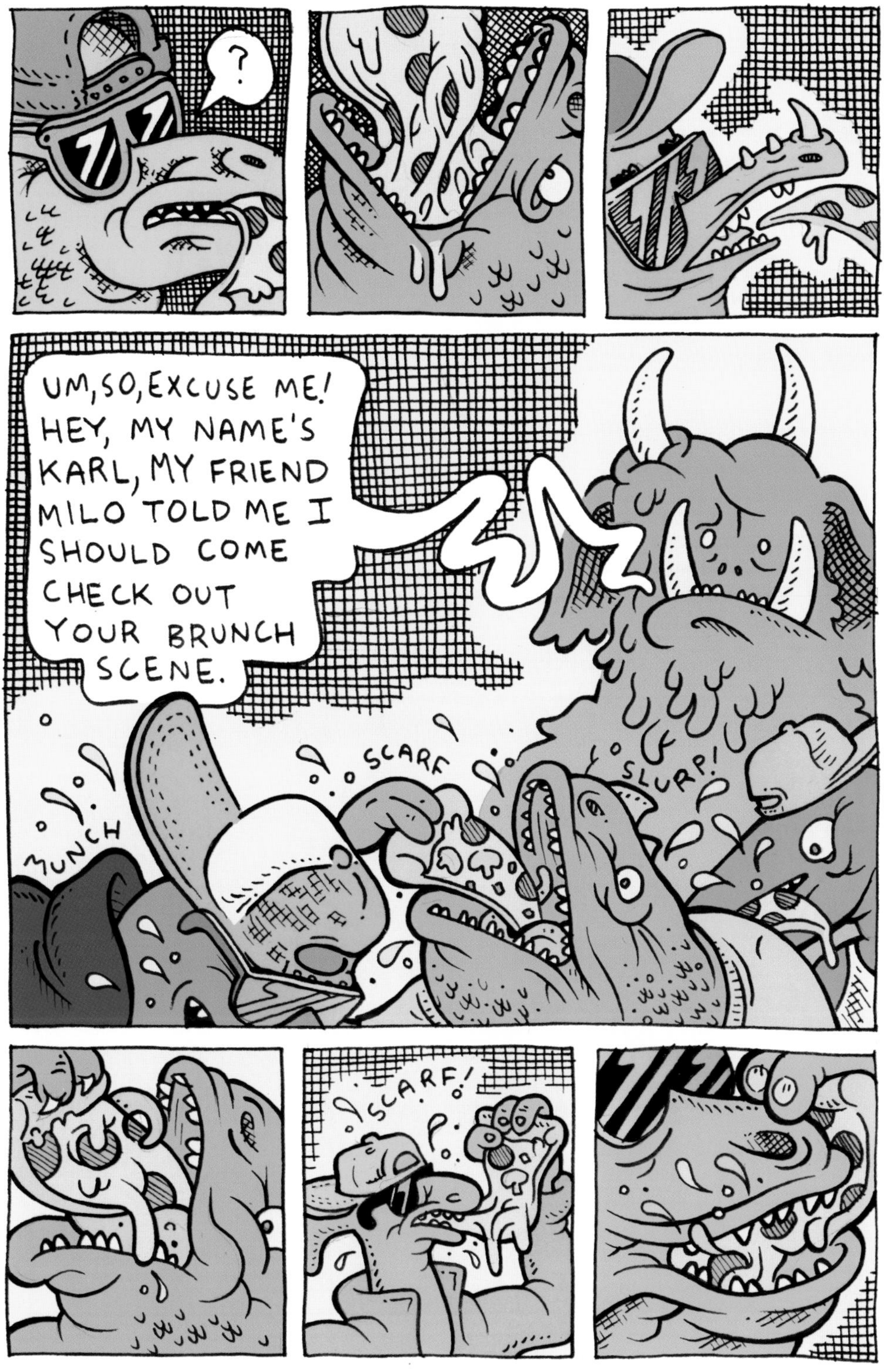
?
UM, SO, EXCUSE ME! HEY, MY NAME'S KARL, MY FRIEND MILO TOLD ME I SHOULD COME CHECK OUT YOUR BRUNCH SCENE.
MUNCH
SCARF
SLURP!
SCARF!

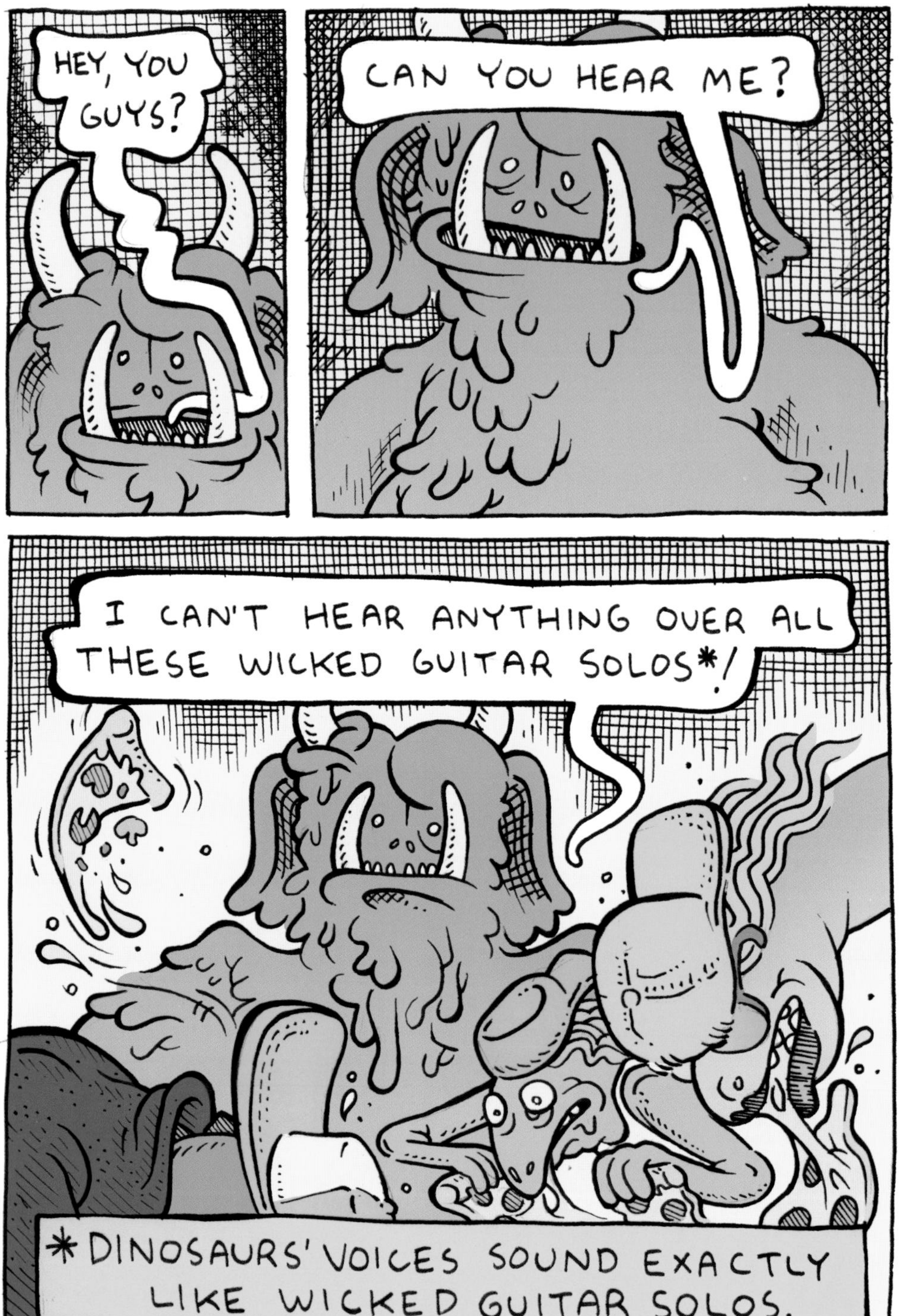
HEY, YOU GUYS?
CAN YOU HEAR ME?
I CAN'T HEAR ANYTHING OVER ALL THESE WICKED GUITAR SOLOS*!
* DINOSAURS' VOICES SOUND EXACTLY LIKE WICKED GUITAR SOLOS.

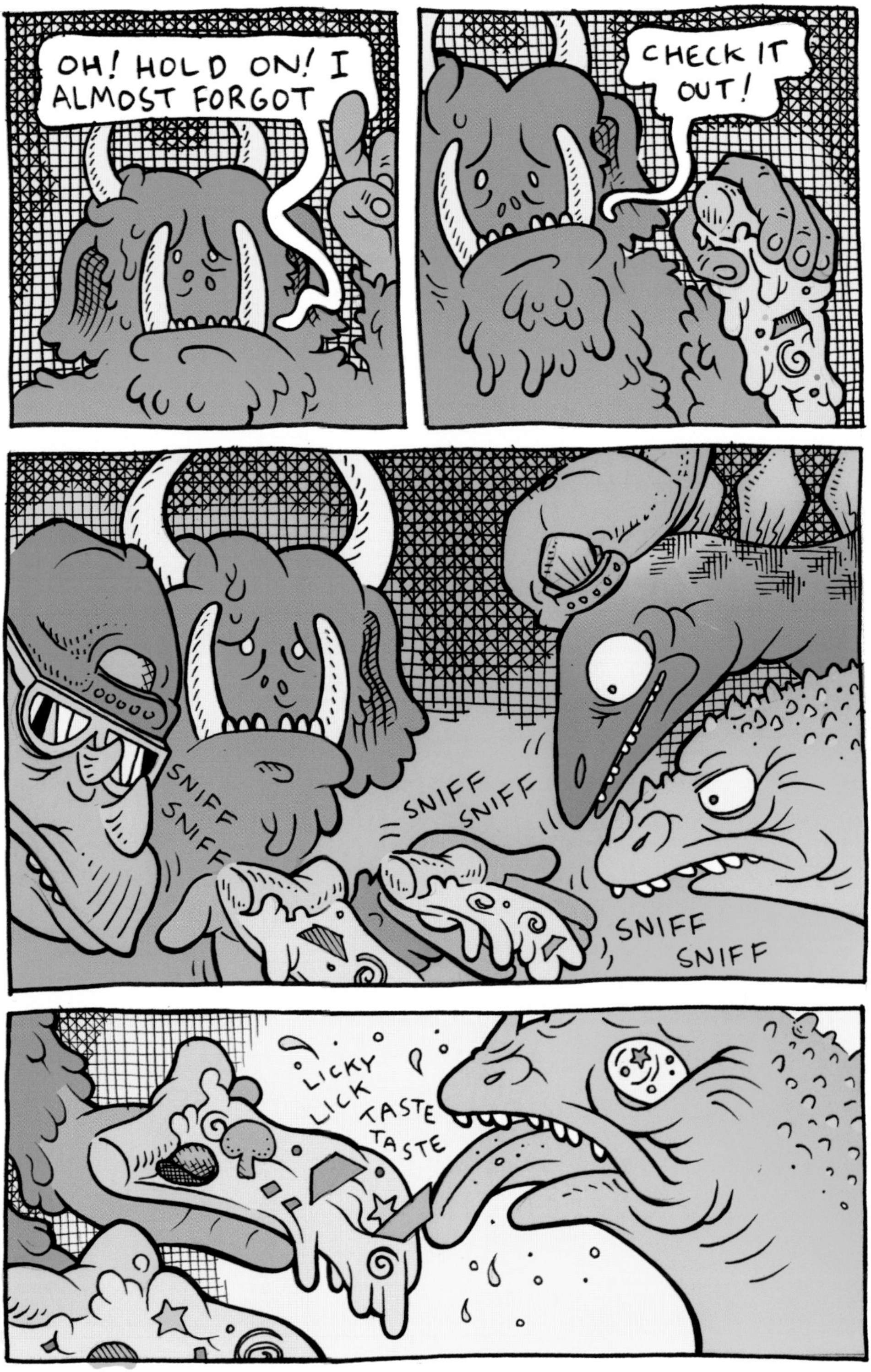
OH! HOLD ON! I ALMOST FORGOT
CHECK IT OUT!
SNIFF SNIFF
SNIFF SNIFF
SNIFF SNIFF
LICKY LICK
TASTE TASTE

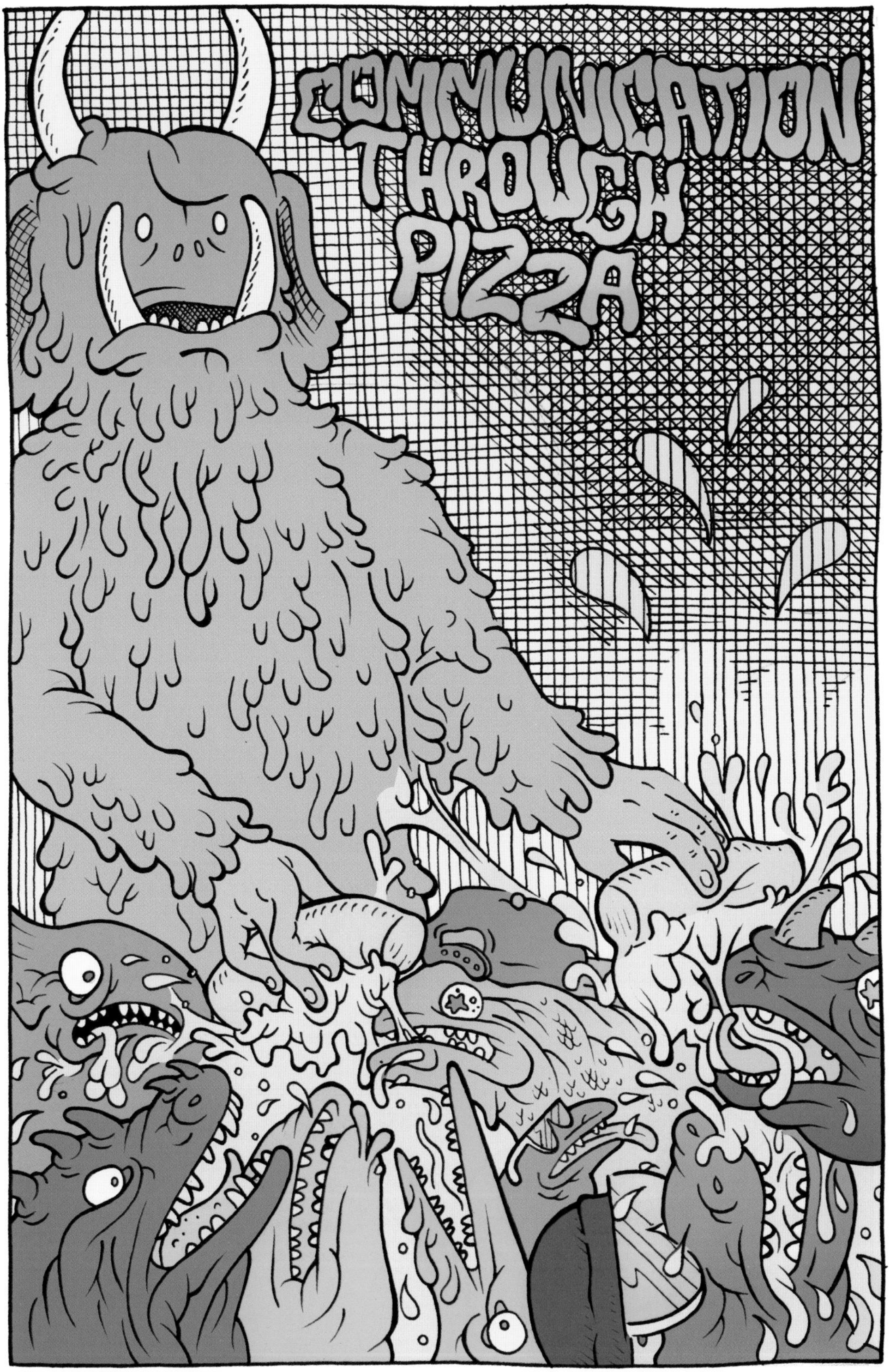
COMMUNICATION THROUGH PIZZA

(PIZZA MEDIUM/MEDIUM PIZZA)

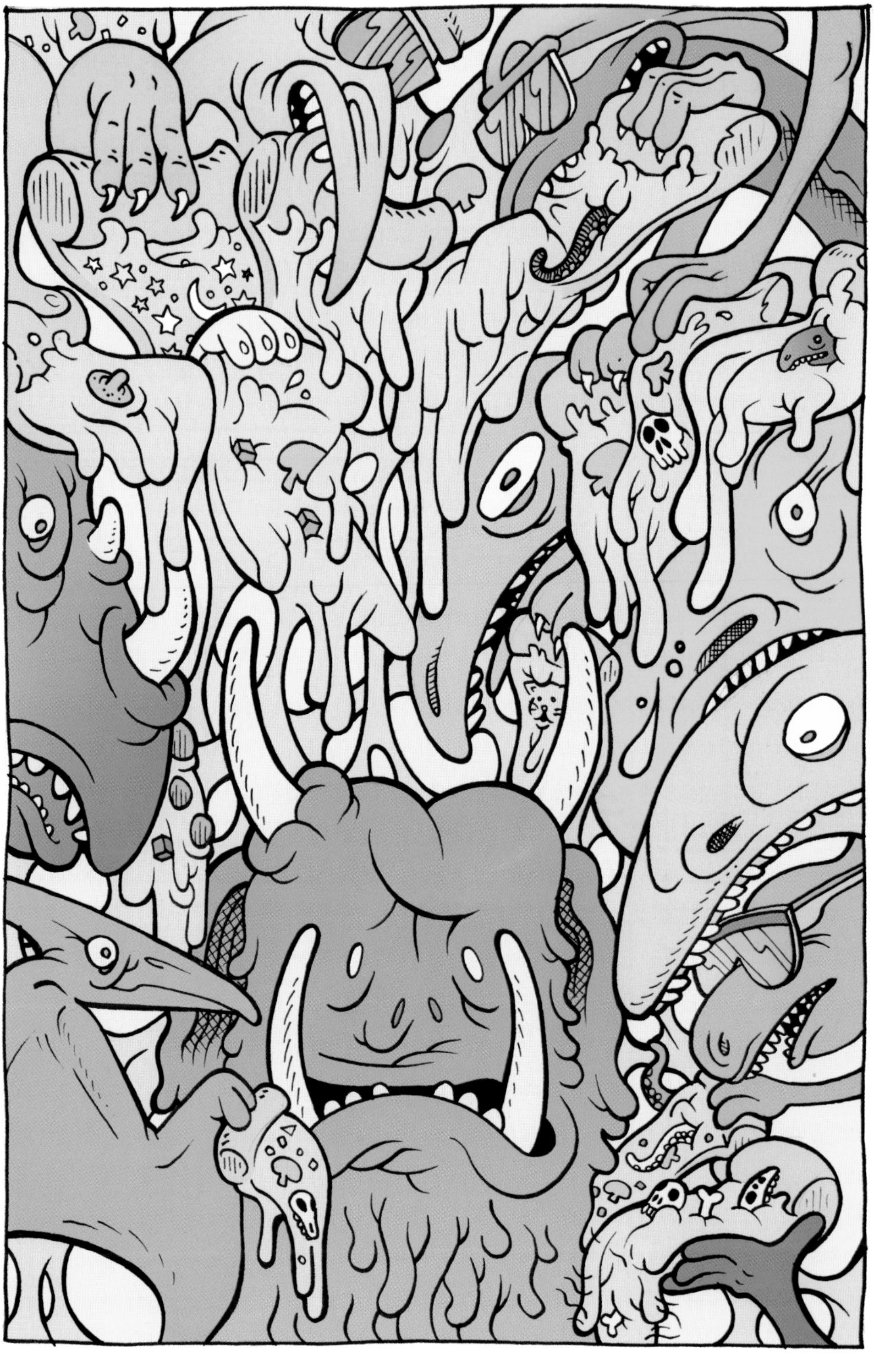

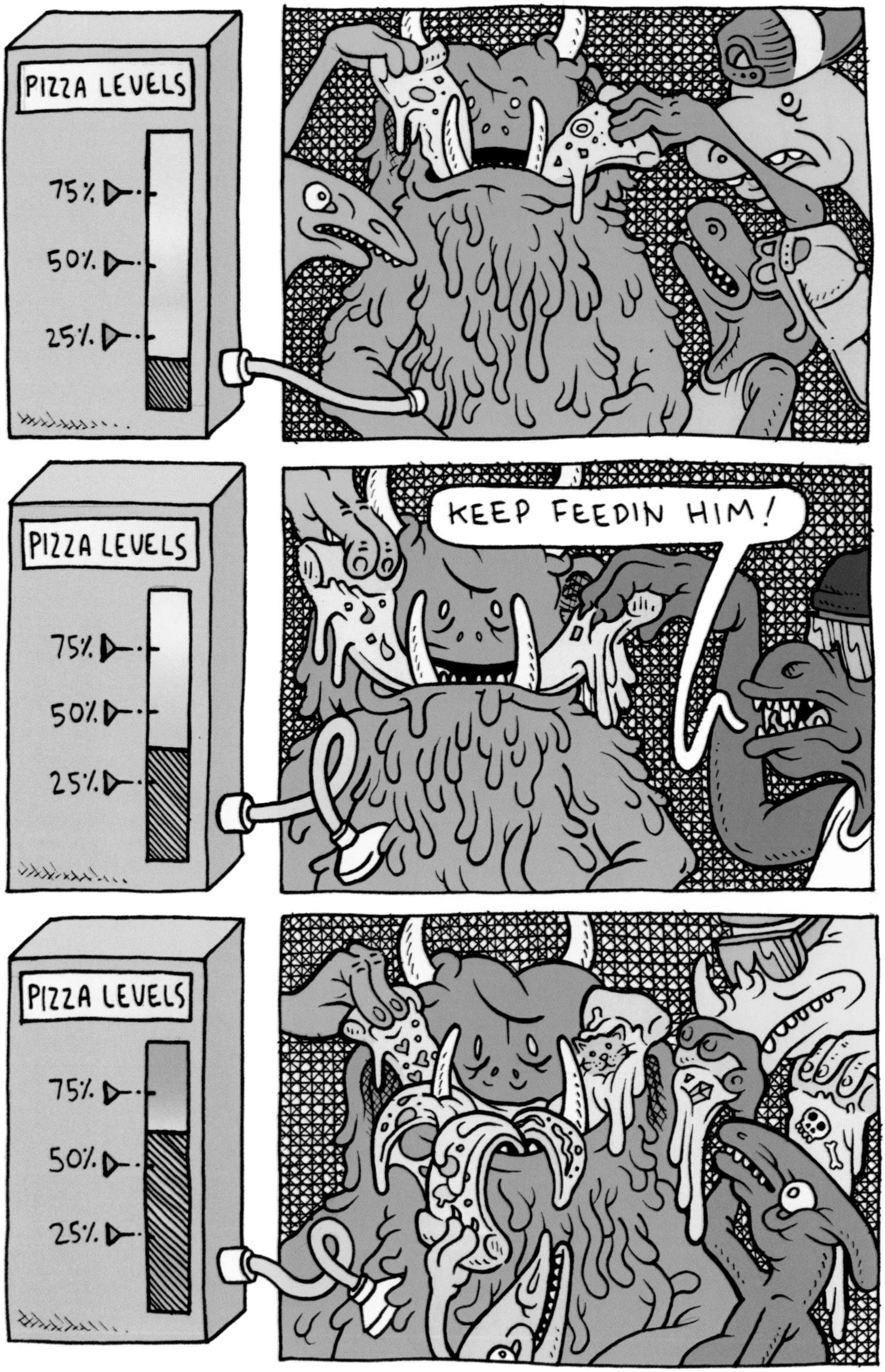
PIZZA LEVELS
75%
50%
25%
PIZZA LEVELS
75%
50%
25%
KEEP FEEDIN HIM!
PIZZA LEVELS
75%
50%
25%

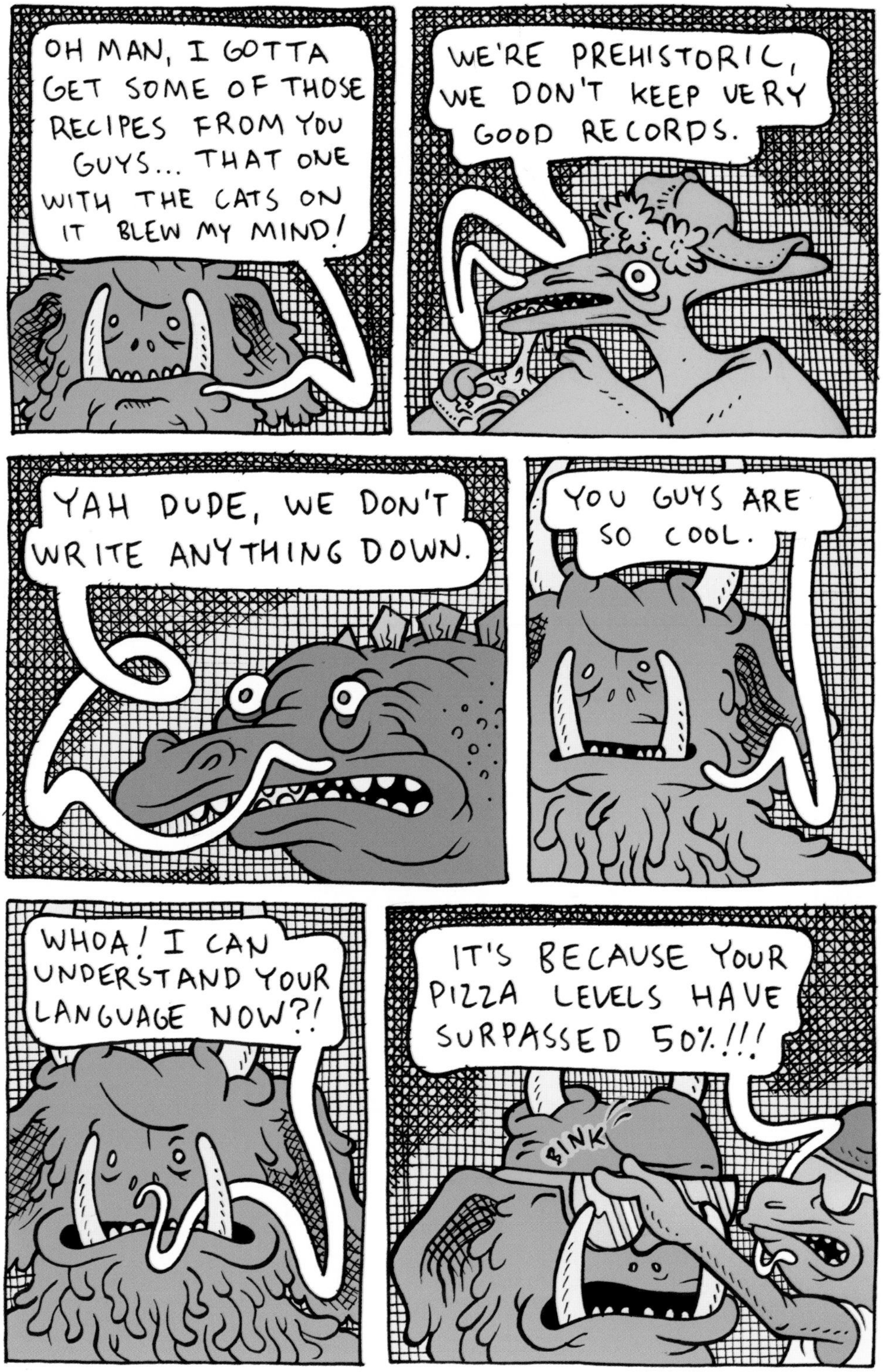
OH MAN, I GOTTA GET SOME OF THOSE RECIPES FROM YOU GUYS... THAT ONE WITH THE CATS ON IT BLEW MY MIND!
WE'RE PREHISTORIC, WE DON'T KEEP VERY GOOD RECORDS.
YAH DUDE, WE DON'T WRITE ANYTHING DOWN.
YOU GUYS ARE SO COOL.
WHOA! I CAN UNDERSTAND YOUR LANGUAGE NOW?!
IT'S BECAUSE YOUR PIZZA LEVELS HAVE SURPASSED 50%!!!
BINK

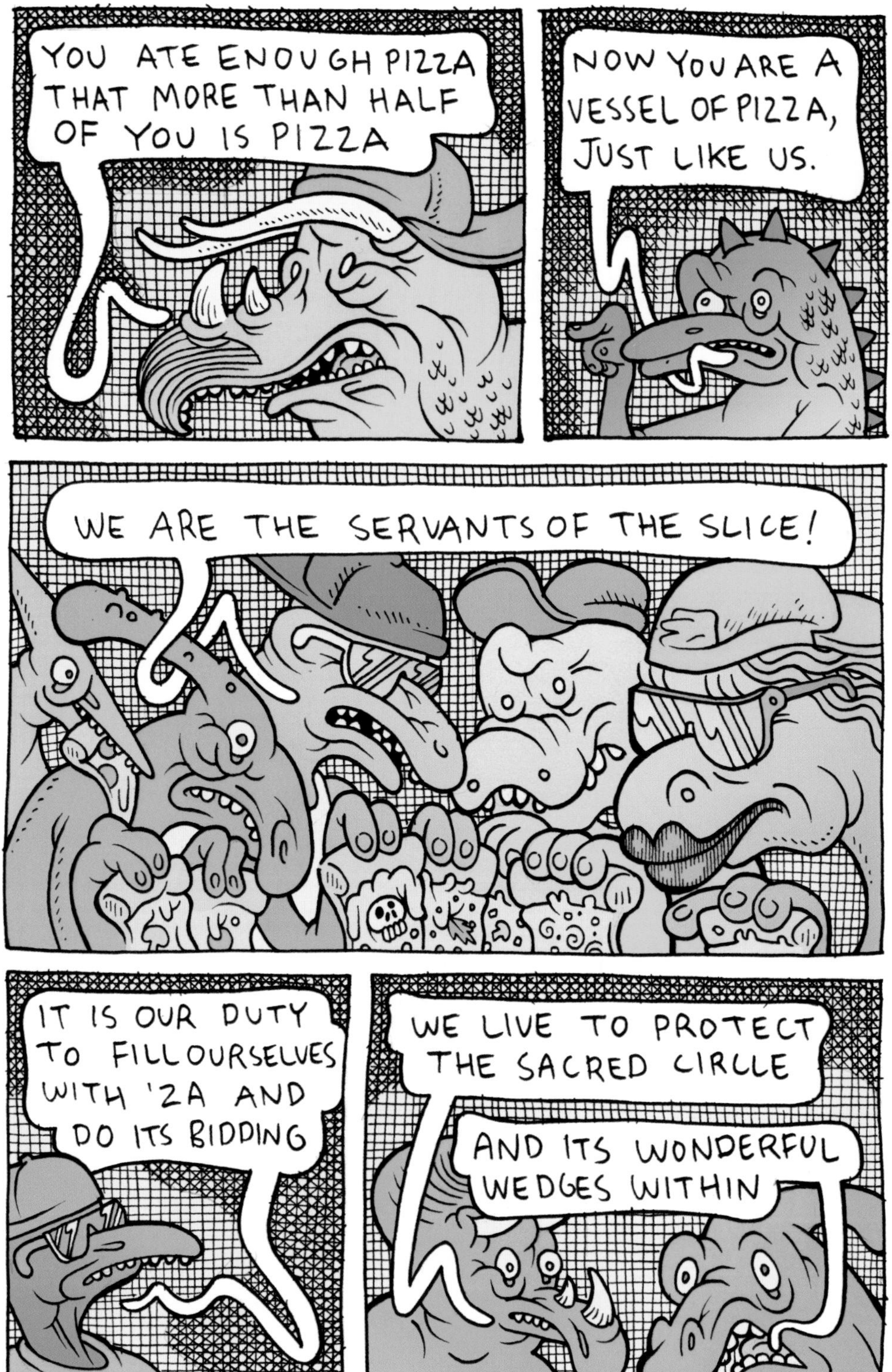
YOU ATE ENOUGH PIZZA THAT MORE THAN HALF OF YOU IS PIZZA
NOW YOU ARE A VESSEL OF PIZZA, JUST LIKE US.
WE ARE THE SERVANTS OF THE SLICE!
IT IS OUR DUTY TO FILL OURSELVES WITH 'ZA AND DO ITS BIDDING
WE LIVE TO PROTECT THE SACRED CIRCLE
AND ITS WONDERFUL WEDGES WITHIN

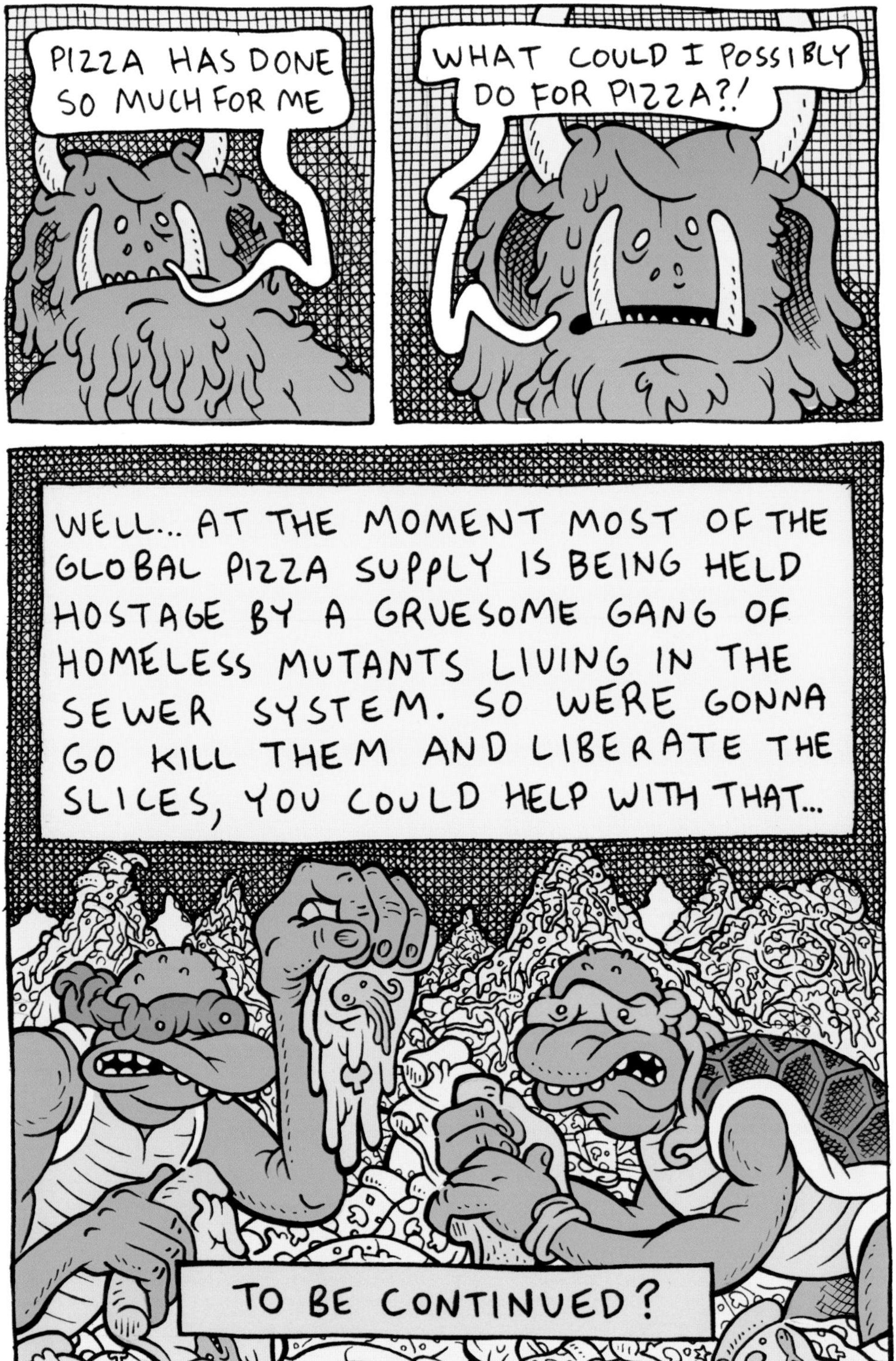
PIZZA HAS DONE SO MUCH FOR ME
WHAT COULD I POSSIBLY DO FOR PIZZA?!
WELL... AT THE MOMENT MOST OF THE GLOBAL PIZZA SUPPLY IS BEING HELD HOSTAGE BY A GRUESOME GANG OF HOMELESS MUTANTS LIVING IN THE SEWER SYSTEM. SO WERE GONNA GO KILL THEM AND LIBERATE THE SLICES, YOU COULD HELP WITH THAT...
TO BE CONTINUED?

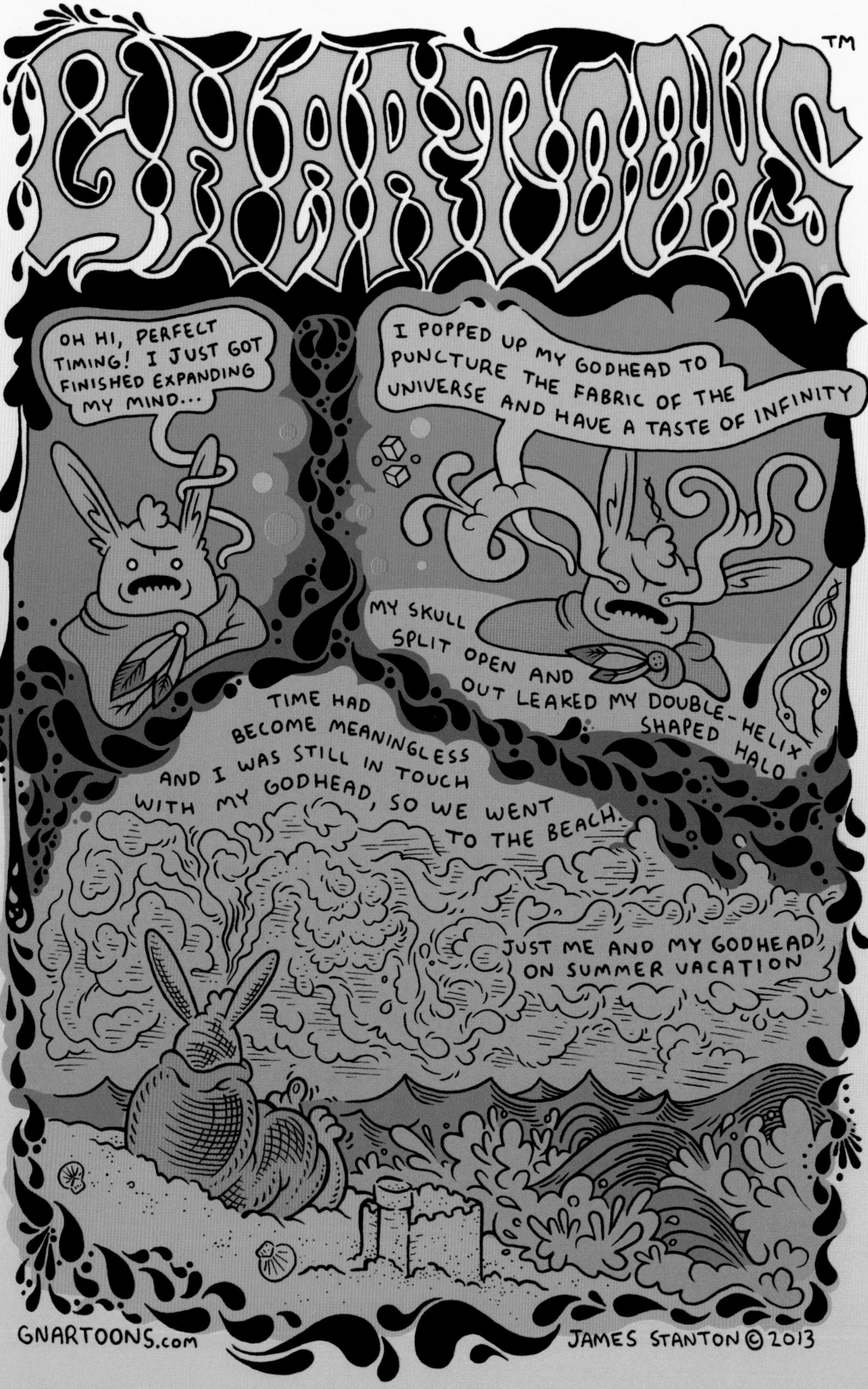
GNARTOONS™
OH HI, PERFECT TIMING! I JUST GOT FINISHED EXPANDING MY MIND...
I POPPED UP MY GODHEAD TO PUNCTURE THE FABRIC OF THE UNIVERSE AND HAVE A TASTE OF INFINITY
MY SKULL SPLIT OPEN AND OUT LEAKED MY DOUBLE-HELIX SHAPED HALO
TIME HAD BECOME MEANINGLESS AND I WAS STILL IN TOUCH WITH MY GODHEAD, SO WE WENT TO THE BEACH.
JUST ME AND MY GODHEAD ON SUMMER VACATION
GNARTOONS.com
JAMES STANTON © 2013

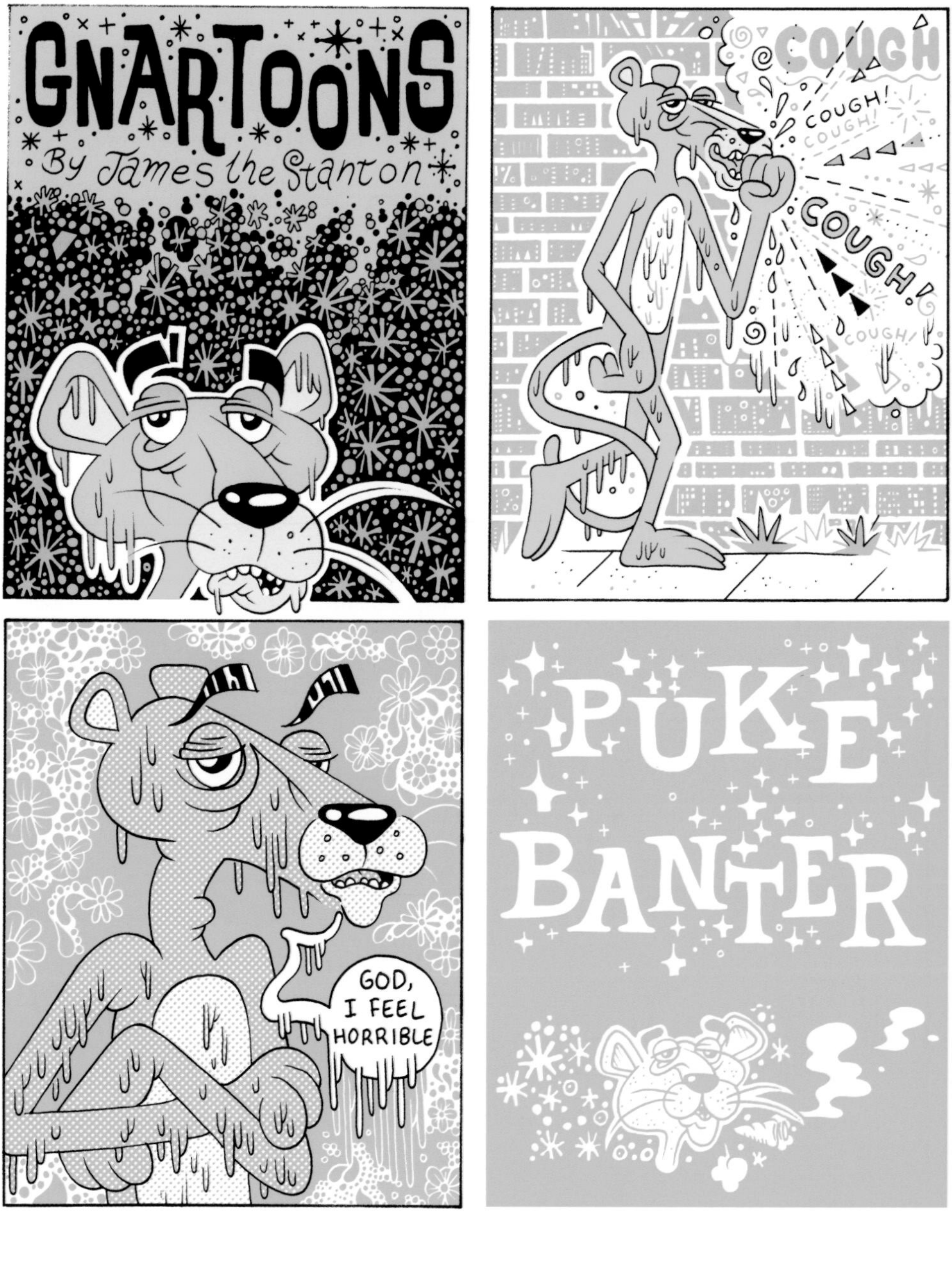
GNARTOONS
By James the Stanton
COUGH
COUGH!
COUGH!
COUGH!
COUGH!
GOD, I FEEL HORRIBLE
PUKE BANTER

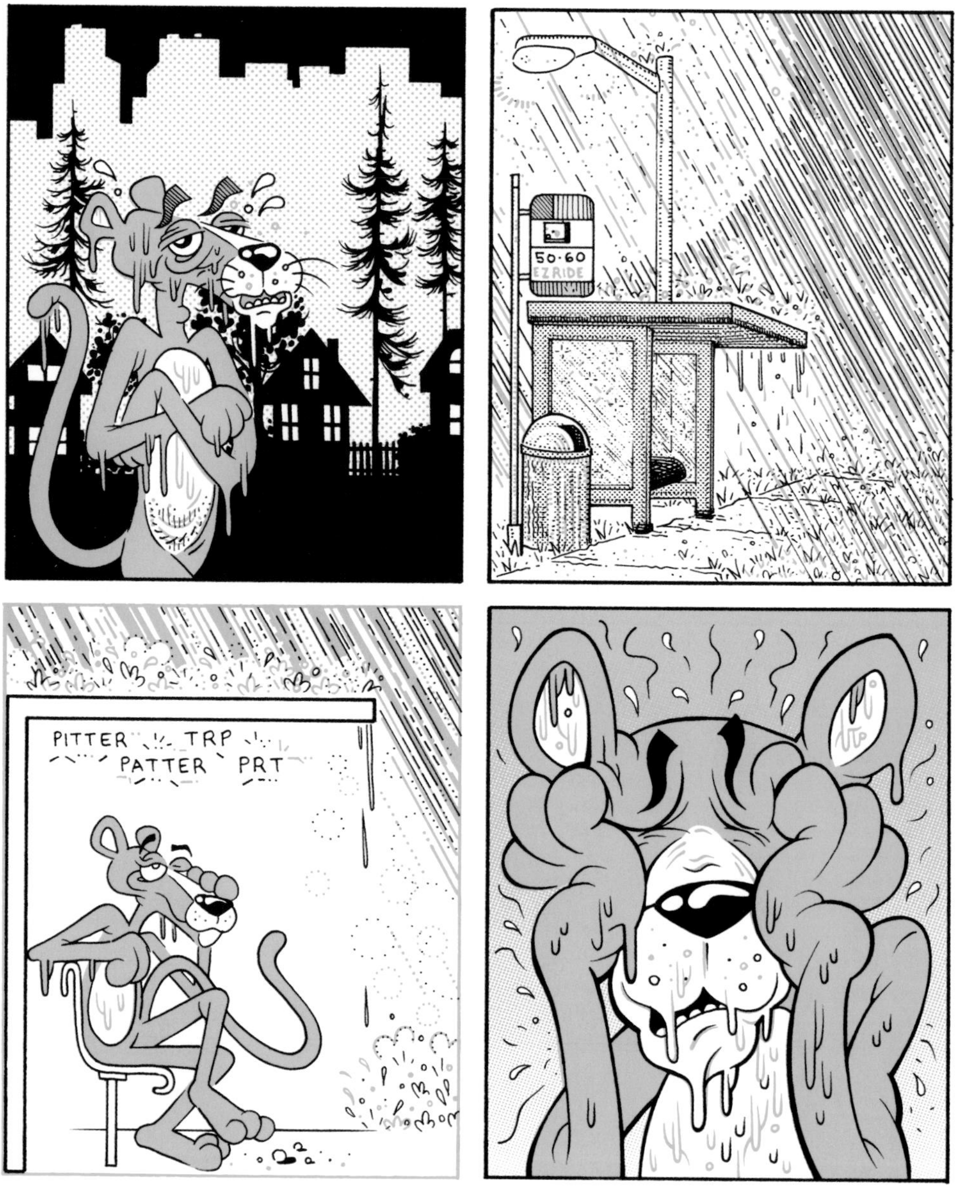
50·60
EZRIDE
PITTER
TRP
PATTER
PRT

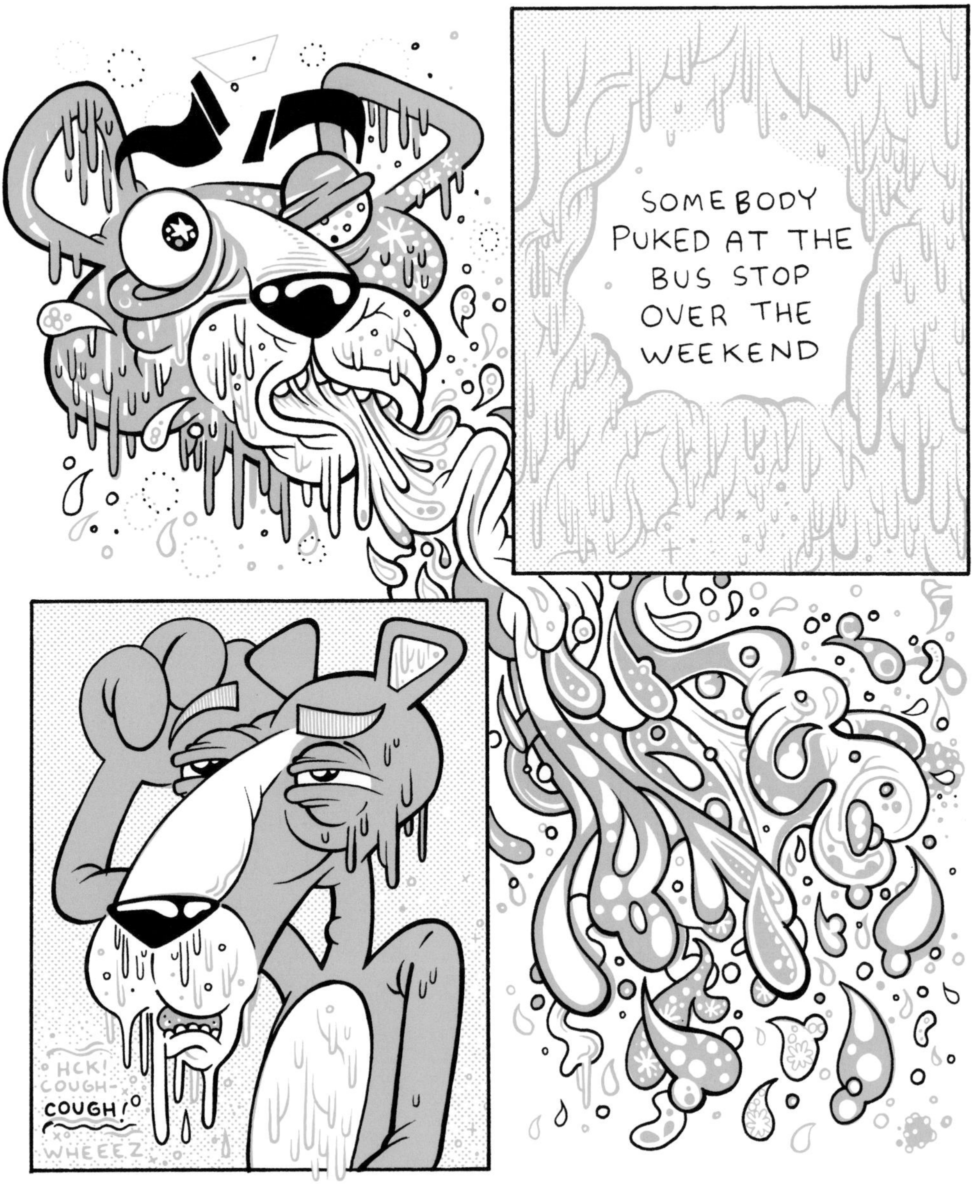
SOMEBODY PUKED AT THE BUS STOP OVER THE WEEKEND
HCK! COUGH-
COUGH!
WHEEEZ

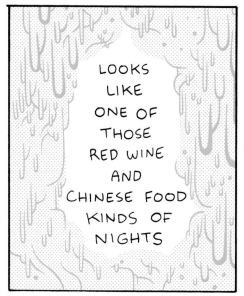

LOOKS
LIKE
ONE OF
THOSE
RED WINE
AND
CHINESE FOOD
KINDS OF
NIGHTS

AND
NOBODY'S
GOING TO
CLEAN
IT UP

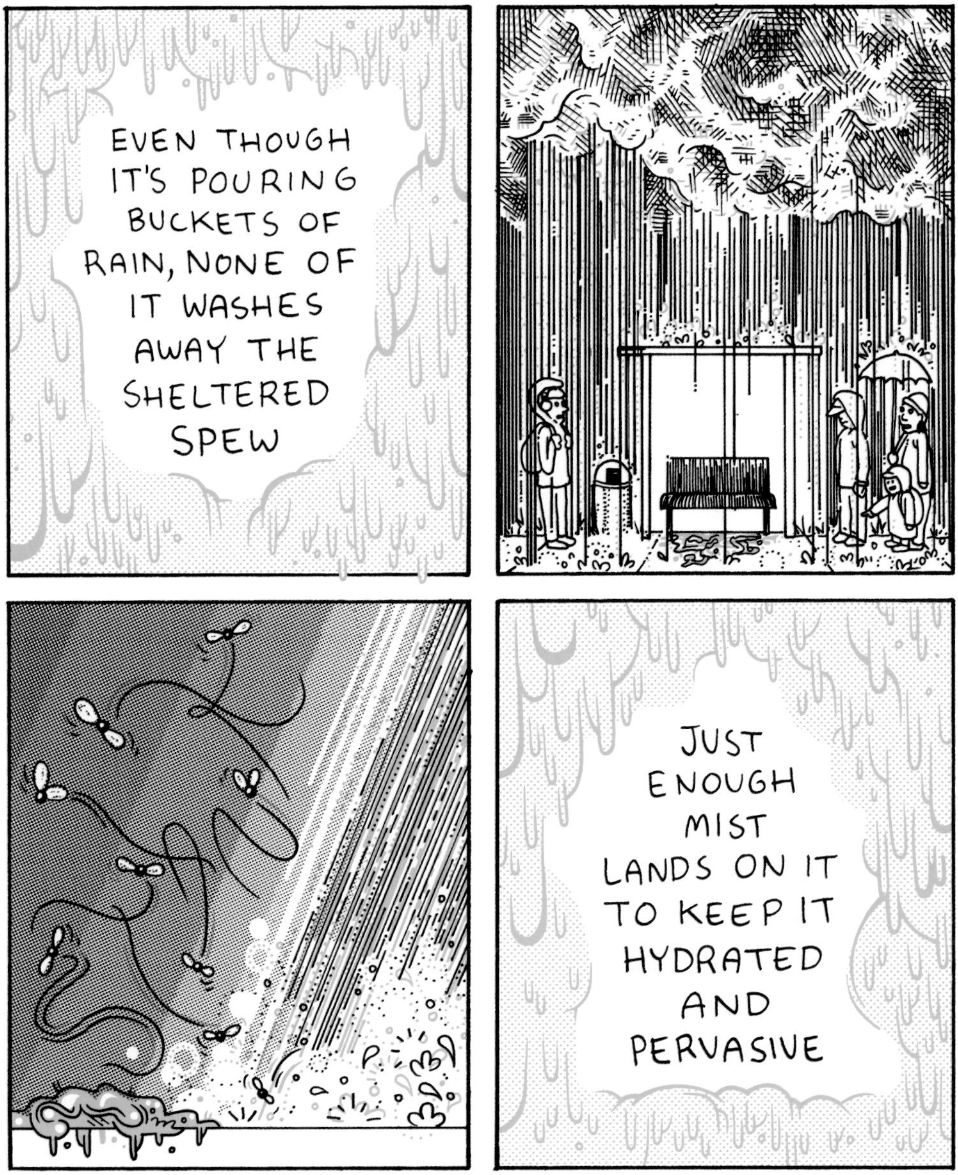
EVEN THOUGH IT'S POURING BUCKETS OF RAIN, NONE OF IT WASHES AWAY THE SHELTERED SPEW
JUST ENOUGH MIST LANDS ON IT TO KEEP IT HYDRATED AND PERVASIVE

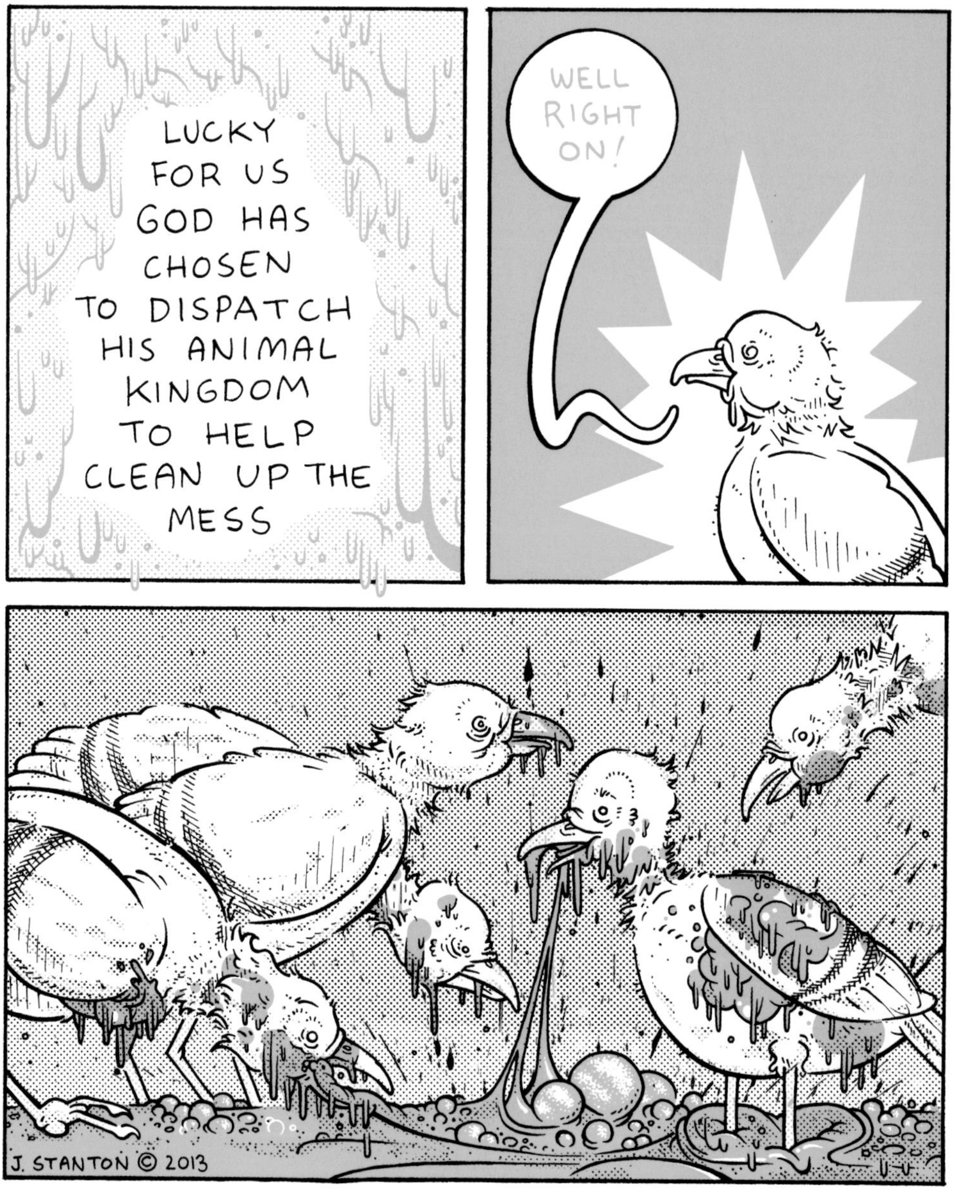
LUCKY FOR US GOD HAS CHOSEN TO DISPATCH HIS ANIMAL KINGDOM TO HELP CLEAN UP THE MESS
WELL RIGHT ON!
J. STANTON © 2013

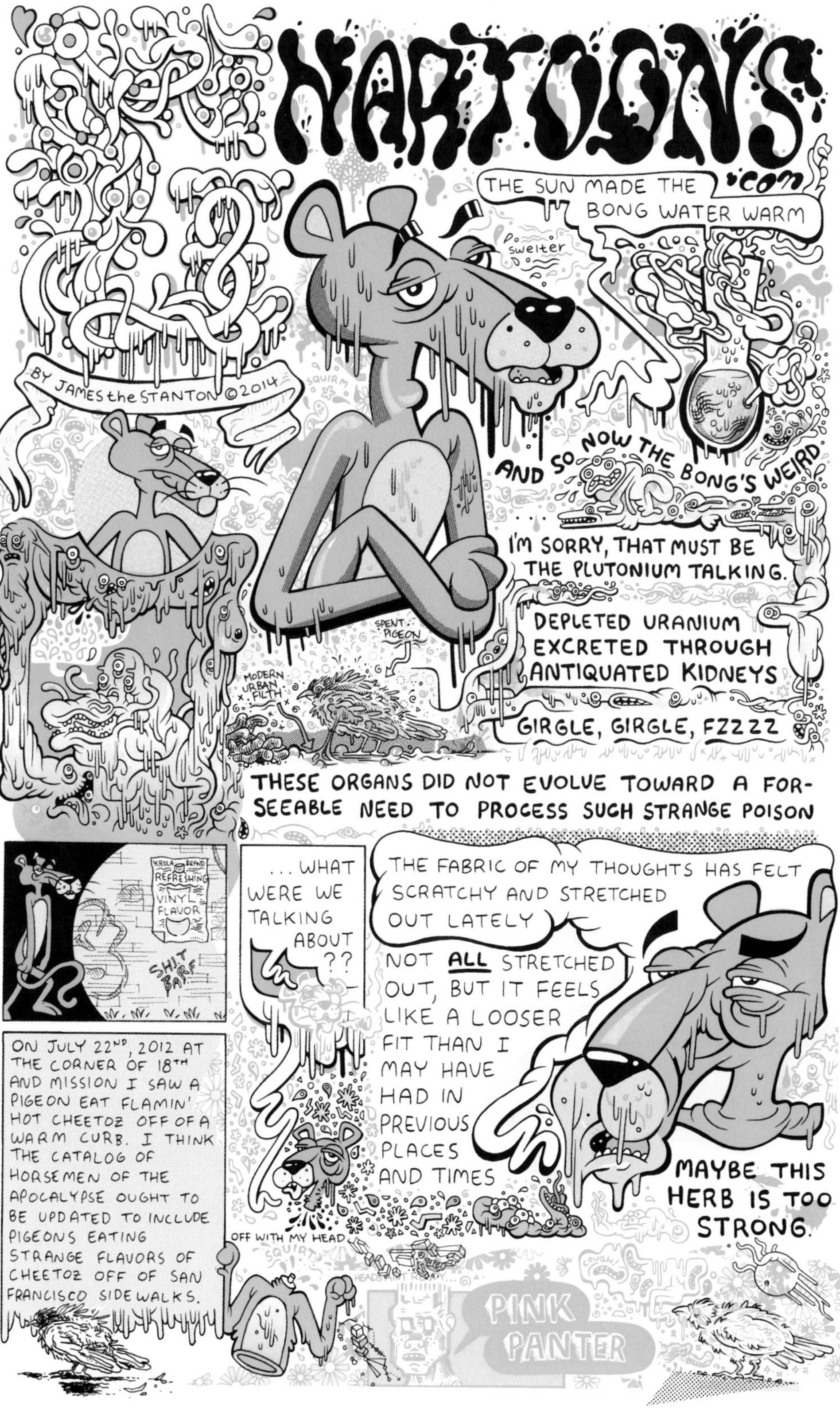

WARTOONS .com
BY JAMES the STANTON © 2014
THE SUN MADE THE BONG WATER WARM
swelter
SQUIRM
AND SO NOW THE BONG'S WEIRD
I'M SORRY, THAT MUST BE THE PLUTONIUM TALKING.
DEPLETED URANIUM EXCRETED THROUGH ANTIQUATED KIDNEYS
SPENT PIGEON
MODERN URBAN FILTH
GIRGLE, GIRGLE, FZZZZ
THESE ORGANS DID NOT EVOLVE TOWARD A FOR-SEEABLE NEED TO PROCESS SUCH STRANGE POISON
KROLA BRAND
REFRESHING VINYL FLAVOR
SHIT BARF
...WHAT WERE WE TALKING ABOUT ??
THE FABRIC OF MY THOUGHTS HAS FELT SCRATCHY AND STRETCHED OUT LATELY
NOT ALL STRETCHED OUT, BUT IT FEELS LIKE A LOOSER FIT THAN I MAY HAVE HAD IN PREVIOUS PLACES AND TIMES
MAYBE THIS HERB IS TOO STRONG.
ON JULY 22ND, 2012 AT THE CORNER OF 18TH AND MISSION I SAW A PIGEON EAT FLAMIN' HOT CHEETOZ OFF OF A WARM CURB. I THINK THE CATALOG OF HORSEMEN OF THE APOCALYPSE OUGHT TO BE UPDATED TO INCLUDE PIGEONS EATING STRANGE FLAVORS OF CHEETOZ OFF OF SAN FRANCISCO SIDEWALKS.
OFF WITH MY HEAD
SQUIRT
PINK PANTER

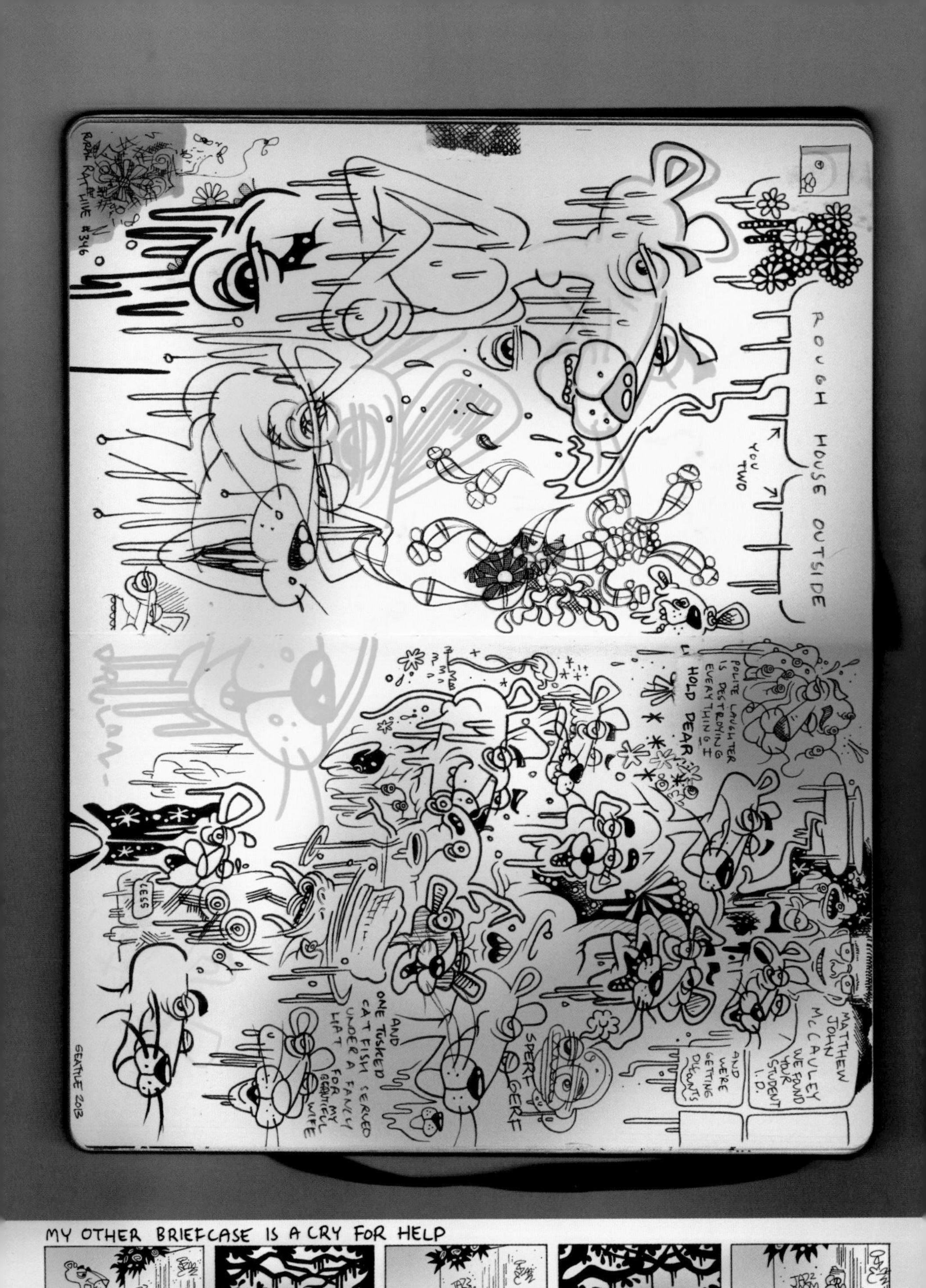
ROUGH HOUSE OUTSIDE
YOU TWO
POLITE LAUGHTER IS DESTROYING EVERYTHING I HOLD DEAR
MATTHEW JOHN McCAULEY WE FOUND YOUR STUDENT I.D.
AND WE'RE GETTING DISCOUNTS
AND ONE TUSKED CAT FISH SERVED UNDER A FANCY HAT FOR MY BEAUTIFUL WIFE
SPERT GERT
SEATTLE 2013

MY OTHER BRIEFCASE IS A CRY FOR HELP

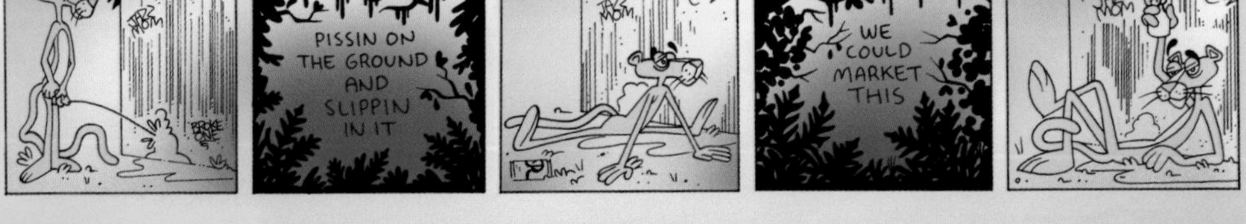
PISSIN ON THE GROUND AND SLIPPIN IN IT
WE COULD MARKET THIS

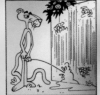

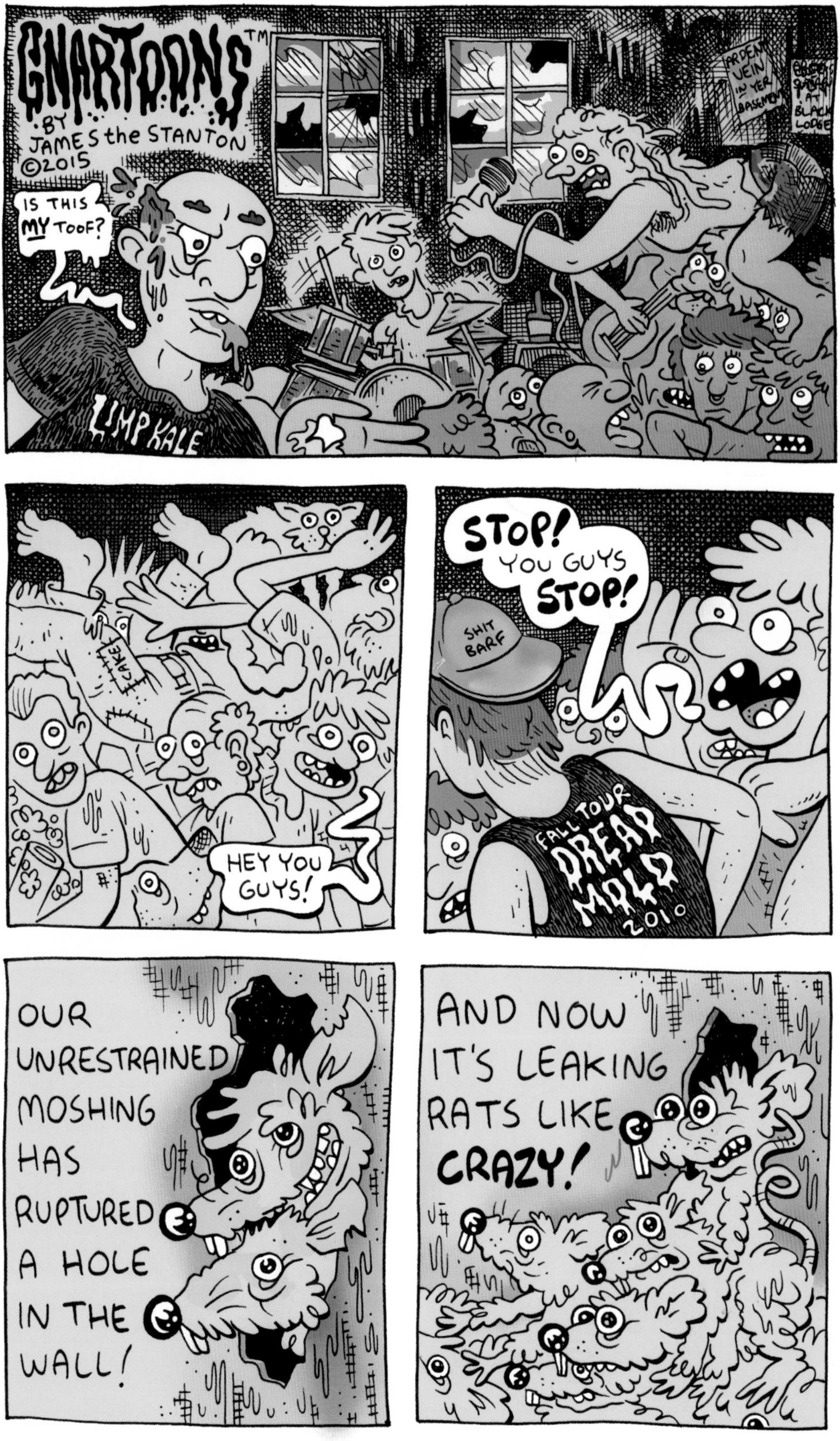
GNARTOONS™
BY JAMES the STANTON ©2015
IS THIS MY TOOF?
ARDENT VEIN IN YER BASEMENT
AT BLACK LODGE
LIMP KALE
CAKE
HEY YOU GUYS!
STOP! YOU GUYS STOP!
SHIT BARF
FALL TOUR DREAD MOLD 2010
OUR UNRESTRAINED MOSHING HAS RUPTURED A HOLE IN THE WALL!
AND NOW IT'S LEAKING RATS LIKE CRAZY!

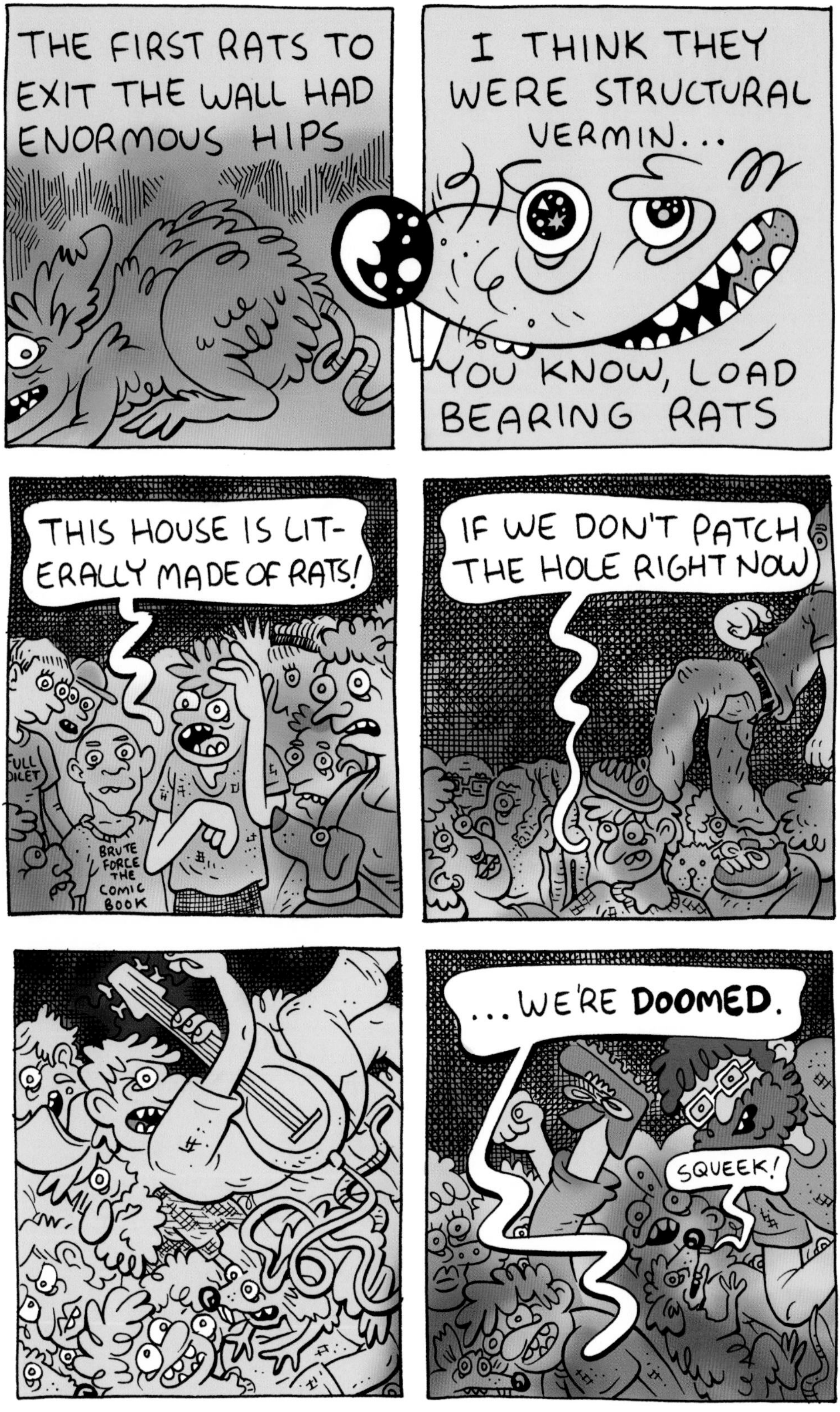
THE FIRST RATS TO EXIT THE WALL HAD ENORMOUS HIPS
I THINK THEY WERE STRUCTURAL VERMIN...
YOU KNOW, LOAD BEARING RATS
THIS HOUSE IS LIT-ERALLY MADE OF RATS!
FULL
OILET
BRUTE FORCE THE COMIC BOOK
IF WE DON'T PATCH THE HOLE RIGHT NOW
...WE'RE DOOMED.
SQUEEK!

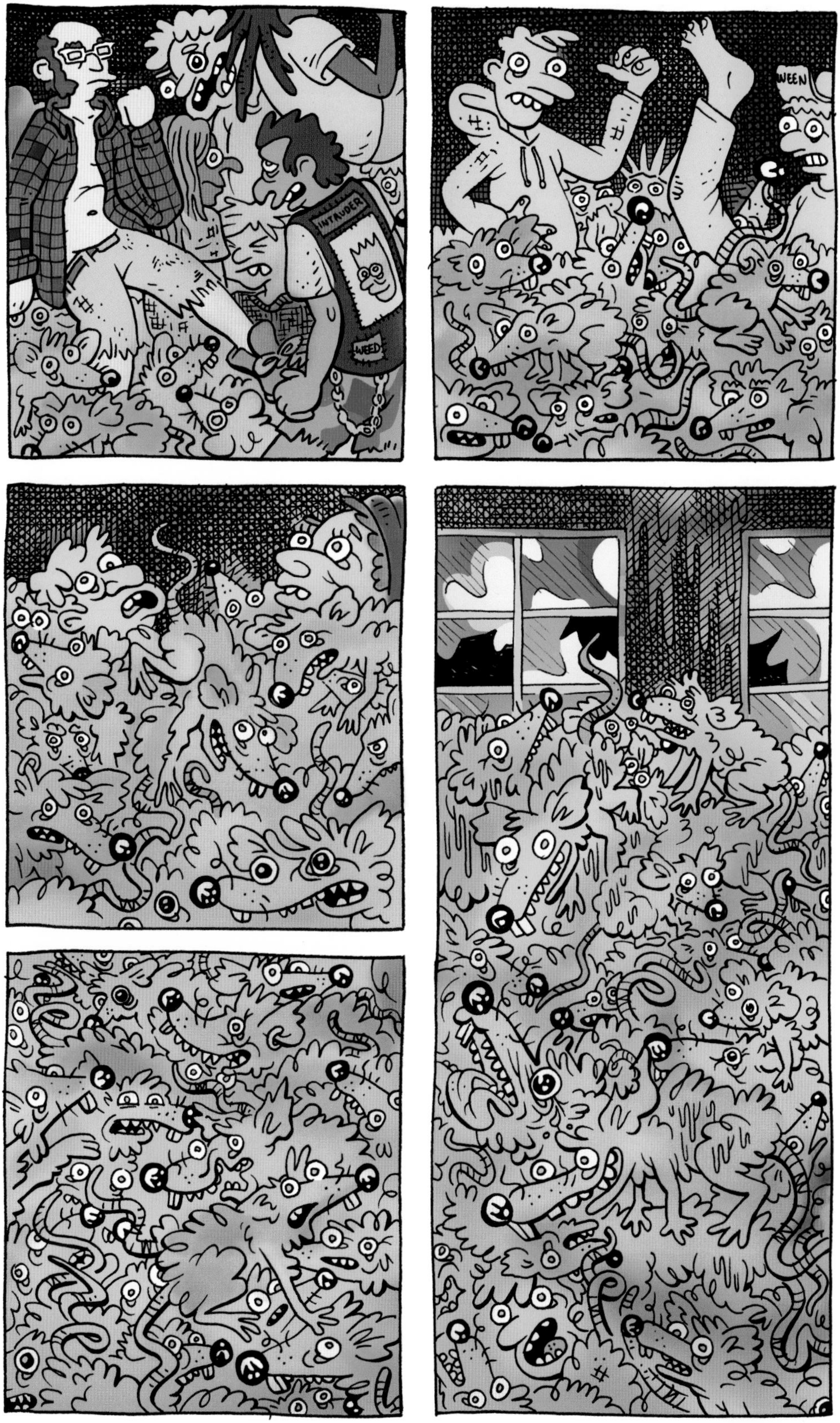
INTRUDER
WEED
WEEN

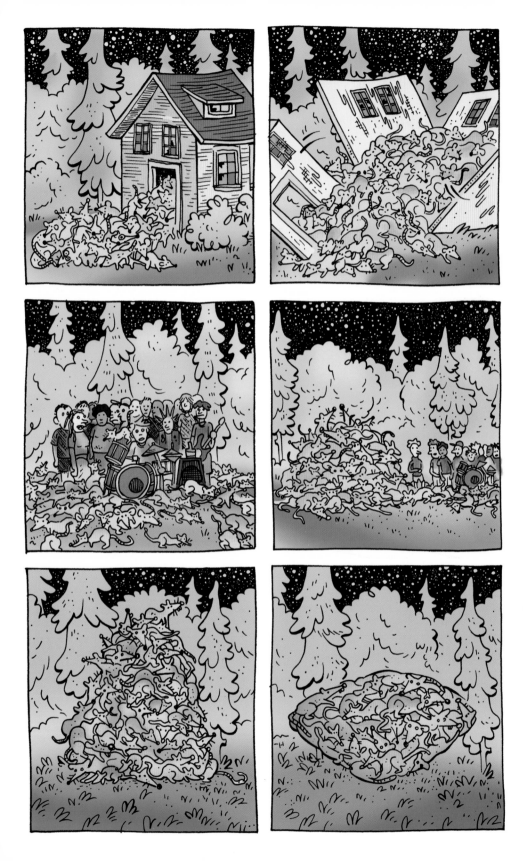

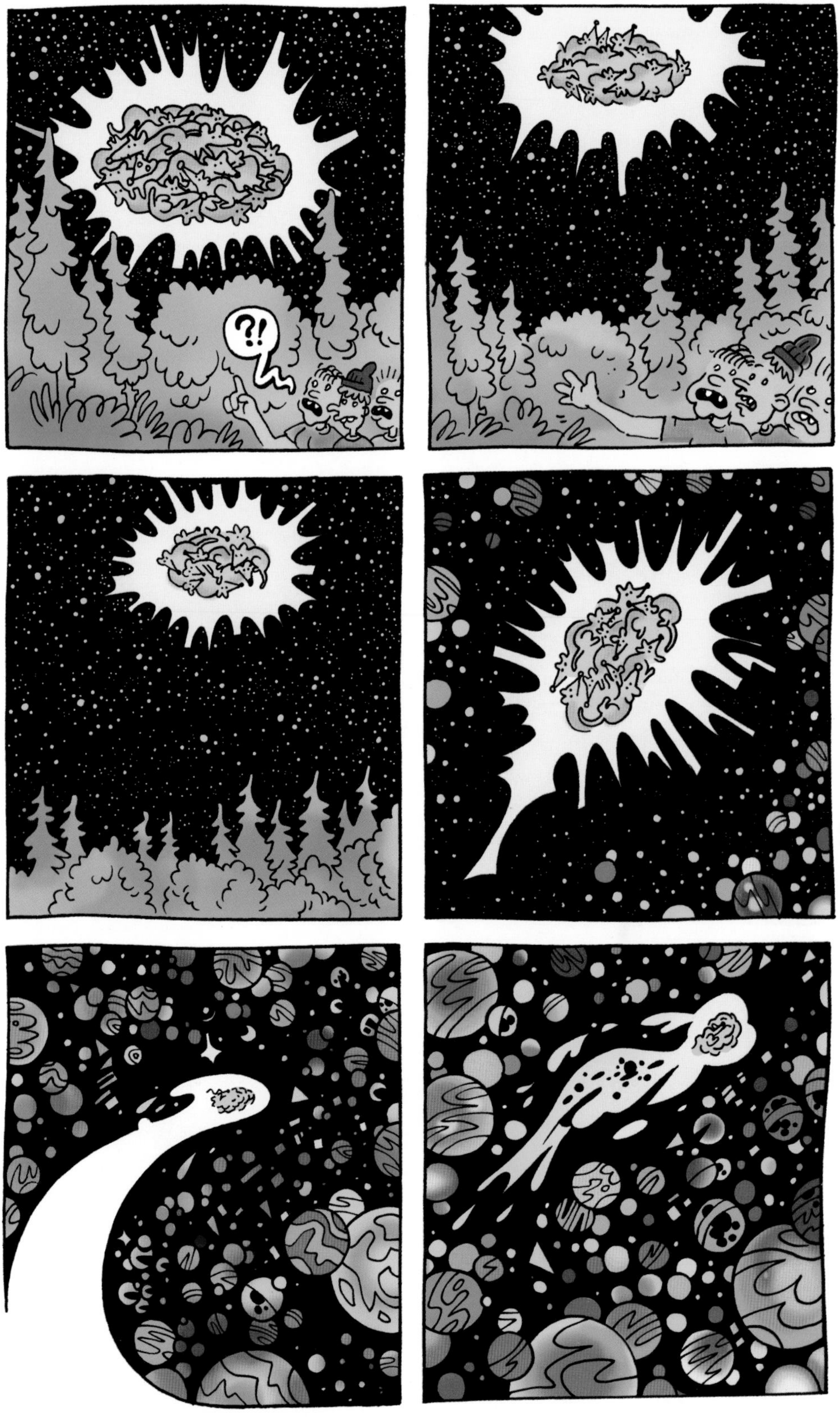
?!

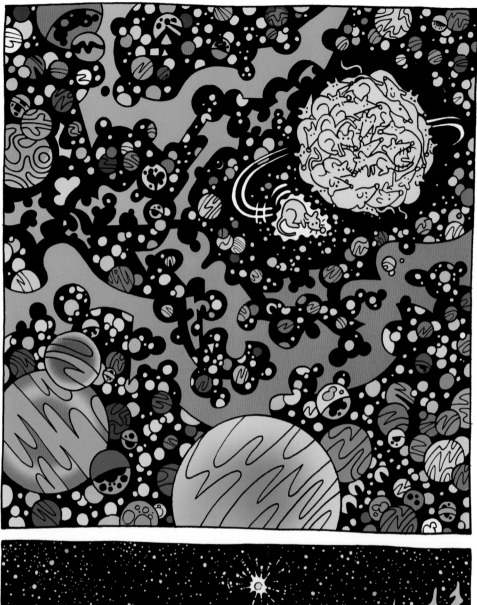

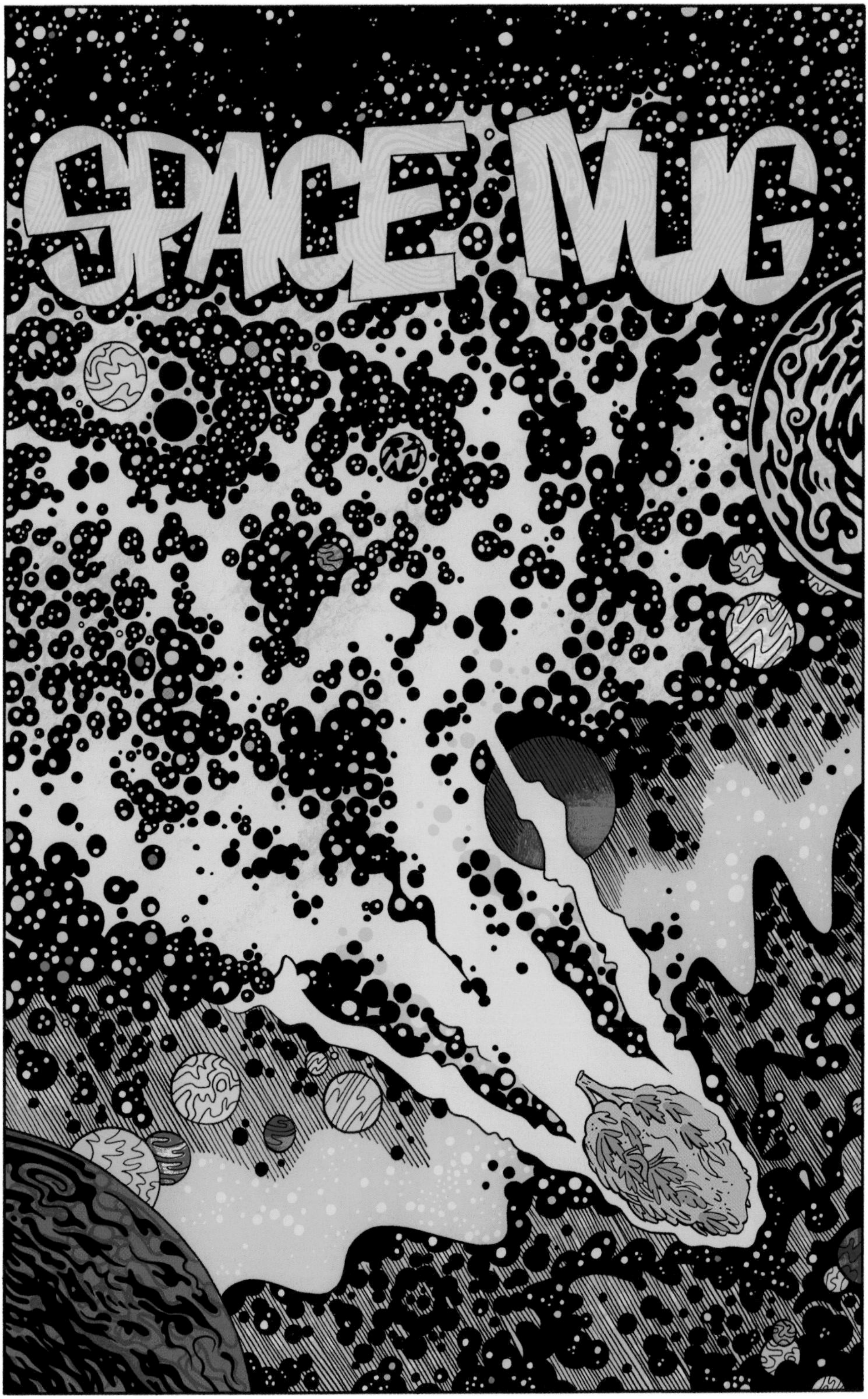
SPACE MUG

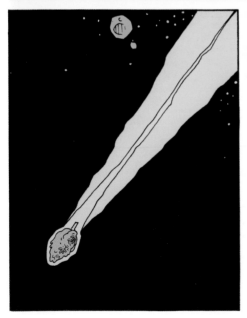

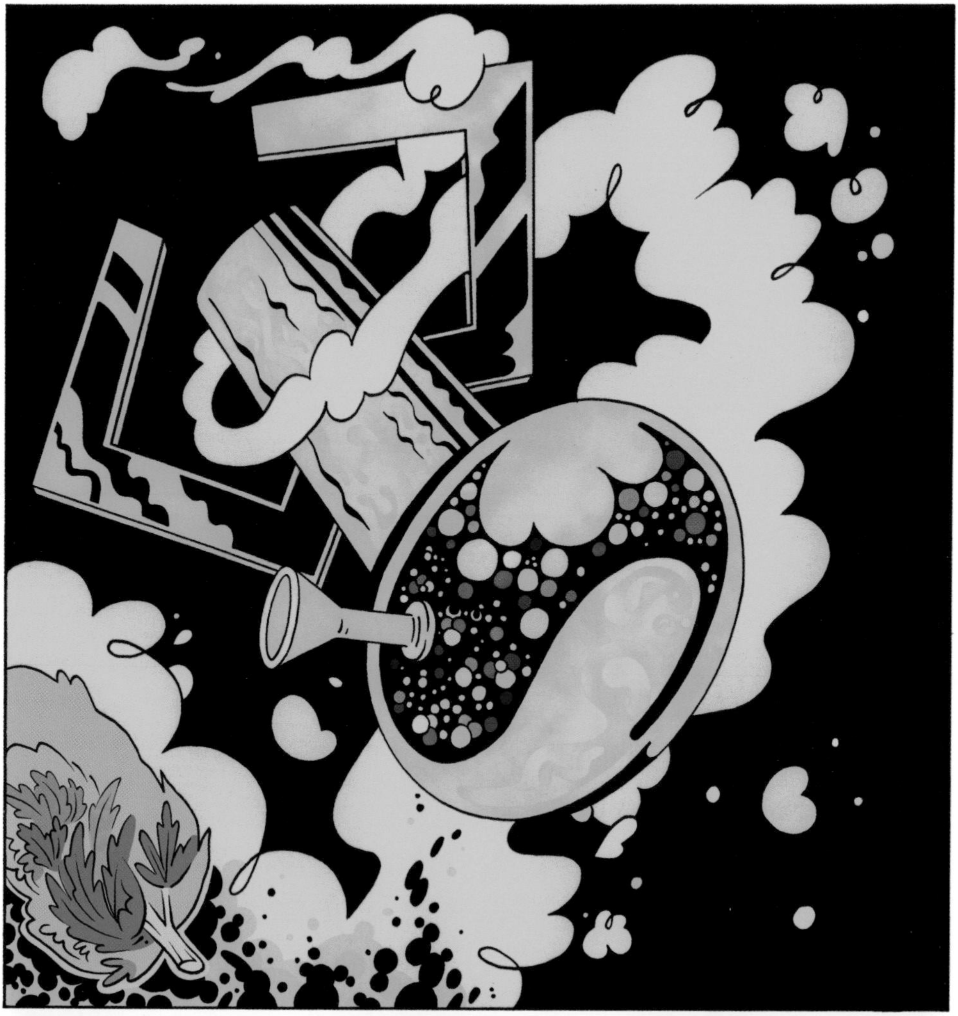

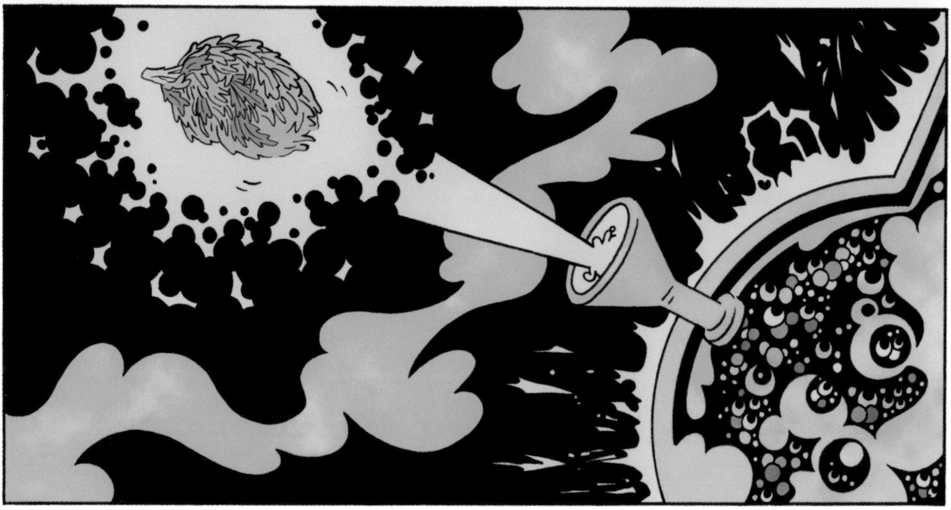

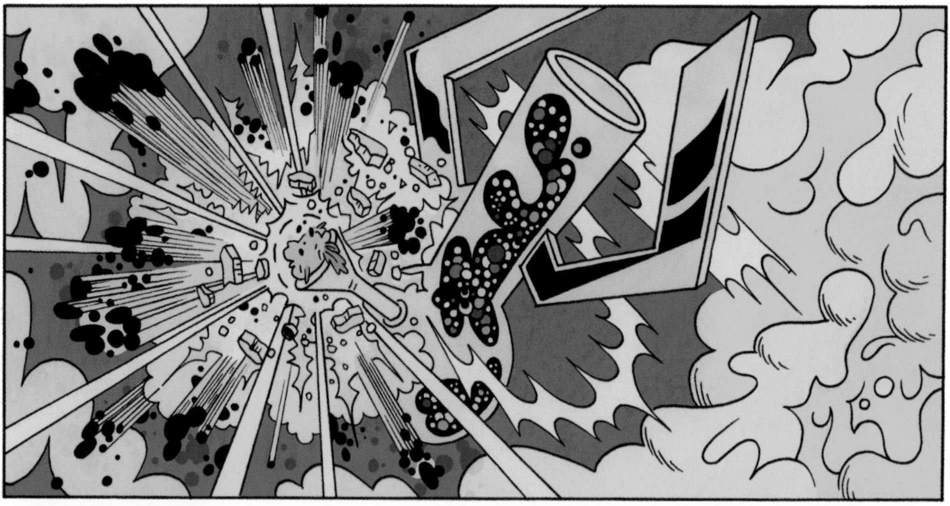

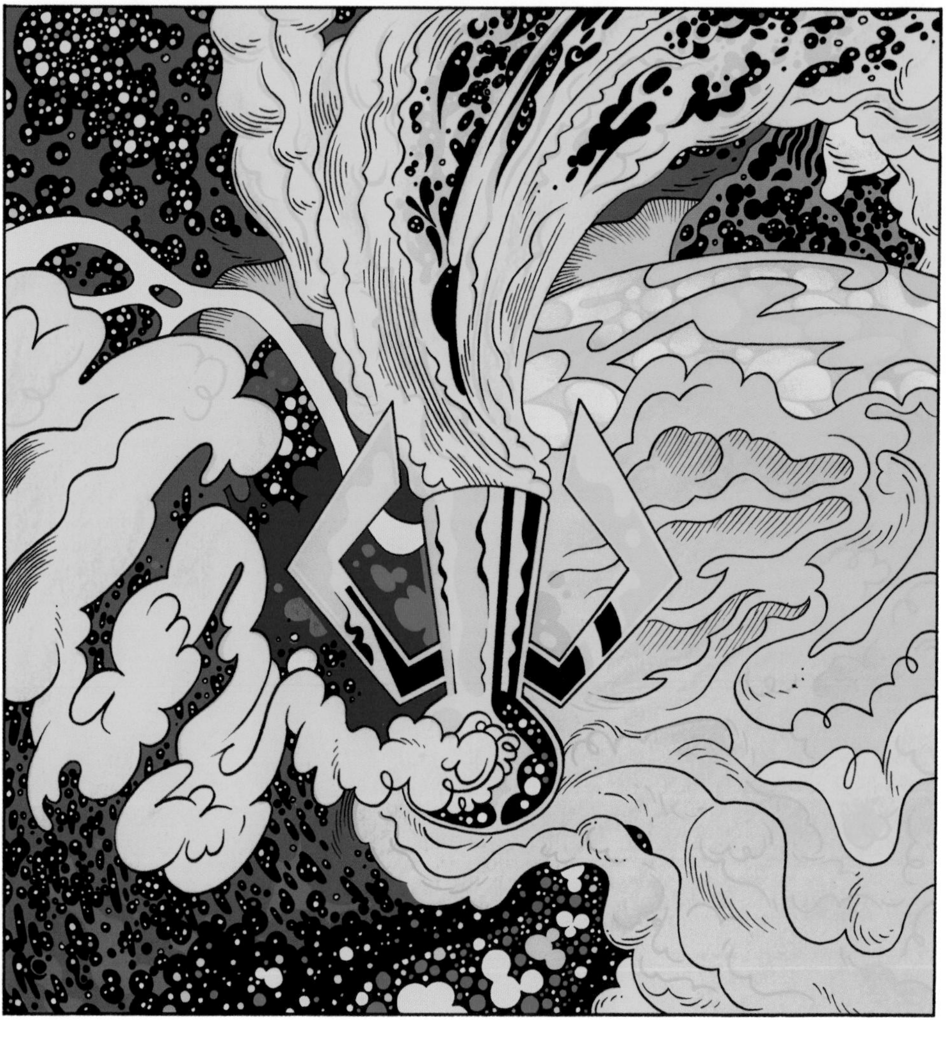

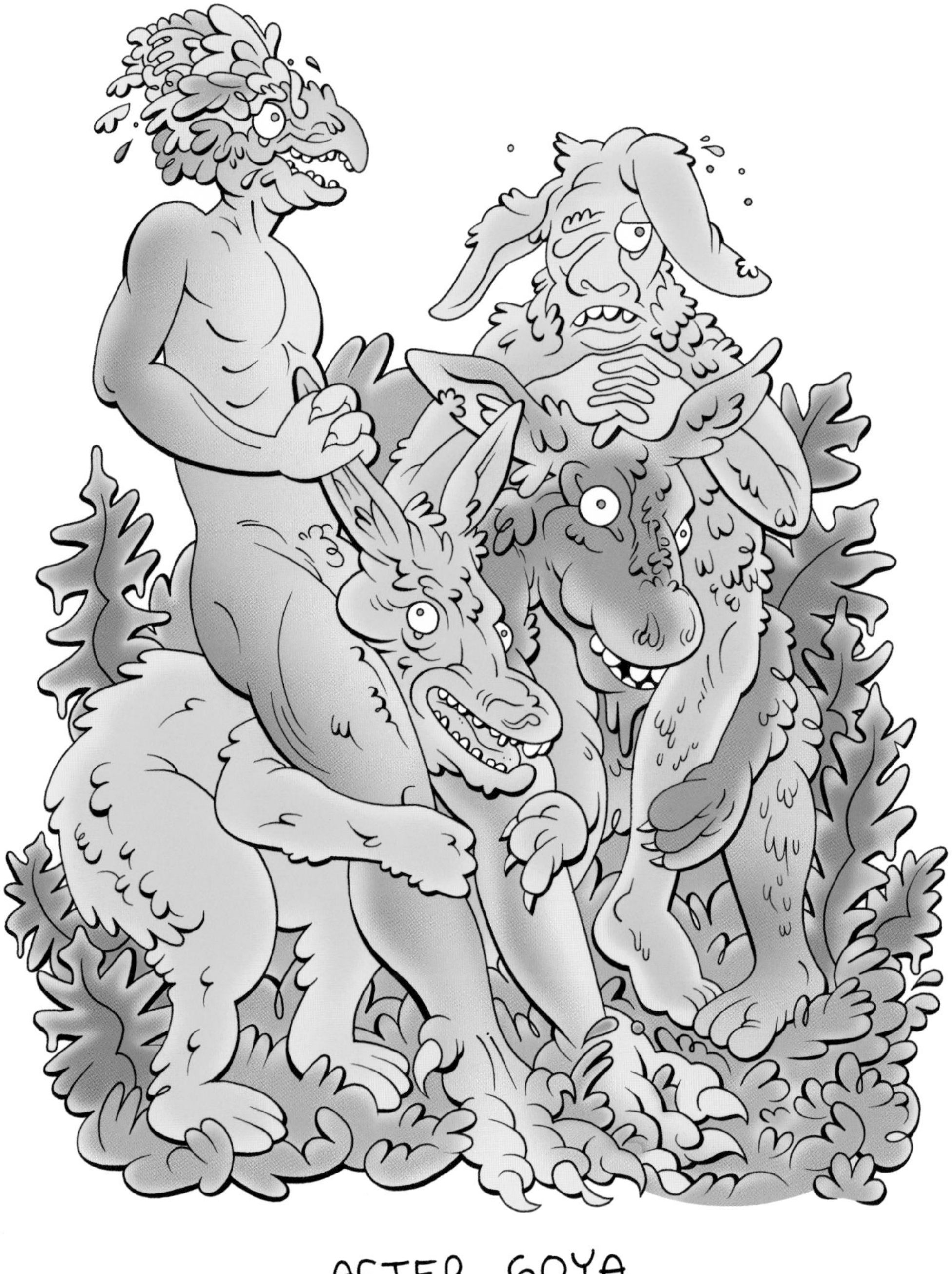

AFTER GOYA.

I THINK OUR FRIEND DAN MIGHT BE A DOLPHIN.

I FIRST NOTICED THE BLOWHOLE STAINS WHEN I RAN INTO HIM AT **HOT-WING CITY** LAST MONDAY

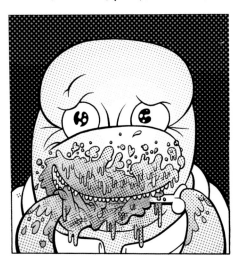

HE TRIED TO PASS IT OFF AS BACK SWEAT, BUT THERE'S REALLY NO MISTAKING A BLOW HOLE STAIN ON THE BACK OF A SHIRT

"SOME **HEAT WAVE** WE'RE HAVING, AM I RIGHT?"

—DAN

I ACTUALLY JUST READ ON THE INTERNET THAT BLOW HOLE STAINS ON CLOTHING ARE THE #1 REASON FOR DOLPHINS WHO THINK THEY'RE PEOPLE TO BE DISCOVERED AS ACTUALLY JUST DOLPHINS.

AND THERE WAS SOMETHING GLISTENING IN HIS EYE ON MONDAY THAT FELT EXPLICITLY NAUTICAL. SEEING HIM THERE, CATATONICALLY

SLATHERING HIMSELF IN HOT SAUCE, IT WAS CLEAR TO ME THAT HE WAS BUILT FOR THE SEA.

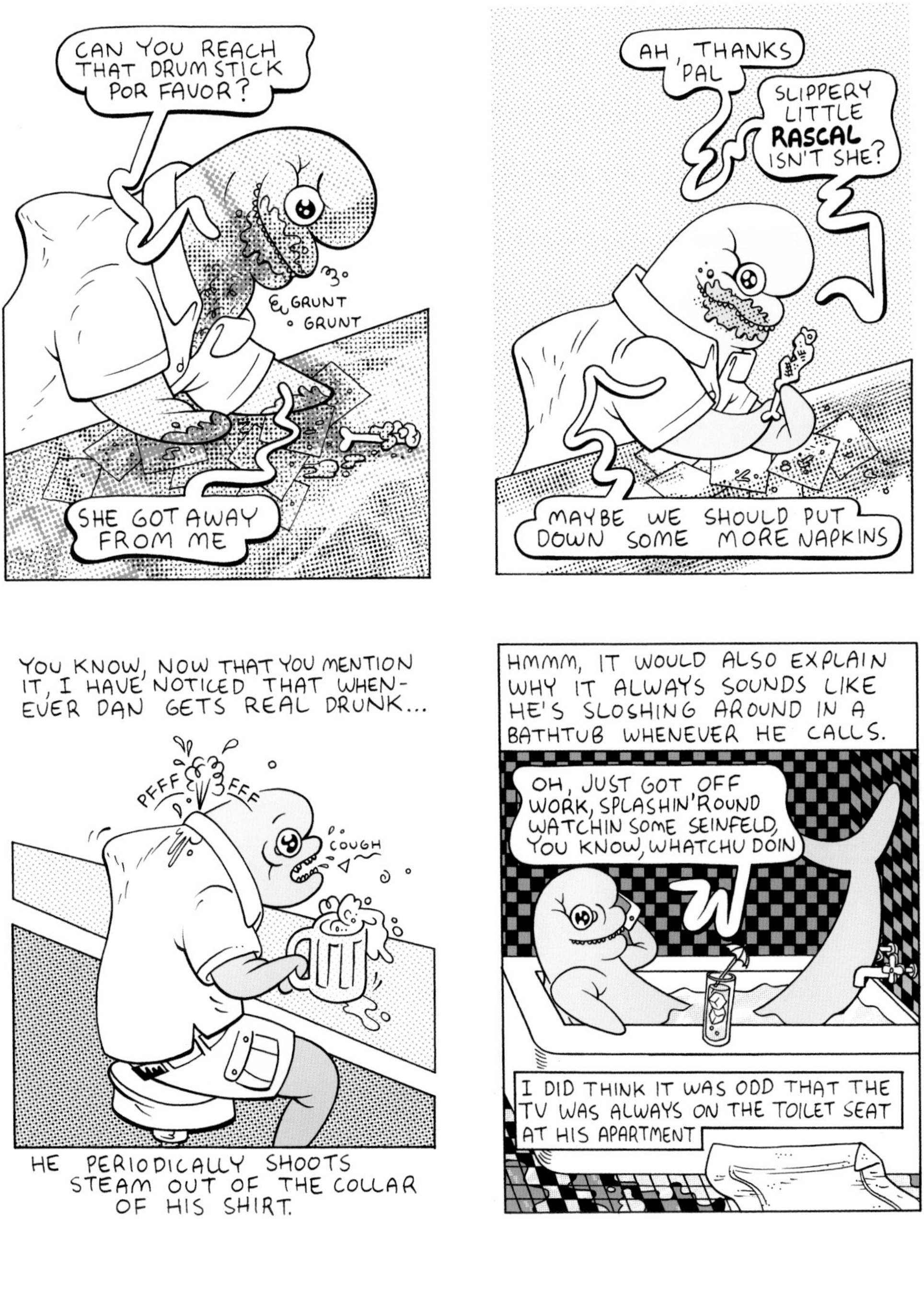
CAN YOU REACH THAT DRUM STICK POR FAVOR?
GRUNT GRUNT
SHE GOT AWAY FROM ME
AH, THANKS PAL
SLIPPERY LITTLE **RASCAL** ISN'T SHE?
MAYBE WE SHOULD PUT DOWN SOME MORE NAPKINS
YOU KNOW, NOW THAT YOU MENTION IT, I HAVE NOTICED THAT WHEN-EVER DAN GETS REAL DRUNK...
PFFFFFF
COUGH
HE PERIODICALLY SHOOTS STEAM OUT OF THE COLLAR OF HIS SHIRT.
HMMM, IT WOULD ALSO EXPLAIN WHY IT ALWAYS SOUNDS LIKE HE'S SLOSHING AROUND IN A BATHTUB WHENEVER HE CALLS.
OH, JUST GOT OFF WORK, SPLASHIN' ROUND WATCHIN SOME SEINFELD, YOU KNOW, WHATCHU DOIN
I DID THINK IT WAS ODD THAT THE TV WAS ALWAYS ON THE TOILET SEAT AT HIS APARTMENT

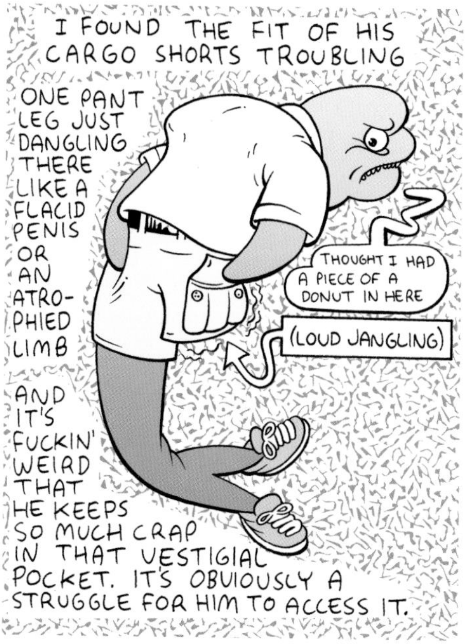
I FOUND THE FIT OF HIS CARGO SHORTS TROUBLING
ONE PANT LEG JUST DANGLING THERE LIKE A FLACID PENIS OR AN ATROPHIED LIMB
THOUGHT I HAD A PIECE OF A DONUT IN HERE
(LOUD JANGLING)
AND IT'S FUCKIN' WEIRD THAT HE KEEPS SO MUCH CRAP IN THAT VESTIGIAL POCKET. IT'S OBVIOUSLY A STRUGGLE FOR HIM TO ACCESS IT.

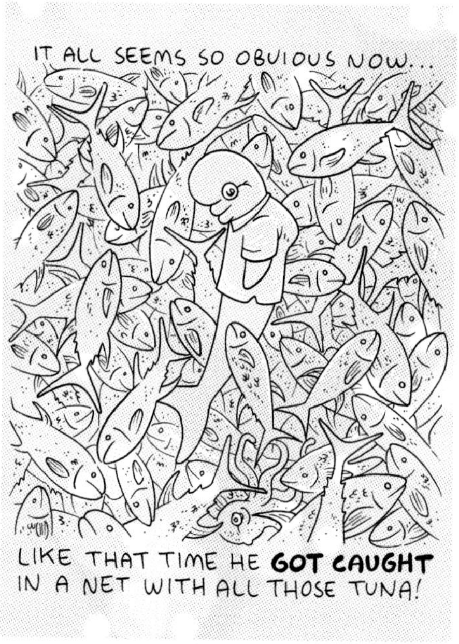
IT ALL SEEMS SO OBVIOUS NOW...
LIKE THAT TIME HE GOT CAUGHT IN A NET WITH ALL THOSE TUNA!

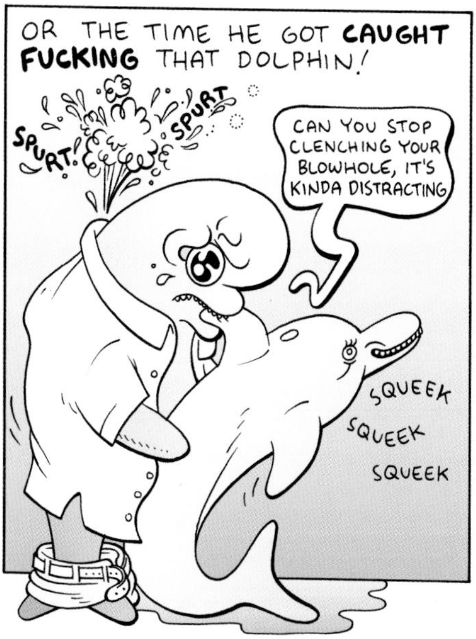
OR THE TIME HE GOT CAUGHT FUCKING THAT DOLPHIN!
SPURT!
SPURT
CAN YOU STOP CLENCHING YOUR BLOWHOLE, IT'S KINDA DISTRACTING
SQUEEK
SQUEEK
SQUEEK

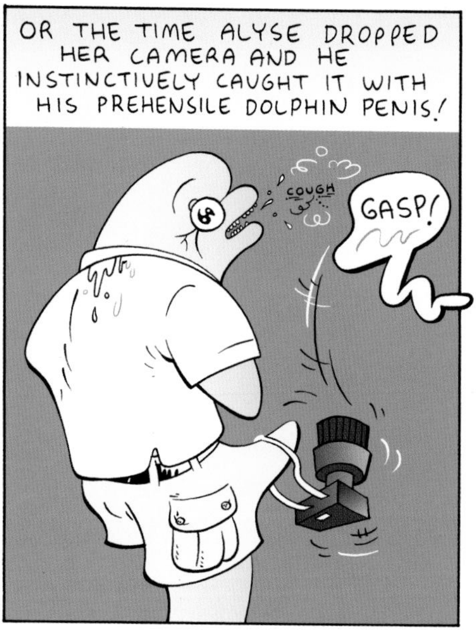
OR THE TIME ALYSE DROPPED HER CAMERA AND HE INSTINCTIVELY CAUGHT IT WITH HIS PREHENSILE DOLPHIN PENIS!
COUGH
GASP!

BOY OH BOY, OUR OLD PAL DAN—A DOLPHIN, HOW ABOUT THAT, EH? NEVER SAW IT COMING.

TOO MUCH?

WELL WHAT ARE WE GONNA DO NOW THAT WE KNOW HE'S A DOLPHIN? WE CAN'T VERY WELL TURN HIM IN AND SUBJECT HIM TO CAPTIVITY, HE'S BECOME SO ACCUSTOMED TO THE HUMAN WORLD...

DO THOSE GUYS FEEDIN US FISH EVER TOSS DOWN ANY CIGARETTES OR CANDY OR ANYTHING COOL? MAYBE SOME BEER OR A SKYMALL MAG?

this fuckin dolfin fuckin sux!

HE COULD NEVER ADAPT TO AQUARIUM CULTURE AT THIS POINT.

WE CAN'T SET HIM FREE, HE'S GOT A ONE YEAR LEASE AND CAR PAYMENTS TO MAKE—

UGH! IS THAT DOLPHIN STUFFING STARFISH INTO HIS CARGO POCKETS ?!? WHO DOES HE THINK HE IS, I'M GONNA EAT HIM

AND THE SHARKS WOULD EAT HIM ALIVE.

OKAY, WELL NOW THAT WE KNOW HE'S A DOLPHIN, ARE WE STILL GONNA LET HIM DRIVE US TO THE BOOM BOOM ROOM?

HOOOONNK!

SQUEEK SQUEEK SQUEEK

YAH I MEAN, IT'S HIS TURN AND I DON'T WANNA **FUGGIN DRIVE!**

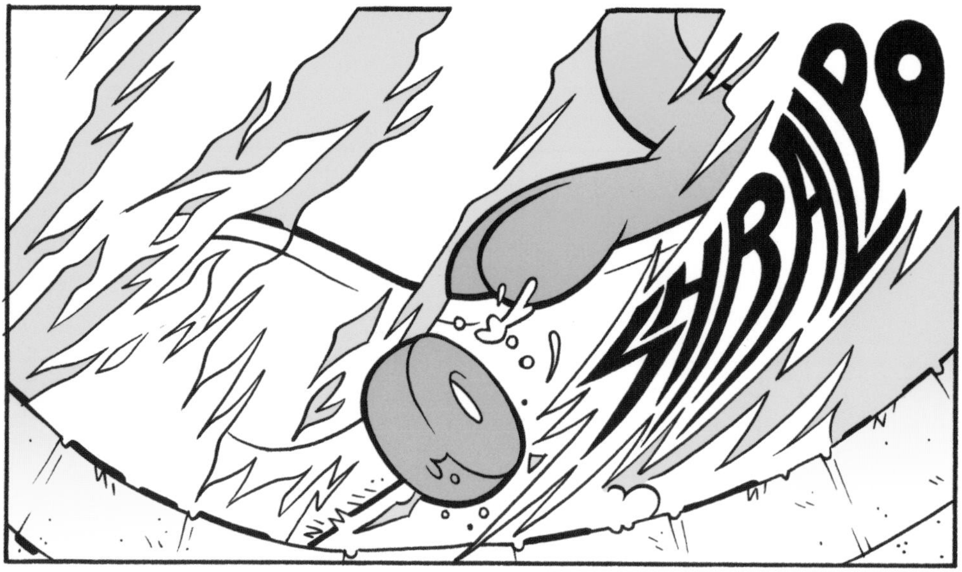
SHRALPO

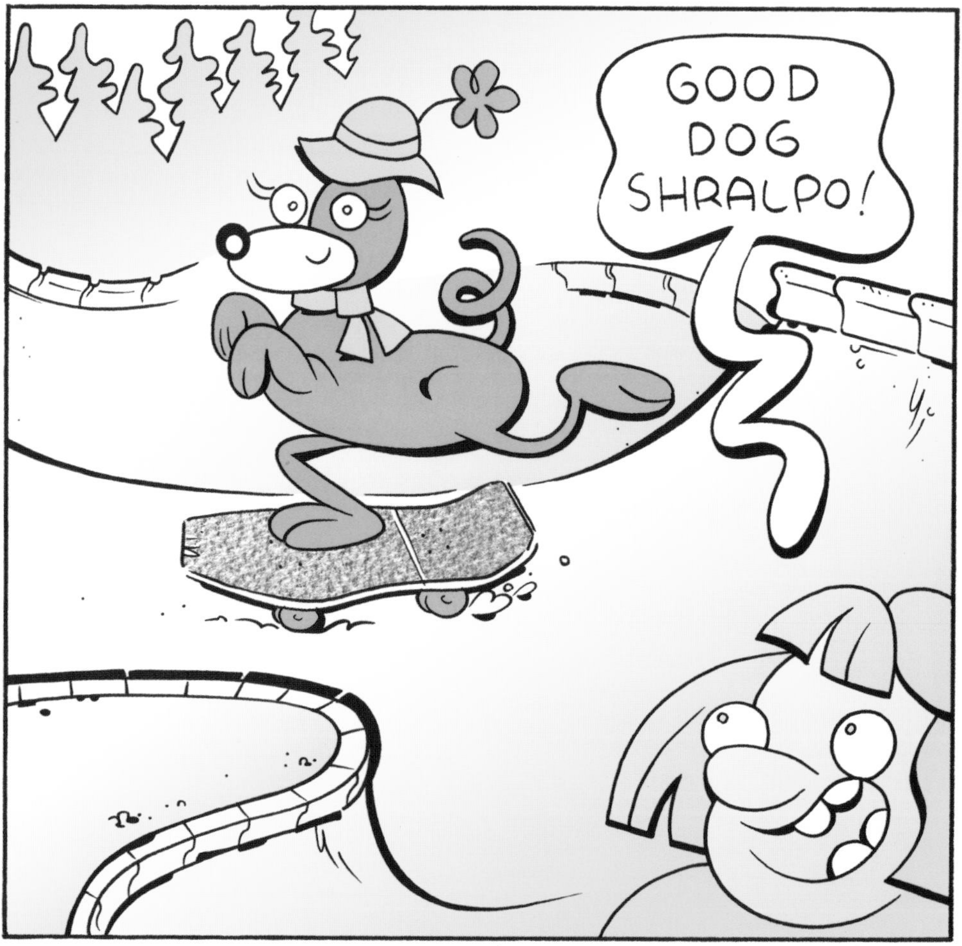
GOOD DOG SHRALPO!

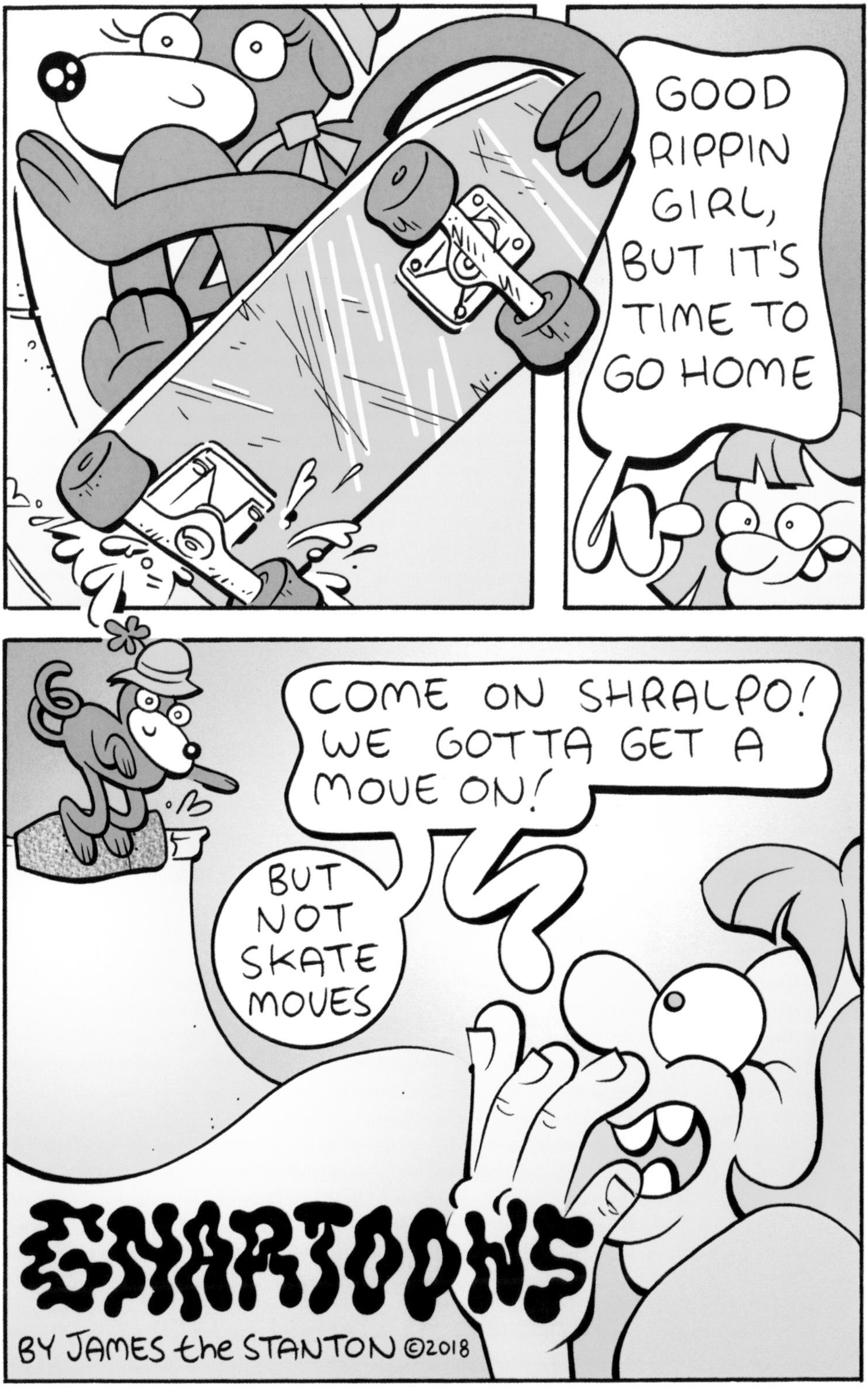
GOOD RIPPIN GIRL, BUT IT'S TIME TO GO HOME
COME ON SHRALPO! WE GOTTA GET A MOVE ON!
BUT NOT SKATE MOVES
GNARTOONS
BY JAMES the STANTON ©2018

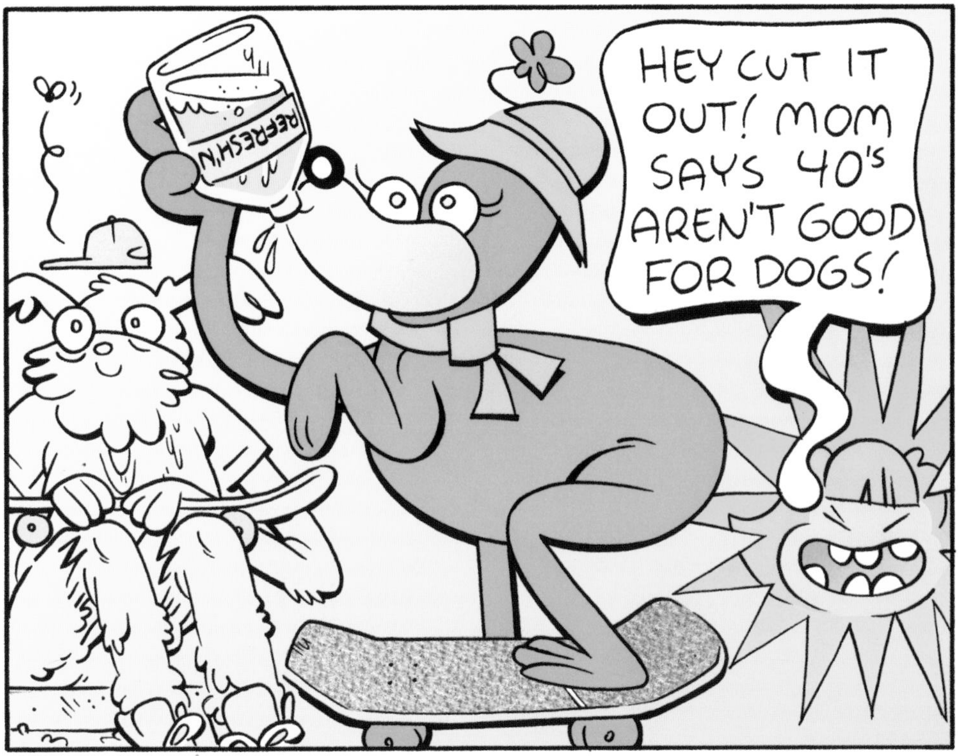
HEY CUT IT OUT! MOM SAYS 40's AREN'T GOOD FOR DOGS!

YOU'RE GETTING TOO OLD FOR NEW TRICKS SHRALPO!

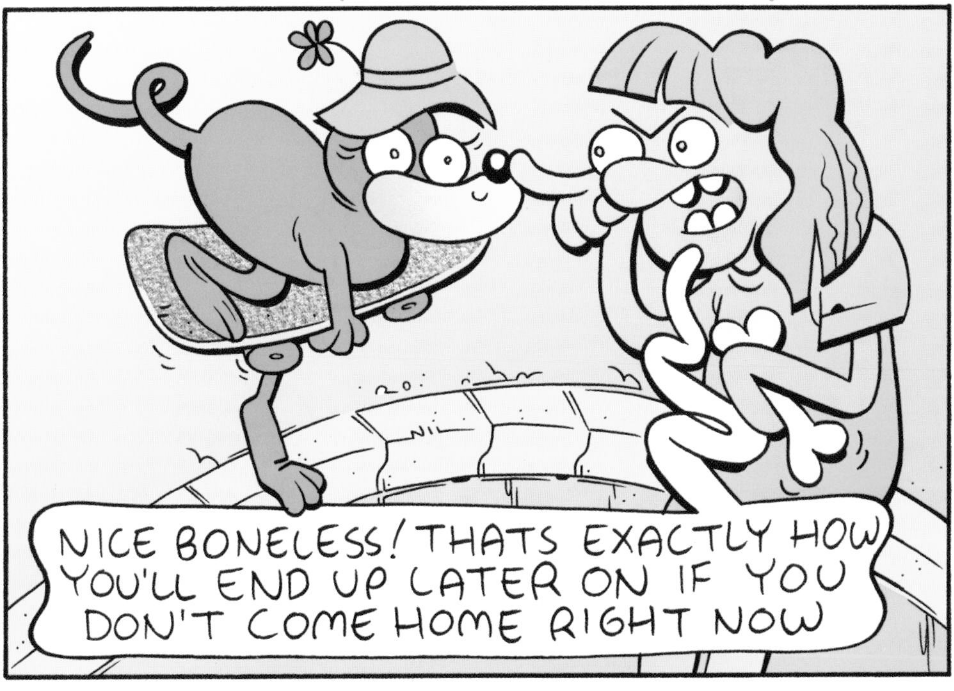
NICE BONELESS! THATS EXACTLY HOW YOU'LL END UP LATER ON IF YOU DON'T COME HOME RIGHT NOW

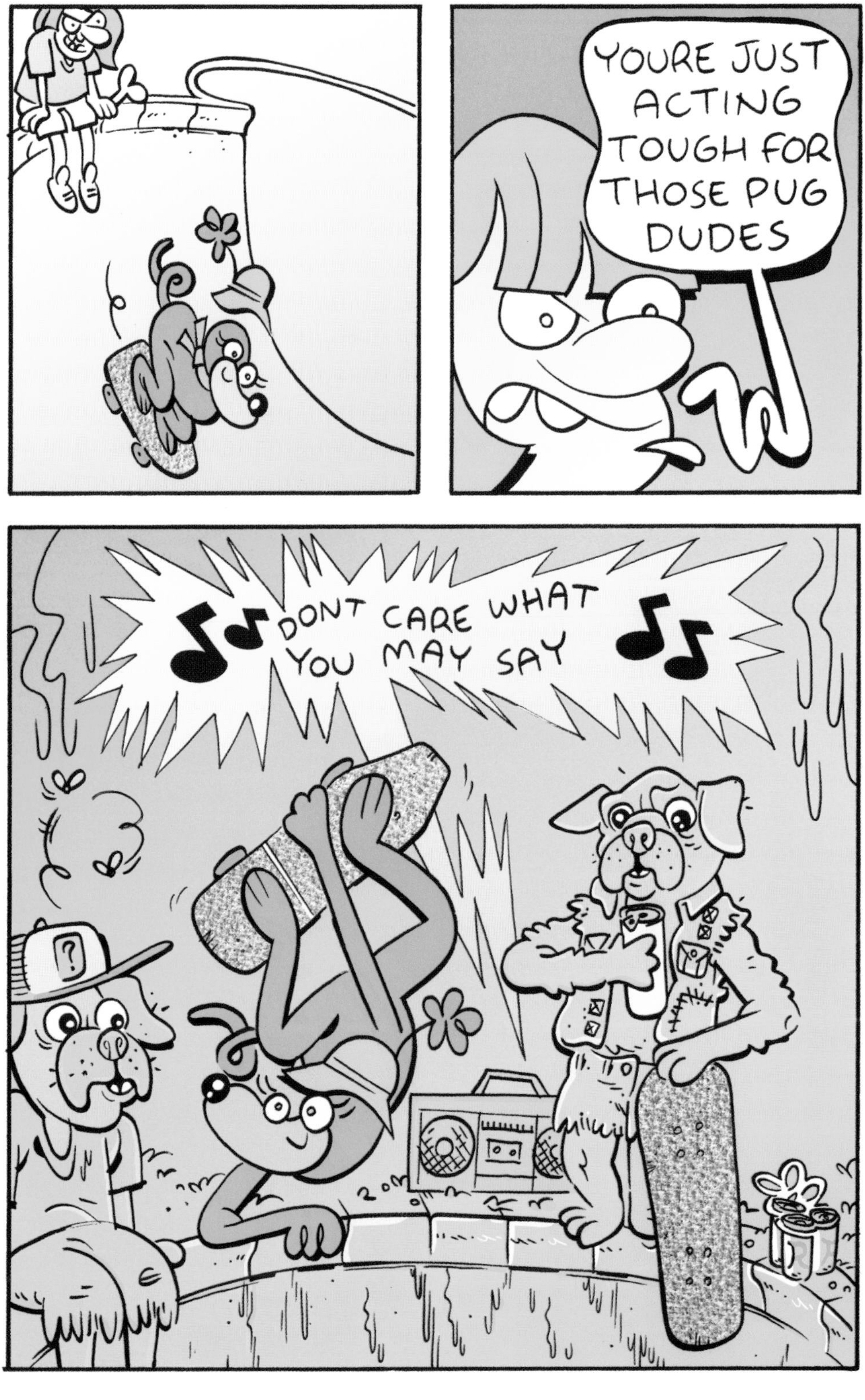
YOURE JUST ACTING TOUGH FOR THOSE PUG DUDES
DONT CARE WHAT YOU MAY SAY

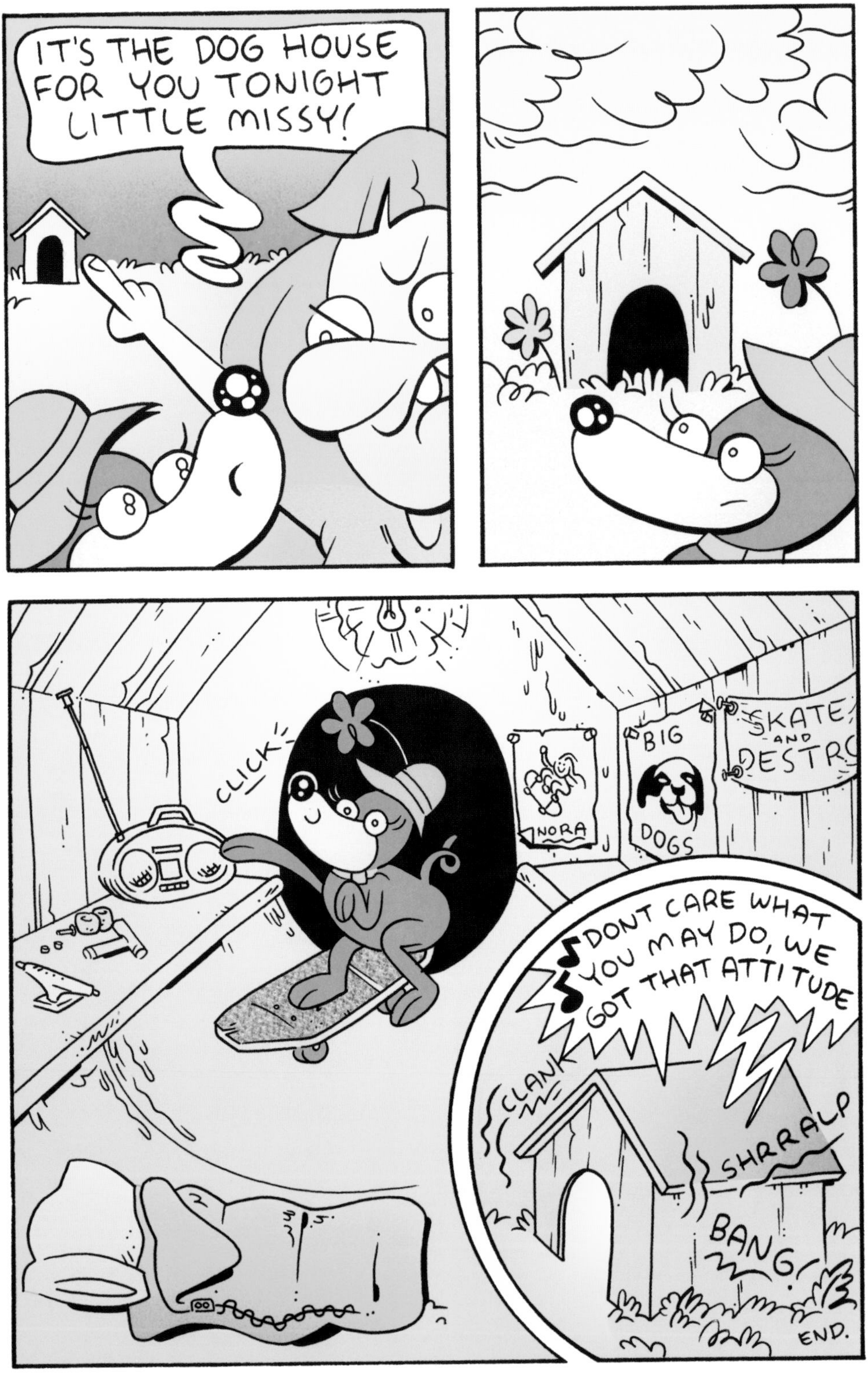

IT'S THE DOG HOUSE FOR YOU TONIGHT LITTLE MISSY!
CLICK
NORA
BIG DOGS
SKATE AND DESTR
DONT CARE WHAT YOU MAY DO, WE GOT THAT ATTITUDE
CLANK
SHRRALP
BANG!
END.

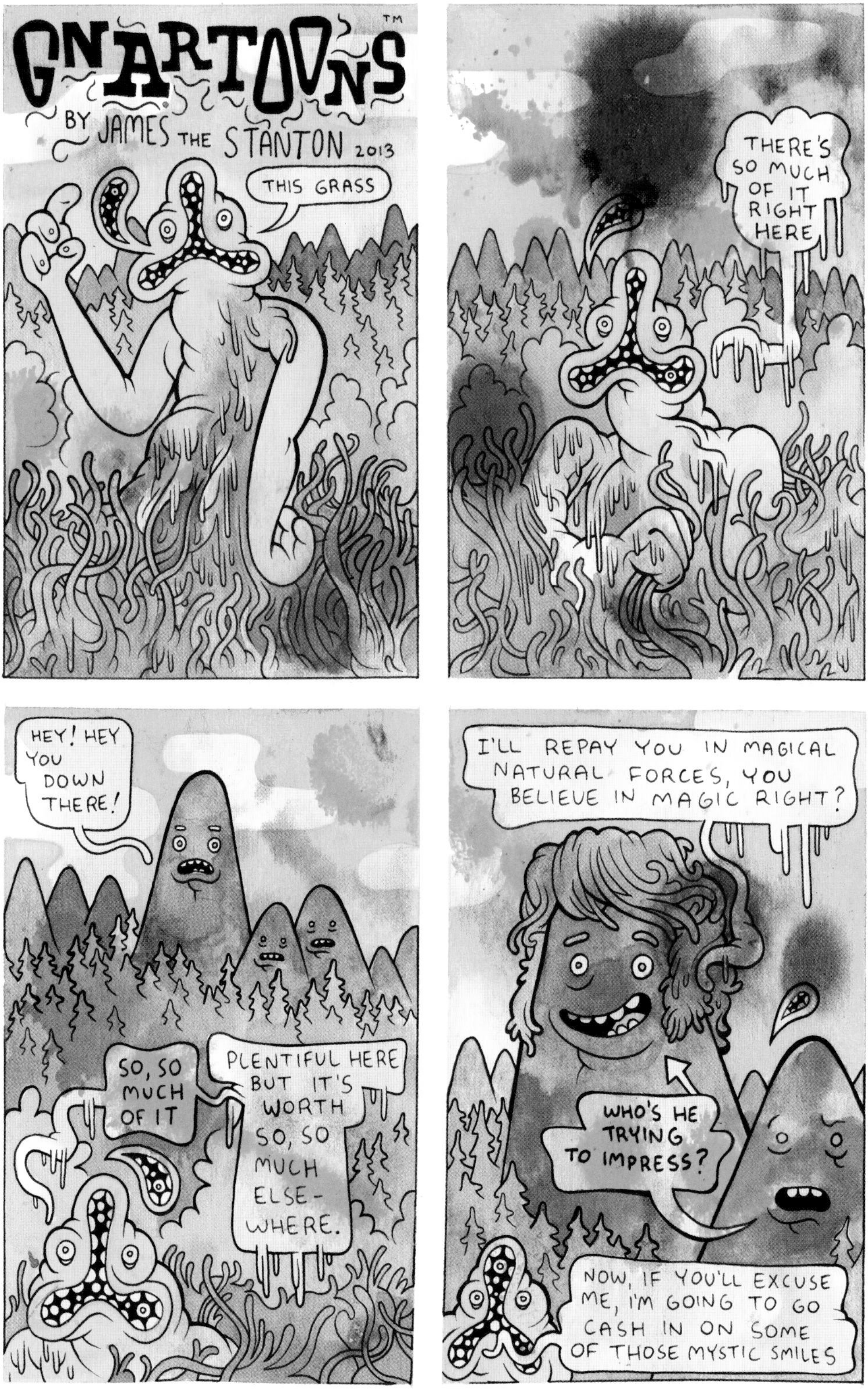
GNARTOONS™
BY JAMES THE STANTON 2013
THIS GRASS
THERE'S SO MUCH OF IT RIGHT HERE
HEY! HEY YOU DOWN THERE!
SO, SO MUCH OF IT
PLENTIFUL HERE BUT IT'S WORTH SO, SO MUCH ELSE-WHERE.
I'LL REPAY YOU IN MAGICAL NATURAL FORCES, YOU BELIEVE IN MAGIC RIGHT?
WHO'S HE TRYING TO IMPRESS?
NOW, IF YOU'LL EXCUSE ME, I'M GOING TO GO CASH IN ON SOME OF THOSE MYSTIC SMILES

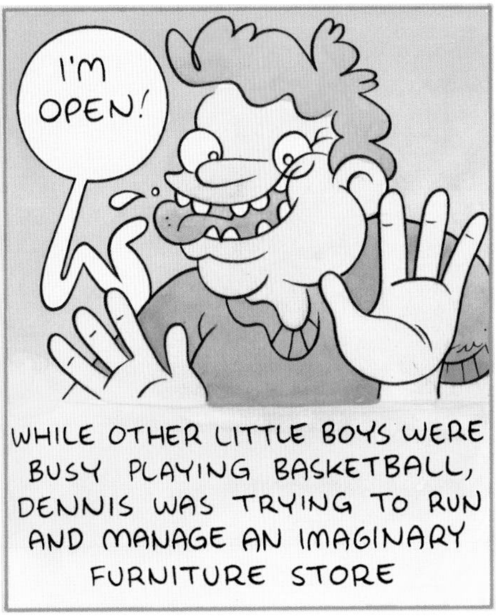
I'M OPEN!
WHILE OTHER LITTLE BOYS WERE BUSY PLAYING BASKETBALL, DENNIS WAS TRYING TO RUN AND MANAGE AN IMAGINARY FURNITURE STORE

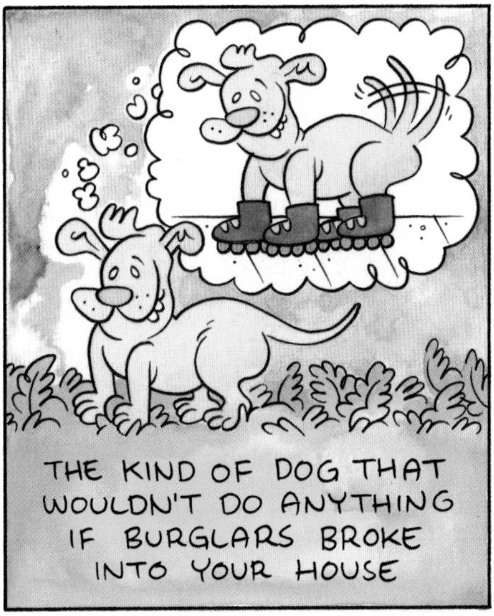
THE KIND OF DOG THAT WOULDN'T DO ANYTHING IF BURGLARS BROKE INTO YOUR HOUSE

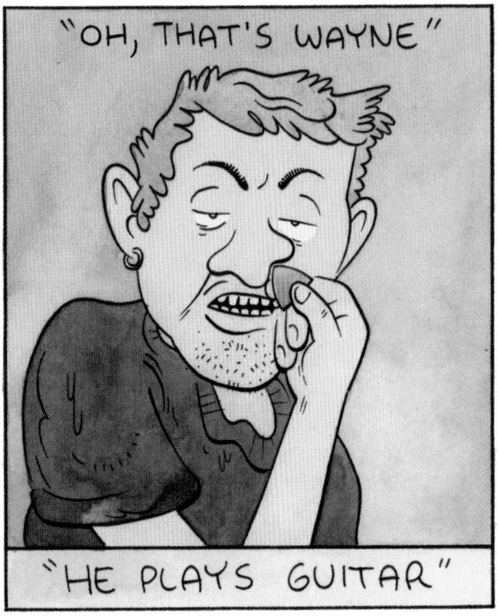
"OH, THAT'S WAYNE"
"HE PLAYS GUITAR"

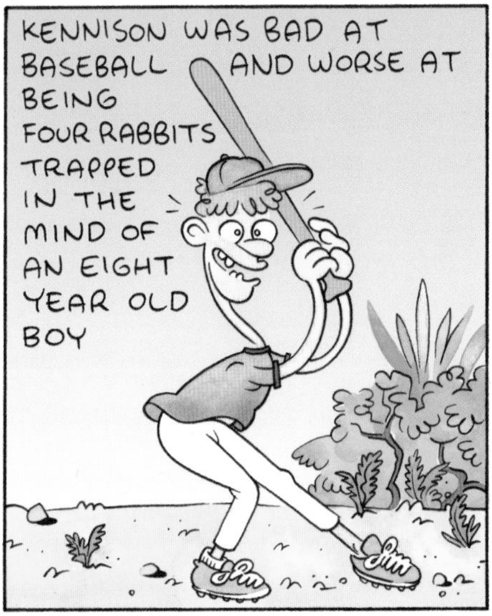
KENNISON WAS BAD AT BASEBALL AND WORSE AT BEING FOUR RABBITS TRAPPED IN THE MIND OF AN EIGHT YEAR OLD BOY

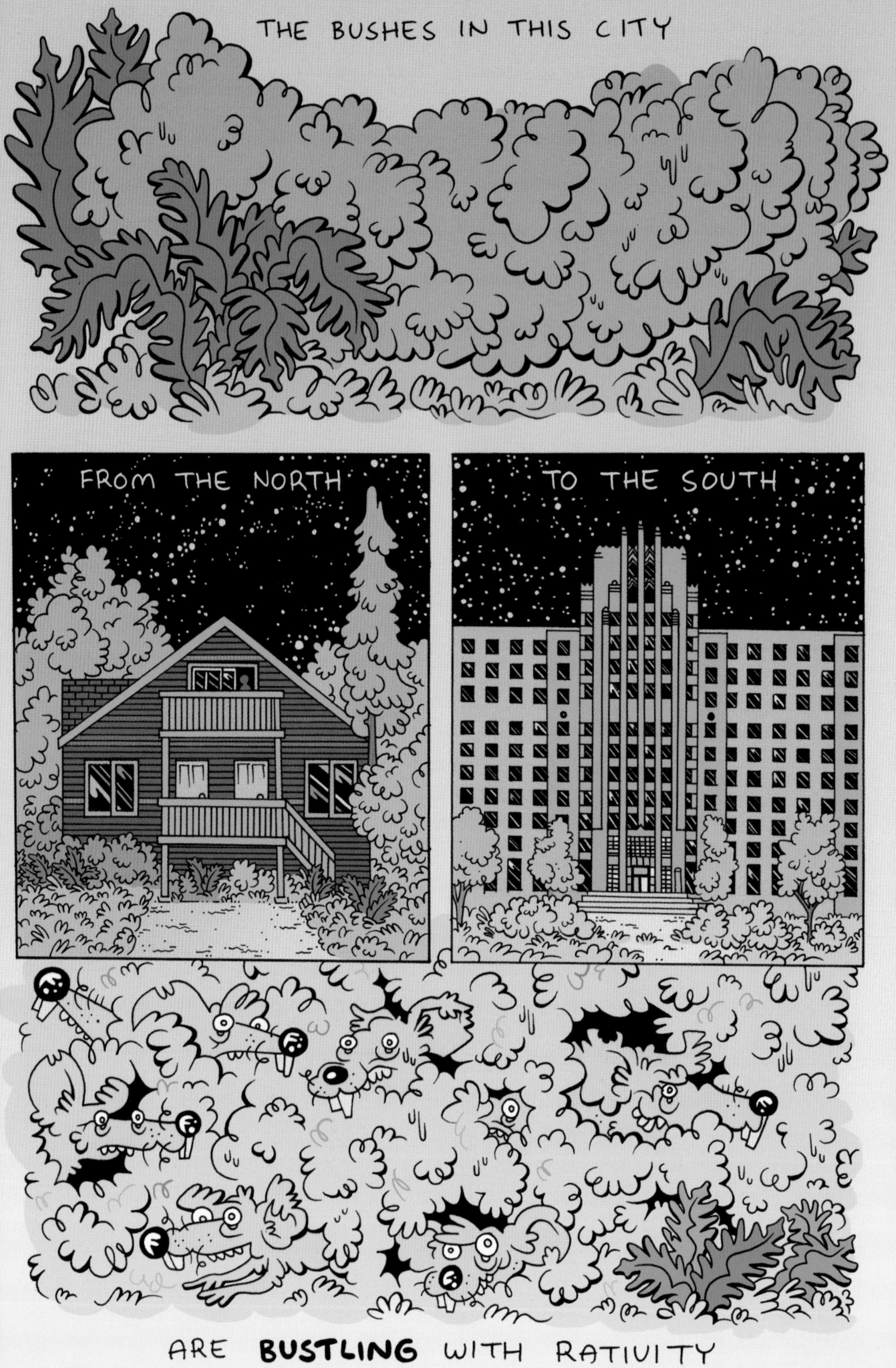
THE BUSHES IN THIS CITY
FROM THE NORTH
TO THE SOUTH
ARE BUSTLING WITH RATIVITY

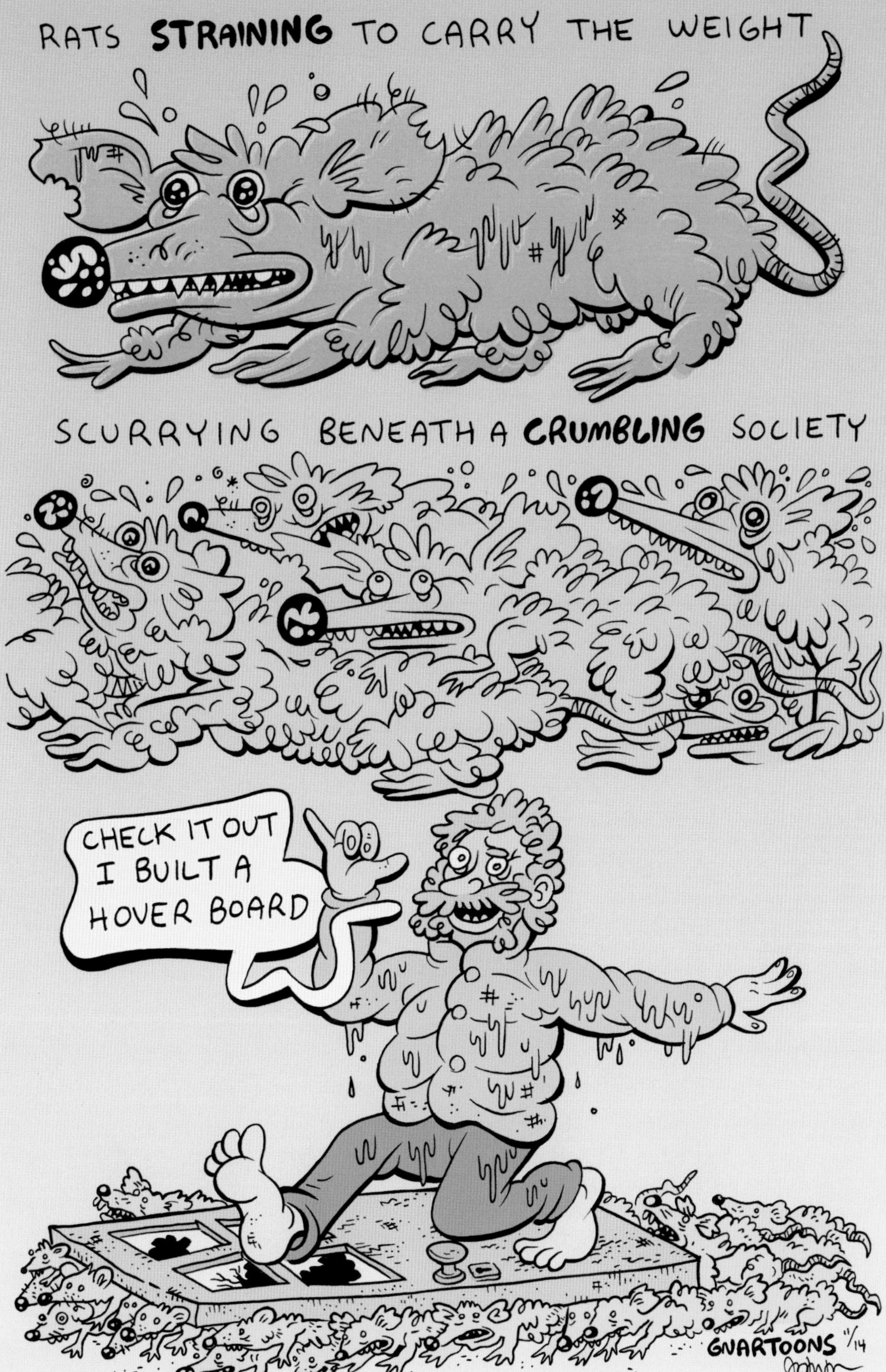
RATS STRAINING TO CARRY THE WEIGHT
SCURRYING BENEATH A CRUMBLING SOCIETY
CHECK IT OUT I BUILT A HOVER BOARD
GNARTOONS 11/14

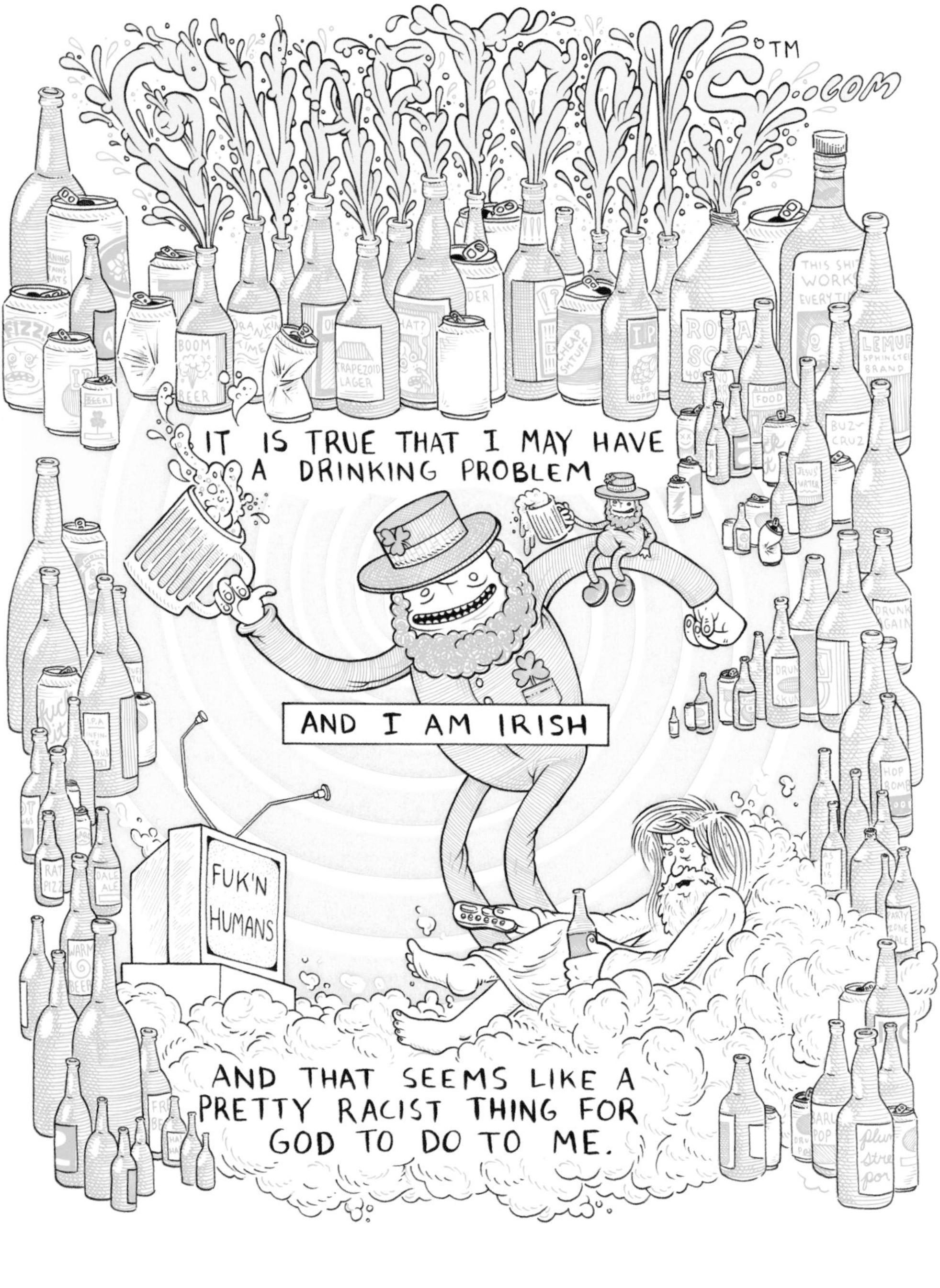
SNARTOONS™ .COM
IT IS TRUE THAT I MAY HAVE A DRINKING PROBLEM
AND I AM IRISH
FUK'N HUMANS
AND THAT SEEMS LIKE A PRETTY RACIST THING FOR GOD TO DO TO ME.

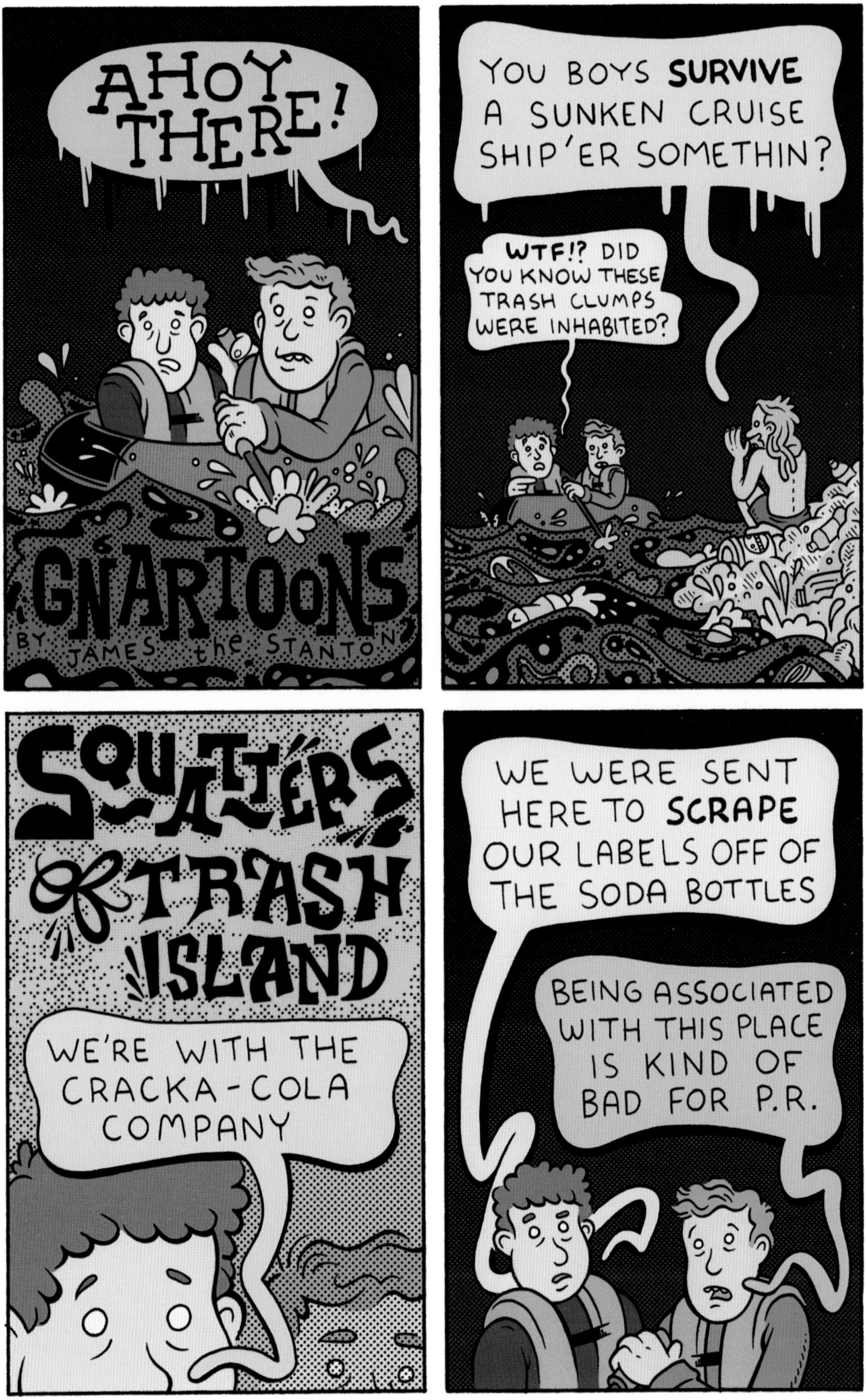
AHOY THERE!
GNARTOONS
BY JAMES the STANTON
YOU BOYS SURVIVE A SUNKEN CRUISE SHIP'ER SOMETHIN?
WTF!? DID YOU KNOW THESE TRASH CLUMPS WERE INHABITED?
SQUATTERS OF TRASH ISLAND
WE'RE WITH THE CRACKA-COLA COMPANY
WE WERE SENT HERE TO SCRAPE OUR LABELS OFF OF THE SODA BOTTLES
BEING ASSOCIATED WITH THIS PLACE IS KIND OF BAD FOR P.R.

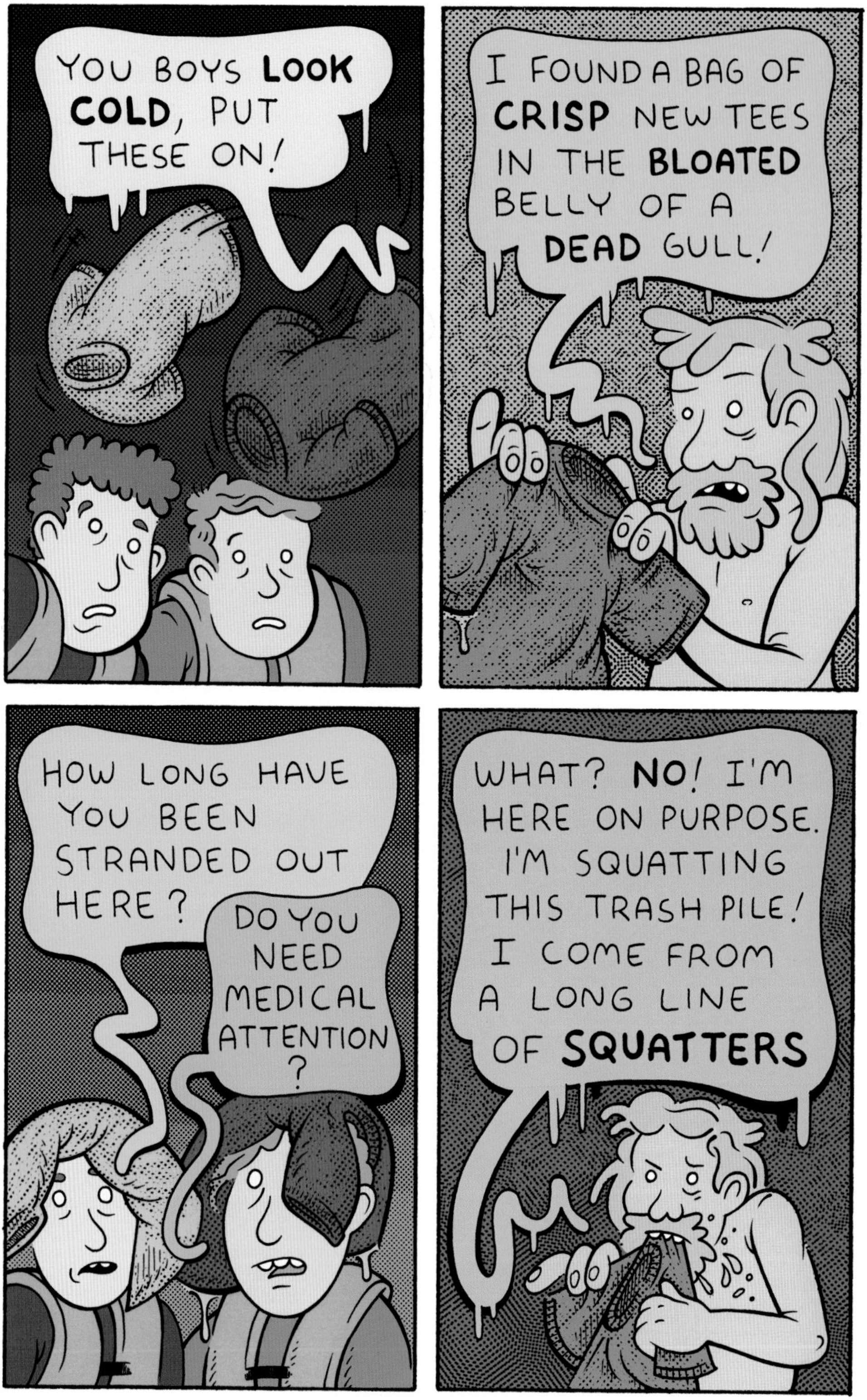
YOU BOYS **LOOK COLD**, PUT THESE ON!
I FOUND A BAG OF **CRISP** NEW TEES IN THE **BLOATED** BELLY OF A **DEAD** GULL!
HOW LONG HAVE YOU BEEN STRANDED OUT HERE?
DO YOU NEED MEDICAL ATTENTION?
WHAT? **NO**! I'M HERE ON PURPOSE. I'M SQUATTING THIS TRASH PILE! I COME FROM A LONG LINE OF **SQUATTERS**

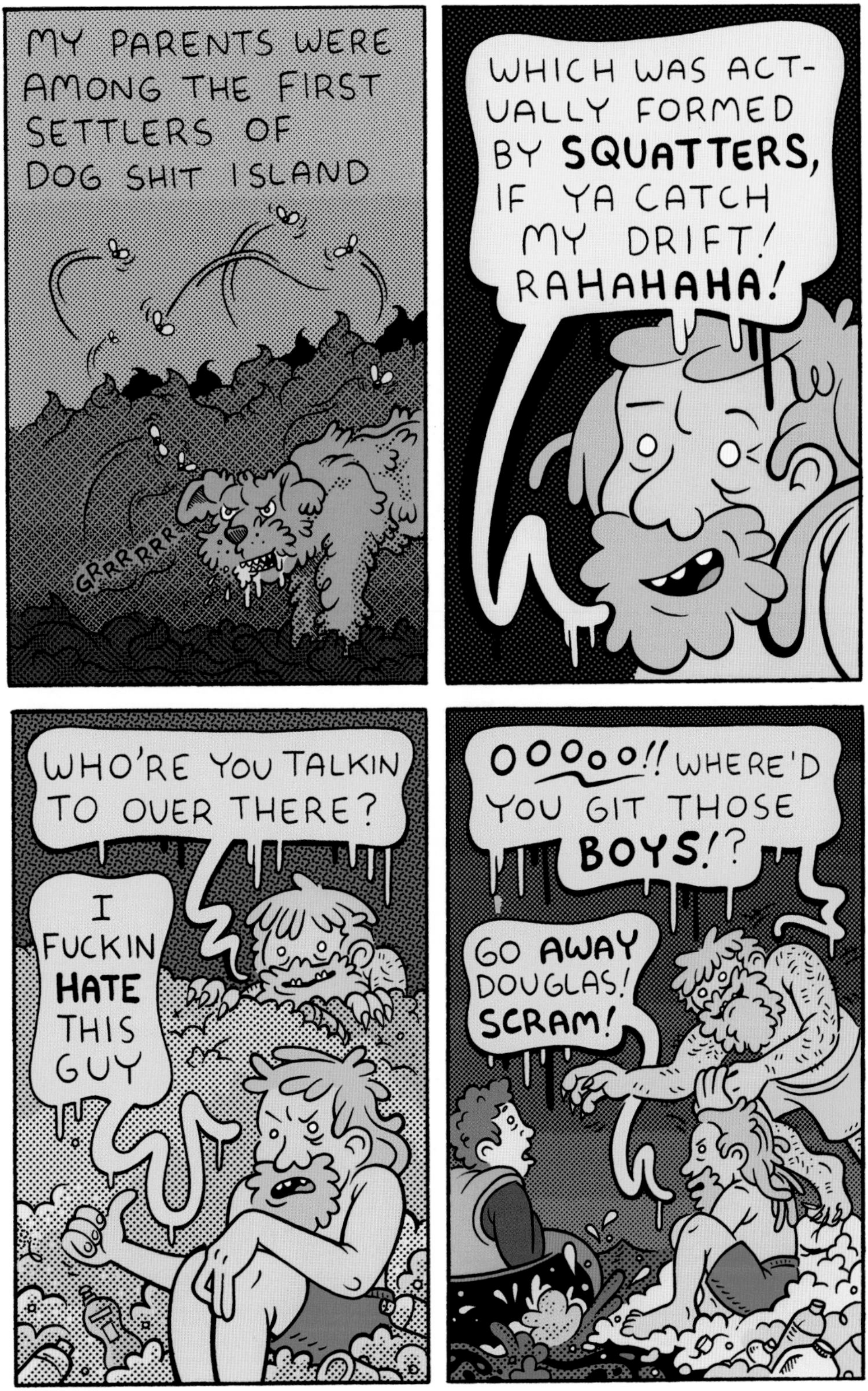
MY PARENTS WERE AMONG THE FIRST SETTLERS OF DOG SHIT ISLAND
GRRRRRR
WHICH WAS ACT-UALLY FORMED BY SQUATTERS, IF YA CATCH MY DRIFT! RAHAHAHA!
WHO'RE YOU TALKIN TO OVER THERE?
I FUCKIN HATE THIS GUY
OOOOO!! WHERE'D YOU GIT THOSE BOYS!?
GO AWAY DOUGLAS! SCRAM!

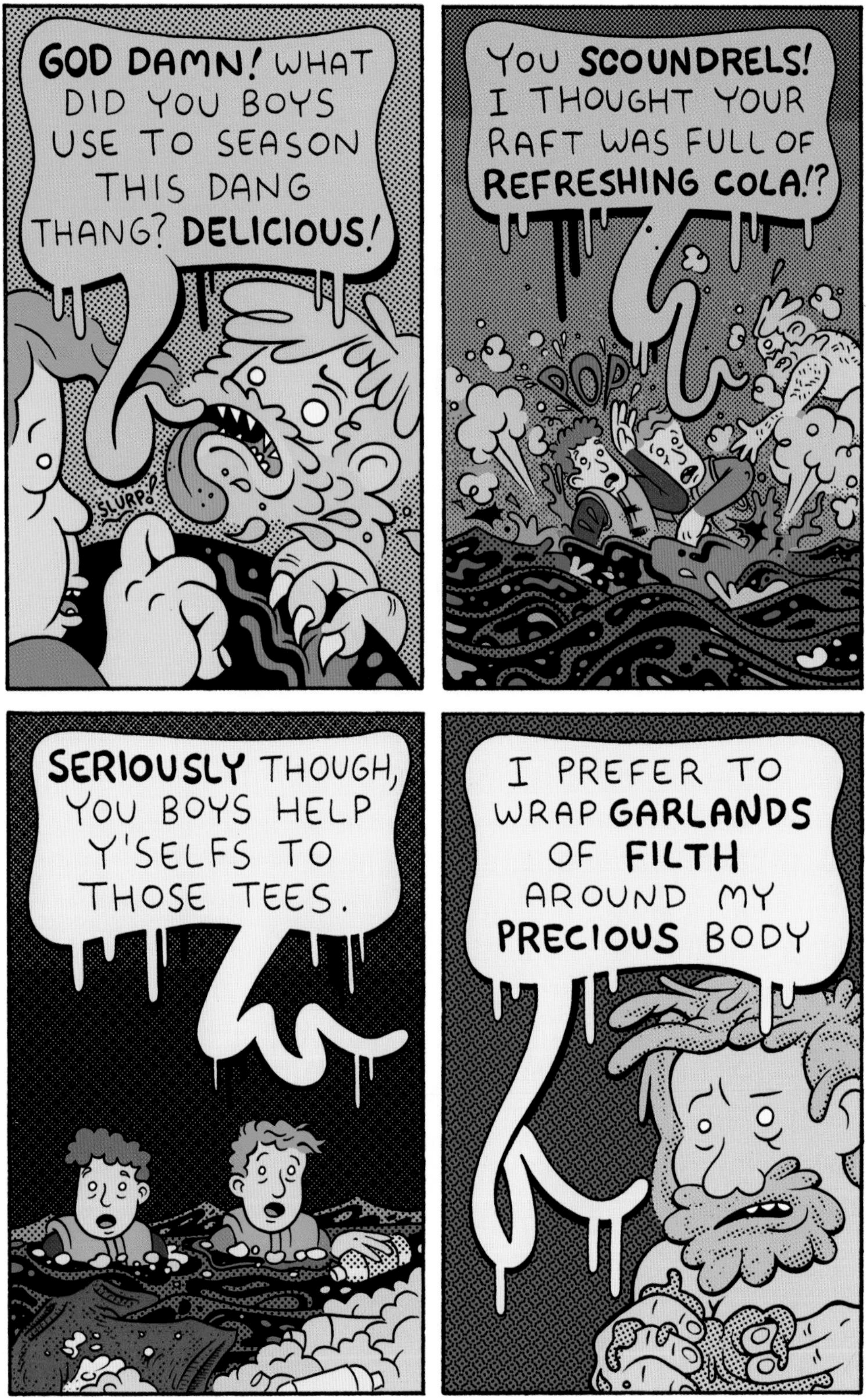
GOD DAMN! WHAT DID YOU BOYS USE TO SEASON THIS DANG THANG? DELICIOUS!
SLURP!
YOU SCOUNDRELS! I THOUGHT YOUR RAFT WAS FULL OF REFRESHING COLA!?
POP
SERIOUSLY THOUGH, YOU BOYS HELP Y'SELFS TO THOSE TEES.
I PREFER TO WRAP GARLANDS OF FILTH AROUND MY PRECIOUS BODY

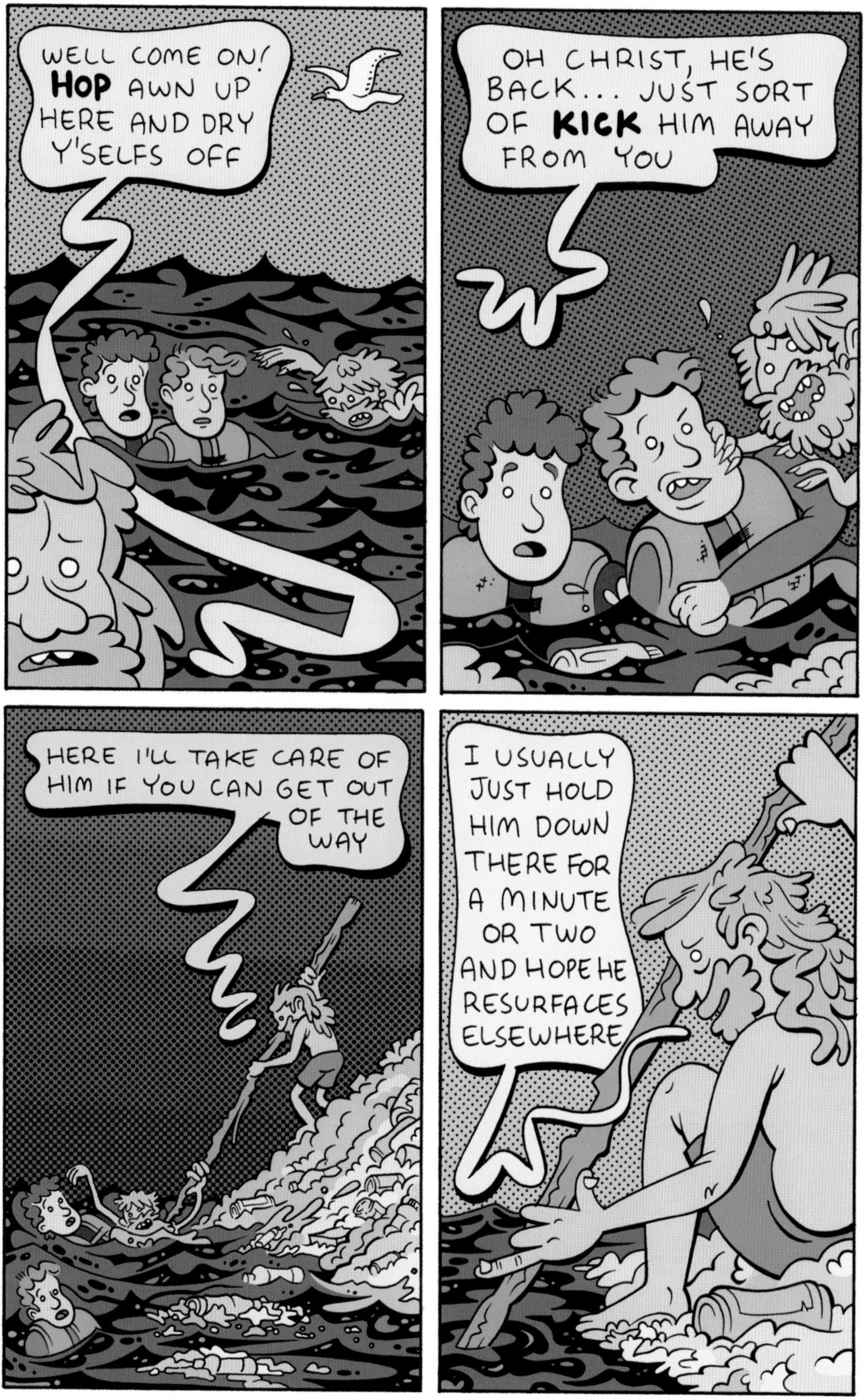
WELL COME ON! HOP AWN UP HERE AND DRY Y'SELFS OFF
OH CHRIST, HE'S BACK... JUST SORT OF KICK HIM AWAY FROM YOU
HERE I'LL TAKE CARE OF HIM IF YOU CAN GET OUT OF THE WAY
I USUALLY JUST HOLD HIM DOWN THERE FOR A MINUTE OR TWO AND HOPE HE RESURFACES ELSEWHERE

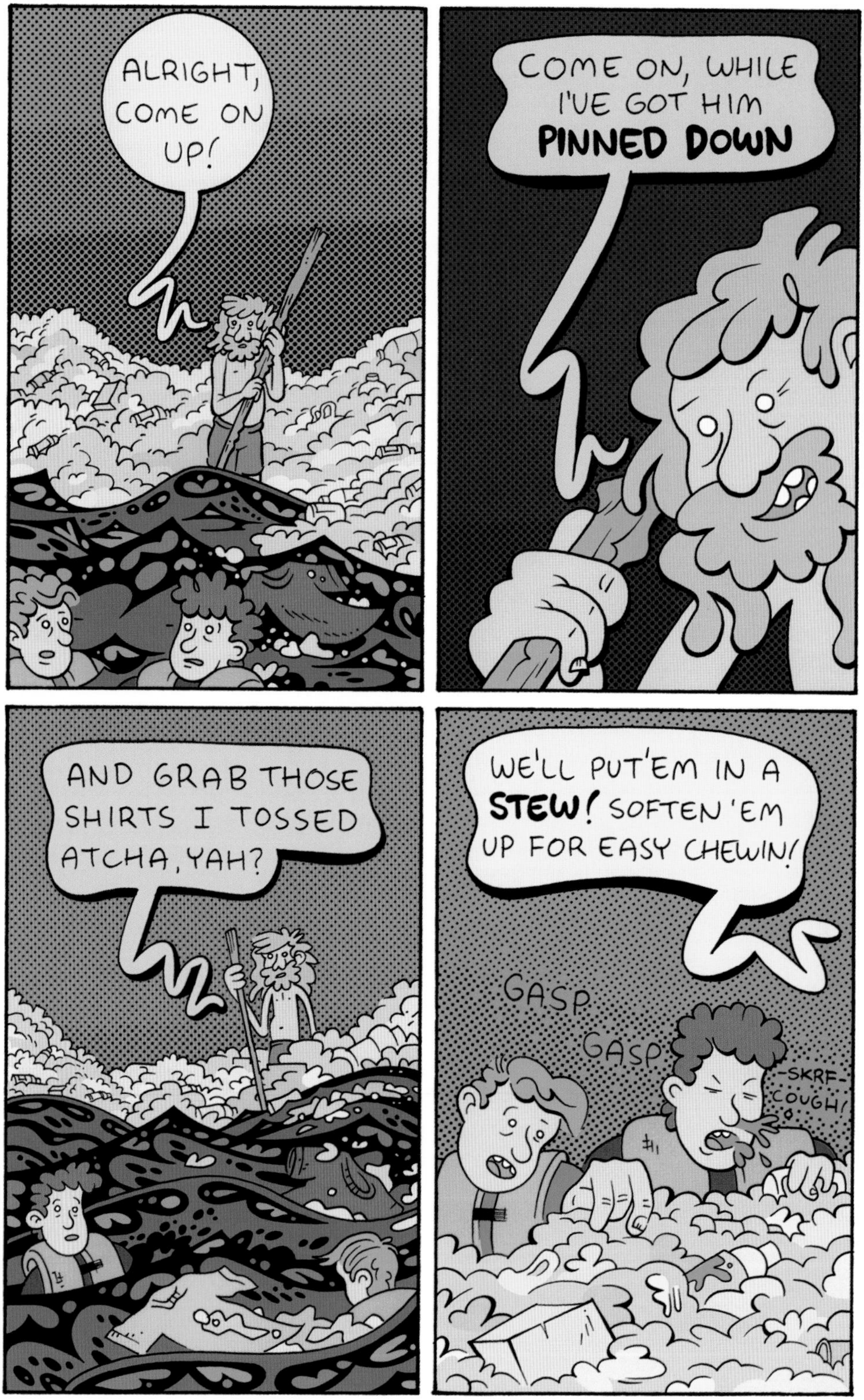
ALRIGHT, COME ON UP!
COME ON, WHILE I'VE GOT HIM **PINNED DOWN**
AND GRAB THOSE SHIRTS I TOSSED ATCHA, YAH?
WE'LL PUT'EM IN A **STEW!** SOFTEN 'EM UP FOR EASY CHEWIN!
GASP
GASP
-SKRF-
COUGH!

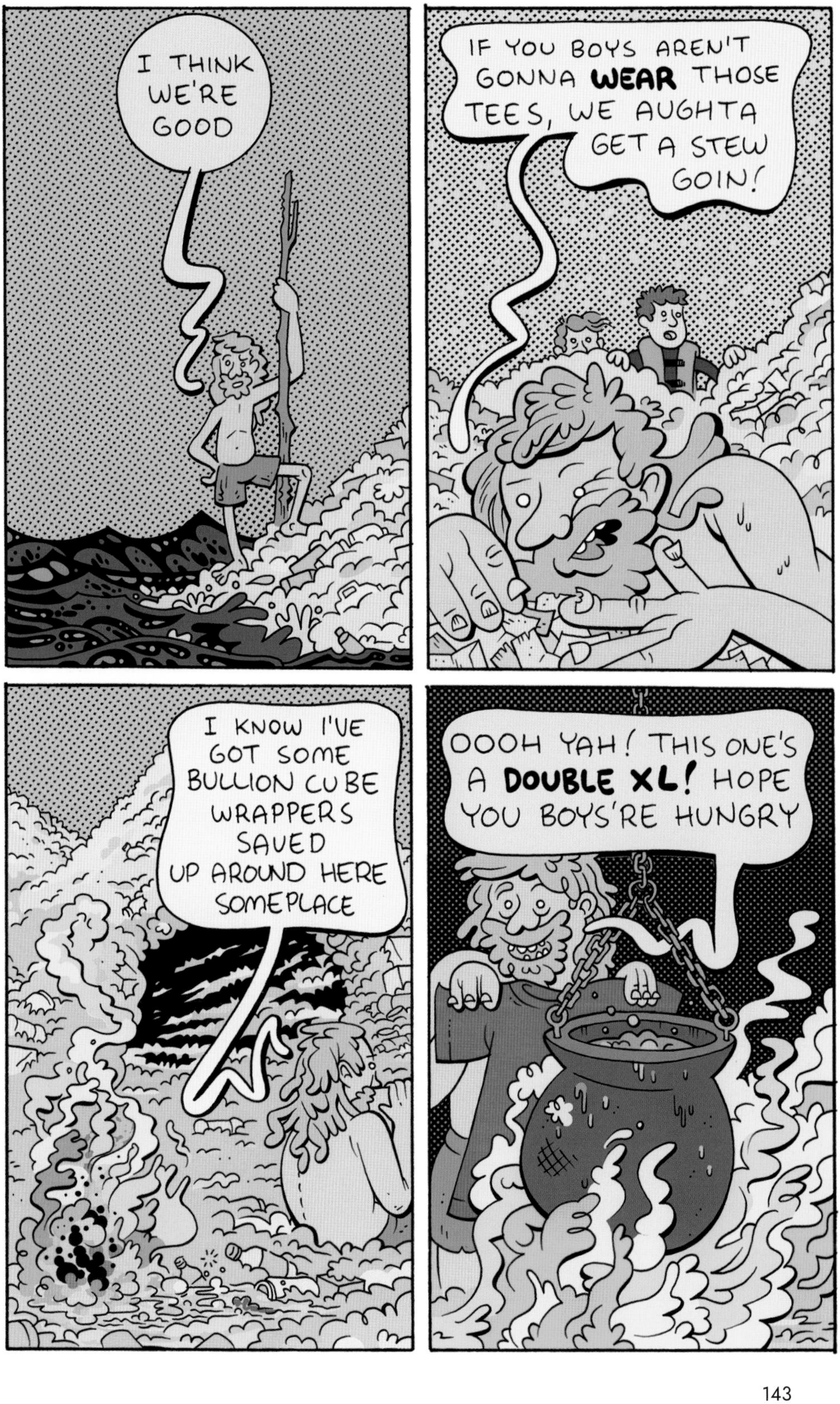
I THINK WE'RE GOOD
IF YOU BOYS AREN'T GONNA **WEAR** THOSE TEES, WE AUGHTA GET A STEW GOIN!
I KNOW I'VE GOT SOME BULLION CUBE WRAPPERS SAVED UP AROUND HERE SOMEPLACE
OOOH YAH! THIS ONE'S A **DOUBLE XL**! HOPE YOU BOYS'RE HUNGRY

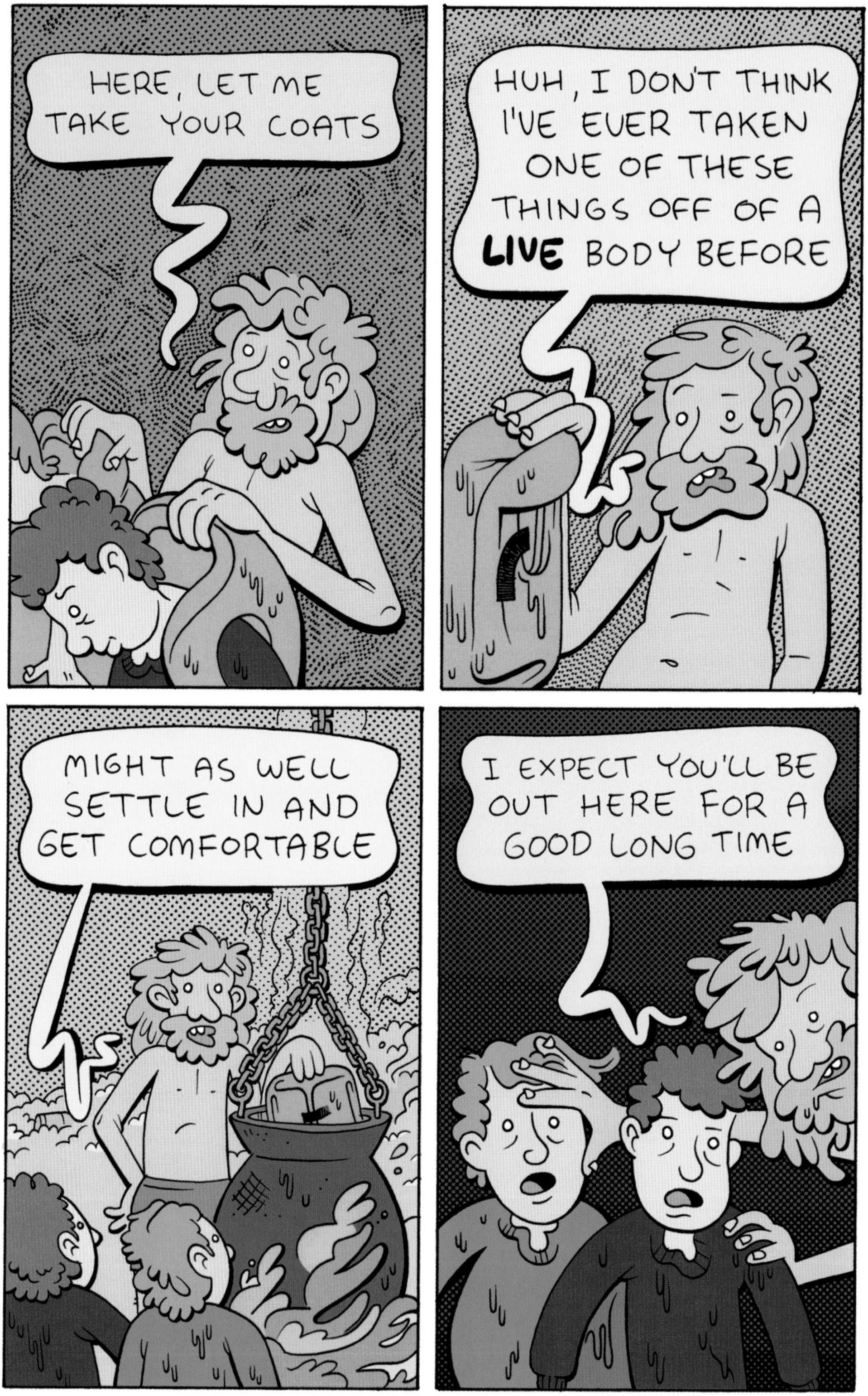
HERE, LET ME TAKE YOUR COATS
HUH, I DON'T THINK I'VE EVER TAKEN ONE OF THESE THINGS OFF OF A LIVE BODY BEFORE
MIGHT AS WELL SETTLE IN AND GET COMFORTABLE
I EXPECT YOU'LL BE OUT HERE FOR A GOOD LONG TIME

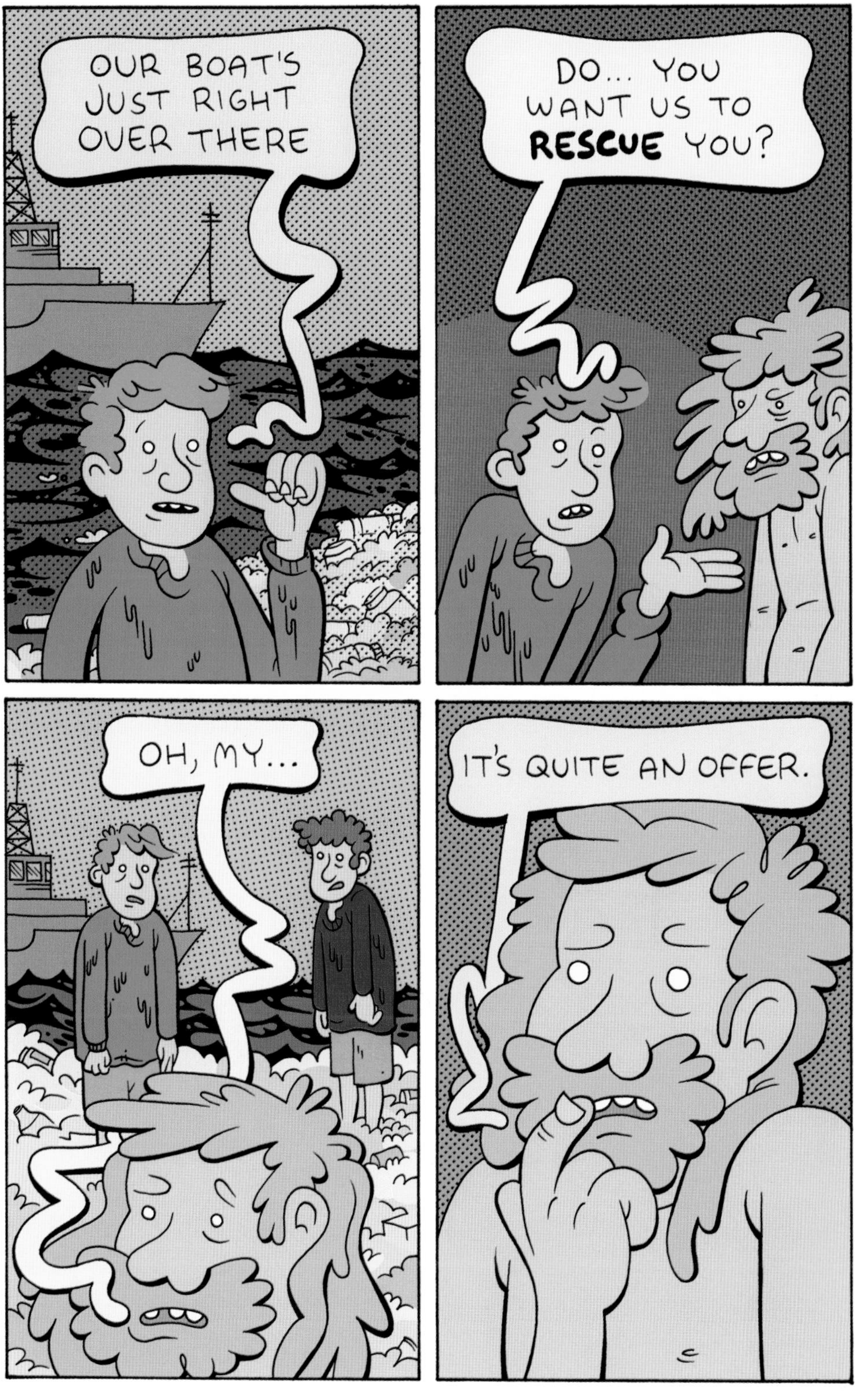
OUR BOAT'S JUST RIGHT OVER THERE
DO... YOU WANT US TO **RESCUE** YOU?
OH, MY...
IT'S QUITE AN OFFER.

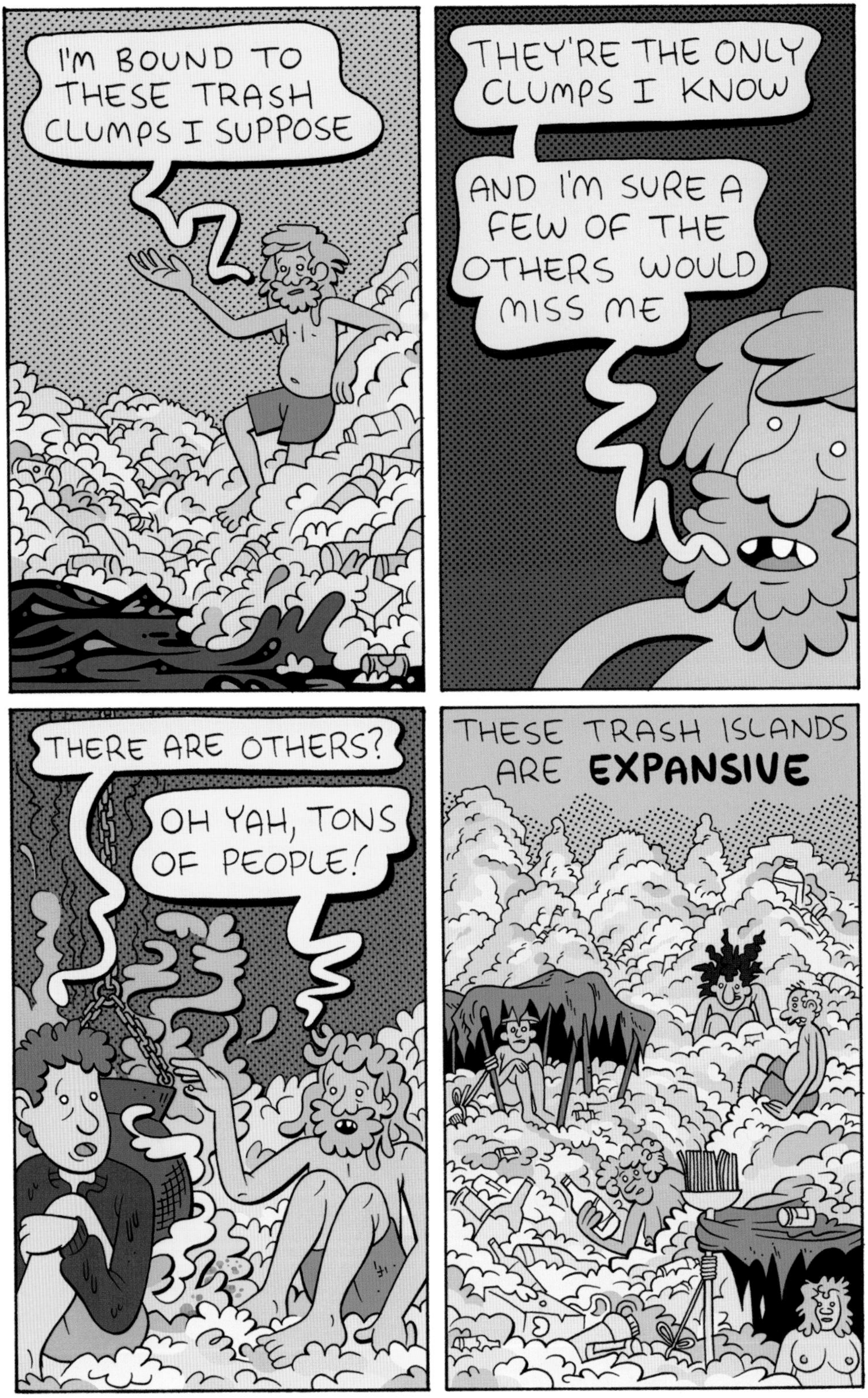
I'M BOUND TO THESE TRASH CLUMPS I SUPPOSE
THEY'RE THE ONLY CLUMPS I KNOW
AND I'M SURE A FEW OF THE OTHERS WOULD MISS ME
THERE ARE OTHERS?
OH YAH, TONS OF PEOPLE!
THESE TRASH ISLANDS ARE **EXPANSIVE**

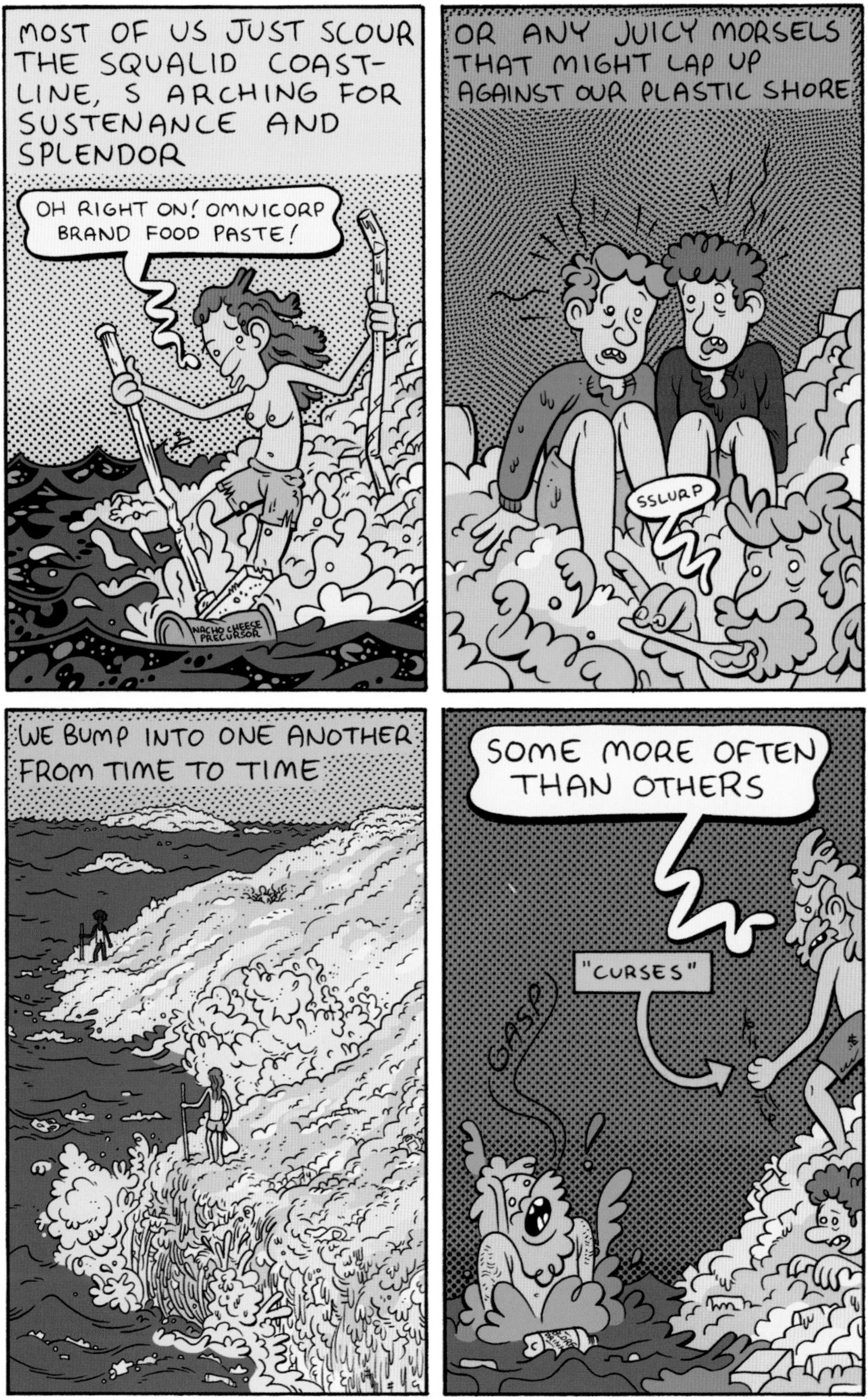
MOST OF US JUST SCOUR THE SQUALID COAST-LINE, S ARCHING FOR SUSTENANCE AND SPLENDOR
OH RIGHT ON! OMNICORP BRAND FOOD PASTE!
NACHO CHEESE PRECURSOR
OR ANY JUICY MORSELS THAT MIGHT LAP UP AGAINST OUR PLASTIC SHORE
SSLURP
WE BUMP INTO ONE ANOTHER FROM TIME TO TIME
SOME MORE OFTEN THAN OTHERS
"CURSES"
GASP
!

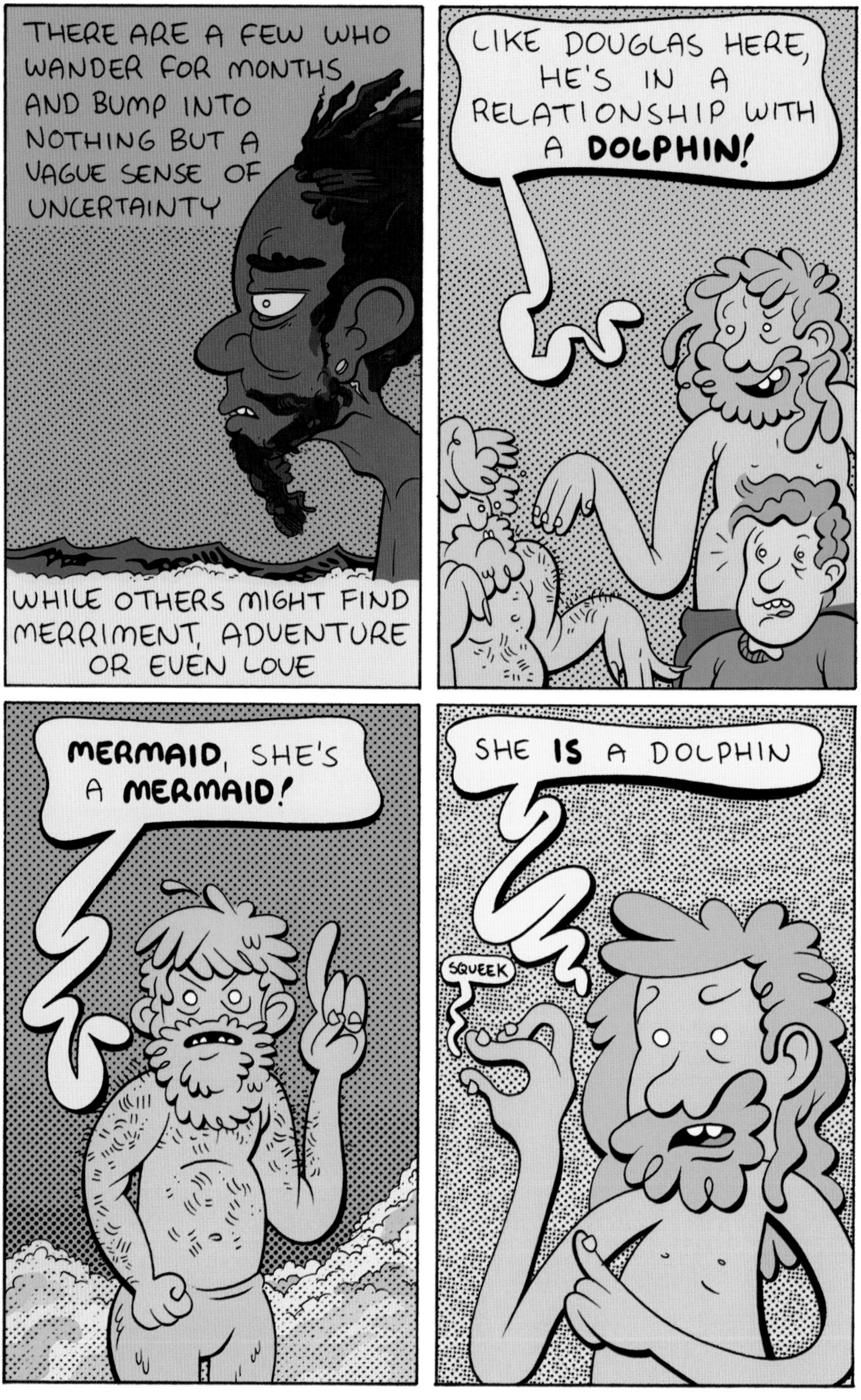
THERE ARE A FEW WHO WANDER FOR MONTHS AND BUMP INTO NOTHING BUT A VAGUE SENSE OF UNCERTAINTY
WHILE OTHERS MIGHT FIND MERRIMENT, ADVENTURE OR EVEN LOVE
LIKE DOUGLAS HERE, HE'S IN A RELATIONSHIP WITH A **DOLPHIN**!
MERMAID, SHE'S A **MERMAID**!
SHE **IS** A DOLPHIN
SQUEEK

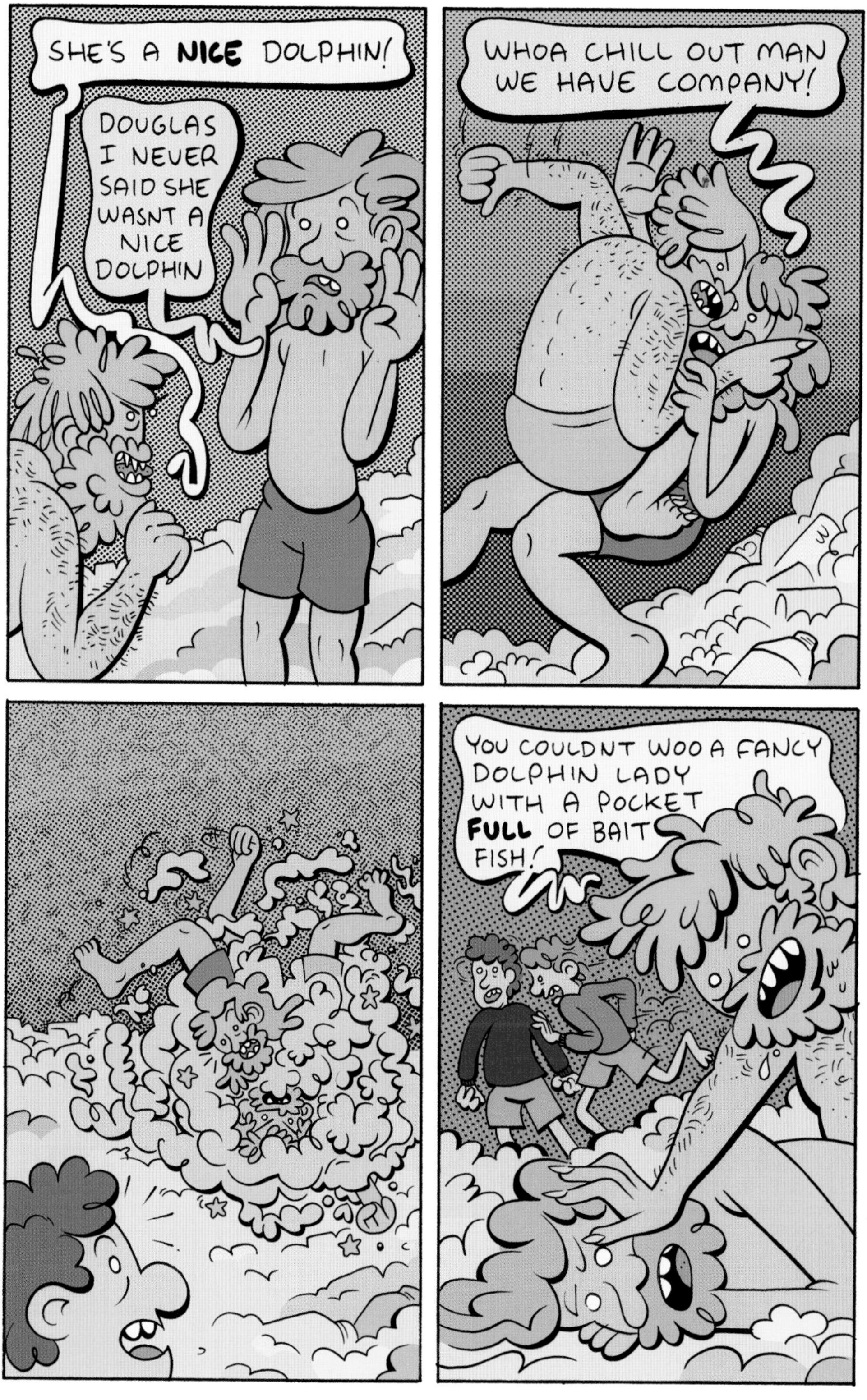
SHE'S A **NICE** DOLPHIN!
DOUGLAS I NEVER SAID SHE WASNT A NICE DOLPHIN
WHOA CHILL OUT MAN WE HAVE COMPANY!
YOU COULDNT WOO A FANCY DOLPHIN LADY WITH A POCKET **FULL** OF BAIT FISH!

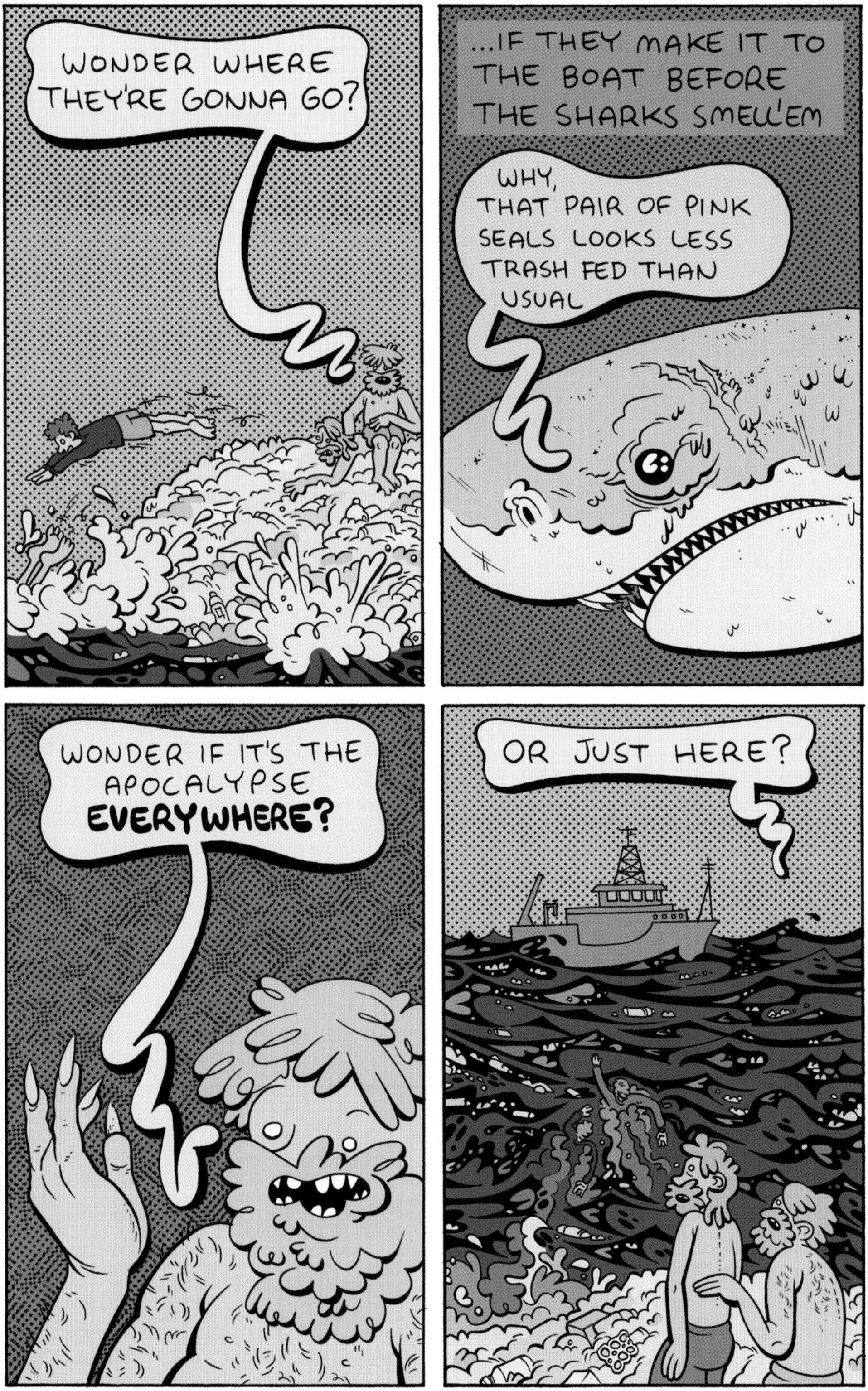
WONDER WHERE THEY'RE GONNA GO?
...IF THEY MAKE IT TO THE BOAT BEFORE THE SHARKS SMELL'EM
WHY, THAT PAIR OF PINK SEALS LOOKS LESS TRASH FED THAN USUAL
WONDER IF IT'S THE APOCALYPSE **EVERYWHERE?**
OR JUST HERE?

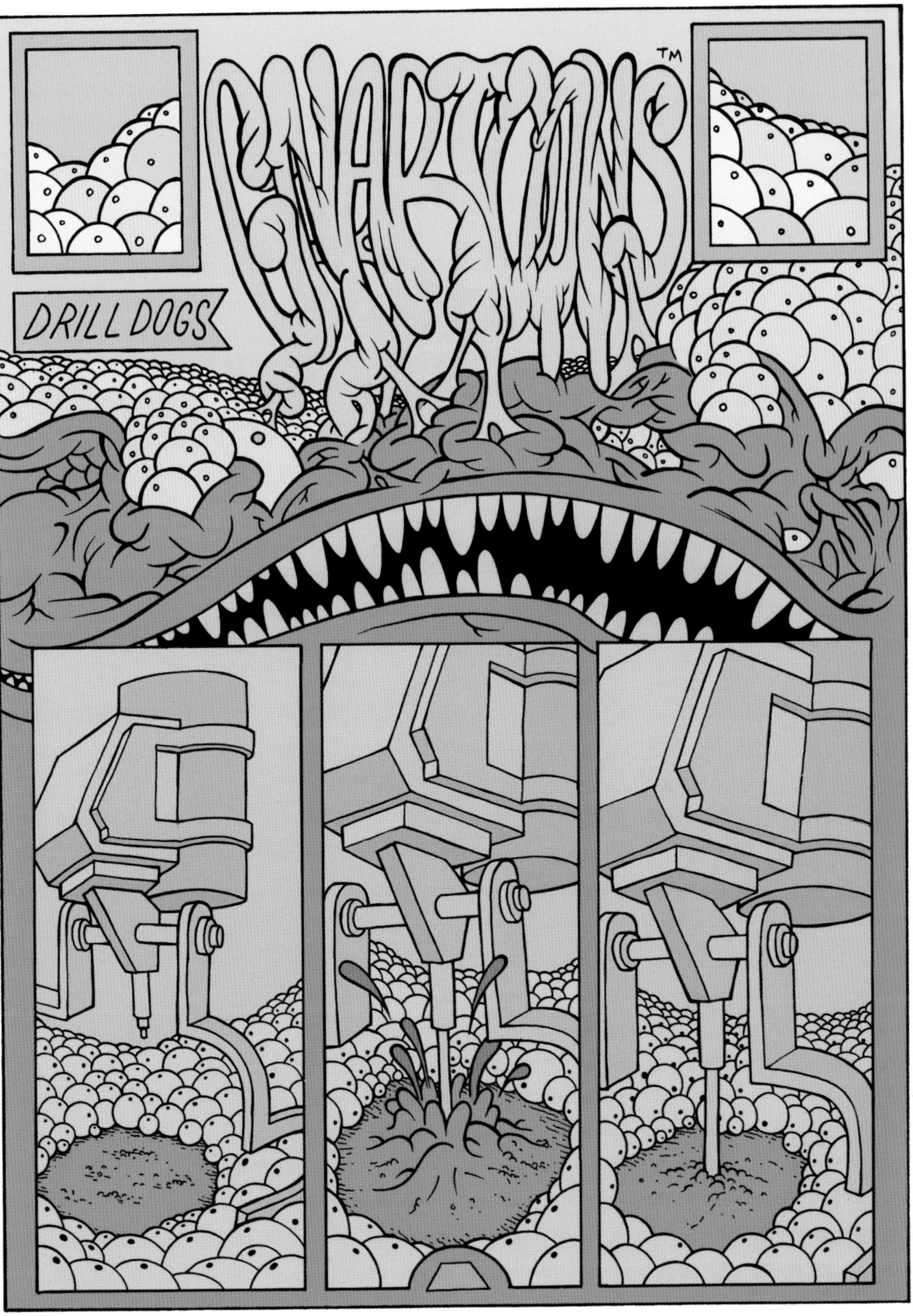
GNARTOONS™
DRILL DOGS

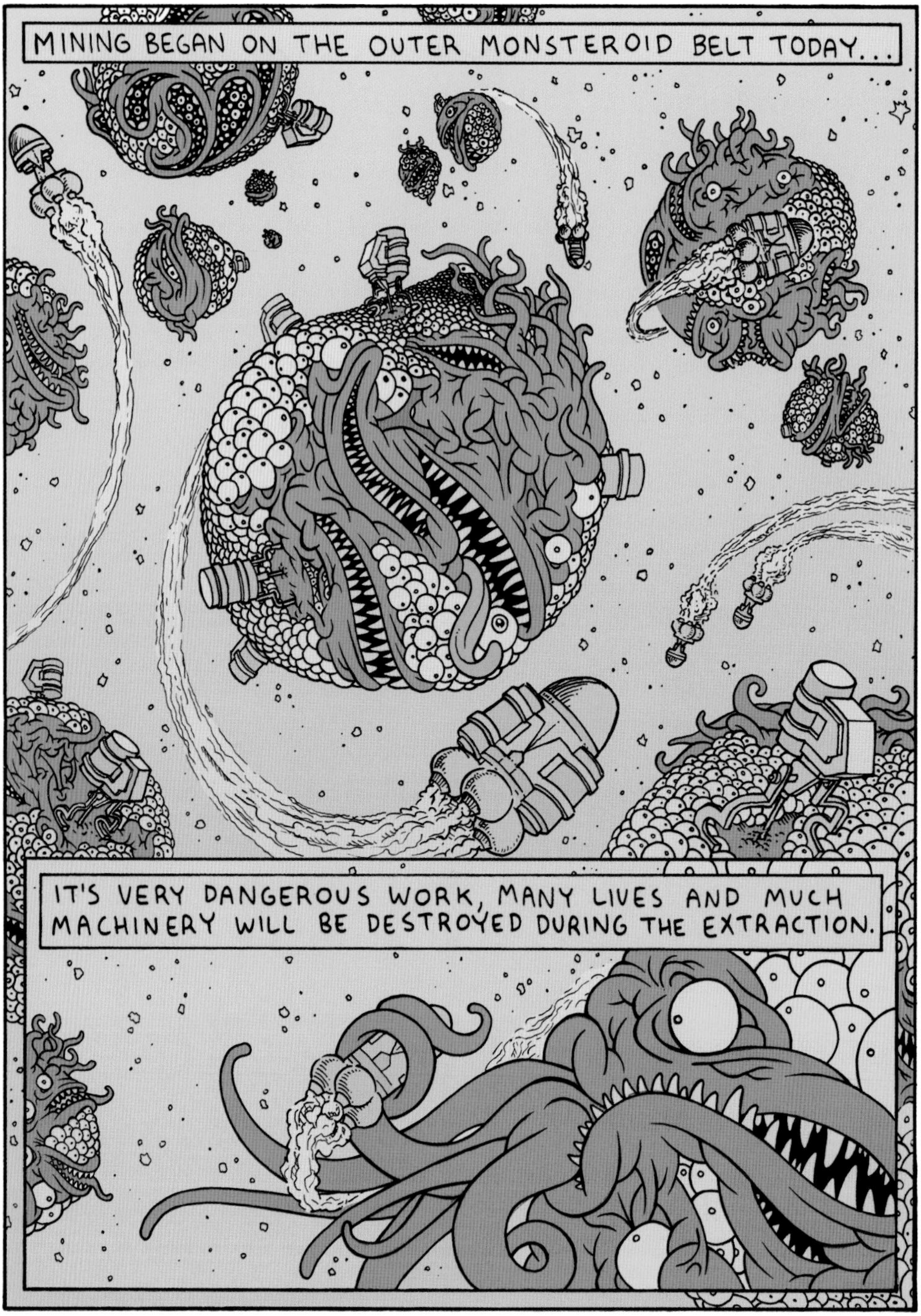
MINING BEGAN ON THE OUTER MONSTEROID BELT TODAY...
IT'S VERY DANGEROUS WORK, MANY LIVES AND MUCH MACHINERY WILL BE DESTROYED DURING THE EXTRACTION.

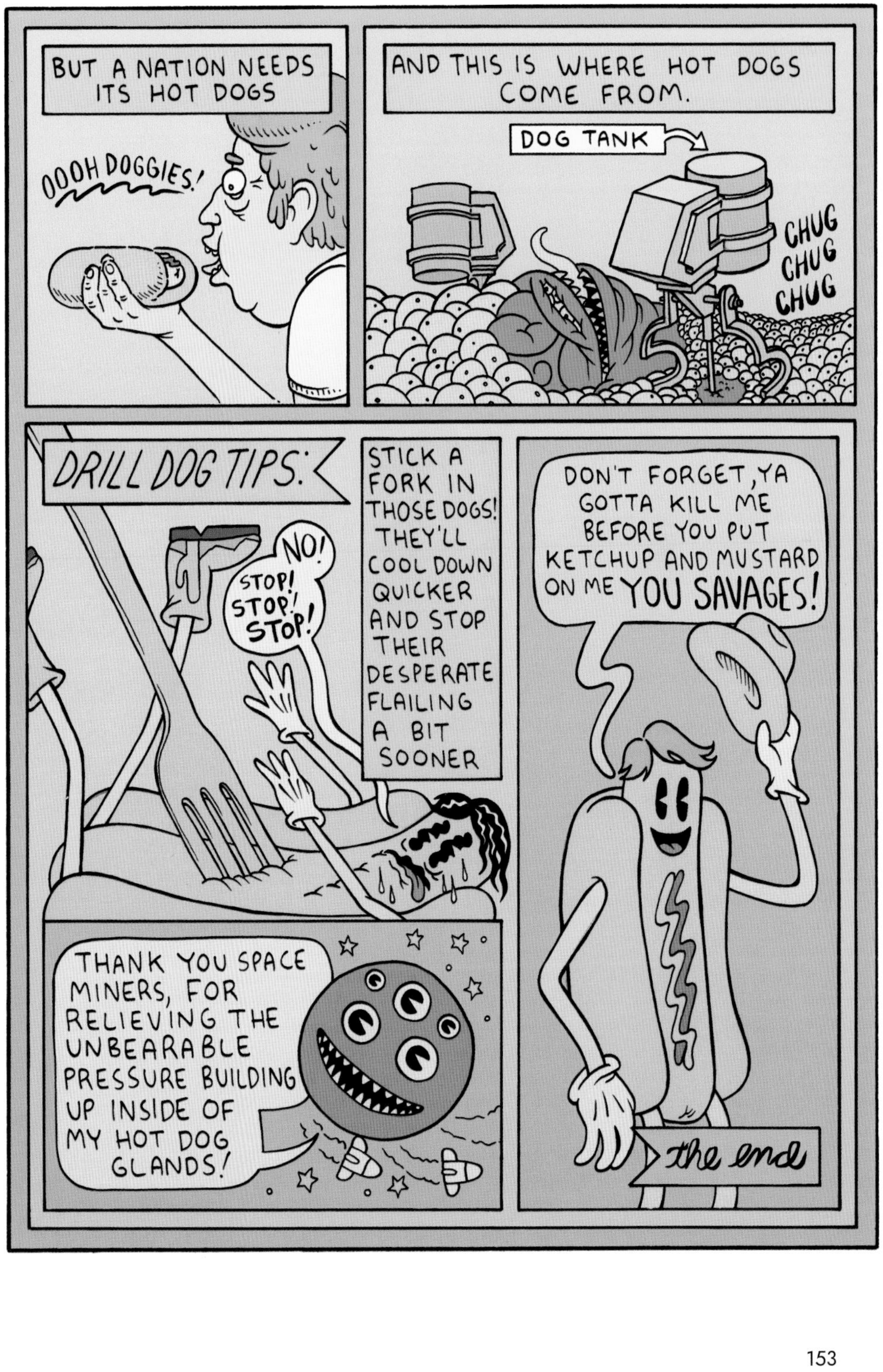
BUT A NATION NEEDS ITS HOT DOGS
OOOH DOGGIES!
AND THIS IS WHERE HOT DOGS COME FROM.
DOG TANK
CHUG CHUG CHUG
DRILL DOG TIPS:
STICK A FORK IN THOSE DOGS! THEY'LL COOL DOWN QUICKER AND STOP THEIR DESPERATE FLAILING A BIT SOONER
NO!
STOP! STOP! STOP!
THANK YOU SPACE MINERS, FOR RELIEVING THE UNBEARABLE PRESSURE BUILDING UP INSIDE OF MY HOT DOG GLANDS!
DON'T FORGET, YA GOTTA KILL ME BEFORE YOU PUT KETCHUP AND MUSTARD ON ME YOU SAVAGES!
the end

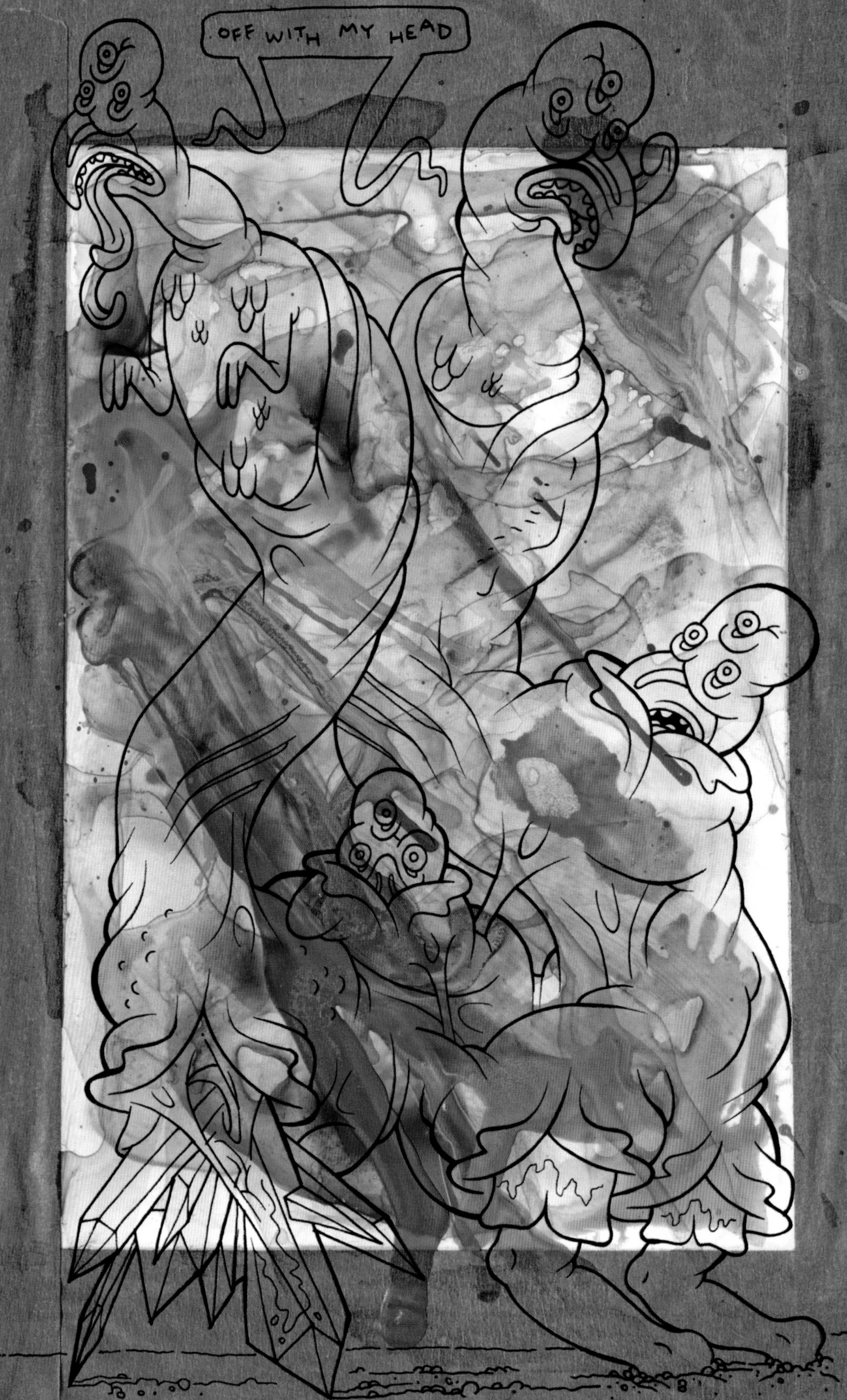
OFF WITH MY HEAD

 I THINK IT'S MY ROOMMATE'S SHE JUST GOT BACK FROM JAPAN.

 I HAVE NO IDEA WHAT'S IN THERE.

THE ONLY CLUE IS THAT ORANGE BLOB

 MY THEORY IS THAT

THE CARTON IS COMPLETELY FULL OF EGG YOLKS

AND THAT IF THE CARTON WERE TO BE

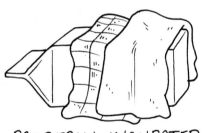

PROPERLY INCUBATED

A MUTANT CHICKEN WOULD HATCH FROM THE CARTON

1/20/15

A CHICKEN FORMED FROM A HUNDRED SWIRLED EMBRYOS

TURNS OUT IT'S SOY SAUCE

-GNARTOONS

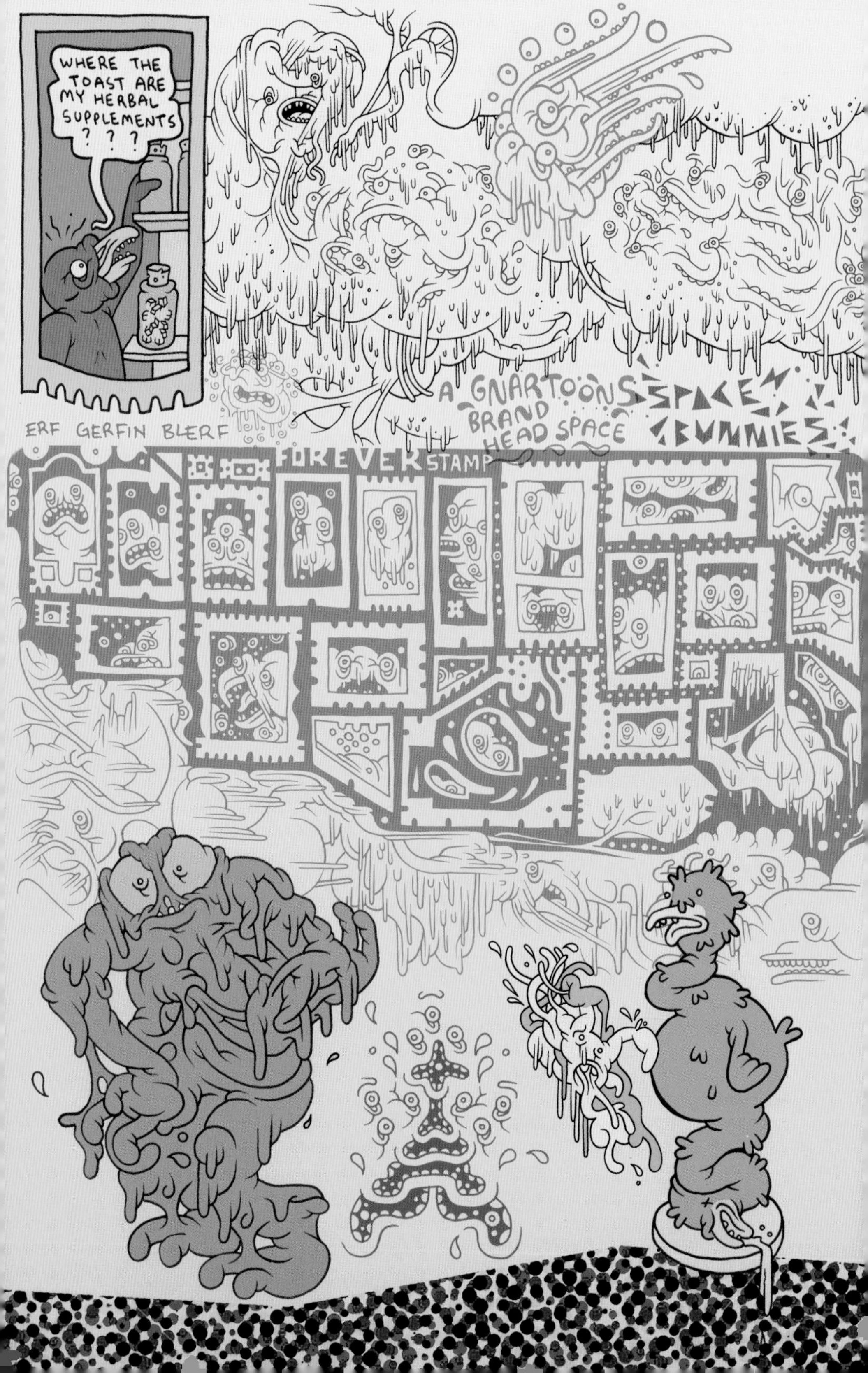
WHERE THE TOAST ARE MY HERBAL SUPPLEMENTS ? ? ?
A GNARTOONS BRAND HEAD SPACE
SPACE BUNNIES
ERF GERFIN BLERF
FOREVER STAMP

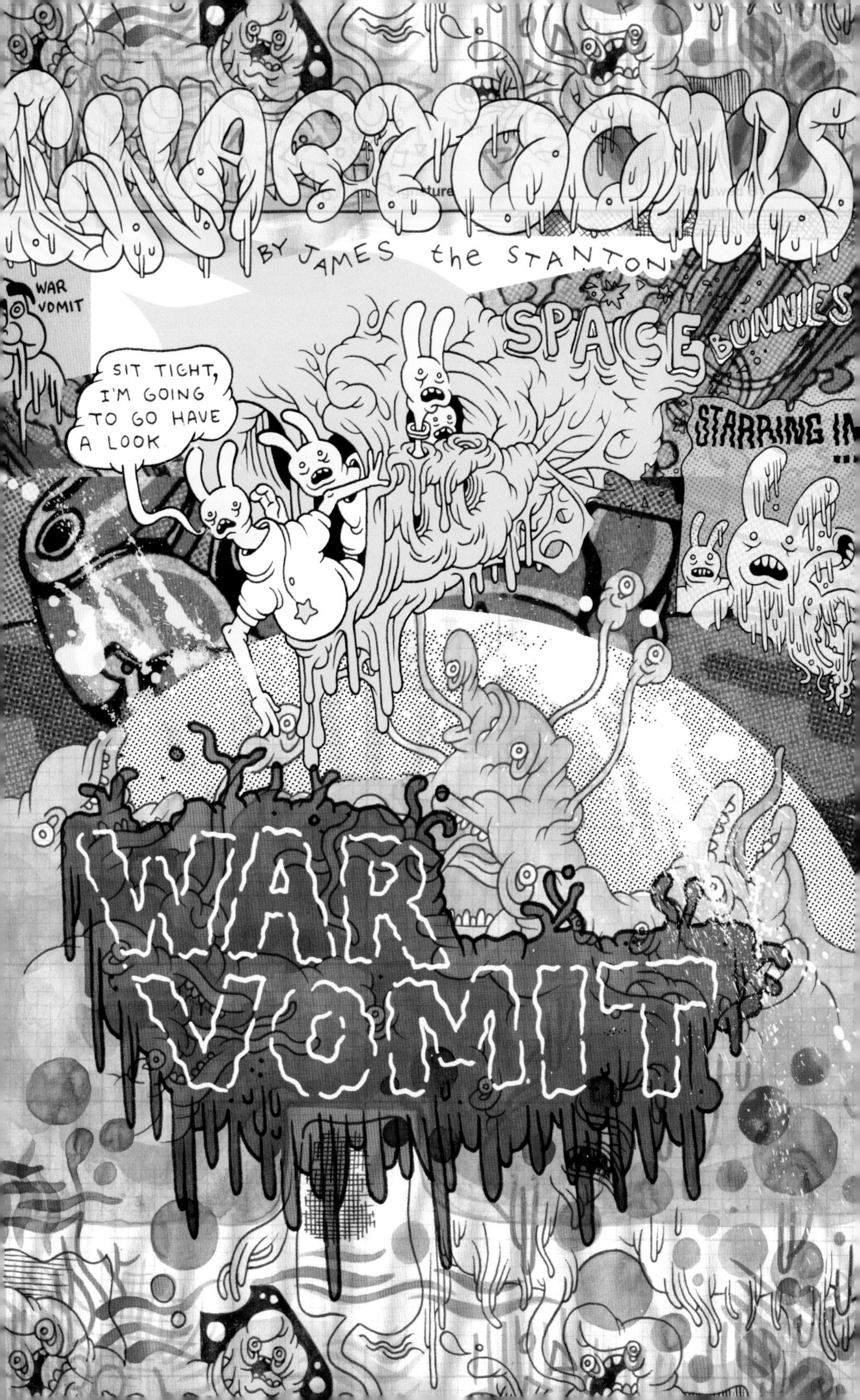
BY JAMES the STANTON
WAR VOMIT
SPACE BUNNIES
SIT TIGHT, I'M GOING TO GO HAVE A LOOK
STARRING IN ...
WAR VOMIT

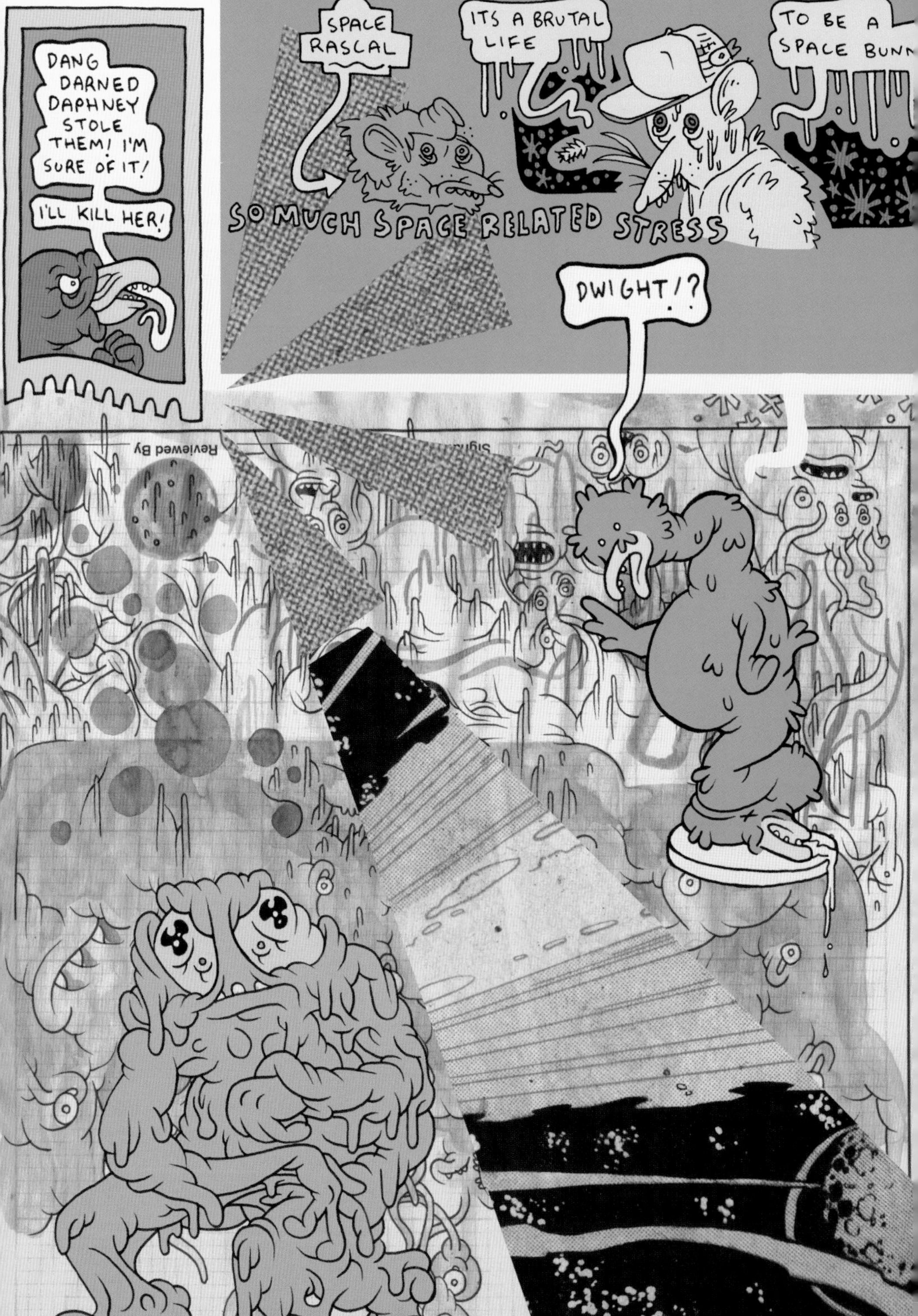

DANG DARNED DAPHNEY STOLE THEM! I'M SURE OF IT!
I'LL KILL HER!
SPACE RASCAL
ITS A BRUTAL LIFE
TO BE A SPACE BUNN
SO MUCH SPACE RELATED STRESS
DWIGHT!?

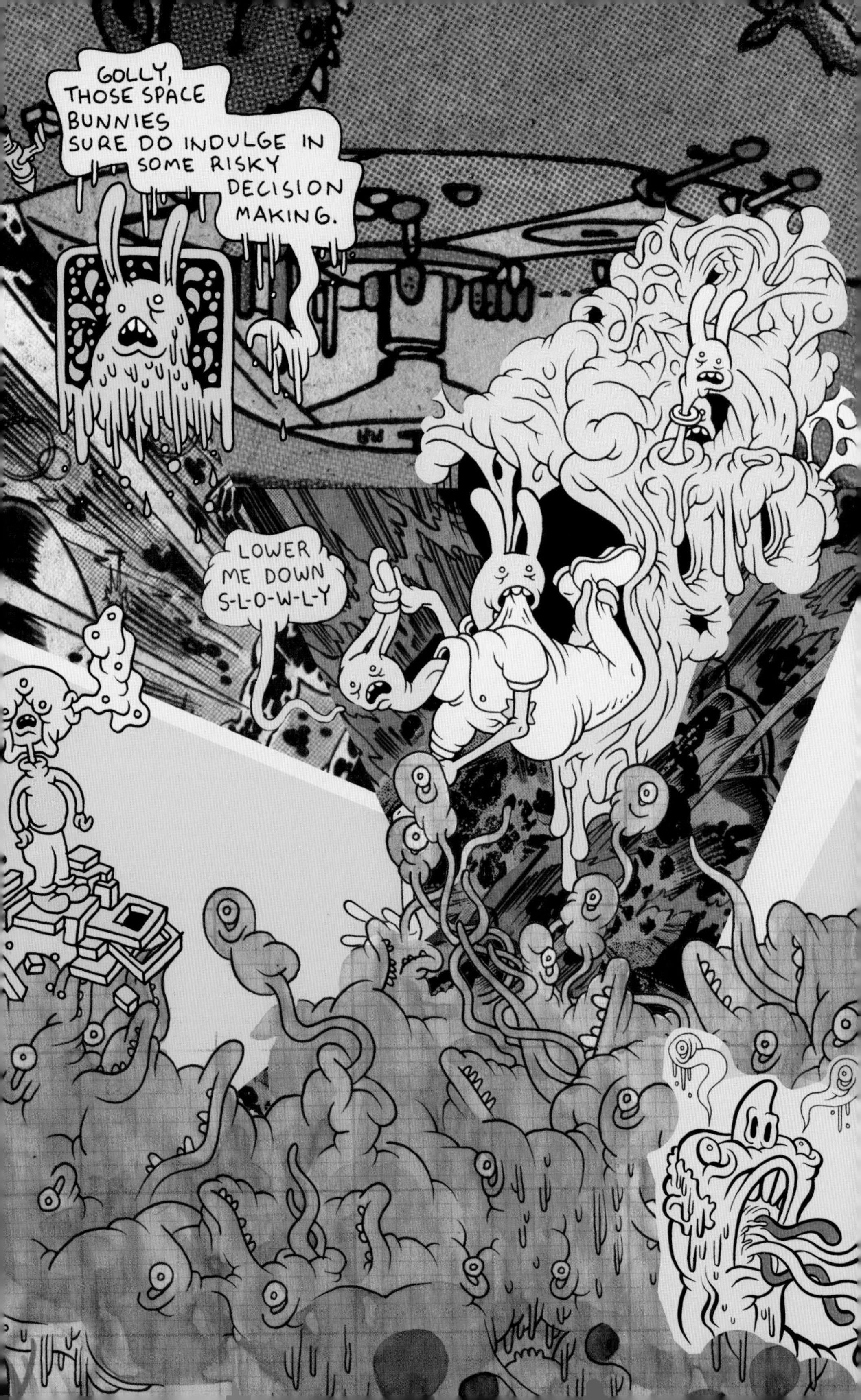
GOLLY, THOSE SPACE BUNNIES SURE DO INDULGE IN SOME RISKY DECISION MAKING.
LOWER ME DOWN S-L-O-W-L-Y

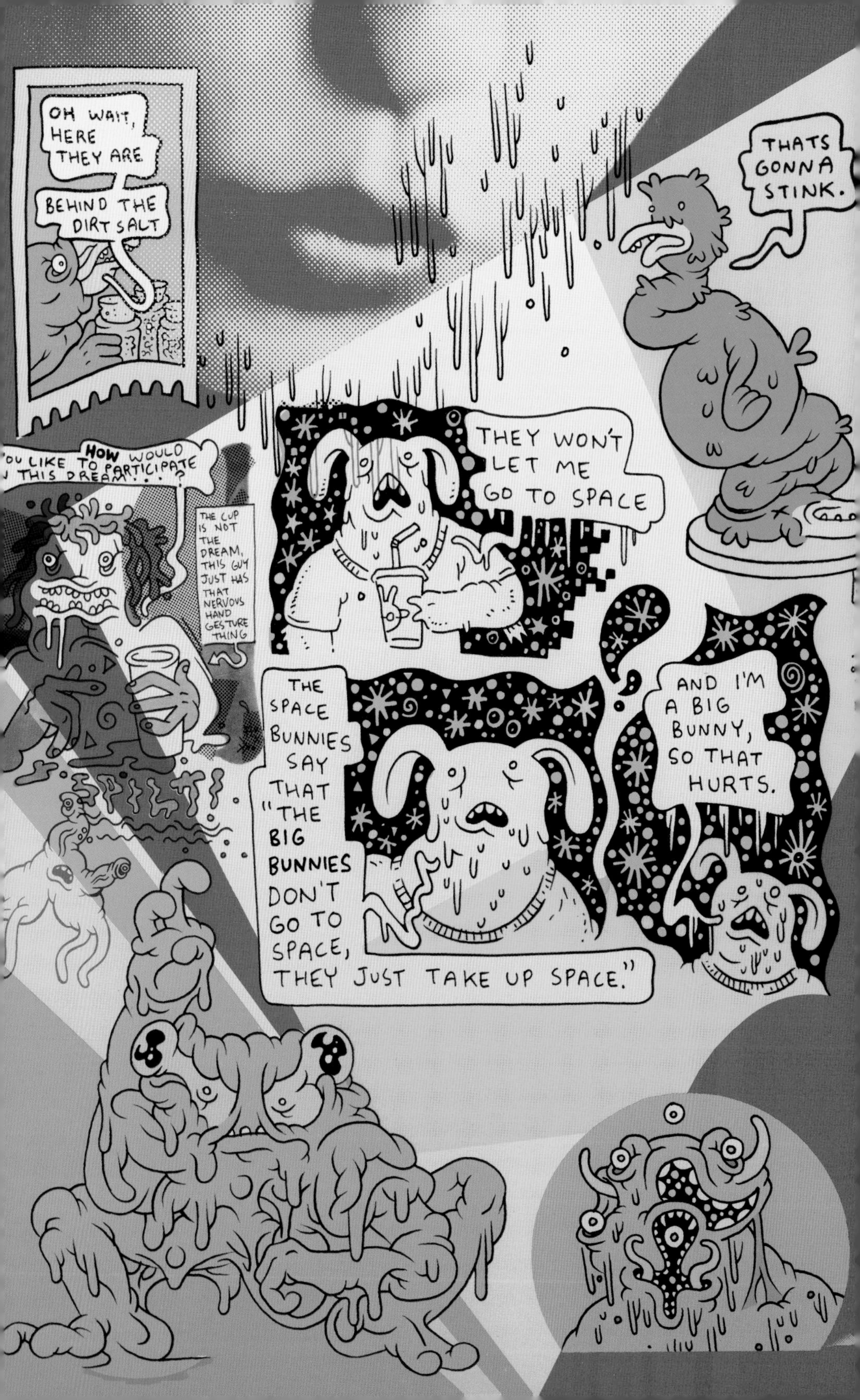
OH WAIT, HERE THEY ARE
BEHIND THE DIRT SALT
THATS GONNA STINK.
HOW WOULD OU LIKE TO PARTICIPATE N THIS DREAM. . . ?
THE CUP IS NOT THE DREAM, THIS GUY JUST HAS THAT NERVOUS HAND GESTURE THING
SPILT!
THEY WON'T LET ME GO TO SPACE
THE SPACE BUNNIES SAY THAT "THE BIG BUNNIES DON'T GO TO SPACE, THEY JUST TAKE UP SPACE."
AND I'M A BIG BUNNY, SO THAT HURTS.

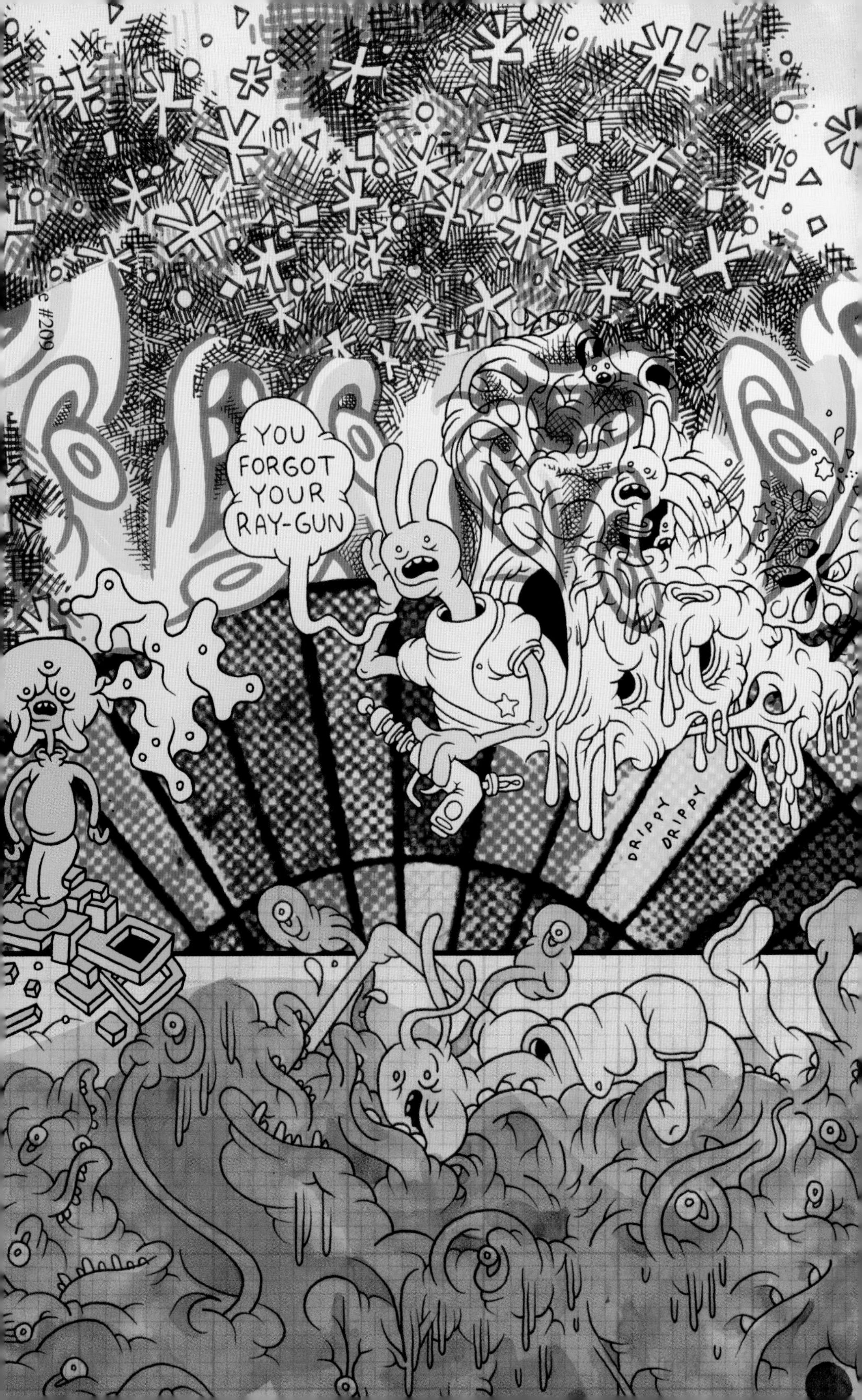
YOU FORGOT YOUR RAY-GUN
DRIPPY DRIPPY

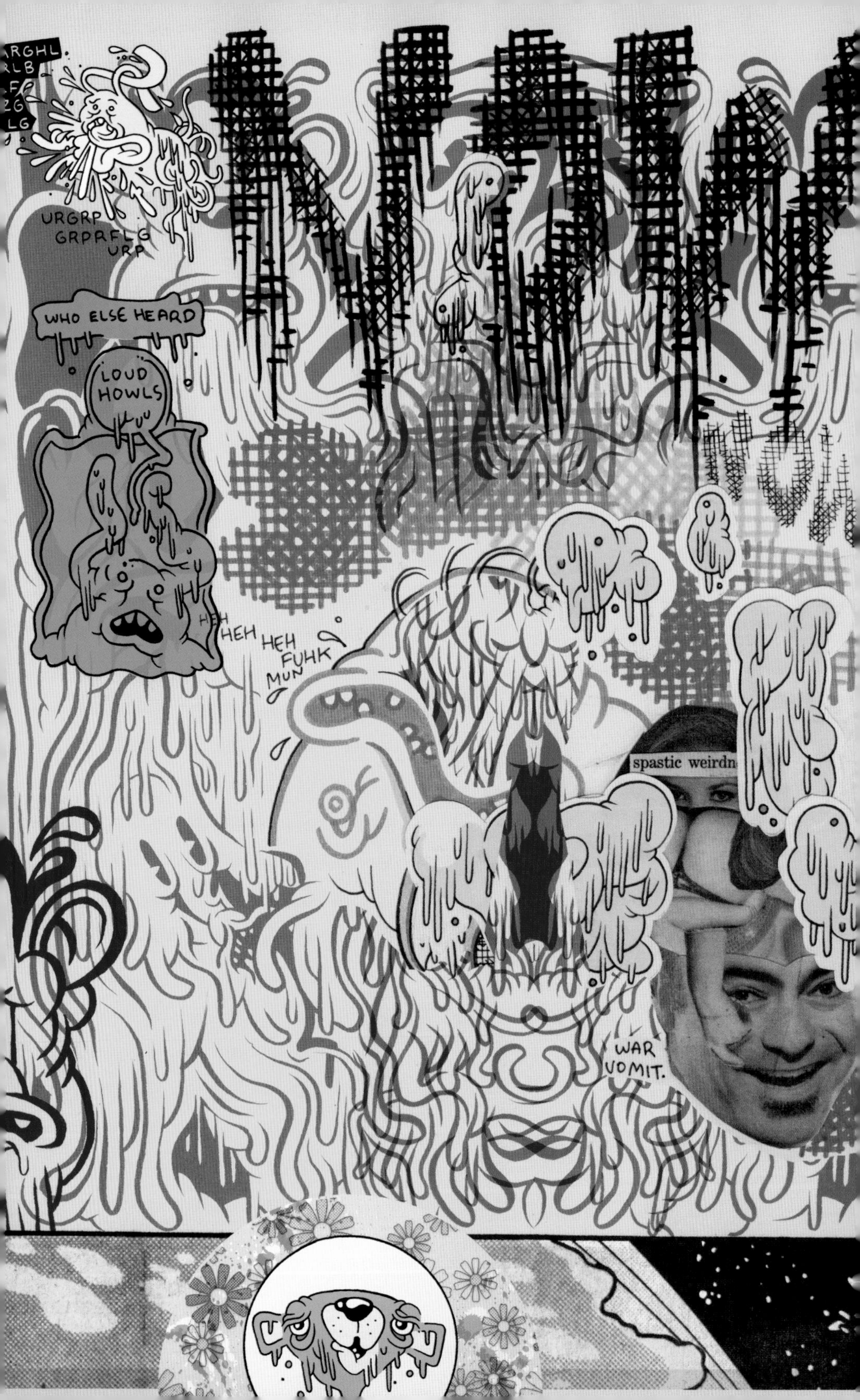
URGRP
GRPRFLG
URP
WHO ELSE HEARD
LOUD HOWLS
HEH HEH
HEH
FUHK
MUN
spastic weirdn
WAR VOMIT.

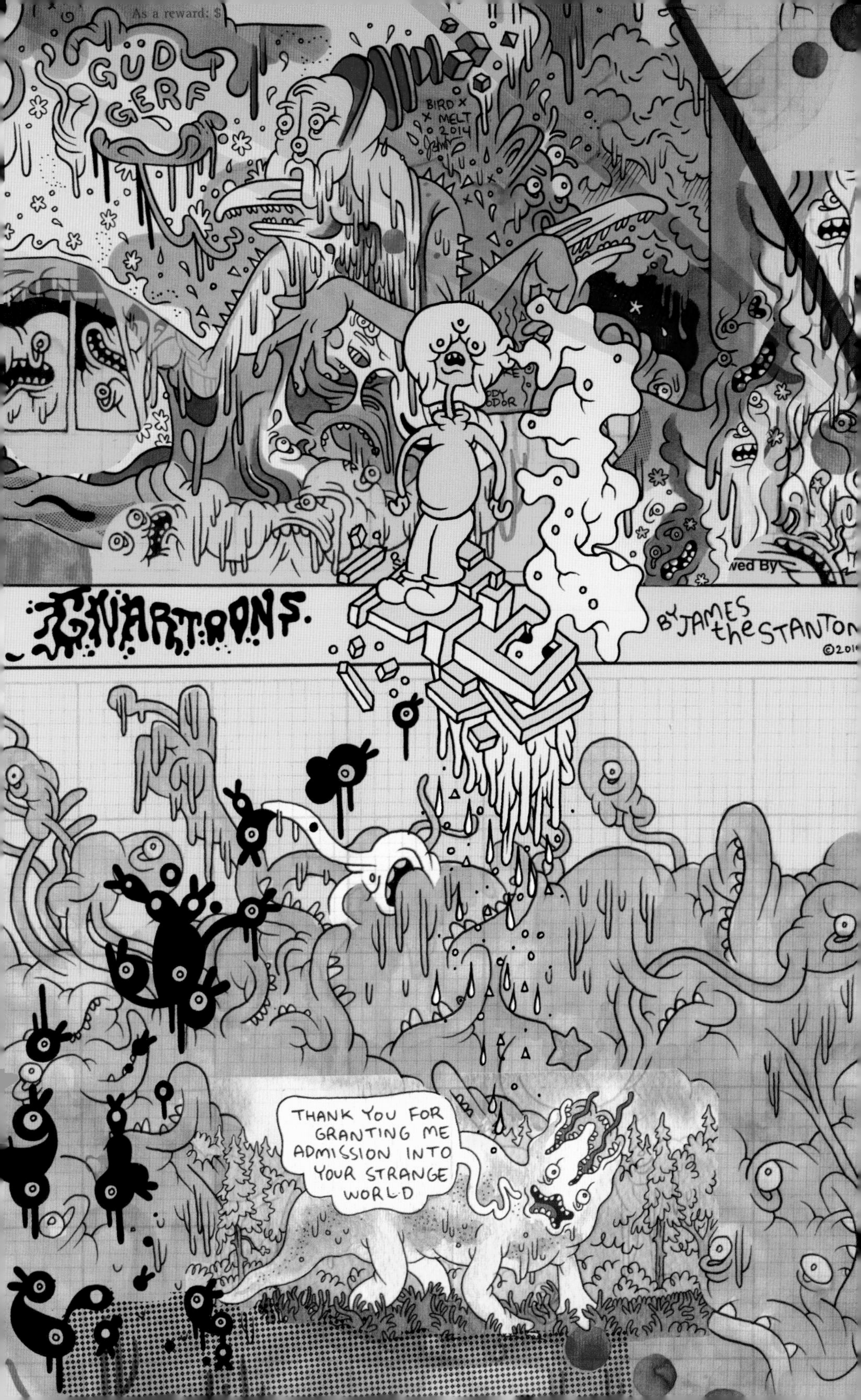
As a reward: $
GUD GERF
BIRD X MELT 2014
GNARTOONS
BY JAMES the STANTON
THANK YOU FOR GRANTING ME ADMISSION INTO YOUR STRANGE WORLD

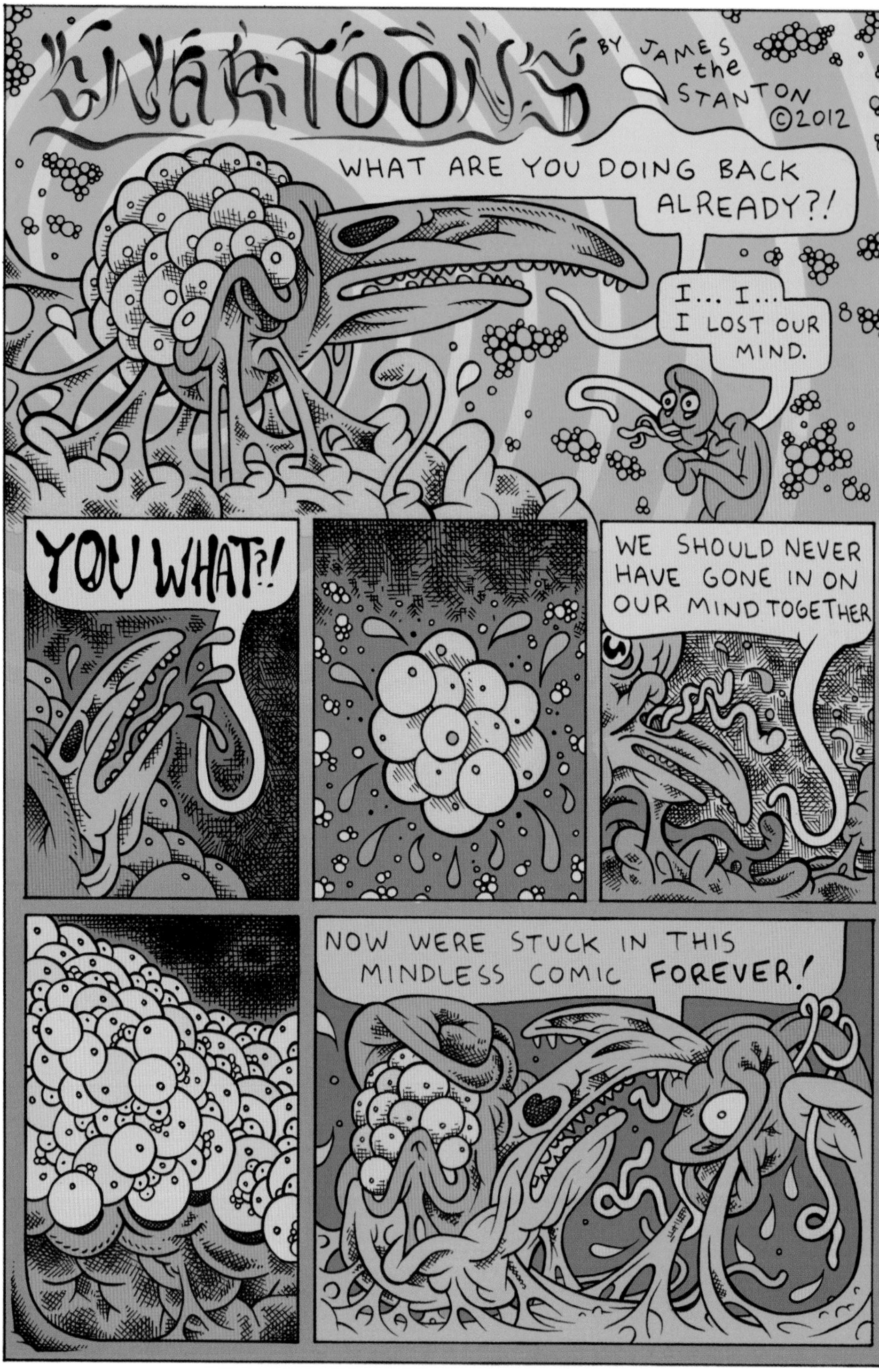
GNARTOONS
BY JAMES the STANTON ©2012
WHAT ARE YOU DOING BACK ALREADY?!
I... I... I LOST OUR MIND.
YOU WHAT?!
WE SHOULD NEVER HAVE GONE IN ON OUR MIND TOGETHER
NOW WERE STUCK IN THIS MINDLESS COMIC FOREVER!

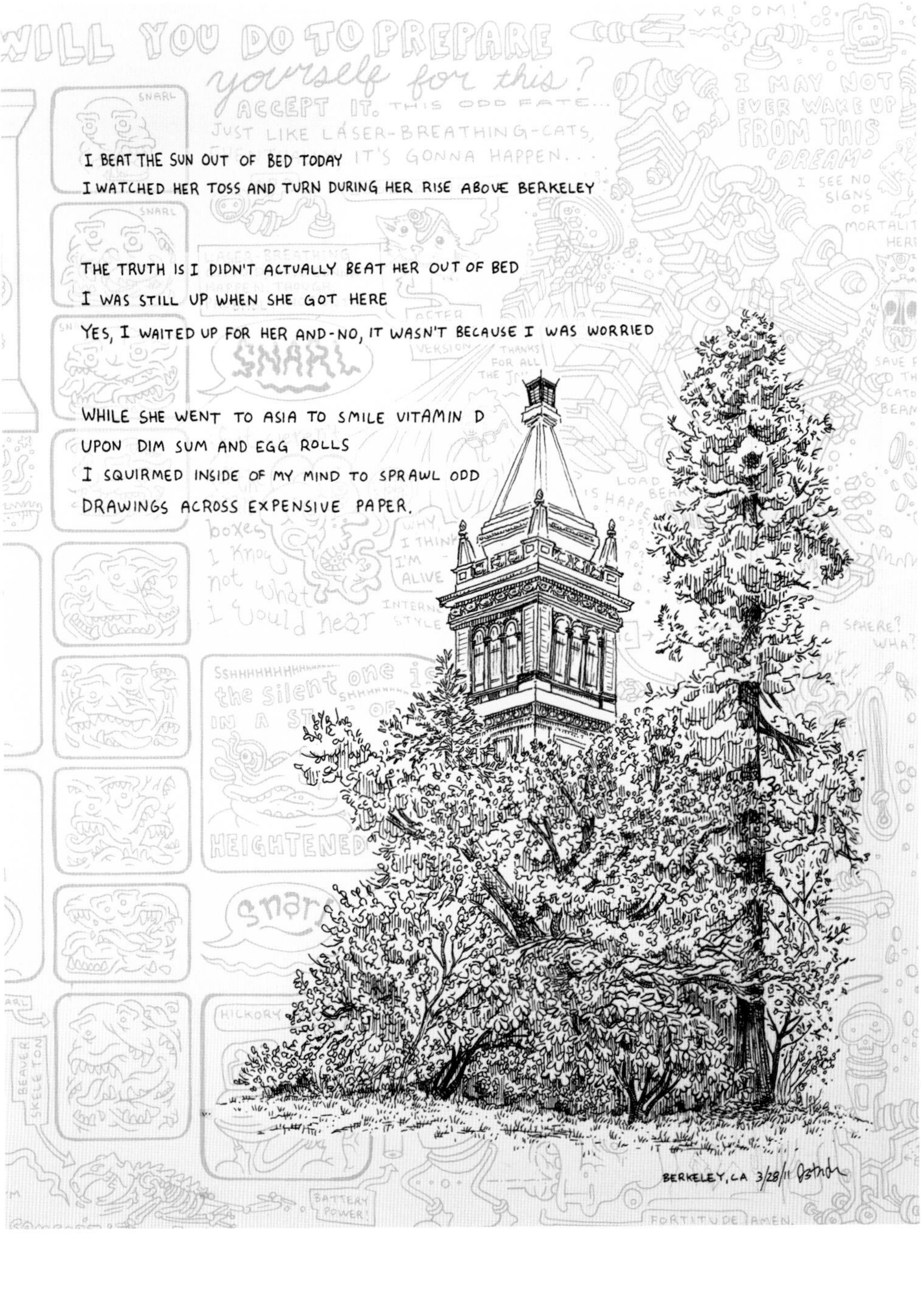

I BEAT THE SUN OUT OF BED TODAY
I WATCHED HER TOSS AND TURN DURING HER RISE ABOVE BERKELEY
THE TRUTH IS I DIDN'T ACTUALLY BEAT HER OUT OF BED
I WAS STILL UP WHEN SHE GOT HERE
YES, I WAITED UP FOR HER AND-NO, IT WASN'T BECAUSE I WAS WORRIED
WHILE SHE WENT TO ASIA TO SMILE VITAMIN D
UPON DIM SUM AND EGG ROLLS
I SQUIRMED INSIDE OF MY MIND TO SPRAWL ODD
DRAWINGS ACROSS EXPENSIVE PAPER.
BERKELEY, CA 3/28/11

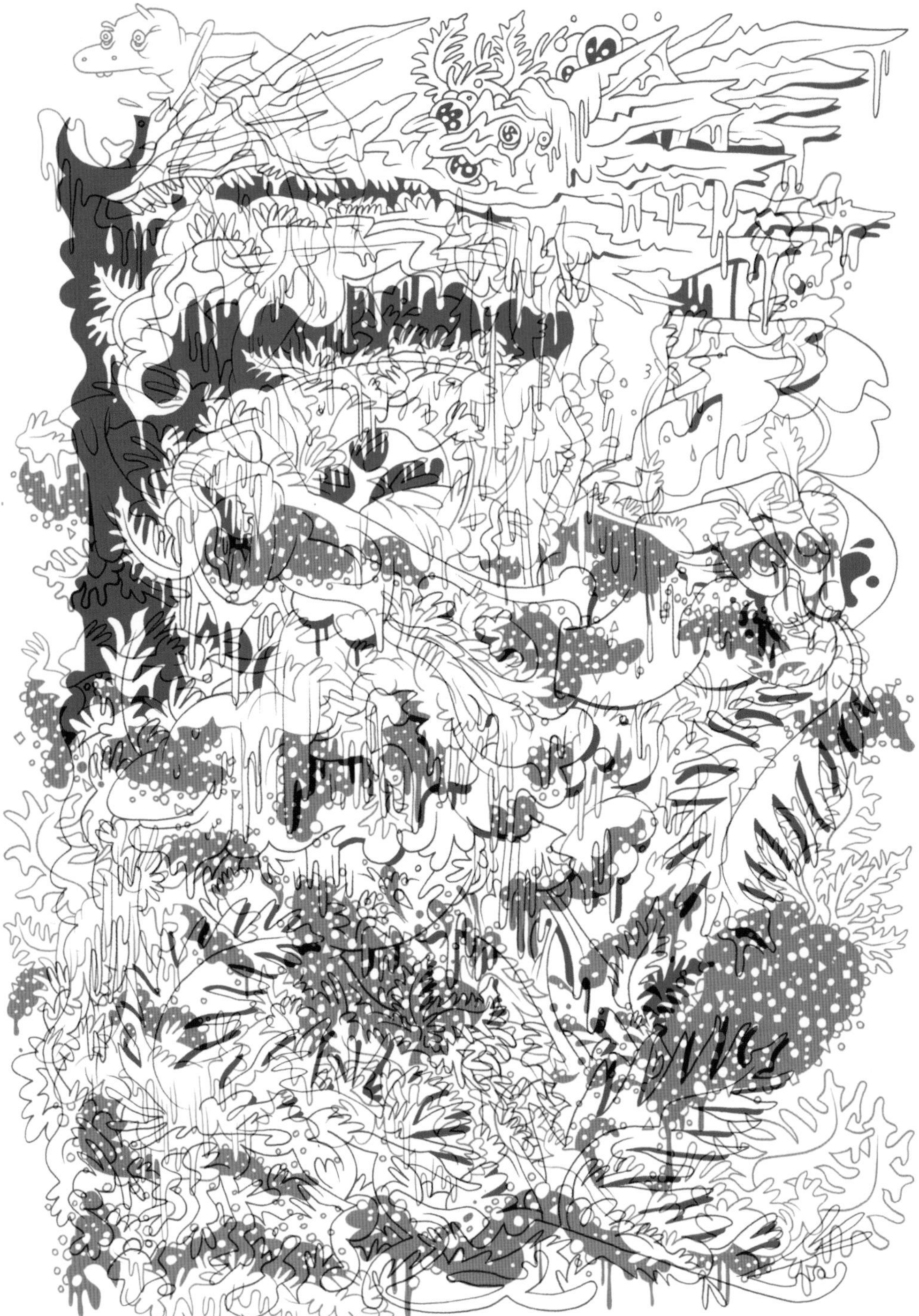

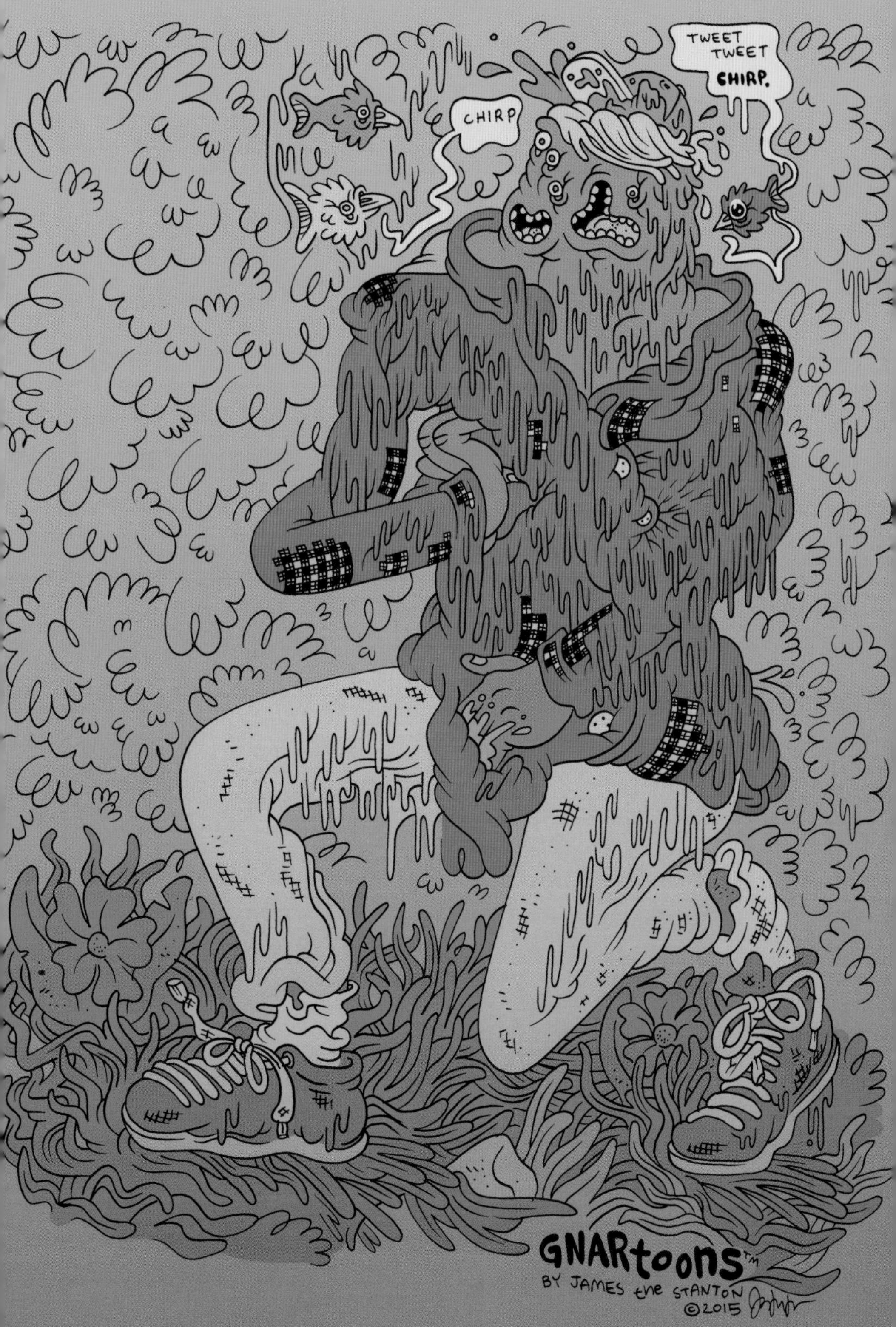
CHIRP
TWEET
TWEET
CHIRP.
GNARtoons™
BY JAMES the STANTON
©2015

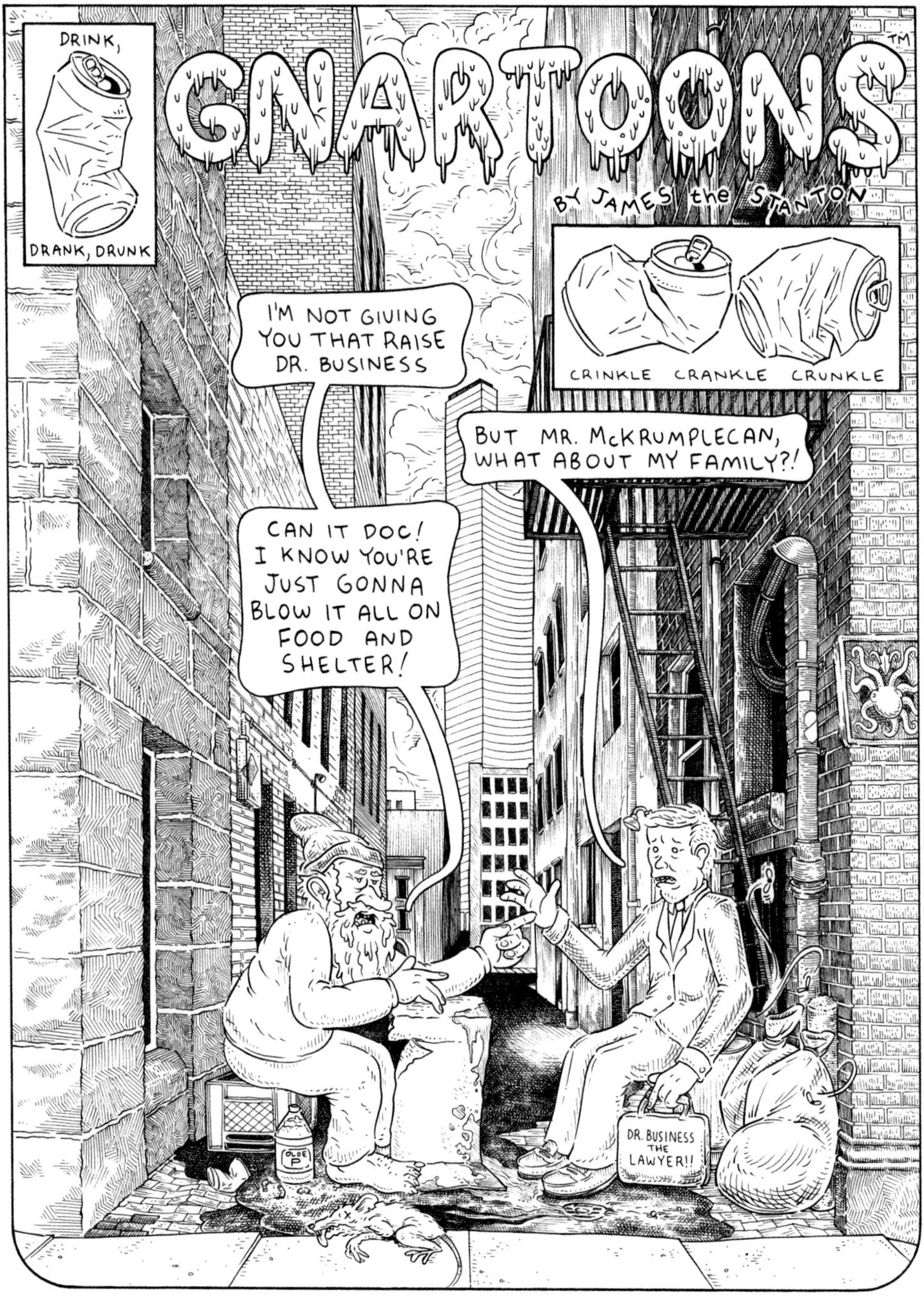
GNARTOONS™
BY JAMES the STANTON
DRINK,
DRANK, DRUNK
CRINKLE CRANKLE CRUNKLE
I'M NOT GIVING YOU THAT RAISE DR. BUSINESS
BUT MR. McKRUMPLECAN, WHAT ABOUT MY FAMILY?!
CAN IT DOC! I KNOW YOU'RE JUST GONNA BLOW IT ALL ON FOOD AND SHELTER!
OLDE P
DR. BUSINESS THE LAWYER!!

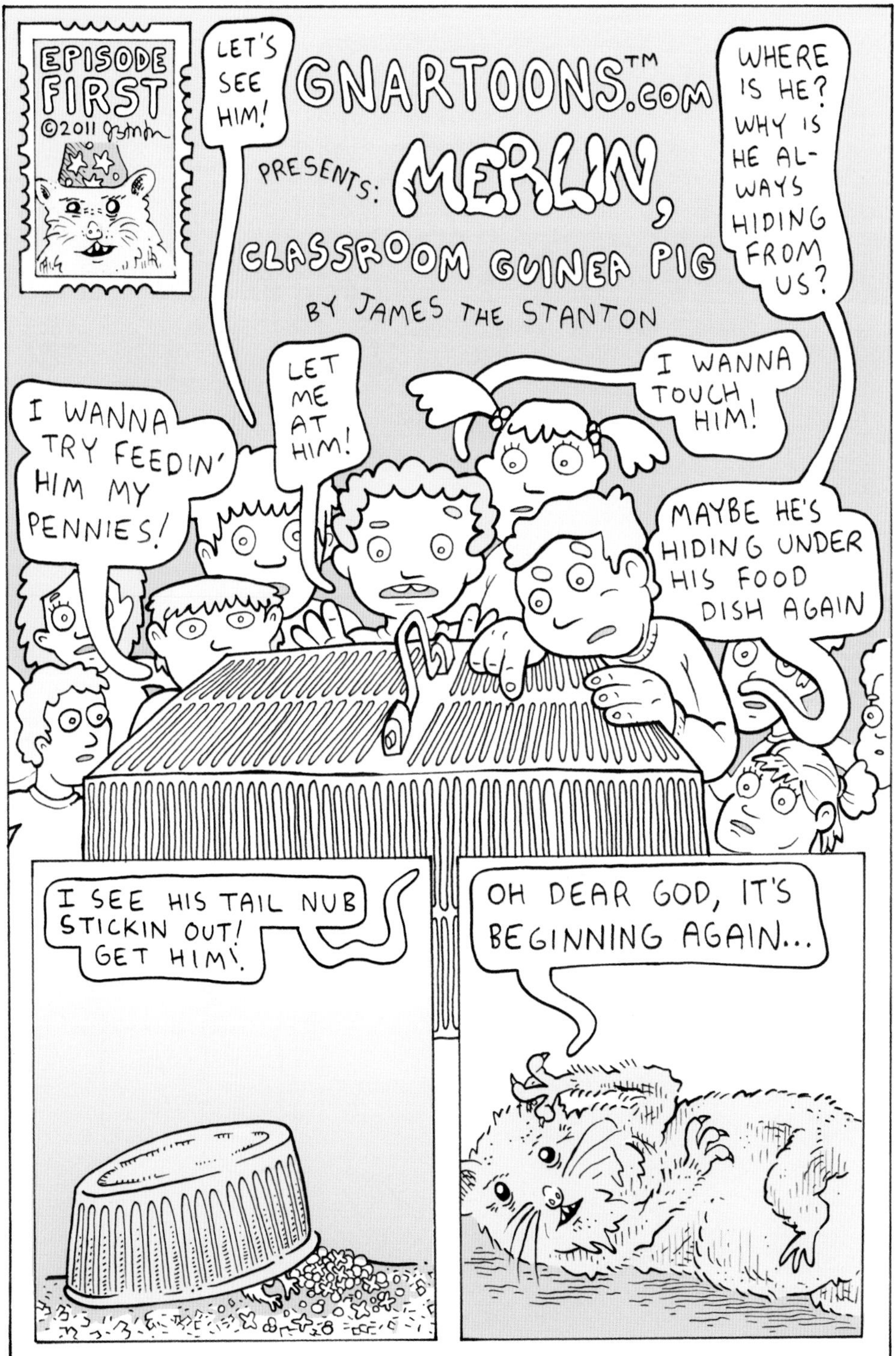
EPISODE FIRST
©2011
LET'S SEE HIM!
GNARTOONS™.com
PRESENTS: MERLIN, CLASSROOM GUINEA PIG
BY JAMES THE STANTON
WHERE IS HE? WHY IS HE AL- WAYS HIDING FROM US?
LET ME AT HIM!
I WANNA TOUCH HIM!
I WANNA TRY FEEDIN' HIM MY PENNIES!
MAYBE HE'S HIDING UNDER HIS FOOD DISH AGAIN
I SEE HIS TAIL NUB STICKIN OUT! GET HIM!
OH DEAR GOD, IT'S BEGINNING AGAIN...

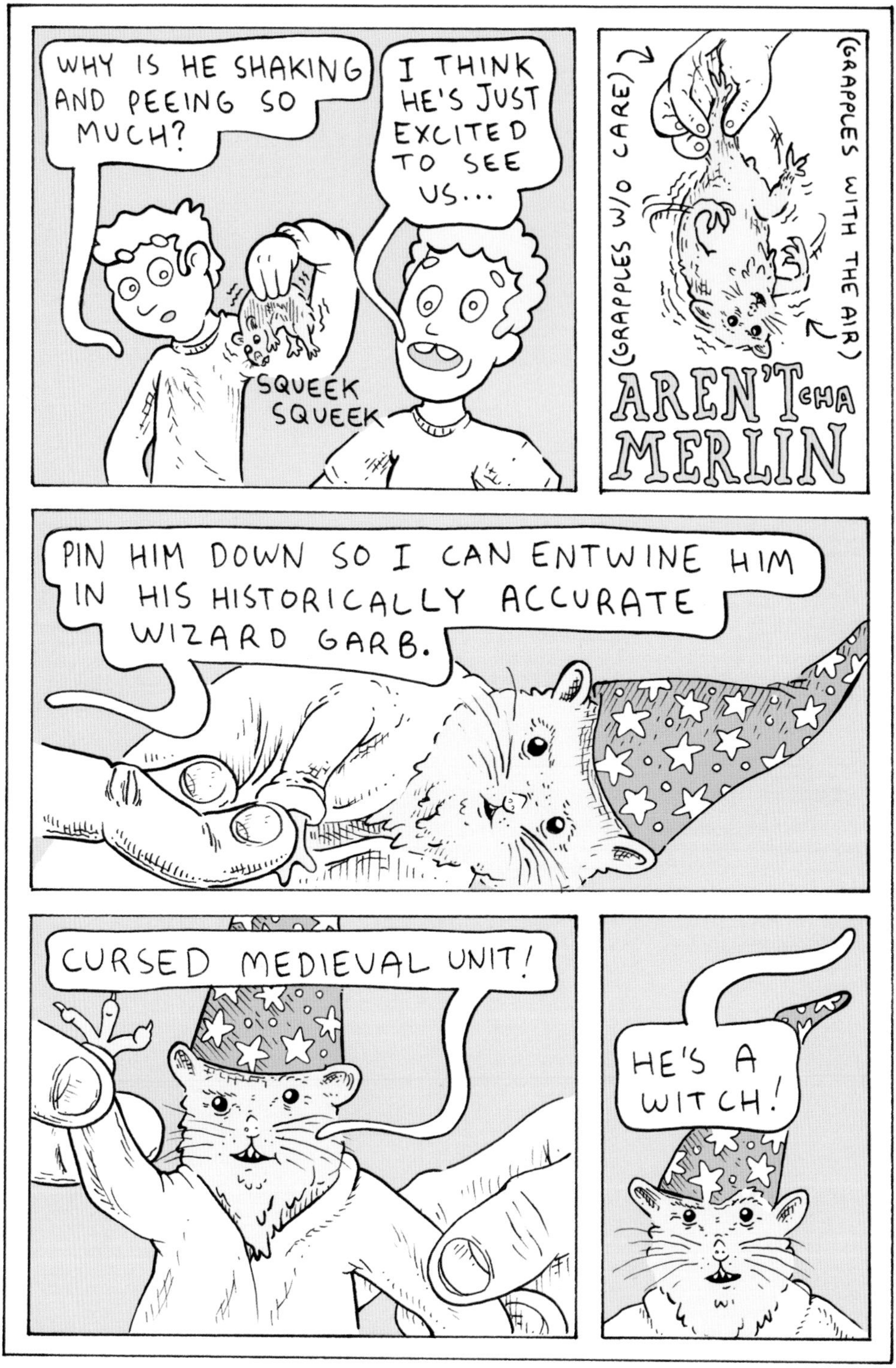
WHY IS HE SHAKING AND PEEING SO MUCH?
I THINK HE'S JUST EXCITED TO SEE US...
SQUEEK SQUEEK
(GRAPPLES W/O CARE)
(GRAPPLES WITH THE AIR)
AREN'Tcha MERLIN
PIN HIM DOWN SO I CAN ENTWINE HIM IN HIS HISTORICALLY ACCURATE WIZARD GARB.
CURSED MEDIEVAL UNIT!
HE'S A WITCH!

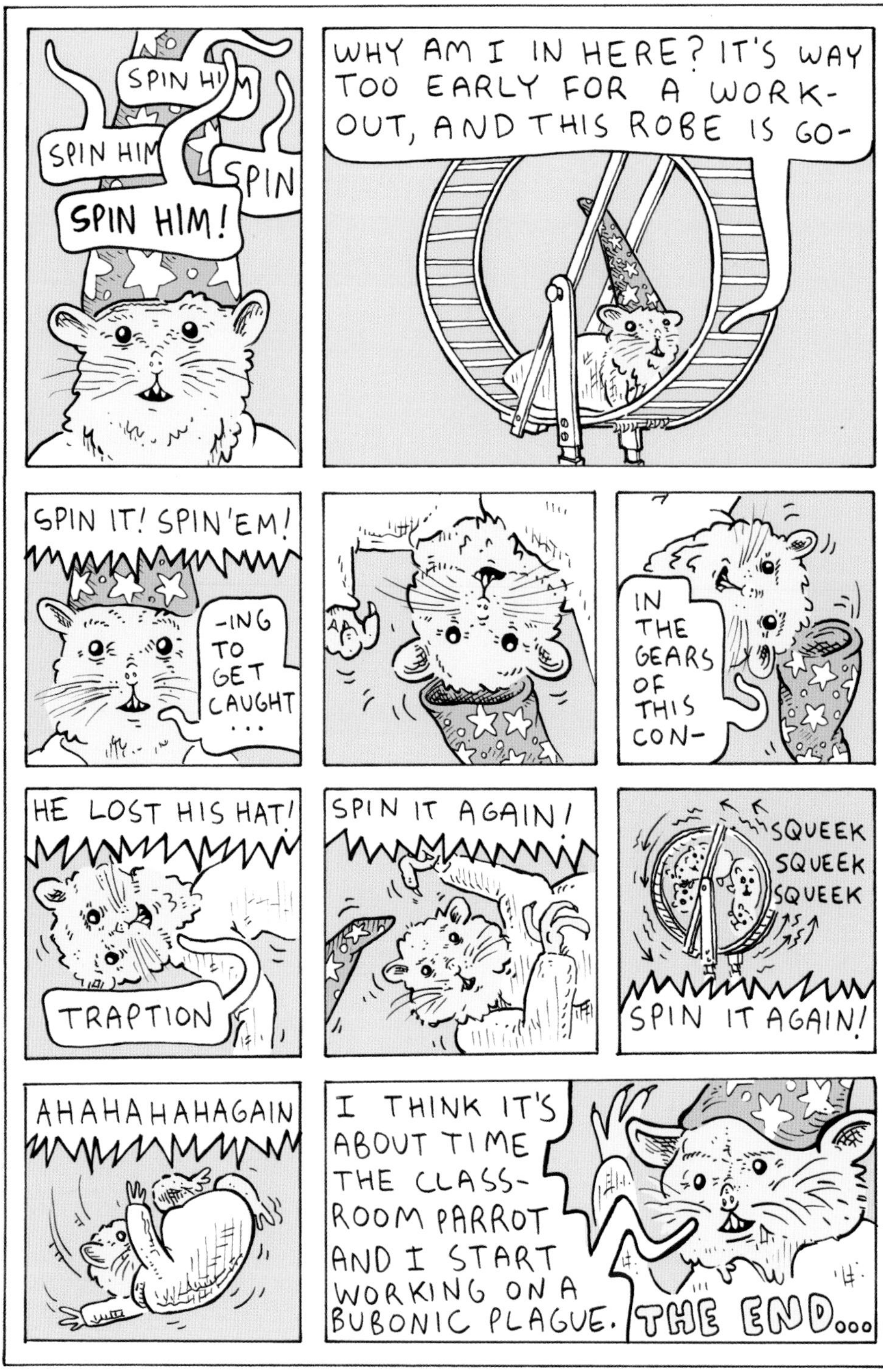
SPIN HIM
SPIN HIM
SPIN
SPIN HIM!
WHY AM I IN HERE? IT'S WAY TOO EARLY FOR A WORK-OUT, AND THIS ROBE IS GO-
SPIN IT! SPIN 'EM!
-ING TO GET CAUGHT ...
IN THE GEARS OF THIS CON-
HE LOST HIS HAT!
TRAPTION
SPIN IT AGAIN!
SQUEEK SQUEEK SQUEEK
SPIN IT AGAIN!
AHAHAHAHAGAIN
I THINK IT'S ABOUT TIME THE CLASS-ROOM PARROT AND I START WORKING ON A BUBONIC PLAGUE.
THE END...

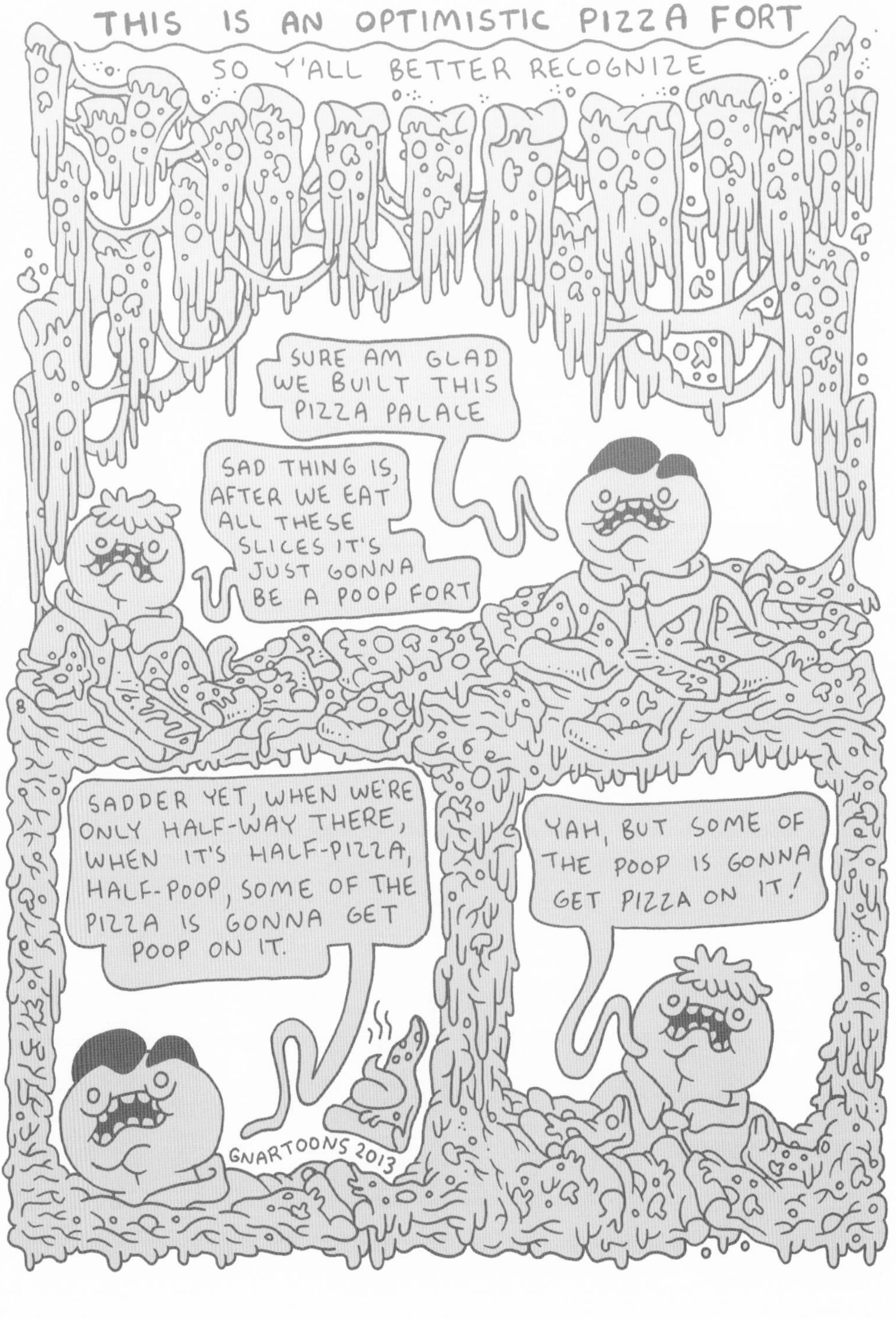
THIS IS AN OPTIMISTIC PIZZA FORT
SO Y'ALL BETTER RECOGNIZE
SURE AM GLAD WE BUILT THIS PIZZA PALACE
SAD THING IS, AFTER WE EAT ALL THESE SLICES IT'S JUST GONNA BE A POOP FORT
SADDER YET, WHEN WE'RE ONLY HALF-WAY THERE, WHEN IT'S HALF-PIZZA, HALF-POOP, SOME OF THE PIZZA IS GONNA GET POOP ON IT.
YAH, BUT SOME OF THE POOP IS GONNA GET PIZZA ON IT!
GNARTOONS 2013

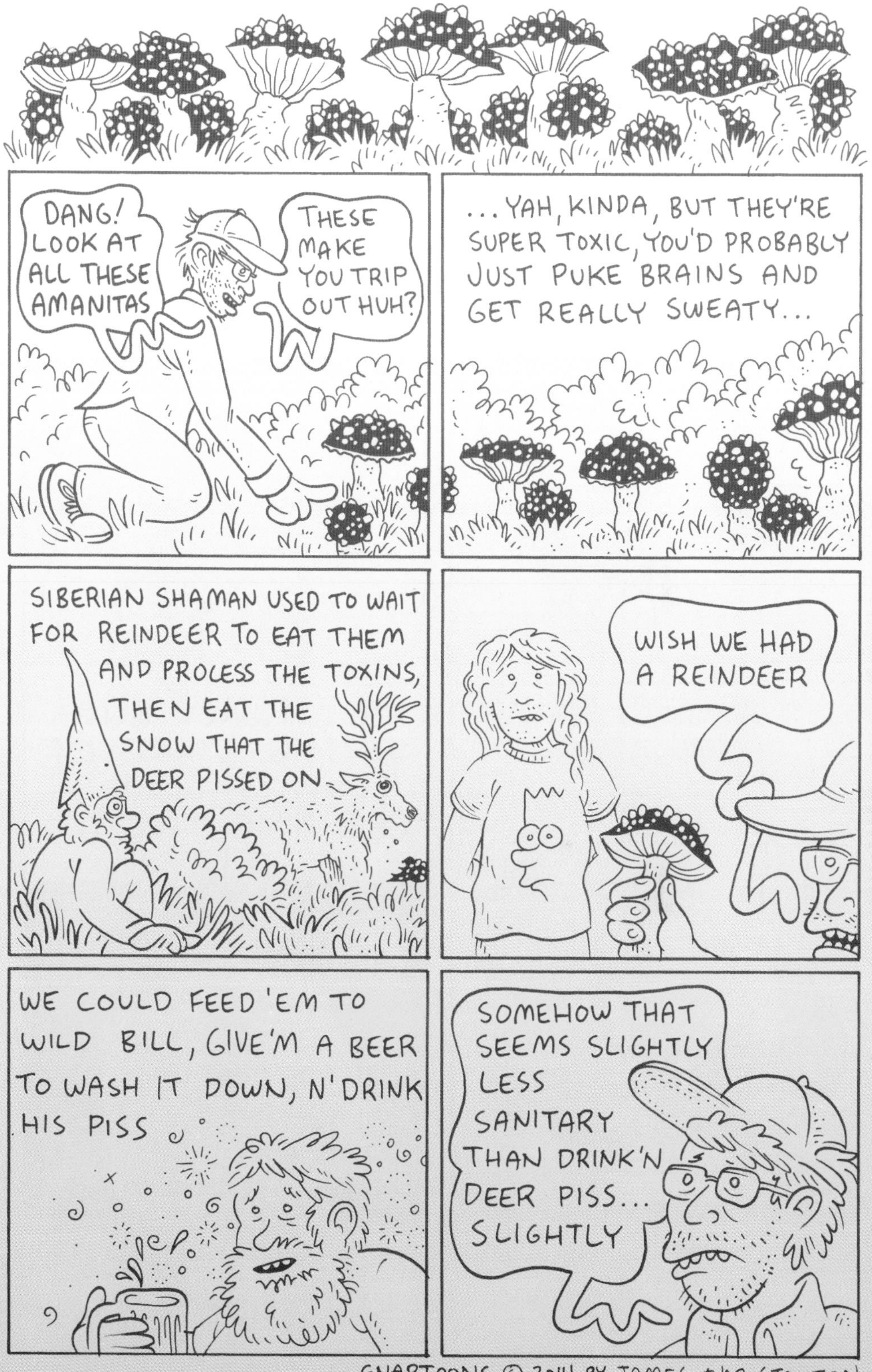
DANG! LOOK AT ALL THESE AMANITAS
THESE MAKE YOU TRIP OUT HUH?
...YAH, KINDA, BUT THEY'RE SUPER TOXIC, YOU'D PROBABLY JUST PUKE BRAINS AND GET REALLY SWEATY...
SIBERIAN SHAMAN USED TO WAIT FOR REINDEER TO EAT THEM AND PROCESS THE TOXINS, THEN EAT THE SNOW THAT THE DEER PISSED ON
WISH WE HAD A REINDEER
WE COULD FEED 'EM TO WILD BILL, GIVE'M A BEER TO WASH IT DOWN, N'DRINK HIS PISS
SOMEHOW THAT SEEMS SLIGHTLY LESS SANITARY THAN DRINK'N DEER PISS... SLIGHTLY

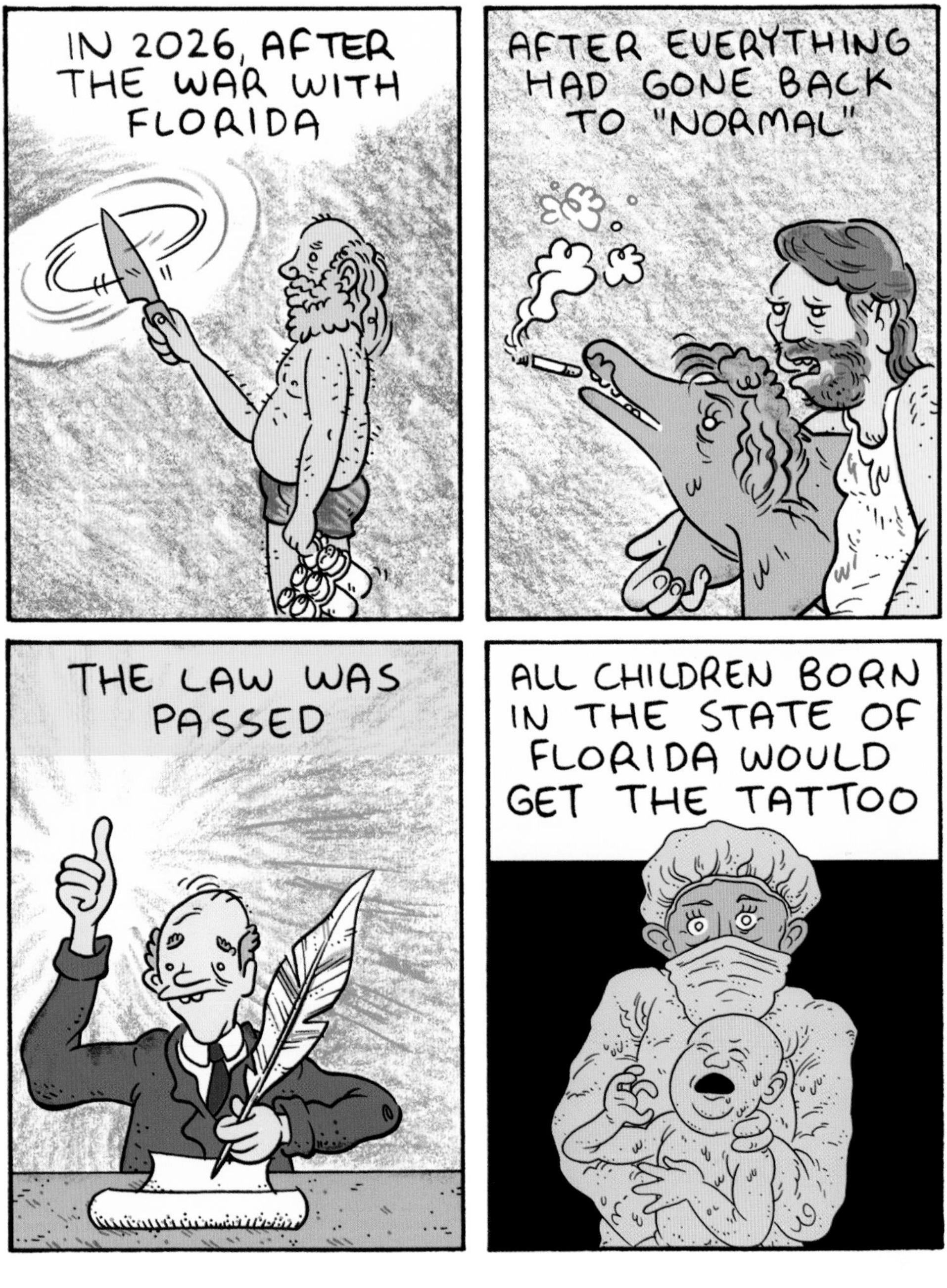
IN 2026, AFTER THE WAR WITH FLORIDA
AFTER EVERYTHING HAD GONE BACK TO "NORMAL"
THE LAW WAS PASSED
ALL CHILDREN BORN IN THE STATE OF FLORIDA WOULD GET THE TATTOO

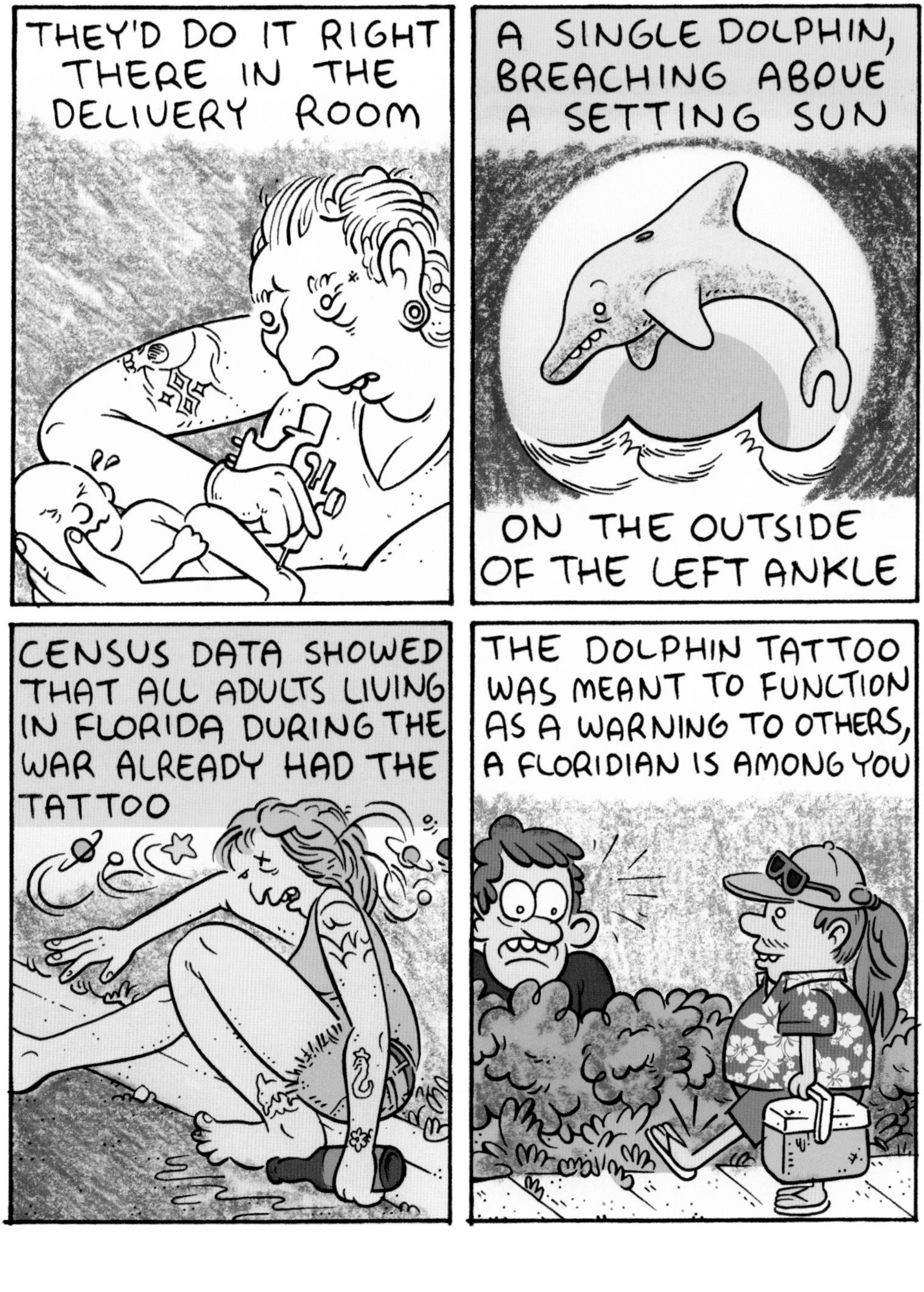
THEY'D DO IT RIGHT THERE IN THE DELIVERY ROOM
A SINGLE DOLPHIN, BREACHING ABOVE A SETTING SUN
ON THE OUTSIDE OF THE LEFT ANKLE
CENSUS DATA SHOWED THAT ALL ADULTS LIVING IN FLORIDA DURING THE WAR ALREADY HAD THE TATTOO
THE DOLPHIN TATTOO WAS MEANT TO FUNCTION AS A WARNING TO OTHERS, A FLORIDIAN IS AMONG YOU

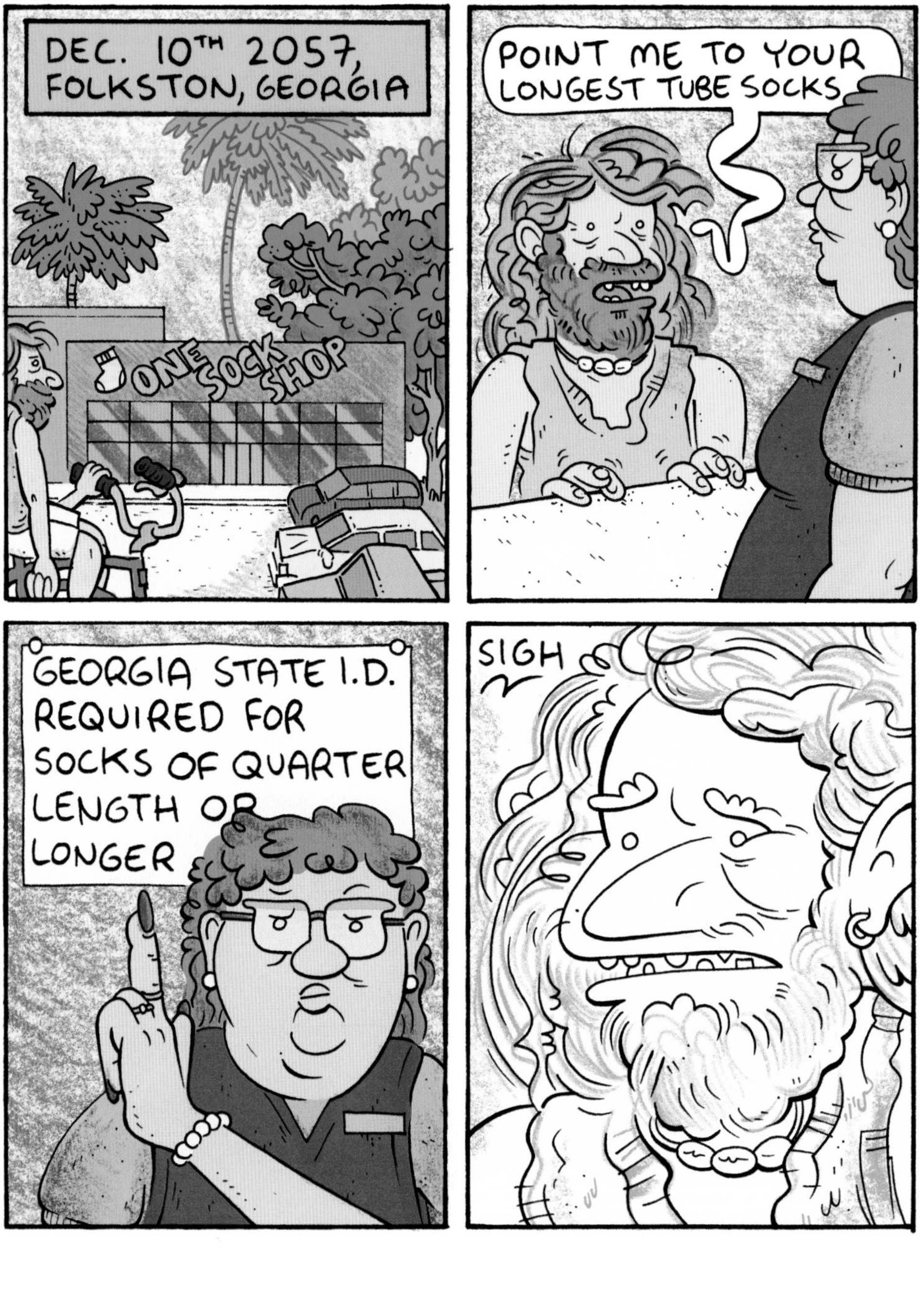
DEC. 10TH 2057,
FOLKSTON, GEORGIA
ONE SOCK SHOP
POINT ME TO YOUR LONGEST TUBE SOCKS
GEORGIA STATE I.D. REQUIRED FOR SOCKS OF QUARTER LENGTH OR LONGER
SIGH

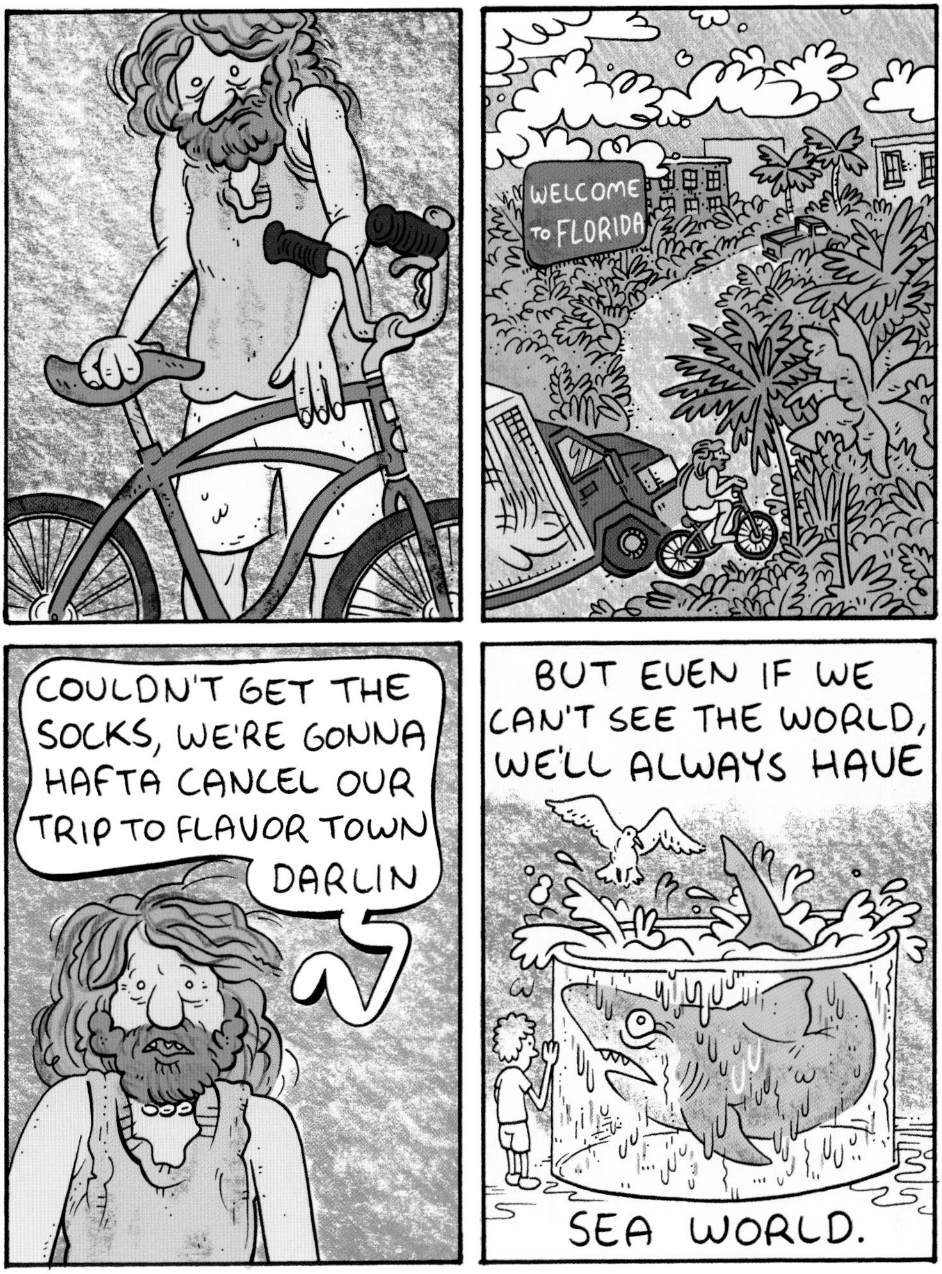
WELCOME TO FLORIDA
COULDN'T GET THE SOCKS, WE'RE GONNA HAFTA CANCEL OUR TRIP TO FLAVOR TOWN DARLIN
BUT EVEN IF WE CAN'T SEE THE WORLD, WE'LL ALWAYS HAVE
SEA WORLD.

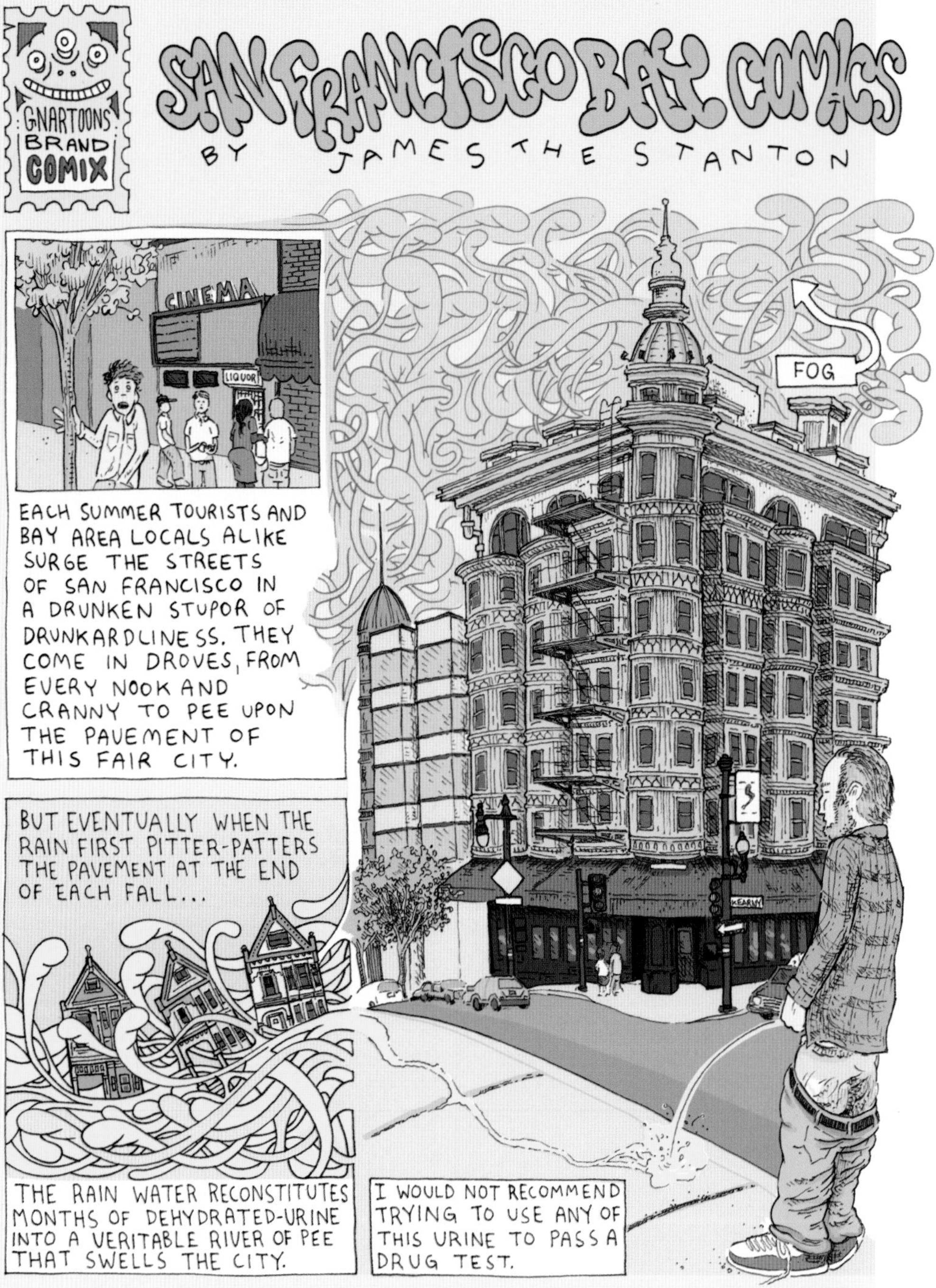
GNARTOONS BRAND COMIX
SAN FRANCISCO BAY COMICS
BY JAMES THE STANTON
CINEMA
LIQUOR
EACH SUMMER TOURISTS AND BAY AREA LOCALS ALIKE SURGE THE STREETS OF SAN FRANCISCO IN A DRUNKEN STUPOR OF DRUNKARDLINESS. THEY COME IN DROVES, FROM EVERY NOOK AND CRANNY TO PEE UPON THE PAVEMENT OF THIS FAIR CITY.
FOG
BUT EVENTUALLY WHEN THE RAIN FIRST PITTER-PATTERS THE PAVEMENT AT THE END OF EACH FALL...
KEARNY
THE RAIN WATER RECONSTITUTES MONTHS OF DEHYDRATED-URINE INTO A VERITABLE RIVER OF PEE THAT SWELLS THE CITY.
I WOULD NOT RECOMMEND TRYING TO USE ANY OF THIS URINE TO PASS A DRUG TEST.

THE LOVELY BUILDING PICTURED BEHIND THE GENTLEMAN WHO'S RELIEVING HIMSELF IS CALLED THE COLUMBUS TOWER. IT WAS DESIGNED BY ARCHITECTS SALFIELD AND KOHLBERG, CONSTRUCTION WAS COMPLETED IN 1907 AND IT IS LOCATED AT 916 KEARNY ST.

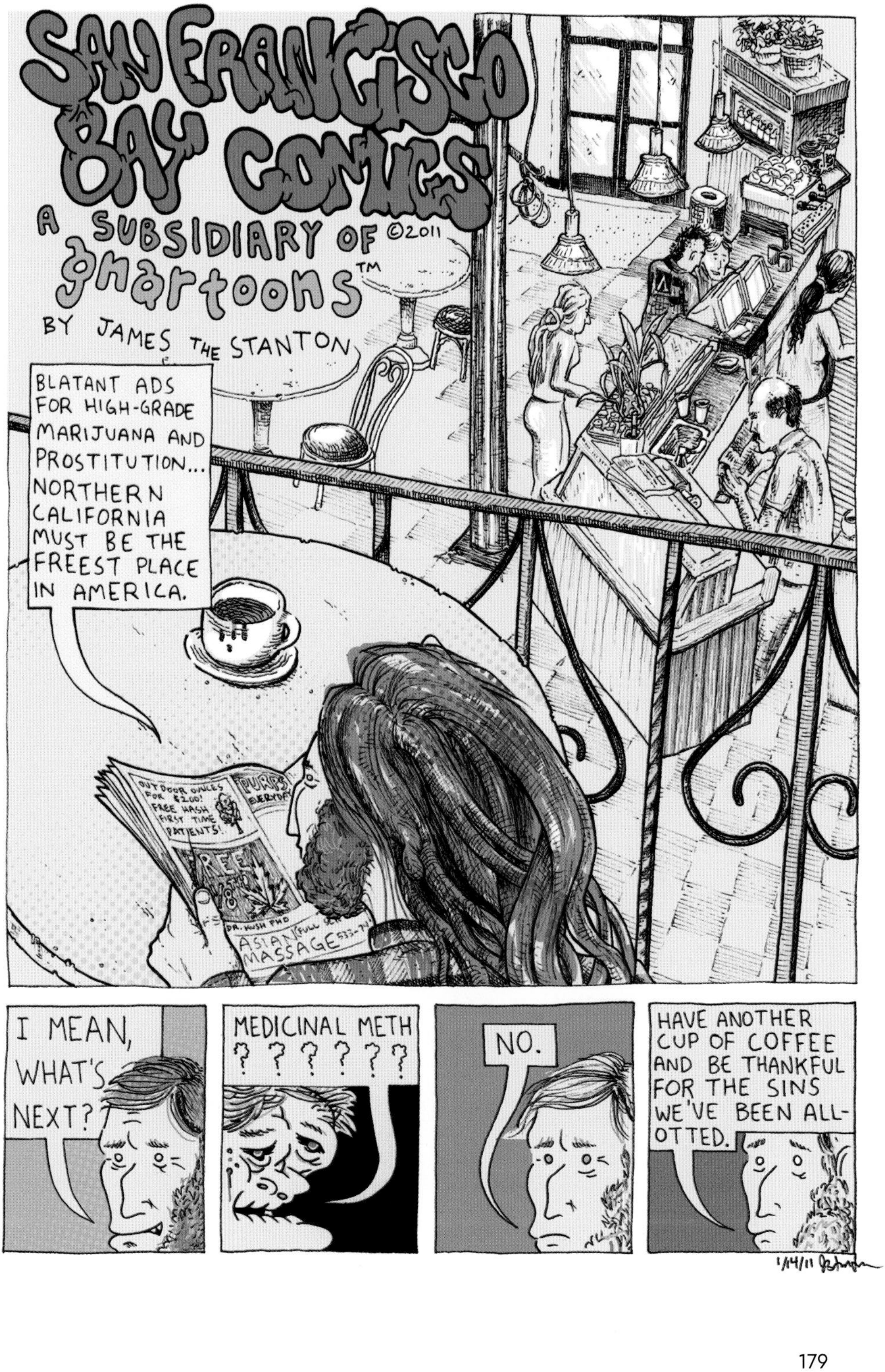

SAN FRANCISCO BAY COMICS
A SUBSIDIARY OF ©2011 gnartoons™
BY JAMES THE STANTON
BLATANT ADS FOR HIGH-GRADE MARIJUANA AND PROSTITUTION... NORTHERN CALIFORNIA MUST BE THE FREEST PLACE IN AMERICA.
OUTDOOR OUNCES FOR $200! FREE HASH FIRST TIME PATIENTS!
PURPS EVERYDAY
DR. KUSH PHD
ASIAN MASSAGE
I MEAN, WHAT'S NEXT?
MEDICINAL METH ??????
NO.
HAVE ANOTHER CUP OF COFFEE AND BE THANKFUL FOR THE SINS WE'VE BEEN ALL-OTTED.
1/14/11

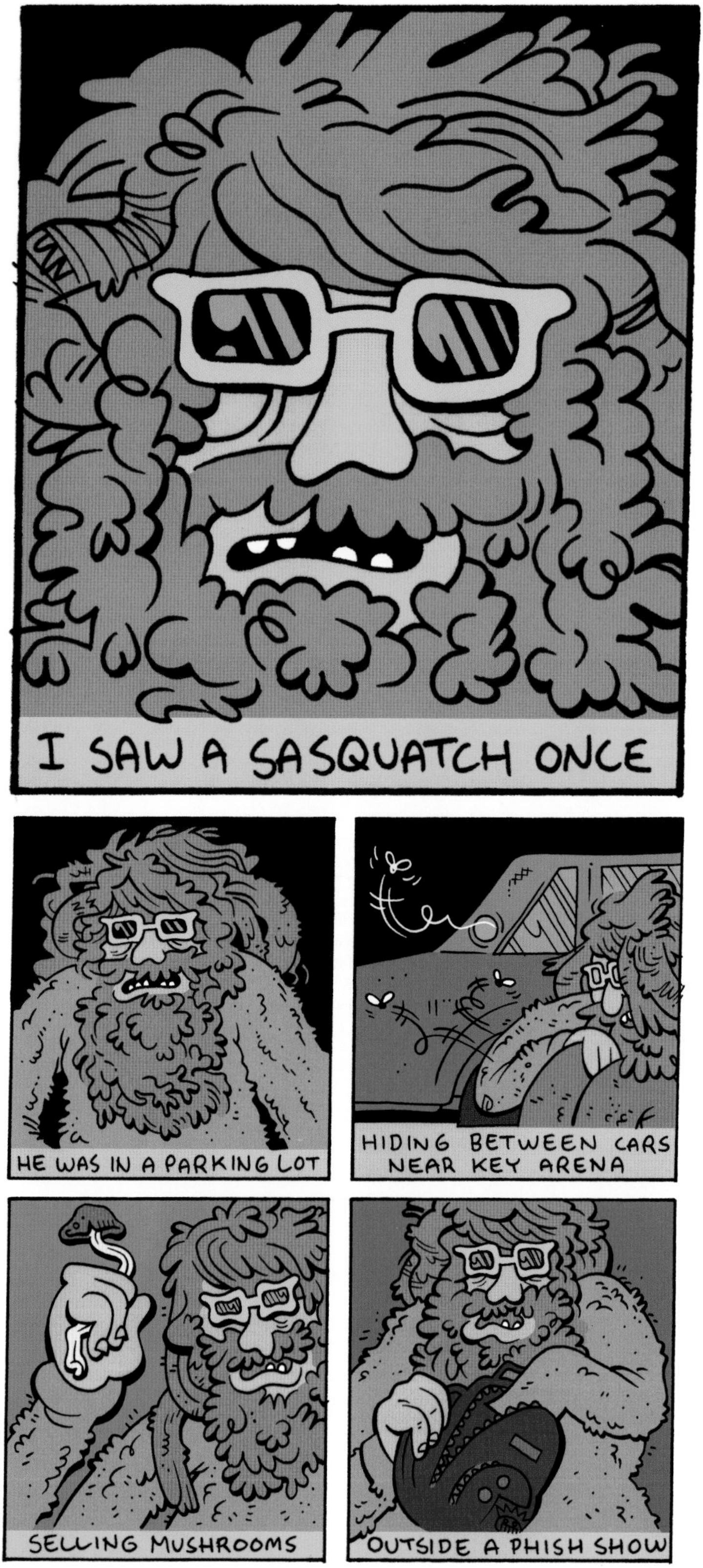

I SAW A SASQUATCH ONCE
HE WAS IN A PARKING LOT
HIDING BETWEEN CARS NEAR KEY ARENA
SELLING MUSHROOMS
OUTSIDE A PHISH SHOW

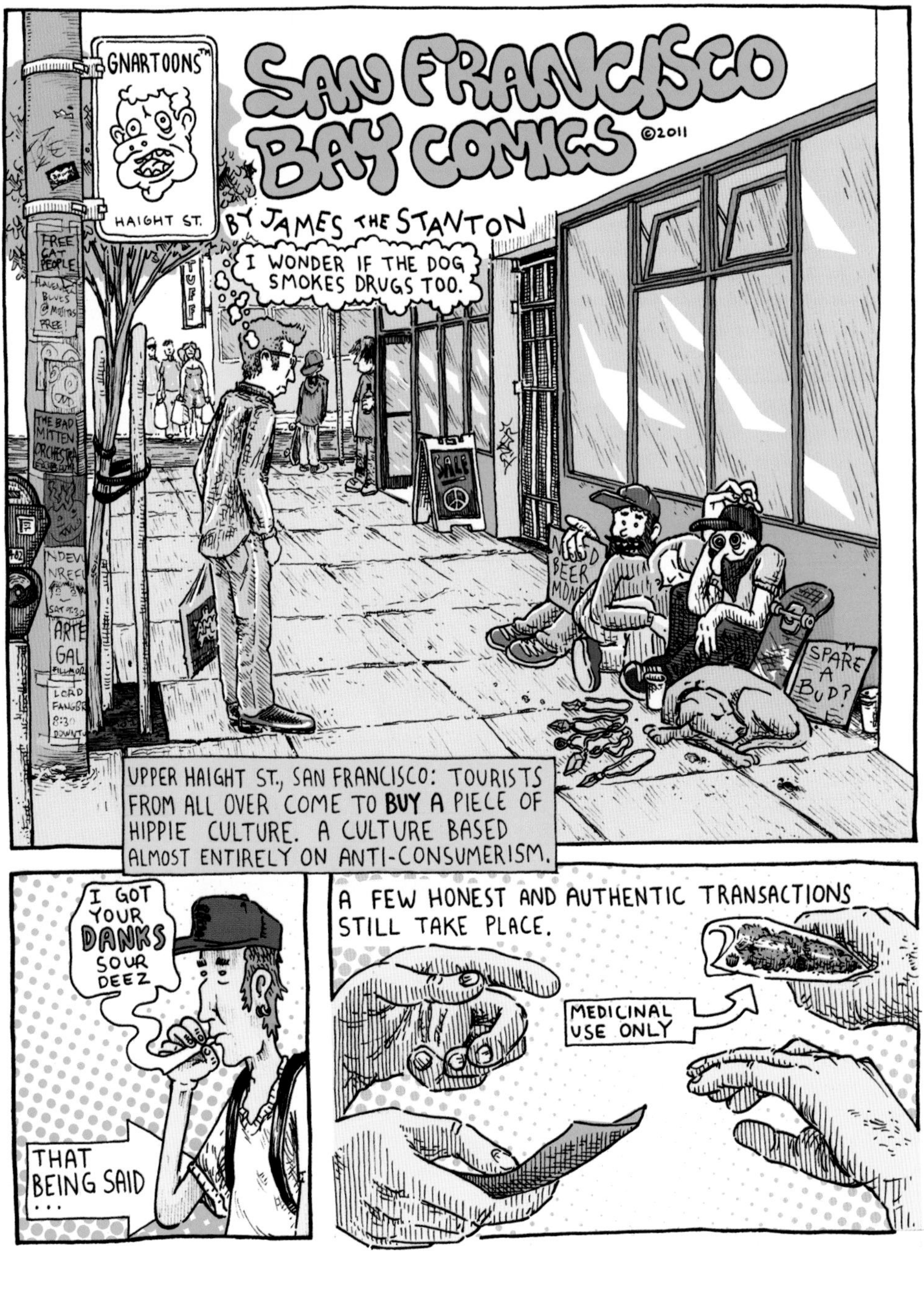
GNARTOONS™
HAIGHT ST.
SAN FRANCISCO BAY COMICS ©2011
BY JAMES THE STANTON
I WONDER IF THE DOG SMOKES DRUGS TOO.
SALE
NEED BEER MONEY
SPARE A BUD?
UPPER HAIGHT ST., SAN FRANCISCO: TOURISTS FROM ALL OVER COME TO BUY A PIECE OF HIPPIE CULTURE. A CULTURE BASED ALMOST ENTIRELY ON ANTI-CONSUMERISM.
I GOT YOUR DANKS SOUR DEEZ
THAT BEING SAID . . .
A FEW HONEST AND AUTHENTIC TRANSACTIONS STILL TAKE PLACE.
MEDICINAL USE ONLY

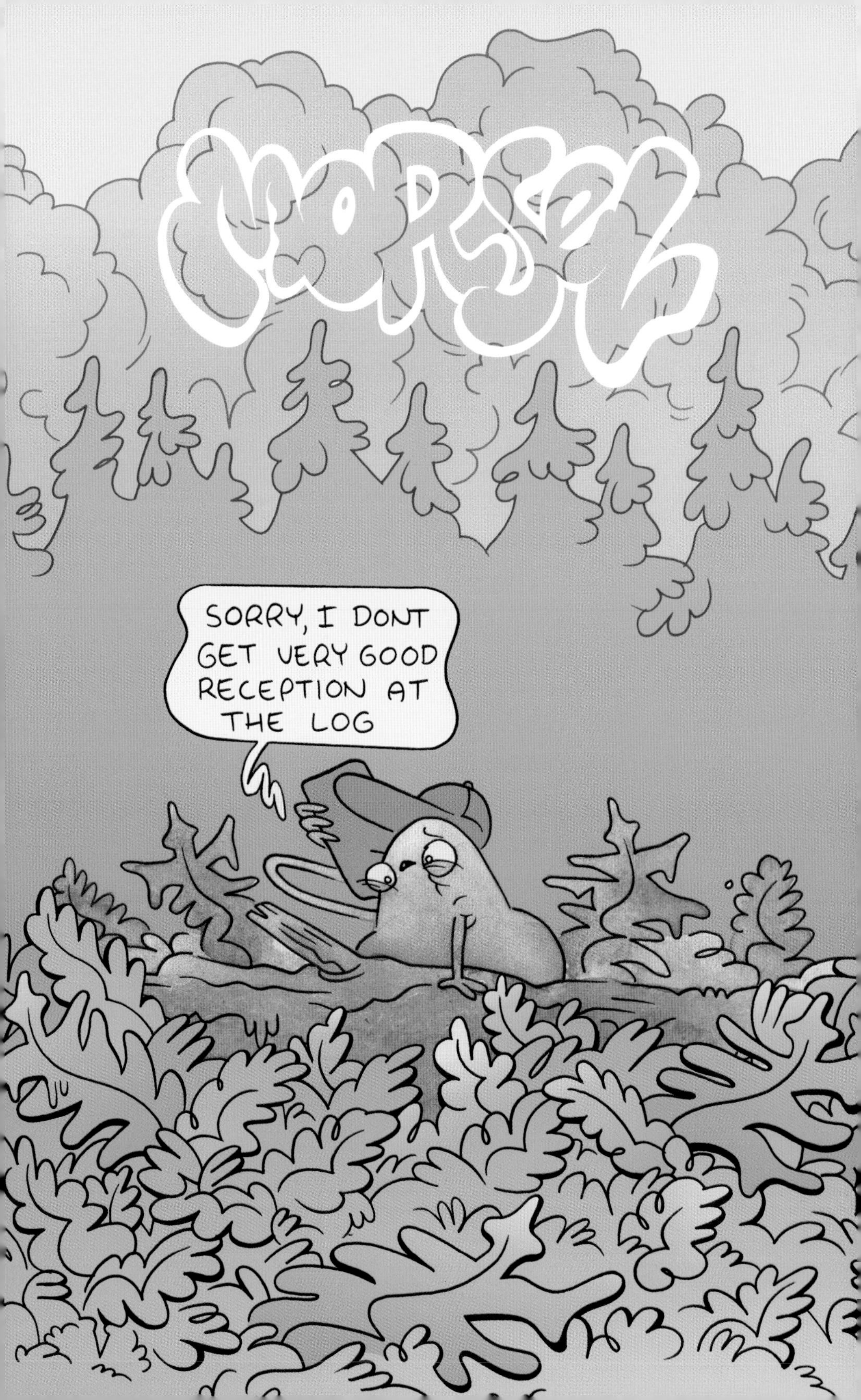
SORRY, I DONT GET VERY GOOD RECEPTION AT THE LOG

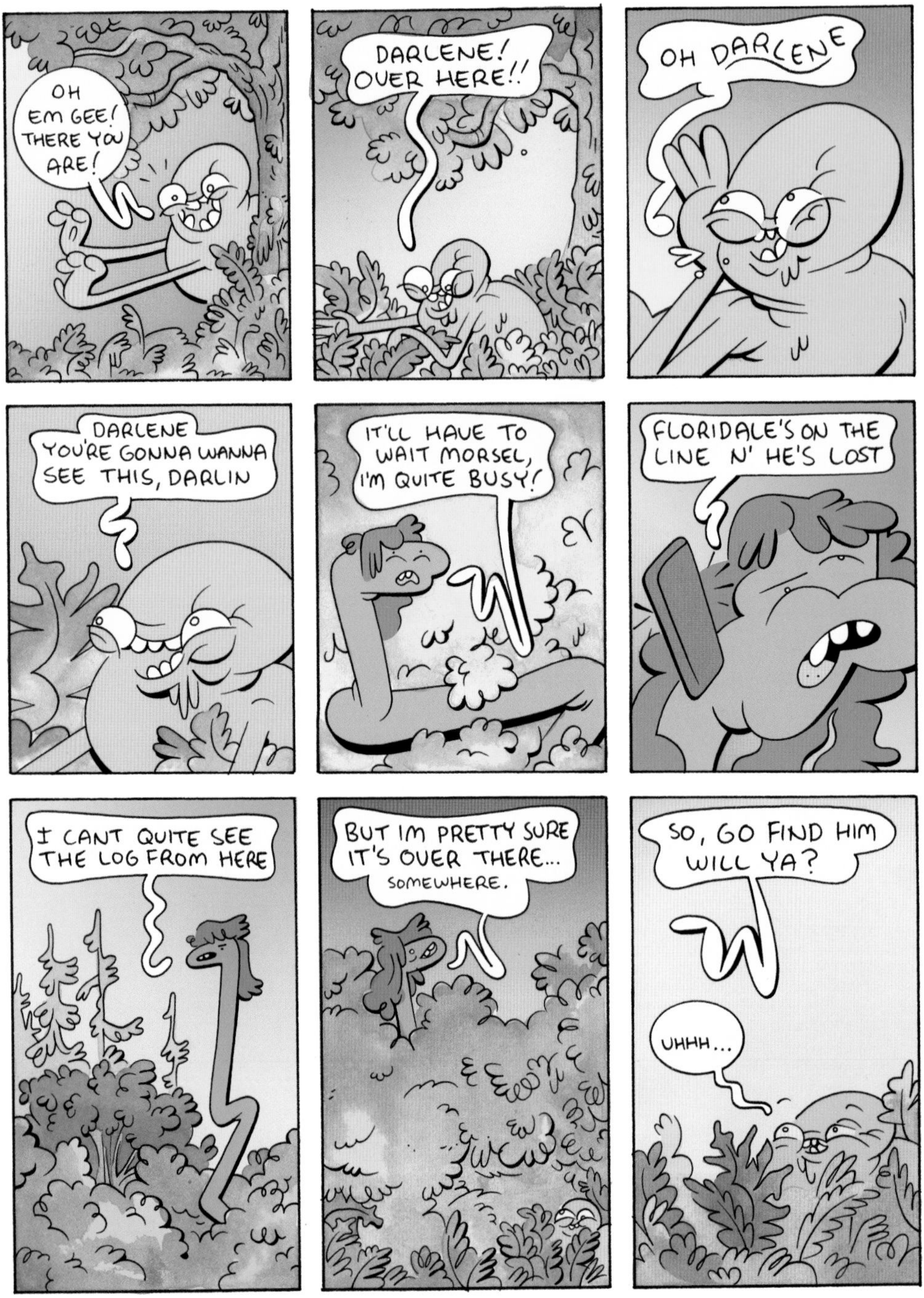
OH EM GEE! THERE YOU ARE!
DARLENE! OVER HERE!!
OH DARLENE
DARLENE YOU'RE GONNA WANNA SEE THIS, DARLIN
IT'LL HAVE TO WAIT MORSEL, I'M QUITE BUSY!
FLORIDALE'S ON THE LINE N' HE'S LOST
I CANT QUITE SEE THE LOG FROM HERE
BUT IM PRETTY SURE IT'S OVER THERE... SOMEWHERE.
SO, GO FIND HIM WILL YA?
UHHH...

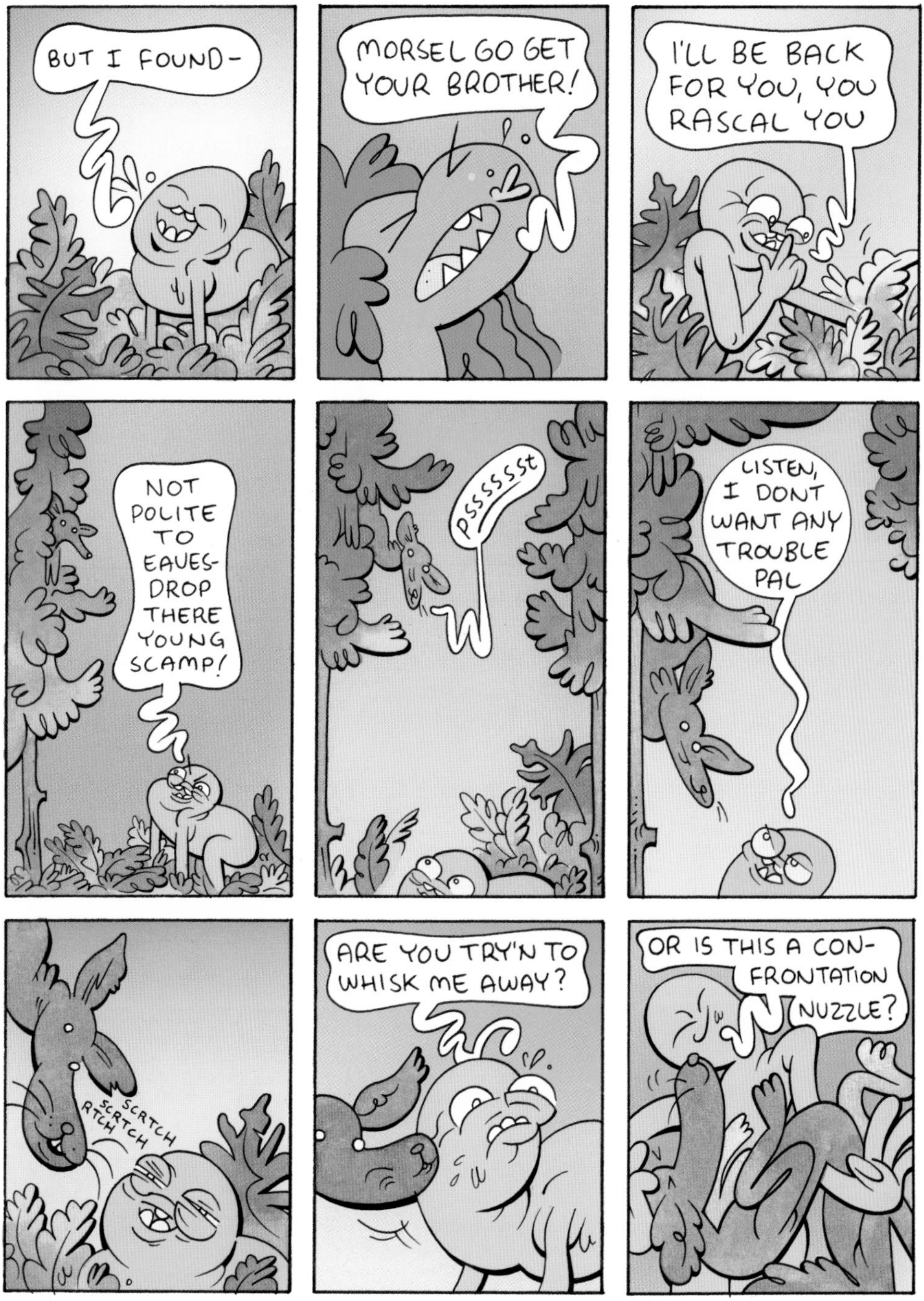
BUT I FOUND-
MORSEL GO GET YOUR BROTHER!
I'LL BE BACK FOR YOU, YOU RASCAL YOU
NOT POLITE TO EAVES-DROP THERE YOUNG SCAMP!
PSSSSSSt
LISTEN, I DONT WANT ANY TROUBLE PAL
SCRTCH SCRTCH RTCH
ARE YOU TRY'N TO WHISK ME AWAY?
OR IS THIS A CON-FRONTATION NUZZLE?

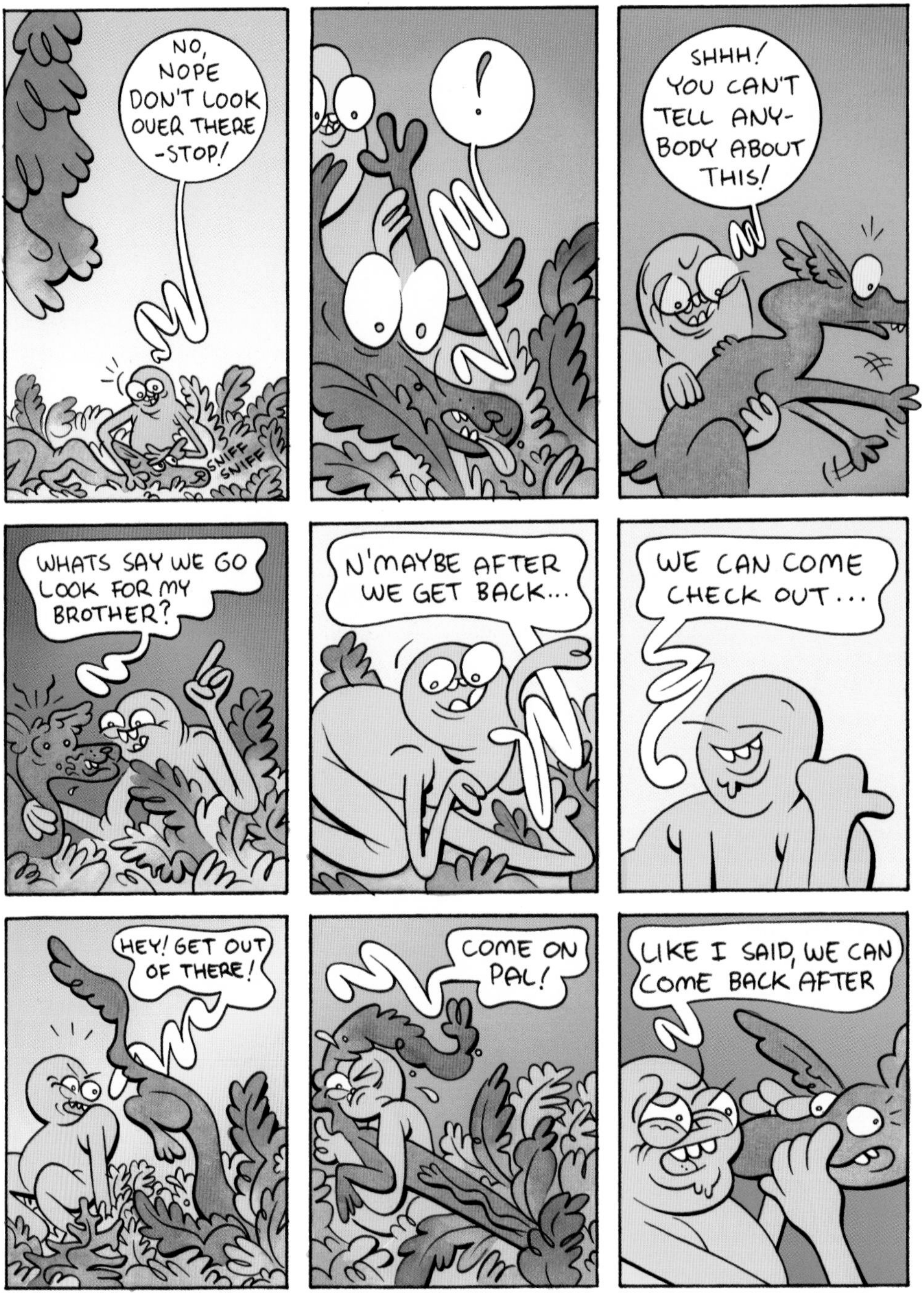
NO, NOPE DON'T LOOK OVER THERE -STOP!
SNIFF SNIFF
!
SHHH! YOU CAN'T TELL ANY-BODY ABOUT THIS!
WHATS SAY WE GO LOOK FOR MY BROTHER?
N'MAYBE AFTER WE GET BACK...
WE CAN COME CHECK OUT...
HEY! GET OUT OF THERE!
COME ON PAL!
LIKE I SAID, WE CAN COME BACK AFTER

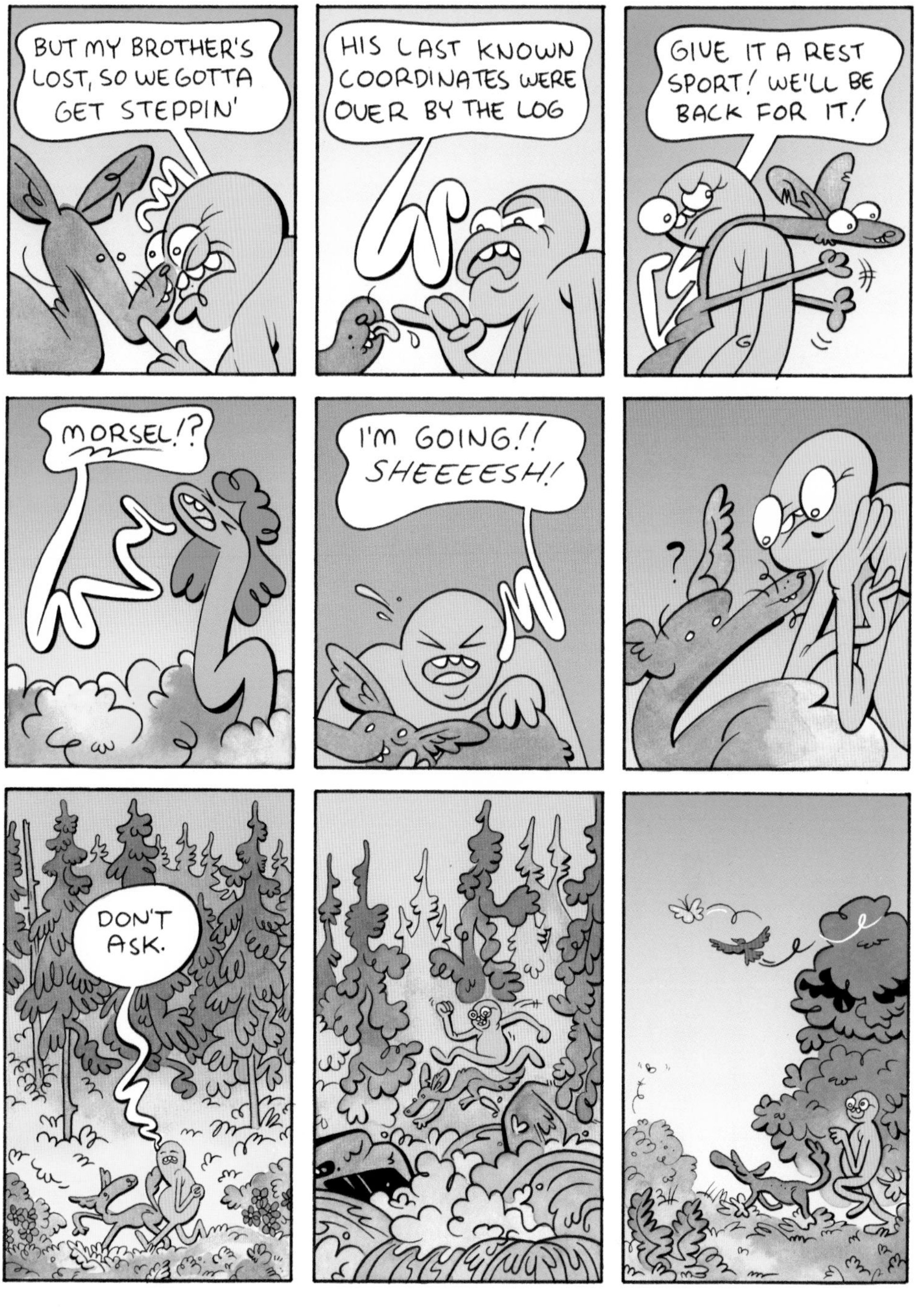
BUT MY BROTHER'S LOST, SO WE GOTTA GET STEPPIN'
HIS LAST KNOWN COORDINATES WERE OVER BY THE LOG
GIVE IT A REST SPORT! WE'LL BE BACK FOR IT!
MORSEL!?
I'M GOING!! SHEEEESH!
?
DON'T ASK.

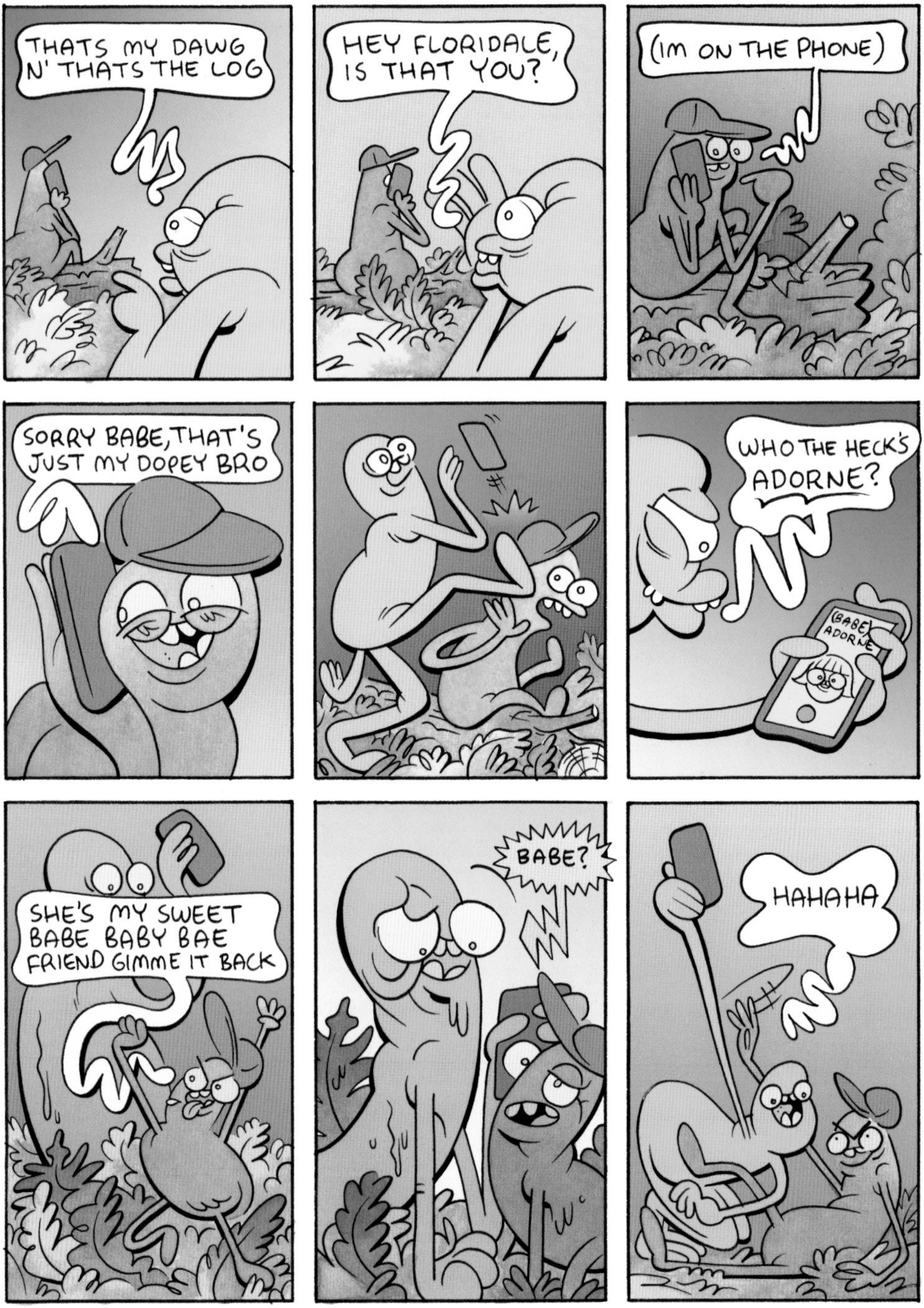
THATS MY DAWG N' THATS THE LOG
HEY FLORIDALE, IS THAT YOU?
(IM ON THE PHONE)
SORRY BABE, THAT'S JUST MY DOPEY BRO
WHO THE HECK'S ADORNE?
(BABE) ADORNE
SHE'S MY SWEET BABE BABY BAE FRIEND GIMME IT BACK
BABE?
HAHAHA

WE CAME TO RESCUE YOU!

HUH?

YOU'RE LOST! AND— SO **HERE I AM**

BABE?

I'M NOT LOST YOU KNUCKLE- HEAD

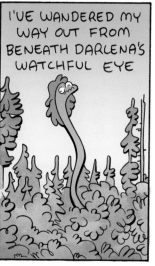

I'VE WANDERED MY WAY OUT FROM BENEATH DARLENA'S WATCHFUL EYE

TRY'N TO FIND A LITTLE PRIVACY

N' SOME SCREENTIME WITH M' BABE

YOU'RE TRIPPIN'

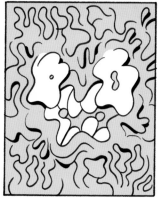

HAVE YOU SEEN...

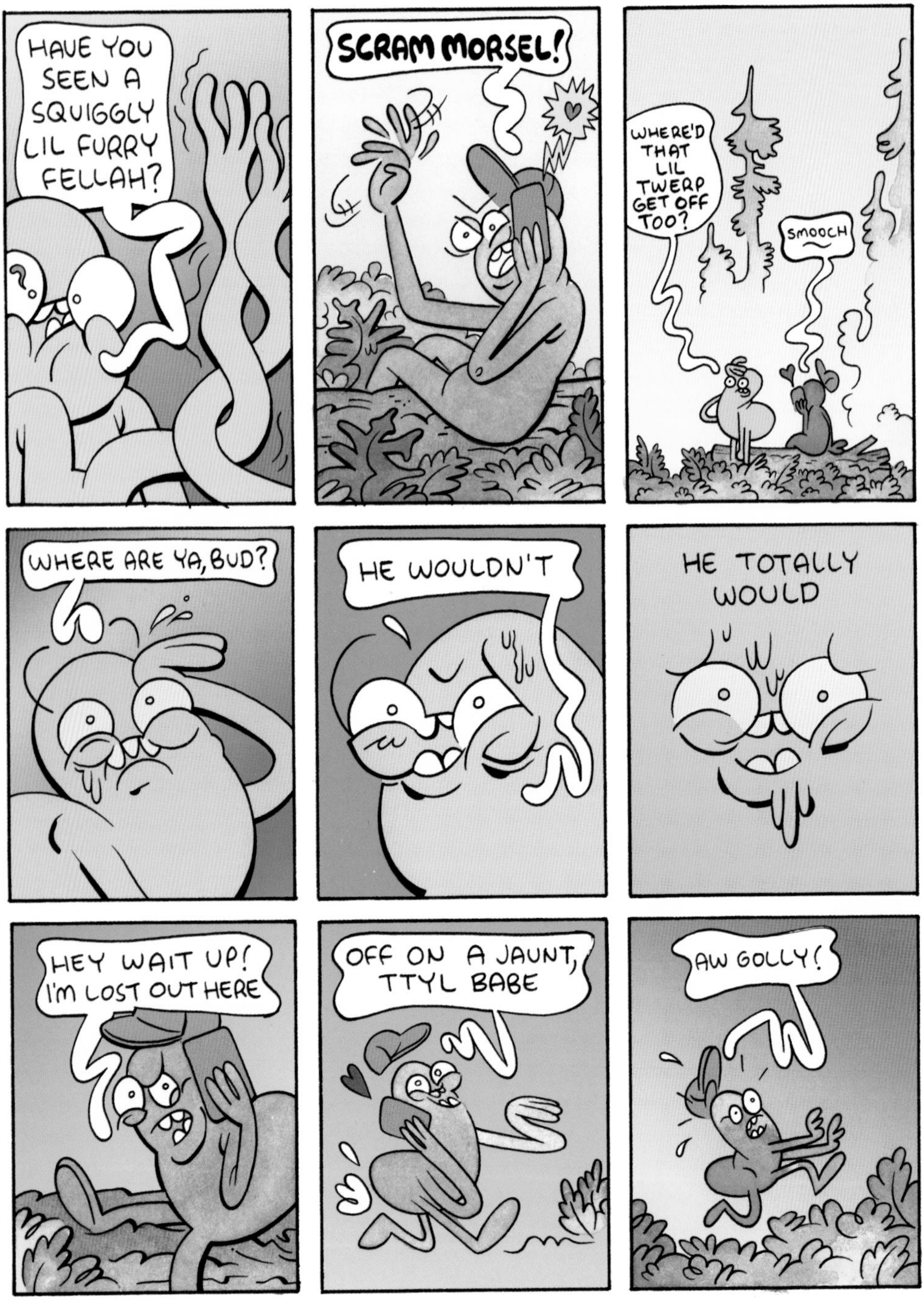
HAVE YOU SEEN A SQUIGGLY LIL FURRY FELLAH?
SCRAM MORSEL!
WHERE'D THAT LIL TWERP GET OFF TOO?
SMOOCH
WHERE ARE YA, BUD?
HE WOULDN'T
HE TOTALLY WOULD
HEY WAIT UP! I'M LOST OUT HERE
OFF ON A JAUNT, TTYL BABE
AW GOLLY!

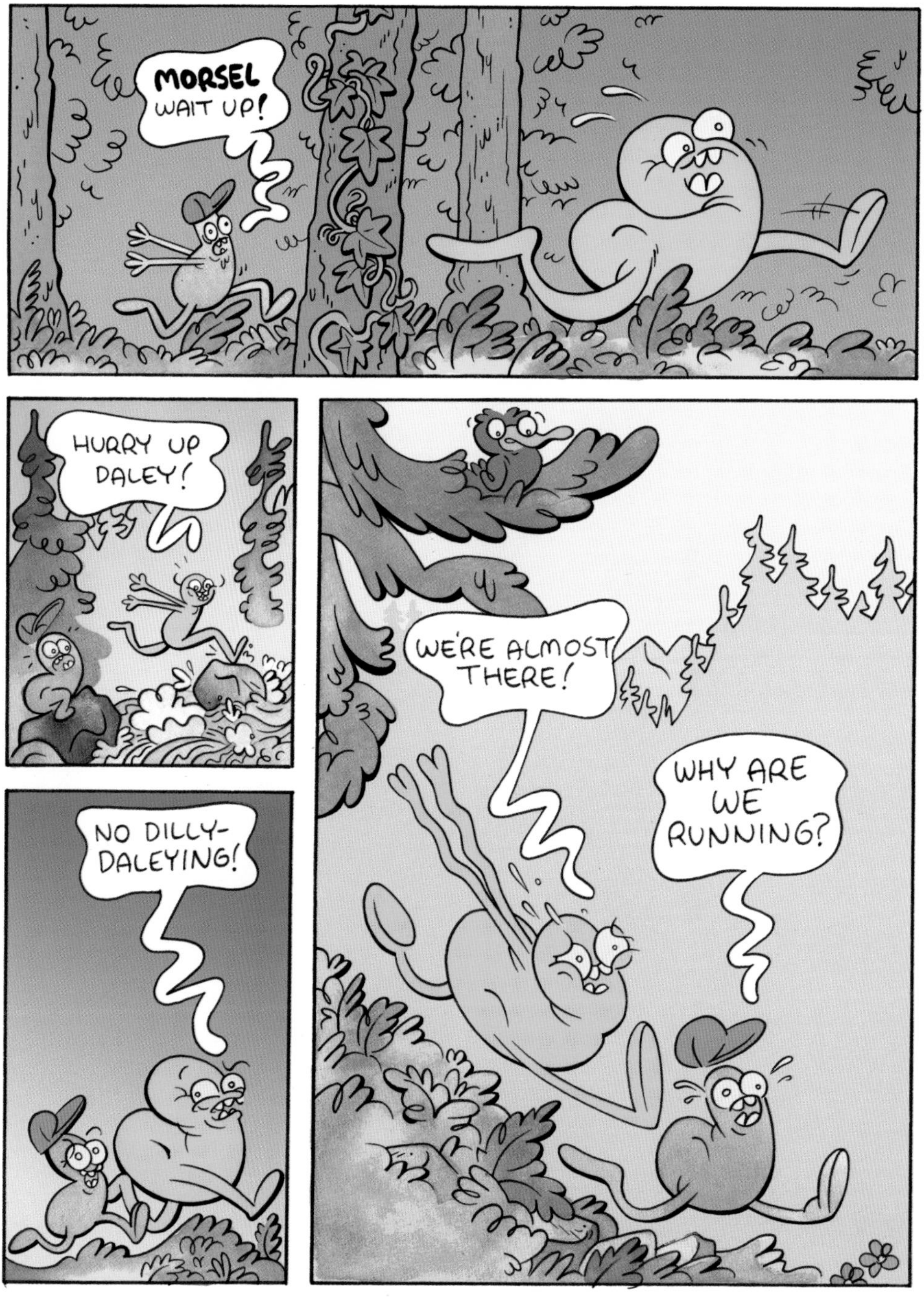
MORSEL WAIT UP!
HURRY UP DALEY!
NO DILLY-DALEYING!
WE'RE ALMOST THERE!
WHY ARE WE RUNNING?

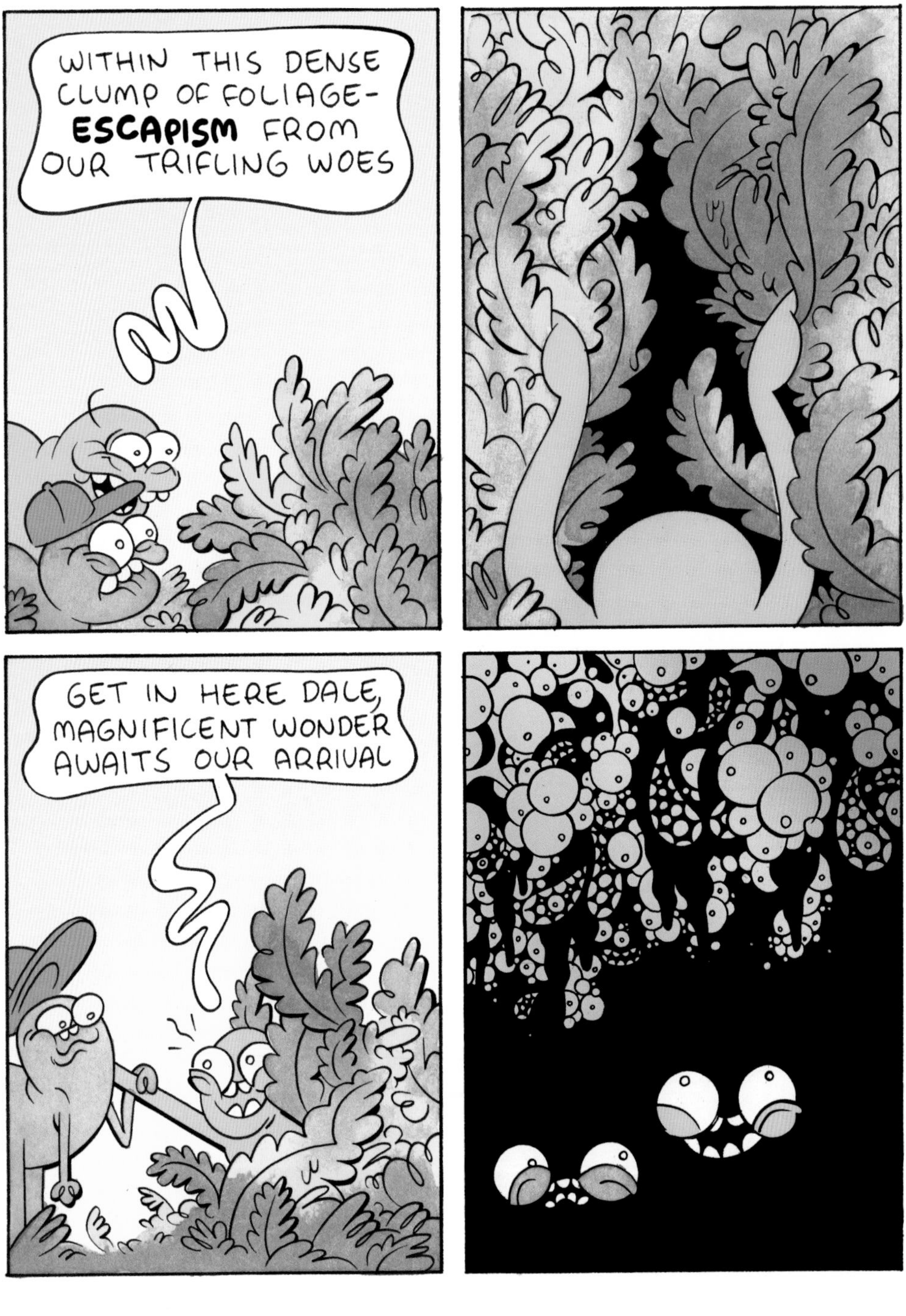
WITHIN THIS DENSE CLUMP OF FOLIAGE- **ESCAPISM** FROM OUR TRIFLING WOES
GET IN HERE DALE, MAGNIFICENT WONDER AWAITS OUR ARRIVAL

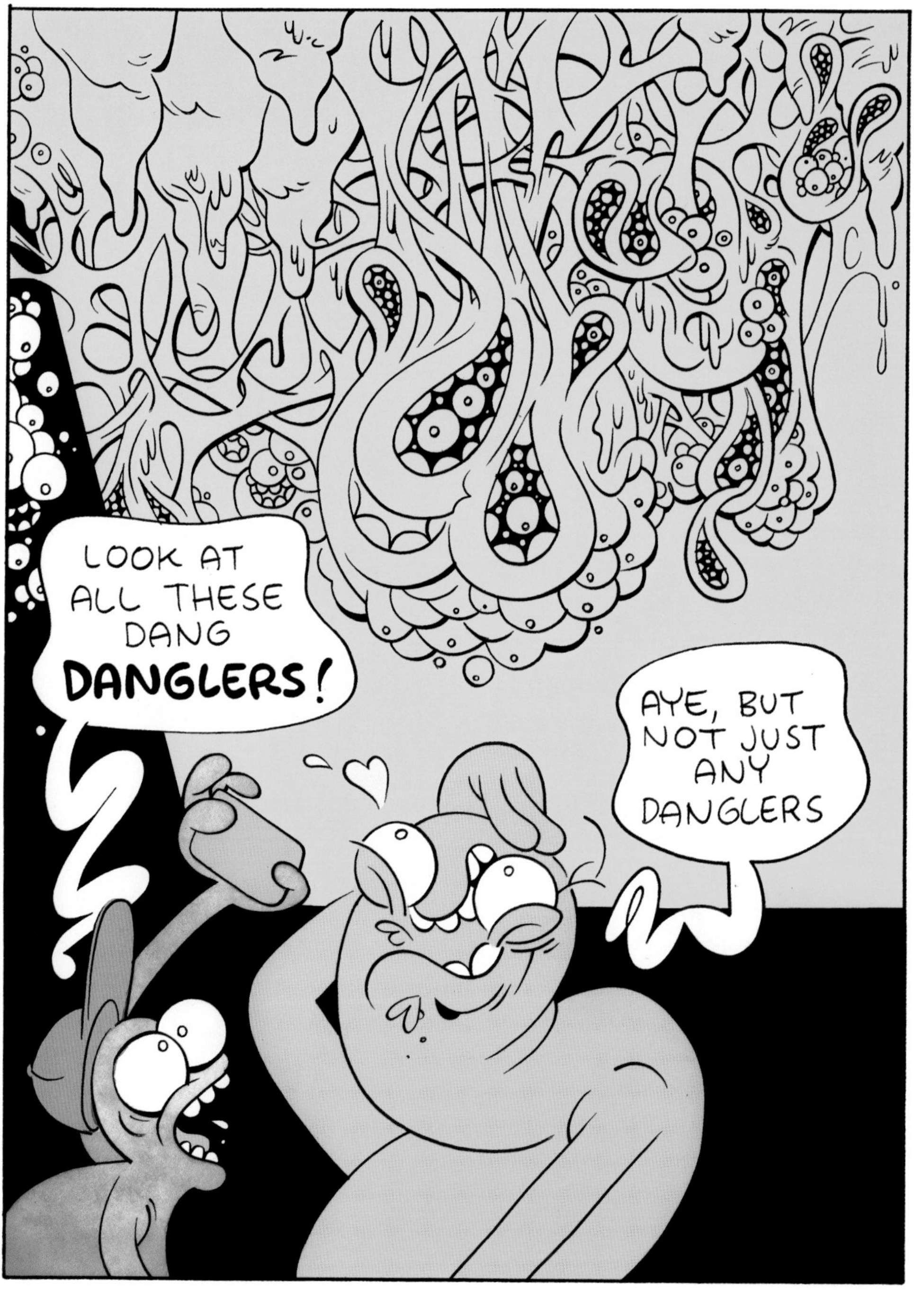
LOOK AT ALL THESE DANG **DANGLERS**!
AYE, BUT NOT JUST ANY DANGLERS

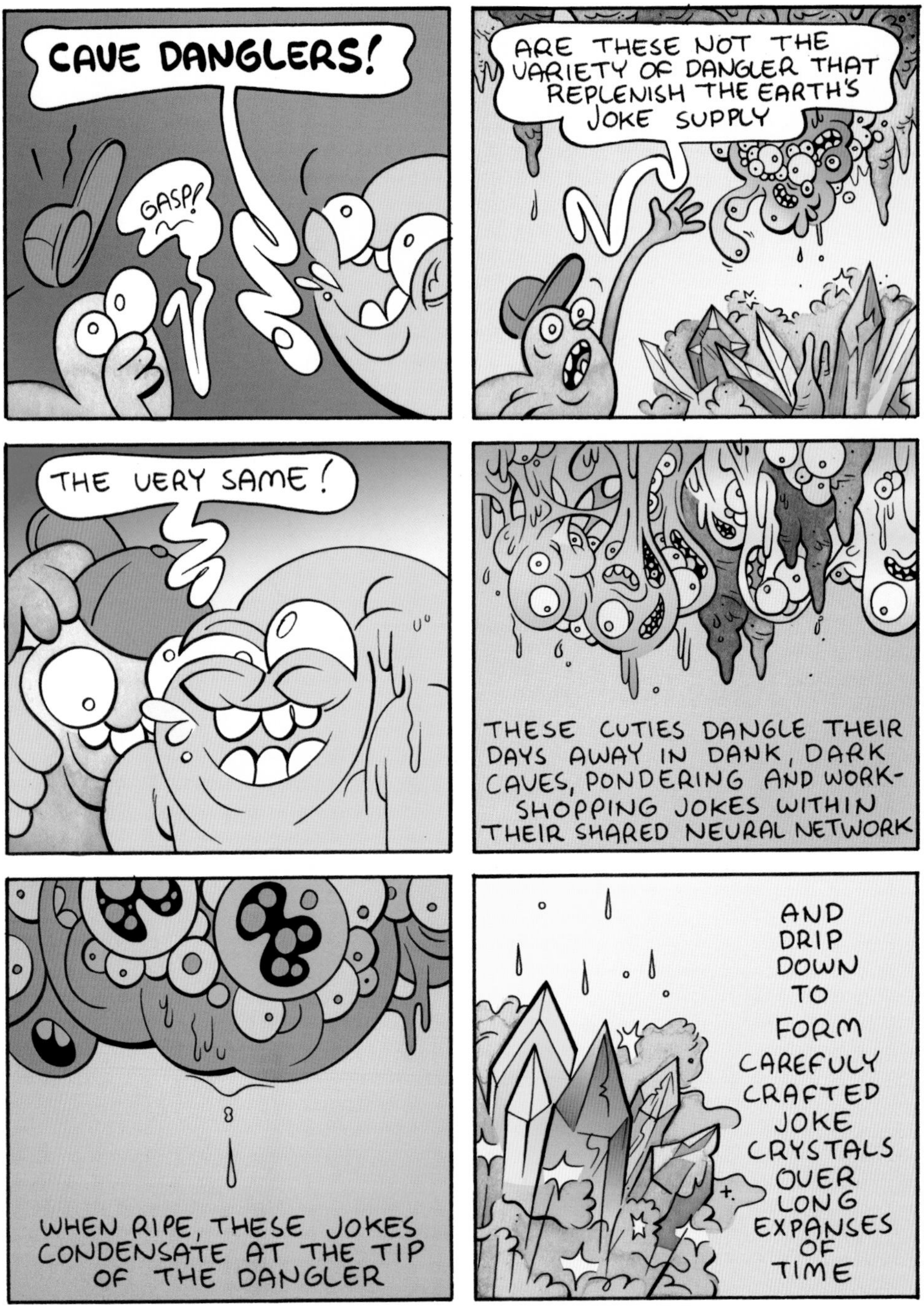
CAVE DANGLERS!
GASP!
ARE THESE NOT THE VARIETY OF DANGLER THAT REPLENISH THE EARTH'S JOKE SUPPLY
THE VERY SAME!
THESE CUTIES DANGLE THEIR DAYS AWAY IN DANK, DARK CAVES, PONDERING AND WORK-SHOPPING JOKES WITHIN THEIR SHARED NEURAL NETWORK
WHEN RIPE, THESE JOKES CONDENSATE AT THE TIP OF THE DANGLER
AND DRIP DOWN TO FORM CAREFULY CRAFTED JOKE CRYSTALS OVER LONG EXPANSES OF TIME

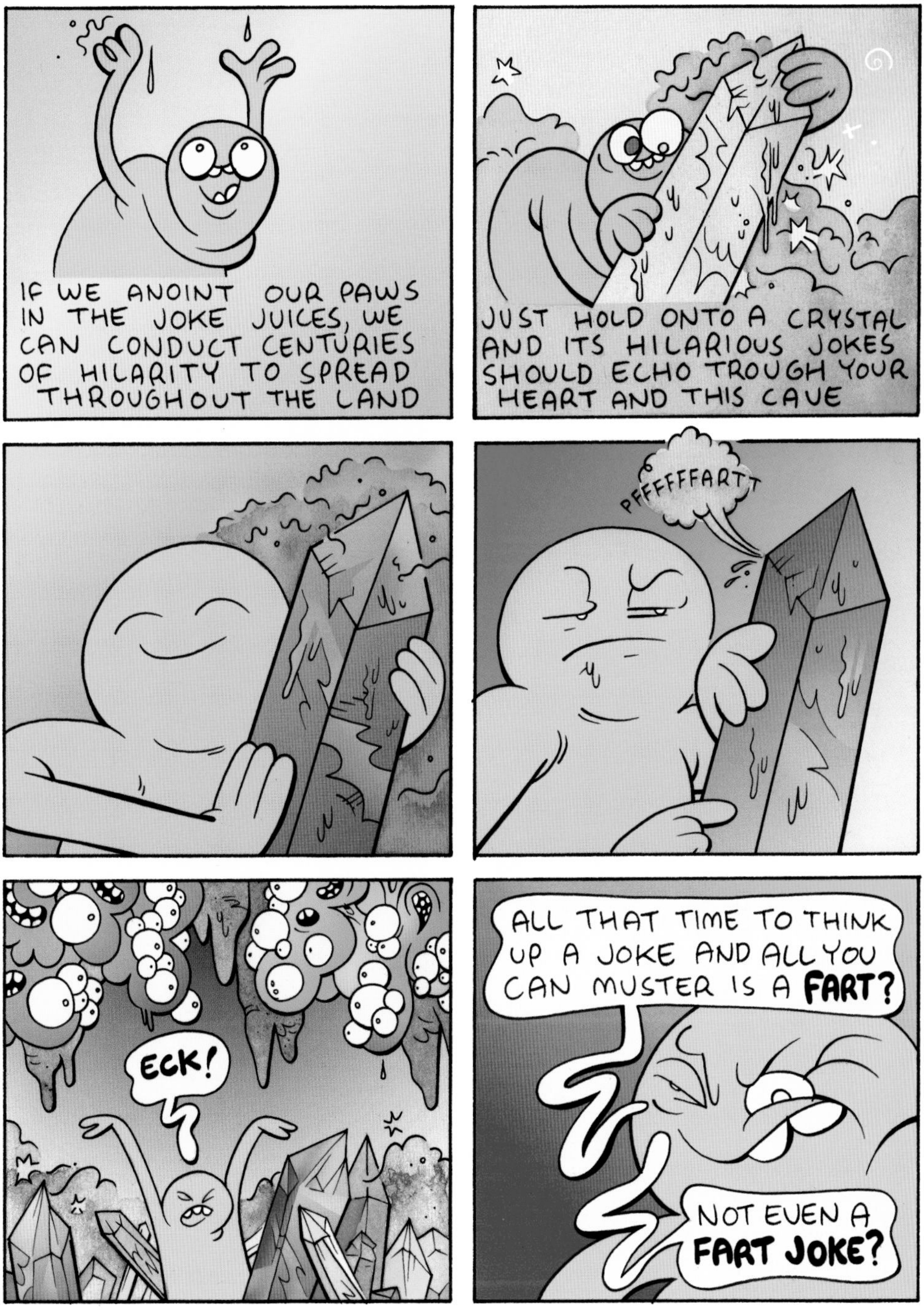
IF WE ANOINT OUR PAWS IN THE JOKE JUICES, WE CAN CONDUCT CENTURIES OF HILARITY TO SPREAD THROUGHOUT THE LAND
JUST HOLD ONTO A CRYSTAL AND ITS HILARIOUS JOKES SHOULD ECHO TROUGH YOUR HEART AND THIS CAVE
PFFFFFFARTT
ECK!
ALL THAT TIME TO THINK UP A JOKE AND ALL YOU CAN MUSTER IS A FART?
NOT EVEN A FART JOKE?

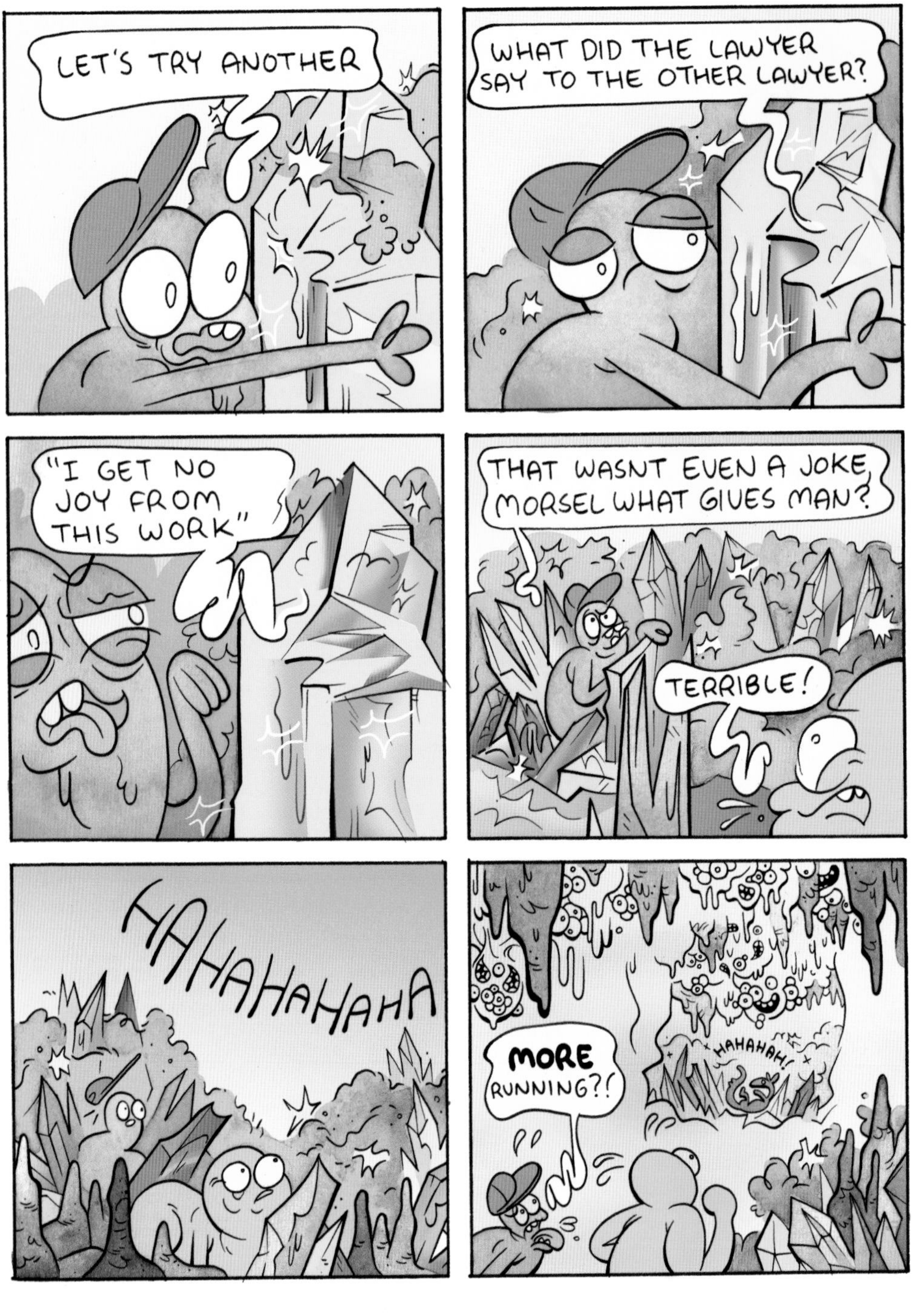
LET'S TRY ANOTHER
WHAT DID THE LAWYER SAY TO THE OTHER LAWYER?
"I GET NO JOY FROM THIS WORK"
THAT WASNT EVEN A JOKE, MORSEL WHAT GIVES MAN?
TERRIBLE!
HAHAHAHAHAHA
MORE RUNNING?!
HAHAHAH!

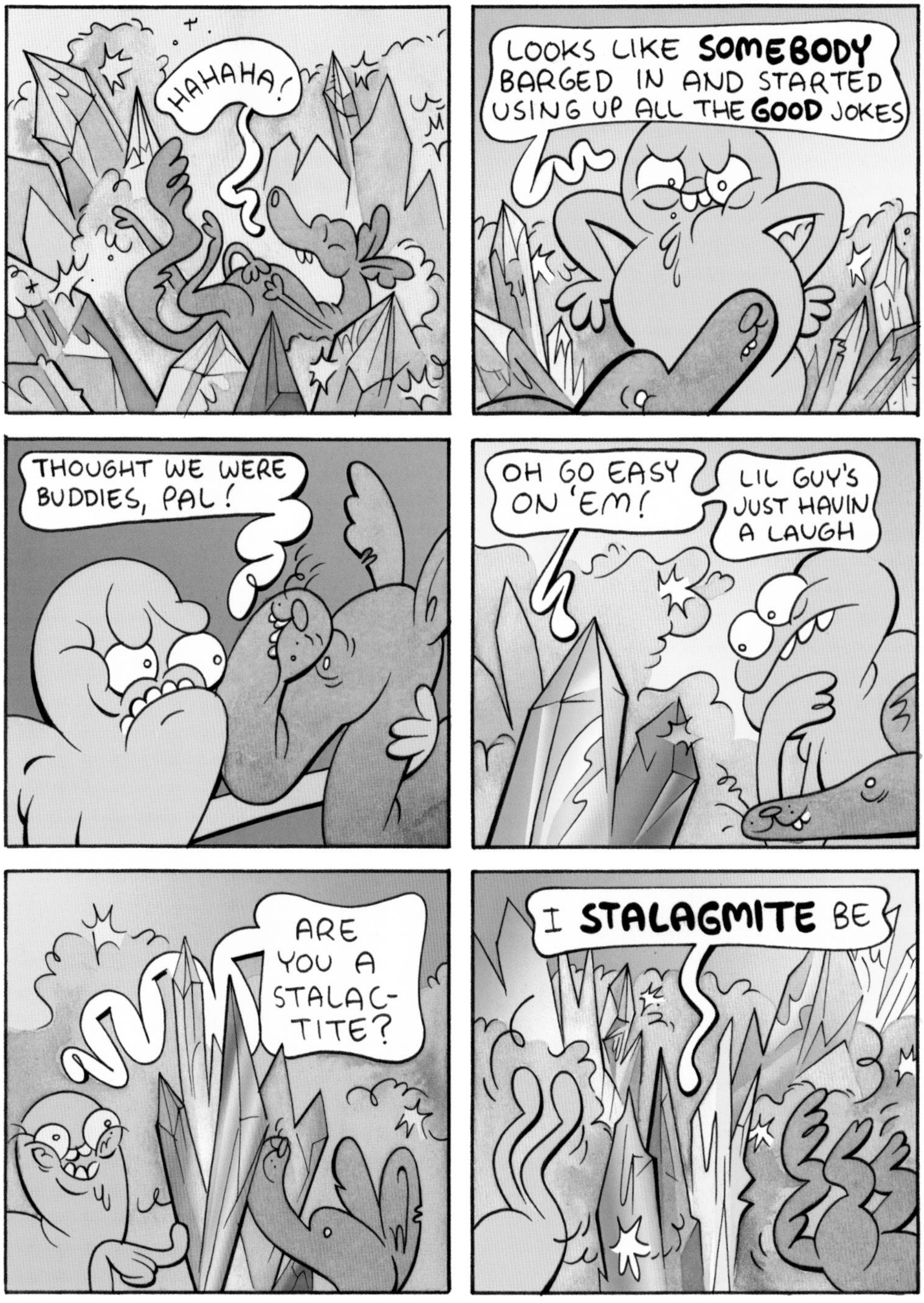
HAHAHA!
LOOKS LIKE SOMEBODY BARGED IN AND STARTED USING UP ALL THE GOOD JOKES
THOUGHT WE WERE BUDDIES, PAL!
OH GO EASY ON 'EM!
LIL GUY'S JUST HAVIN A LAUGH
ARE YOU A STALAC-TITE?
I STALAGMITE BE

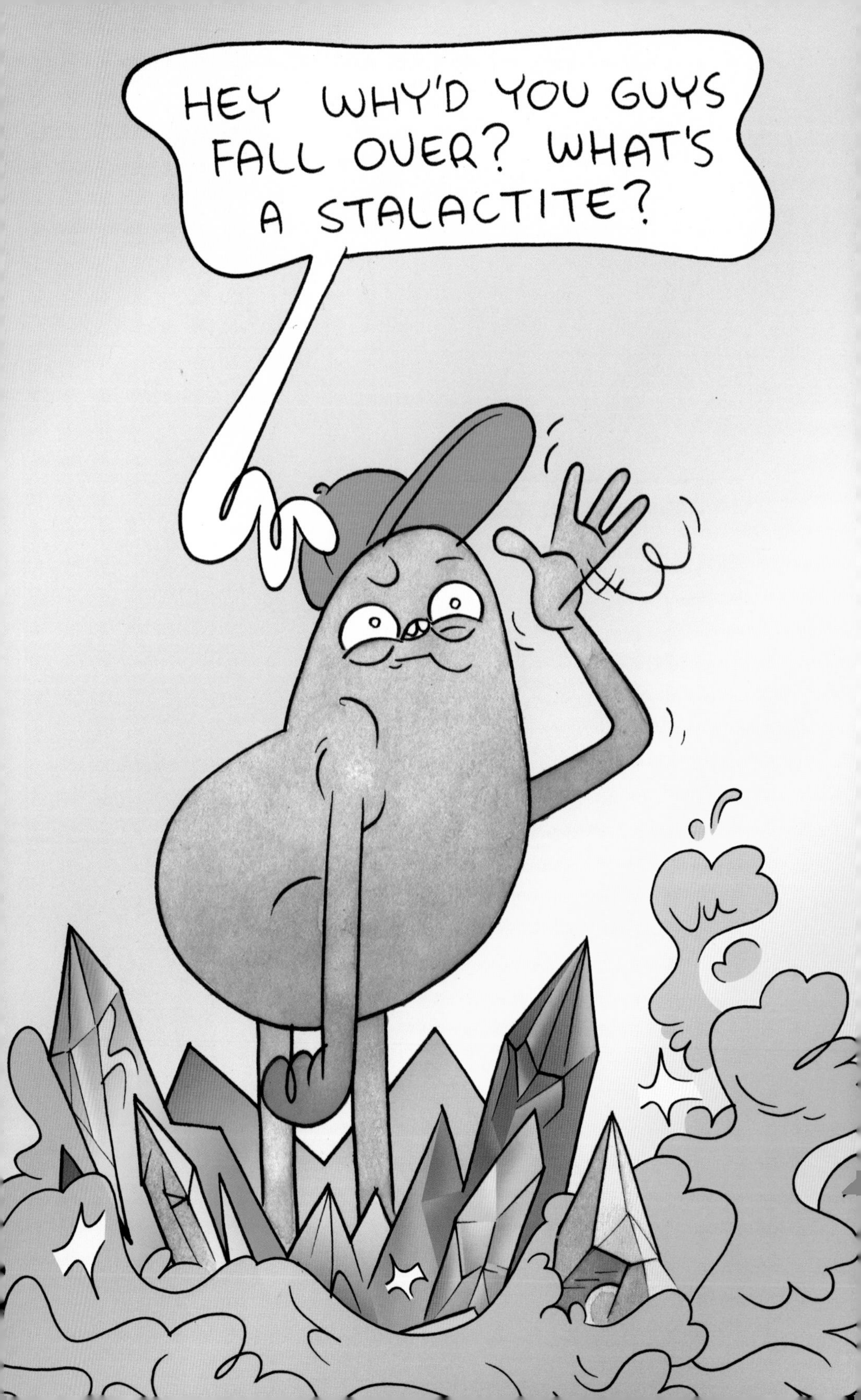
HEY WHY'D YOU GUYS FALL OVER? WHAT'S A STALACTITE?

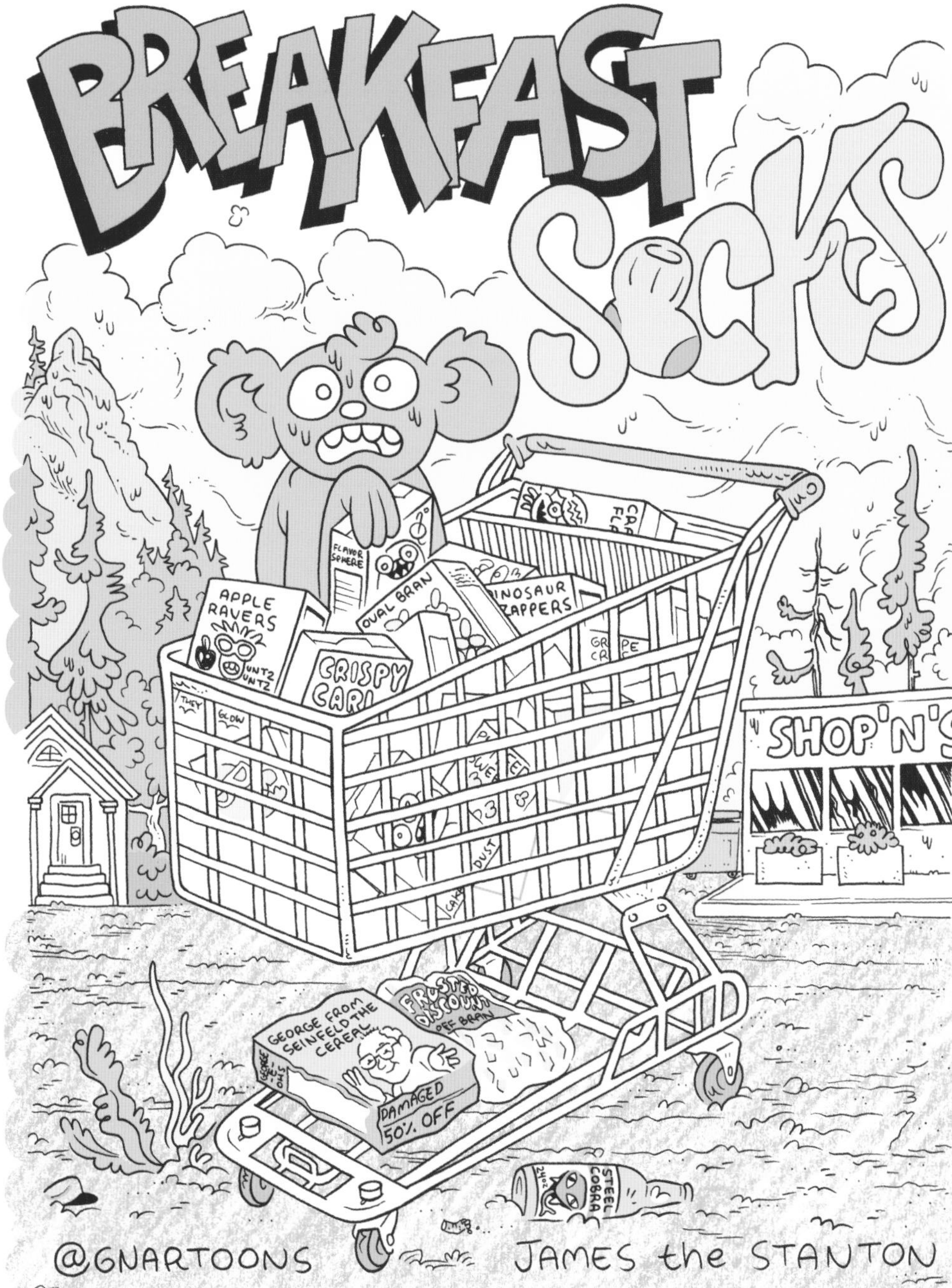
BREAKFAST
SOCKS
APPLE RAVERS
UNTZ UNTZ
FLAVOR SPHERE
OVAL BRAN
INOSAUR ZAPPERS
CRISPY CARL
SHOP'N'S
GEORGE FROM SEINFELD THE CEREAL
DAMAGED 50% OFF
FROSTED DISCOUNT
STEEL COBRA
@GNARTOONS
JAMES the STANTON

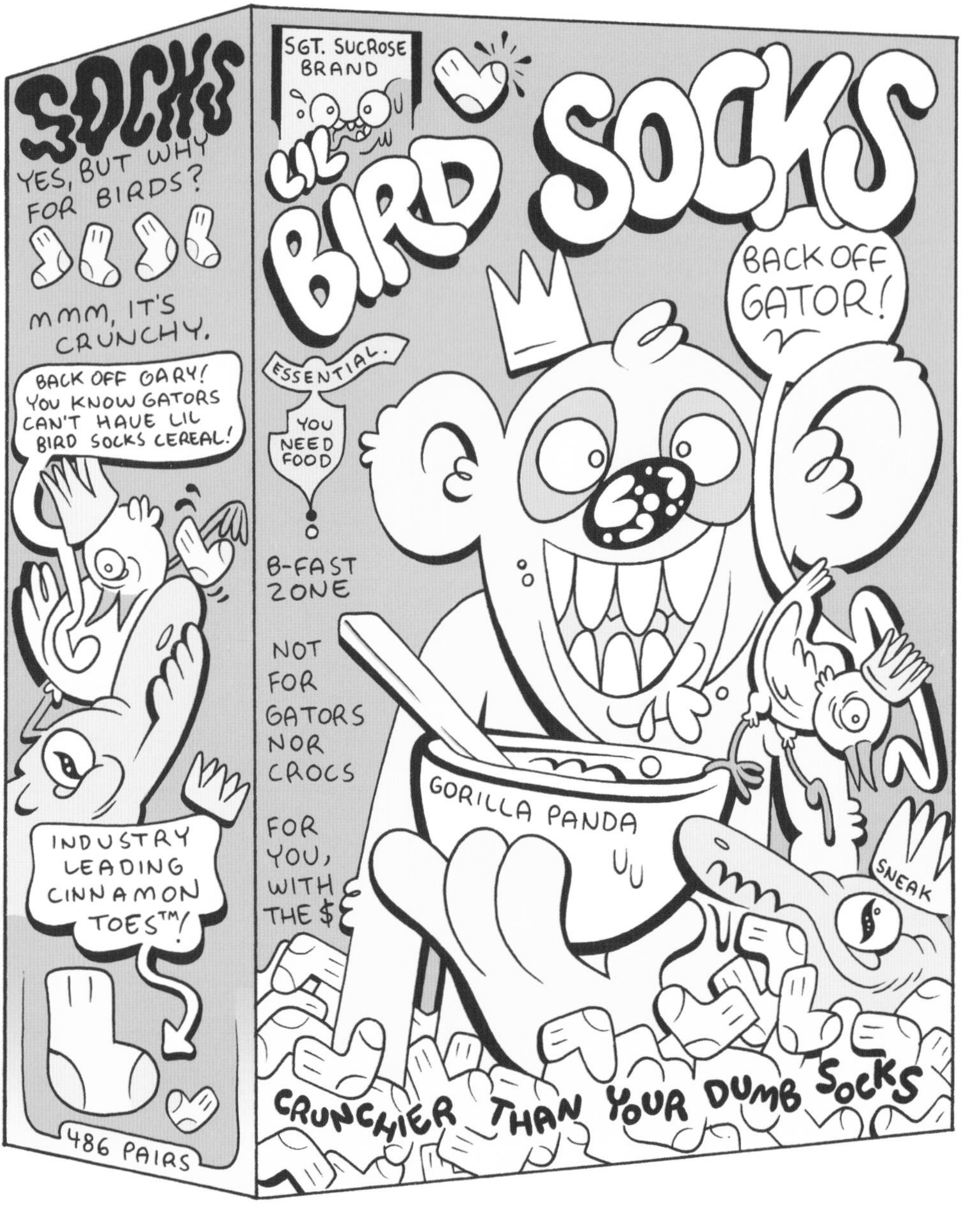
SOCKS
YES, BUT WHY FOR BIRDS?
mmm, IT'S CRUNCHY.
BACK OFF GARY! YOU KNOW GATORS CAN'T HAVE LIL BIRD SOCKS CEREAL!
INDUSTRY LEADING CINNAMON TOES™!
486 PAIRS
SGT. SUCROSE BRAND
LIL BIRD SOCKS
ESSENTIAL.
YOU NEED FOOD
B-FAST ZONE
NOT FOR GATORS NOR CROCS
FOR YOU, WITH THE $
BACK OFF GATOR!
GORILLA PANDA
SNEAK
CRUNCHIER THAN YOUR DUMB SOCKS

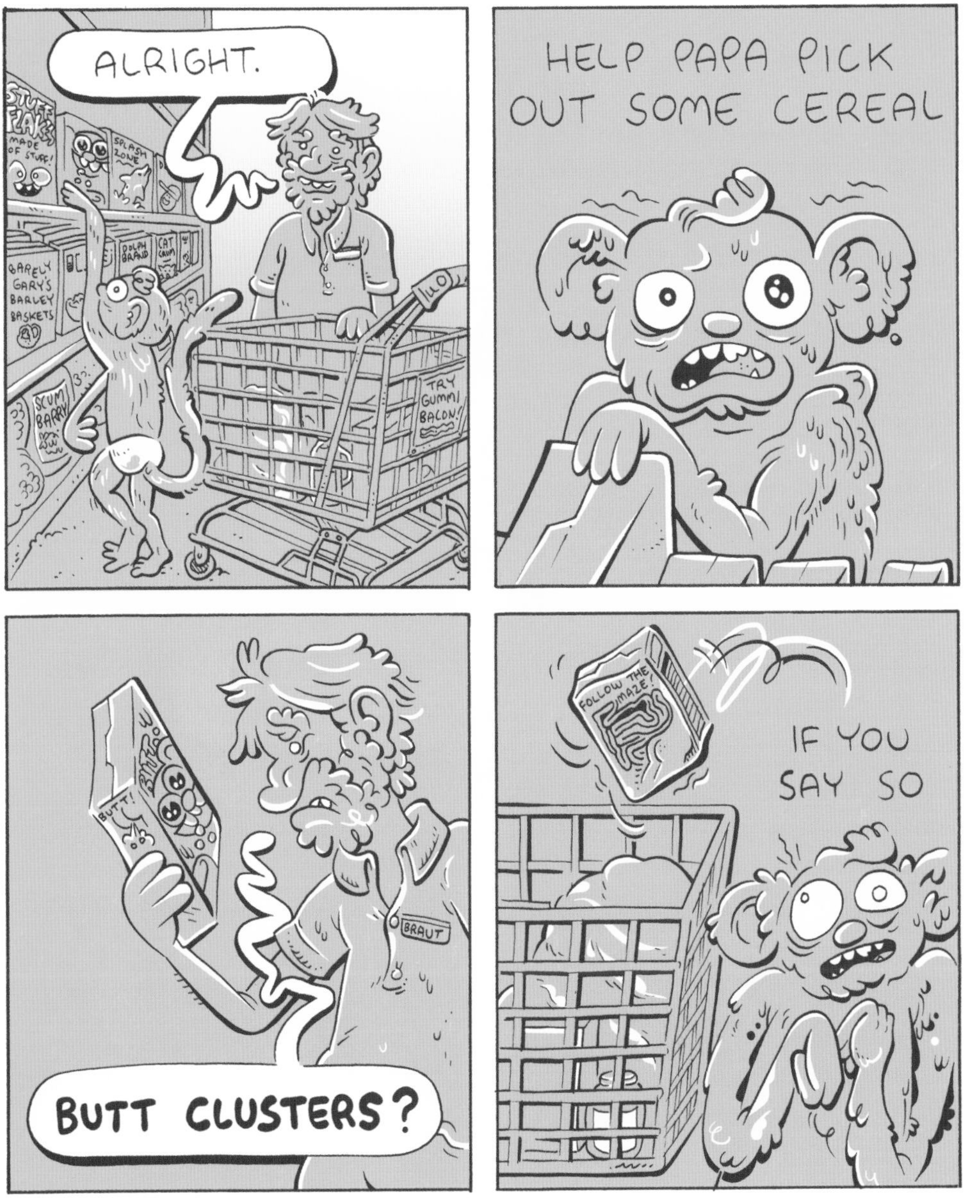
ALRIGHT.
STUFF FLAKES
MADE OF STUFF!
SPLASH ZONE
DOLPH BRAND
BARELY GARY'S BARLEY BASKETS
SCUM BARRY
TRY GUMMI BACON!
HELP PAPA PICK OUT SOME CEREAL
BUTT!
BRAUT
BUTT CLUSTERS?
FOLLOW THE MAZE!
IF YOU SAY SO

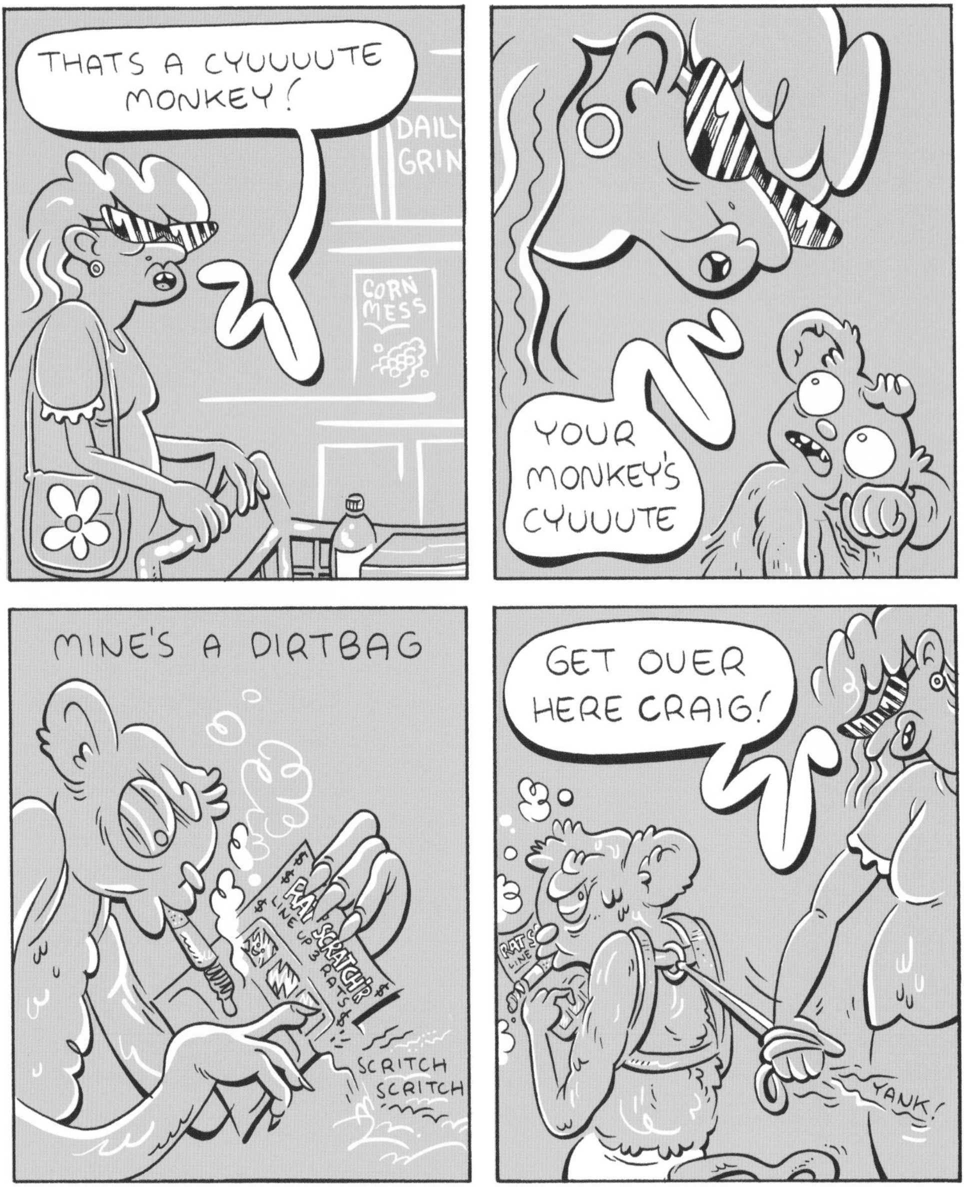
THATS A CYUUUUTE MONKEY!
DAILY GRIN
CORN MESS
YOUR MONKEY'S CYUUUTE
MINE'S A DIRTBAG
RAT SCRATCH'R
LINE UP 3 RATS
SCRITCH SCRITCH
GET OUER HERE CRAIG!
YANK!

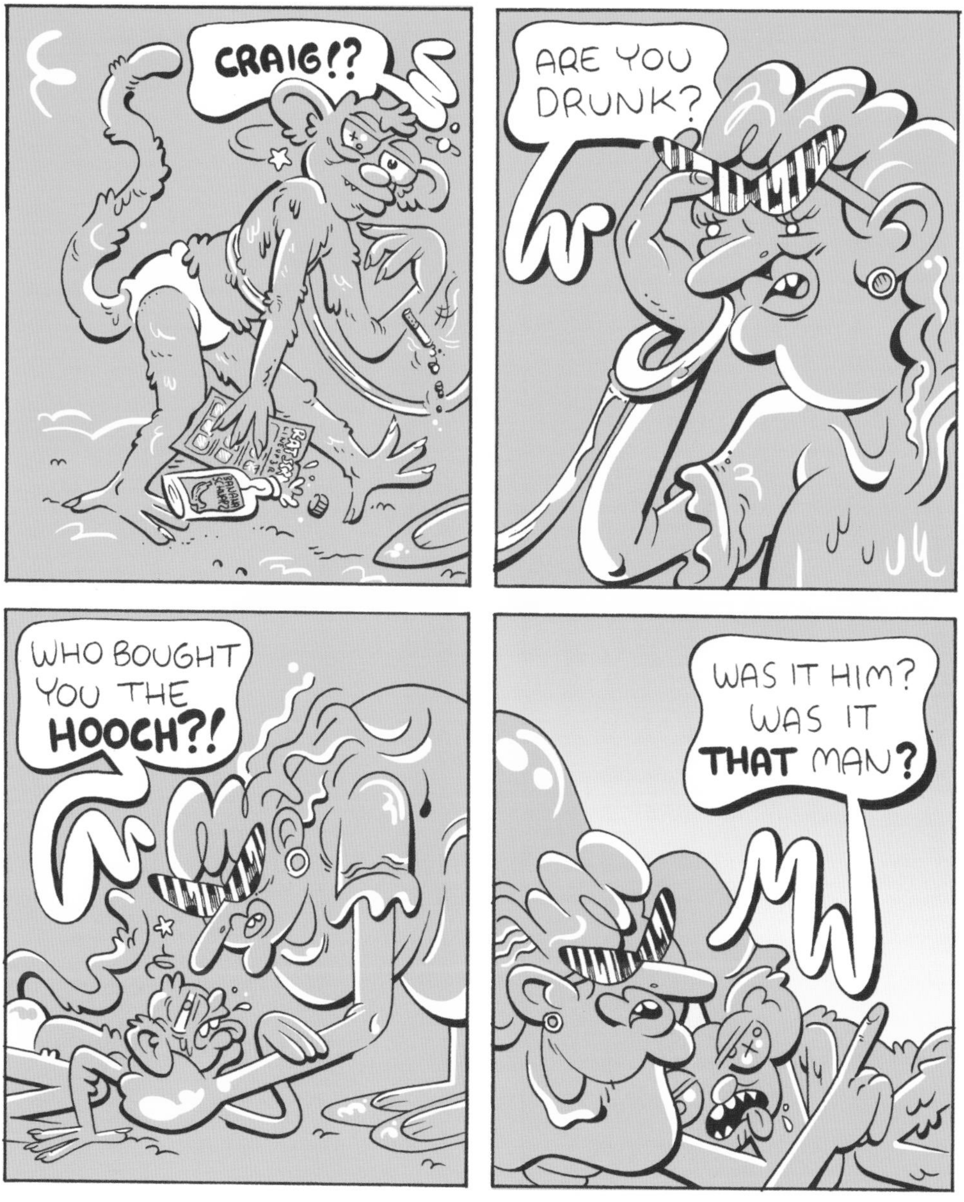
CRAIG!?
ARE YOU DRUNK?
WHO BOUGHT YOU THE **HOOCH?!**
WAS IT HIM? WAS IT **THAT** MAN?

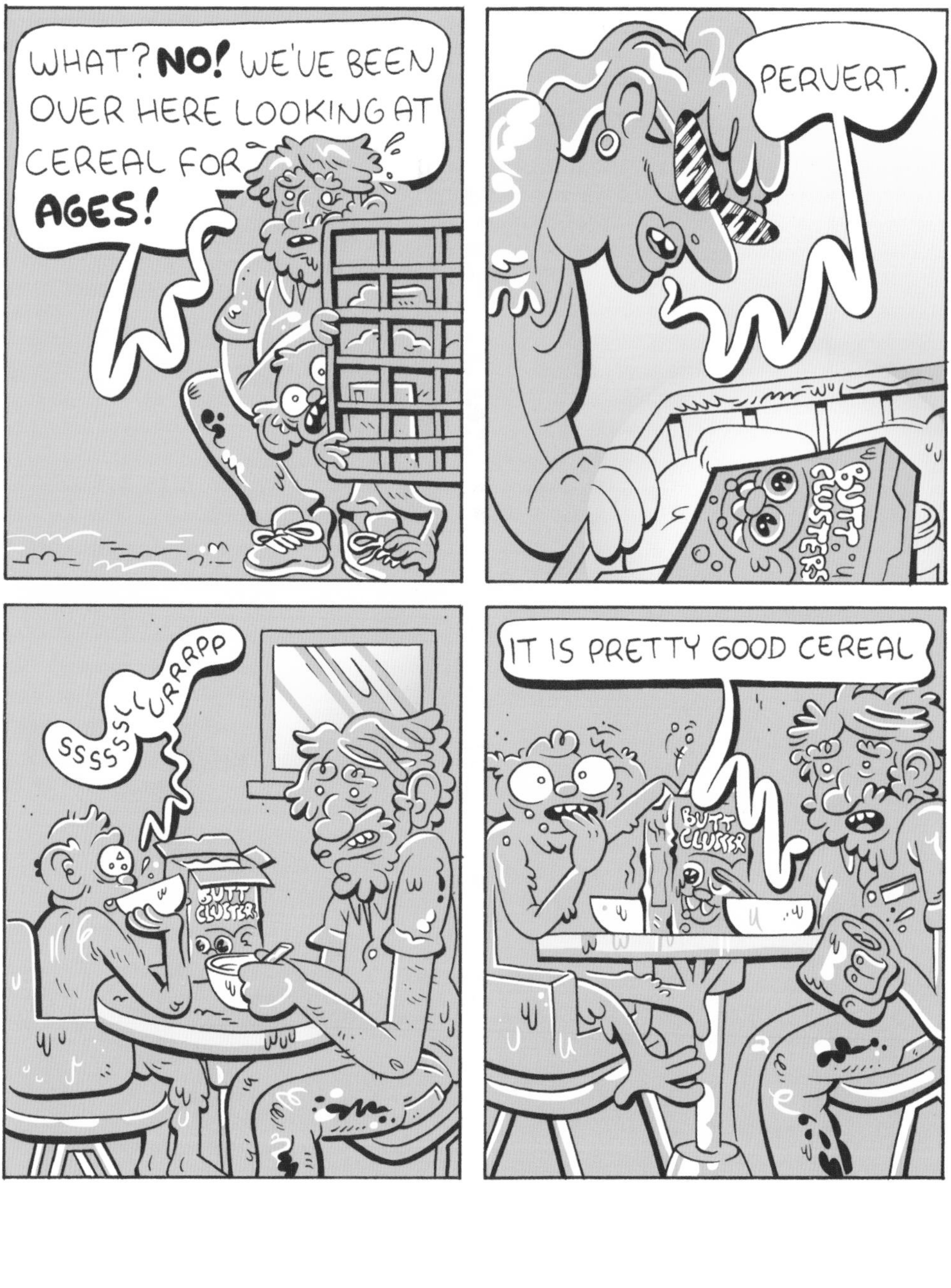
WHAT? NO! WE'VE BEEN OVER HERE LOOKING AT CEREAL FOR AGES!
PERVERT.
BUTT CLUSTERS
SSSSSSLLURRRPP
BUTT CLUSTER
IT IS PRETTY GOOD CEREAL
BUTT CLUSTER

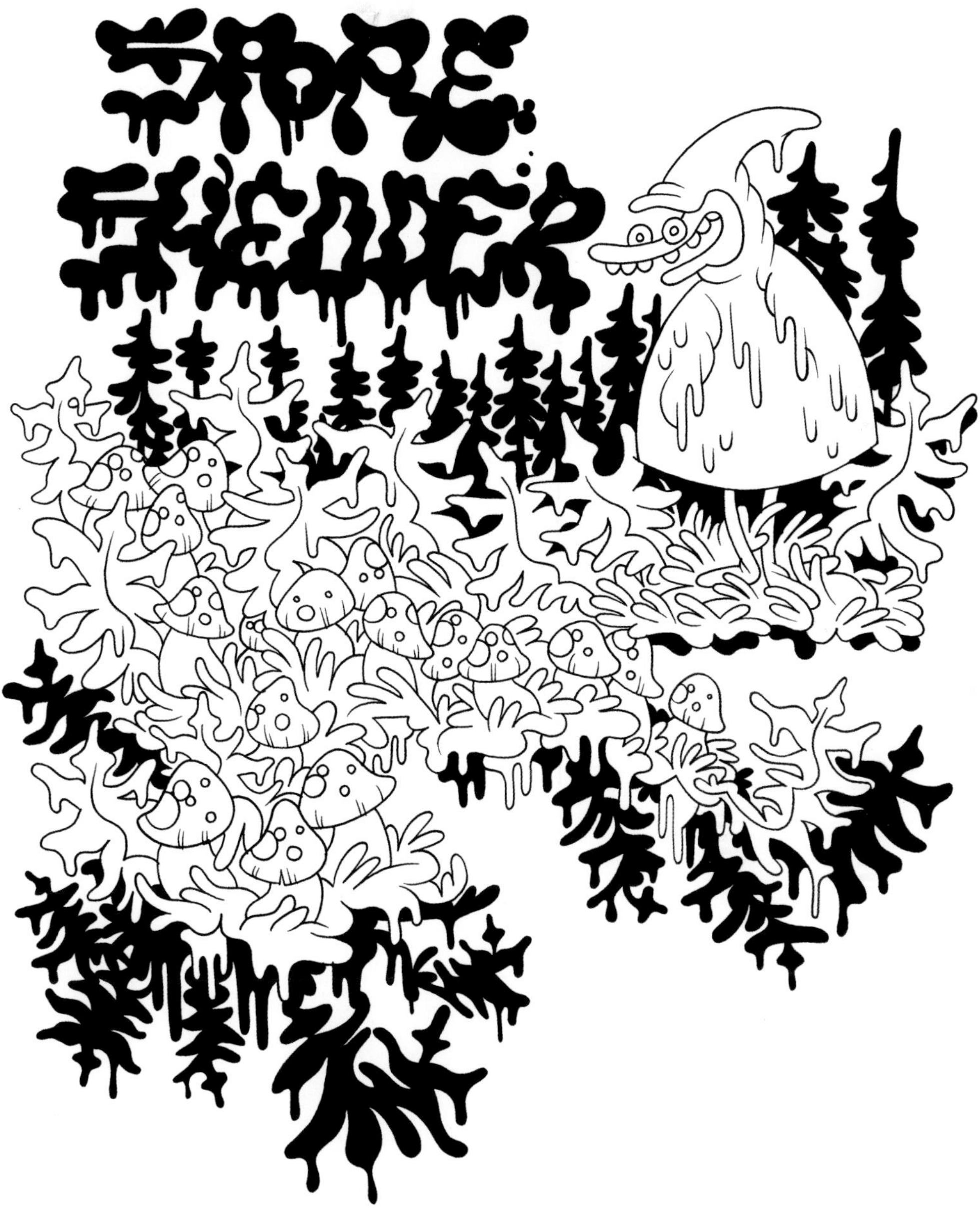
SPORE SHEDDER

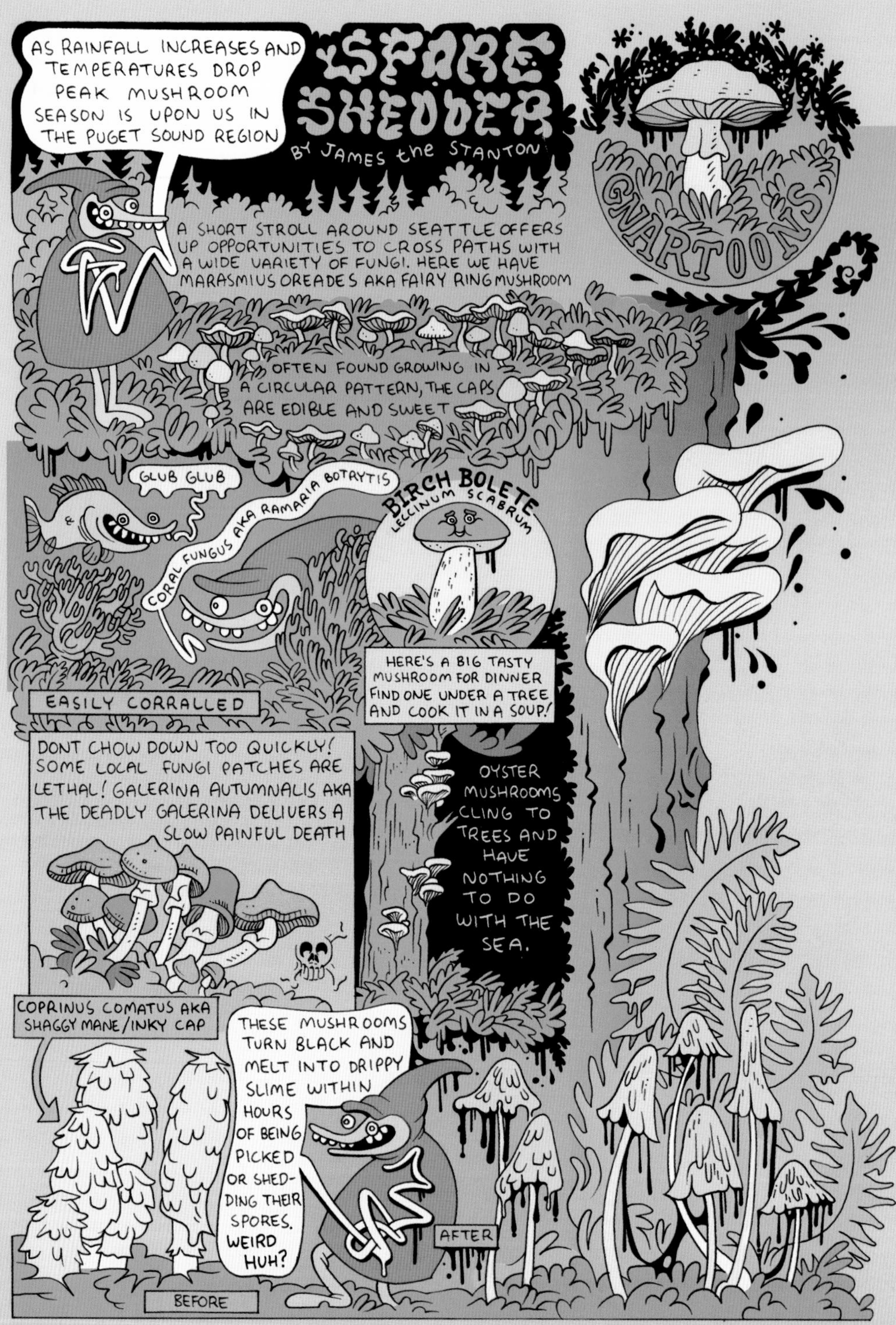
AS RAINFALL INCREASES AND TEMPERATURES DROP PEAK MUSHROOM SEASON IS UPON US IN THE PUGET SOUND REGION
SPORE SHEDDER
BY JAMES the STANTON
GNARTOONS
A SHORT STROLL AROUND SEATTLE OFFERS UP OPPORTUNITIES TO CROSS PATHS WITH A WIDE VARIETY OF FUNGI. HERE WE HAVE MARASMIUS OREADES AKA FAIRY RING MUSHROOM
OFTEN FOUND GROWING IN A CIRCULAR PATTERN, THE CAPS ARE EDIBLE AND SWEET
GLUB GLUB
CORAL FUNGUS AKA RAMARIA BOTRYTIS
BIRCH BOLETE
LECCINUM SCABRUM
EASILY CORRALLED
HERE'S A BIG TASTY MUSHROOM FOR DINNER FIND ONE UNDER A TREE AND COOK IT IN A SOUP!
DONT CHOW DOWN TOO QUICKLY! SOME LOCAL FUNGI PATCHES ARE LETHAL! GALERINA AUTUMNALIS AKA THE DEADLY GALERINA DELIVERS A SLOW PAINFUL DEATH
OYSTER MUSHROOMS CLING TO TREES AND HAVE NOTHING TO DO WITH THE SEA.
COPRINUS COMATUS AKA SHAGGY MANE/INKY CAP
THESE MUSHROOMS TURN BLACK AND MELT INTO DRIPPY SLIME WITHIN HOURS OF BEING PICKED OR SHEDDING THEIR SPORES. WEIRD HUH?
AFTER
BEFORE

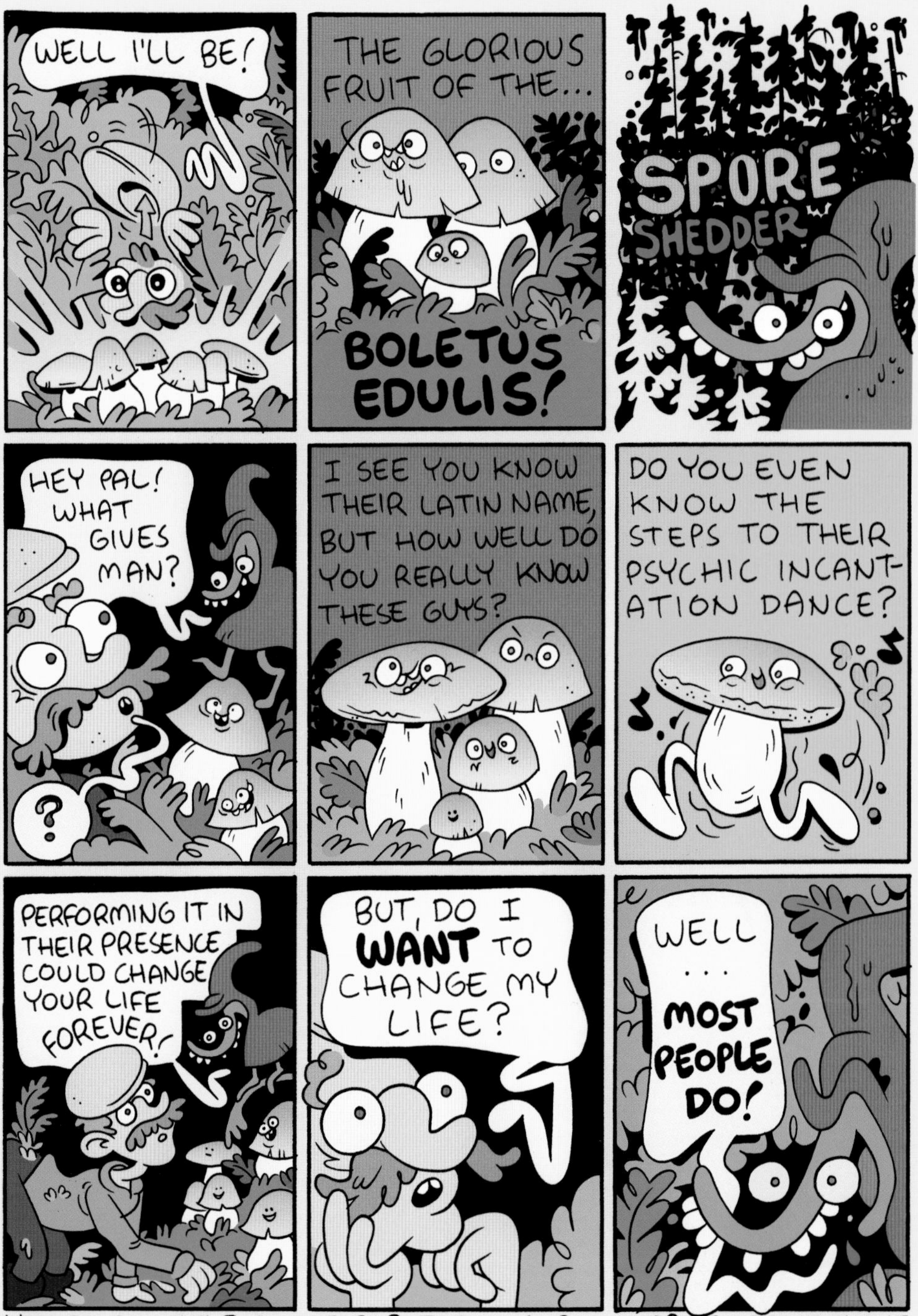
WELL I'LL BE!
THE GLORIOUS FRUIT OF THE...
BOLETUS EDULIS!
SPORE SHEDDER
HEY PAL! WHAT GIVES MAN?
?
I SEE YOU KNOW THEIR LATIN NAME, BUT HOW WELL DO YOU REALLY KNOW THESE GUYS?
DO YOU EVEN KNOW THE STEPS TO THEIR PSYCHIC INCANTATION DANCE?
PERFORMING IT IN THEIR PRESENCE COULD CHANGE YOUR LIFE FOREVER!
BUT, DO I **WANT** TO CHANGE MY LIFE?
WELL ... **MOST PEOPLE DO!**

YOU DO A LITTLE DANCE FOR THE MUSHROOM - OR YOU DON'T PICK IT

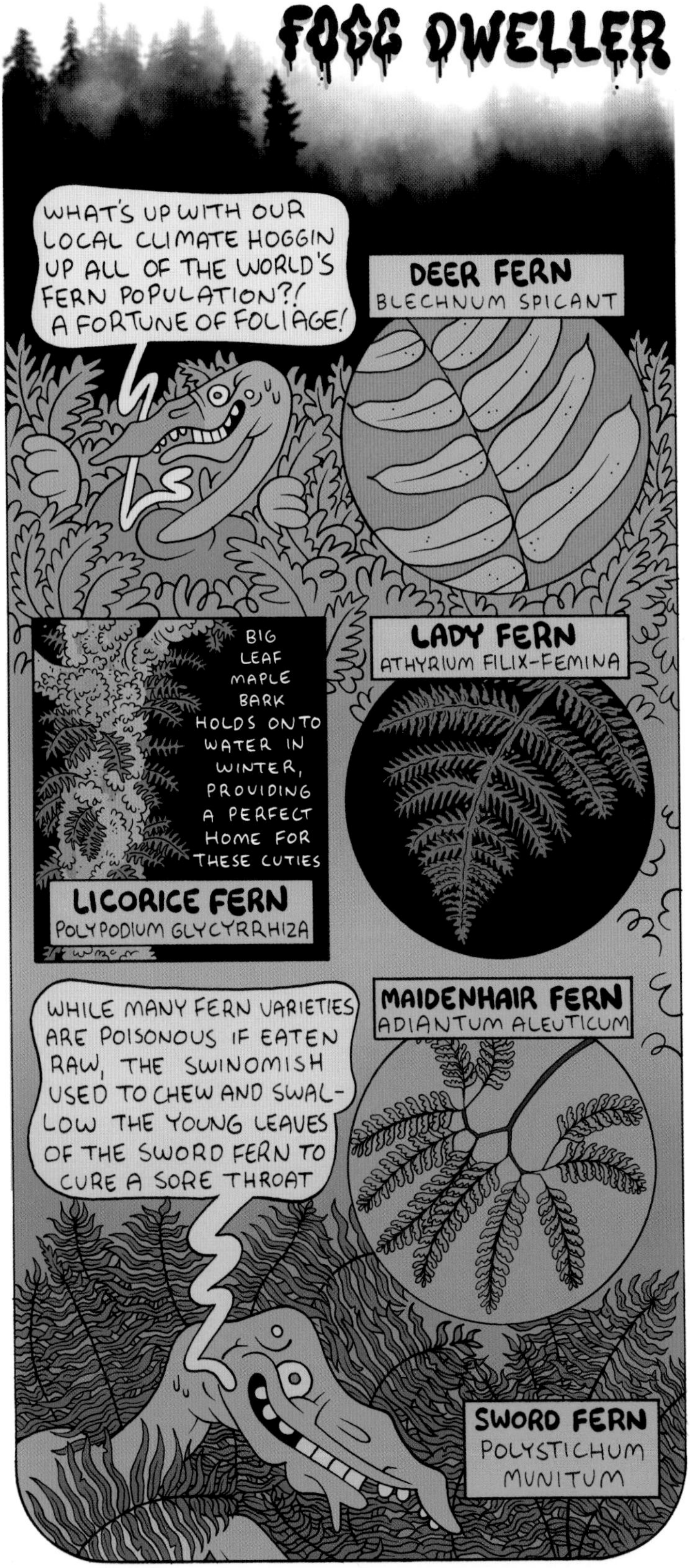
FOGG DWELLER
WHAT'S UP WITH OUR LOCAL CLIMATE HOGGIN UP ALL OF THE WORLD'S FERN POPULATION?! A FORTUNE OF FOLIAGE!
DEER FERN
BLECHNUM SPICANT
BIG LEAF MAPLE BARK HOLDS ONTO WATER IN WINTER, PROVIDING A PERFECT HOME FOR THESE CUTIES
LICORICE FERN
POLYPODIUM GLYCYRRHIZA
LADY FERN
ATHYRIUM FILIX-FEMINA
WHILE MANY FERN VARIETIES ARE POISONOUS IF EATEN RAW, THE SWINOMISH USED TO CHEW AND SWALLOW THE YOUNG LEAVES OF THE SWORD FERN TO CURE A SORE THROAT
MAIDENHAIR FERN
ADIANTUM ALEUTICUM
SWORD FERN
POLYSTICHUM MUNITUM

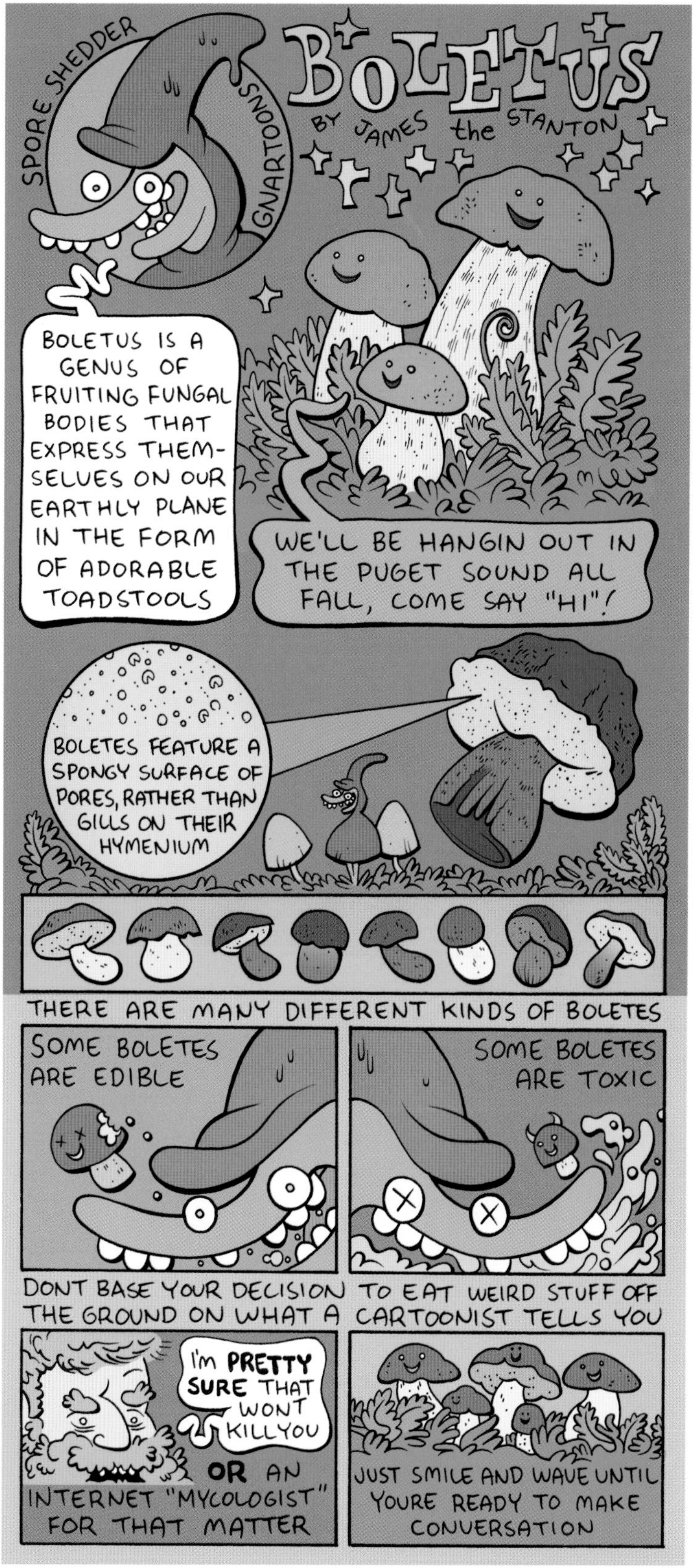

SPORE SHEDDER GNARTOONS
BOLETUS
BY JAMES the STANTON
BOLETUS IS A GENUS OF FRUITING FUNGAL BODIES THAT EXPRESS THEMSELVES ON OUR EARTHLY PLANE IN THE FORM OF ADORABLE TOADSTOOLS
WE'LL BE HANGIN OUT IN THE PUGET SOUND ALL FALL, COME SAY "HI"!
BOLETES FEATURE A SPONGY SURFACE OF PORES, RATHER THAN GILLS ON THEIR HYMENIUM
THERE ARE MANY DIFFERENT KINDS OF BOLETES
SOME BOLETES ARE EDIBLE
SOME BOLETES ARE TOXIC
DONT BASE YOUR DECISION TO EAT WEIRD STUFF OFF THE GROUND ON WHAT A CARTOONIST TELLS YOU
I'm PRETTY SURE THAT WONT KILLYOU
OR AN INTERNET "MYCOLOGIST" FOR THAT MATTER
JUST SMILE AND WAVE UNTIL YOURE READY TO MAKE CONVERSATION

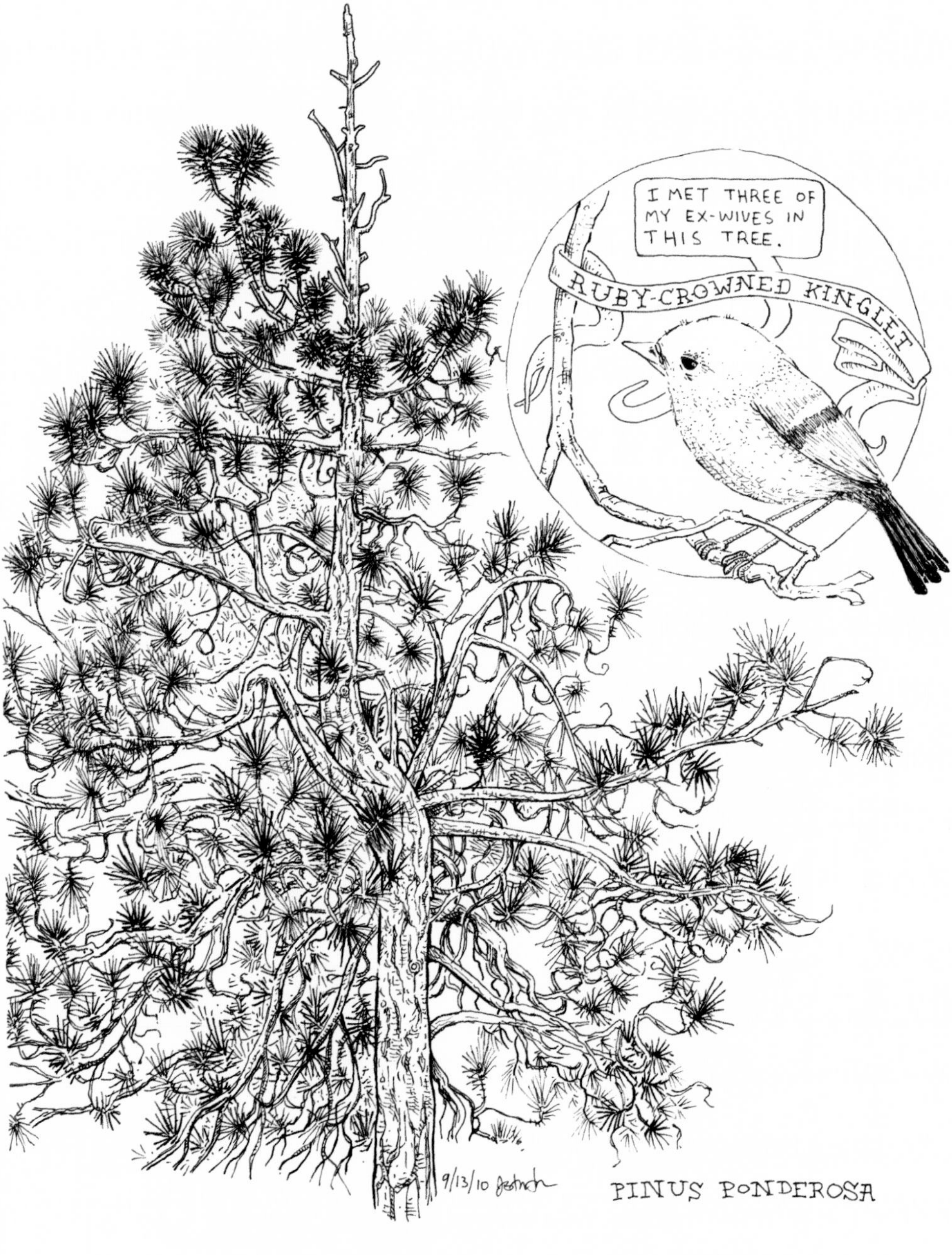
I MET THREE OF
MY EX-WIVES IN
THIS TREE.
RUBY-CROWNED KINGLET
9/13/10
PINUS PONDEROSA

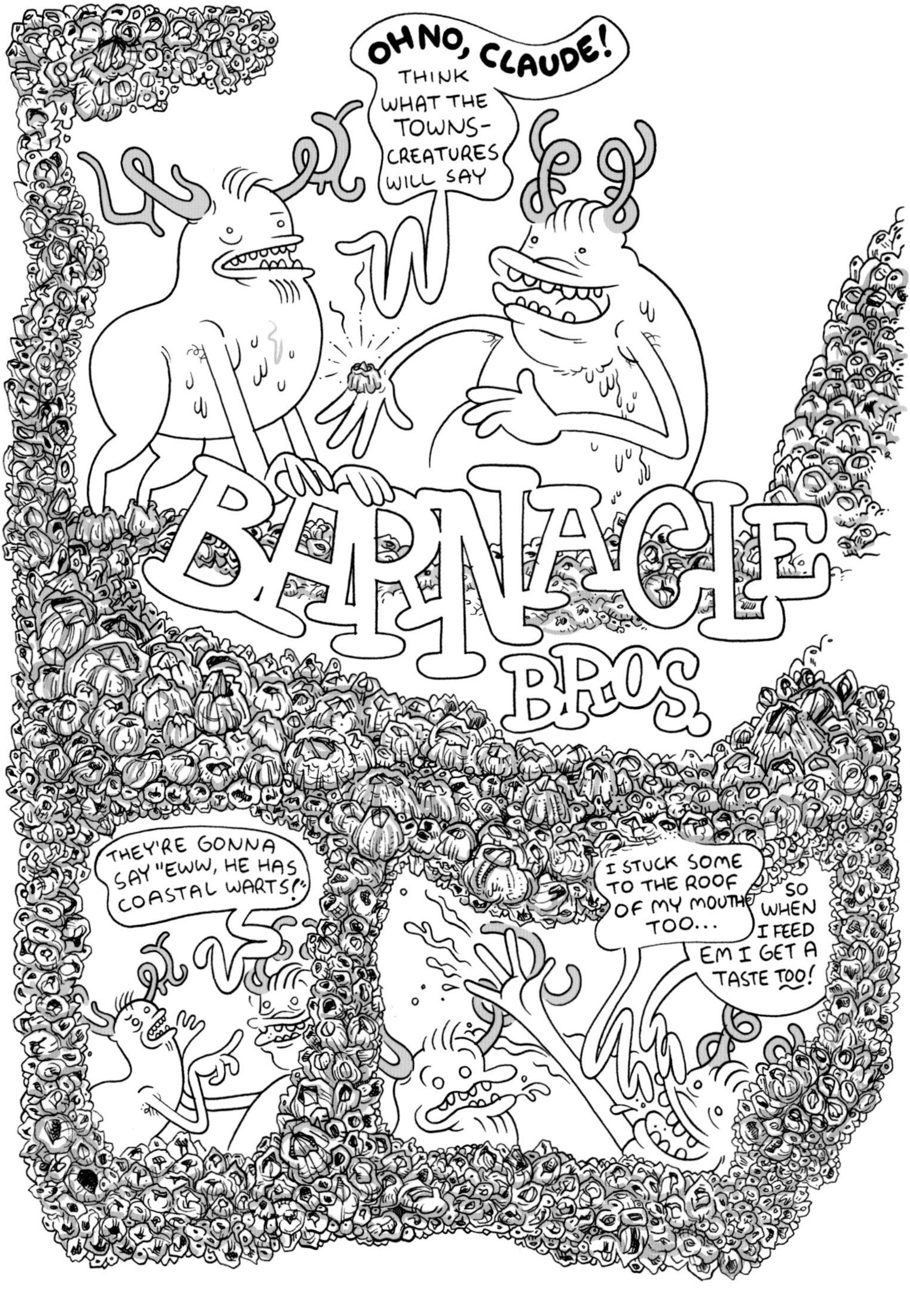
OH NO, CLAUDE! THINK WHAT THE TOWNS-CREATURES WILL SAY
BARNACLE BROS
THEY'RE GONNA SAY "EWW, HE HAS COASTAL WARTS!"
I STUCK SOME TO THE ROOF OF MY MOUTH TOO...
SO WHEN I FEED EM I GET A TASTE TOO!

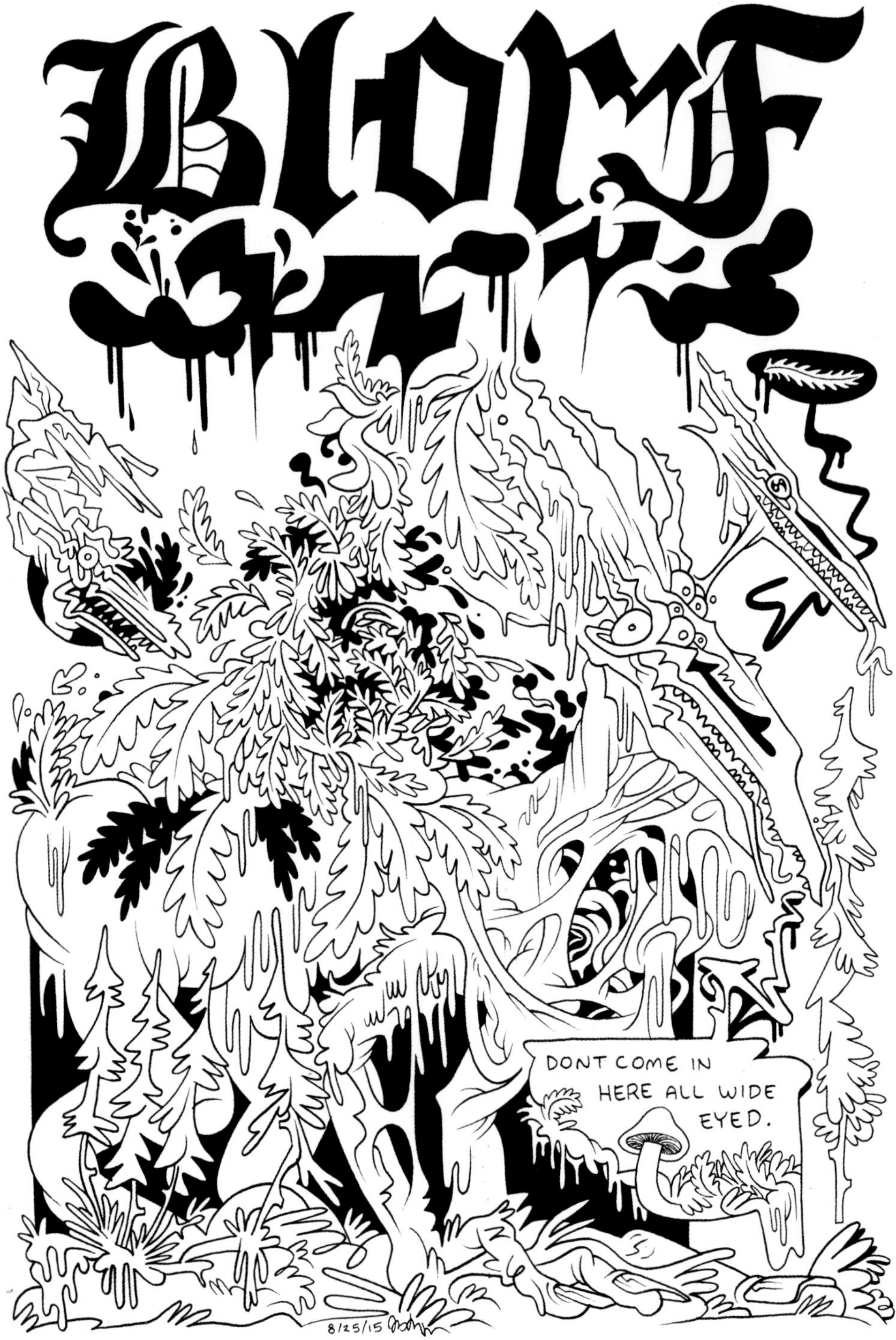
DONT COME IN
HERE ALL WIDE
EYED.
8/25/15

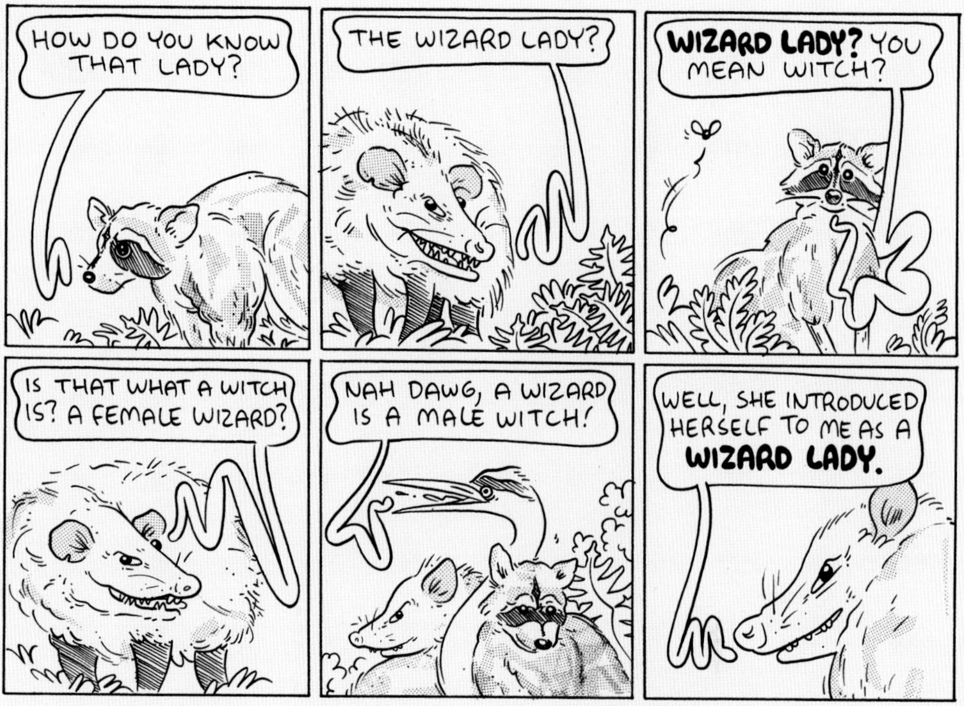
HOW DO YOU KNOW THAT LADY?
THE WIZARD LADY?
WIZARD LADY? YOU MEAN WITCH?
IS THAT WHAT A WITCH IS? A FEMALE WIZARD?
NAH DAWG, A WIZARD IS A MALE WITCH!
WELL, SHE INTRODUCED HERSELF TO ME AS A WIZARD LADY.

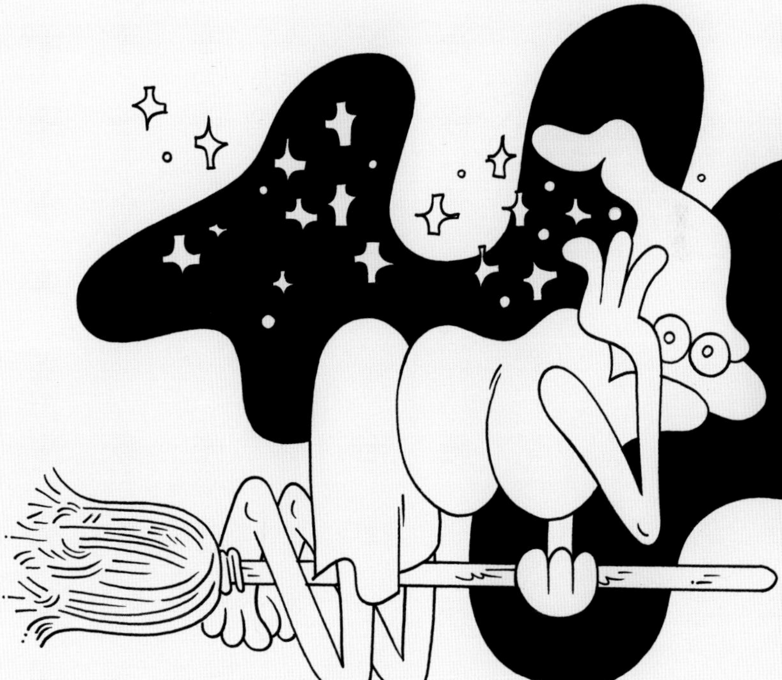

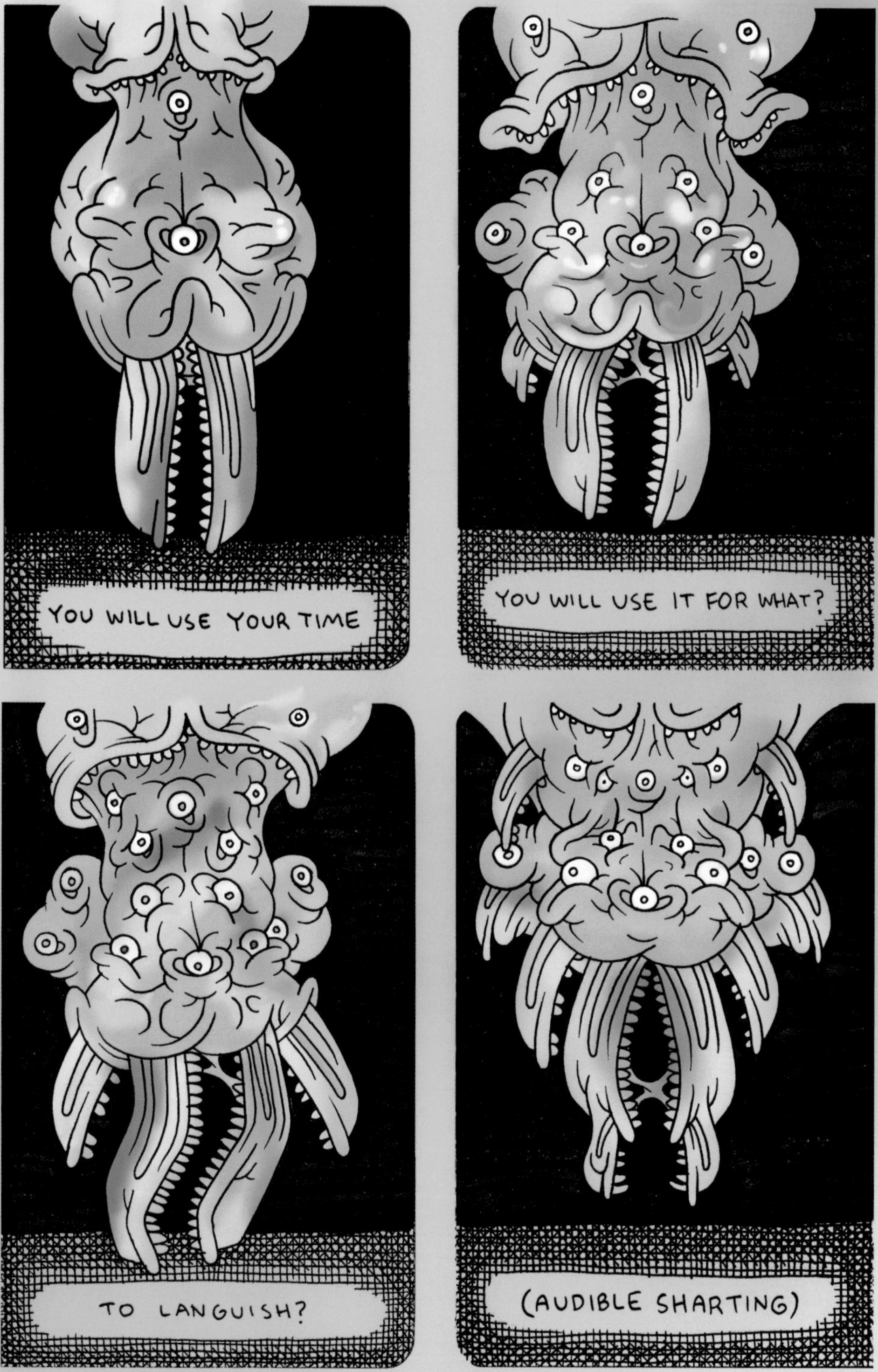
YOU WILL USE YOUR TIME
YOU WILL USE IT FOR WHAT?
TO LANGUISH?
(AUDIBLE SHARTING)

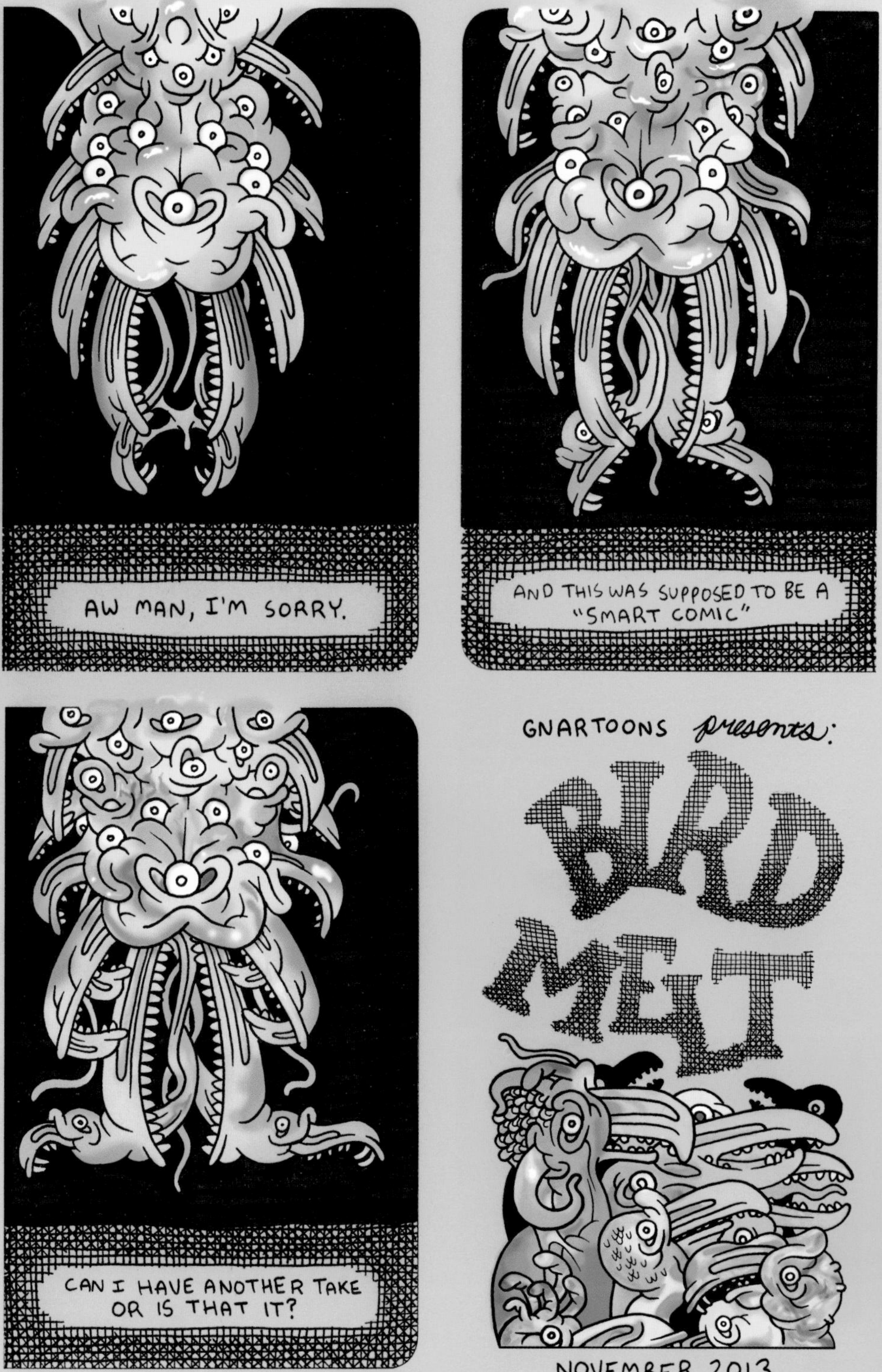
AW MAN, I'M SORRY.
AND THIS WAS SUPPOSED TO BE A "SMART COMIC"
CAN I HAVE ANOTHER TAKE OR IS THAT IT?
GNARTOONS presents:
BIRD MELT
NOVEMBER 2013

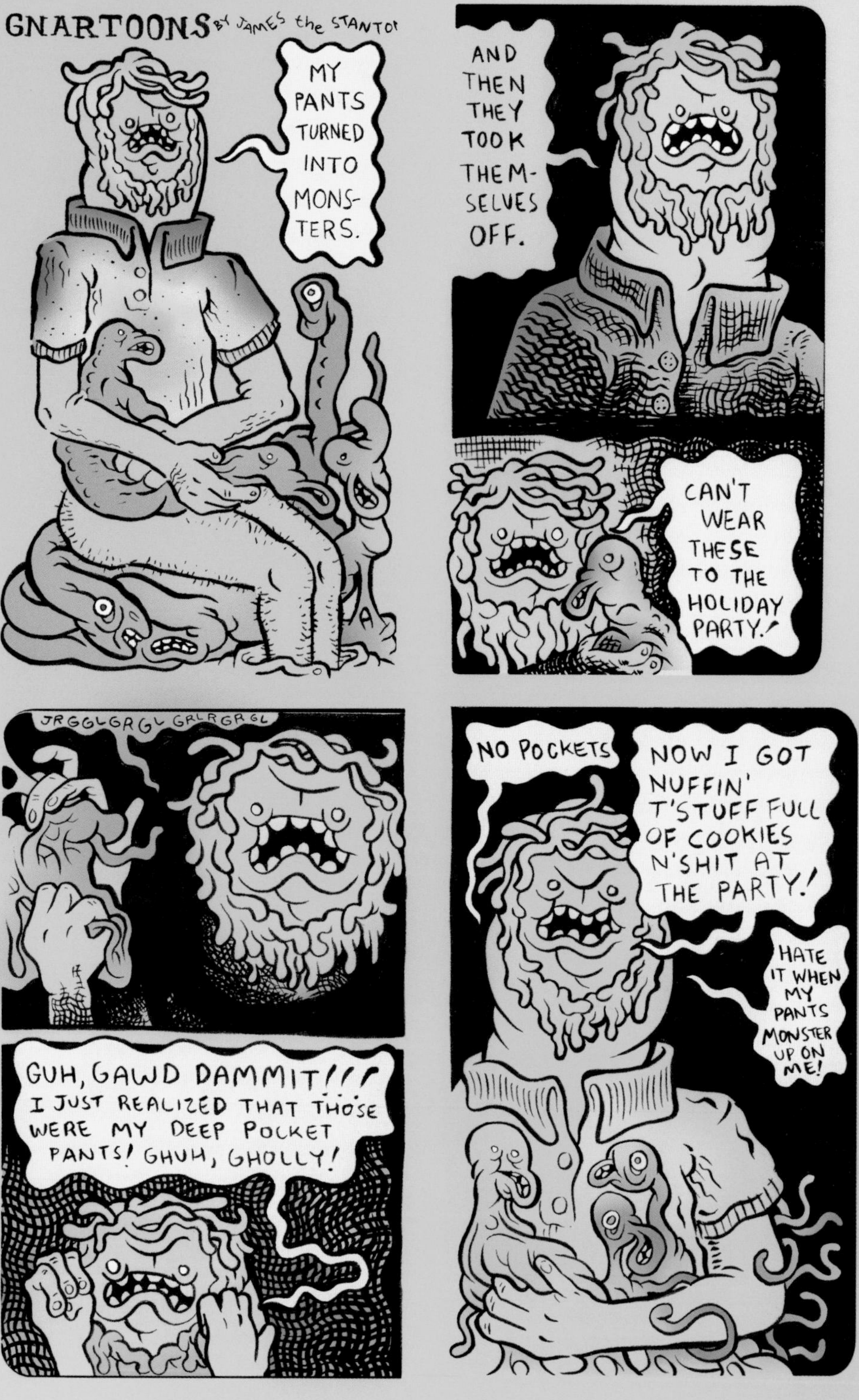
GNARTOONS BY JAMES the STANTON
MY PANTS TURNED INTO MONSTERS.
AND THEN THEY TOOK THEMSELVES OFF.
CAN'T WEAR THESE TO THE HOLIDAY PARTY!
JRGGLGRGL GRLRGRGL
GUH, GAWD DAMMIT!!! I JUST REALIZED THAT THOSE WERE MY DEEP POCKET PANTS! GHUH, GHOLLY!
NO POCKETS
NOW I GOT NUFFIN' T'STUFF FULL OF COOKIES N'SHIT AT THE PARTY!
HATE IT WHEN MY PANTS MONSTER UP ON ME!

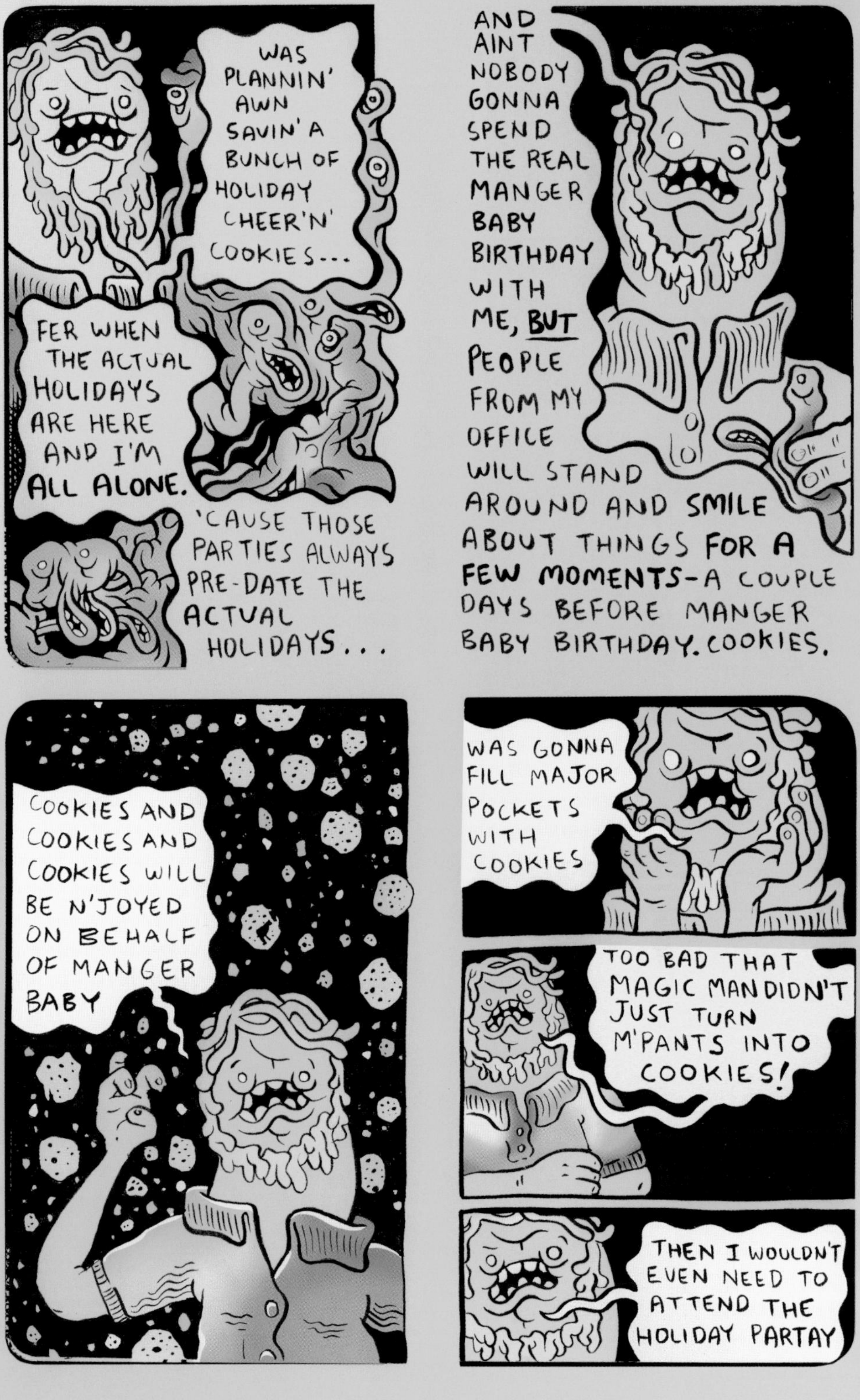
WAS PLANNIN' AWN SAVIN' A BUNCH OF HOLIDAY CHEER'N' COOKIES...
FER WHEN THE ACTUAL HOLIDAYS ARE HERE AND I'M ALL ALONE.
'CAUSE THOSE PARTIES ALWAYS PRE-DATE THE ACTUAL HOLIDAYS...
AND AINT NOBODY GONNA SPEND THE REAL MANGER BABY BIRTHDAY WITH ME, BUT PEOPLE FROM MY OFFICE WILL STAND AROUND AND SMILE ABOUT THINGS FOR A FEW MOMENTS-A COUPLE DAYS BEFORE MANGER BABY BIRTHDAY. COOKIES.
COOKIES AND COOKIES AND COOKIES WILL BE N'JOYED ON BEHALF OF MANGER BABY
WAS GONNA FILL MAJOR POCKETS WITH COOKIES
TOO BAD THAT MAGIC MAN DIDN'T JUST TURN M'PANTS INTO COOKIES!
THEN I WOULDN'T EVEN NEED TO ATTEND THE HOLIDAY PARTAY

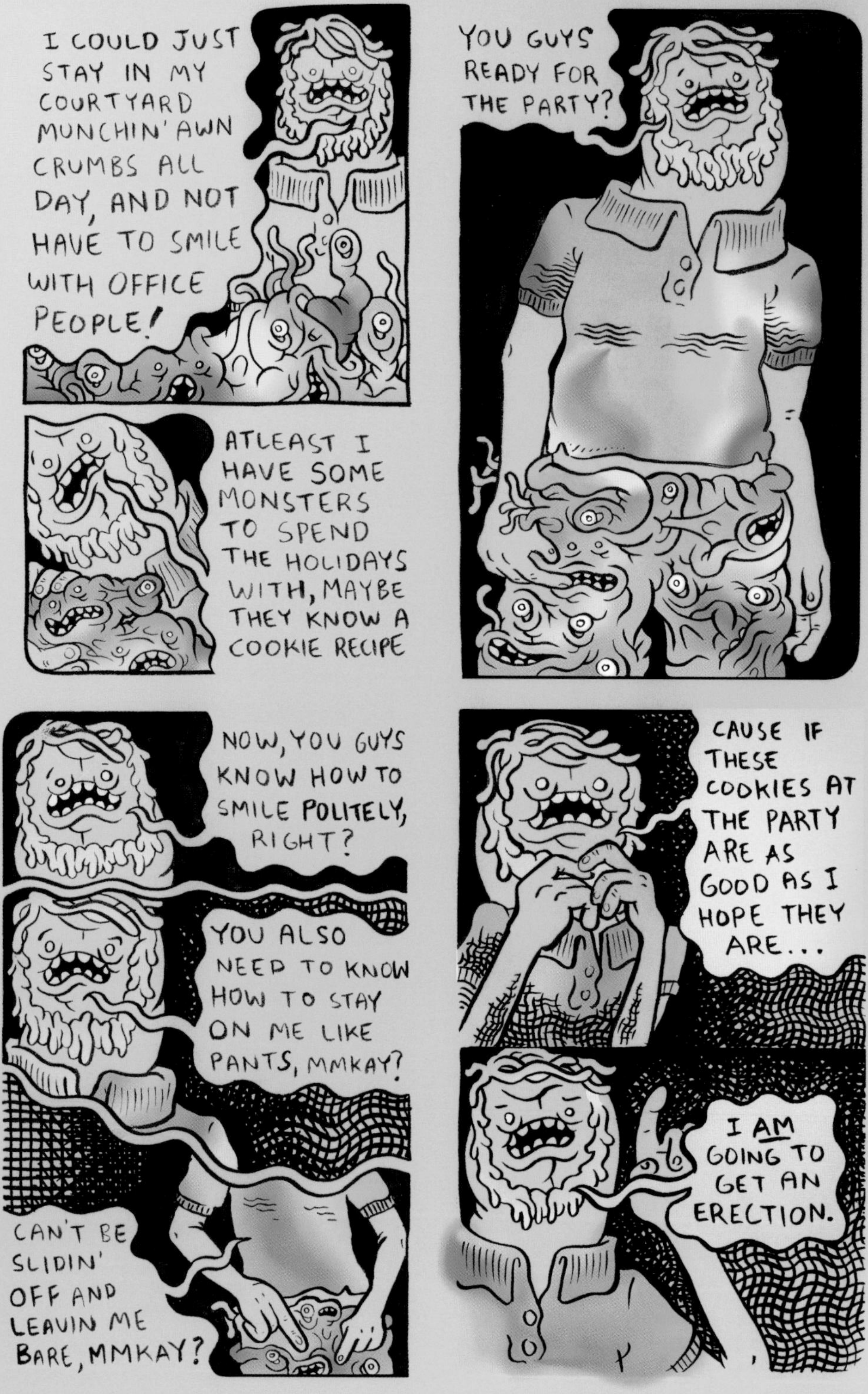
I COULD JUST STAY IN MY COURTYARD MUNCHIN' AWN CRUMBS ALL DAY, AND NOT HAVE TO SMILE WITH OFFICE PEOPLE!
ATLEAST I HAVE SOME MONSTERS TO SPEND THE HOLIDAYS WITH, MAYBE THEY KNOW A COOKIE RECIPE
YOU GUYS READY FOR THE PARTY?
NOW, YOU GUYS KNOW HOW TO SMILE POLITELY, RIGHT?
YOU ALSO NEED TO KNOW HOW TO STAY ON ME LIKE PANTS, MMKAY?
CAN'T BE SLIDIN' OFF AND LEAVIN ME BARE, MMKAY?
CAUSE IF THESE COOKIES AT THE PARTY ARE AS GOOD AS I HOPE THEY ARE...
I AM GOING TO GET AN ERECTION.

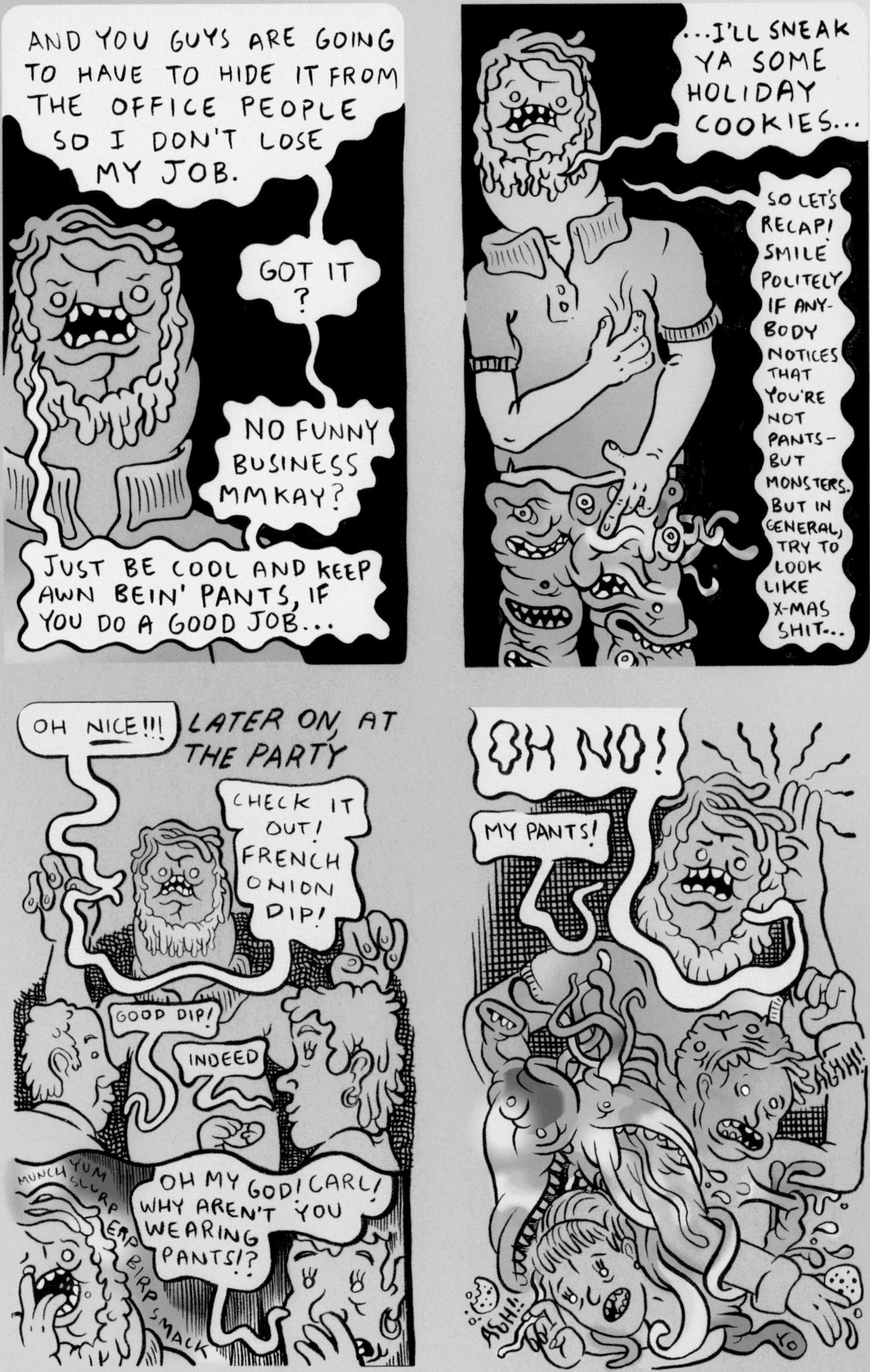
AND YOU GUYS ARE GOING TO HAVE TO HIDE IT FROM THE OFFICE PEOPLE SO I DON'T LOSE MY JOB.
GOT IT ?
NO FUNNY BUSINESS MMKAY?
JUST BE COOL AND KEEP AWN BEIN' PANTS, IF YOU DO A GOOD JOB...
...I'LL SNEAK YA SOME HOLIDAY COOKIES...
SO LET'S RECAP! SMILE POLITELY IF ANYBODY NOTICES THAT YOU'RE NOT PANTS-BUT MONSTERS. BUT IN GENERAL, TRY TO LOOK LIKE X-MAS SHIT...
OH NICE!!!
LATER ON, AT THE PARTY
CHECK IT OUT! FRENCH ONION DIP!
GOOD DIP!
INDEED
MUNCH YUM SLURP ERP BIRP SMACK
OH MY GOD! CARL! WHY AREN'T YOU WEARING PANTS!?
OH NO!
MY PANTS!
AGHH!
AGH!!

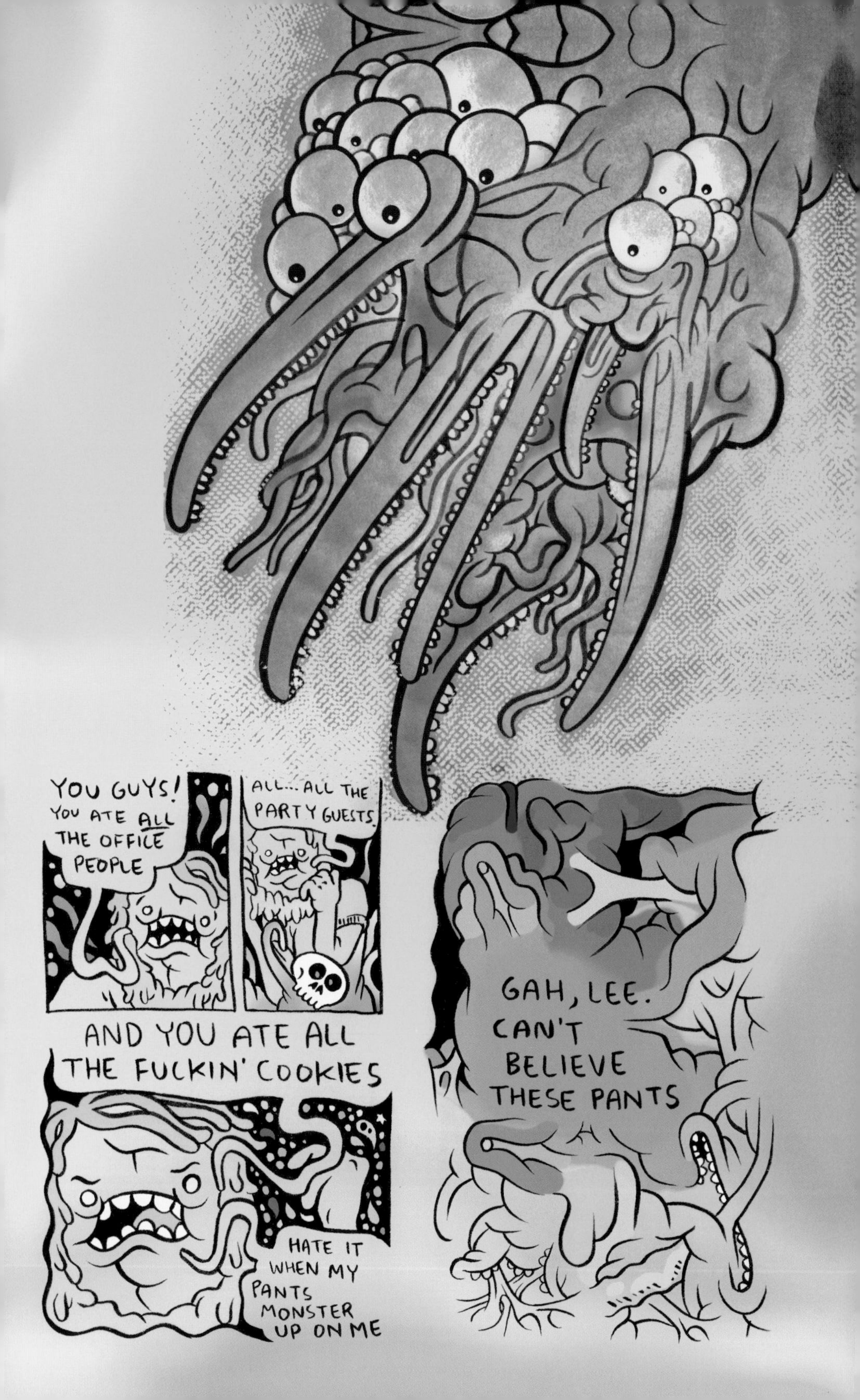
YOU GUYS! YOU ATE ALL THE OFFICE PEOPLE
ALL... ALL THE PARTY GUESTS.
AND YOU ATE ALL THE FUCKIN' COOKIES
HATE IT WHEN MY PANTS MONSTER UP ON ME
GAH, LEE. CAN'T BELIEVE THESE PANTS

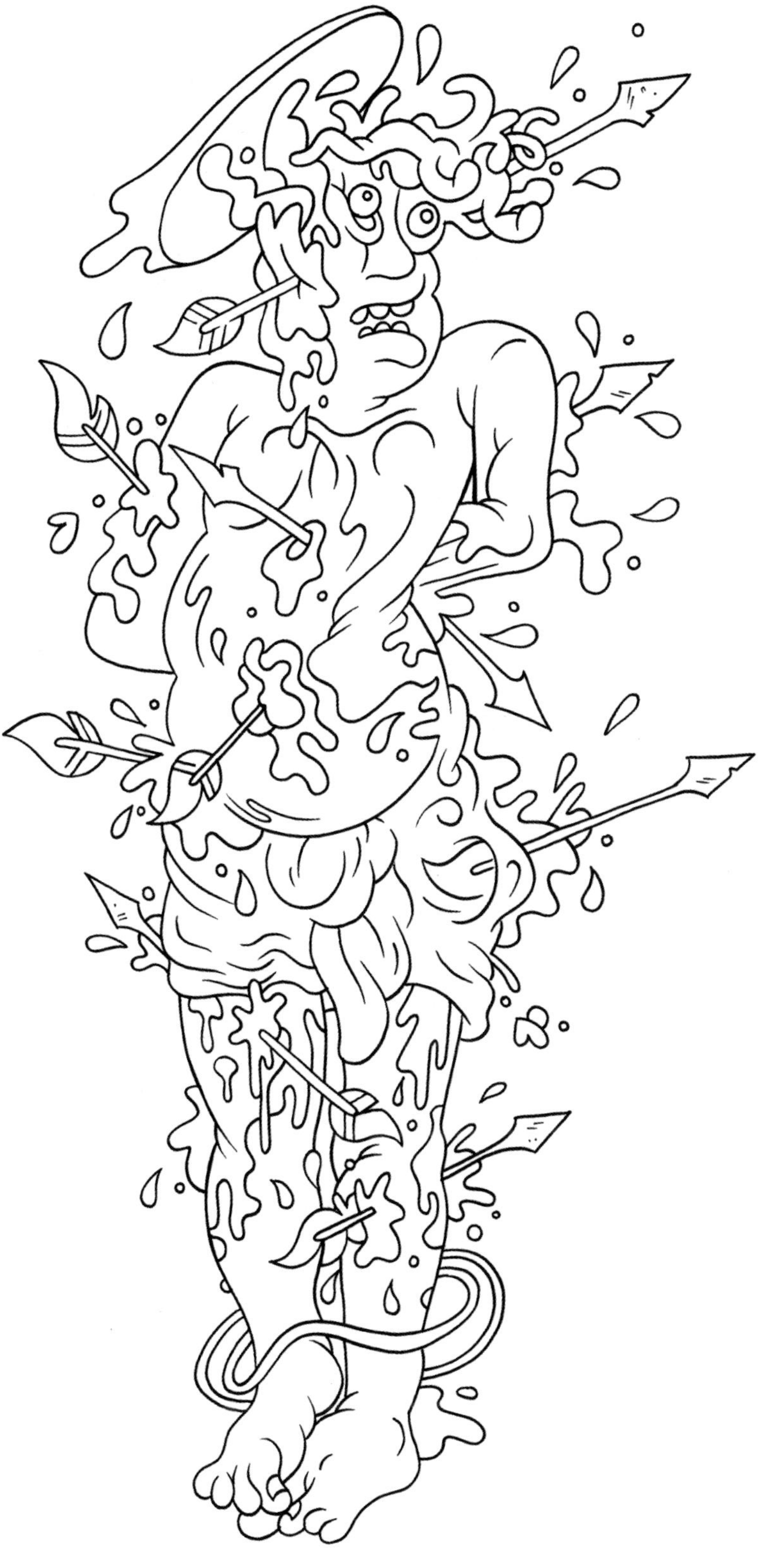

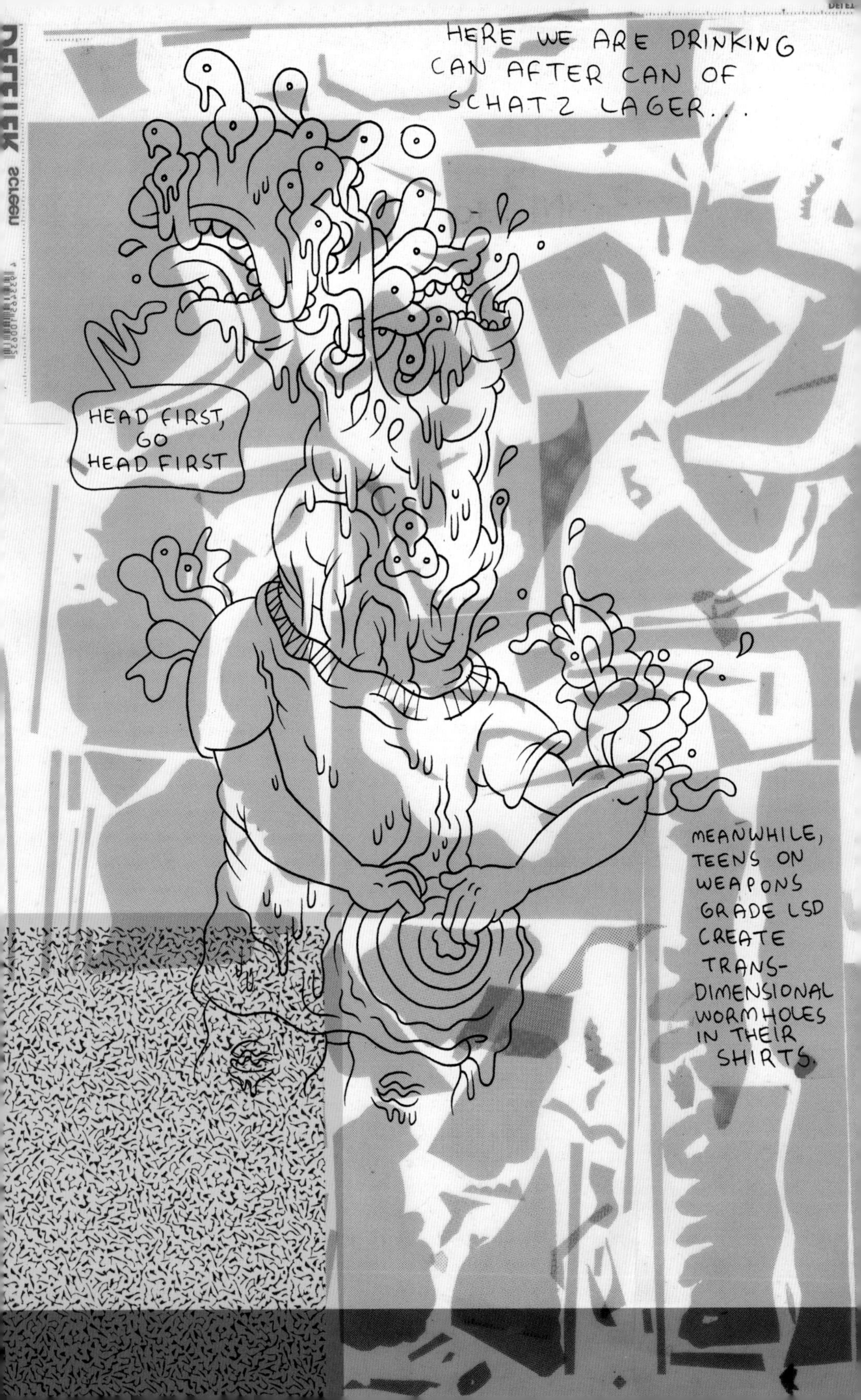
HERE WE ARE DRINKING CAN AFTER CAN OF SCHATZ LAGER...
HEAD FIRST, GO HEAD FIRST
MEANWHILE, TEENS ON WEAPONS GRADE LSD CREATE TRANS-DIMENSIONAL WORMHOLES IN THEIR SHIRTS.

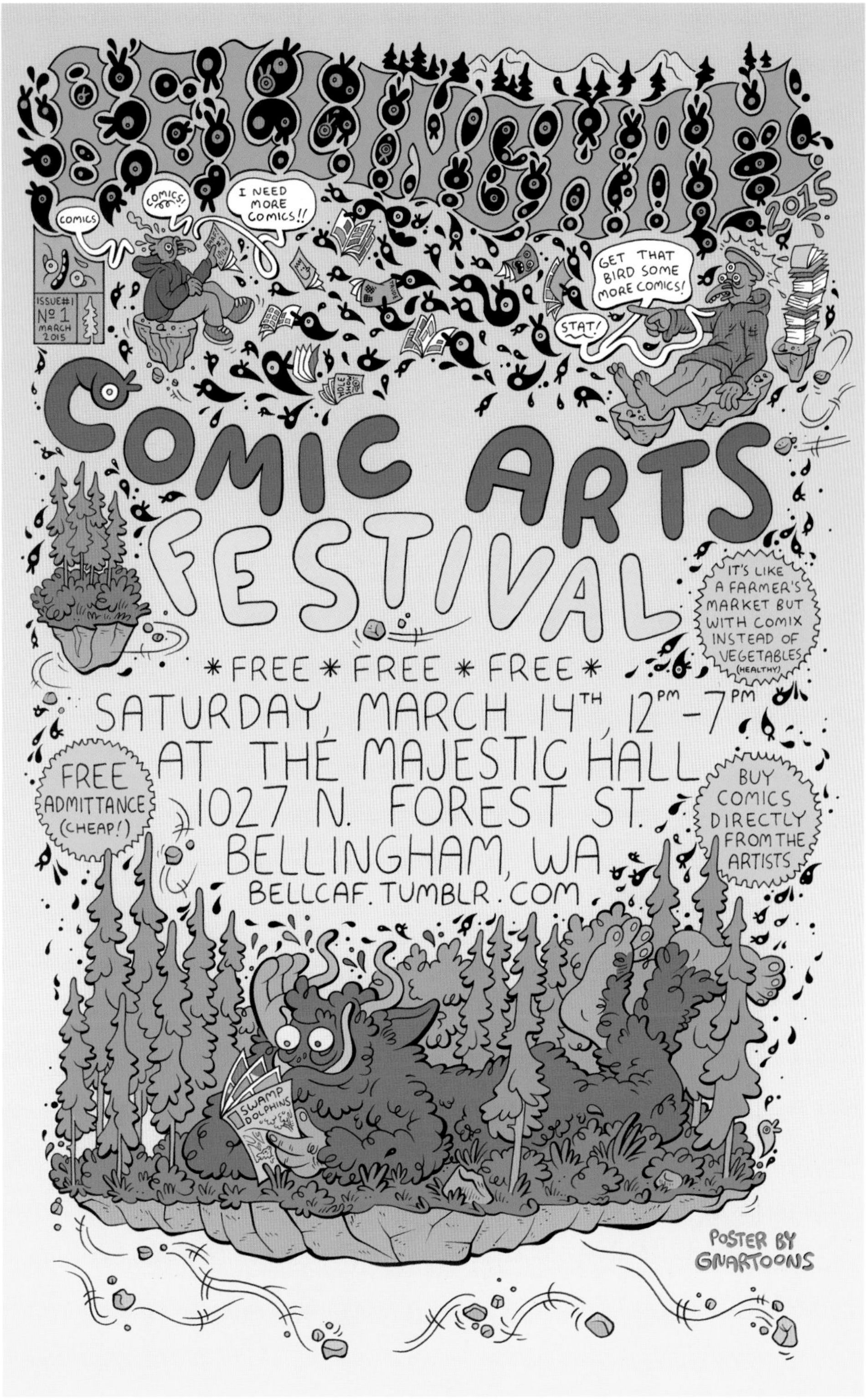

2015
COMICS
COMICS!
I NEED MORE COMICS!!
ISSUE#1 №1 MARCH 2015
GET THAT BIRD SOME MORE COMICS!
STAT!
HOLE SHOW
COMIC ARTS FESTIVAL
IT'S LIKE A FARMER'S MARKET BUT WITH COMIX INSTEAD OF VEGETABLES (HEALTHY)
* FREE * FREE * FREE *
SATURDAY, MARCH 14TH, 12PM-7PM
AT THE MAJESTIC HALL
1027 N. FOREST ST.
BELLINGHAM, WA
BELLCAF.TUMBLR.COM
FREE ADMITTANCE (CHEAP!)
BUY COMICS DIRECTLY FROM THE ARTISTS
SWAMP DOLPHINS
POSTER BY GNARTOONS

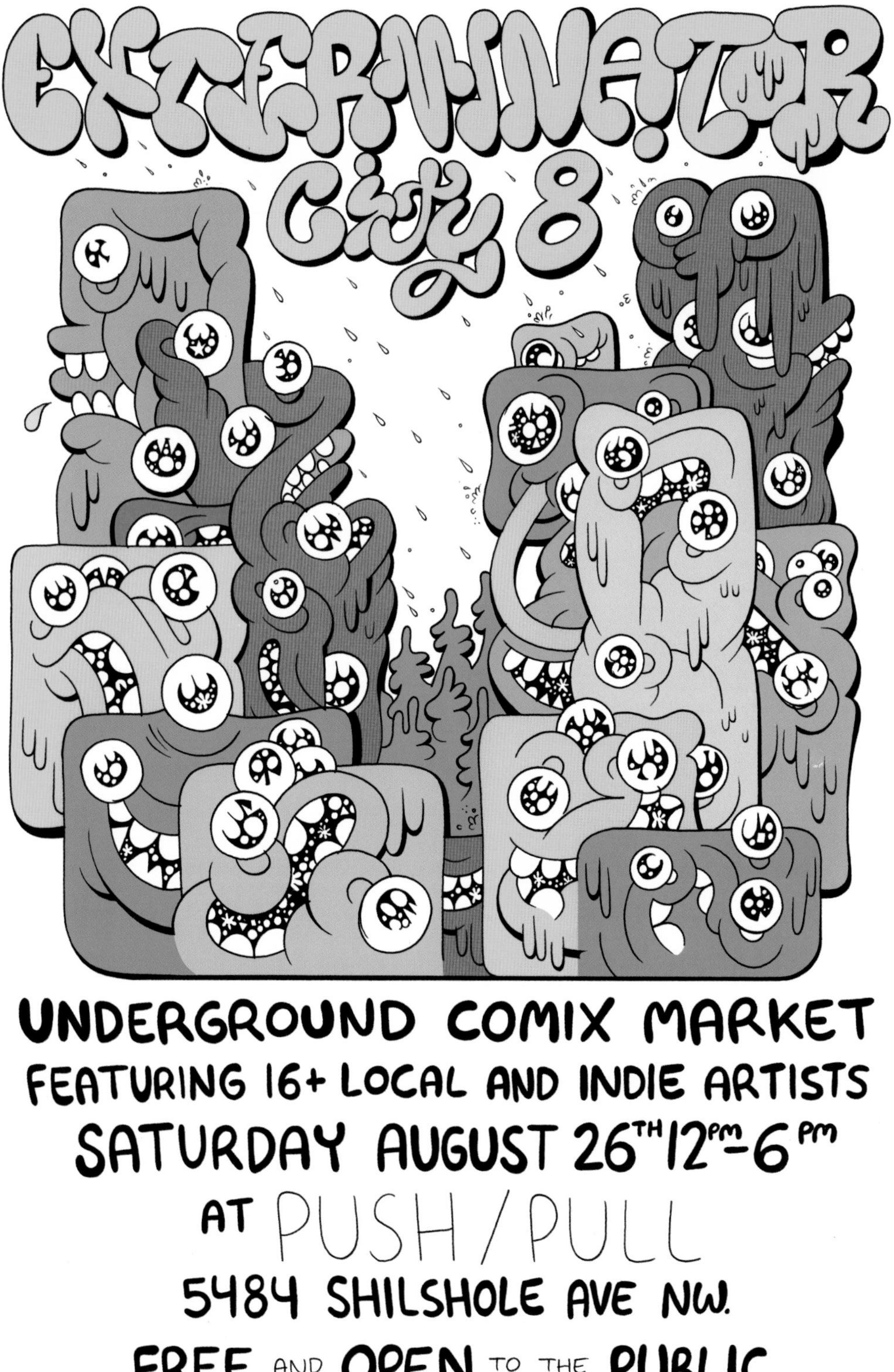
EXTERMINATOR
City 8
UNDERGROUND COMIX MARKET
FEATURING 16+ LOCAL AND INDIE ARTISTS
SATURDAY AUGUST 26TH 12PM–6 PM
AT PUSH/PULL
5484 SHILSHOLE AVE NW.
FREE AND OPEN TO THE PUBLIC

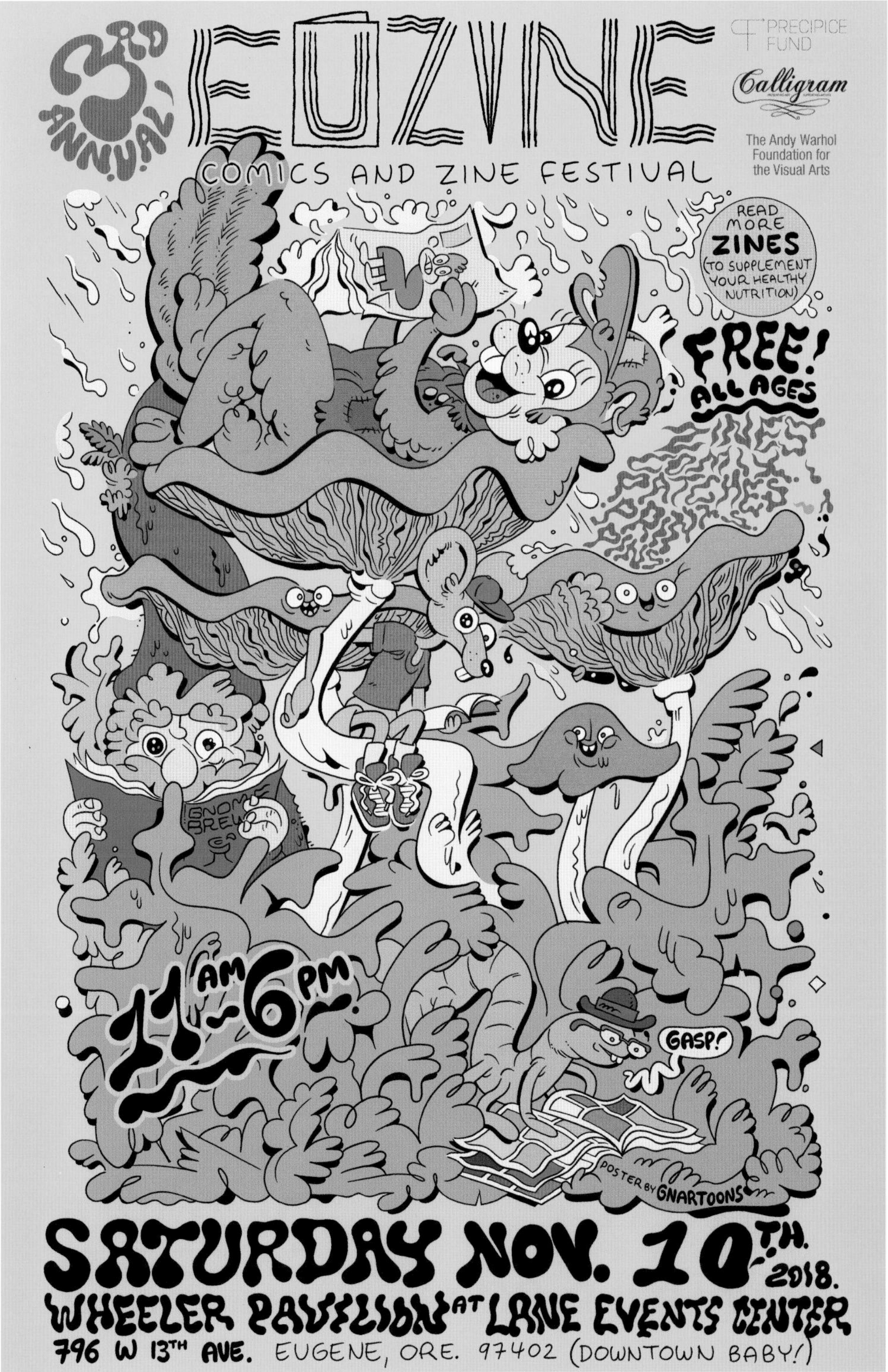
3RD ANNUAL
EUZINE
COMICS AND ZINE FESTIVAL
PRECIPICE FUND
Calligram
The Andy Warhol Foundation for the Visual Arts
READ MORE ZINES (TO SUPPLEMENT YOUR HEALTHY NUTRITION)
FREE! ALL AGES
GNOME BREW
11 AM - 6 PM
GASP!
POSTER BY GNARTOONS
SATURDAY NOV. 10TH. 2018.
WHEELER PAVILION AT LANE EVENTS CENTER
796 W 13TH AVE. EUGENE, ORE. 97402 (DOWNTOWN BABY!)

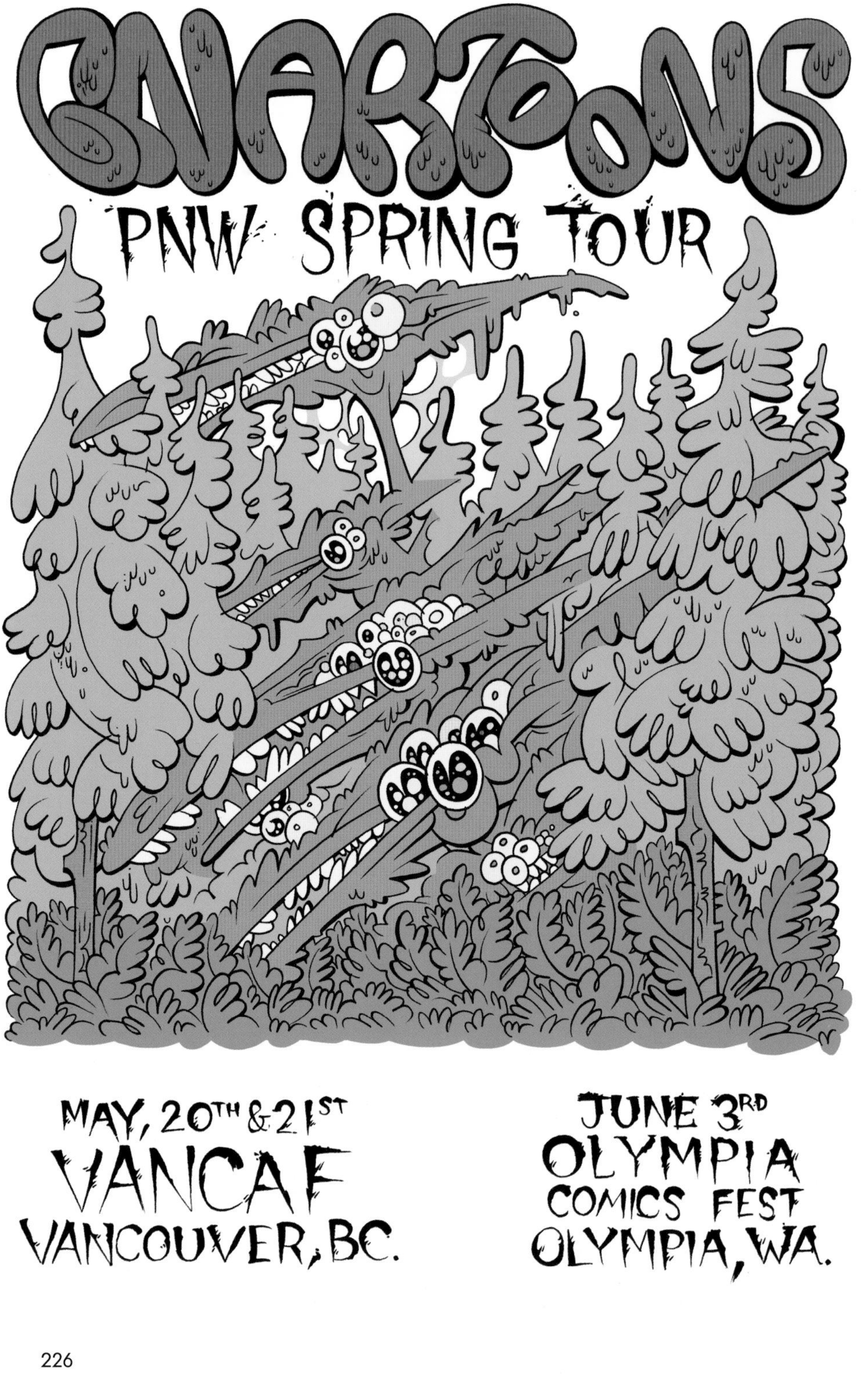
GNARTOONS
PNW SPRING TOUR
MAY, 20TH & 21ST
VANCAF
VANCOUVER, BC.
JUNE 3RD
OLYMPIA
COMICS FEST
OLYMPIA, WA.

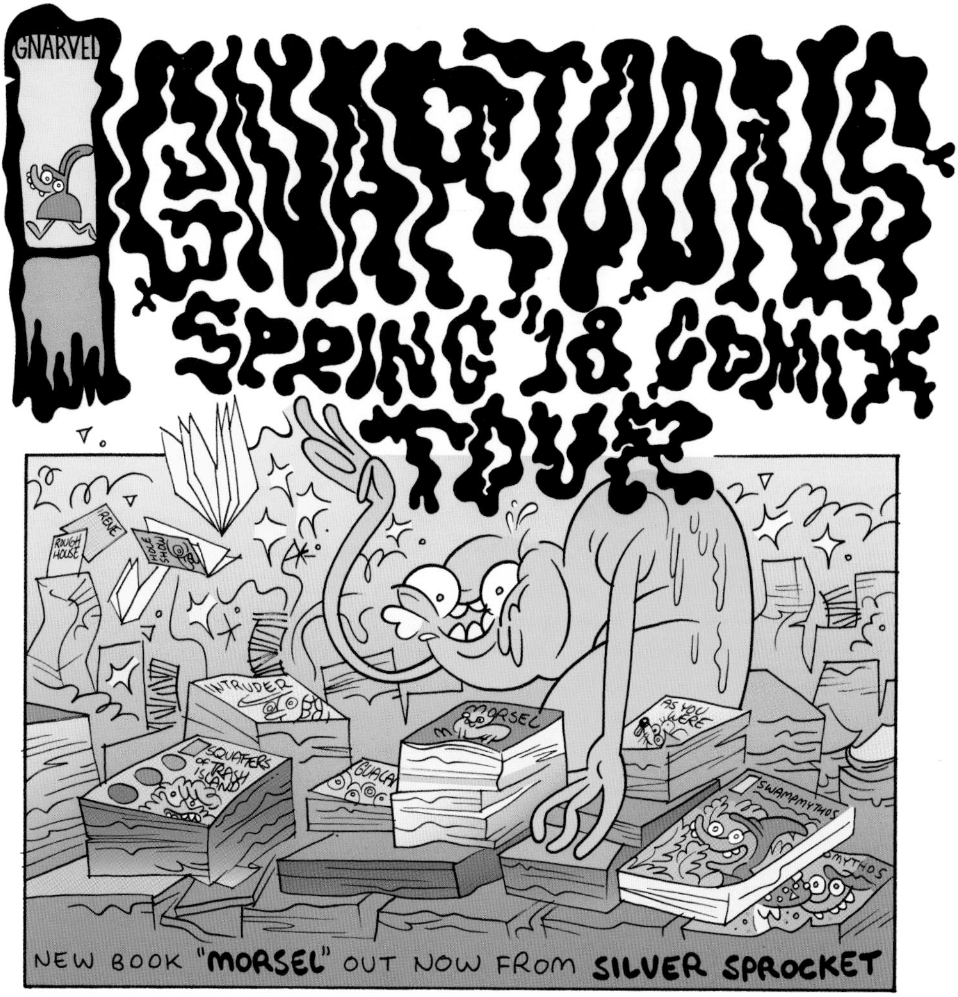
GNARVED
GNARTOONS
SPRING '18 COMIX TOUR
ROUGH HOUSE
IRENE
HOLE SHOW
INTRUDER
MORSEL
AS YOU WERE
SQUATTERS OF TRASH ISLAND
SWAMPMYTHOS
NEW BOOK "MORSEL" OUT NOW FROM SILVER SPROCKET

EMERALD CITY COMICON
MARCH 1-4
SEATTLE, WASH

BELLINGHAM COMIC ARTS FESTIVAL
MARCH 31ST
BELLINGHAM, WASH

VANCOUVER COMIC ARTS FESTIVAL
MAY 19-20
VANCOUVER, BC

CHICAGO ALTERNATIVE COMICS EXPO
JUNE 2ND
CHICAGO, IL

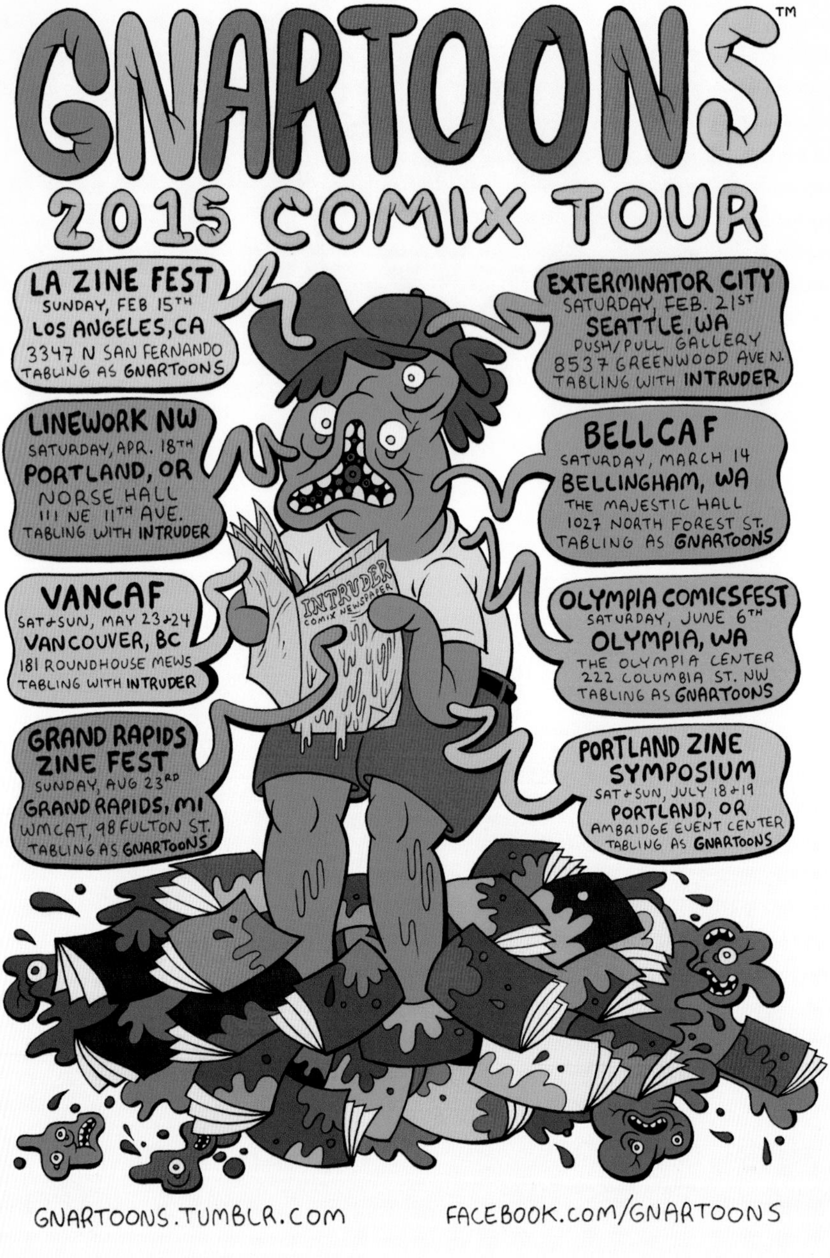
GNARTOONS™
2015 COMIX TOUR
LA ZINE FEST
SUNDAY, FEB 15TH
LOS ANGELES, CA
3347 N SAN FERNANDO
TABLING AS GNARTOONS
EXTERMINATOR CITY
SATURDAY, FEB. 21ST
SEATTLE, WA
PUSH/PULL GALLERY
8537 GREENWOOD AVE N.
TABLING WITH INTRUDER
LINEWORK NW
SATURDAY, APR. 18TH
PORTLAND, OR
NORSE HALL
111 NE 11TH AVE.
TABLING WITH INTRUDER
BELLCAF
SATURDAY, MARCH 14
BELLINGHAM, WA
THE MAJESTIC HALL
1027 NORTH FOREST ST.
TABLING AS GNARTOONS
VANCAF
SAT+SUN, MAY 23+24
VANCOUVER, BC
181 ROUNDHOUSE MEWS
TABLING WITH INTRUDER
INTRUDER COMIX NEWSPAPER
OLYMPIA COMICSFEST
SATURDAY, JUNE 6TH
OLYMPIA, WA
THE OLYMPIA CENTER
222 COLUMBIA ST. NW
TABLING AS GNARTOONS
GRAND RAPIDS ZINE FEST
SUNDAY, AUG 23RD
GRAND RAPIDS, MI
WMCAT, 98 FULTON ST.
TABLING AS GNARTOONS
PORTLAND ZINE SYMPOSIUM
SAT+SUN, JULY 18+19
PORTLAND, OR
AMBRIDGE EVENT CENTER
TABLING AS GNARTOONS
GNARTOONS.TUMBLR.COM
FACEBOOK.COM/GNARTOONS

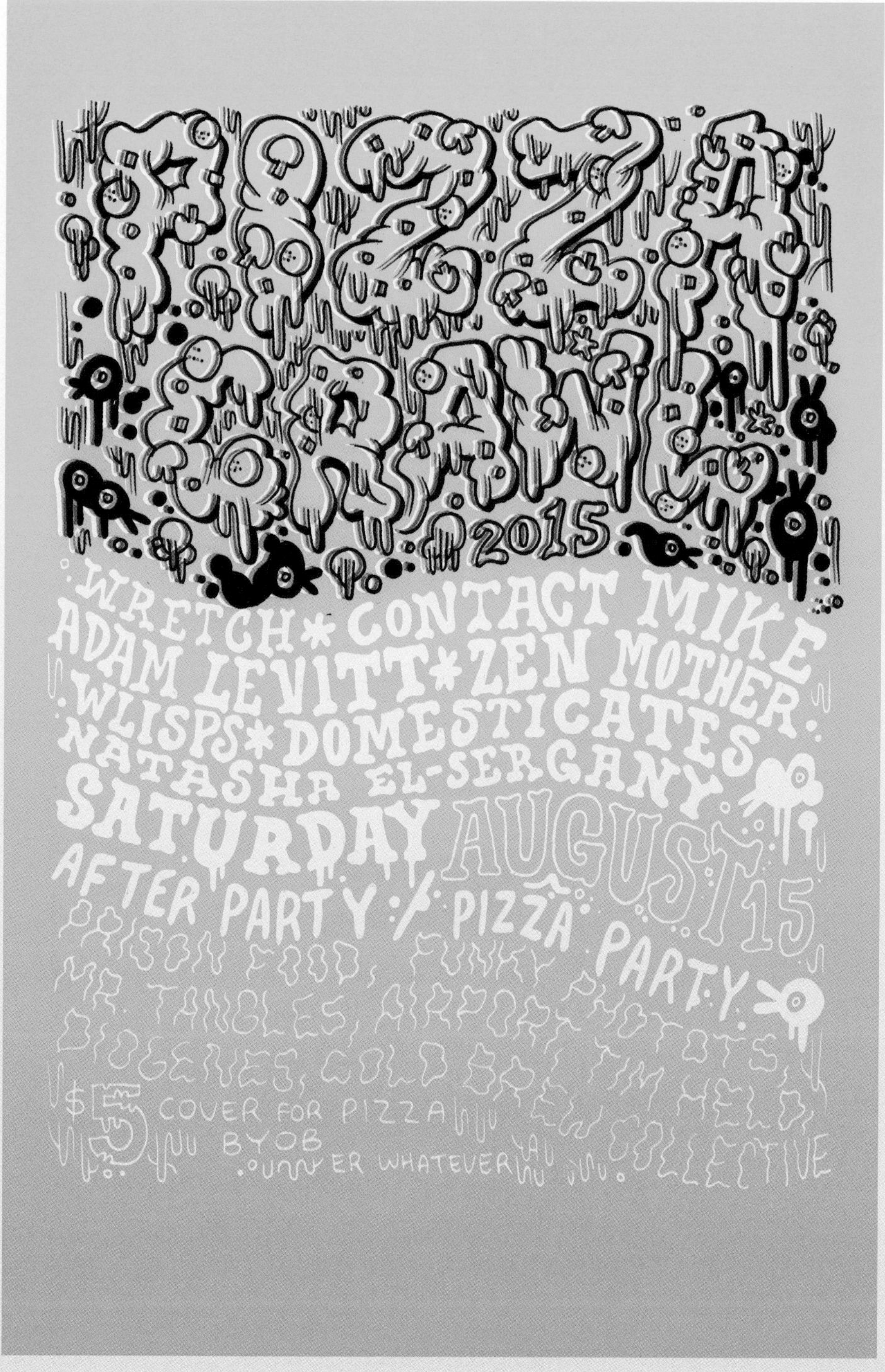

PIZZA BRAWL
2015
WRETCH * CONTACT MIKE
ADAM LEVITT * ZEN MOTHER
WLISPS * DOMESTICATES
NATASHA EL-SERGANY
SATURDAY AUGUST 15
AFTER PARTY // PIZZA PARTY
MR. TANGLES,
$5 COVER FOR PIZZA
BYOB
ER WHATEVER
COLLECTIVE

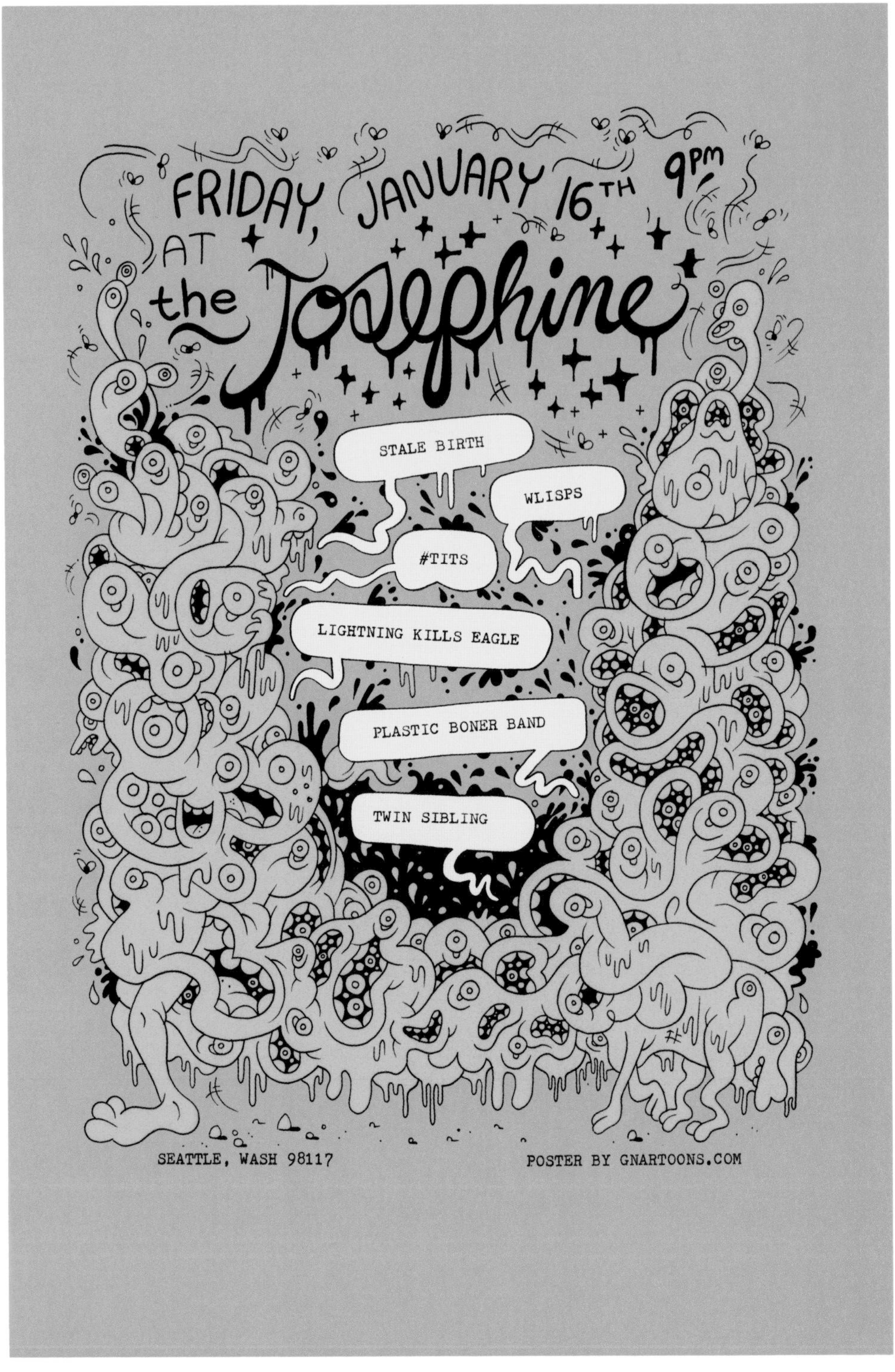
FRIDAY, JANUARY 16TH 9PM
AT
the Josephine
STALE BIRTH
WLISPS
#TITS
LIGHTNING KILLS EAGLE
PLASTIC BONER BAND
TWIN SIBLING
SEATTLE, WASH 98117
POSTER BY GNARTOONS.COM

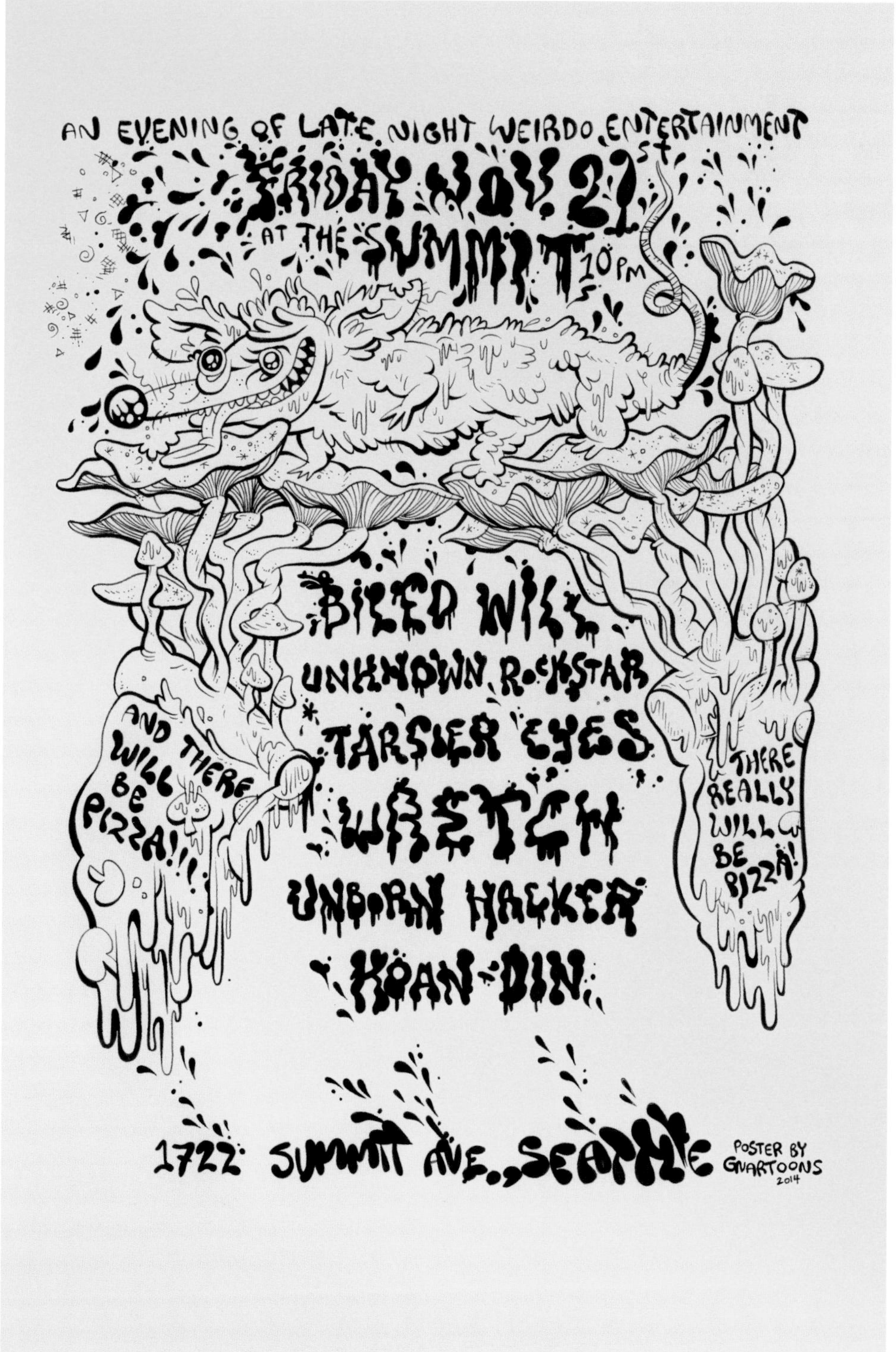
AN EVENING OF LATE NIGHT WEIRDO ENTERTAINMENT
FRIDAY NOV 21st
AT THE SUMMIT 10 PM
BILED WILL
UNKNOWN ROCKSTAR
TARSIER EYES
WRETCH
UNBORN HACKER
KOAN-DIN
AND THERE WILL BE PIZZA!!!
THERE REALLY WILL BE PIZZA!
1722 SUMMIT AVE., SEATTLE
POSTER BY GNARTOONS 2014

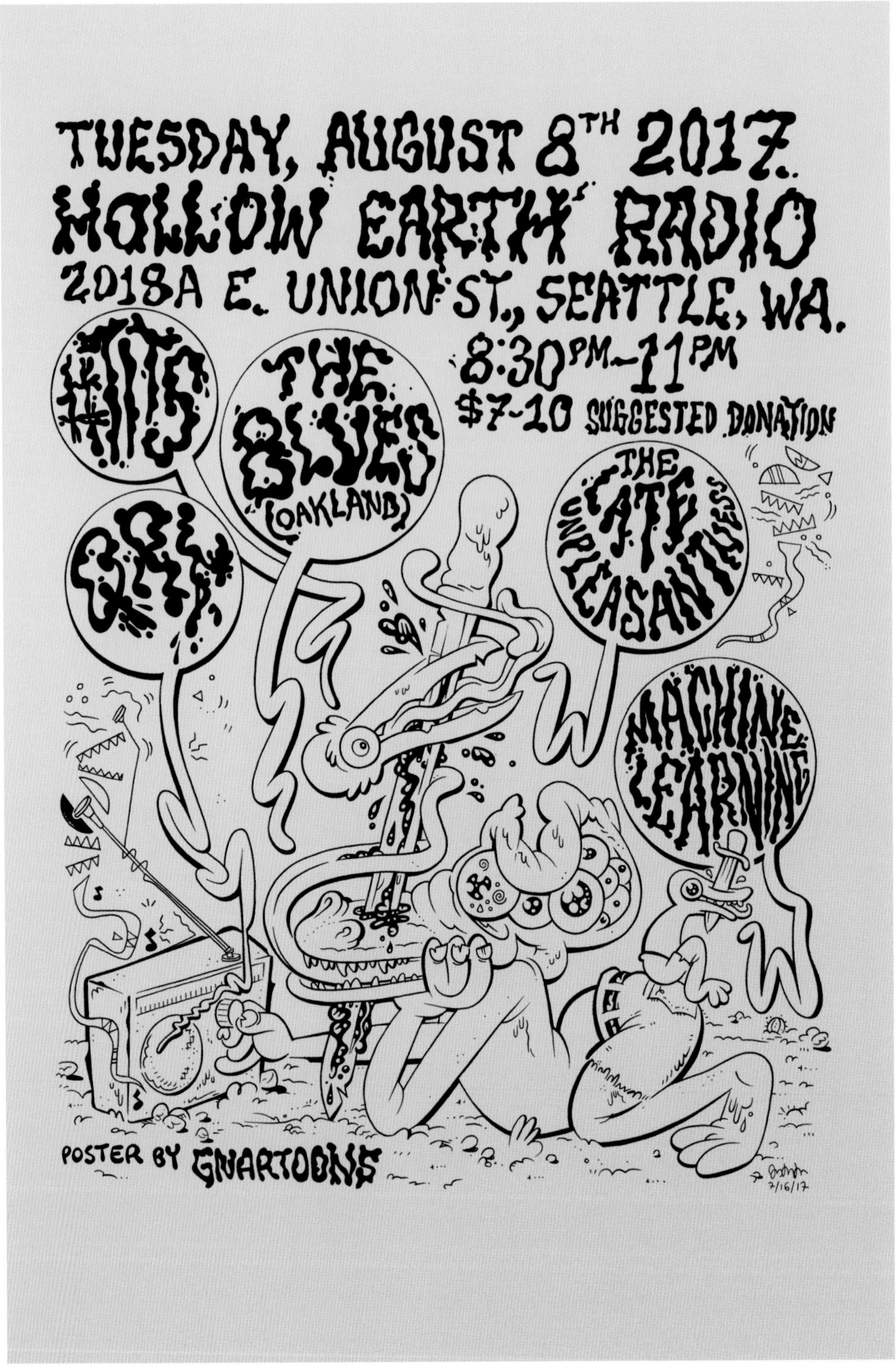
TUESDAY, AUGUST 8TH 2017.
HOLLOW EARTH RADIO
2018A E. UNION ST., SEATTLE, WA.
8:30PM–11PM
$7-10 SUGGESTED DONATION
THE BLUES (OAKLAND)
THE LATE UNPLEASANTNESS
MACHINE LEARNING
POSTER BY GNARTOONS
7/16/17

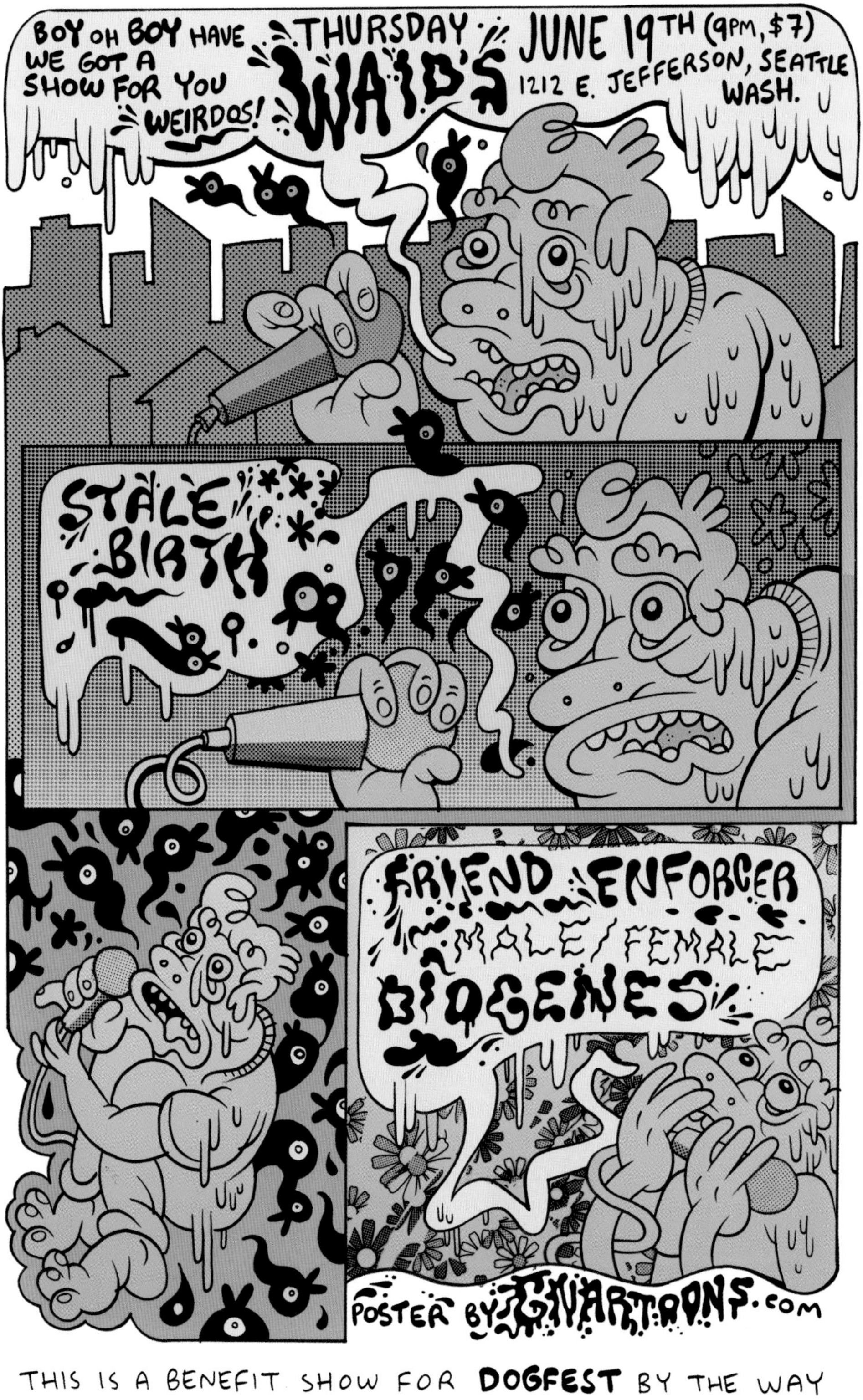
BOY OH BOY HAVE WE GOT A SHOW FOR YOU WEIRDOS!
THURSDAY
WAID'S
JUNE 19TH (9PM, \$7)
1212 E. JEFFERSON, SEATTLE WASH.
STALE BIRTH
FRIEND ENFORCER
MALE/FEMALE
DIOGENES
POSTER BY GNARTOONS.com

THIS IS A BENEFIT SHOW FOR **DOGFEST** BY THE WAY

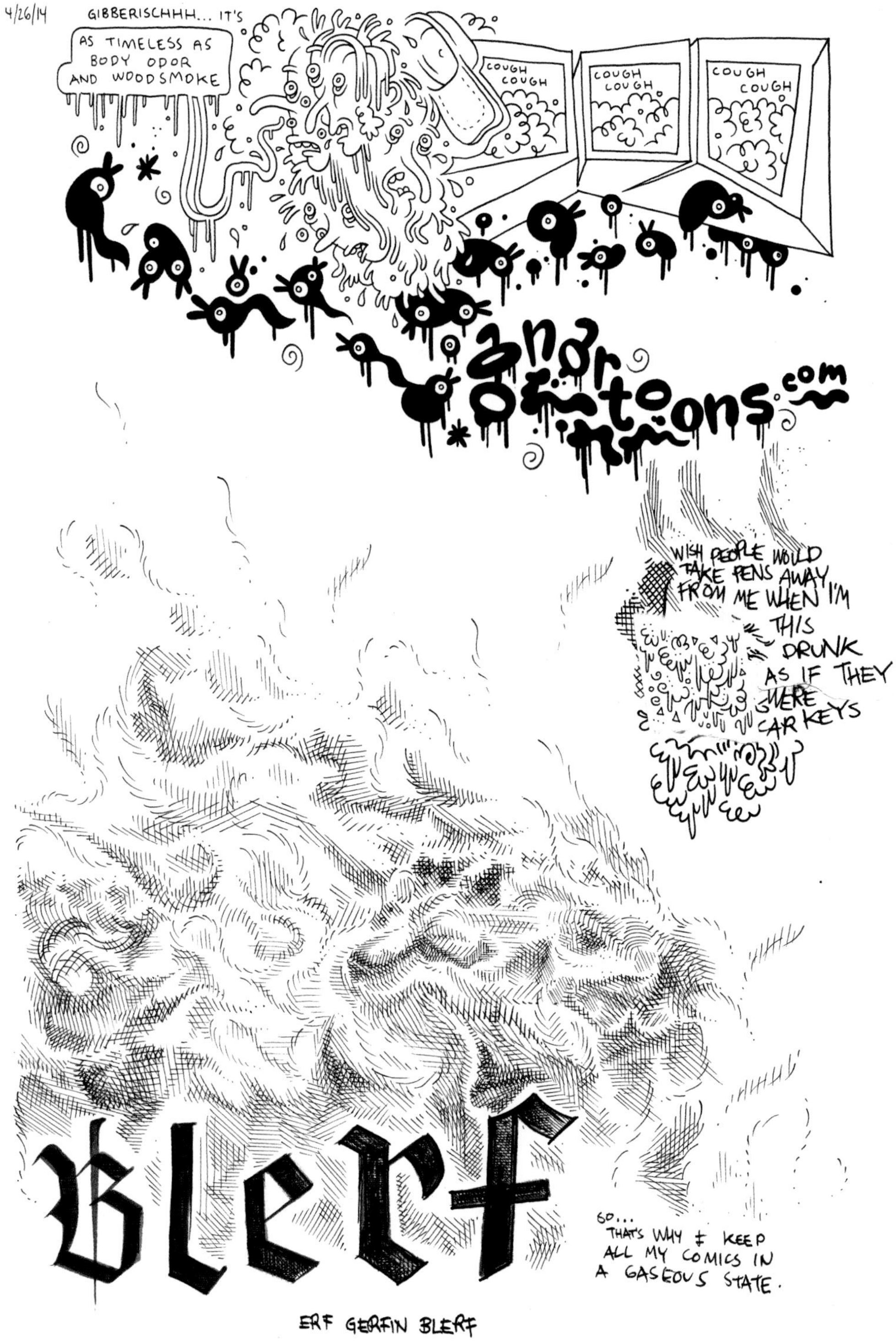
4/26/14
GIBBERISCHHH... IT'S
AS TIMELESS AS BODY ODOR AND WOODSMOKE
COUGH COUGH
COUGH COUGH
COUGH COUGH
WISH PEOPLE WOULD TAKE PENS AWAY FROM ME WHEN I'M THIS DRUNK AS IF THEY WERE CAR KEYS
Blerf
SO... THAT'S WHY I KEEP ALL MY COMICS IN A GASEOUS STATE.
ERF GERFIN BLERF

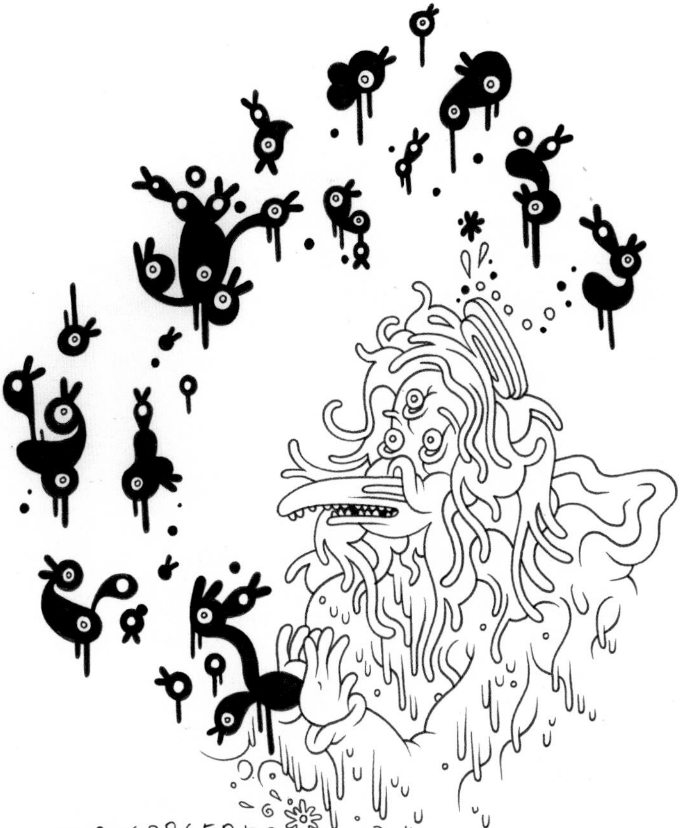

A SORCERER MAKING FART NOISES WITH HIS HANDS.

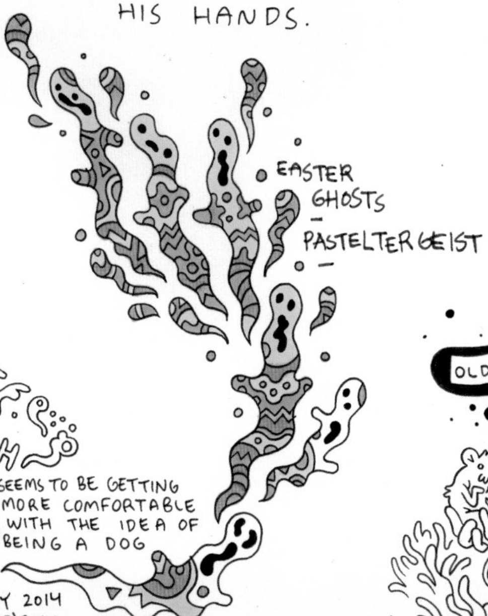
EASTER GHOSTS
-
PASTELTERGEIST
-

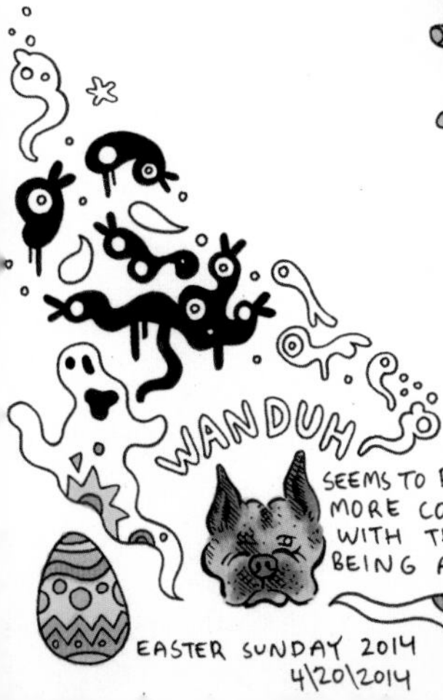
WANDUH

SEEMS TO BE GETTING MORE COMFORTABLE WITH THE IDEA OF BEING A DOG

EASTER SUNDAY 2014
4\20\2014

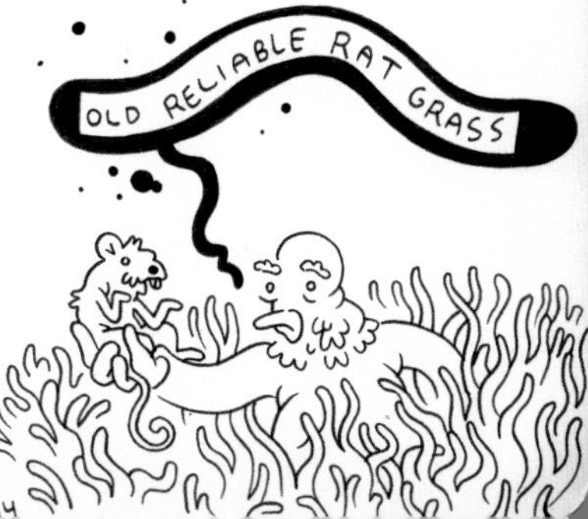
OLD RELIABLE RAT GRASS

4/22/14

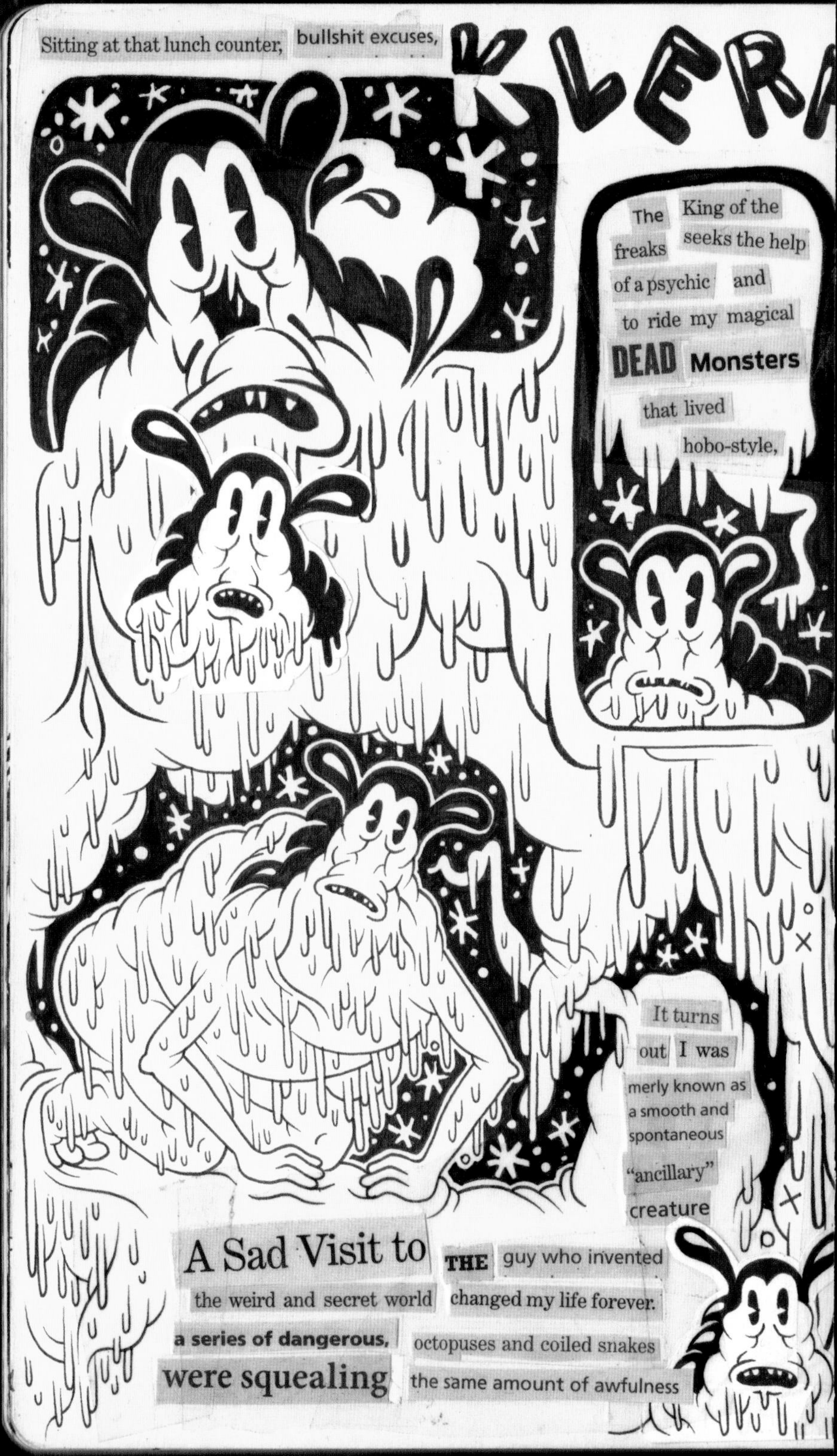
Sitting at that lunch counter,
bullshit excuses,
KLER
The freaks
King of the seeks the help
of a psychic
and
to ride my magical
DEAD
Monsters
that lived
hobo-style,
It turns out
I was
merly known as a smooth and spontaneous
"ancillary"
creature
A Sad Visit to
THE
guy who invented
the weird and secret world
changed my life forever.
a series of dangerous,
octopuses and coiled snakes
were squealing
the same amount of awfulness

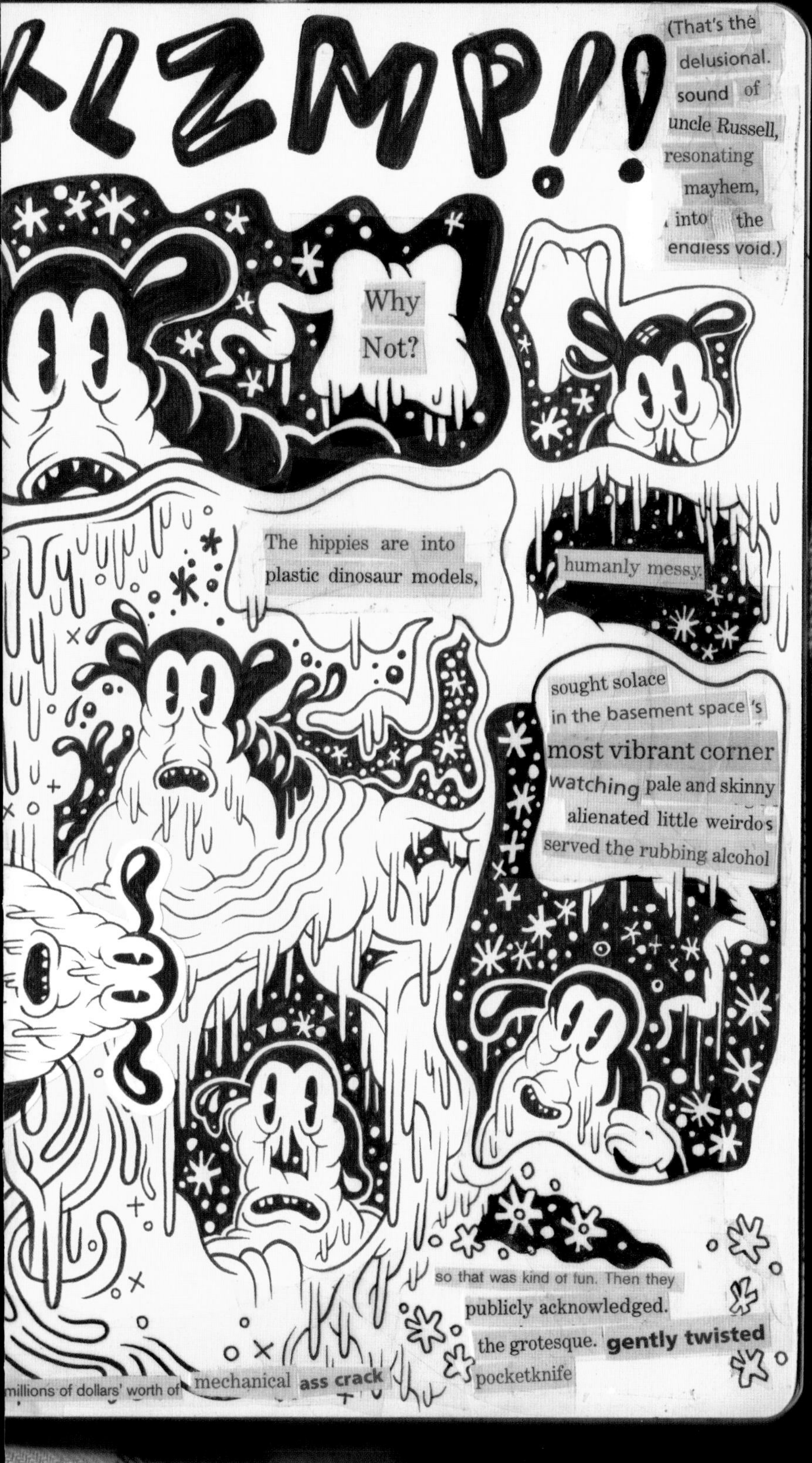

LZMP!!
(That's the delusional. sound of uncle Russell, resonating mayhem, into the endless void.)
Why Not?
The hippies are into plastic dinosaur models,
humanly messy.
sought solace in the basement space 's most vibrant corner watching pale and skinny alienated little weirdos served the rubbing alcohol
so that was kind of fun. Then they publicly acknowledged. the grotesque. gently twisted pocketknife
millions of dollars' worth of mechanical ass crack

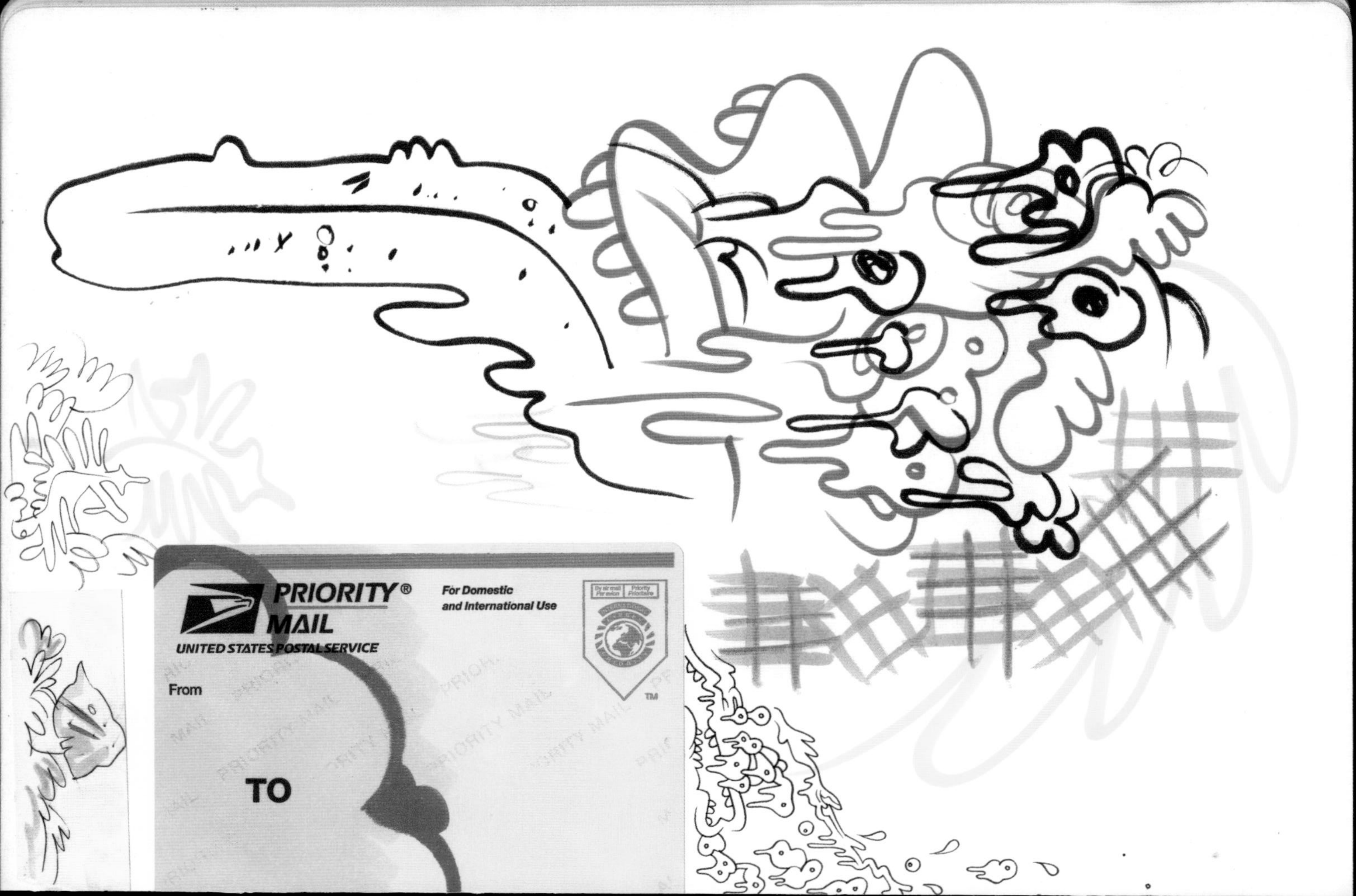
PRIORITY®
MAIL
UNITED STATES POSTAL SERVICE
For Domestic
and International Use
From
TO

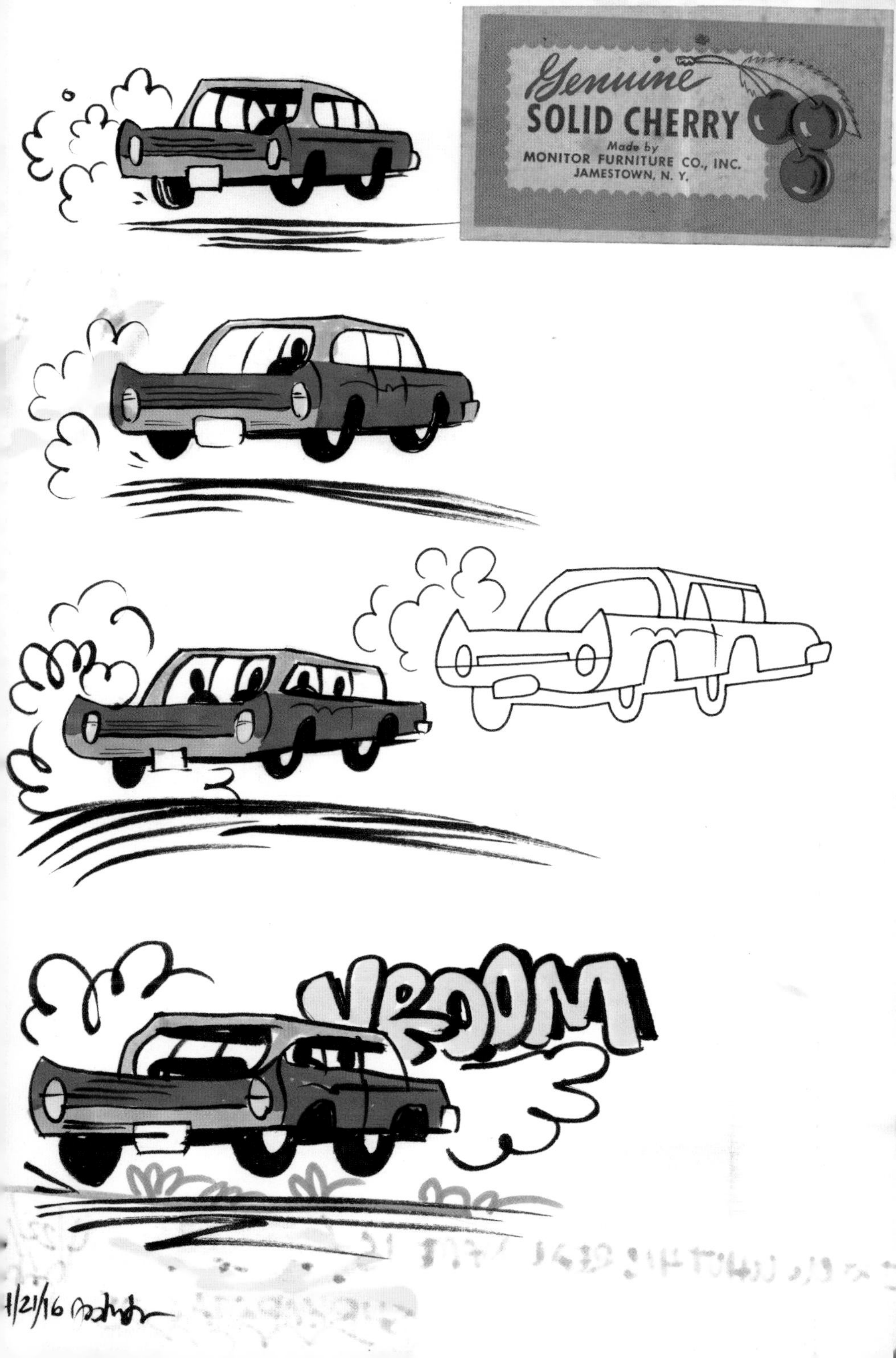
Genuine
SOLID CHERRY
Made by
MONITOR FURNITURE CO., INC.
JAMESTOWN, N. Y.
VROOM

1/21/16

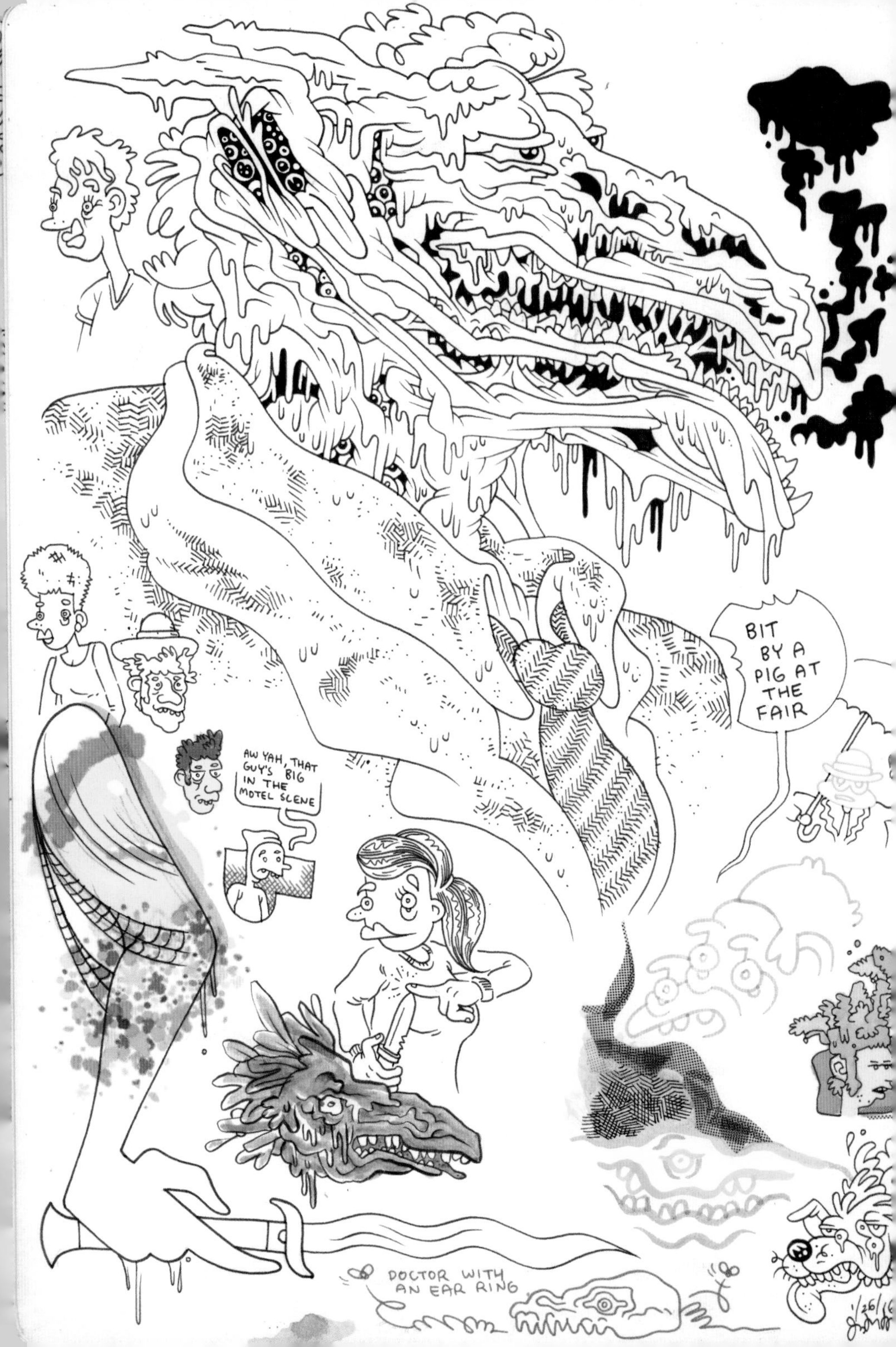
BIT BY A PIG AT THE FAIR
AW YAH, THAT GUY'S BIG IN THE MOTEL SCENE
DOCTOR WITH AN EAR RING
1/26/16

E-ROLL YOUR ROACHES GENTLE PEOPLE, SUPPLIES ARE RUNNING OUT.

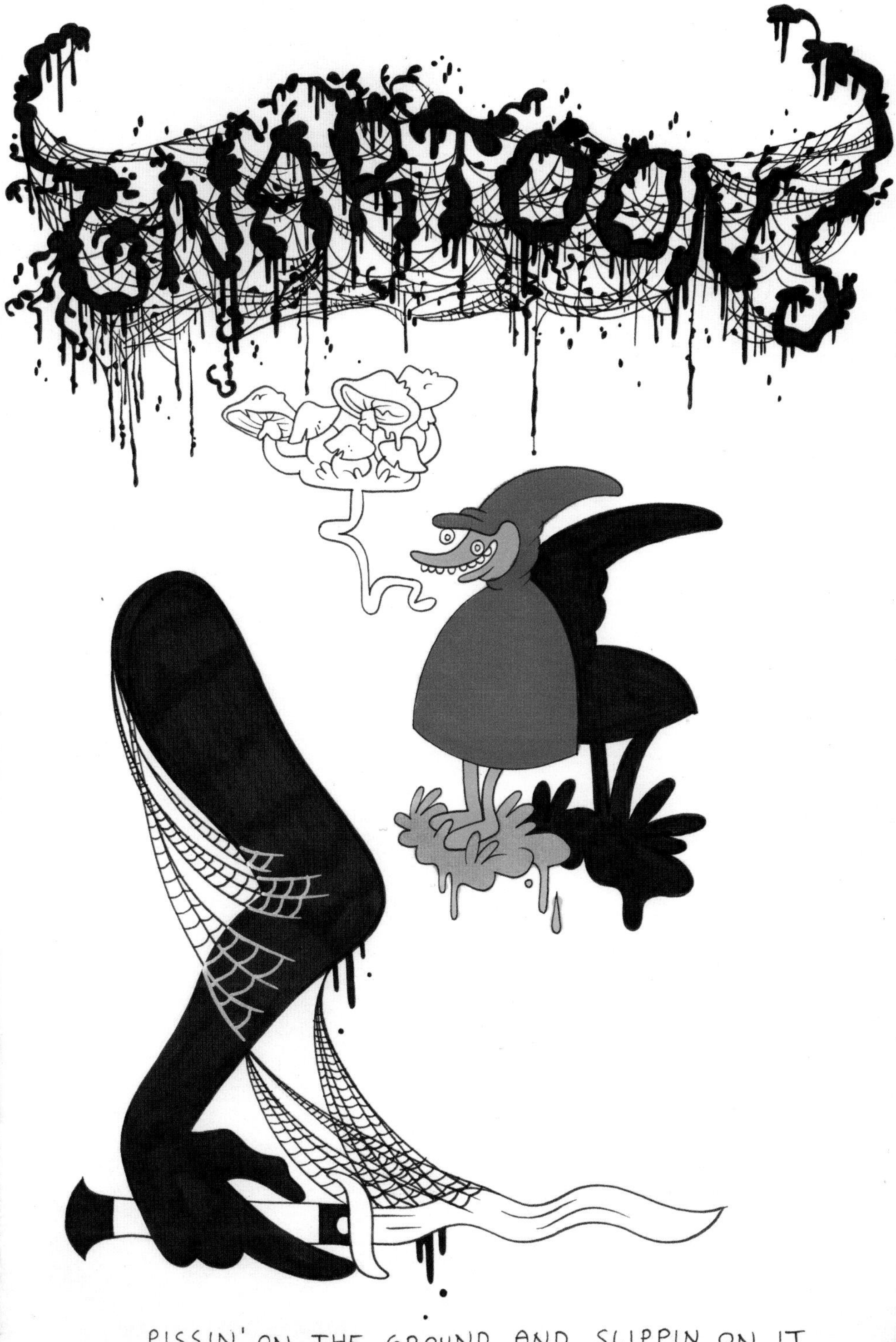
GNARTOONS

PISSIN' ON THE GROUND AND SLIPPIN ON IT

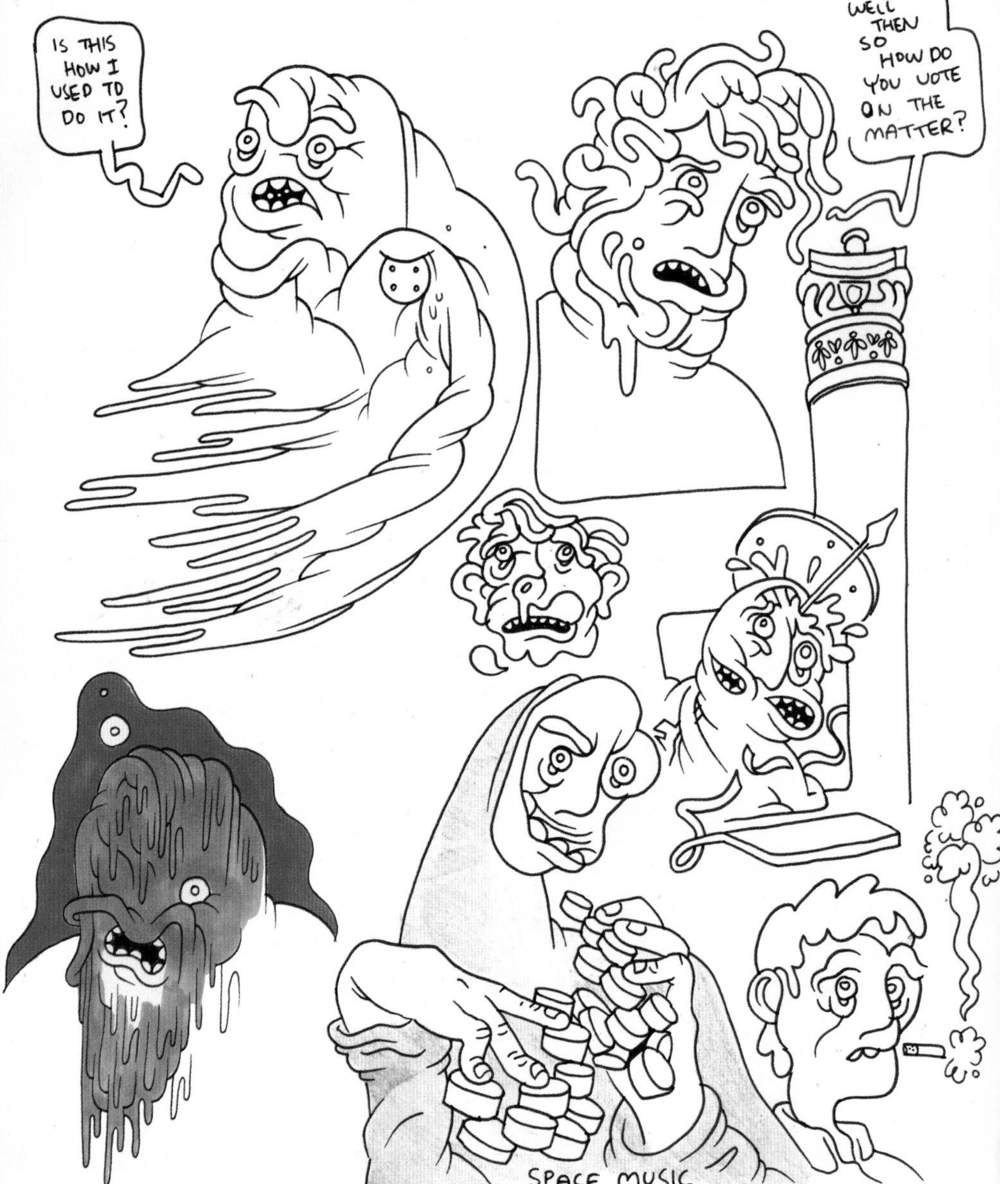
IS THIS HOW I USED TO DO IT?
WELL THEN SO HOW DO YOU VOTE ON THE MATTER?
SPACE MUSIC
3/4/15

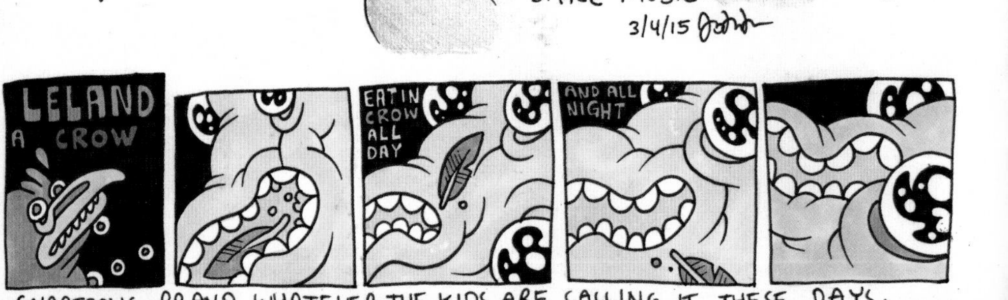
LELAND A CROW
EATIN CROW ALL DAY
AND ALL NIGHT

GNARTOONS BRAND WHATEVER THE KIDS ARE CALLING IT THESE DAYS.

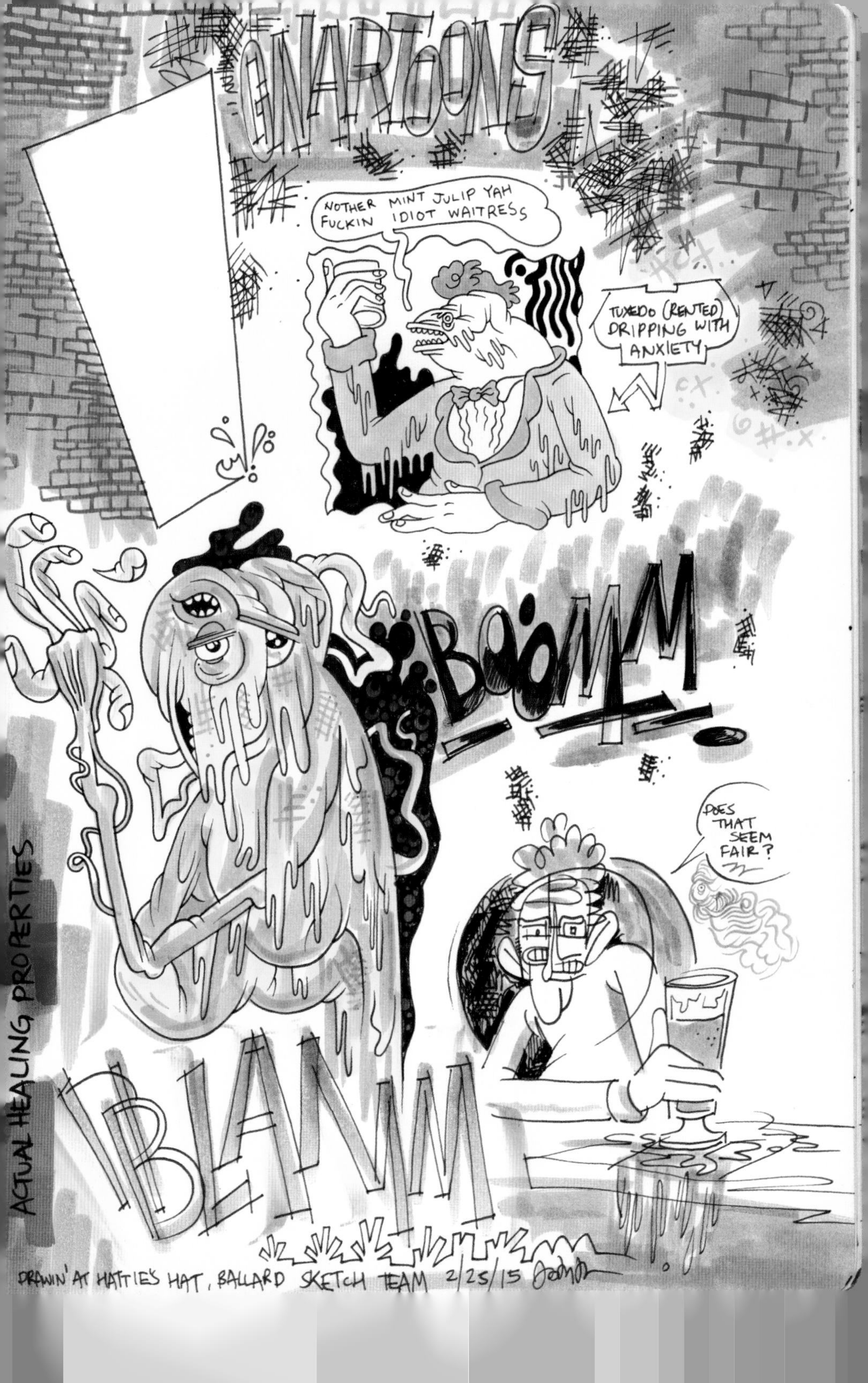
GNARTOONS
NOTHER MINT JULIP YAH FUCKIN IDIOT WAITRESS
TUXEDO (RENTED) DRIPPING WITH ANXIETY
BOOM!
DOES THAT SEEM FAIR?
ACTUAL HEALING PROPERTIES
BLAMM!
DRAWIN' AT HATTIE'S HAT, BALLARD SKETCH TEAM 2/25/15

ACTUAL HEALING POWERS OF CORNDOGS WILL GO ON UNRECOGNIZED BY THE NEW AGE COMMUNITY UNTIL LONG AFTER THE DECLINE OF CRYSTAL POPULARITY.

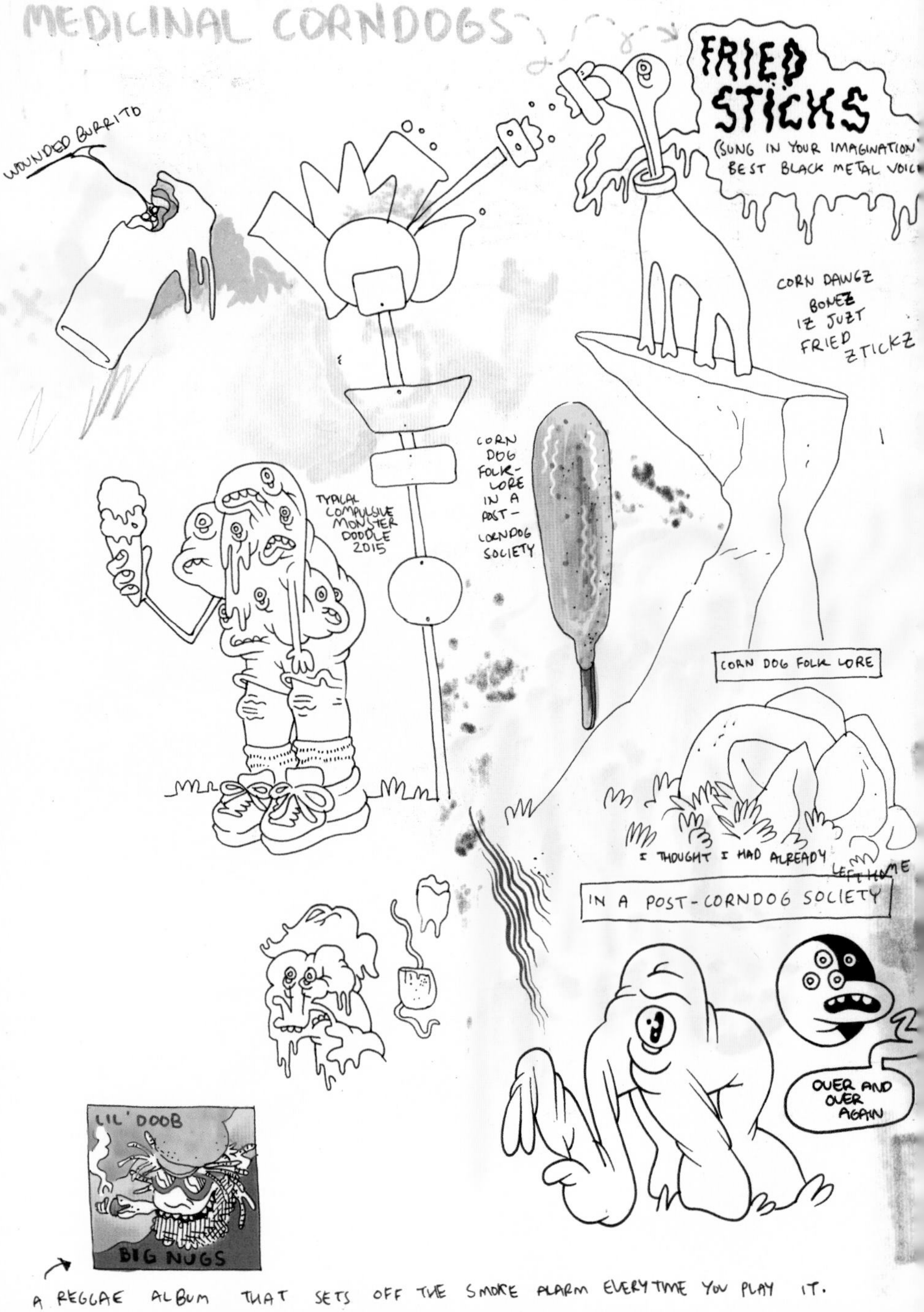
MEDICINAL CORNDOGS
FRIED STICKS
(SUNG IN YOUR IMAGINATION' BEST BLACK METAL VOIC
WOUNDED BURRITO
CORN DAWGZ BONEZ IZ JUZT FRIED ZTICKZ
CORN DOG FOLK-LORE IN A POST-CORNDOG SOCIETY
TYPICAL COMPULSIVE MONSTER DOODLE 2015
CORN DOG FOLK LORE
I THOUGHT I HAD ALREADY LEFT HOME
IN A POST-CORNDOG SOCIETY
OVER AND OVER AGAIN
LIL' DOOB
BIG NUGS

A REGGAE ALBUM THAT SETS OFF THE SMOKE ALARM EVERYTIME YOU PLAY IT.

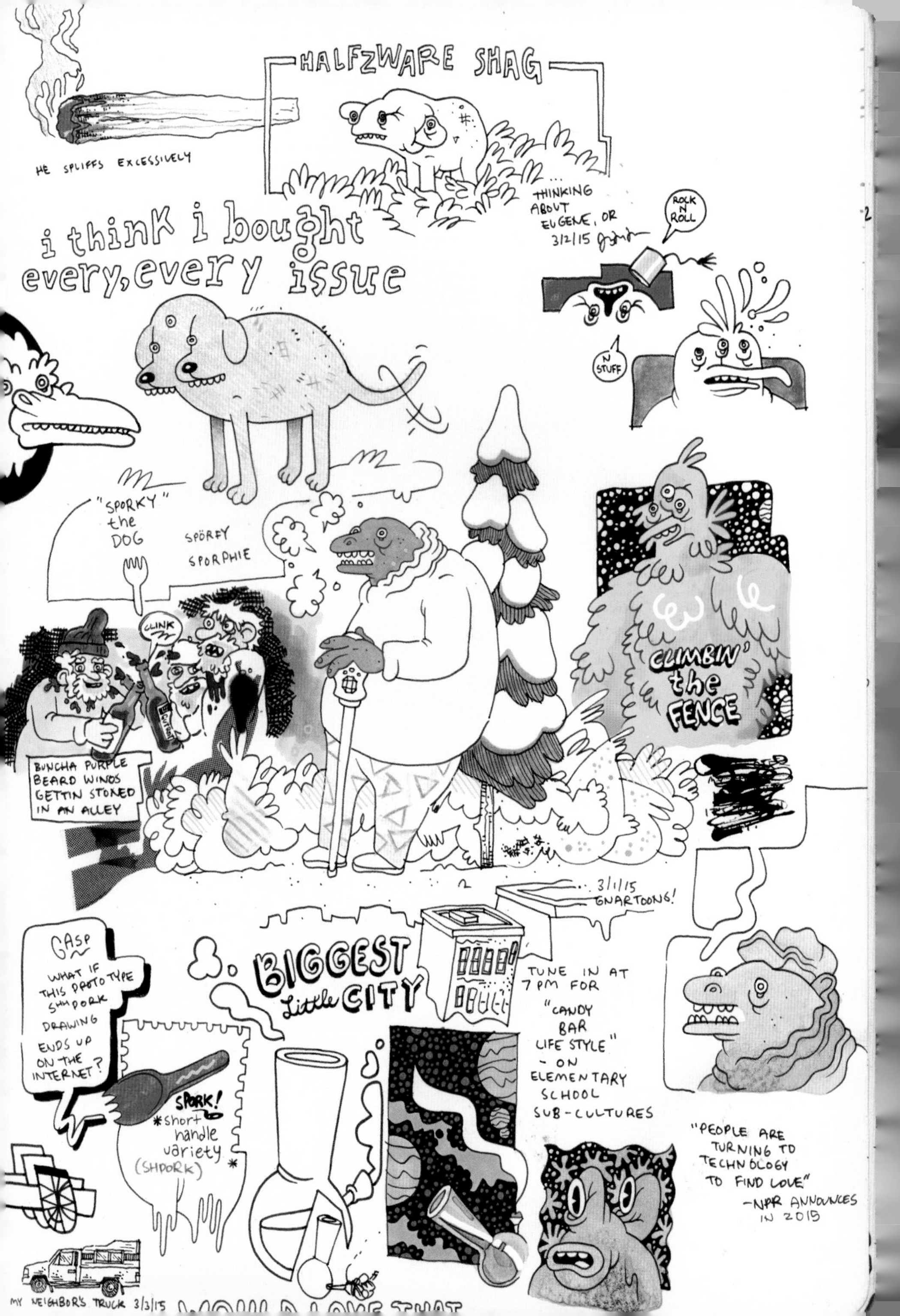
HE SPLIFFS EXCESSIVELY
HALFZWARE SHAG
... THINKING ABOUT EUGENE, OR 3/2/15
ROCK N ROLL
i think i bought every, every issue
N STUFF
"SPORKY" the DOG
SPÖRFY
SPORPHIE
CLINK
BUNCHA PURPLE BEARD WINOS GETTIN STONED IN AN ALLEY
CLIMBIN' the FENCE
3/1/15 GNARTOONS!
GASP
WHAT IF THIS PROTOTYPE SHPORK DRAWING ENDS UP ON THE INTERNET?
BIGGEST Little CITY
TUNE IN AT 7PM FOR "CANDY BAR LIFE STYLE" - ON ELEMENTARY SCHOOL SUB-CULTURES
SPORK!
short handle variety (SHPORK)
"PEOPLE ARE TURNING TO TECHNOLOGY TO FIND LOVE" -NPR ANNOUNCES IN 2015
MY NEIGHBOR'S TRUCK 3/3/15

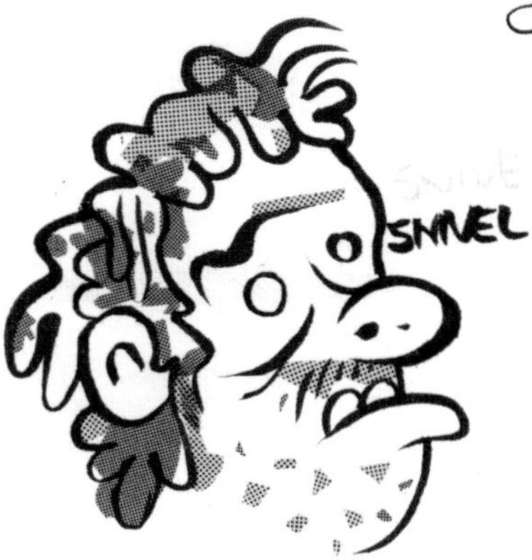
SNIVEL

DUCK SHART

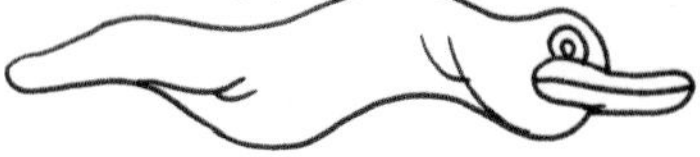

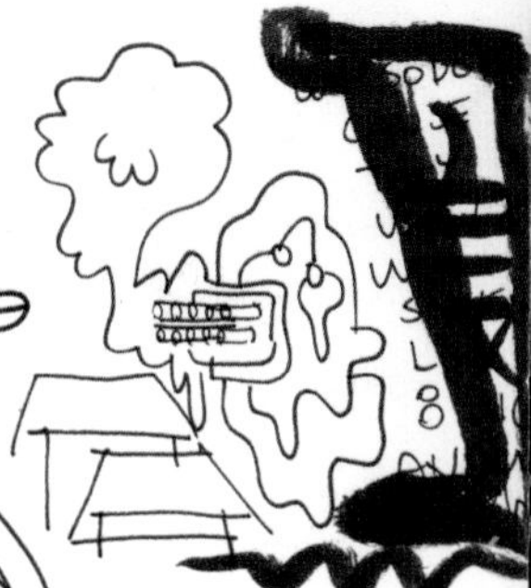

LAKE HOUSE

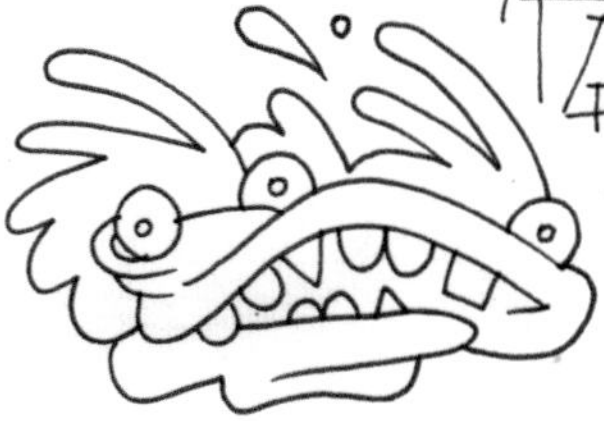

SLINKIN OFF FOR A NIGHTCAP...

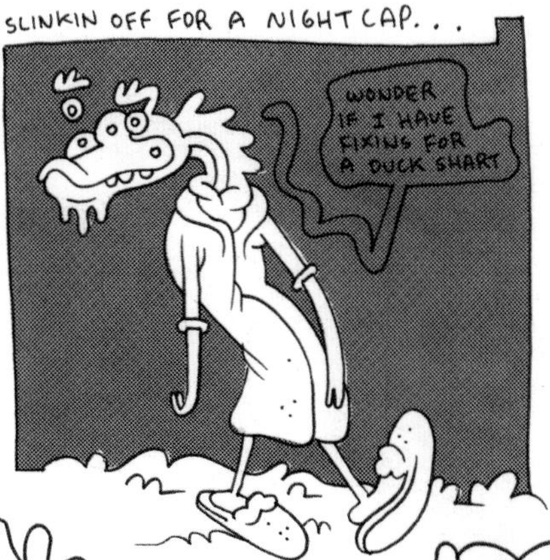
WONDER IF I HAVE FIXINS FOR A DUCK SHART

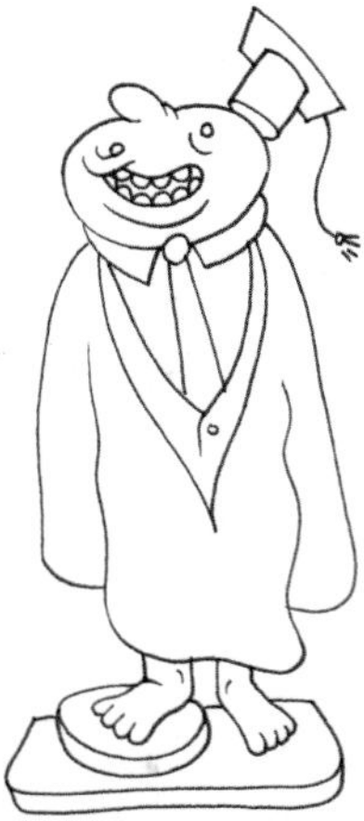

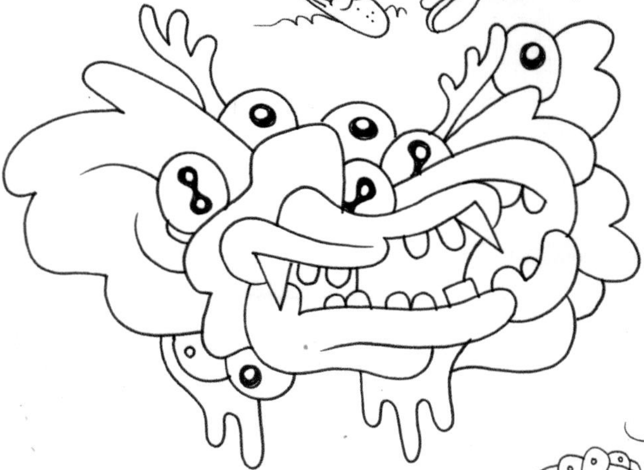

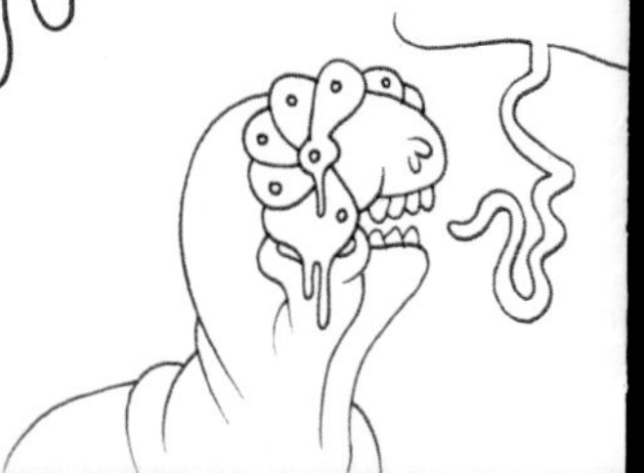

E.T. the EXTRA TESTICAL

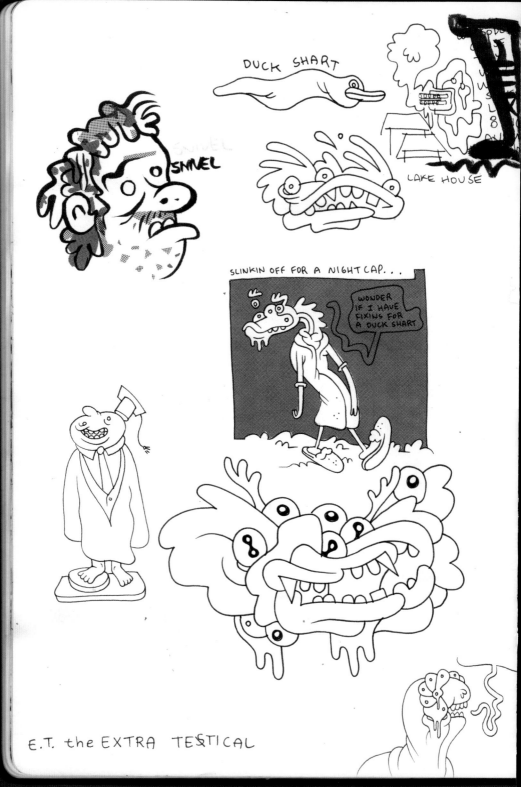

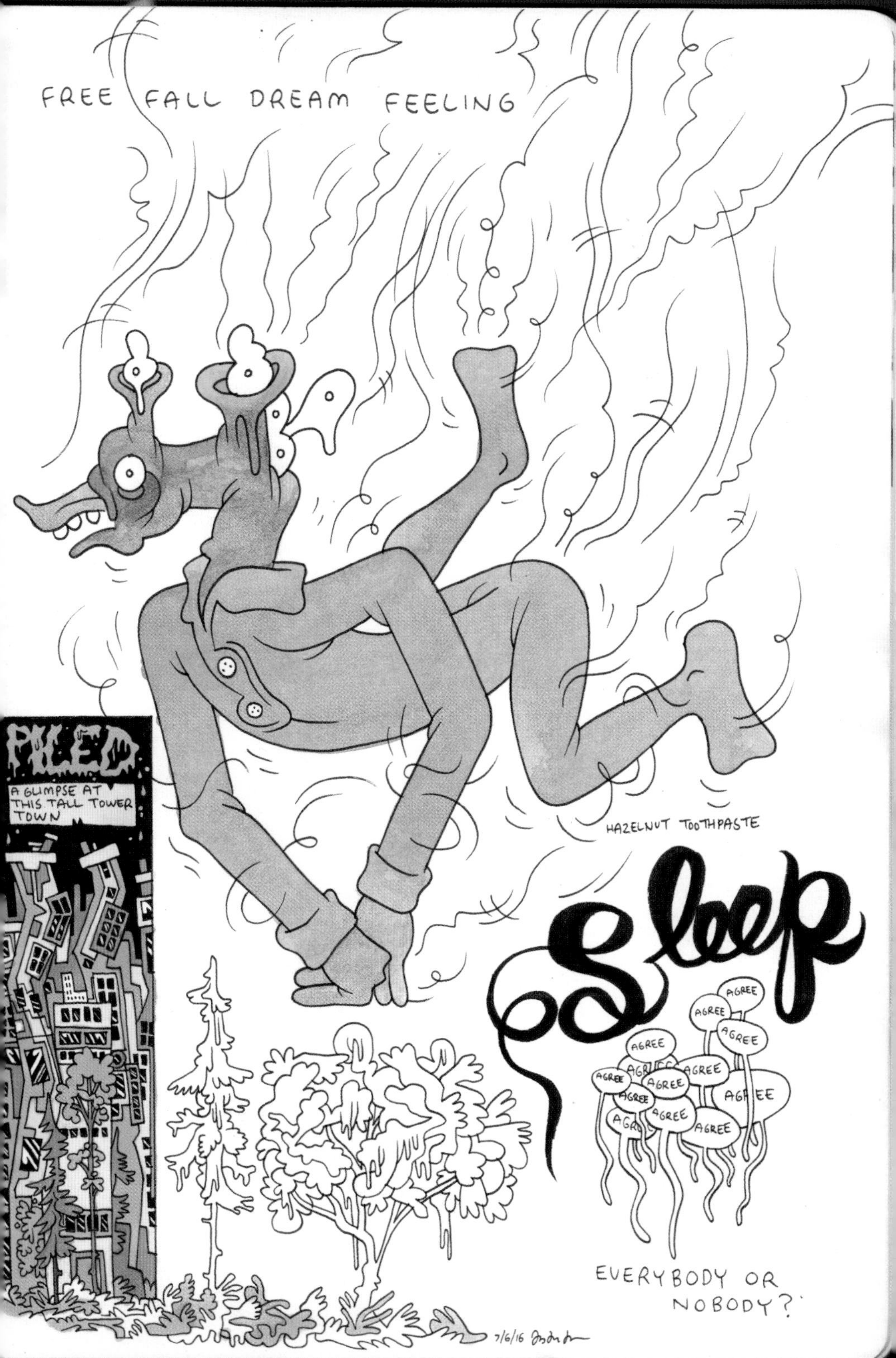
FREE FALL DREAM FEELING
PILED
A GLIMPSE AT THIS TALL TOWER TOWN
HAZELNUT TOOTHPASTE
Sleep
AGREE
AGREE
AGREE
AGREE
AGREE
AGREE
AGREE
AGREE
AGREE
EVERYBODY OR NOBODY?
7/6/16

BZZZZ

I'D PREFER TO LIVE AT THE END OF A LONG DIRT ROAD

PAN

SIGHT
FOR
SORE
EYES

A
FIGHT
FOR
FOUR
GUYS

RE-
DISTRI-
BUTED
TENDER-
NESS

POCKET FULL OF FROND

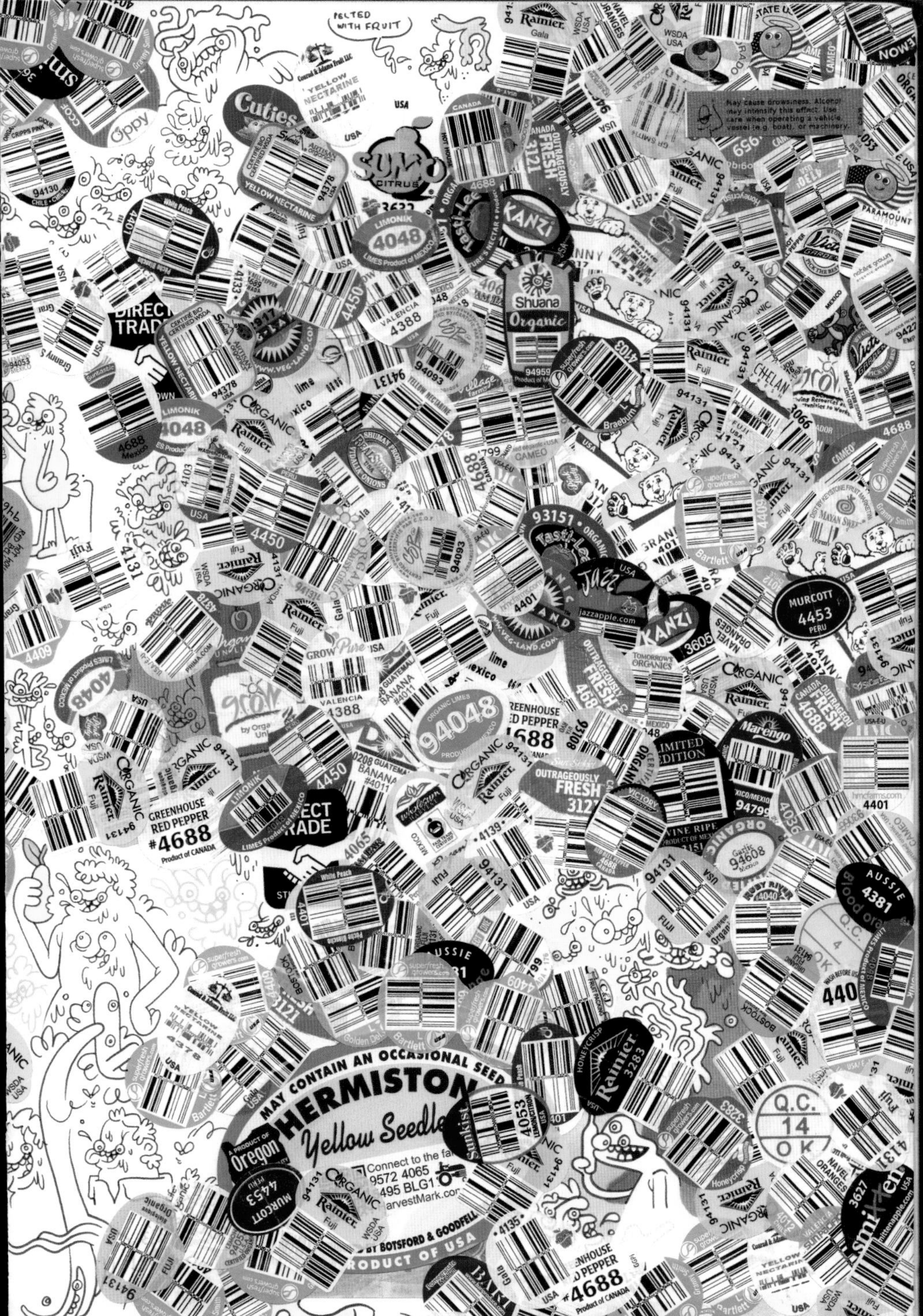
PELTED WITH FRUIT
May cause drowsiness. Alcohol may intensify this effect. Use care when operating a vehicle, vessel (e.g. boat), or machinery.
MAY CONTAIN AN OCCASIONAL SEED
HERMISTON
Yellow Seedle
A PRODUCT OF Oregon
PRODUCT OF USA
GREENHOUSE RED PEPPER #4688 Product of CANADA
MURCOTT 4453 PERU
AUSSIE 4381
Q.C. 14 OK
jazzapple.com
ORGANIC LIMES 94048
LIMONIK 4048
VALENCIA 4388
OUTRAGEOUSLY FRESH
Cuties
SUMO CITRUS
KANZI
Shuana Organic
DIRECT TRADE

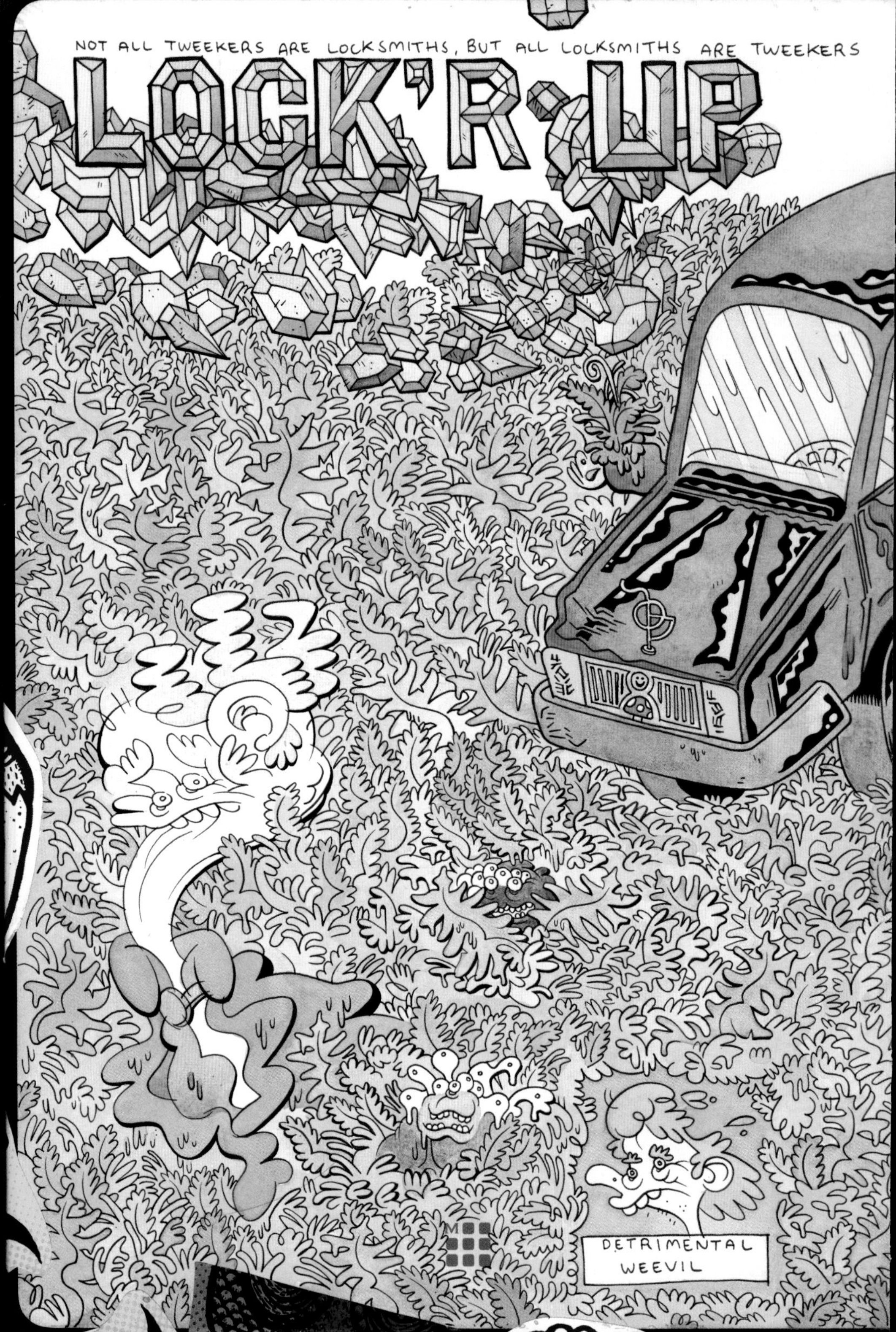
NOT ALL TWEEKERS ARE LOCKSMITHS, BUT ALL LOCKSMITHS ARE TWEEKERS
LOCK'R'UP
DETRIMENTAL WEEVIL

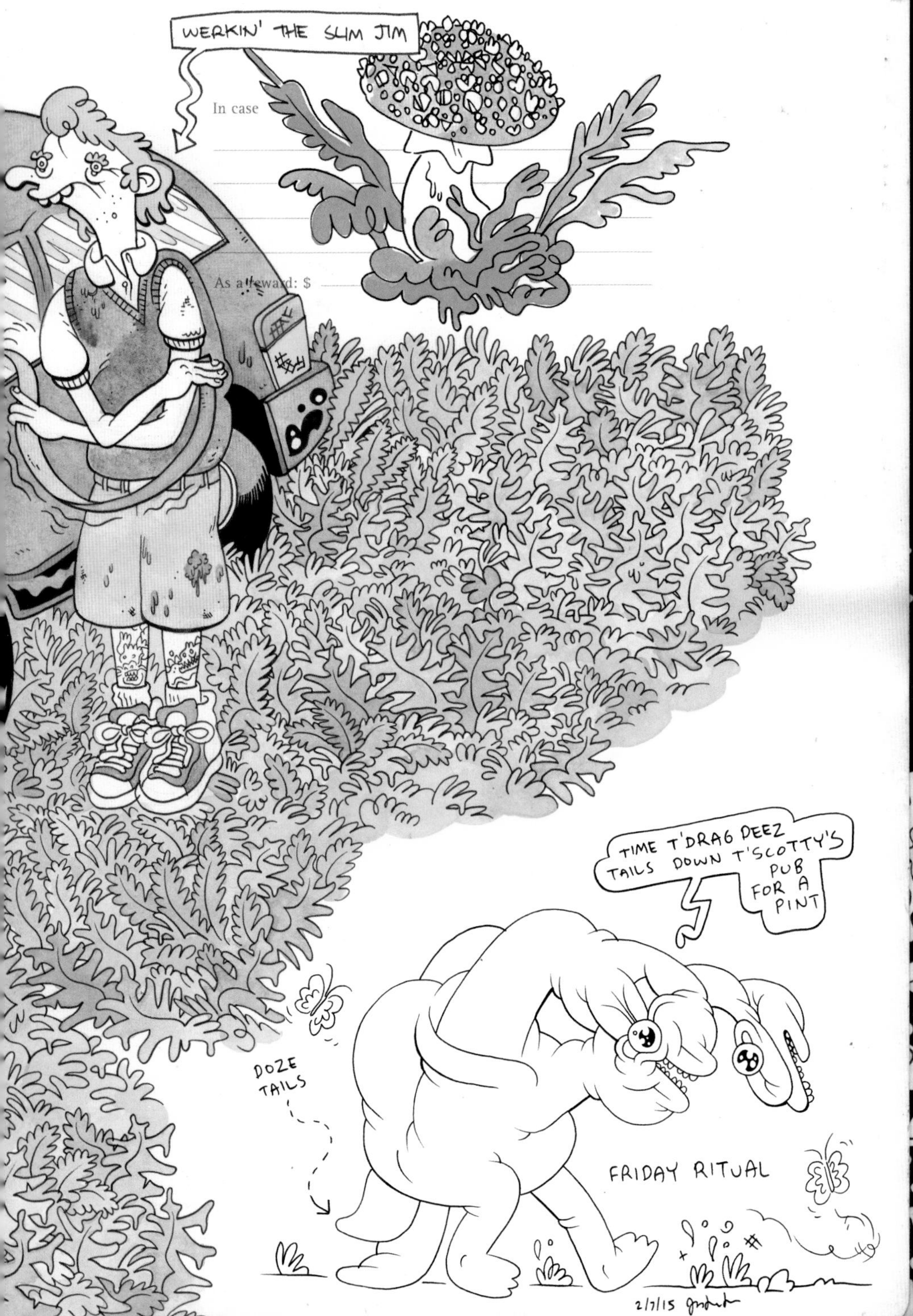
WERKIN' THE SLIM JIM
In case
As a reward: $
TIME T'DRAG DEEZ TAILS DOWN T'SCOTTY'S PUB FOR A PINT
DOZE TAILS
FRIDAY RITUAL
2/7/15

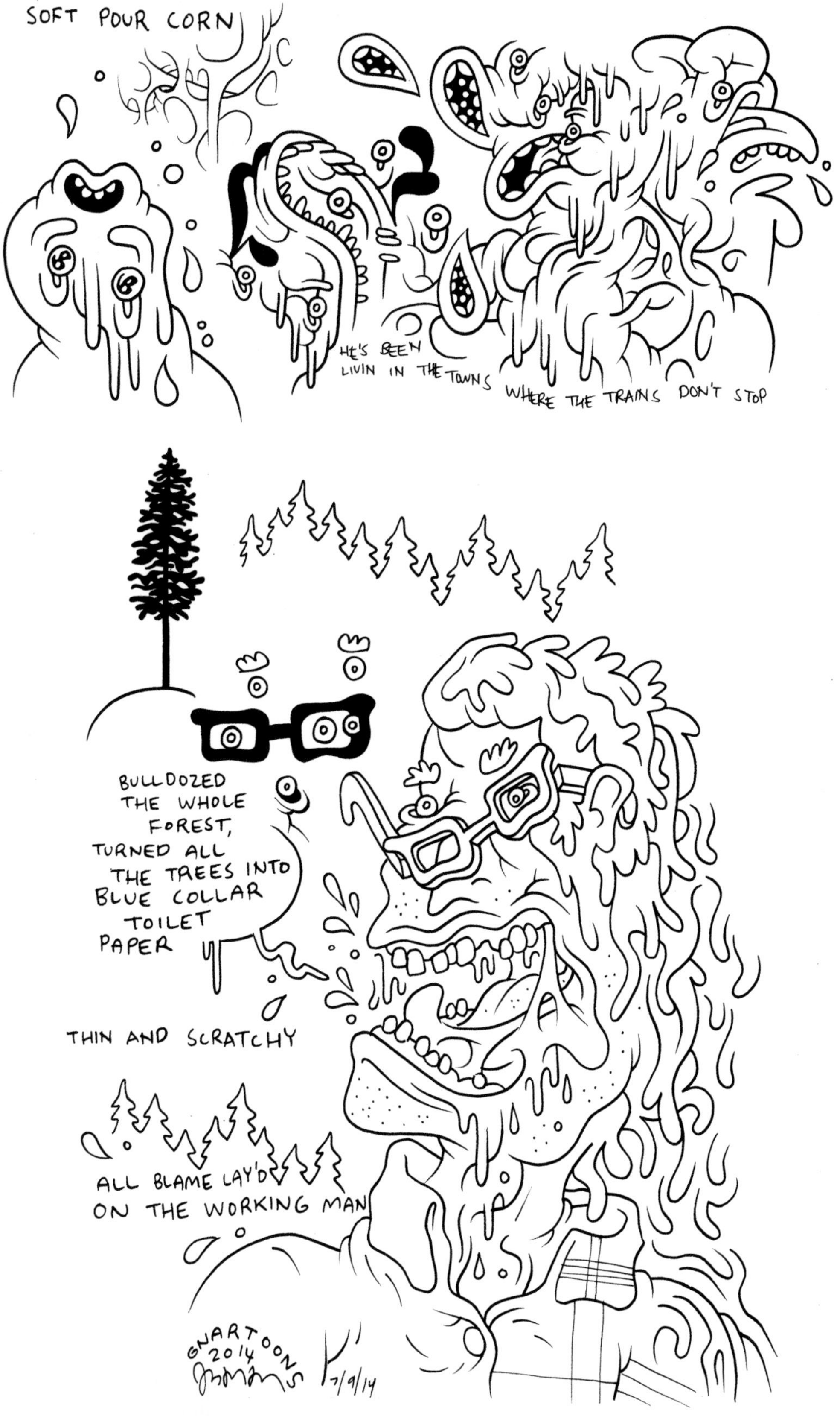
SOFT POUR CORN
HE'S BEEN LIVIN IN THE TOWNS WHERE THE TRAINS DON'T STOP
BULLDOZED THE WHOLE FOREST, TURNED ALL THE TREES INTO BLUE COLLAR TOILET PAPER
THIN AND SCRATCHY
ALL BLAME LAY'D ON THE WORKING MAN
GNARTOONS 2014
7/9/14

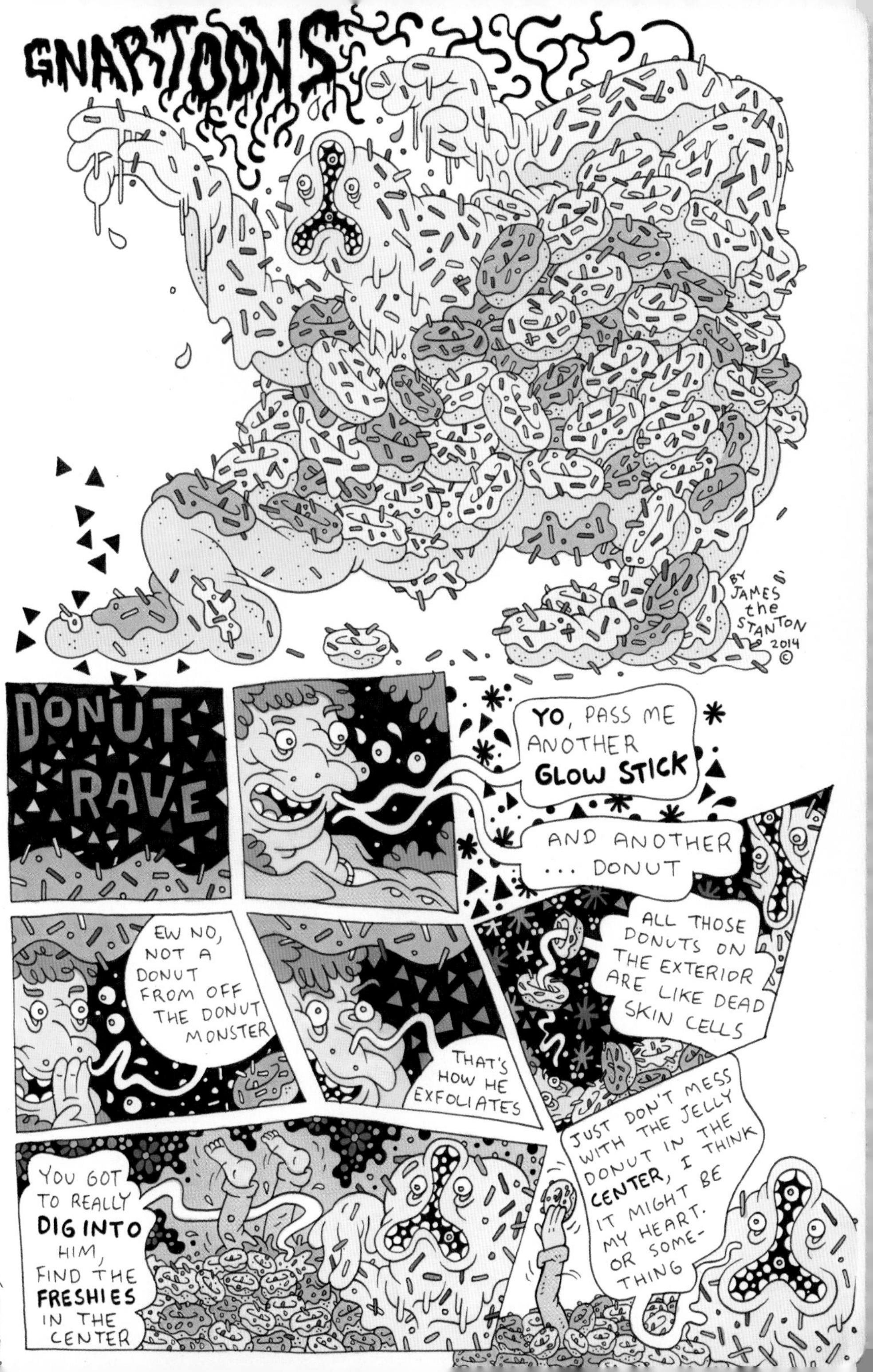
GNARTOONS
BY JAMES the STANTON 2014 ©
DONUT RAVE
YO, PASS ME ANOTHER GLOW STICK
AND ANOTHER ... DONUT
ALL THOSE DONUTS ON THE EXTERIOR ARE LIKE DEAD SKIN CELLS
EW NO, NOT A DONUT FROM OFF THE DONUT MONSTER
THAT'S HOW HE EXFOLIATES
YOU GOT TO REALLY DIG INTO HIM, FIND THE FRESHIES IN THE CENTER
JUST DON'T MESS WITH THE JELLY DONUT IN THE CENTER, I THINK IT MIGHT BE MY HEART. OR SOME-THING

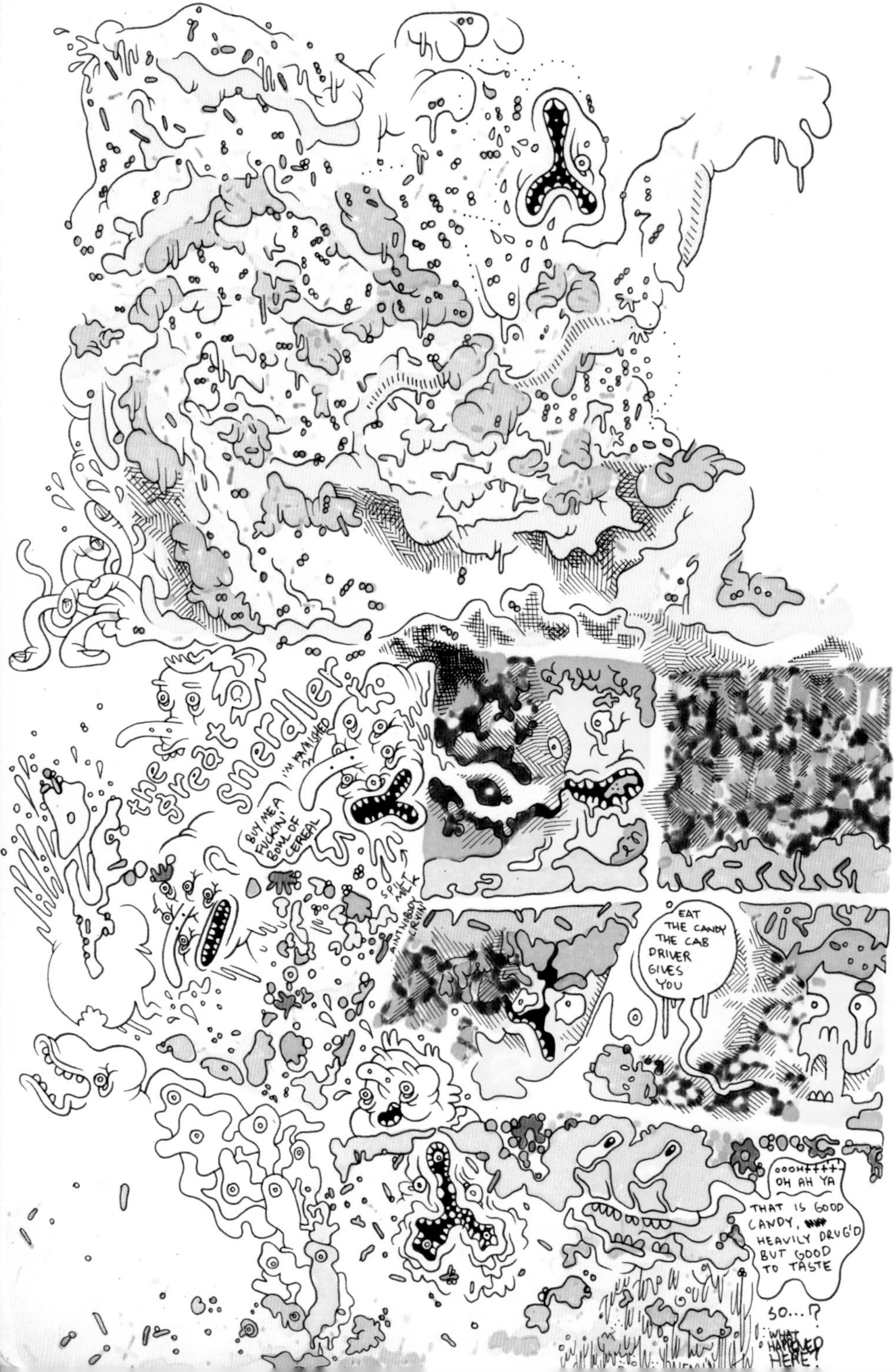
the great snerdler
I'M FAMISHED
BUY ME A FUCKIN' BOWL OF CEREAL
SPILT MILK AIN'T NOBODY CRYIN'
EAT THE CANDY THE CAB DRIVER GIVES YOU
OOOH+++++ OH AH YA
THAT IS GOOD CANDY, HEAVILY DRUG'D BUT GOOD TO TASTE
SO...?
WHAT HAPPENED HERE?

"HEY SUGAR"
3/5/15 John

GNARTOONS

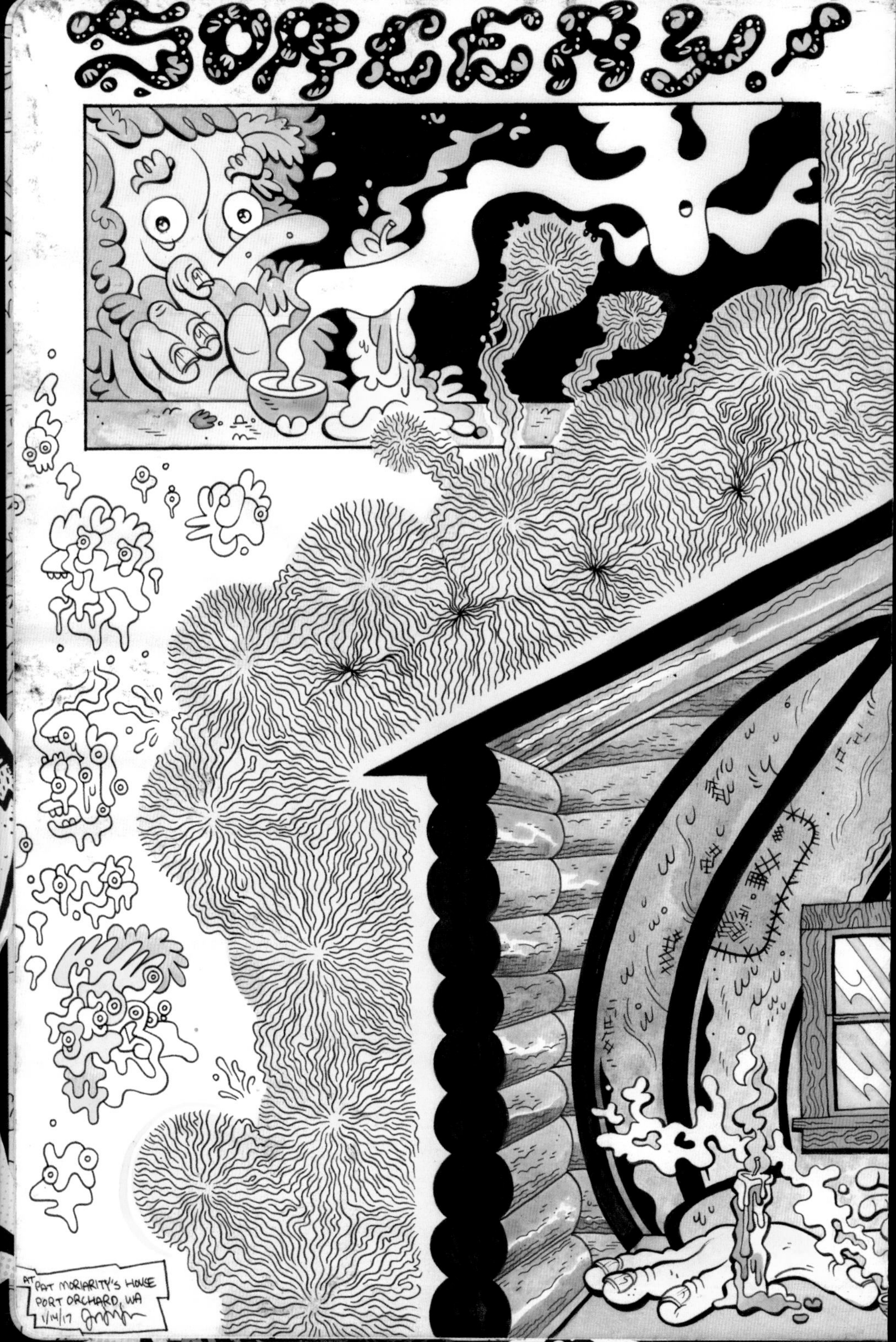
SORCERY!
AT PAT MORIARITY'S HOUSE
PORT ORCHARD, WA
1/14/17

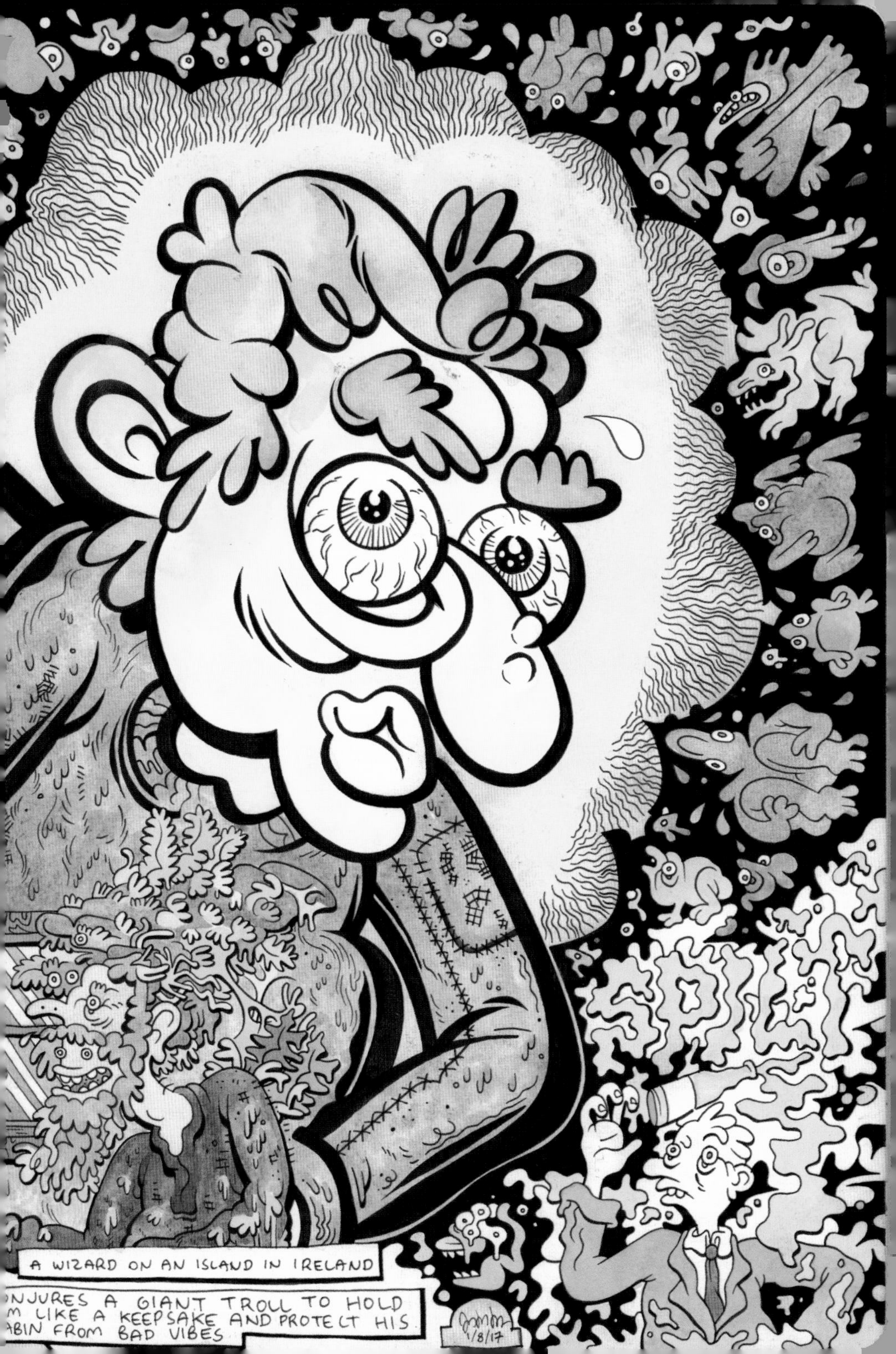
A WIZARD ON AN ISLAND IN IRELAND
ONJURES A GIANT TROLL TO HOLD
M LIKE A KEEPSAKE AND PROTECT HIS
ABIN FROM BAD VIBES
1/8/17

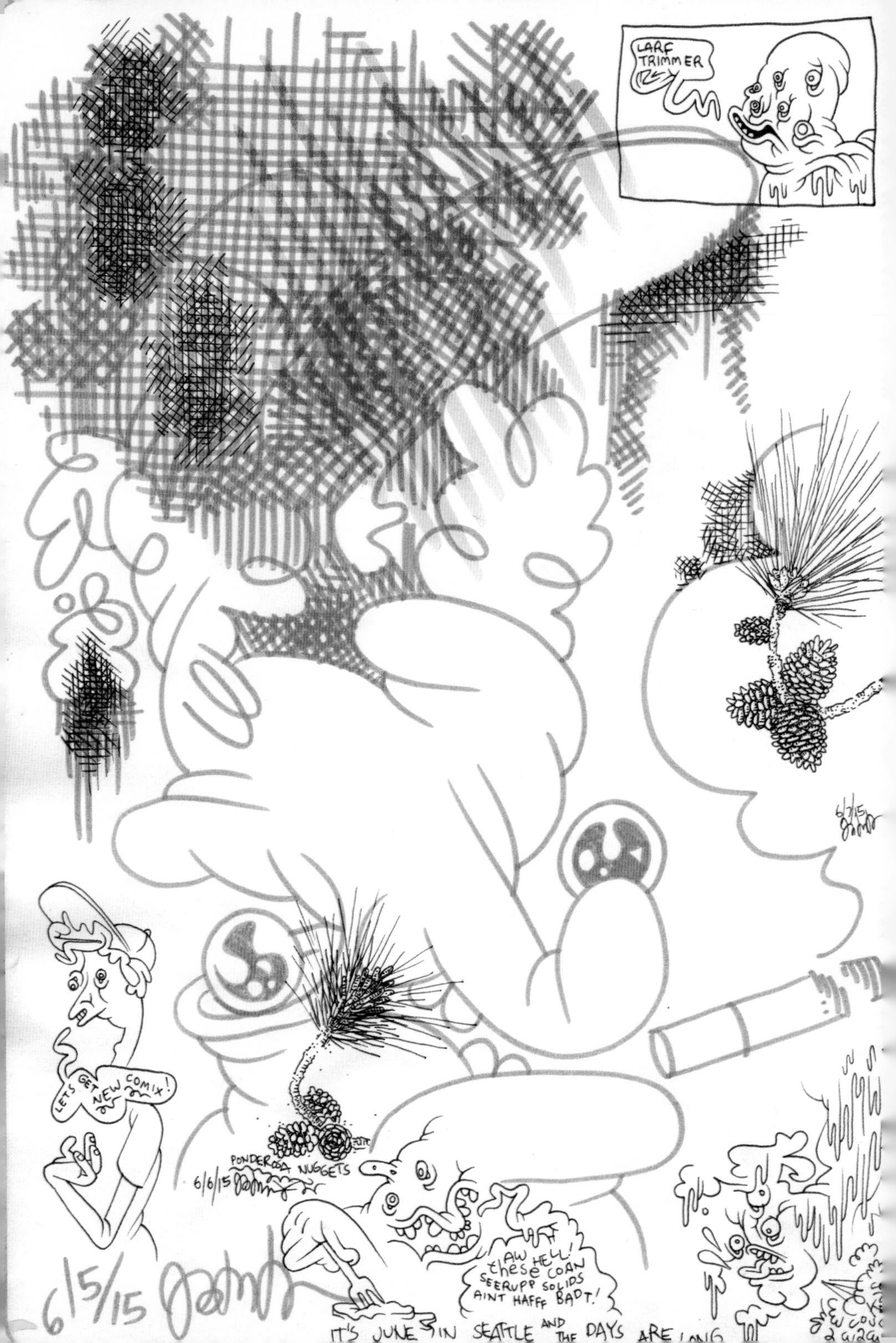
LARF TRIMMER
6/7/15
LET'S GET NEW COMIX!
PONDEROSA NUGGETS
6/6/15
AW HELL! these COAN SEERUPP SOLIDS AINT HAFFF BADT!
6/5/15
IT'S JUNE IN SEATTLE AND THE DAYS ARE LONG

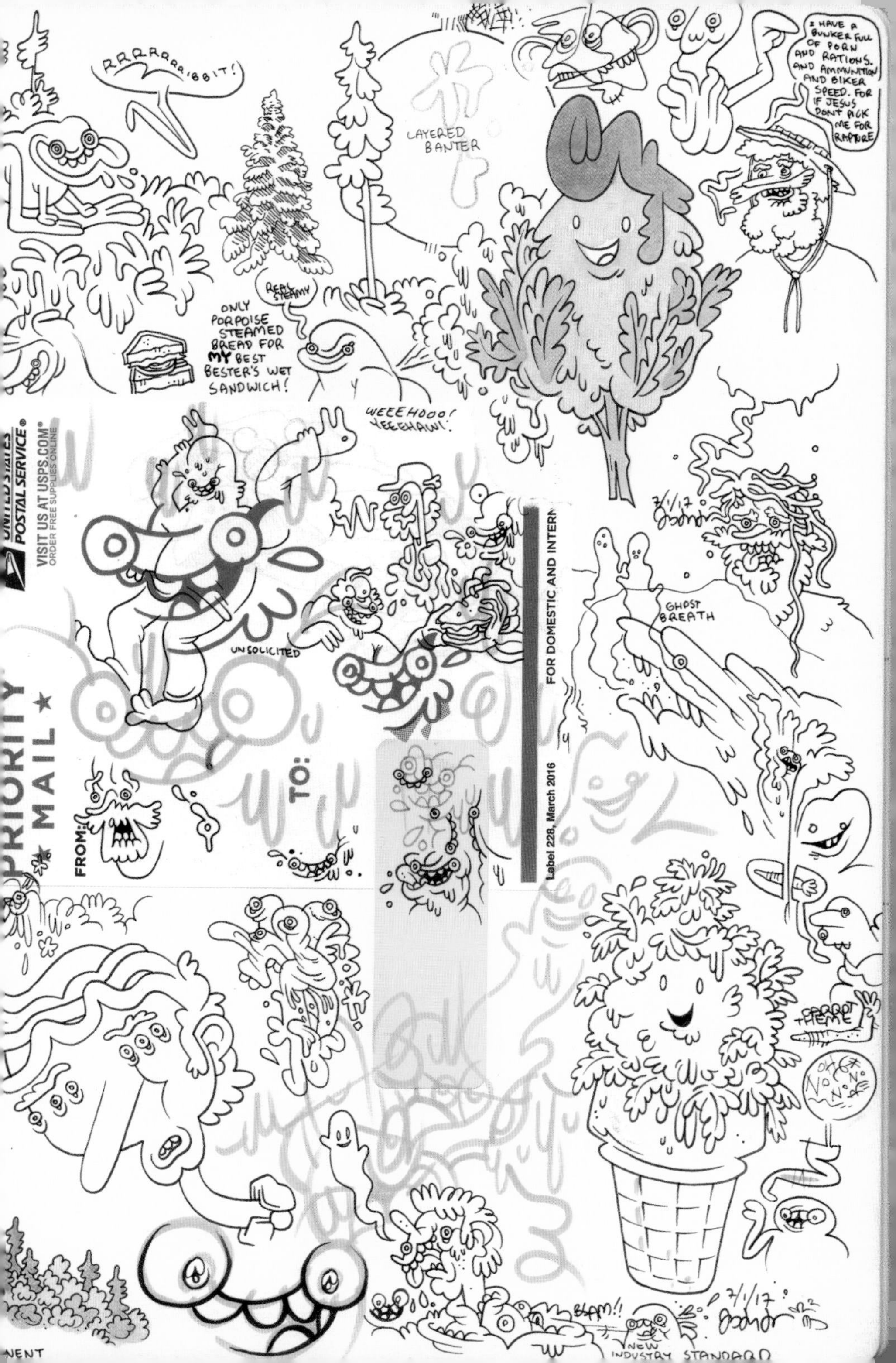
LAYERED BANTER
I HAVE A BUNKER FULL OF PORN AND RATIONS. AND AMMUNITION AND BIKER SPEED. FOR IF JESUS DON'T PICK ME FOR RAPTURE
REAL STEAMY
ONLY PORPOISE STEAMED BREAD FOR MY BEST BESTER'S WET SANDWICH!
WEEEHOOO! YEEEHAW!
UNITED STATES POSTAL SERVICE®
VISIT US AT USPS.COM®
ORDER FREE SUPPLIES ONLINE
PRIORITY ★ MAIL ★
FROM:
TO:
UNSOLICITED
FOR DOMESTIC AND INTERN
Label 228, March 2016
7/1/17
GHOST BREATH
CARROT THEME
BLAM!!
7/1/17
NEW INDUSTRY STANDARD

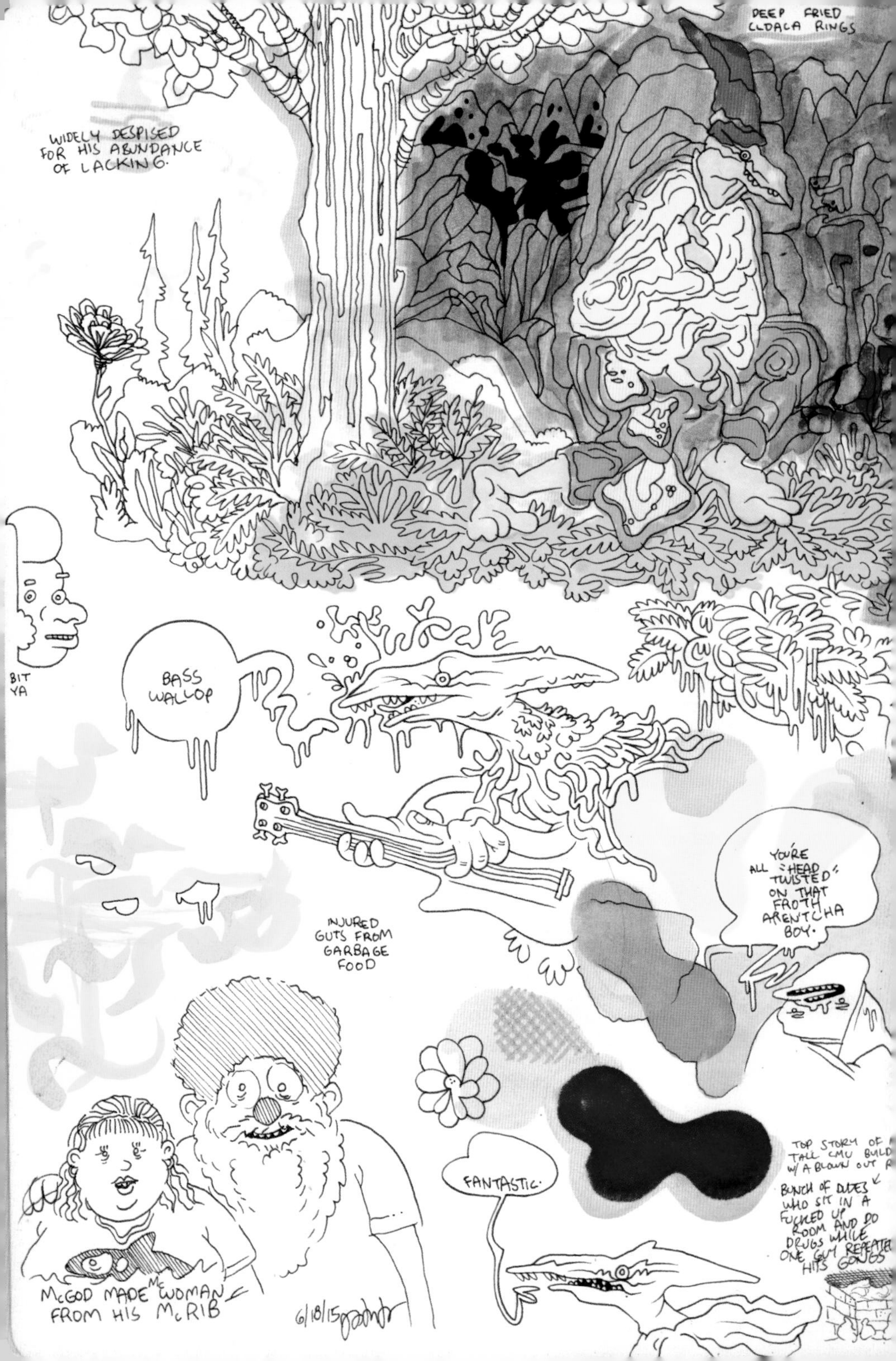
DEEP FRIED CLOACA RINGS
WIDELY DESPISED FOR HIS ABUNDANCE OF LACKING.
BIT YA
BASS WALLOP
YOU'RE ALL "HEAD TWISTED" ON THAT FROTH AREN'TCHA BOY.
INJURED GUTS FROM GARBAGE FOOD
TOP STORY OF TALL CMU BUILD W/ A BLOWN OUT R
BUNCH OF DUDES WHO SIT IN A FUCKED UP ROOM AND DO DRUGS WHILE ONE GUY REPEATED HITS GONGS
FANTASTIC.
McGOD MADE McWOMAN FROM HIS McRIB
6/18/15

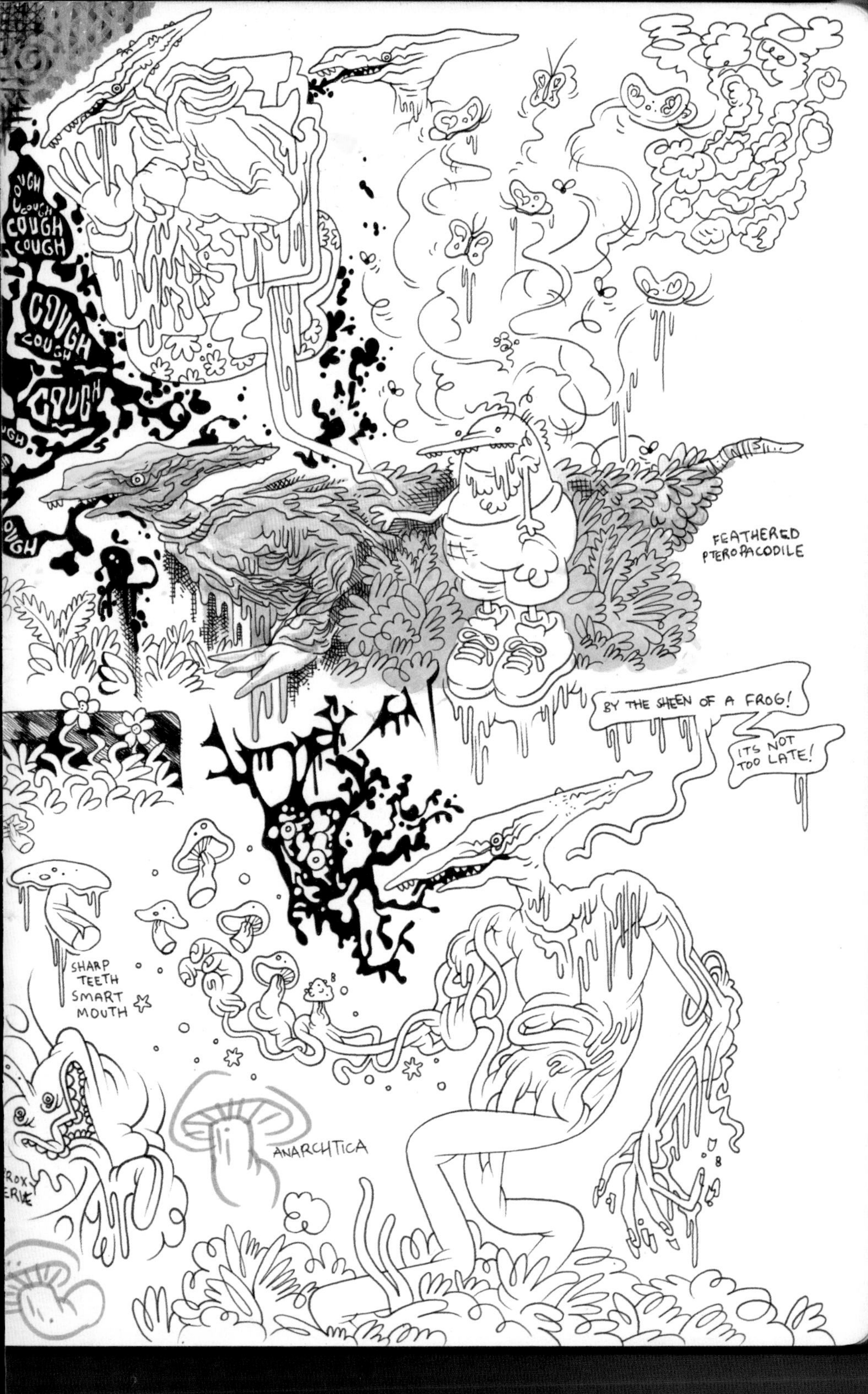
COUGH COUGH COUGH COUGH
COUGH COUGH
COUGH
FEATHERED PTEROPACODILE
BY THE SHEEN OF A FROG!
ITS NOT TOO LATE!
SHARP TEETH SMART MOUTH
ANARCHTICA

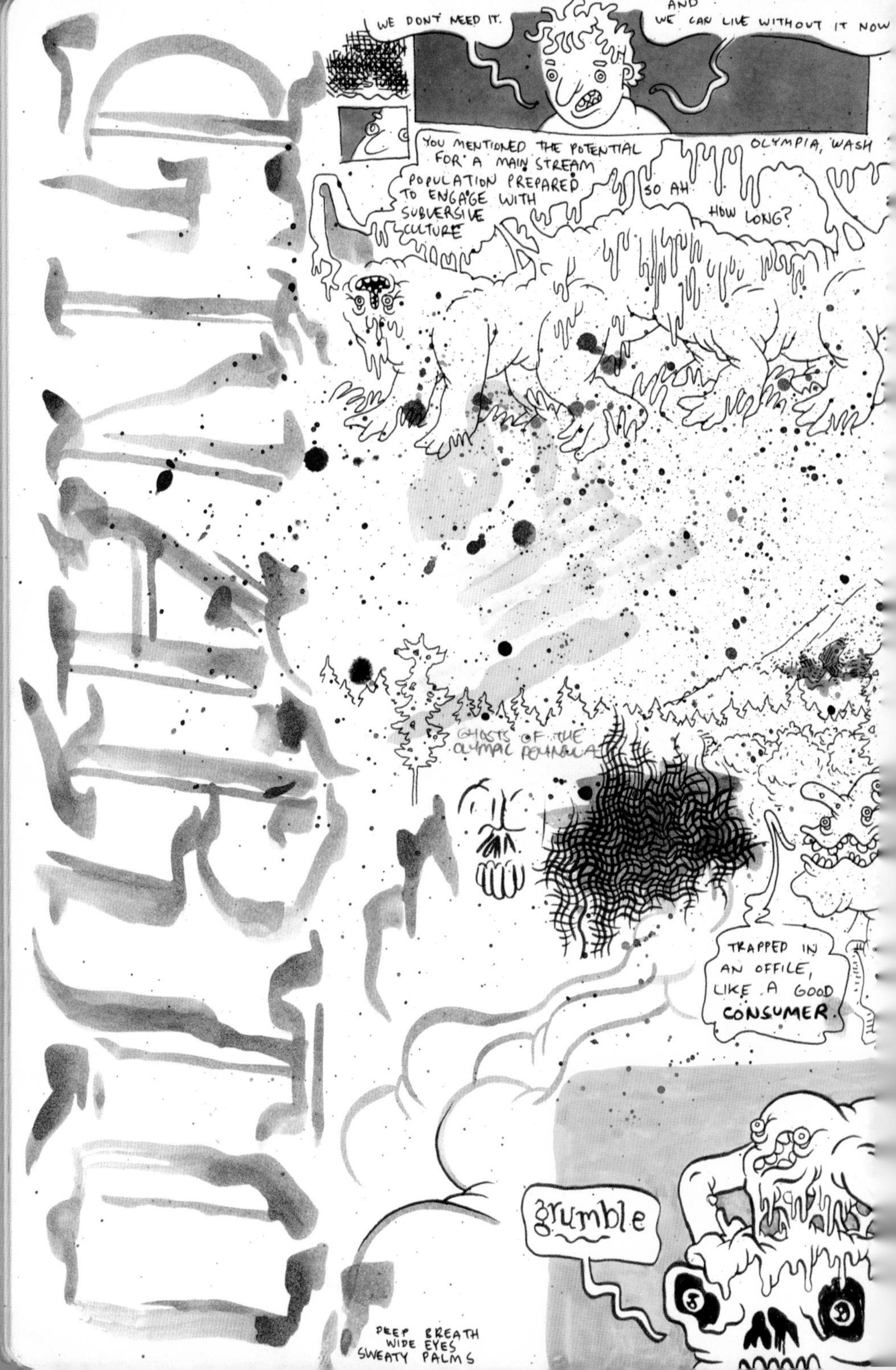

WE DONT NEED IT.
AND WE CAN LIVE WITHOUT IT NOW
YOU MENTIONED THE POTENTIAL FOR A MAIN STREAM POPULATION PREPARED TO ENGAGE WITH SUBVERSIVE CULTURE
SO AH
OLYMPIA, WASH
HOW LONG?
GHOSTS OF THE
TRAPPED IN AN OFFILE, LIKE A GOOD CONSUMER.
grumble
DEEP BREATH
WIDE EYES
SWEATY PALMS

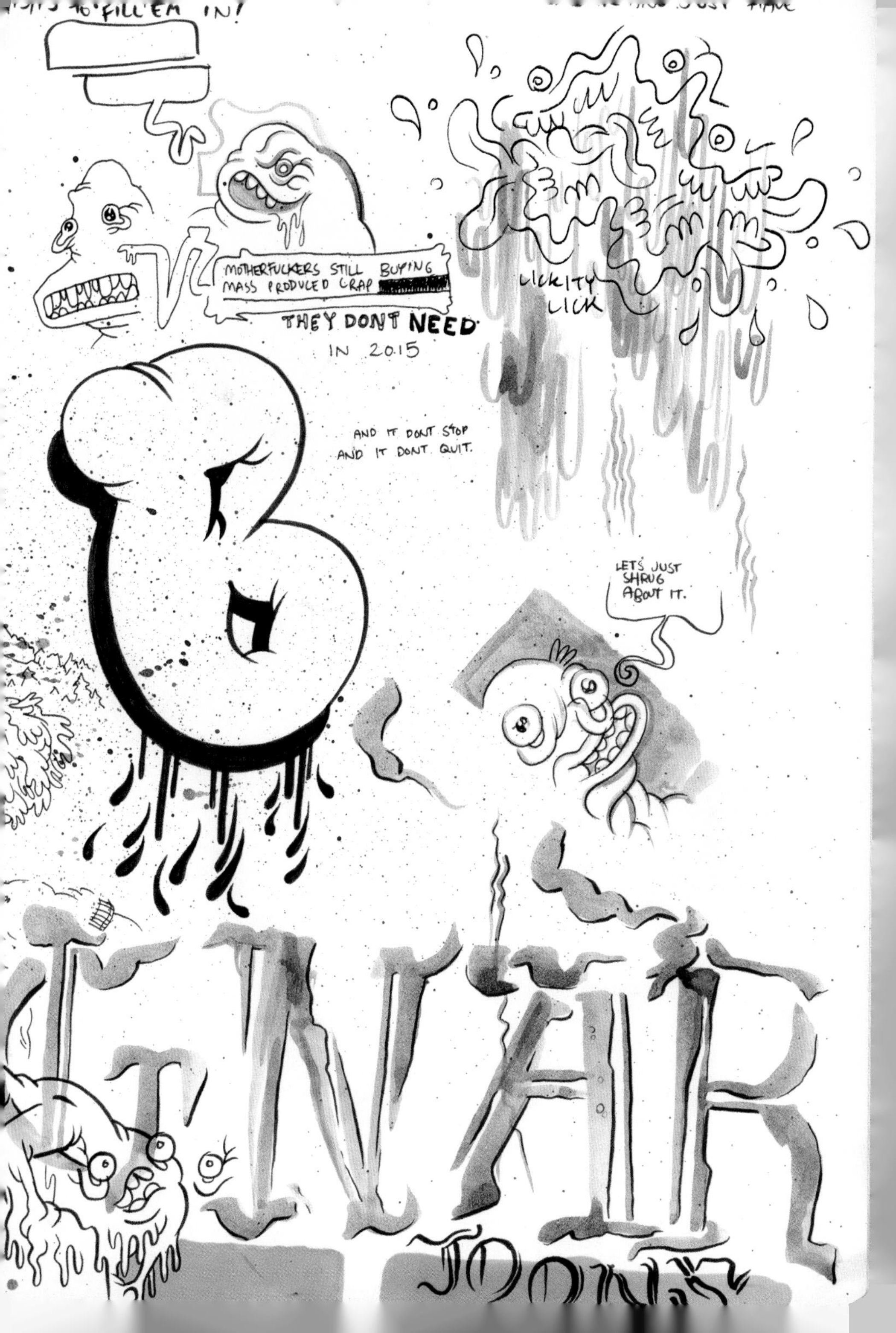
FILL'EM IN!
MOTHERFUCKERS STILL BUYING MASS PRODUCED CRAP [redacted]
THEY DONT NEED
IN 2015
LICKITY LICK
AND IT DONT STOP AND IT DONT QUIT.
LETS JUST SHRUG ABOUT IT.

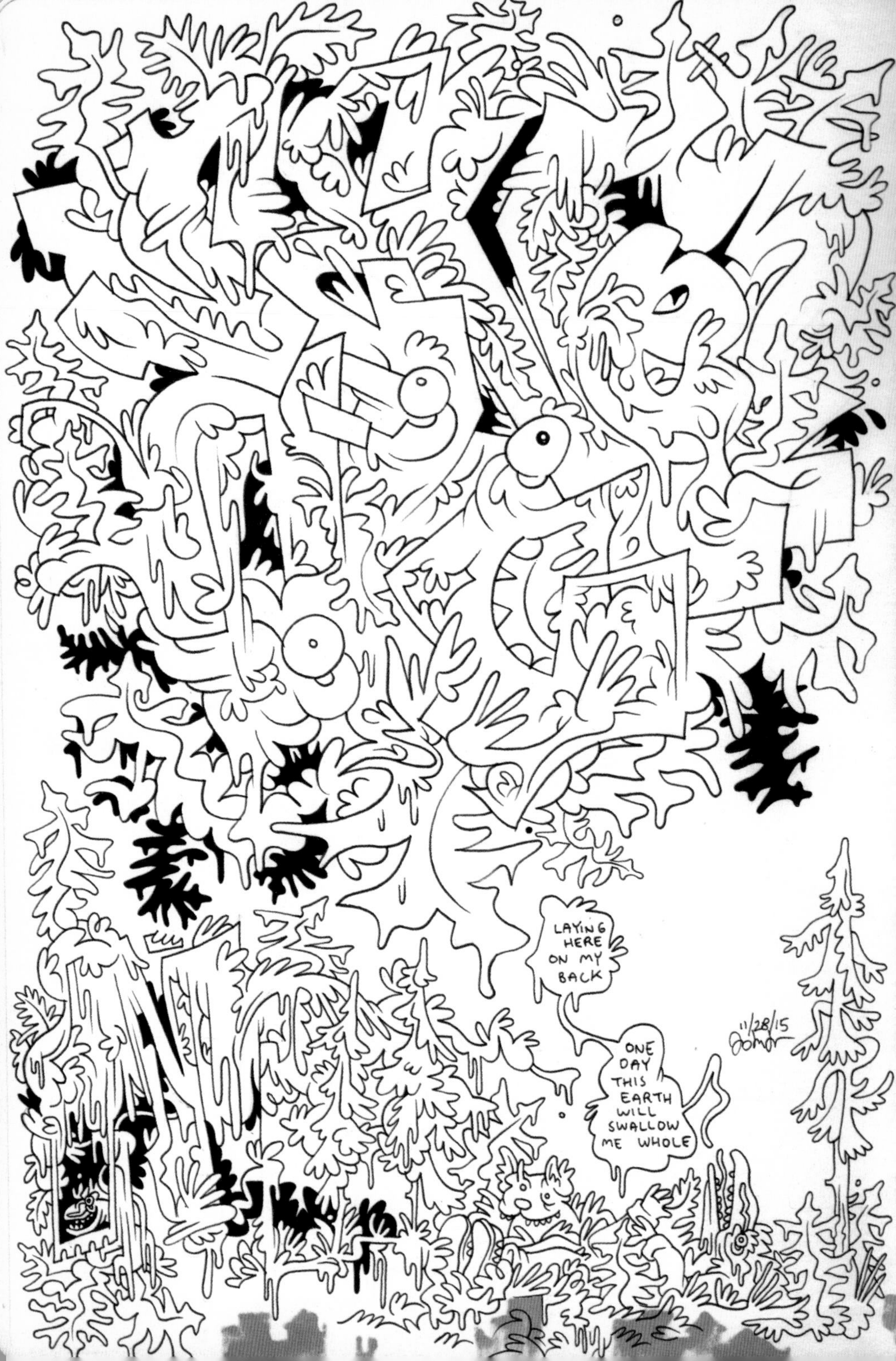
LAYING HERE ON MY BACK
ONE DAY THIS EARTH WILL SWALLOW ME WHOLE
11/28/15

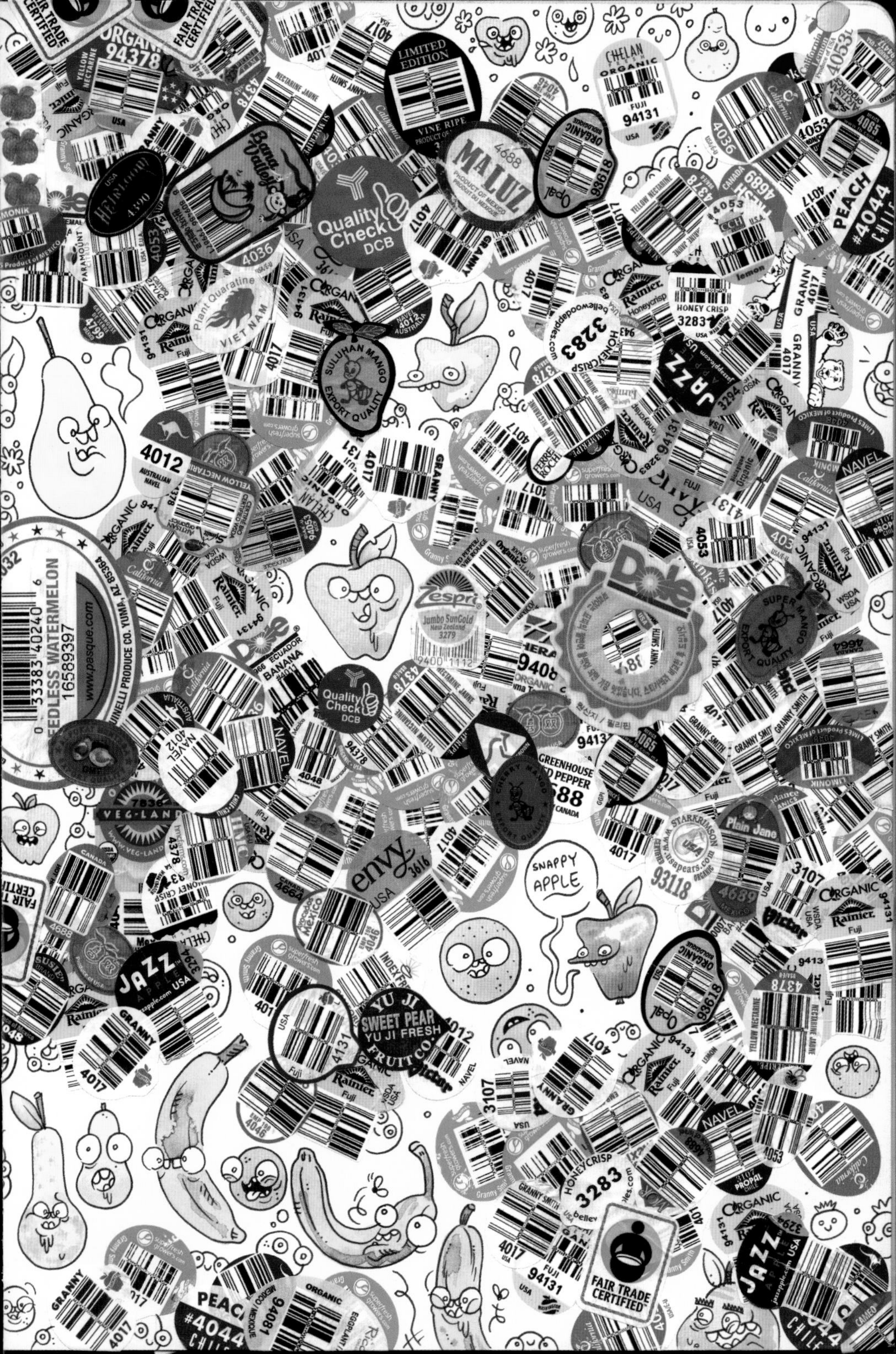

FAIR TRADE CERTIFIED
ORGANIC 94378
YELLOW NECTARINE
LIMITED EDITION
VINE RIPE
CHELAN FRESH ORGANIC
FUJI 94131
MALUZ 4688
PRODUCT OF MEXICO
Quality Check DCB
HEIRLOOM 4390
Plant Quarantine VIET NAM
SULUHAN MANGO EXPORT QUALITY
4012 AUSTRALIAN NAVEL
HONEY CRISP 3283
JAZZ
PEACH #4044 CHILE
SEEDLESS WATERMELON
www.pasque.com
Zespri Jumbo SunGold New Zealand 3279
Dole
SUPER MANGO EXPORT QUALITY
BANANA #4011 ECUADOR
VEG-LAND
GREENHOUSE RED PEPPER CANADA
CHERRY MANGO EXPORT QUALITY
envy USA 3616
SNAPPY APPLE
STARKRIMSON 93118
Plain Jane
YU JI SWEET PEAR YU JI FRESH FRUIT CO.
Rainier Fuji
ORGANIC
GRANNY SMITH 4017
HONEYCRISP 3283
NAVEL
94081 ORGANIC EGGPLANT
superfresh growers.com

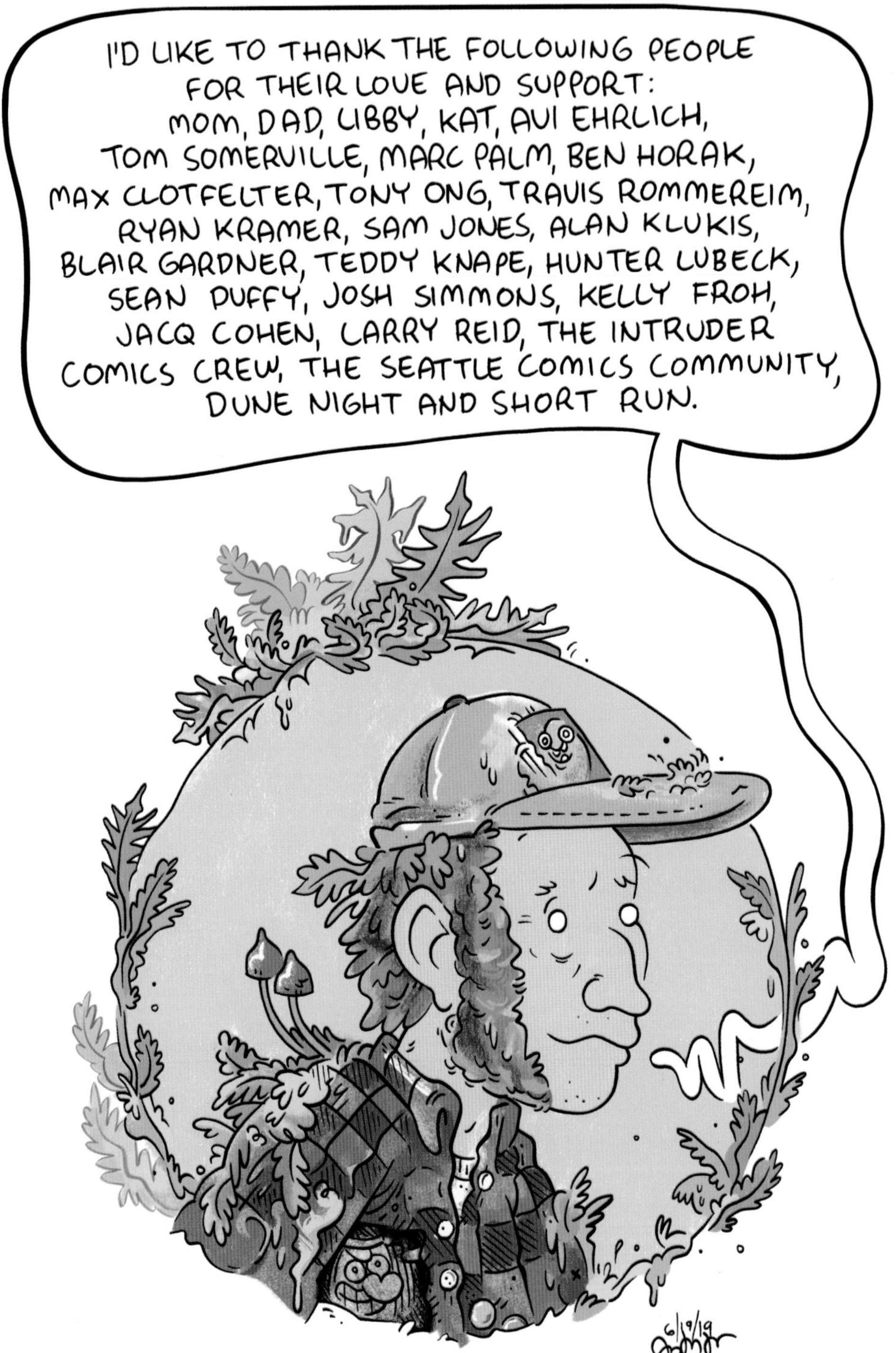
I'D LIKE TO THANK THE FOLLOWING PEOPLE FOR THEIR LOVE AND SUPPORT: MOM, DAD, LIBBY, KAT, AVI EHRLICH, TOM SOMERVILLE, MARC PALM, BEN HORAK, MAX CLOTFELTER, TONY ONG, TRAVIS ROMMEREIM, RYAN KRAMER, SAM JONES, ALAN KLUKIS, BLAIR GARDNER, TEDDY KNAPE, HUNTER LUBECK, SEAN PUFFY, JOSH SIMMONS, KELLY FROH, JACQ COHEN, LARRY REID, THE INTRUDER COMICS CREW, THE SEATTLE COMICS COMMUNITY, DUNE NIGHT AND SHORT RUN.
6/19/19

CONTENTS

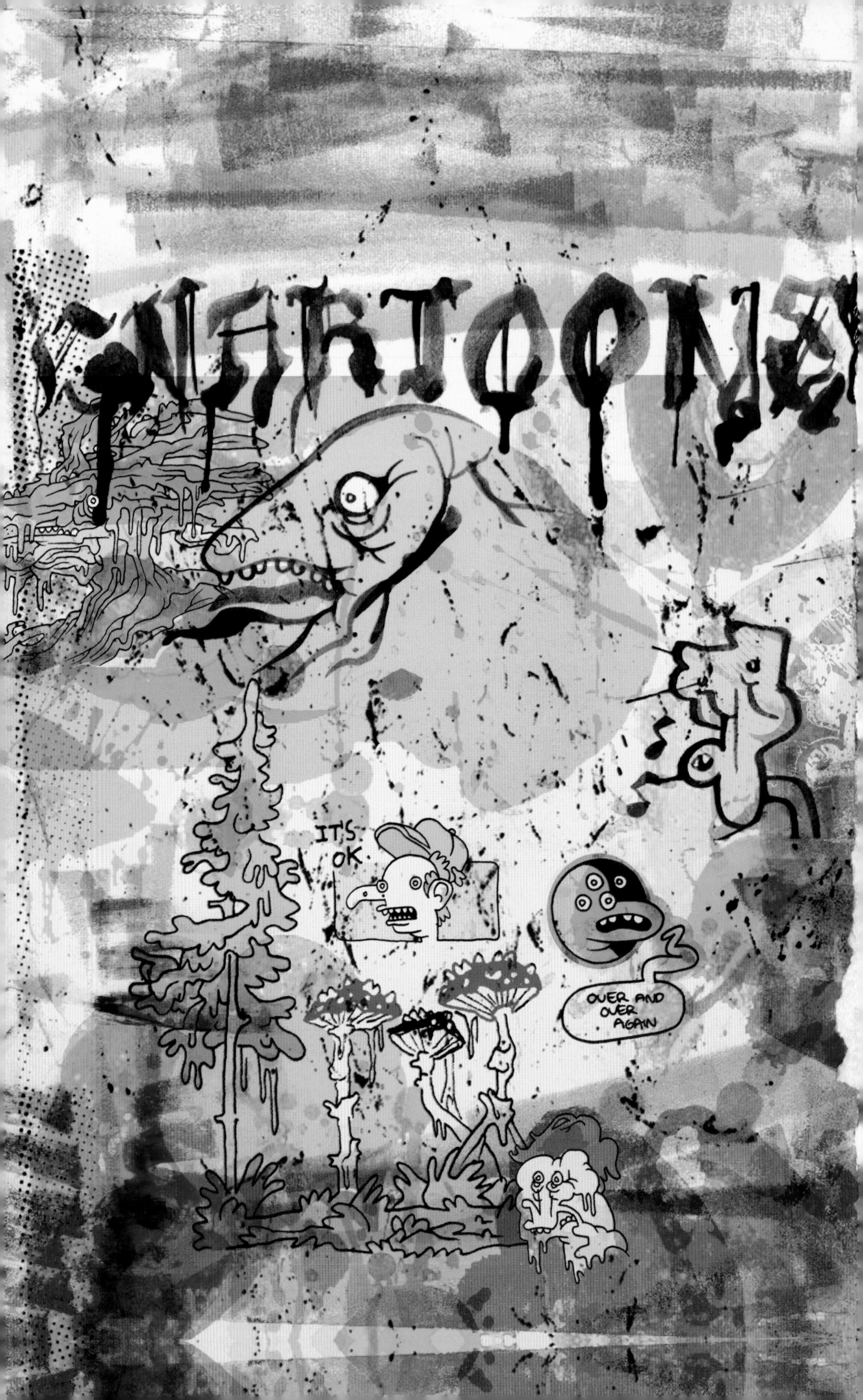
IT'S OK
OVER AND OVER AGAIN

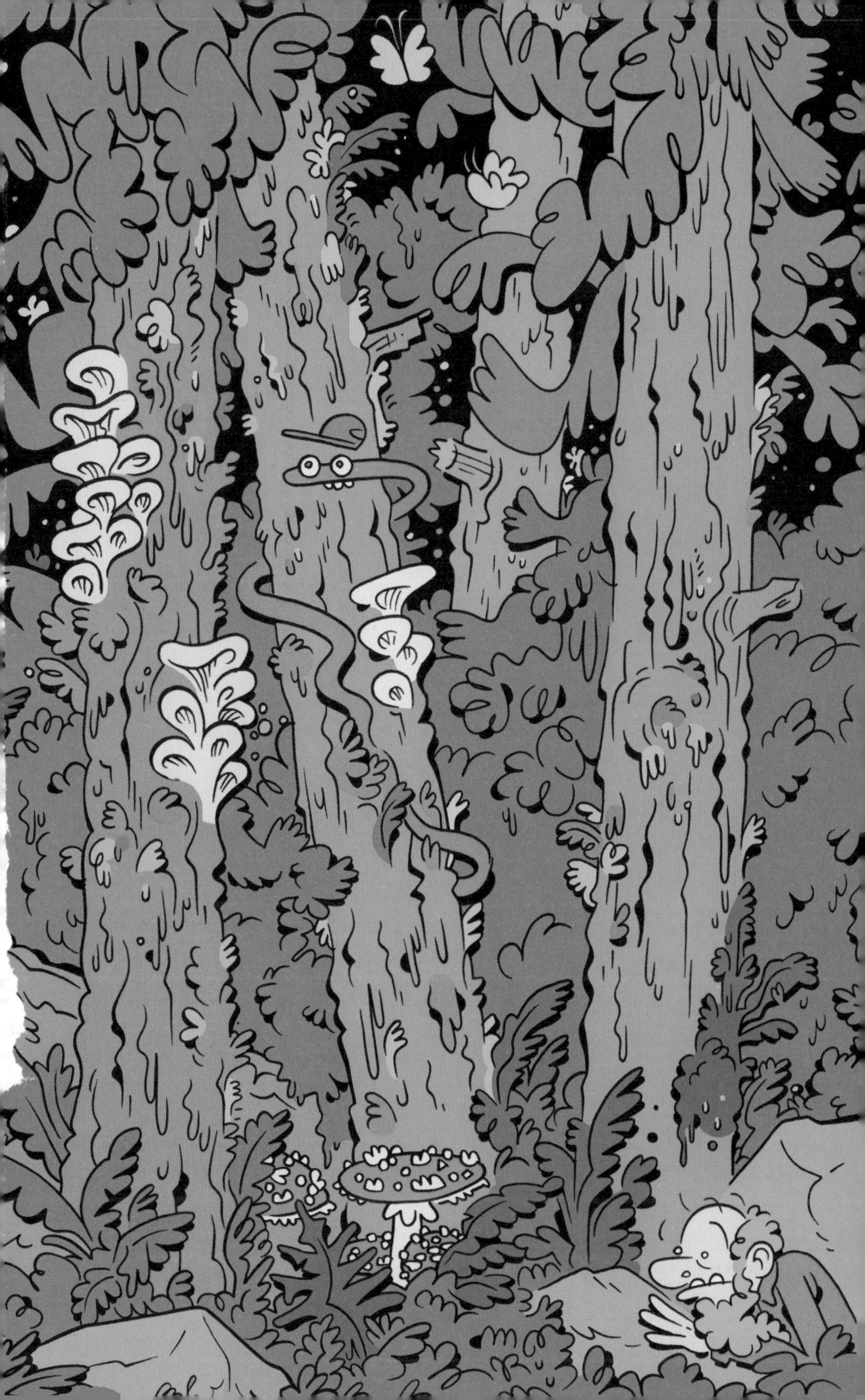

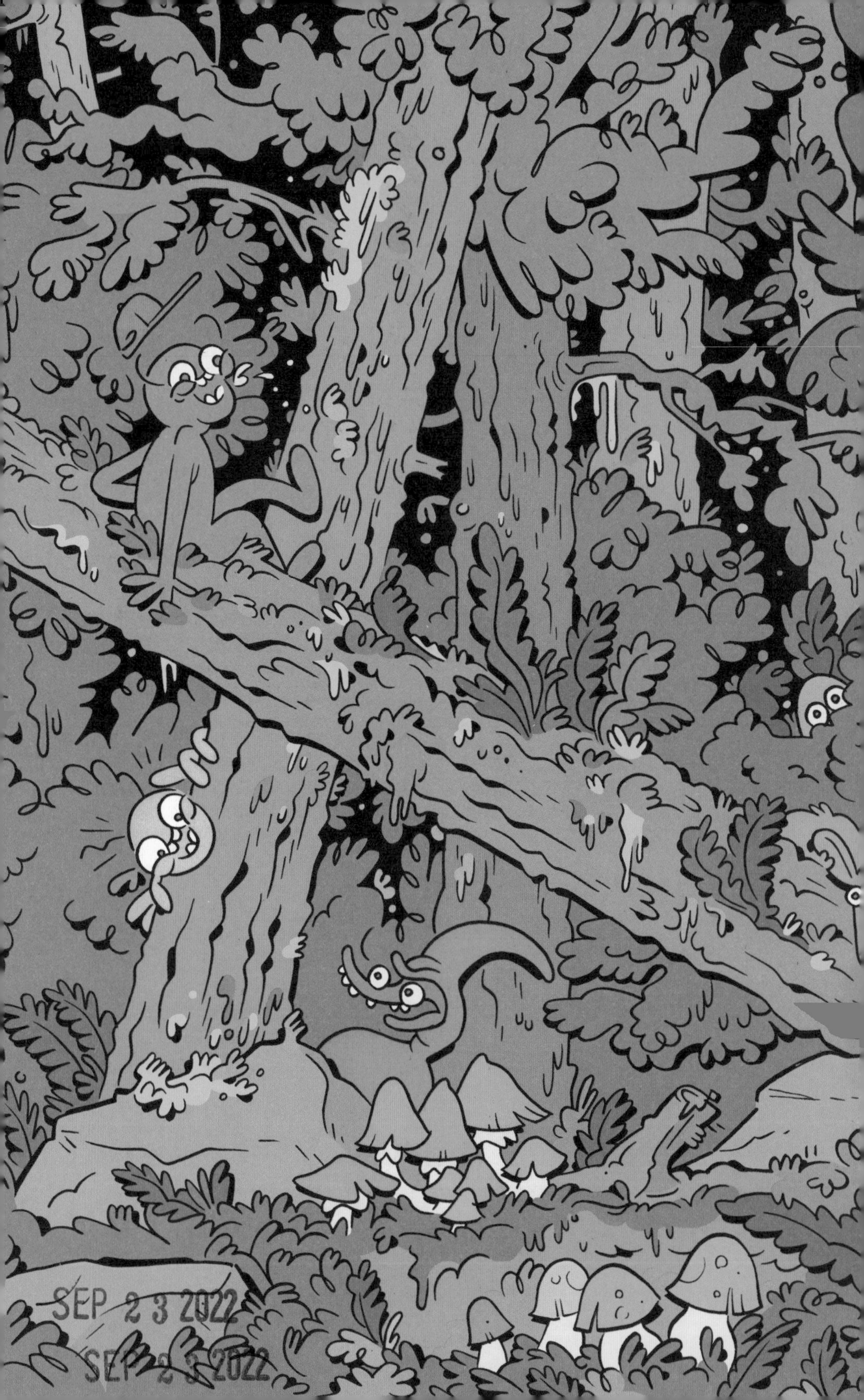

SEP 2 3 2022